A HISTORY OF THE
ANCIENT WORLD

PLATE I

A PORTION OF THE PARTHENON AND ITS FRIEZE

A HISTORY OF THE ANCIENT WORLD

BY

GEORGE STEPHEN GOODSPEED, Ph.D.

LATE PROFESSOR OF ANCIENT HISTORY IN THE UNIVERSITY OF CHICAGO

REVISED BY

WILLIAM SCOTT FERGUSON, Ph.D.

PROFESSOR OF HISTORY, HARVARD UNIVERSITY

AND

STILLMAN PERCY ROBERT CHADWICK, A.M.

INSTRUCTOR IN HISTORY, PHILLIPS EXETER ACADEMY

WITH ILLUSTRATIONS, MAPS, AND PLANS

CHARLES SCRIBNER'S SONS

NEW YORK   CHICAGO   BOSTON

PREFACE

It is now eight years since my father, Professor Good-speed, wrote "A History of the Ancient World" Had he lived it would have been his first care to follow the results of historical research and advancing methods of teaching history in secondary schools by frequent revisions of the subject-matter of the text. Recognizing the growing faith in the book on the part of those who have come to know and teach it. and the value and necessity of a revision at the present time, the family of the author have secured the services of Professors Ferguson and Chadwick to make such changes as the author himself would have considered as adding to the value of the book.

It is believed that the book in its present form will perpetuate that spirit of usefulness and the genuine scholarly feeling which characterized the author's life and work.

T. H. GOODSPEED.

DEPARTMENT OF BOTANY,
UNIVERSITY OF CALIFORNIA

REVISERS' NOTE

We have been led to make this revision of the late Professor Goodspeed's "History of the Ancient World" mainly by three considerations· its use of an easy, graceful, yet clean-cut and vigorous, English; its firm grasp of the great main lines of historical development, and its high excellence in respect of type, paper, and illustrations. There seemed to us to be no necessity that a text-book should be trivial in style, weak in coherence, or inferior in presswork Accordingly, we have been careful to preserve in the revision the character of the original. The book remains in essentials the work of Professor Goodspeed.

On the other hand, we have by no means contented ourselves with the correction of verbal inaccuracies. While at our work we have had constantly in mind the possibility, by making additions, expansions, and other modifications, of meeting more closely all reasonable demands of experienced teachers. And at the same time we have tried to make the text a faithful exponent of the views now held in the most authoritative scientific circles. It is our hope that the book, as revised, will be found—in its comparative neglect of the growth of constitutions, and the comparative fulness with which it treats the matured governments of Sparta, Athens, and Rome; in its care for the transitions from the old world of the East to Greece and from Greece via Sicily and M. ...

Græcia to Italy; in its reduction of the political history
of Egypt and Babylonia and of later Rome to a mere outline; and, above all, in its effort to interpret historically
the Hellenistic Age—a fairly close approach to the ideal
as stated in the recent report of the Committee of Five
of the American Historical Association.   As for its scientific quality, it will suffice to say that nowhere else in
English, so far as we know, can the teacher find so closely
followed the general conception of ancient history which
we owe to the epoch-making work of Professor Eduard
Meyer, of the University of Berlin

Attention may be called to a number of pedagogical
improvements.

(1) At the head of each section we have set in bold-
faced type its general contents, and in the margins we
have given a more detailed analysis of the text.

(2) The pronunciation of difficult words has been indicated on their first occurrence in the narrative as well
as in the index.

(3) The index has been arranged so as to enable the
student to find place-names on the maps without difficulty.

(4) A select list for reading has been added.   This has
been compiled almost exclusively from five single-volume
works   It makes it possible for teachers in schools with
large classes and small library funds to attend to col-
lateral reading.   For the small sum of eighty dollars,
ten copies of each of these five books can be procured.
The topics for this list have been chosen and the references made by a successful and experienced teacher—
Miss Margaret McGill, Head of the History Department
of the Newton High School, Massachusetts.

(5) By the use of strong colors, as well as by additions and corrections in details, the value of the maps taken from the first edition has been enhanced substantially. Four new maps have been added   The number of full-page illustrations has been nearly doubled.

(6) A table of dates and events has been added.   This contains the chronological data found indispensable during many years' experience in college preparatory work.

(7) The material set into the text in smaller type has been expanded (*a*) by a number of significant Greek and Roman legends; (*b*) by occasional explanations of difficult matters.   The latter are intended primarily for the teacher, upon whom, as Professor Goodspeed wrote in some omitted Suggestions to Teachers, "the usefulness of this book will depend largely."

WILLIAM SCOTT FERGUSON.
S. PERCY R CHADWICK.

PREFACE TO FIRST EDITION

This volume owes much to a wide variety of helpers. Doubtless, what may be original in it is of least value. Accordingly, the author wishes, first of all, to make general confession of having drawn upon any stores of pedagogical widsom and any treasures of scholarship which seemed to contribute to his subject In particular, however, special acknowledgments are due to some who have given personal assistance in the preparation of the book. Professors F. B Tarbell and Gordon J Laing, of the University of Chicago, have made helpful suggestions regarding the illustrations. Frances Ada Knox, Assistant in History in the University of Chicago, has given important aid in the preparation of the manuscript and in other ways. The maps, charts, and plans have had the skilful and scholarly attention of Mr. Harold H. Nelson, now of the Syrian Protestant College, of Beyrout. The book has also profited from the suggestions of a number of teachers in East and West who have read it in whole or in part. Nor should the share of the publishers be forgotten, whose warm interest and generous co-operation have made work with them a pleasure. If the book succeeds in serving the cause of sound historical learning in high-schools and academies, their share in making this possible is no small one.

G. S. G.

THE UNIVERSITY OF CHICAGO,
May, 1904.

CONTENTS

I. THE EASTERN EMPIRES

PAGE

PRELIMINARY SURVEY 1

1. THE FIRST KINGDOMS IN EGYPT AND BABYLONIA . . 5

2. THE EARLY BABYLONIAN EMPIRE 10

3. EGYPTIAN AND BABYLONIAN CULTURE 14

4. THE EGYPTIAN (NEW) EMPIRE. 29

5. THE SYRIAN STATES 39

6. THE EMPIRE OF ASSYRIA 48

7. THE MEDIAN, CHALDEAN (NEW BABYLONIAN) AND
   LYDIAN EMPIRES 54

8. THE EMPIRE OF PERSIA: ITS FOUNDING AND ORGANI-
   ZATION. 57

II. THE GREEK STATES

PRELIMINARY SURVEY 65

1. THE ÆGEAN WORLD AND THE BEGINNINGS OF GREECE 70

2. THE MIDDLE (HOMERIC) AGE 79

3 THE DEVELOPMENT OF CONSTITUTIONAL STATES . . 91

4. SPARTA AND ATHENS 109

5. THE GREEK EMPIRES: ATHENIAN, SPARTAN, THEBAN
   AND MACEDONIAN 126

6. ALEXANDER THE GREAT 231

7. THE HELLENISTIC AGE 248

8. THE WESTERN GREEKS: THE TRANSITION TO ROME . 270

III. THE EMPIRE OF ROME

PAGE

PRELIMINARY SURVEY 276

1. THE MAKING OF ROME 284

2. ROME'S DEFENCE AGAINST HER NEIGHBORS 299

3. THE UNIFICATION AND ORGANIZATION OF ITALY . . . 318

4. THE STRUGGLE WITH CARTHAGE FOR THE WESTERN MEDITERRANEAN 343

5. ROME'S CONQUEST OF THE EAST 365

6. THE DECLINE OF THE ROMAN REPUBLIC 375

7. THE ROMAN EMPIRE (PRINCIPATE) 425

8. THE LATER ROMAN EMPIRE (DESPOTISM) 491

9. THE BREAKING UP OF THE ROMAN EMPIRE AND THE END OF THE ANCIENT PERIOD 502

CHRONOLOGICAL TABLE 524

BIBLIOGRAPHIES FOR STUDENTS

1. ORIENTAL HISTORY 4

2. GREEK HISTORY 69

3. ROME—GENERAL 283

4. ROME—THE EMPIRE 425

5. ROME—CLOSING PERIOD 502

APPENDICES

I BIBLIOGRAPHY FOR ADVANCED STUDENTS AND TEACHERS 531

II. NOTES ON THE ILLUSTRATIONS 538

GENERAL INDEX 555

MAPS, PLANS AND CHARTS

FULL-PAGE AND DOUBLE-PAGE MAPS

		PAGE
THE ANCIENT EAST	*facing*	3
EMPIRES OF THE ANCIENT EASTERN WORLD	*following*	60
ANCIENT GREECE	*following*	66
CENTRES OF MYCENÆAN CIVILIZATION	*facing*	77
COLONIES OF PHŒNICIA AND GREECE	*facing*	89
LANDS OF THE ÆGEAN	*following*	128
ATHENS	*facing*	147
ATHENIAN EMPIRE AT ITS HEIGHT	*facing*	171
GREECE AT THE TIME OF THE PELOPONNESIAN WAR	*facing*	180
ALEXANDER'S EMPIRE AND KINGDOMS OF HIS SUCCESSORS	*following*	234
ANCIENT ITALY	*following*	278
THE PUNIC WARS	*facing*	343
ITALY IN 218 B C	*facing*	350
GAUL AT THE TIME OF CÆSAR	*facing*	412
THE ROMAN STATE AT SUCCESSIVE PERIODS OF ITS DEVELOPMENT TO 44 B.C.	*following*	424
THE ROMAN EMPIRE IN THE TIME OF AUGUSTUS	*following*	434
THE CITY OF ROME	*following*	460
THE MEDITERRANEAN WORLD	*following*	476
THE ROMAN EMPIRE UNDER DIOCLETIAN	*facing*	493
THE BARBARIAN KINGDOMS	*facing*	505
THE ROMAN EMPIRE UNDER JUSTINIAN	*facing*	509
EUROPE ABOUT A.D. 800	*facing*	717

xviii *Maps, Plans, and Charts*

MAPS AND PLANS IN THE TEXT

	PAGE
THE BATTLE OF SALAMIS	137
THE WORLD ACCORDING TO HERODOTUS	157
PYLOS AND SPHACTERIA	181
THE HELLESPONT, PROPONTIS AND BOSPORUS	197
THE BATTLE OF LEUCTRA	209
THE BATTLE OF ISSUS	235
ALEXANDRIA AT THE TIME OF CHRIST	237
THE WORLD ACCORDING TO ERATOSTHENES, 235 B.C.	241
THE EARLIEST PEOPLES OF ITALY	281
EARLY ROME	286
THE ENVIRONS OF ROME	301
THE BATTLE OF CANNÆ	351
CARTHAGE	371
THE BATTLE OF PHARSALUS	416
THE WORLD ACCORDING TO PTOLEMY, A.D. 150	463

CHRONOLOGICAL CHART

THE ANCIENT ORIENTAL EMPIRES	*facing*	57

ILLUSTRATIONS

PLATE
I. A Corner of the Parthenon and a Portion of Its Frieze   Color   . . *Frontispiece*

PAGE

II. Typical Oriental Heads. . . . *facing* 5

III. The Sumerian Army in Action . . *facing* 8

IV. Painting from the Wall of an Egyptian Tomb . . . . *facing* 15

V. Swamp-Hunting in a Reed Boat (Egypt) *facing* 24

VI. Babylonian and Egyptian Temples *facing* 26

VII Ancient Systems of Writing . . *facing* 42

VIII Typical Assyrian Scenes . . . *facing* 52

IX and X Decoration of a Cretan Sarcophagus. Color . . . . *facing* 70

XI. Kamares Pottery. Color . . . *facing* 72

XII Throne of Minos and Pillar of the Double-Axes . . . . . . *facing* 73

XIII. Lion Gate and Bee-Hive Tomb . *facing* 74

XIV. Reliefs from Gold Cups of the Mycenæan Age . . . . *facing* 75

XV. Wild Goat and Young—Cretan Art of the Twentieth Century B C   Color *facing* 123

XVI. Art of Greece in the Time of the Persian War . . . . *facing* 141

XVII. The Acropolis of Athens (restored) *facing* 164

XVIII Typical Greek Heads . . . . . *facing* 189

XIX. The Hermes of Praxiteles . . . *facing* 215

XX. The Alexander Mosaic   Color   *f. .* 1

PLATE   PAGE

XXI. REALISTIC AND ROMANTIC ART OF HELLENISTIC PERIOD . . . . . . facing 257

XXII. TYPICAL SCULPTURED FIGURES: KHAFRE AND POSIDIPPUS . . . . . facing 265

XXIII. THE LAOCOÖN GROUP . . . . . facing 267

XXIV. CLASSICAL TEMPLES . . . . . . facing 271

XXV. TYPICAL SCULPTURED FIGURES: ASHURNATSIRPAL AND TRAJAN . . . . facing 287

XXVI. WALL PAINTINGS FROM CAMPANIAN TOMBS facing 321

XXVII. TYPICAL COINS: ORIENT AND GREECE

XXVIII. TYPICAL COINS: ROME   } . following 332

XXIX. THE ROMAN FORUM AND THE SURROUNDING BUILDINGS (RESTORED) . . . facing 358

XXX. TYPICAL ROMAN HEADS . . . . facing 409

XXXI. ART OF THE AUGUSTAN AGE . . . facing 435

XXXII. RELIEF FROM THE ARCH OF TITUS . facing 454

XXXIII. A ROOM IN THE HOUSE OF THE VETTII, POMPEII . . . . facing 458

XXXIV. ROMAN PORTRAITURE . . . . . facing 472

XXXV. A RELIEF FROM THE COLUMN OF TRAJAN facing 475

XXXVI. CASTLE OF ST. ANGELO: HADRIAN'S MOLE facing 478

XXXVII. THE PANTHEON AND THE WALL OF AURELIAN . . . . facing 488

XXXVIII. EARLY CHRISTIAN ART. COLOR . . facing 490

XXXIX. CHARACTERISTIC ROMAN ARCHITECTURE facing 496

XL. BYZANTINE ART: CHRIST ENTHRONED. COLOR facing 509

A HISTORY OF THE ANCIENT WORLD

I. THE EASTERN EMPIRES

TO 500 B C.

PRELIMINARY SURVEY

1. The Field of Oriental History.—The earliest seats of ancient civilization are found in Egypt and Bab-y-lo′-ni-a. Egypt lies in the lower valley of the river Nile; Babylonia in the lowland where the rivers Tigris and Eu-phra′tes unite to flow into the Persian gulf. Both these river-systems have their sources in high mountain regions. At regular periods in the spring of each year their waters are swollen by the melting snows or winter rains. These floods pour over the plain and carry with them masses of earth which they deposit along the banks and at the mouths of the rivers. Thus in the course of time they have piled up layers of soil which, regularly irrigated by the overflowing waters, are marvellously fertile. Between the Nile valley and the Tigris-Euphrates basin direct communication is cut off by the Arabian desert; the upper Euphrates, however, bending westward, connects the Tigris-Euphrates basin with the series of fertile valleys and plateaus made by the mountain ranges which run from north to south, parallel with the eastern shore of the Mediterranean. Thus this middle region, known in general as Syria, is the connecting link between

The River Valleys.

Syria.

the two river-systems, since its southern boundary is separated from the Nile valley only by a comparatively narrow stretch of sandy desert.

2. **Its Physical Unity.**—Looking at the whole region thus bound together, we observe that it has somewhat the character of a crescent. The two extremities are the lands at the mouths of the two river-systems— Egypt and Babylonia. The upper central portion is called Mes-o-po-ta'mi-a. The outer border consists of mountain ranges which pass from the Persian gulf north- ward and westward until they touch the northeast cor- ner of the Mediterranean, from which point the boun- dary is continued by the sea itself. The inner side is

The Cres- cent.

made by the desert of Arabia. The crescent-shaped stretch of country thus formed is the field of the history of the ancient eastern world. It consisted of two primi- tive centres of historic life connected by a strip of hab- itable land of varying width.

3. **Its Peoples.**—The inhabitants of this region were peoples who spoke dialects of a common language. Most of them are named in the book of Genesis as

Semites.

descended from Shem (Sem), the son of Noah. The accepted name for them, therefore, is the "Semitic" peoples, and the languages they spoke are called the "Semitic" languages.

4. **Their Distribution.**—The original home of the prim- itive Semites was probably northern Arabia. From here, when the scanty sustenance afforded by the desert could not supply their needs, they poured out on every side into the fertile valleys that bordered upon their home. Thus, from this natural centre they went forth into the lower Tigris-Euphrates valley to master the civiliza-

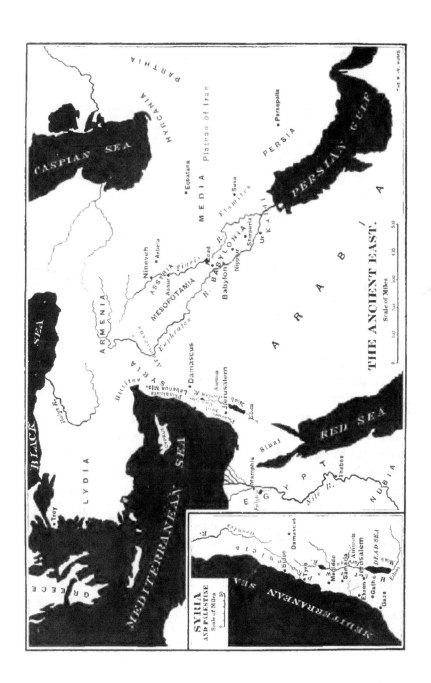

PARTHIA

BACTRIA

CASPIAN SEA

MEDIA   Plateau of Iran

Ecbatana

Susa   PERSIA   Persepolis

Elam   Ulai R.

Nineveh   Asshur   Arbela

ASSYRIA   Akkad   BABYLONIA

MESOPOTAMIA   R. Babylon   Sippar

Tigris   Nippur

R. Euphrates   PERSIAN GULF

ARMENIA   A   R   A   B   I   A

Halys R.

BLACK SEA

LYDIA   SYRIA   Damascus

Ammon

Lebanon Mts.   Jordan R.   Jerusalem

Troy   Anti-Lebanon Mts.   Moab

CYPRUS

GREECE   MEDITERRANEAN SEA   Sinai   RED SEA

Memphis   Thebes

E   G   Y   P   T   Nile R.   NUBIA

THE ANCIENT EAST.

Scale of Miles

0   100   200   300   400   500

SYRIA
AND PALESTINE
Scale of Miles
0   50

Orontes R.

Damascus

PHOENICIA

Sidon

Tyre   Megiddo   Samaria

Ammon

Ekron   Jerusalem   DEAD SEA

Gath   Moab

Gaza   Edom

MEDITERRANEAN SEA

tion which we know as the Babylonian; farther to the
north, on the upper Tigris, they became the Assyrians;
roaming back and forth in the wide regions between the
upper Euphrates and Tigris, they were known as the
Ar′a-me′ans; farther to the west, in the region bordering
on the Mediterranean, they formed communities known
as the Canaanites, the Phœnicians and the Hebrews.
Pushing on to the south and southwest, some of them
made their homes on the fertile coasts of southern Arabia. Others passed over into the Nile valley and made
up the most important element of the peoples who settled in Egypt.

5. The Surrounding Peoples.—Occupying the upper
valleys and plateaus of the northern mountain ranges
that border the crescent of this Semitic world was a
variety of tribes and peoples without unity of language
or civilization. From time to time they fell upon the
Semites of the river-valleys and established their authority more or less permanently and extensively over them.
Such were the Elamites occupying the high table-lands
to the east of Babylonia, and the Hittites, or Khati, whose
original home was in the mountains to the northwest of
the upper waters of the Euphrates. From the same Indo-Eu-
mountain regions came, toward the close of the history ropeans.
of the ancient east, the Medo-Persians, by language a
branch of the family to which the historical peoples of
western Europe and North America belong—the Indo-
European or Indo-Germanic family of languages.* They

* This family, clearly distinguished from the Semitic (§ 3), comprised
peoples whose homes were as far distant from one another as India and
England. Its chief branches were spoken by the people of India, the
Persians, the Greeks, the Romans, the Teutons, the Celts and the
Slavs.

had their homes in the lofty plateaus far to the east of the Tigris-Euphrates valley. Thence by slow degrees they pushed westward until, descending upon the plains, they absorbed the ancient Semitic civilization and established the Persian empire.

5a. Grand Divisions.—The grand divisions of this long development are the following:

1. The First Kingdoms in Egypt and Babylonia.
2. The Early Babylonian Empire (2500–1600 B.C.).
3. Egyptian and Babylonian Culture.
4. The Egyptian (New) Empire (1580–1150 B.C.).
5. The Syrian States (1150–900 B.C.).
6. The Empire of Assyria (900–606 B.C.).
7. The Median, Chaldean (New Babylonian) and Lyd· ian Empires (606–539 B.C.).
8. The Empire of Persia: its founding and organiza· tion (539–500 B.C.).

BIBLIOGRAPHY OF ORIENTAL HISTORY *

BREASTED. *A History of the Ancient Egyptians.* Scribners. The best one-volume history of Egypt.

ERMAN. *Life in Ancient Egypt.* Macmillan. Graphic account, richly illustrated, of public and private life.

GOODSPEED. *History of the Babylonians and Assyrians.* Scribners. The only one-volume history in moderate compass.

KENT. *History of the Hebrew People.* Scribners, 2 vols. An attractively written account on the basis of modern biblical learning.

KING. *A History of Sumer and Akkad.* Stokes Company. Volume I of a history of Babylonia and Assyria. The most recent and authoritative work on the subject.

MASPERO. *Ancient Egypt and Assyria.* Chapman and Hall. Sketches of the life of these peoples. Pleasantly written and instructive.

* An additional bibliography for advanced students and teachers will be found in Appendix I.

PLATE II

Hammurabi

Rameses II

Esarhaddon

A Syrian

A Philistine

A Hittite

TYPICAL ORIENTAL HEADS

Murison. 1. *Babylonia and Assyria*. 2. *History of Egypt*. Both imported by Scribners. Excellent little sketches for school use.

Ragozin. 1. *The Story of Chaldea*. 2. *The Story of Assyria*. 3. *The Story of Media, Babylon and Persia*. Putnams. Well-written, full, not abreast of the most recent discoveries, but modern enough to be very useful.

Sayce. *Ancient Empires of the East*. Scribners. A collection of detached histories of the oriental peoples not altogether up to date and with no sense of the unity of ancient oriental history.

Sayce. *Babylonians and Assyrians· Life and Customs*. Scribners. Deals with the life of these peoples fully and interestingly.

Tarbell. *A History of Greek Art*. Chautauqua Press. Has an introductory chapter on oriental art.

Wendel. *History of Egypt*. History Primer Series. American Book Company.

1.—THE FIRST KINGDOMS IN EGYPT AND BABYLONIA

6. Beginnings of Egypt.—The darkness that covers the beginnings of man's life on the earth lifts from the valley of the Nile about five thousand years before the birth of Christ. Then, and for a long time thereafter, Egypt was in the stone age and made its chief weapons, instruments and ornaments of stone. It was apparently not till at least one thousand years had passed that the use of copper ushered in a new epoch. In the interval, a number of petty districts, called nomes, divided the Nile valley between them. Their history was doubtless full of incident, but it is a sealed book to us It is not even clear whether they were distinct states or administrative districts of larger kingdoms, such as those of Upper and Lower Egypt—the two which finally emerged and for many centuries prior to 3400 B.C. dominated the one south, the other north, of a point not far

The Nomes.

up the river from Memphis. Many names, customs and institutions existed in after ages to bear witness to the long duration and high achievements in government and civilization of the two-kingdom period.

7. **The Old Kingdom.**—Not later than 3400 B C. the people of the Nile valley were united by Menes into one state with its capital at Memphis, and subsequently during three epochs they were ruled over by great kings whose official title was the "Pharaoh."* The first epoch
is that of the Old Kingdom (2980-2475 B.C.). In this early period the most important dynasty was the fourth (2900-2750 B C.). Its kings left their inscriptions on the cliffs of the peninsula of Sinai, east of Egypt. There one of them is pictured in the act of striking down an enemy with his mace. Another remarkable memorial of them is the mighty Pyramids, the wonder and admiration of travellers in all ages. In the time of the sixth dynasty, commerce with the rich lands of central Africa was flourishing. Sea-voyages, the first that history records, were made upon the Red sea. Yet the crowning achievement of these kings was their successful rule of the state with its loyal and devoted officials and its contented and prosperous people. From all parts of the realm nobles came to live in Memphis, the king's seat, and to serve him. When they died, they desired above all else to be buried near his tomb.

8. **The Middle Kingdom.**—The second epoch of Egyptian unity and prosperity—the Middle Kingdom (2160-

---

* An Egyptian historian named Manetho, writing in Greek, has left a list of the Pharaohs organized in thirty-one successive groups called by him "dynasties"—a most convenient arrangement followed by all la.....

1788 B C)—reached its acme under the twelfth dynasty (2000–1788 B.C.). A thousand years had passed and many changes had taken place. Princes of Thebes were on the throne, and the capital of the state was removed farther to the south. The nobles no longer flocked to the court, but preferred to dwell on their own domains. They recognized the Pharaoh's authority and did his bidding, but lived and died and were buried at home. The following utterance of one of them is an evidence of their authority as well as of the character of their rule:

"No daughter of a citizen have I injured, no widow have I mo- **A Prince's**
lested, no laborer have I arrested, no shepherd have I banished, **Boast**
no superintendent of workmen was there whose laborers I have
taken away from their work. In my time there were no poor, and
none were hungry in my day When the years of famine came I
ploughed all the fields of the nome from the southern to the northern boundary; I kept the inhabitants alive and gave them food, so
that not one was hungry. I gave to the widow even as to her who
had a husband, and I never preferred the great to the small "

9. Feudalism in Egypt.—In the period of this Middle Kingdom Egypt developed and perfected a feudal organization much like that which William the Conqueror established in England. By this is meant a political system in which the land is divided into lots of varying size, and let out to tenants who owe certain obligations such as rent in kind and military service to the owner of the land who is their political superior. The twelfth dynasty is the first example of feudal government in history. Rulers in such circumstances have to be able and active to keep the nobles obedient. The Pharaohs **Cultural** of this dynasty were equal to the task. Under them the **Contact with Eu-** culture of Egypt became familiar to the people of far- **rope**

distant Crete.   They extended the state up the Nile by
the conquest of Nubia (Ethiopia), the quartz mines of
which yielded much gold.   A series of successful engineering works on the lower Nile, by which a marshy district in the west, now called the Fa-yum' was drained,
added a wide and fertile tract to the kingdom.   The
Pharaohs of this dynasty adorned it with palaces and
temples and lived in it or on its border.   One of these
structures was so elaborate that it was called by Herod'o-tus, the Greek historian and traveller, a "labyrinth," and in his judgment it surpassed the Pyramids.

The Sume-
rians

10. The Beginnings of Babylonia.—There was a long
period of material and political development in the valley
of the Tigris-Euphrates rivers before the Su-me'ri-ans
make their appearance as lords of the southern portion of it, which we call Babylonia (about 2800 B C).
They were a round-headed, clean-shaven people who
fought in a close formation and created the system of
writing as well as the main elements of culture which
subsequently existed in this district.

11. Sumer and Accad.—Their chief cities were Opis,
Kish and Uruk.*   Nippur was the leading religious centre
where stood a famous temple to the god Ellil (Bel).   The
others were in turn the seats of kingdoms, which ruled
the whole region for about two hundred and fifty years.
Uruk's one emperor, Lu'gal-zag-gi'si, claims, in fact, to
have led his armies from the Persian gulf to the Med-

The Acca-
dians.

iterranean.   Then at about 2500 B C. the suzerainty
passed into the possession of the men of Ag'a-de'—a
long-headed, black haired and bearded people of Semitic
stock whose great king, Sargon, not only conquered all

* The *u* in all these words is pronounced like *oo.*

PLATE III

THE SUMERIAN ARMY IN ACTION

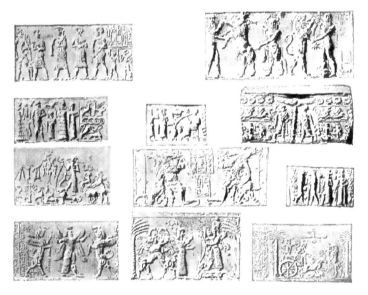

BABYLONIAN CYLINDERS

Babylonia but also extended his authority over the conglomerate of kinsmen peoples who inhabited the arable
lands between his home and the Mediterranean sea. He
probably reaped where his predecessor of Uruk had
sown.

An interesting account of Sargon's early life has come down to us
in his own words· "Sargon, the powerful king, am I. My mother
was of low degree, my father I did not know. The brother of my
father dwelt in the mountain. My city was Azupirani, situated on the
bank of the Euphrates. [My] humble mother in secret brought me
forth. She placed me in a basket-boat of rushes, with pitch she
closed my door. She gave me over to the river, which did not [rise]
over me. The river bore me along; to Akki, the irrigator, it carried
me. Akki, the irrigator, brought me to land. Akki, the irrigator,
reared me as his own son. Akki, the irrigator, appointed me his
gardener. While I was gardener, the goddess Ishtar looked on me
with love [and] . . . four years I ruled the kingdom." *Sargon's Autobiography.*

An ancient record reads as follows: "The moon was favorable
to Sargon, who at this season was highly exalted, and a rival, an
equal, there was not. His own land was quiet Over the countries
of the sea of the setting sun [the Mediterranean sea] he passed,
and for three years at the setting sun [the west] all lands his hand
subdued. Every place he formed into one [*i.e.*, he organized all into
an empire] His images at the setting sun he erected [*i e.*, as a sign
of authority in the west]." *The Conquests of Sargon.*

12. Accad and Sumer.—Sargon was succeeded by his
vigorous son Naram Sin, and he in turn by ten other
Accadian kings; but at the end of one hundred and
ninety-seven years the empire of Agade fell (2300 B.C.).
A period of confusion and invasion followed. Then the
Sumerians, now largely Semitized, seized the government
again and for over two hundred years kings of Ur
and Isin ruled in turn over the cities of Sumer and

Accad. Of the governors (pa-te′sis) whom they installed in their dependencies none was more energetic than Gud′e-a of Shir-pur′la (La′gash).

2.—THE EARLY BABYLONIAN EMPIRE
2500–1600 B.C.

13. The Kingdom of Babylon.—Isin at length failed to keep down the subject cities. Civil wars followed accompanied by invasions from Elam (§ 5). About the same time some Arabian kings seized the northern city of Babylon. The two invaders fought each other, and the kings of Babylon drove out the Elamites and got possession of the whole country. Thus a strong and permanent state was founded with its capital at Babylon.

Union under Babylon.

14. The Expansion of Babylonia.—To the east, west and south, with their barriers of mountain, desert and sea, there was small prospect of extension. Elam and the districts lying on the slopes of the eastern ranges marked the limit in this direction. But to the north and northwest, the rivers Tigris and Euphrates opened up highways to the Mesopotamian and Syrian regions as far as the northern mountains and the Mediterranean. Thither, as we have just seen, the kings of Uruk and Agade had led their armies and laid the foundations of an empire.* Of its organization and history we know nothing.

15. The First Babylonian Empire.—When the kings of Babylon (§ 13) had united all Babylonia under their

---

* An empire (Latin, *imperium*) is a state made by the supremacy of one city or state over several others. Such a policy of making a great state is called imperialism

sway, they, too, followed the imperial policy and founded the first Babylonian empire—the earliest enduring state that covered the larger part of the known world. In extent it did not surpass the limits which tradition assigns to Sargon, but the long and abundant series of written documents which have come from its kings bears undoubted testimony to their rule. The founder of the empire was Ham-mu-ra'bi. a brilliant warrior and statesman (about 1950 B.C.). An inscription illustrates his care for the canal-system of Babylonia: *King Hammurabi.*

"When Anu and Bel [great gods of Babylonia] gave me the land of Babylonia to rule and intrusted their sceptre to my hands, I dug out the Hammurabi canal, nourisher of men, which brings abundance of water to the Babylonian lands. Both its banks I changed into fields for cultivation, and I gathered heaps of grain, and I procured unfailing water for the Babylonian lands."

For his empire the king published a code of laws which contains some 280 statutes and reveals a high ideal of justice. Some of the more striking and instructive of the laws are the following: *His Law-code*

1 If a man bring an accusation against a man and charge him with a crime, but cannot prove it, he, the accuser, shall be put to death.

8. If a man steal ox or sheep, ass or pig or boat—if it be from a god (temple) or a palace, he shall restore thirty-fold; if it be from a freeman, he shall render tenfold. If the thief have nothing wherewith to pay, he shall be put to death.

21. If a man make a breach in a house, they shall put him to death in front of that breach, and they shall thrust him therein

25. If a fire break out in the house of a man, and a man who goes to extinguish it cast his eye on the furniture of the owner of the house, and take the furniture of the owner of the house, that man shall be thrown into that fire.

57. If a shepherd have not come to an agreement with the owner of a field to pasture his sheep on the grass and pasture his sheep on the field without the owner's consent, the owner of the field shall harvest his field, the shepherd who has pastured his sheep on the field without the consent of the owner of the field shall give over and above twenty *gur* of grain per *gan* to the owner of the field

117. If a man be in debt and sell his wife, son or daughter, or bind them over to service, for three years they shall work in the house of their purchaser or master; in the fourth year they shall be given their freedom.

195-199 If a son strike his father, they shall cut off his fingers. If a man destroy the eye of another man, they shall destroy his eye. If one break a man's bone, they shall break his bone. If one destroy the eye of a freeman or break the bone of a freeman, he shall pay one mina of silver. If one destroy the eye of a man's slave or break a bone of a man's slave, he shall pay one-half his price.

206. If a man strike another man in a quarrel and wound him, he shall swear "I struck him without intent," and he shall be responsible for a physician.

251. If a man's bull has been wont to gore and they have made known to him its habit of goring, and he has not protected its horns, or has not tied it up, and that bull gores the son of a man and brings about his death, he shall pay one-half mina of silver.

In his concluding words the king says: "Let any oppressed man, who has a cause, come before my image as king of righteousness! Let him read the inscription on my monument! Let him give heed to my mighty words! And may my monument enlighten him as to his cause and may he understand his case! May he set his heart at ease! (and he will exclaim·) 'Hammurabi is indeed a ruler who is like a real father to his people.'"

16. The Decline of Babylon.—For two centuries kings continued to rule in peace and prosperity over the empire founded by Hammurabi. Even when rude tribes from the eastern mountains, called the Kassites, entered the Babylonian plain and their chieftains (about 1750 B.C.) seated themselves on the throne of Babylon, the structure

of the state remained firm. The new people accepted
the civilization, and the new kings ruled by the customs
and laws of the old Babylonian empire. For the temple at Nippur (§ 11) gypsum came from Mesopotamia,
marble, cedar and cypress from the eastern mountains,
lapis lazuli from Bactria in the far east, magnesite from
the island of Eu-bœ'a in the Ægean sea, and cobalt,
possibly, from China, besides copper, gold and precious
stones from other regions Nevertheless, the Kassite
period was one of stagnation. Babylonia ceased to
develop and no longer gave an impulse for progress to
other peoples.

The Com
merce of
Babylon

17. The Heirs of Babylon.—The Kassites were not
the only foreigners who coveted the rich land of the two
rivers.' They had rivals in the Hittites from Asia Minor
and the Arians of Indo-European stock (§ 5) from the
east. The whole world of the Babylonian empire seems
to have been a prey in this epoch to captains and soldiers
of fortune from diverse parts. The Kassite rule was
merely nominal in many districts. About 1650 B.C. the
Semitic city of Assur on the upper Tigris threw off the
yoke of Babylon and founded the kingdom of Assyria.
For a long time it fought with varying fortune against
Kassites, Hittites and Arians. Elam, too, became independent. The whole region beyond the Euphrates
passed into the hands of Egypt (§ 38) and thus the early
Babylonian empire perished (about 1600 B C.).

Fall of
First Baby
lonian
Empire

REVIEW EXERCISES. 1. Who were the Elamites? 2. For
what are the following places noted. Memphis, Agade, Nippur,
Thebes, Babylon? 3. For what were the following famous:
Hammurabi, Sargon of Agade? 4. Who were the Semites,
the Kassites? 5. What is meant by empire, lapis lazuli,
tradition? 6. When did Hammurabi live?

SELECT LIST FOR READING. 1. The Land of the Egyptians. Breasted, A History of the Ancient Egyptians, pp. 3–13. 2. The Tigris-Euphrates Valley. Goodspeed, A History of the Babylonians and Assyrians, pp 5–13. 3. Sources of Information of the Tigris-Euphrates People. Goodspeed, pp. 14–24, 37–43. 4. The Cuneiform Inscriptions. Goodspeed, pp 25–36. 5. Chronology of Egyptian History. Breasted, pp 23–28. 6. The Earliest Egyptians. Breasted, pp. 30–39 7. Sargon of Agade. Goodspeed, pp 61–63. 8. Khammurabi. Goodspeed, pp. 107–117. 9. The Kassites. Goodspeed, pp 121–126.

TOPICS FOR READING AND ORAL REPORT. 1. The Fourth Egyptian Dynasty. Wendel, pp. 39–41; Murison, Egypt, §§ 22–24; Rawlinson, Story of Egypt, chs. 3–4. 2. The Twelfth Egyptian Dynasty. Wendel, pp. 50–57; Murison, Egypt, §§ 32–35; Rawlinson, Story of Egypt, chs 5–7. 3. Sargon of Agade. Ragozin, Chaldea, pp 205–214, Murison, Babylon and Assyria, §§ 6–9 King, Sumer and Akkad, pp. 238–252. 4. The Fourteenth Chapter of Genesis, verses 1–5. Ragozin, Chaldea, pp. 221–224; Murison, Babylon and Assyria, §§ 13–14. 5. The Reign of Hammurabi. Murison, Babylon and Assyria, § 15. 6. The Code of Hammurabi. The Biblical World, March, 1903, March 1904. 7. The Kassites. Murison, Babylon and Assyria, § 16. 8. The Cuneiform Inscriptions. Encyclopedia Britannica, article "Inscriptions."

3.—EGYPTIAN AND BABYLONIAN CULTURE

18. Agriculture the Chief Occupation.—In that far-off period when the primitive inhabitants settled in the Tigris-Euphrates and Nile basins, the first and easiest things they found to do were the raising of cattle and the growing of grain. The wonderfully rich and well-watered soil produced for man and beast all kinds of plants for food. The cattle could be pastured in the luxuriant marshes by the river-banks. Seed sown in moist spots produced wonderful harvests, sometimes two

PLATE IV

PAINTING FROM THE WALL OF AN EGYPTIAN TOMB

hundred-fold and more. Soon a system of canals, dykes Systems of Irrigation. and reservoirs was created to distribute the inundating waters. By this means larger tracts of land were obtained for cultivation, until the entire valley was one vast garden. The majority of the people were farmers; the chief products of the lands were cattle and grain. The regular yearly inundations of the rivers kept the land fertile, and the bountiful soil continued from generation to generation to pour its wealth into the arms of the cultivators. Its abundant products not merely supplied their needs, but furnished a surplus which they could store away or sell to other peoples less favored. It was this surplus that made the nations in these river-valleys rich and gave them their commanding position in the ancient world.

19. Industry.—These lands were also the earliest seats of industry. The records show that already there were carpenters, blacksmiths, weavers, goldsmiths, silversmiths, leather workers, potters, dyers, masons, miners, vintners, jewellers, and brickmakers. Each trade appears to have been organized as a guild or union with a chief officer. Egypt was specially famous for its wonderfully fine white linen, Babylonia for its woollens woven into cloths and rugs of various colors. Pa-py'-rus,* a tall reed growing in profusion in the Nile, was used by the Egyptians to make mats, rope, sandals, boats and writing material. Long strips of it were laid Paper. crosswise, pressed together and the surfaces polished off to make a rude kind of paper. The most important industry to the Babylonians was brickmaking. Stone was hard to get and clay was abundant. Hence all

* From this word our "paper" is derived.

Babylonian buildings were of brick. Clay was the chief

Clay Tab-
lets.

writing material of Babylonia. It was moulded, when soft, into cakes, into these the characters were pressed with a tool, and then the cakes were dried in the sun or in a kiln. One of their months, corresponding to our June, had a name which meant "the month of bricks," because it was the best time of the year for brickmaking.

20. Commerce and Trade.—Trading was another ac-

Of Egypt

tivity of these peoples. The Egyptians traded chiefly among their own people up and down the Nile. Yet sea-voyages also were undertaken from an early period; and a regular maritime traffic, especially in lumber, was conducted by the Egyptians with the coast of Phœnicia whence they got the cedars of Lebanon which were greatly in demand in woodless Egypt. They obtained ivory, incense and spices, ostrich feathers and panther skins from the far south. They delighted also in strange animals, and made a specialty of importing apes and

Of Baby-
lonia.

monkeys. But it was the Babylonians who were the chief traders They extended their commercial operations throughout the ancient eastern world. Having no stone and little wood in their own land they imported them. Cedar was brought from the Mediterranean coast, teak from India; stone came from the eastern mountains and even from western Arabia. They got gold and silver from the east in exchange for their grain and cloth. Their merchants ventured into the borders of distant countries with their wares, and carried thither knowledge of the Babylonian civilization.

21. Organization of Society.—Men engaged in so many varied pursuits would very early be organized into communities. We have already said that our first glimpse of the peoples in the Tigris-Euphrates river-valley finds them living in city-states. The head of the state was the king. He seems to have been first a priest, occupied with religious duties, and to have risen from the priesthood to the kingship. He was closest to the gods, as was also the king in Egypt, who was regarded as divine and called "the good god." Hence his power was supreme and absolute; he had "divine right" Obedience to him was the first duty of his subjects. But he must also be the benefactor of his people. He was the one who hunted and killed the wild animals that preyed upon the land; he led his people in war against their enemies. He was the source of law and the fountain of justice. Any subject could appeal to him for deliverance. Next, but far below him, came the nobility. The greatest noble in Egypt must fall on his face and "snuff the ground" before the king; the highest honor was to be called the king's "friend" The land had been divided among the nobles by the king, the sole owner; they held it at his will and paid him tribute and military service in return. They were his counsellors and assistants in government, the governors, the judges and the general of the army. Often they lived on their own estates in fine palaces surrounded by gardens; they ruled over their dependants as the king over the state. There was always danger that some one among them would become strong enough to aspire to the throne and rebel against his lord. The kingship was too glittering a prize not to attract an ambitious noble. Hence the king had to be strong and watchful.

22. The People.—The common people played no part in public life, and it is hard to discover and to describe their place in this ancient world. Probably very few of them owned land. That belonged to the king and nobles, who rented it out to tenant farmers. The latter cultivated the land personally or by means of free laborers or slaves, and usually paid one-third of the yearly crop as rent to the proprietor. Slaves were not very numerous in this early period and were well treated. In Babylonia most slaves were the property of the temples and were hired out by the priests to the farmers, who had to care for them if sick or injured; the free hired laborers had to look out for themselves.

Slaves.

23. Merchants.—The artisans and tradesmen were not very highly regarded by the upper classes, but their growing wealth gave them increasing importance in the cities where they naturally gathered Babylonian merchants began early to form an important class. Some trading families carried on mercantile operations from generation to generation, amassed riches, and engaged in banking. At first all trade was in natural products; cattle were exchanged for wheat or dates. But standards of value began to be set up by the use of the precious metals. They were fashioned in bars or rings and went by weight. In Babylonia the standard was the *she'kel* of half an ounce avoirdupois; sixty of these made a *mi'na*, and sixty minas a *talent*. In Egypt the *deb'en*, weighing three and a quarter ounces, was the standard. In those days silver was more precious than gold and copper was the commonest metal. Iron was rarer. It was possible to estimate the value of natural products in these standards, and thus mercantile operations on a much greater scale could be engaged in Soon the Babylonian merchants began to make loans, usually at a high rate of

Means of Exchange.

interest Their security was often the person or family of the borrowers, who were ruthlessly seized and sold as slaves if payment was not made. Thus the merchant came to be more and more a power in the ancient world.

24. **Supremacy of Law.**—One of the most wonderful things about this early world is that all these various activities of ancient life were firmly established on a basis of law. The chief reason for the organization and continuance of the state was that it secured justice for its members. Not violence but order was the rule. The symbol of rank was the staff, not the sword. The highest official in Egypt under the Pharaoh was the Chief Justice. The Babylonians were particularly given to legal forms. When one sold his grain, or hired a laborer, or made a will, or married a wife, or adopted a son, he went before the judge, and a document recording the transaction was written out and signed by the contracting parties in his presence. The document was then filed away in the public archives. In the case of a dispute arbitrators were employed or the matter was brought before the court. The opposing parties were sworn, and after the case was heard, a written verdict was rendered and accepted by the disputants, or an appeal was made to a higher tribunal. Thousands of these legal documents, decisions, bills, drafts, sales, orders, wills, etc., have been preserved to the present day.

The Judge.

25. **The Family.**—The family was already a well-recognized institution The father was its acknowledged head, but the mother was highly honored. No family was regarded as complete without children. In Babylonia it was common to adopt sons by process of law.

Respect and love for parents was taught and practised. "Thou shalt never forget what thy mother has done for thee," says Ani, the sage of Egypt, and another declares, "I have caused the name of my father to increase." Giving in marriage was the father's privilege and was arranged on a money basis. The wooer paid for his **Marriage.** bride according to his wealth. Usually the marriage ceremony was both civil and religious. The wife brought a marriage portion to her husband, which he had to return if he divorced her. A man might buy more than one wife, but this was a luxury reserved for the rich and was of doubtful advantage to the peace of the home life. In the king's "harem" were gathered as many princesses as there were political alliances with neighboring rulers or nobles. The sense of family unity seems to have been stronger in Babylonia than in Egypt. The Babylonian father had the power of life and death over wife and children; the children called themselves after the names of their ancestors. In Egypt names were individual, containing no reference to family relations, nor do funeral epitaphs usually glorify the ancestors of the dead.

26. Writing.—Both Babylonians and Egyptians had already invented systems of writing. These systems sprang out of the attempt to represent objects and ideas by pictures—a circle standing for "sun," or a winged creature for "flying," etc. Two changes took place in **Picto-** course of time. The pictures began to have various **graphs.** meanings and they came to lose their original form as pictures. So in Babylonia we have words represented by a series of lines thickened into a wedge at the end. Hence these signs are called, from the Latin word *cu'-*

ne-us, "a wedge," *cu'nei-form.* The Egyptians regarded their picture-signs as "divine" and "holy"; hence they are called hi'er-o-glyph'ics, from the Greek word *hi'er-os,* "holy." All these systems of writing, which seem to us so cumbrous and difficult, are nevertheless the foundation of our own alphabet, and in their day were a wonderful achievement which contributed immensely to human progress.

27. The Scribe.—To master these methods of writing required special study, to which only a few could give themselves. These began as boys under the teacher, usually in the temple school, and graduated as *scribes.* To be a scribe was to enjoy an honorable and useful career in government employ, with the prospect of riches and advancement. To every king, prince, noble, governor or judge a scribe was indispensable for preparing his despatches or decisions; indeed, everybody who wished to write a letter or to read one was dependent on the scribe.

28. Literature.—Songs, stories and records had also been written In other words, these peoples had a literature. It started with the priests, who were the learned men of the time; therefore it was chiefly made up of religious books, such as prayers and hymns for public worship. But there were also tales in prose and verse about divine heroes and their wonderful adventures. The most striking of these is the Babylonian epic of the Hero Gilgamesh, who seeks the fountain of immortality. In the eleventh book of this poem is the account of the deluge and the building of the ship in which one family of all human kind is saved—wonderfully like the Bible story in Genesis The Egyptians had

Its Religious Element.

a fondness for stories o magic and fairy tales. Their poetry also was sometimes touching and thoughtful.

> "Mind thee of the day when thou too shalt start for the land
> To which one goeth never to return.
> Good for thee then will have been an honorable life;
> Therefore be just and hate transgressions,
> For he who loveth justice will be blessed;
> Then give bread to him who has no field
> And create for thyself a good name for posterity forever"

29. Historical Literature.—A sense for literature and history is shown in the desire of kings and nobles to preserve memorials of themselves. Long autobiographies are found in the tombs of Egyptian officials, and Babylonian kings proclaim their own deeds in inscriptions upon slabs and images. King Sargon of Agade (§ 11) is said to have formed a library in his capital and to have collected hymns and rituals in a great work called *The Illumination of Bel*. Every Babylonian temple also had its library where the temple documents and sacred books were placed. Many of these have only recently been unearthed. History involves more, however, than the making and keeping of records. They must be knit together so as to make a connected and intelligible whole. This was not done by either the ancient Egyptians or Babylonians; it was done imperfectly by the Hebrews. The Greeks were the real creators of history.

30. Arts of Life.—No little degree of comfort in living was enjoyed. The country houses of the aristocracy were roomy and surrounded by gardens in which trees, flowers and running water were found. The Egyptians had a passion for flowers, and at the banquets

[margin notes: Libraries.　Lack of Real History.　The House.]

the guests were garlanded with wreaths. The walls of
the house were hung with brilliant tapestries Stools
and couches, the forms of which are still copied among
us, constituted the furniture. In the Babylonian cities
the palaces of the king and his officials were built on
platforms or mounds raised high above the plain, while
the houses of the common people were crowded together below them. The latter were simple and low,
with thick mud walls and flat roofs. The streets were
narrow and dirty. The fire was started with a fire-
stick and bow. The dining-table was a low bench, Food and
around which the family squatted and partook of the Drink.
usual meal of dried fish, dates and cakes of ground
grain. Beer was the universal drink, though wine was
also very common. When an Egyptian gave an entertainment he usually invited his friends to a "house of
beer," or a roast goose. They slept on low couches or
on mats spread on the floor. The Egyptian's pillow was
a wooden head-rest, which, though hard, was cool and
did not disarrange his wig. The priests shaved their
heads, other people wore their hair short, and all well-
to-do persons wore wigs. Although the beard was
shaven, the pictures represent the nobles with false
beards as a sign of dignity. In Babylonia, on the contrary, the prevailing fashion was to wear hair and
beard long. The fundamental article of dress was the Dress.
cloth that was wrapped about the middle of the body.
Additions were made to this by the better classes; the
cloth was lengthened to the knees or a quilted skirt was
worn. The Egyptian was most careful about cleanliness
in dress, and the laundryman is a conspicuous figure on
the monuments. In Egypt nothing was worn on the

head; the Babylonian aristocracy are represented with flat caps. To go barefoot was customary, or, at most, sandals were worn. Ointments and cosmetics were used by men and women alike and for the entire body. A man's street costume was not complete without a cane; in Babylonia everyone carried a seal, which served him when he wished to sign his name. A variety of recreations is illustrated by the Egyptian monuments. Hunting birds and hippopotami in the Nile marshes was the favorite sport of the nobles. Bull-fights, wrestling, dancing, singing and playing on musical instruments were greatly enjoyed; even games of checkers and chess are found.

Amusements

31. The Higher Arts.—Thus the higher arts were early reached. Both peoples accomplished much in architecture. Although the Babylonians had only bricks as building material, they erected massive and effective temples and palaces. A mighty terrace forty or more feet high was first built and on this rose the temple which usually culminated in a tower made of solid stories of brick placed one above another, each successive story smaller than the one beneath it—the whole often reaching one hundred feet in height. Egypt's most splendid structures were the Pyramids, built to serve as tombs of the kings. The pyramid of the Pharaoh Khu'fu of the fourth dynasty was a mass of limestone and granite over 755 feet square at the base, thus covering 13 acres, and rising to a point at a height of 481 feet; the sides were faced with blocks so nicely fitted together as to look like a single mighty surface smooth and shining In the heart of it was the funeral chamber, the roof of which was so carefully adjusted to bear the enormous

Architecture.

The Pyramids.

SWAMP-HUNTING IN A REED BOAT (EGYPT)

weight above it as not to have yielded an inch in the course of the ages.*

32. Sculpture.—In the little as well as the great the ancients of these days showed remarkable skill. In the engraving of hard stones, the Babylonian artists excelled, while the gold and brightly colored inlay work of the Egyptians is surprising. The pottery is both useful and artistic, and the furniture affords models for the present day. The statues from hard granite, or harder diorite, were cut and polished with amazing fineness. It is true that grace and naturalness are rarely found in the pose and modelling of the figures. The Egyptians not only did not understand perspective, but they mixed up the profile and front views of their human figures in a grotesque manner The statues, however, from both peoples, while stiff, are strong, real and impressive You feel that they are for eternity.

33. Science.—What was known of the natural world, its laws and its forces, was a strange compound of truth and error. Many of nature's secrets had been pierced. The movements of the heavenly bodies were Astronomy mapped out. The year of $365\frac{1}{4}$ days was determined. Eclipses were calculated. Men were familiar with the points of the compass and the signs of the Zodiac. The decimal system was employed, and joined with it was the sexagesimal system (10×6) Weights and measures were carefully worked out on the basis of the hand-breadth. The sun-dial and the water-clock measured time. The mechanical skill shown in building is amaz- Mechanics. ing. The arch, the lever and the inclined plane were known. Engineers of to-day, if they had only the means

* The roof-beams of granite were cracked by the earthquake of 27 B.C.

then available, would have serious difficulty in putting some of the stones of the Pyramids into their places, if indeed they could accomplish it at all. On the other hand, the earth was regarded by the Babylonians as an inverted bowl, its edges resting on the great watery deep On its outer surface dwelt mankind. Within its crust was the dark abode of the dead. Above and about it, resting on the ocean of waters, was the heaven, another inverted bowl or disk, on the under side of which moved the heavenly bodies; on the outer side lay another ocean beyond which dwelt the gods in eternal light. The stars were thought to have influence, either good or bad, on the life of men, and hence were carefully studied. The study of medicine consisted of a search for strange combinations of incongruous substances, in which a wise prescription or a useful discovery came only by chance. The blood of lizards, the teeth of swine, putrid meat, the moisture from pigs' ears are among Egyptian remedies for illness. No study of Nature for her own sake, but only for practical ends or from religious motives—this was the vital weakness of the science of the ancient east.

34. Religion.—The main factor in the life of these peoples was their religion It inspired their literature, their science and their art. It was the foundation of their social and political life. Priests were judges, scribes, teachers and authors. Temples were treasuries, fortresses and colleges as well as places of worship. All this means that one of the first problems that these men had to face was their relation to the world about and above them. They sought to solve this problem by believing that they were surrounded by higher beings with whom it was possible to get on in peace and harmony.

PLATE V

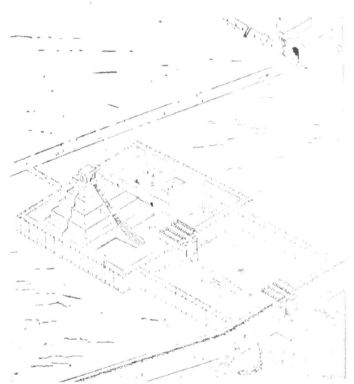

A Babylonian Temple (Nippur)

An Egyptian Temple (Luxor)

ORIENTAL TEMPLES

This belief, and the worship that sprang out of it, was religion; it had everything to do with primitive society. In the periods which we are studying, religion was far advanced. Had you gone into a city of Egypt or Babylonia and talked with a priest of the temple, he would have told you that, as there were gods for every city, so his city had its god who cared for and watched over its people; the king was his representative or even his son God gave rain and fruitful seasons to the farmer and prosperity to the merchant; he saved from sickness and calamity; he appointed judges to give true judgments and governors to rule uprightly. In turn the king reared the temple to the glory of the gods and established the priesthood to offer daily sacrifice of grain and cattle to them; he gave to the gods of the spoils of war and of the harvest, and hither the people brought their gifts and paid their vows. Had you asked the Babylonian who was this God, he would have replied: "Bel, 'the Lord'; or the Sun, or the Moon, or the Storm Wind, or the Watery Deep—all gods of power afar off. Nevertheless they are very watchful of man, who, often sinful and deserving of punishment, feels himself dependent on them, and comes to them with psalms and prayers of penitence when they have brought plague and sorrow upon him for his sin." To the same question the Egyptian would have replied: "Re,* the Sun, who moves daily over the sky in his boat scattering blessings upon his children, before whom flowers spring up and fields bloom, whom we praise in the morning at his rising and at even in his setting—and a thousand other gods of animals and plants who love us and are ever

General Ideas of Gods.

The Babylonian Gods.

The Egyptian Gods.

* Pronounced *Ray.*

near to bless us by their mysterious presence and favor."

The Future Life. And had you asked about the life after death the Babylonian would have shaken his head and spoken of the future as dark and sad when the spirit, torn from the body, goes down to the dusky abode of the dead, to drag out a miserable existence. But the Egyptian, with hopeful face, would have told you how to keep the body as an eternal abode of the spirit by mummifying it and putting it in a deep tomb far from decay and disturbance; or he would have spoken of the fields of Aaru, a happier Egypt beyond the sky, where, after passing through the trials of the underworld, by the aid of the god Osiris and the power of the Book of the Dead, or in the sunboat of the god Re, the soul would at last be united with the body in a blissful immortality.

REVIEW EXERCISES. 1. Mention some things peculiar to Egyptian culture? 2. Why were the scribes important? 3. What is meant by papyrus, deben, nome, cuneiform, feudal, shekel, hieroglyphic, dynasty? 4. Name with dates the grand divisions of ancient history. 5. At about what time were the Pyramids built?

SELECT LIST FOR READING. 1. The Early Babylonian Cities. Goodspeed, pp. 49-53. 2. Elamite Invasions of Babylonia. Goodspeed, pp 66-70. 3. Babylonian Civilization. (*a*) Family Life Government, Goodspeed, pp 79-85. (*b*) Industries, Goodspeed, pp 73-79. (*c*) Literature, Goodspeed, pp 31-36, 86-91. (*d*) Babylonian Art, Goodspeed, pp. 94-101. 4. How the Early Egytians Lived. (*a*) Industries and Sources of National Income, Breasted, pp 30-33, 88-92 (*b*) Family and Homes, Breasted, pp 83-88. (*c*) Burial Customs, Breasted, pp. 36-38, 65-73. (*d*) Religion, Breasted, pp. 47-48, 55-73. (*e*) The Egyptian Art, Breasted, pp. 95-102. 5. Growth and Change in the First Period of the Empire in Egypt. Breasted, pp. 195-206.

TOPICS FOR READING AND ORAL REPORT. 1. Egyptian Agriculture and Arts and Crafts. Erman, Life in Ancient

Egypt, pp. 425-520. 2. Babylonian Civilization. Murison, Babylonia and Assyria, ch 15. 3. Relations between Egypt and Babylonia. King, Sumer and Akkad, pp. 321 348. 4. What Countries Have Once Had a Feudal System? See Encyclopedia Britannica, articles "Feudalism" and "Japan." 5. Modern Irrigation in Egypt: the Assouan Dam. Cosmopolitan, Aug, 1901; Idler, 22, 257; Nature, 67, 184.

MAP AND PICTURE EXERCISES. 1. Draw a rough map of the ancient oriental world illustrating the crescent-shaped formation suggested in § 2   Locate as many countries and cities as possible. 2. From plate II, 1-4, try to enumerate the physical characteristics of the Semitic type of man. 3. From plate IV find as many illustrations as possible of the life described in §§ 18-34.

4.—THE EGYPTIAN (NEW) EMPIRE

1580-1150 B.C.

35. The Hyksos Invade Egypt.—The feudal kingdom of Egypt, after the brilliant days of the twelfth dynasty (§ 8), fell into decay. The nobles gained more power and rose up against their kings. Foreign peoples invaded the land and added to the confusion. Finally, not long after the Kassites entered Babylonia (§ 16), invaders from western Arabia and Syria burst into Egypt through the isthmus of Suez and took possession of the northern half of the land. They also made southern Egypt tributary, though the seat of their own power was in the north   From the name given to their leaders they are usually called the Hyksos.

Man'e-tho (§ 7n), as quoted in a writing of Josephus the Jew, tells among other things why this name was given to them. He says: "There came up from the east in a strange manner men of an ignoble race, who had the confidence to invade our country, and

easily subdued it by their power without a battle And when they
had our rulers in their hands, they burnt our cities and demolished
the temples of the gods and inflicted every kind of barbarity upon
the inhabitants, slaying some and reducing the wives and children
of others to a state of slavery. At length they made one of themselves king . . . He lived at Memphis and rendered both the upper
and the lower regions of Egypt tributary and stationed garrisons in

The Shep-
herd (?)
Kings.

places which were best adapted for that purpose. All this nation
was styled Hyksos, that is, Shepherd Kings; for the first syllable,
Hyk, in the sacred dialect denotes 'king,' and *sos* signifies 'shepherd,'
but this only according to the vulgar tongue; and of these is com-
pounded the name *Hyksos*."

36. Expulsion of the Hyksos.—The Hyksos ruled over
Egypt for a century (about 1675–1575 B.C.). The people adopted the manners and customs of the Egyptians,
and the kings ruled like the native Pharaohs. Yet the
Egyptians could not forget that they were foreigners
A rebellion broke out in the south, gathered strength, and
war was waged for years   The princes of Thebes were
leaders of the rebels, fighting for the deliverance of their
country and their gods. It was a fierce struggle. The
mummy of one of these princes, now in the Cairo Museum, shows a great slash on the head received appar-

The Siege
of Avaris.

ently in one of these battles. After, perhaps, half a century of fighting, the foreign princes who had made their
last stand in their capital A-va′ris, and had sustained there
a siege of many years' duration, were driven out of
Egypt into the northeast whence they had come. The
native Egyptians recovered their land, and the princes
of Thebes, who had led them so valiantly, had their reward. They became kings of Egypt.

37. The New Warlike Spirit.—The Egyptians hitherto
had been a peaceful people. They had enlarged their

domains in the early days chiefly by entering the penin- sula of Sinai and making expeditions up the Nile into Nubia. But now circumstances made it possible for them to do greater things. The Hyksos had brought the horse The Horse with them into Egypt,* and in war much more could be done by means of horses. Chariots could be employed, longer marches made. The Egyptian army had been trained in the new art of war and seasoned by the long and fierce struggle with the Hyksos The Pharaoh, their leader, had become a warrior eager for military glory. The gods of Egypt, represented by their priests, called for vengeance on their enemies and for the extension of their divine sway over the distant lands. So the Egyp- tians embarked on a new career—a career of conquest. Thereby they transformed Egypt from a kingdom into an Egypt an Empire empire, the second empire of the ancient world (§ 15).

38. The Eighteenth Dynasty. Thutmose III.—The conquering monarchs make up the eighteenth dynasty (1580–1350 B C.). The greatest of them was Thut'mose III, who ruled in the sixteenth century. He made at least sixteen campaigns into the northeast through the regions on the eastern coast of the Mediterranean. Twice, perhaps thrice, he reached the Euphrates, and The Eu- phrates an Egyptian River. even crossed the river into Mesopotamia. The Egyp- tian empire reached from central Nubia in the south to the northern mountains and the Euphrates. Egypt suc- ceeded Babylonia in supremacy over Syria.

Thutmose III had a long account of his expeditions written on the walls of one of his temples in Thebes. His first campaign lasted

* The horse had been known in Egypt and in Europe at some period exceedingly remote, but it disappeared in both places before the dawn of history.

about six months, from April to October, during which he covered about two thousand miles and fought at least one great battle at Megiddo. The following is the king's description of the battle:

"Command was given before his whole army, saying, 'Prepare ye, make ready your weapons, for we move to fight with the vile enemy to-morrow.' The baggage of the chiefs was prepared and the provisions of the followers, and the sentinels of the army were spread abroad; they said 'Firm of heart, firm of heart, watchful of head, watchful of head' On the twenty-first day of the month, even the same as the royal coronation, early in the morning command was given to the entire army to advance. His Majesty went forth in his chariot of electrum adorned with his weapons of war. His Majesty was in the midst of them, the god Amon being the protection to his body and strength to his limbs. Then his Majesty prevailed over them at the head of his army When they saw his Majesty prevailing over them, they fled headlong to Megiddo, as if terrified by spirits; they left their horses and their chariots of silver and gold, and were drawn up by hauling them by their clothes into this city, for the men shut the gates of this city upon them. The fear of his Majesty entered their hearts, their arms failed, their mighty men lay along like fishes on the ground. The great army of his Majesty drew around to count their spoil. The whole army rejoiced, giving praise to Amon for the victory that he had given to his son, and they glorified his Majesty, extolling his victories."

39. Wars with the Hittites.—The victorious kings of the eighteenth dynasty held this region for a century. Their rule culminated in the reign of Ikh-na'ton (1375–1358 B.C.) who, breaking free from all the national traditions, founded a new religion and a new capital and tried in vain to recast Egyptian art, society and customs. Then a new enemy came down from the north, the Hittites, who began to contest the possession of the northern half of Syria. The famous Pharaohs, Se'ti I (about 1313–1292 B.C.) and Ram'ses II (1292–1225 B C), of the nineteenth dynasty, fought with them for many years.

Ramses II.

At last Ramses made a treaty with their king, Khe-ta'sar, which was the basis of a lasting peace between the two peoples. From this time the Egyptian empire practically extended only to the Lebanon mountains. A century later the Hittite kingdom in Syria disappeared before the advance of a horde of peoples migrating down the coast of the Mediterranean from Asia Minor (about 1170 B.C.). Ramses III, of the twentieth dynasty, was then on the Egyptian throne. He summoned all his forces to withstand the invaders, and dispersed them in a great battle on the northern border of his empire. Pharaohs continued to rule in the Nile valley, but their power over Syria was soon lost. Thus the second imperial state of the ancient east disappeared (1150 B.C.). Ramses III. Decline of the Egyptian Empire.

40. Results of Empire upon Egypt.—As a result of its conquests, Egypt had become very rich in gold and slaves. Hence, money and cheap laborers were plentiful for building operations Temples of unequalled grandeur were reared. The capital city, Thebes, was the scene of the most splendid exhibition of this architecture. The temples on the sites now known as Karnak and Luxor (parts of the city of Thebes) were and have ever since remained among the wonders of the world. Every great king of these dynasties enlarged and beautified them, wrote an account of his exploits upon their walls and enriched their priests by splendid offerings. The Karnak temple—the work mainly of Seti I and Ramses II—was a quarter of a mile long and 379 feet wide at the main front—more than twice as large as St. Peter's Church at Rome. Am'on, the god specially worshipped at Thebes, became the great god of Egypt, beside whom other gods seemed of no account. The kings set up colossal statues Architecture.

of themselves in the temples.   One of Ramses II, found in northern Egypt, was some ninety feet high and weighed about nine hundred tons.   Abundant wealth gave also the leisure to study and write; hence the literature of the Egyptian empire is most abundant.   Love-songs, hymns to the gods, theological works, romances, and letters are among the writings preserved.   One of the most famous is a kind of epic history describing the deeds of Ramses II in a battle with the Hittites.   From the name of the scribe who copied it, it is called the Poem of Pentaur.

The most stirring part of it presents Ramses II cut off from his army and surrounded by the enemy.   Ramses calls upon his god· "How is this, my father Amon?   Does a father then forget his son? I have done nothing, indeed, without thee.   He is miserable who knows not god.   Have I not erected to thee many monuments, in order to fill thy temple with my spoil?   I call to thee, my father Amon   I am in the midst of many people, I am quite alone, my foot-soldiers and my chariot force have forsaken me.   When I called to them, I found that Amon was better to me than millions of foot-soldiers and hundreds of thousands of chariots.   The works of men are as nothing;   Amon is more precious than they.   Do I not call from the ends of the world?   Yet Re has heard me, he comes to me when I call.   He calls from behind me 'Thou art not alone, I am with thee, I, thy father Re;   my hand is with thee.'   I take heart again.   What I desire to do, that happens.   Behold, none of them are able to fight before me, their hearts melt, their arms fall, they cannot shoot   I slay them according to my will.   Not one of them looks behind him and not one of them turns round.   He who falls of them rises no more."

41. The Weakness of Egypt.—Yet in the higher arts Egypt in this period was not superior.   Bigness rather than beauty was the ideal of art and architecture.   Fine writing and swelling words rather than clear and deep thought were the rule. Indeed, the whole structure of the state and society was artificial and not a natural growth. The building was made great and splendid by slave labor and foreign money; the Egyptians were enfeebled by the luxury which they enjoyed. In all that constitutes true greatness Egypt was not so strong as in the earlier days

42. **Organization of the Empire.**—Egypt in these centuries better deserved the name of an empire than did its predecessor, Babylonia. It was more thoroughly organized. Whenever the Pharaoh conquered a city-state of Syria, he laid upon its king the obligation to pay a yearly sum as tribute. Sometimes he took the king's eldest son to his court to be educated. Garrisons of Egyptian troops were placed in some cities, and governors were appointed in certain districts. Even communities of Egyptian people went out to dwell in towns of Syria. Such bodies of settlers are called *colonies*. The Pharaoh kept in close relations with his governors and subject-kings through constant correspondence with them and by sending out inspectors from time to time to examine into their affairs.

43. A mass of this official correspondence with two kings of the eighteenth dynasty was discovered in Egypt recently at Tel-el-Amarna, and is called the Tel-el-Amarna Letters. They contain despatches from governors and princes of Syria. Some are from the king of Jerusalem; other letters are from the rulers of Babylonia and Assyria, with replies from the Pharaoh. All of these are written in the Babylonian character—a fact which shows how deeply Babylonian civilization had influenced the ancient world. Even Egyptian kings wrote to their Syrian subjects in Babylonian. It was the diplomatic* language of the day

Tel-el-
Amarna
Letters.

* The language which different states use in dealing with each other. Diplomacy is the science of *international* relations.

44. The Home Government.—Egypt as an empire was very different from the Egypt of the preceding feudal period. The feudal nobility had been wiped out by the invasion of the Hyksos and the wars of deliverance. Their property fell into the hands of the king, who now became the one proprietor of all Egypt. This property he rented out to the people for a percentage of its product. Some of it he gave to the generals of his armies. They were

The Army. his officials, governors and judges. The army was now a standing institution, under arms at all times. Though not so at first, it gradually came to be made up in large part of foreigners who were paid for their military service. Such soldiers are called "mercenaries." A mercenary army was a dangerous machine, since the soldiers were held to the imperial service only by the money that they gained from it. The spoils of the wars made

The Priests. many of them very rich. The religious officials, the priests, also profited by the wars, since a part of the spoils of victory was given to the gods of Egypt, whose ministers they were. The temples became wealthy and powerful establishments. Their property was not taxed, and their people did not have to perform military service. Thus it came about that the chief elements in the state were now three—the king, the army and the priests.

45. An Ancient "Corner" in Wheat.—In the Old Testament the change in the position of the king is said to have been brought about by a foreign prime minister, the Israelite statesman and hero, Joseph. The Book of Genesis says: "He gathered up food in the cities, corn as the sand of the sea And there was famine and the people cried unto Pharaoh for bread, and Pharaoh said: 'Go unto Joseph; what he saith to you, do.' And Joseph sold unto the Egyptians. And when the money was all spent, Joseph said 'Give your cattle.' And they brought their cattle and Joseph gave them bread in exchange. And they said: 'Buy us and our land for bread, and we and our land will be servants unto Pharaoh.' So Joseph bought all the land of Egypt for Pharaoh Only the land of the priests he bought not; for the priests had a portion from Pharaoh, and did eat their portion: wherefore they sold not their land. Then Joseph said unto the people: 'At the harvests ye shall give a fifth unto Pharaoh and four parts shall be your own.' And Joseph made it a statute concerning the land of Egypt unto this day that Pharaoh should have the fifth; only the land of the priests alone became not Pharaoh's."

46. Later Egypt—to Alexander.—While the empire of Egypt was falling away the priests got the upper hand. After ruling for about a century by the side of a series of weakling kings, they finally seized the government (1090 B.C.) and reigned openly. Next came the turn of the army and for over two hundred years (945-712 B C.) the Libyan mercenaries lorded it vigorously over Egypt. An end was put to their domination by the Nubians (Ethiopians) who, pushing down the valley, mastered it to the mouth of the Nile; but their sway was still insecure when the Assyrians came and added Egypt to their dominions (670 B.C.). In the interval between the dissolution of the Assyrian and the rise of the Persian empire, Egypt enjoyed a brief period of independence, and under the intelligent rule of Psam-met'i-cus I and II and A-ma'sis of Sa'is, the valley of the Nile was opened to Greek enterprise and the Milesian colony of Nau'cra-tis was planted in the delta. This settlement might have anticipated the later prosperity of Alexandria had it not been that in 525 B.C. Cam-by'ses, the second Persian king, conquered Egypt, and, making it into a province of his vast empire, postponed by two centuries the Greek exploitation of the Nile valley. A new chapter in the history of

Rule of the Priests, Soldiers and Foreigners.

ancient Egypt was opened on its occupation by Alexander the Great in 332 B.C.

47. Egypt a Mummy.—The period of one thousand years from the death of Ikhnaton onward was one of utter stagnation in Egypt. For generation after generation life followed the old forms. Dynasty after dynasty came and went, but the great body of the people remained unchanged in their ideas and habits. The last word had been said on all the problems of human life by religion. To change any custom was sacrilege. Freedom of thought and invention there was none. The nation itself was mummified. It had nothing to teach the Greeks when they came in contact with it: at most it offered an impressive and suggestive spectacle for their curious observation.

REVIEW EXERCISES. 1. For what were the following famous: Ramses II, Thutmose III, Ramses III? 2. Who were the Hyksos, the Hittites? 3. What is meant by Tel-el-Amarna Letters, nome, empire? 4. For what are the following places noted: Karnak, Assur, Memphis, Luxor, Nippur, Meggido? 5. When did Ramses II live? 6. At about what date was the departure of the Israelites from Egypt? 7. Describe the causes for and the events in Egypt's period of decline. 8. How was Egypt mummified? 9. Through what channels did the Greeks have intercourse with the Egyptians?

SELECT LIST FOR READING. 1. The Hyksos: Their Effect upon Egypt. Breasted, pp. 175-184. 2. Amenhotep III, the Last Great Egyptian Emperor. Breasted, pp 248-263. 3. Ikhnaton, an Individual. Breasted, pp. 269-289 4. The Influence of Asiatic Conditions upon Egypt. Breasted, pp 373-383. 5. The "Downfall of Egypt." Breasted, pp 412-418.

TOPICS FOR READING AND ORAL REPORT. 1. Invasion of the Hyksos. Murison, Egypt, §§ 36-40, Rawlinson, Story of Egypt, chs. 8-9. 2. Thutmose III. Murison, Egypt, §§ 45-47; Rawlinson, Story of Egypt, pp. 189-206 3. Ramses II. Murison, Egypt, § 55; Wendel, pp. 87-95, Rawlinson, Story of Egypt,

pp 238–252, Sayce, Ancient Empires, pp 43–46   **4. The Hittites
and Their Empire.** Encyclopedia Britannica, article "Hittites."
5. The Temples of Thebes. Rawlinson, Story of Egypt, see index under "Temple of Ammon," of "Karnak"   **6. Egyptian
Civilization.** Munson, Egypt, chs 13–15.   **7. The Book of the
Dead.** Munson, Egypt, ch. 12   **8. Apply the following utterance of an Egyptian Sage to Egyptian history of this Epoch:**
"If thou hast become great after having been little, harden not thy
heart.   Thou art only become the steward of the good things of
God."

5.—THE SYRIAN STATES
1150–900 B.C.

48. New Immigrations.—The passing away of the
Egyptian empire about 1150 B.C. was not followed—as
might have been expected—by the advance of the states
of Assyria and Babylonia to seize her lost supremacy.
One of those tremendous overflows of people from central and northern Arabia, such as took place from time
to time when there was not food enough in the desert to
supply the population, flooded the northern districts of
Mesopotamia and Syria.   These peoples, called the Ara- The
means, thus cut off communication between east and Arameans
west.   At the same time a similar horde, called the The Chal
Chaldeans (Kaldi), entered southern Babylonia.   Both deans.
Assyria and Babylonia, therefore, had all they could do
to defend themselves and could not advance westward.

49. The Opportunity of Syria.—One region of the ancient world had now the opportunity to assert itself—
that between the Nile and the Euphrates—Syria.   Here
was the scene of the attempts at empire in the next two
centuries (1150–900 B C).   During this time Syria was
the real centre of historical life.   Four peoples of this

region came forward and made up the history of the time. These were the Phœnicians, the Philistines, the Israelites and the Arameans of Damascus.

50. The Phœnicians.—The Lebanon mountains, as they run down along the eastern Mediterranean from the north for two hundred miles, throw out spurs from time to time into the sea and leave here and there spaces of coast from one to five miles wide and six to twenty

Land. miles long. In these petty patches of earth, with the high mountains at their back and the blue sea before them, the Phœnicians cultivated the fertile soil, built

Occupa-
tions. cities and learned to sail the sea. Beginning by trading with each other and with the people of the interior, they went on to make voyages to more distant parts and to carry the wares of the east to the less advanced western lands. When the Egyptian kings ceased to rule over

Tyre's
Commercial
Supremacy. them, they were free to act for themselves. At first their most important city was Si'don, but at an early date Tyre, situated on a rocky island about half a mile from shore, obtained the leadership among them and became the commercial centre of the east and west. The merchandise of Babylonia, Assyria, Egypt, Arabia, Armenia, not to speak of the lesser peoples, was brought to Tyre. Raw materials were received and turned into manufactured articles in Tyrian workshops—metal into arms, toilet articles and furniture; wool into cloths which were marvellously colored by means of the dye made from shell-fish found on the Phœnician coast. All these materials were taken out in Phœnician ships and exchanged for native products at trading posts established at dif-

Phœnician
Coloniza-
tion. ferent points on the Mediterranean. Already the Phœnicians had settled in the island of Cyprus, seventy miles

to the west. Some points in the Ægean sea were touched, but the Greeks were too strong there, and the Phœnicians went on to the regions of the western Mediterranean. The north African coast, Malta, Sicily, Sardinia, the Bal'e-ar'ic islands, were occupied. Spain, with its mines of precious metal, was a rich centre of Phœnician enterprise. Out into the Atlantic fared their adventurous ships, southward to the latitude of the Canary islands and northward to Britain.

51. **Phœnician Trading.**—Herodotus describes a typical instance of Phœnician trading: "When they have come to a land and un-load the merchandise from their ships, they set it in order along the beach and return aboard their ships. Then they raise a smoke, and the natives of the land, seeing the smoke, come to the shore and lay down gold as much as they think the goods are worth; then they withdraw quite a distance. The Carthaginians upon that come ashore again and look; if they think the gold enough, they take it and go their way; but if not, they go on board again and wait. The others approach and add more gold till they satisfy them They say that neither party wrongs the other; for they themselves do not touch the gold till it comes up to the value of their wares, nor do the others lay hands on the goods till the gold has been taken away."

52. **The Chief Colonies.**—Most of their settlements were temporary trading posts, but in some districts, where wealth and prosperity seemed to be constant, they established permanent colonies. The most famous of these were Cit'i-um in Cyprus, Utica and Carthage in north Africa, Ga'des (Cadiz) in Spain and the cities of western Sicily. The tie between the colony and the home-land was close. The mother city usually main-tained a political and religious supremacy. Thus Tyre under its kings was during these centuries the head of a flourishing colonial empire.

A Colonial Empire.

53. Phœnician Services to Civilization.—The Phœnicians carried things more valuable than the merchandise of the east to the western world, for they also made known to it the higher arts of life. Thus the systems of weights and measures, the achievements of eastern art, and, above all, the alphabet, became the possession of the peoples of the Mediterranean The Phœnicians improved upon these things before they handed them

The Alphabet.

on. This is especially true of the alphabet. In the interests of their business activities they so simplified and modified the various modes of writing acquired by them from the eastern nations, that we are not able to say from which one of the eastern systems, whether the Egyptian, or the Babylonian, or the Arabian, the Phœnician alphabet is derived We only know that the Phœnician alphabet with its twenty-two phonetic characters is the basis of ours.

54. The Philistines.—The Phœnicians made their conquests upon the shores of the Mediterranean in the peaceful ways of trade. Not so arose the other great

Origin.

states of Syria. Closely connected with the mighty migration from the coast of Asia Minor in the time of Ramses III (§ 39), a new people came, possibly from Crete, and seized the broad plain which lies at the southeastern corner of the Mediterranean. The Philistines —called by Ramses III the Peleset—though they were evidently not Semites, accepted the language and customs of the Semitic cities which they ruled.* As these cities lay on the main routes of trade from Egypt into Asia, their lords, the Philistines, were rich and power-

* The five cities of the Philistines were Gaza, Gath, Ashdod, Askalon and Ekron.

PLATE VII

Brick of Hammurabi, Recording
the Building of a Temple

Cretan Pictographic Writing from
Phæstos

Clay Tablet, with Linear Script,
Palace of Minos, Cnossos, Crete

The Rosetta Stone

ANCIENT SYSTEMS OF WRITING

ful and flourished exceedingly. They were a fighting folk, far superior in weapons and the arts of war to the peaceful Semites about them, and soon began to make their power felt throughout the whole maritime plain from Mt. Carmel in the north to the highlands in the east. They began to push up into the interior and came _{Expansion} into conflict with a people that had settled the mountain valleys some time after they themselves had conquered the plain. This people was Israel, one of the tribes known as the Hebrews (§ 4).

55. The Hebrews Appear.—At first the Hebrews had wandered through the southern part of Syria (Palestine), but in the time of the Hyksos kings they entered northern Egypt. There, after the Hyksos had been driven out, they were oppressed, by Ramses II, it is thought, and in the last years of the nineteenth dynasty, led by the hero Moses, they escaped into the eastern desert, delivered from the Egyptians by Jehovah their god at the crossing of the Red sea (about 1200 B.C.). Israel, after escaping from Egypt and wandering for a Israel. generation in the desert south of Syria, moved to the east of the Dead sea, crossed the Jordan river and burst into the highlands of Palestine about 1150 B.C. Here, as we have seen, he came into collision with the Philistines.

In the first encounters Israel was badly beaten, although in fact, as will soon appear, the Philistine victories were only temporary. A Palestine. proof of the importance and renown of the Philistines is seen in the fact that the name by which southern Syria is known—Palestine— is derived from the Philistines.

The Israelites were a wild, wandering folk with a Religion. simple faith in their god, Jehovah, who had given them, through Moses his servant, the Ten Commandments, and was for them the one supreme lord of justice and truth, their deliverer and friend. From him they derived their moral law which they have passed on to the Christian world.

The Ten Commandments are the noblest brief collection of the laws of right living that has come down from the ancient world. They are the following:

I am Jehovah thy God:

1. Thou shalt have none other gods before me.
2. Thou shalt not make unto thee a graven image.
3. Thou shalt not take the name of Jehovah thy god in vain.
4. Remember the Sabbath day to keep it holy.
5. Honor thy father and thy mother.
6. Thou shalt do no murder.
7. Thou shalt not commit adultery.
8. Thou shalt not steal.
9. Thou shalt not bear false witness.
10. Thou shalt not covet.

56. National Feeling.—After a century occupied in overcoming the people of the region, called the Canaanites, and settling down as farmers, they began to desire a national life and an organized government. What brought this to a head was the attack and temporary supremacy of the Philistines (§ 55). A religious leader, Samuel, organized a band of prophets who went about preaching deliverance through Jehovah and stirred up the people to rebellion. He also presented to them a king whom Jehovah had chosen, Saul, a frank, impetuous, mighty man of valor. He became the first king of Israel (about 1050 B.C.), and beat back the Philistines.

Samuel the Prophet.

Saul the Warrior.

57. David the Hero.—After his death David was chosen king, another heroic and magnetic warrior, who was also a man of genius and statesmanship. He built up an army with which he defeated his enemies, extended the authority of Israel over neighboring peoples and made its influence felt as far north as the Euphrates river. His greatest work was the establishment of the national capital at Jerusalem, where the king dwelt, the

Jerusalem.

court assembled, justice was administered and Jehovah was worshipped as the national god.

58. Solomon the Organizer.—David was followed by his son Solomon (about 975 B.C.). As his father had been the founder of the state, so he became its organizer. He had a masterly mind for politics and administration. To break up sectional feeling and to weld the state firmly together, he divided the land into twelve districts as the basis for his administration. He instituted regular taxes, had a standing army, entered into alliances with neighboring states. One of the most important of these alliances was that with Hiram, king of Tyre, the most brilliant of the Phœnician rulers. Together they made commercial expeditions on the Red sea and the Indian ocean. Solomon also allied himself with the king of Egypt and married his daughter. He made trading alliances with the peoples of the north. Thus Israel became a nation among the other nations of the world. Solomon used his abundant wealth to strengthen and beautify his kingdom, building cities and fortresses at strategic points for trade and defence. Jerusalem was the object of his special attention. There he built palaces, walls and the famous Temple, the wonder and pride of his people, for the worship of Jehovah. When he died, Israel was the leading state of Syria, and a splendid future seemed to be assured. *Partnership with Hiram.* *The Temple.*

59. Weakness of Solomon's Régime.—But Solomon was in advance of his people and his time. The people resented his strict government with its taxes, its military service, its forced labor on the palaces and forts. They had been only two centuries out of the free life of the desert, and the memory of it remained. They did

not care to play the imperial rôle which Solomon de-
signed for them.　When after his death his son continued his father's policy, the northern tribes refused to
recognize him and elected another king, leaving him to
The Dis-　be king over his own tribe, Judah.　This event is known
ruption.　as the Disruption (about 930 B.C); it was the death-
blow to the position of Israel as a world-power.　Henceforth there were two kingdoms on the highlands of Palestine—Israel in the north and Judah in the south.
The capital of Judah remained at Jerusalem.　Israel's
new capital was placed at Samaria.　Israel's kings tried
to play the part of David and Solomon on a smaller
scale, while Judah was content to lead a quiet and secluded life under the descendants of those great rulers.

60. The Arameans.—By this time (925 B.C) the Arameans, who had migrated into Syria (§ 48), had become settled.　Both David and Solomon had come into
At　contact with them.　One of their leaders got possession
Damascus.　of the city of Damascus, where he set up a kingdom
(about 975 B.C.).　Damascus was the chief trading
centre of Syria, the halting-place of caravans, where
merchants from Egypt and the east met to exchange
their wares and to supply the wandering tribes that
came in from the neighboring desert.　The city was
beautiful for situation, lying in the midst of a well-
watered and fertile valley on the edge of the desert, midway between the Mediterranean and the Mesopotamian
Growth.　valley, between Egypt and the Euphrates.　The Aramean kingdom planted at this strategic point soon be·
came powerful and began to lay its hand upon the dis-
Wars with　tricts round about.　Soon it came into touch with Israel,
Israel.　and the relations, at first friendly, passed later into en-

mity, each power striving for mastery over the land of Syria.

61. The End of Syrian Greatness.—Neither of these states, however, was destined for empire. The troubles that had held back the greater powers on the Euphrates and Tigris were over; the brief career of splendor for the kingdoms of Syria was at an end. Already Assyria was knocking at the gates of the west, and the conflicts of Philistia, Judah, Israel and Damascus were swallowed up in the fiercer struggle of all against the oncoming Assyrian might. Thus a new period of the history of the ancient east was ushered in.

During the period of the Assyrian advance into Syria a series of great political and religious leaders appeared among the Jews These men were known as the Prophets They taught that Jehovah was the Lord, not of Judah alone, but of the whole world; that He was using the Assyrian [and afterward the Chaldean and Persian] kings as instruments to punish the Jews for their sins. They, therefore, preached not resistance to their national foes but righteousness, repentance of sins and careful observance of the will of God. The Prophets were the greatest thinkers which the world of the ancient east produced.

The Prophets.

REVIEW EXERCISES. 1. Who were the Arameans, the Kassites, the Canaanites, the Chaldeans? 2. For what were the following places noted: Carthage, Damascus, Jerusalem, Thebes, Gades, Tyre, Gaza? 3. For what were the following persons famous: Solomon, Hammurabi, Thutmose? 4. Prepare a map showing the extent of Phœnician colonization.

SELECT LIST FOR READING. 1. Syria's International Relations. Goodspeed, pp. 131–136. 2. The Philistines. Goodspeed, pp. 182–184. 3. Conquests in Syria by Shalmaneser II. Goodspeed, pp. 213–216. 4. Sennacherib's Excursion against Syria. Goodspeed, pp. 268–272.

TOPICS FOR READING AND ORAL REPORT. 1. The Phœnicians. Sayce, Ancient Empires, pp. 178–209, Ragozin, Assyria,
ch. 3. 2. Moses and His Work. Encyclopedia Britannica, article "Moses." 3. The Reign of David. Encyclopedia Britannica,
article "David"; Kent, History of Hebrew People, United Kingdom, pp. 136–168. 4. The Story of the Disruption. 1 Kings,
ch. 12, Kent, Divided Kingdom, pp. 1–25. 5. The Temple at
Jerusalem. Encyclopedia Britannica, article "Temple", International Encyclopedia, article "Temple", Kent, United Kingdom, ch. 13.

6.—THE EMPIRE OF ASSYRIA

900–606 B.C.

Early
Conditions.

62. Assyria.—The kingdom of Assyria since the days
of its beginning (§ 17) had fought with Babylonia, at
first for its own existence and then for mastery in the
Mesopotamian valley.　Meanwhile it had pushed up the
Tigris and taken firm possession of the country between
the upper course of the river and the eastern mountains.
Besides the city of Assur, its chief centre was Nin'e-veh,
destined to be the capital of the empire.　In the northeastern upland corner of Mesopotamia, life was not so
easy as in Babylonia; the climate was colder, the land
less fertile, wild beasts plentiful, the mountaineers threatening.　Hence, the Assyrians had to fight with nature
and man for their life, and by this training became
hardy and warlike.　They had to make their way by
sword and spear rather than by plough and spade.

63. Assyrian Expansion.—Their early efforts at expansion were checked by the Aramean migration into
Mesopotamia (§ 48), which forced them back into their
own borders and thus gave Syria its opportunity for independent empire.　But by 900 B.C. the Arameans had

settled down and Assyria lifted her head. Under a vig- Advance toward the West.
orous and fearless king, whose name was Ash'ur-nats'ir-
pal', the conquering movement began anew. He brought
northern Mesopotamia, as far as the Euphrates, and
southern Armenia under the yoke. His son crossed the
Euphrates and made northern Syria subject. His great-
grandson carried the Assyrian arms to the southwest as
far as Philistia. Thus by 800 B.C. the Assyrian armies
had marched throughout the length and breadth of Syria.

64. **Conquest of Babylon.**—The next century saw the
downfall of Babylonia, when the Assyrian conqueror,
Tig'lath-pi-le'zer III, in 728 B.C., became king in Baby-
lon. Fifty years later Egypt became subject (670 B.C.); Occupation of Egypt and of the North.
in another generation Elam was conquered (645 B.C.).
Meanwhile Assyrian armies had marched into the
mountains surrounding the Mesopotamian plain. In
the northwest they penetrated into Asia Minor; in the
northeast they reached the Caspian sea. In extent and
power Assyria was the mightiest empire that the ancient
world had known.

65. **Assyria at Its Height.**—Assyria reached this splendid height during the reigns of four rulers, the first
of whom was Sargon (722–705 B.C.), who was followed
in regular succession by Sen-nach'er-ib (705–681 B.C.),
E'sar-had'don (681–668 B.C.), and Ash'ur-ban'i-pal'
(668–626 B.C.), each the son of his predecessor. Under An Empire
these kings Assyria became an imperial state. Conquered
countries were organized into districts under the rule
of an imperial officer who had a military force at his
command and was responsible for order and peace; he
collected the taxes and administered justice   Such districts we call provinces. Assyria was the first to intro-

duce provincial government—a great advance in im
perial administration. The Assyrians also invented the
plan of removing the inhabitants of a city or district
from their homes and putting in their places other people
from a distant part of the empire. This is called deportation. It destroyed the old feeling of local patriotism
and made people more willing to accept the rule of the
central government. Thus the empire was built up
solidly and all parts of it united under the rule of the
great king at Nineveh.

66. Rebellions of Vassals.—That Assyria's government of conquered countries was not perfect is shown
by the many rebellions that arose among them. Whenever they had the slightest encouragement to revolt,
they flew to arms. Thus Syria was constantly being
stirred up by Egypt, which during these centuries was
under the rule of the Libyan kings, and was trying to
get back its lost empire. In 745 B.C. Damascus and
Israel joined in such rebellion; as a result Tiglathpileser
III put an end to Damascus and severely punished Israel
The latter, however, rebelled again, and perished at the
hands of Sargon in 722 B.C. All the better classes of
citizens were deported and the state became an Assyrian province.

The king describes his capture of Samaria and punishment of
Israel in these words: "The city of Samaria I besieged; 27,290
inhabitants of it I carried away captive; fifty chariots in it I took
for myself, but the remainder (of the people) I allowed to retain their
possessions   I appointed my governor over them, and the tribute
of the preceding king I imposed upon them."

67. Rebellions in Judah.—Judah's king, Ahaz, had
already submitted to Assyria, but his son and successor,

Hez'e-ki'ah, joined in a rebellion of the Syrian states,
which brought Sennacherib on the scene in 701 B.C.
He punished the rebels severely, but met with a disaster
which compelled him to retire without capturing Jerusalem.

The Old Testament describes the disaster thus: "It came to pass
that night that the angel of Jehovah went forth and smote in the
camp of the Assyrians an hundred fourscore and five thousand:,
and when men arose early in the morning, behold, they were all
dead corpses. So Sennacherib, king of Assyria, departed, and went
and returned and dwelt at Nineveh" (2 Kings 19: 35, 36).

68. Rebellions in Babylonia.—A mighty revolt arose
in Babylonia against Ashurbanipal. The Chaldeans
(§ 48) had been unceasing enemies of Assyria ever since
her entrance into Babylonia, and now secured the aid
of the Elamites (§ 5). At this time a brother of the Assyrian king was governor of Babylonia; he made common cause with them and invited other subject peoples
to join the conspiracy. The storm broke in 652 B.C.;
only by the most tremendous efforts did Ashurbanipal
gain the victory. The faithless brother perished in the
flames of his palace, and the other rebels, with their
allies, were fearfully punished.

69. Assyrian Civilization.—The kings of the family of
Sargon were wealthy and proud monarchs. Magnificent Architect
palaces were built by them at Nineveh. Sargon founded ure.
in connection with his palace a city capable of holding
eighty thousand people. The palace itself filled twenty-
five acres and had at least two hundred rooms. The Sculpture.
halls were lined with sculptured slabs of alabaster picturing the king's campaigns; at either side of the great
door-ways stood mighty winged bulls carved in stone.

The royal temple-tower with seven stories, each story faced with tiles of a color different from that of the others, rose out of the palace court one hundred and forty feet high.   Inscriptions describing the mighty deeds of the kings in war and peace were written on the palace

Libraries. walls or on great monuments standing in the courts.   In the palace of Ashurbanipal at Nineveh was a library consisting of tens of thousands of clay books arranged on shelves.   They consisted in part of official documents and also of the choicest religious, historical and scientific literature of the Babylonian and Assyrian world Ashurbanipal tells us of his youthful training, how "he acquired the wisdom of (the god) Nabu, learned all the knowledge of writing of all the scribes, and learned how to shoot with the bow, to ride on horses and in chariots

The Debt to and to hold the reins."   The Assyrians, however, were
Babylon. a practical, not a literary, people; they were content to accept all the learning of the Babylonians and did not add to it.   Their language and religion follow Babylonian models.   The god Ashur, the lord and patron of the state, the leader of the armies in war, stood at the head of the gods, the rest of whom have the same names and characteristics as those of Babylonia.   It is only just to add, however, that nothing comparable in vigor and composition to the Assyrian reliefs was produced by the earlier people.

70. **Assyrians as Administrators.**—The Assyrians were good warriors and excellent administrators.   They knew how to conquer and how to rule better than any people that had hitherto appeared   They broke down the separate nations of the east and welded them into a unity.   They spread abroad the civilization of the east

PLATE VII

An Assyrian Relief. Hunting Scene

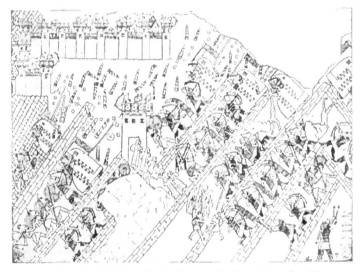

An Assyrian Relief. Battle Scene, the Storming of a City
TYPICAL ASSYRIAN SCENES

throughout the empire and extended commerce. But they did not know how to attach conquered peoples to themselves and give them something to do beyond paying taxes. They were just, but not generous; toward rebels and obstinate enemies they were outrageously cruel. Hence their empire, although superior to all its predecessors, did not endure.

Ashurnatsirpal describes the punishment of a rebellious city as follows: "I drew near to the city of Tela The city was very strong, three walls surrounded it The inhabitants trusted to their strong walls and numerous soldiers; they did not come down or embrace my feet With battle and slaughter I assaulted and took the city Three thousand warriors I slew in battle Their booty and possessions, cattle, sheep, I carried away; many captives I burned with fire. Many of their soldiers I took alive; of some I cut off hands and limbs; of others the noses, ears, and arms; of many soldiers I put out the eyes I reared a column of the living and a column of heads. I hung up on high their heads on trees in the vicinity of their city Their boys and girls I burned up in the flame I devastated the city, dug it up, in fire burned it; I annihilated it."

71. The Fall of the Assyrian Empire.—The fall of Assyria was sudden and startling. At the death of Ashurbanipal, in 626 B.C., the empire seemed strong But on the eastern mountains the Medes had been gathering from the far east, ready to descend upon the plains in irresistible power. For a time Assyria beat them off, but they returned. At last the province of Babylonia broke away and allied itself with the Medes. This was the finishing stroke. The next assault was successful. Nineveh was taken in 606 B.C., and, with its capture, Assyria vanished So complete was its collapse that the very site and name of Nineveh disappeared from the knowledge of mankind, only to be re-

covered by the investigations of scholars and travellers
in the last century

REVIEW EXERCISES. 1. For what were the following places
noted: Samaria, Assur, Nineveh, Tyre? 2. For what were
the following famous: Sargon of Assyria, Sargon of Agade,
Ashurbanipal, Ramses II? 3. What is meant by province,
colony, shekel? 4. When did Sargon of Assyria live? 5.
What is the date of the fall of Nineveh? 6. What is the difference between Syria and Assyria?

SELECT LIST FOR READING. 1. Earliest Assyria. Goodspeed, pp. 127–130 2. The Expansion under Tiglathpileser I.
Goodspeed, pp 160–172. 3. The Kings of the House of Ashurnatsirpal. Goodspeed, pp. 185–222 4. The Rule of Sargon II.
Goodspeed, pp. 243–264 5. The Fall of Assyria. Goodspeed,
pp. 320–330 6. The Palace of Sargon. Goodspeed, pp. 259–
261. 7. The Heirs of Assyria. Goodspeed, pp. 333–336.

TOPICS FOR READING AND ORAL REPORT. 1. The Rise of
Assyria. Murison, Babylonia and Assyria, ch. 3. 2. The Dynasty
of Sargon. Murison, Babylonia and Assyria, §§ 36–38 3. The
Fall of Assyria. Murison, Babylonia and Assyria, §§ 59–61 4.
The Palace of Sargon. Ragozin, Assyria, pp 278–294, Maspero,
Ancient Egypt and Assyria, ch 11. 5. The Library of Ashurban-
ipal. Ragozin, Chaldea, Introduction, ch 4; Maspero, Ancient
Egypt and Assyria, ch. 16. 6. "The Assyrian came down like
a wolf on the fold:" Does this line of Byron justly characterize
Assyrian warfare?

7.—THE MEDIAN, CHALDEAN (NEW BABY-
LONIAN) AND LYDIAN EMPIRES

606–539 B.C.

72. Medes and Babylonians Heirs of Assyria.—The
Medes, whose sudden attack overthrew the Assyrian
empire, had been sifting into the eastern mountains for
more than a century. They were the rear guard of a

migration of Indo-European peoples (§ 5) which was to overwhelm the Semitic world (§ 3) and usher in a new era. Their alliance with the rebellious province of Babylonia brought about Assyria's fall and meant the division of the world between the two victors. The Medes received the eastern and northern mountain regions, stretching from the Persian gulf to Asia Minor. The Babylonians obtained the Mesopotamian valley west of the Tigris and the Mediterranean coast-lands. Thus two empires sprang up where Assyria had once ruled.

73. The Chaldean Empire.—Babylonia's rebellion against Assyria really marked the victory of the Chaldeans (§ 48) in their long struggle with the Assyrians. The new Babylonian empire therefore was a Chaldean empire. It had a short career of splendor under its greatest king, Neb'u-chad-rez'zar (605–562 B.C.), who, secure from outside attack by his alliance with the Medes, devoted himself to the strengthening of his empire and the restoration of the land and cities of Babylonia. He had trouble with the subject kingdom of Judah, which rebelled several times and was finally destroyed, its capital, Jerusalem, burned to the ground and the Jews deported to Babylonia (586 B.C.). There they soon became an industrious and wealthy part of the population The king spent vast sums of money in fortifying and beautifying the city of Babylon. He surrounded it with a triple wall, built splendid palaces and made magnificent gardens for his Median wife. Babylon in his time was the largest, richest and most wonderful city of the ancient world. *Nebuchad-rezzar.* *End of Judah.*

74. The Median Empire.—Meanwhile the Median empire had been having a checkered experience. In the far northwest it had come into conflict with the expanding empire of Lydia, which had reduced all Asia Minor under its yoke. From the north new migrations of Scythians, a wild nomadic folk from central Asia, poured over the borders In the east and south a people closely related to the Medes was growing in numbers and importance. This people, called the Persians, was for a time in subjection to the Medes. Under the leadership of a great prince called Cyrus they rose up against their Median lords and succeeded in overthrowing them. In the year 550 B.C Cyrus became king of the combined peoples and founded the Persian empire.

Overthrown by Cyrus.

75. The Kingdom of Lydia.—The Babylonian rulers that followed Nebuchadrezzar set themselves with the other powers of the world in opposition to Cyrus. Of these the most important was the kingdom of Lydia. It owed its greatness to the dynasty of Gy′ges who at about 700 B.C. had set aside the old ruling family of Midas and put himself in its place. Gyges and his successors —in particular Crœ′sus (560–546 B.C)—conquered the entire coast of Asia Minor, making all the Greek cities, except Mi-le′tus, tributary. They also extended their sway to the Hellespont and in the interior to the Ha′lys river, thus becoming by far the most powerful and opulent state in the peninsula. The fame of Crœsus for wealth was so great that his name has become a synonym for riches. Through his realm lay a main highway from Assyria and Babylon to the Ægean sea and a mixed culture developed in Lydia which was at once sympathetic to Greece and the orient. The father of Crœsus had fought with the Medes but later had made a peace with them (585 B C) Now Crœsus joined with Egypt,

Crœsus

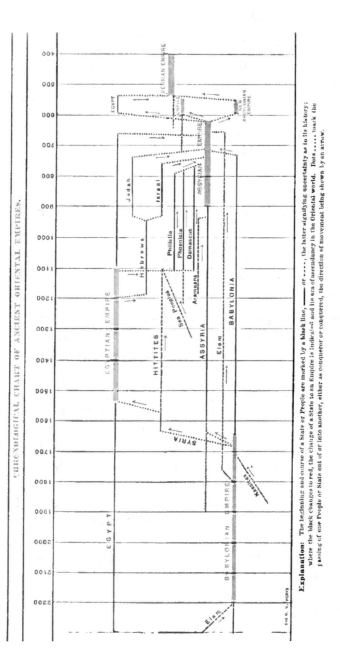

CHRONOLOGICAL CHART OF ANCIENT ORIENTAL EMPIRES.

Explanation: The beginning and course of a State or People are marked by a black line, ——— or ....., the latter signifying uncertainty as to its history; where the black changes to red, the change of a State to an Empire is indicated and its era of ascendancy in the Oriental world. Dots ..... mark the passing of one People or State out of or into another, either as conqueror or conquered, the direction of movement being shown by an arrow.

and even the leading Greek state, Sparta, in the endeavor to put a stop to the victorious career of Cyrus. It was all in vain. Cyrus defeated Crœsus, king of Lydia, and captured him and his capital, Sardis (546 B.C.). His Over-throw.

76. Fall of Babylon.—Babylon was then attacked, and yielded to him in 539 B.C. Thus the last Semitic empire of the Mesopotamian valley passed away and a new race took the reins of government over a wider world than had ever fallen within the bounds of an ancient state.

8.—THE EMPIRE OF PERSIA: ITS FOUNDING AND ORGANIZATION

550–500 B C.

77. The Persian Land and People.—Not only did the Persians belong to another race than the Semites of the Tigris-Euphrates valley, but the centre of empire was shifted by them farther to the east. This centre was the broad and lofty region east of the Tigris, from which the Za'gros mountains rise. These consist of a series of high ridges running north and south with fertile valleys between. The whole country lay on an average four thousand feet above the sea and suffered from wide extremes of climate. The people who inhabited it were vigorous and hardy, simple in manners, given to the raising of cattle and horses, or, in the few fertile valleys, to agriculture. Such were the Medes and Persians. Their capitals lay in this region—Ec-bat'a-na in the north, Per-sep'o-lis in the east and Susa in the west From this lofty land they went forth east and west to conquest and the founding of their empire.

78. Their Outlook.—To the east lay the mighty table-land of I'ran—1,000 miles long and 700 miles wide—girt about with high mountains. The greater part of it is desert; only in the north and northeast are fertile districts. On the slopes of the northern range along the southeastern coast of the Caspian sea lay Hyrcania; farther to the east was Parthia; far to the northeast in the valleys of the lofty eastern mountains on the route leading from Eastern Turkestan over to India was the rich land of Bactria. The western lands are familiar to us—the Mesopotamian valley, the coast-lands of the eastern Mediterranean leading down to Egypt, and in the northwest, Armenia, stretching away to the table-land of Asia Minor and the coasts of the Ægean sea. Such was the prospect opening before the Persians, eager to enter into the struggle for the possession of these broad lands

79. Cyrus.—Cyrus, as we have seen, was the leader of the Persians in this world-campaign; his conquest of the empires of Media, Lydia and Babylonia has already

been described During the remainder of his career he seems to have added the eastern lands to his domain and is said to have died in battle with an insignificant folk on the far northeastern borders (530 B.C.). At the time of his death his eldest son, Cambyses, was the heir to the throne, and a younger son, Bard'i-ya, was governor of the

northeastern lands. Cyrus made a deep impression upon the men of his own and of later times. A Jewish prophet hailed him as the one called by Jehovah to deliver the Jews from their Babylonian captivity. The Greek, Herodotus, calls him the father of his people, and says that in the estimation of the Persians he was above all comparison, being of all those of his time the bravest and the best beloved.

80. Cambyses.—For Cambyses, his successor (530–522 B.C.), one region remained unconquered—Egypt. This he added to his domains. Before departing for Egypt he had caused Bardiya to be put to death for fear of his attempting to seize the throne. But this did not prevent a pretender named Gau'ma-ta from stirring up rebellion during his absence in Egypt, and Cambyses died while returning to punish him. It seemed that the **Darius** pretender might succeed, but Darius, a cousin of Cambyses, was able to kill the rebel and to secure the throne after fierce struggles in the heart of the realm. He ruled for thirty-six years (521–485 B.C.) with splendid vigor and wise statesmanship.

81. The Organization of the Empire.—Persia, on the accession of Darius, occupied the entire known world of the east. This world was a natural geographical whole, some 3,000 miles in length and from 500 to 1,500 miles in width, surrounded for the most part by seas, mountains or deserts—"more than half the size of modern Europe." But little attention as yet had been given to its organization. This was the first and most memorable work of Darius. He followed the Assyrian system (§ 65) and improved upon it. The empire was divided into about **Officials** twenty provinces, each in charge of an official called the satrap. Two assistants were given him, a secretary and a general. All were appointed by the king; each was independent of the others and kept watch upon them. This arrangement made the three efficient and kept them faithful. Each province had to pay taxes according to **Taxes** its ability; so wisely was the income from all sources

organized that the sum realized may have been worth
fifty million dollars yearly. A system of coinage was instituted and three royal coins were minted—the gold daric
($5), the silver stater (50 cents) and the silver drachma
(25 cents)   The army was made up of an imperial guard,
of native Medes and Persians, the "Immortals," and of
troops from the various provinces. The strongest corps
of the service was the cavalry armed with the bow. In one
thing especially the Persian government was superior to
those that had gone before—in its provincial system. The
kings took special interest in the affairs of the province to
secure its peace and prosperity. Its customs and religion
were not interfered with. The satrap was enjoined to
secure justice and protection to the inhabitants   Trade
was encouraged. Roads were built and travel was made
safe and comfortable. A royal post carried messages from
the capital over these roads to the ends of the empire.

Herodotus describes the royal post in these words: "There is nothing mortal which accomplishes a journey with more speed than these
messengers, so skilfully has this been invented by the Persians; for
they say that according to the number of the days of which the entire journey consists, so many horses and men are set at intervals,
each man and horse appointed for a day's journey   Neither snow
nor rain nor heat nor darkness of night prevents each one of these
from accomplishing the task proposed to him with the very utmost
speed. The first rides and delivers the message with which he is
charged to the second, and the second to the third; and so it goes
through handed from one to the other "

82. The Early Persians.—Physically the early Persians were great, strong men, with thick hair and beard,
clear-eyed and active, in character they were pure-
hearted and brave. The common people were intensely

Army.

*Care of
Provinces.*

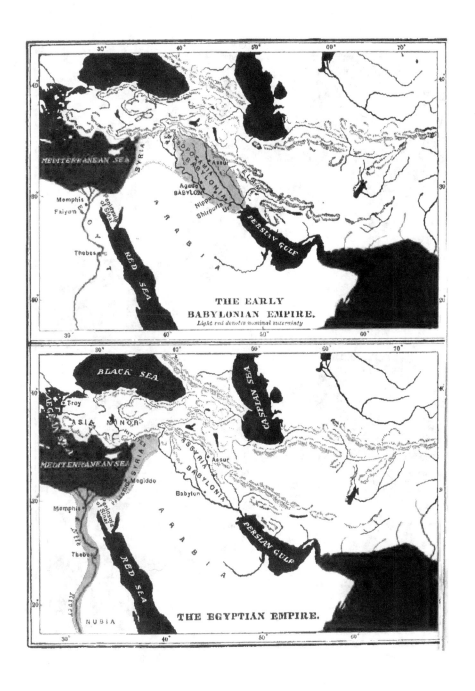

MEDITERRANEAN SEA

SYRIA

MESOPOTAMIA
BABYLONIA

Assur

ELAM

Agade
BABYLON

Nippur

Shirpurla

Memphis

Faiyum

Peninsula of Sinai

E G Y P T

A R A B I A

RED SEA

Thebes

PERSIAN GULF

THE EARLY
BABYLONIAN EMPIRE.

Light red denotes nominal suzerainty

BLACK SEA

CASPIAN SEA

Troy

AEGEAN SEA

ASIA MINOR

MEDITERRANEAN SEA

PALESTINE SYRIA

ASSYRIA

Assur

BABYLONIA

Megiddo

Babylon

Memphis

Peninsula of Sinai

Nile River

A R A B I A

RED SEA

PERSIAN GULF

Thebes

NUBIA

THE EGYPTIAN EMPIRE.

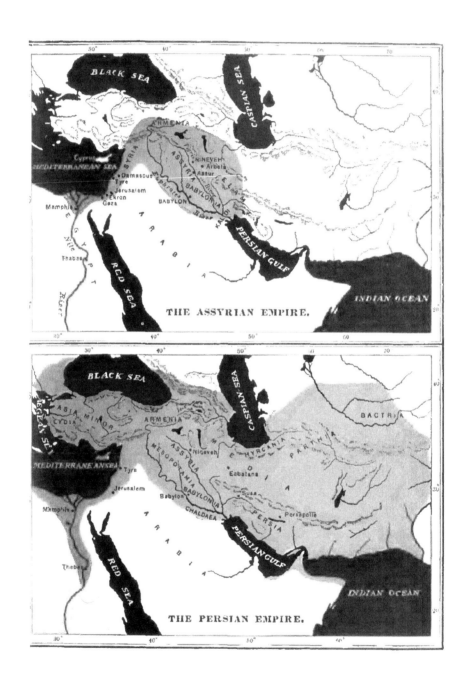

BLACK SEA

CASPIAN SEA

ARMENIA

MEDITERRANEAN SEA

Cyprus

SYRIA

Damascus
Tyre
Jerusalem
Ekron
Gaza

Memphis

NINEVEH
Arbela
Assur

ASSYRIA

ELAM

BABYLONIA

BABYLON

Euphrates

Tigris

E G Y P T

Nile River

Thebes

RED SEA

A R A B I A

PERSIAN GULF

INDIAN OCEAN

THE ASSYRIAN EMPIRE.

BLACK SEA

CASPIAN SEA

AEGEAN SEA

ASIA MINOR

LYDIA

ARMENIA

BACTRIA

MEDITERRANEAN SEA

Tyre

Jerusalem

Memphis

MESOPOTAMIA

ASSYRIA

Nineveh

HYRCANIA

PARTHIA

Ecbatana

BABYLONIA

Babylon

Susa

CHALDAEA

PERSIA

Persepolis

A R A B I A

RED SEA

Thebes

PERSIAN GULF

INDIAN OCEAN

THE PERSIAN EMPIRE.

devoted to their chiefs, who exhibited the characteristic Persian virtues at their highest. Herodotus tells us that the training of the sons of the nobles consisted in riding, shooting the bow and speaking the truth. Their relig- Their Religion. ion was lofty and inspiring. By their prophet, Zo'ro- as'ter, who lived about 1000 B.C., they were taught that two supreme divine Powers were in conflict for the mastery of the world—the Power of Good and the Power of Evil. Zoroaster called upon them to choose the Good and fight for him against the Evil, to hate the Lie and to love the Truth. Thus, all life was for them a moral conflict, brightened by the faith that the Good and True would finally be victorious. This simple and sublime doctrine made them men of courage, nobility and virtue, conscious of a mission to fulfil in the world.

83. Effect of Culture on the Persians.—But they were still an uncultivated folk. When they came into possession of the wide eastern world with its higher culture and its lower morals, they were gradually corrupted. They accepted the higher culture, but they were also affected by the lower morality. This change appears prominently in the royal court. The Babylonian forms of court life were adopted. Persian devotion to the chief became slavish subjection to the Great King, whose slightest wish was law. The sudden increase of Loss of Manly Vigor. wealth, following upon the possession of the world, produced luxury and feebleness. In the realm of art and architecture the ideals and achievements of Assyria and Egypt were the models. Magnificent royal palaces at Susa and Persepolis show little if anything that is new in artistic style. An imposing grandeur appears, rising out of the combination of all the old forms that the ar-

tists of the Semitic world had worked out, but that is all.
Of course these changes in manners and culture came
slowly.   Later history was to reveal how low the Persians were to fall before their work was done and their
empire was swept away.

84. **Wars of Darius.**—Besides his scheme of organization, Darius extended his empire by means of war.
In the far east he advanced into India and added the
valley of the Indus river to his dominions.   In the west
he marched through Asia Minor across the Bosporus

Contact
with
Greece.

to attack the Scythians (about 510 B C.)   This expedition brought him into close contact with the Greeks.
It was the most important among a series of events
which led to the wars between the Persian empire and
the Greek states.   With these wars the Greeks came
fully into the current of the world's history, to hold,
henceforth, the commanding position.   Hence the centre
of our study shifts from the east to the west, from Persia

A New Age.

to Greece.   The old world of Asia falls back; the new
world of Europe takes its place (500 B.C.).

REVIEW EXERCISES. 1. For what were the following famous:
   Cyrus, Nebuchadrezzar, Darius? 2. Who were the Scythians,
   the Lydians, the Jews, the Chaldeans? 3. For what are the
   following noted: Sardis, Carthage, Susa, Tyre, Persepolis?
   4. What is meant by drachma, papyrus, satrap, province?
   5. When did Nebuchadrezzar live? 6. When did Cyrus live?

SELECT LIST FOR READING. 1. The Medo-Persian Tradition.
   Goodspeed, pp 320–326. 2. Nebuchadrezzar and Judah. Goodspeed, pp 337–347. 3. The Renaissance of Babylonia under
   the Chaldeans. Goodspeed, pp. 353–360. 4. The City of Babylon. Goodspeed, pp. 360–366 5. Cyrus, the Enemy of Babylon. Goodspeed, pp. 372–376.

TOPICS FOR READING AND ORAL REPORT. 1. The Babylon of Nebuchadrezzar. Murison, Babylonia and Assyria, § 67;

Ragozin, Media, etc , ch. 9. 2. The Victories of Cyrus. Ragozin, Media, etc., ch. 11. 3. The Story of the Accession of Darius.
Herodotus, Book II, pp. 67-88; Ragozin, Media, etc., ch. 13. 4.
The Organization of the Persian Empire. Encyclopedia Britannica, article "Persia"; Sayce, Ancient Empires, pp. 247-250;
Ragozin, Media, etc., pp. 384-391. 5. The Scythian Expedition
of Darius. Herodotus, Book IV, pp. 1-142, Ragozin, Media, etc.,
pp. 412-429. 6. The Palaces of Persepolis. Sayce, Ancient Empires, pp. 270-272; Ragozin, Media, etc., pp. 391-411.

GENERAL REVIEW OF PART I

TOPICS FOR CLASS DISCUSSION. 1. What were the chief influences of the geography of the oriental world upon its history? See §§ 1, 2, 4, 13, 50, 62, 77, 78. 2. How did the invasions of the desert and mountain tribes affect the history
of the oriental world? See §§ 5, 16, 35, 48, 55, 72, 74. 3. What
were the chief commercial products of the oriental world
and from what countries did each come? See §§ 18, 19, 20,
52, 53. 4. What special contribution to modern civilization
was made by each of the great peoples studied? 5. Trace
the growth of government in the oriental world, showing how
new ideas were added from time to time. See §§ 6-9, 11, 12,
15, 21, 37, 42, 52, 58, 65, 81. 6. What were the main points
of difference between the various religions of the oriental
world? See §§ 34, 40, 55, 82

MAP AND PICTURE EXERCISES.* 1. Compare Babylonian-
Assyrian and Egyptian architecture as illustrated in Plate VI.
2. Enumerate such defects in Egyptian art as appear in Plates
IV, XXII. 3. From a study of Plate VIII, what subjects were
most successfully treated by the Assyrian artists? How does
this illustrate the national character? 4. What conclusions
as to mode of fighting may be drawn from Plate III? 5. Draw
an outline map from memory of the field of ancient oriental
history, locating as many places and countries mentioned as
possible.

TOPICS FOR WRITTEN PAPERS. 1. The Pyramids. Maspero,
Dawn of Civilization, pp. 363-377, Egyptian Archæology, ch. 3;

* See Appendix II and Tarbell, *History of Greek Art*, pp. 1-46.

Rawlinson, Story of Egypt, ch 4; History of Egypt, ch 7; Encyclopedia Britannica, article "Egypt" (sub-division "Pyramids"). 2. Compare the laws of Hammurabi given in the text with the laws of the Hebrews contained in Exodus, chs. 21-23, Deuteronomy 15 : 12-14; 19 · 16-21   See also The Biblical World, March, 1903, pp. 175-190   3. What did the ancient oriental people think of the world?   Maspero, Dawn of Civilization, pp. 16-22; Encyclopedia Britannica, article "Cosmology."   4. Write an account of the departure of the Israelites from Egypt from the standpoint of an Egyptian, using the account given in Exodus, chs. 1-14, as the basis of your study.   5. What nations had stories of the flood?   Ragozin, Story of Chaldea, ch 6; Encyclopedia Britannica, article "Cosmology," also "Deluge" 6. What did the Nile do for Egypt?   Maspero, Dawn of Civilization, ch 1, Rawlinson, Story of Egypt, ch. 1; Encyclopedia Britannica, article "Egypt."   7. The Education of an Assyrian Boy. Sayce, Babylonians and Assyrians, ch. 3; Goodspeed, History of Babylonians and Assyrians, § 261.   8. Life and Times of Nebuchadrezzar.   Goodspeed, Part IV, chs 2-3; Maspero, Passing of the Empires, pp. 513-568; Harper, in Biblical World, July, 1899; Ragozin, Media, etc., ch. 9.

II. THE GREEK STATES

2500-200 B. C.

PRELIMINARY SURVEY

85. Physical Geography of Greece.—From .the vast
plains, broad rivers, mighty mountain chains, trackless
deserts, high table-lands, magnificent empires of the ancient east—where the works of nature and man alike
are huge, massive, steadfast and overpowering, and history is measured by centuries or even millenniums—
we turn to a very different scene in passing westward
across the Ægean sea to Greece. A petty peninsula, its
rivers are rushing torrents on which no ship can sail, and
its plains are deep, narrow basins between high ridges
and peaks. Taken in its fullest extent it is less than half The Home
as large as the state of Illinois. Still, though Greece is Land.
small, it has striking natural characteristics. The lack
of rivers is made up by innumerable bays and inlets
from the sea, so that there is no spot of land which is
more than forty miles from it. Half-way down the
peninsula on its western side a deep gulf—the gulf of
Corinth—almost cuts off the southern part, the Peloponnesus, while on the south are two bays, and on the east
five, one of which actually parts Eubœa from the mainland. Its mountains, though pursuing a general course
from northwest to southeast, fly off in every direction
from the Pindus range in the north to meet the sea, cutting the land up into a variety of independent valleys

and glens, and towering above them in ridges and peaks from five thousand to eight thousand feet in height, sometimes bare and stern, often thickly wooded or crowned with snow. Over sea, valley and mountain gleams a brilliant sky; the play of light and shade upon the varied scene is indescribably beautiful. From the points of bold promontories that stand out into the Ægean sea, islands, large and small, summits of lost mountain-peaks, push forth one after the other toward the eastward and go to meet similar islands that dot the shores of Asia Minor. Far to the south, Crete lies across the foot of the sea, sixty miles from the extremity of the Peloponnesus and barely twice as far from Asia Minor.

The Islands.

86. Its Influence on Greek History.—Observe what the position of Greece and her relation to the sea meant for the life and history of her people. The Ægean, pushing far upward, received the trade of the northwest while it also opened into the Black sea, down to the northern and eastern shores of which came the roads from the far northeast. The bays on the eastern side of Greece, coupled with the innumerable islands that stretched across the sea, made access easy for men coming from the east, the early home of civilization. Thus Greece lay at the very spot where the ways of progress met, from north and east and south, and extended welcoming hands to the bearers of the world's best gifts. Yet the land was also protected. No hostile force could easily come down through the high mountains of the north. Should ships bring enemies, the coasts alone could be seized; the interior remained easily defensible. Moreover, intercourse, by land in Greece, difficult on account of the mountains, was made easy by inlets from

Relations to the World Without.

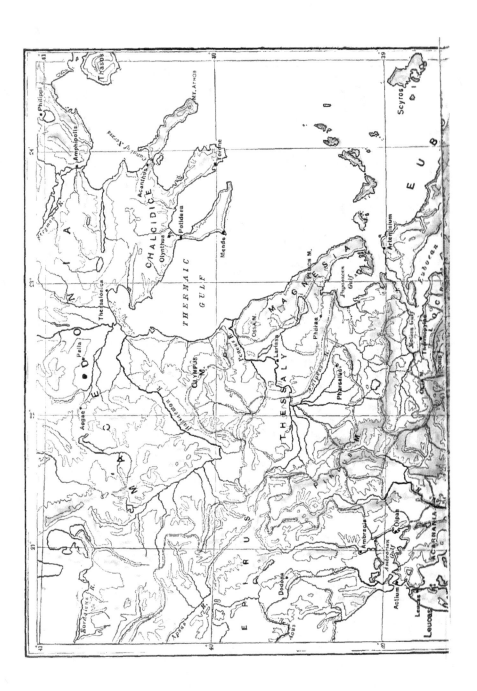

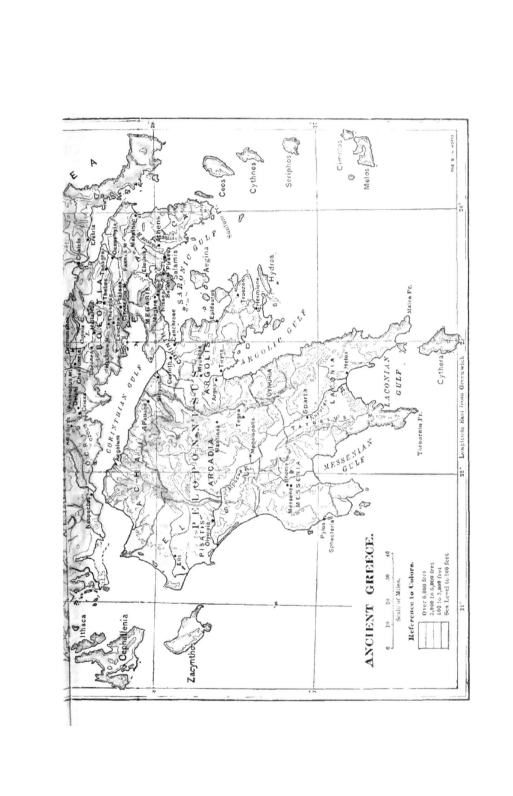

ANCIENT GREECE.

Scale of Miles.

0   10   20   30   40

Reference to Colors.

Over 6,000 feet
3,000 to 6,000 feet
600 to 3,000 feet
Sea Level to 600 feet

the sea. Hence the Greeks, like the Phœnicians of the eastern Mediterranean (§ 50), were early thrust forth on the water, and learned how to defend their shores as well as to engage in commerce with outside peoples. Thus Greece was at the same time an accessible and a defensible land.

87. On the Politics of Greece.—The mountains had another important influence on Greek history. The narrow secluded valleys, into which they broke up the land, became seats of petty communities, each independent of the other, each zealous to maintain its own independence and each protected in its separateness by the mountain barriers which girt it about. Hence, for a long period, the history of Greece is a history of a variety of small states; unity of political life was the last thing secured and, when secured, was with difficulty maintained. On the other hand, this separateness in Greek political life had its advantages. A wonderful variety in forms of society and politics was produced, each state working out its own local problems with substantial freedom from interference and with the incitement of healthy rivalry with its neighbors.

Disunion of Greeks.

88. On the Greek Character.—In such physical conditions and relations a peculiar type of man was produced that the world had not seen before. In these little communities the single man counted for much. The individual was not lost in the crowd; hence individuality was an early trait of the Greek character. Devotion to his own state and pride in its independence gave him patriotism and a love of freedom. The beauty and variety of the natural world all about bred in him sensitiveness to form and color, while its steep, narrow and rugged ways made him healthy, strong and supple. All his circumstances called for quickness of body and mind, stimulated him to thought and action, and brought out a variety of resource and achievement that has been the admiration and the inspiration of mankind. Thus it has been well said that "the Greeks owed their greatness largely to the country in which it was their fortune to dwell."

Greek Traits.

89. The Greek People.—The Greeks belonged by language to the Indo-European family (§ 5). If we may judge from the ancient statues and from the prevailing Greek type of to-day, they were tall and spare in build, with oval face, long straight nose, bright large eyes, fair complexion, of graceful and elastic carriage and a general harmony of form, free from signal excess or defect of any one characteristic. They were, in disposition, genial and sunny, imaginative and inquiring, temperate and chaste, vibrating between reasonableness and emotion, with an ambition which was not always nice about the means to gain its end, and a vivacity which leaned toward fickleness.

89a. Main Divisions of Greek History.—We have the following main divisions of this portion of our history:

1. The Ægean World and the Beginnings of Greece: 2500–1000 B.C.
2. The Middle (Homeric) Age: 1000–550 B.C.
3. The Development of Constitutional States: 700–500 B.C.
4. Sparta and Athens.
5. The Greek Empires — Athenian, Spartan, Theban and Macedonian: 500–336 B.C.

6. Alexander the Great and the World-Empire: 336–323 B.C.
7. The Hellenistic Age: 323–200 B.C.
8. The Western Greeks—The Transition to Rome: 350–275 B.C.

BIBLIOGRAPHY OF GREEK HISTORY*

ABBOTT. *A Skeleton Outline of Greek History.* Macmillan Co. Useful primarily for chronology.

BAIKIE. *Sea-Kings of Crete.* A. & C. Black. Interesting.

BOTSFORD. *A History of Greece.* Macmillan Co. A well-proportioned narrative in moderate compass. Rather radical at times.

BURROWS. *The Discoveries in Crete.* John Murray. An admirable survey of the Cretan civilization.

BURY. *History of Greece.* Macmillan Co. The best single volume, combining a detailed treatment with accurate and up-to-date knowledge. Possibly too full for elementary use.

CAPPS. *From Homer to Theocritus.* Scribners. The most useful single book; contains abundant extracts.

FERGUSON. *Hellenistic Athens.* Macmillan Co. Begins where Bury ends.

FOWLER. *The City-State of the Greeks and Romans.* Macmillan Co. Belongs to the field of political science rather than of history. Interprets as no other book of its size the meaning of ancient political institutions.

FOWLER AND WHEELER. *Greek Archæology.* American Book Co. A simple, abundantly illustrated treatment of architecture, sculpture, terra cottas, metal work, coins, gems, vases and mosaics.

GREENIDGE. *A Handbook of Greek Constitutional History.* Macmillan Co. The only book of moderate size covering the whole field

JEBB. *Greek Literature* (History Primer Series). American Book Co. Brief, but judicious, compact and illuminating.

MAHAFFY. *Old Greek Life.* American Book Co. A convenient primer of antiquities.

MOREY. *Outlines of Greek History.* American Book Co. A little fragmentary, dealing in detail with the growth of civilization rather than with outward history.

* For previous bibliographies, see § 5a. For bibliography for advanced students and teachers, see Appendix I.

MURRAY. *Ancient Greek Literature.* Appleton. Keen, brilliant, fascinating, but takes for granted a general knowledge of Greek life and history.

PLUTARCH. Translation by Dryden, edited by Clough. 5 vols. Little, Brown and Co ; or by Stewart and Long. 4 vols. Bohn.

SHUCKBURGH *History of the Greeks.* Macmillan Co. Conventional in arrangement but clearly and concisely written.

TARBELL. *A History of Greek Art.* Chautauqua Press. The best single book on the subject.

TUCKER *Life in Ancient Athens* Macmillan "An excellent and simply written little book "

ZIMMERN. *Greek History.* Longmans. Emphasizes the picturesque sides of Greek History; written in a simple style for elementary students.

1.—THE ÆGEAN WORLD AND THE BEGINNINGS OF GREECE

2500–1000 B C.

90. The Neolithic Age.—The region of the Ægean sea was the home of the earliest civilization which has left behind it material objects in the land of the Greeks. This was a stone civilization (neolithic), and by the aid of the many islands which make the Ægean seem to the navigator a series of land-locked channels and little lakes, it became fairly uniform in all the region from Troy to Crete. Indeed, it is probable that in the long ago, between 5000 and 2500 B.C., the stone utensils and weapons—the knives, spear and arrow heads, the needles and other instruments used in the Ægean were not dissimilar to those which in general characterize the neolithic age of Europe. Their most distinctive feature is the use of the hard, black stone called obsidian, which is found on the island of Melos.

PLATE IX

DECORATION OF CRETAN SARCOPHAGUS

DECORATION OF CRETAN SARCOPHAGUS

91. Egypt and Crete.—To this world, probably for a long time stagnant, came a strong impulse forward from Egypt, with which, at the time of the Old Kingdom, it came into contact. The entrance from the east and south into the Ægean sea is blocked by the great, long-ranging island of Crete, which is thus determined by geographical position as 'the first of the lands of Europe to receive the culture of the East. Crete was accordingly the forerunner of Greece, and the Cretans, called by the Egyptians the Keftiu, were for about a thousand years (2500–1500 B.C.) the rivals of the Egyptians and Babylonians in the arts and sciences and, indeed, in some respects, their masters.

92. Crete and the Greeks.—The Cretans were apparently not Greeks, but may have been kinsmen of the early inhabitants of Asia Minor. They wrote their language by the means of pictographs like those of Egypt, and of linear characters like those of the Phœnicians. We are as yet unable to read either system, but it seems quite probable that what they conceal is a non-Greek speech like that of the Et'eo-cre'tans, who in later times dwelt on part of the island. The Greeks may have advanced from the region of the lower Danube into the peninsula of Greece as early as 2500–2000 B.C., but it was not till about 1500 B.C. that, after a long period of rude barbarism, they assimilated the high culture radiating from Crete; and it was not till the Cretan age had come to an end that they spread over the insular world and eventually occupied the western coast line of Asia Minor. In fact, the decay of Crete and the destruction by fire of its palaces and towns at about 1350 B.C. may be connected with the stormy advent of the Greeks in what from that

Systems of Writing.

The First Greek Migration.

day to this has been their natural home.   The high civilization common to the entire Ægean world between 1500 and 1150 B.C. we term My′ce-næ′an from Mycenæ in Argolis, where was its most vigorous centre.

93. Cretan Culture.—The Cretan age may be divided into three periods, called Mi-no′an, which correspond closely in time with the Old, Middle and New Kingdoms
in Egypt.   Of these the second (ca. 2200–1600 B.C.) reached its acme in what we may term the Ka-ma′-res epoch (ca. 2200 B C.) from the style of vase painting which characterizes it, while the bloom-time of the third,
commonly called the Palace epoch, coincides with the eighteenth Egyptian dynasty (1580–1350 B C.).

94. Cretan and Mycenæan Pottery.—The Kamares epoch is distinguished from the ages which it followed and preceded by the production of a shapely, thin, wheel-turned pottery with an exclusively linear decoration, and use of many colors—such as reds and whites.   The fondness of the period for grotesque and striking, though rich, effects was but a temporary fashion, however, and it soon yielded to the taste for the sober black through brown to yellow color scheme which characterizes the pottery of the Mycenæan age.   This later ware went directly to nature for its designs, and displaced spirals, circles, scrolls and arabesques with wonderful sketches of animal and vegetable, and especially marine life. Along with painting, the art of frescoing prospered, and with it the art of working and coloring low relief on pottery, stone and metal.   A fine porcelain made its appearance, the several pieces—such as crosses, cows and goats suckling their young, flying fishes—being used for the ornamentation of the interior walls of the houses.

PLATE XI

Middle Minoan Polychrome Pottery (First Palace, Classes) from below Olive Press Room

PLATE XII

PILLAR OF THE DOUBLE AXES

THRONE OF MINOS IN THE COUNCIL ROOM,
PALACE OF CNOSSOS, CRETE

95. The Palace at Cnossus.—All these various arts combined with that of the architect to give shape and beauty to the great palace at Cnossus, which, constructed first at ca. 2200 B.C., was rebuilt in ca. 1900 B.C., and thoroughly remodelled at about 1800 B.C. in the form in which it stood when wiped out by the final conflagration Like all the Cretan palaces it was unfortified. It formed a great complex of rooms, corridors and closets set about a vast central court, and rambled in all directions over an area of five acres. Possessing, as it did, all the conveniences of modern sanitation, it was obviously a comfortable place to live in. Light and airy, it had the same general characteristics as the "Labyrinth" of the twelfth dynasty, in imitation of which it was doubtless erected. In beauty of interior decoration, as well as in size, it probably surpassed all residences built afterward in Greece before the Hellenistic Age. After the conflagration the basement and part of the first story stood half ruined and covered with débris, a maze of passages and chambers—the Labyrinth of the legend of Minos (§ 122). Labyrinth in Egypt and Crete

96. The Lords and Ladies of Cnossus.—We have to conceive of it in the Palace period as the home of a gay and rich court. Then it was tenanted by low-statured slender men with Caucasian features, clad only in a loin-cloth richly decorated but carrying a dagger with inlaid blade in a belt close drawn round the waist. Then it was adorned by a company of ladies dressed in strangely modern, low-necked, short-sleeved, close-fitting bodices with flounced skirts, long flowing and richly embroidered. Its lord was a monarch whose fleets ruled the sea and whose merchant-men went in safety whither they pleased Cretan Dress

97. The Mycenæan World.—Already in the Palace epoch the culture of Crete had been carried north and west into Greece; so that the Mycenæan world reached from Py′los and A-my′clæ north past Tir′yns, Mycenæ, Attica and Orch-om′en-us to the gulf of Pag′a-sæ, and in its later days included the islands on the west coast of Greece and not only Troy, but also the Cyclades and the entire western fringe of Asia Minor; while its pottery and other wares not only reached Egypt, like those of the Cretans, but were also carried as far west as Sicily and Spain. The most important outside contact of this world was with Egypt of the New Empire, of which many monuments have been found at its various centres. Ultimately, moreover, it developed an active commercial and colonizing activity in Cyprus and Asia Minor, thus tapping in both its Syrian and Anatolian channels the stream of culture which had its source in Babylonia.

98. Fortifications and Communications.—Its civilization is in general that of Crete of the Palace epoch. It had the same dress, weapons and habits of life, but, since power was divided between a great many little monarchies, each town had to be strongly fortified. Hence the massive walls twenty to sixty feet thick—with cunningly contrived portals—set around low hills which for greater safety were selected a short distance from the sea, have no parallel in Crete. Within these rugged fortifications stood the palace of the ruler and the houses of his courtiers; outside lay the huts of his subjects.

The whole community centred in the autocrat, who, on occasion, might be the lord of a wide realm. Thus at one time the despots of Mycenæ bound all the territory from their capital to the isthmus of Corinth by a system

PLATE XIII

THE LION GATE: MYCENÆ

BEE HIVE TOMB: TREASURY OF ATREUS

PLATE XIV

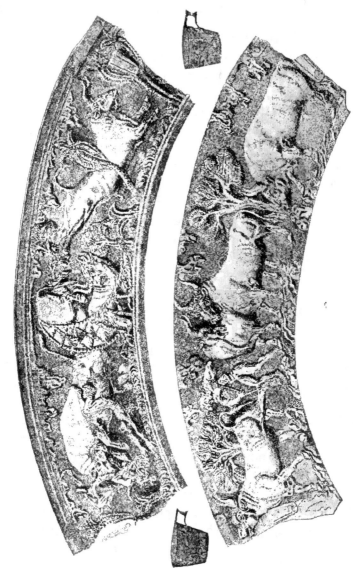

RELIEFS FROM GOLD CUPS OF THE MYCENÆAN AGE

of massive and durable roads. Their use was economic rather than military, since they seem to have been too narrow for the chariots on which the king and his soldiers drove to battle. The land was, accordingly, the scene of a lively traffic; on the sea boats shot like shuttles between the islands. Far beyond the confines of Articles of the Ægean sea sped the articles of Mycenæan commerce. Commerce. The graves disclose what these were; for in them have been found masks of gold, cups of gold and silver, armlets, bracelets, beads, chains, diadems, ear-rings, necklaces, rings, and vases—all of gold. There were bronze swords with inlaid work. There were glazed and painted pottery of various and striking patterns, decorated with scenes from land and sea. There were vases of alabaster, of marble and of terra-cotta. Into the Ægean tract came, on the other hand, the products of far-distant countries, tin, jade, amber, for examples. Like every high culture the Mycenæan had a strong power of attraction for commodities and men, and we may be sure that the faces of many strange peoples were familiar in the country at this time.

99. The Beehive Tombs.—In the earlier age it was Respect for doubtless a general custom to pay respect to the dead, the Dead. but it was not till now that provision for the after-life of the kings became one of the chief public interests of the living. Monarchs now strove to secure great tombs, beehive in shape, comparable, though far from equal, to the pyramids of Egypt, to which a similar regard for the welfare of the departed gave rise. The spirits of the dead were thought to need a habitation near the body and to receive from the living the arms, weapons, utensils, food and drink without which living was unthinkable.

100. Religion.—Quite different from this cult of the dead was the worship of the gods, as to the character of which many relics testify. Primitive man regards nature not merely as a complex of things and processes, but as the abode of spirits (§ 112). These he tries to control by magic. He also tries to placate and propitiate them, and thus singles out specific deities whose characteristics—desires and dislikes—he comes to know. Such deities the Cretans and Mycenæans worshipped, not as idols of human form, but as sacred trees and pillars, in which they thought their deities were permanently or temporarily resident; and long after they came to think of these deities as human in shape they continued to revere the stocks and stones which were from of old set behind the altars and in the precincts or caves where offerings were placed. The most notable of the Cretan and Mycenæan deities were a male god of the Sky, Thunder and War, the prototype of the Greek Zeus, whose attribute was the double axe with which he slew his enemies; and a female goddess whose attribute was the dove, whose province was the mystery of birth, and whose popularity is witnessed by myriads of little clay, stone and metal images which were placed in her shrines by her votaries.

Sacred Trees and Pillars.

Cretan and Mycenæan Deities.

101. The Decline of the Mycenæan World.—About 1150 B.C. this rich Mycenæan civilization declined rapidly. The blight which simultaneously ended a culture epoch in Egypt and Babylon (§§ 17, 39) affected the Ægean district also. The cause was no doubt in each instance internal decay; but this was accompanied, as in the similar case of the Roman empire over fifteen hundred years later, by external invasions.

Causes.

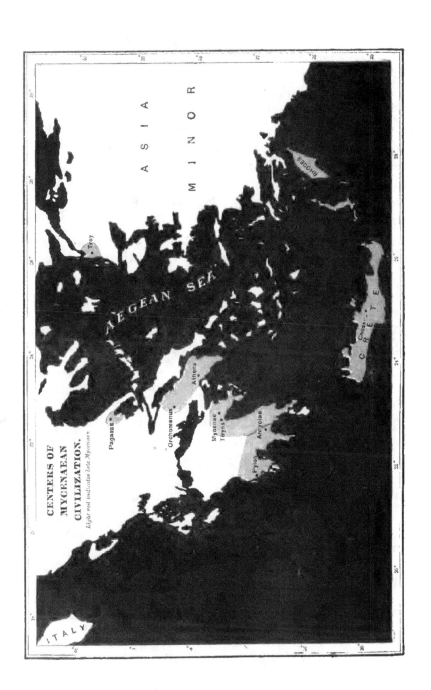

CENTERS OF
MYCENAEAN
CIVILIZATION.

Light red indicates late Mycenaean

ITALY

ASIA

MINOR

AEGEAN SEA

RHODES

CRETE

Cnossus

Troy

Pagasæ

Orchomenus

Athens

Mycenae
Tiryns

Pylos

Amyclae

102. The Second Greek (Dorian) Migration. It was about this time that the so-called northwest Greeks, who had been left behind in the mountains when their kinsmen possessed the areas of Mycenæan culture, and who retained the barbarism which their more fortunate vanguard had lost through contact with Crete, now advanced to the south and east. Subsequently Thessalians appear in Thessaly, Bœotians in Bœotia, Elians and Dorians in the Peloponnesus and Dorians in all the large islands of the south Ægean—Crete inclusive—as well as in the southwestern part of Asia Minor. At Italians. the same time, it may well be, the Italians pushed into the peninsula to which they gave their name, and the Phrygians branched off from their kinsmen in Thrace Phrygians. and advanced violently into the heart of Asia Minor.

103. The Decline of the Ancient Eastern Culture.— The End of the First It was this avalanche pressing on from behind which Culture dislodged Etruscans, Shardani, Danæi, Lycii, Peleset Epoch. and other peoples from their Ægean homes and forced them to seek new abodes for themselves and their families and possessions in Syria, Egypt and the far west (§§ 39, 54, 344). It was this avalanche which overwhelmed the Mycenæan world, and forced fugitives from the east coast of Greece to scurry across the Ægean, thus reinforcing their kinsmen who had earlier settled in central and northern Asia Minor. There—in Æolia and Ionia—Mycenæan Greek life lingered on through the dark age which followed to reach a new bloom in the time of Homer.

REVIEW EXERCISES. 1. What part do the following play in the physical geography of Greece : the Ægean, the Pindus, the gulf of Corinth? 2. For what are the following places noted :

Mycenæ, Troy, Cnossus? 3. Locate from memory on an outline map the chief points at which remains of Mycenæan civilization have been found. 4. At about what time was the Mycenæan civilization at its height? 5. At about what time did the Dorian invasion occur? 6. Describe the conditions in the Ægean world at the time of the advent of the Greeks. 7. What was the position of Crete in this world? 8. Characterize the Cretan pottery. 9. Describe the palace at Cnossus and the people who occupied it. 10. Compare Cretan and Mycenæan architecture. 11. What were the characteristics of the Cretan religion? 12. Describe the Dorian invasion and its effect upon the distribution of Mycenæan civilization.

COMPARATIVE STUDIES. 1. What was going on in the oriental world during the bloom-time of Crete? 2. Compare the articles of commerce of the Mycenæan Greeks with those of the Phœnicians (§ 50). 3. Compare the effect of the Dorian invasion of Greece with that of the Hyksos invasion of Egypt (§§ 35-36).

SELECT LIST FOR READING. 1. The Geography of Greece. Bury, pp. 1-5. 2. The Mycenæan Age : (*a*) Its Remains, Bury, pp. 11-30. (*b*) Its History in Greece, Bury, pp. 31-43. (*c*) Its Expansion, Bury, pp. 43-53. 3. Phœnician Influence on Greece, Bury, pp. 76-78. 4. Early Cretan Civilization, Bury, pp. 7-11 5. The Dorian Invasion and Its Effect upon Greek Migration. Bury, pp. 57-63. 6. The Effect of the Illyrian Pressure upon Thessalians, Ætolians and Bœotians, Bury, pp. 53-57.

TOPICS FOR READING AND ORAL REPORT. 1. The Story of Theseus. Plutarch, Life of Theseus. 2. The Hill of Hagia Triada : Its Treasures. Burrows, pp. 29-39. 3. The Geography of Greece. Morey, pp. 72-77. 4. The Mycenæan Age: (*a*) Its Remains, Morey, pp. 86-91. (*b*) Its History in Greece, Morey, pp. 91-94. (*c*) Its Expansion, Botsford, pp. 8-10. 5. The Earliest History of Greece. Bury, pp. 6-11. 6. Myths and Legends of the Heroic Age. Morey, pp. 83-86. 7. The Epic Poets. Botsford, pp. 10-11; Morey, pp. 94-96; Capps, pp. 14-20. 8. Palaces and Their Contents in the Middle Minoan Period. Burrows, pp. 55-65, 85-92.

2.—THE MIDDLE (HOMERIC) AGE
1000–550 B.C.

104. The New Beginning.—In the new Greece that came into being when the turmoil of the migrations had subsided civilization must in a sense begin all over again. The incomers were numerous; the old civilization was too weak to absorb and win its peaceful victory over them, as was the case in so many similar situations in the ancient east (§§ 16, 36). They came with their flocks and herds and for a time continued the old pastoral life. Apart from the raising and pasturing of their cattle, hunting and fighting were their favorite activities. But as they settled down, agriculture was taken up; fields were sown; vineyards planted; the fig and the olive cultivated. In time industries came in. At first, everything needed was made at home, but gradually the various trades appeared, the blacksmith, the potter, the carpenter, the leatherworker, the bowmaker and the spinner. For a long time any kind of industry was looked upon as unworthy of freemen. Even heralds, physicians, seers, singers, poets and jugglers were together counted as workmen and, though respected, had no social standing. First the warrior, and then the farmer, were the gentlemen of Greece. *Occupations.*

105. Social and Political Elements.—The new-comers brought the tribal system with them into the Peloponnesus. In the tribe the chief subdivision is the brotherhood (phra'try) the members of which are bound together by a tie of blood-relationship. Each is the equal of his brother. He eats at the common table. *The Brotherhood.*

He must be ever ready in arms at the call of the tribe to battle. If slain by an enemy, it rests upon his fellow-brothers to avenge him by killing any and all of the hostile tribe or brotherhood whose member took his life.* At the head of the tribe is the king, the chief among equals, surrounded by his council, the elders, men of valor over sixty years old. He leads the tribe in war; he is the judge and the priest in peace. The tribesmen, gathered in close array, armed for war, constitute the public assembly for the settlement of tribal affairs.

106. Rise of Aristocracy.—When these wandering tribes settled down in the narrow valleys of Greece, tribal unity was broken up. Each petty community began to live for itself. The land was definitely occupied and each family to which a "lot" was assigned came to own it and, where possible, added more. Some families grew great and strong and began to claim superiority thereby. Other families grew poor and became dependent upon their richer neighbors. The strong became proud and called themselves *Ar'is-toi*, "the best" people. Thus an "aristocracy" grew up with its dependents. The noble head of an aristocratic family led his people in war and protected them in peace. He lived on his estates in rude luxury, surrounded by his family The Clan. and dependents. An aggregation such as this consisting of a noble or a group of nobles and their dependents who were at once their serfs and their retainers we call a clan (ge'nos). The members thought they were sprung from a god or demi-god peculiar to themselves and to him as the progenitor of their race they attached

* This is called the law of blood-revenge.

themselves by a pedigree, and in his honor they performed special religious rites in which none but members could participate. The king soon began to find that
these great noble families were too strong for him; in
time he lost his powers, one after the other, keeping at
last only his religious functions The aristocracy stepped
into his place and ruled the state by a council of chiefs,
administering justice and making war. In this new situation the old tribal equality faded away. The public
assembly, though still existent, had no power in the new
aristocratic state. The nobles were the state.

107. The City-State.—The usual and characteristic
form taken by these states was the city, just as in the
primitive east (§ 11). The Greek city came into exist- Its Origin
ence by a union of the petty villages of a district. The
inhabitants for the most part migrated to a common
spot and there took up their residence. The political
powers of the several communities were given to the new
state. There the officials lived and administered justice;
there the public assembly met; there the citizen exercised his rights. There was the centre of political life.
There was set up the worship of the common gods. It
thus resulted that everywhere throughout progressive
Greece the agricultural population was made urban in
its character. The ordinary city was in fact essentially
an aggregate of farmers who tilled the land in its vicinity.
In this way the social and political advantages of city life Its Unique
were brought within the reach of everybody.* Thus a ness.

* The case of Athens is not typical; for Athens is peculiar in that because of the size of its territory (Attica) it absorbed the village population
less completely than any other city-state in Greece. Hence in Attica
many villages inhabited by citizens—such as Acharnæ and Sunium—
continued to exist.

fundamental difference appears between the eastern and the Greek city-state. In the former all power was lodged in a king, and his people were subject to him and dependent upon him for all things (§ 21). But in the Greek city-state there was always a measure of popular freedom; to be a citizen was to have some political rights and duties. The king was never a despot, nor did the rule of the aristocracy destroy the old rights of the freeman, although it often limited his exercise of them. But they were always capable of being revived and enlarged should the proper occasion offer itself. The Greek city was also economically independent. The citizens produced their own wealth and employed it for the city's interest, not for those of a king and his court.

Freedom of the Citizens.

Thucydides, the Athenian historian, gives the following account of the origin of the city-state of Athens:

"In the days of Ce'crops and the first kings, down to the reign of The'seus, Athens was divided into communes, having their own town-halls and magistrates. Except in case of alarm the whole people did not assemble in council under the king, but administered their own affairs, and advised together in their several townships. Some of them at times even went to war with him, as the Eleusinians under Eu-mol'pus with E-rech'theus. But when Theseus came to the throne, he, being a powerful as well as a wise ruler, among other improvements in the administration of the country, dissolved the councils and separate governments, and united all the inhabitants of Attica in the present city, establishing one council and town-hall They continued to live on their own lands, but he compelled them to resort to Athens as their metropolis, and henceforward they were all inscribed on the roll of her citizens. A great city thus arose which was handed down by Theseus to his descendants, and from his day to this the Athenians have regularly celebrated the national festival of the Syn-oi'ki-a, or union of the communes, in honor of the goddess Athena."

Theseus.

108. A New Impulse: Commerce.—The history of the Greek world is henceforth and chiefly the history of these city-states in their growth and relations to one another. The first to become prominent were those on the Asiatic side of the Ægean sea. They had been the least disturbed by the migrations; indeed, by the advent of those who fled out of Greece from before the new-comers they had been distinctly benefited. An activity, new for this age, began to be cultivated among them—commerce. It made them vigorous, enterprising and wealthy. Miletus was the leader, followed by its rivals, Ephesus, Colophon, Magnesia, Samos, Chios and Myt-i-le′ne. Soon the impulse spread to the western side of the sea and commercial cities appeared there— Chalcis and E-re′tri-a upon the island of Eubœa, as well as Meg′a-ra, Corinth and Æ-gi′na. A lively trade, especially in natural products, sprang up between these cities and gave a stimulus to manufacturing, and occasionally some manufactured article was exported. Thus Miletus was famous for its woollen garments, Eubœa for its purple cloths, Chalcis and Corinth for pottery, other cities for metal-work and chariots.

The Eastern Cities.

109. Beginnings of Literature.—But for all this commerce was still in its infancy. Both in the most progressive cities which took part in maritime enterprises and in the great number of smaller states which did not the dominant interest remained agricultural, and it was a nobility of country gentlemen which everywhere formed the highest social class. The nobles and the wealthy sought entertainment for their leisure and found it in music and song. In these cities appeared a class of singers who, accompanying their song with the lyre,

The Singers

produced the first literature of Greece. They sang of
gods and heroes, of battles, sieges and adventures by
land and sea, of the loves and hates, the sins and virtues
of men and gods, of the worlds above and below this
earth and of all the splendid life of the mighty of old.
They laid under contribution all of religion and history
that had come down to them from the dim past.

Such was the singer described in the "Odyssey," viii, 62: "Then
the henchman drew near, leading with him the beloved minstrel, whom
the Muse loved dearly, and she gave him both good and evil; of his
sight she reft him, but granted him sweet song. Then Pon-ton'ous,
the henchman, set for him a high chair inlaid with silver, in the midst
of the guests, leaning it against the tall pillar, and he hung the loud
lyre on a pin, close above his head, and showed him how to lay his
hands on it. The Muse stirred the minstrel to sing the songs of
famous men, even that lay whereof the fame had then reached the
wide heaven, namely, the quarrel between Odysseus and Achilles,
son of Peleus; how once on a time they contended in fierce words at
a rich festival of the gods, but Agamemnon, king of men, was inly
glad when the noblest of the Achæans fell at variance. This song it
was that the famous minstrel sang."

110. The Epics.—In time these songs came to be
woven together into a series of greater poems, in hexameter verse, dealing with particular events, like the story
of the ship "Argo" and its crew of bold heroes led by
Jason (§ 127), or that of the "Seven against Thebes"
(§ 123), or that of the "Siege of Troy" and the "Wanderings of Odysseus." These are called epics, and the
most famous of them are said to have been the work of
Homer and are known to us as the "Iliad" and the
"Odyssey." For centuries these cycles of song passed
down from singer to singer unwritten, until finally, when

Homer.

the age of the singers was passing, they were written down.

111. Life of the Times.—From these epics comes a vivid picture of the life of the times, nowhere more strikingly exhibited than in the description of the scenes on the shield of Achilles in the eighteenth book of the "Iliad" (lines 483–606). There appears city-life, the marriages and the leading of the brides through the city with songs, the public assembly where the judges give justice between the slayer and the slain, the siege and battle, fell Death in the midst, her raiment red with the blood of men, the field ploughed with oxen, the sweet wine given to the laborer, the binding of the sheaves at harvest, the vineyard with its black and luscious grapes and the gatherers listening to the "Linos" song, the cattle in the pasture attacked by lions, the sheep and the sheepfolds, the dance, the maidens clad in fine linen with wreaths on their heads, and the youth in well-woven doublets with golden daggers in silver sheaths, the great company standing round the lovely dance in joy.*

The Shield of Achilles

112. Religion.—As we have already seen (§ 100), the Mycenæan Greek, like the oriental (§ 34), thought of the world as peopled by divine powers that influenced human life. Every spring, every forest, every height, the wind and the storm, the lights flaming in the sky, the deep and rolling sea and the bright heaven revealed

---

* Other passages in which graphic pictures of life in Homeric times are set forth are the following: "Iliad," ii, 211 *ff.* (Thersites—the first demagogue); iii, 120 (Helen describes Greek leaders to Priam); vi. 369 *ff.* (Parting of Hector and Andromache): "Odyssey," xv, 403 *ff.* (Phœnician traders); vii, 81 *ff* (Palace and estate of a king); xiv, 191 *ff.* (Career of an adventurer); vi, 1 *ff.* (Story of Nausicaa); xi, 1 *ff* (Ulysses in the lower world).

the presence and activity of the gods. But in the age of the Epics he was not satisfied until he had formed

clear-cut and vivid ideas of these powers. Above all, he thought of them as looking and acting like himself, only on a grander scale. The best that he could desire himself to be, that he imagined the gods were. When the singers sang of the gods, they pictured them as glorified and beautiful beings. Thereby they gave to Greek religion its most characteristic stamp; they made it a religion of supreme human beauty. Another thing they

did. They organized this vast and confused variety of gods. They sang of the family of the great gods, twelve or more in number, dwelling in the far north on Mt. Olympus, from whose snow-crowned summit they directed the universe. Zeus, the mighty father, was the ruler of gods and men. His wife was He'ra; his brothers, Po-sei'don, whose domain was the sea, and Pluto, lord of the underworld and the dead; his children, A-pol'lo, god of light, A-the'na, goddess of wisdom, Aph'ro-di'te, goddess of love, A'res, god of war, Ar'te-mis, goddess of the forest and the hunt, Her'mes, the divine messenger, and He-phæs'tus, the lame god of fire and the forge; and other notable figures, Her'a-cles, the hero of many labors, E'ros, god of desire, De-me'ter, goddess of the earth and its fruits, her daughter Cora (or Per-seph'o-ne), wife of Pluto, and Di'o-ny'sus, god of the vine. The singers did not much care about the moral character of

these divine beings. They are sometimes represented as quarrelling, lying or deceiving; even worse actions are told of some of them. What the poets saw in them was their human interests, with artistic sense they made them always beautiful and only sometimes good. Yet

Zeus was the judge of human and divine deeds; Apollo punished wrong-doing and was the type of moral beauty. And in those days it was no small boon to turn men's minds away from stocks and stones, and present for their worship, instead of objects of nature, human-like forms, gloriously gracious. Thus one could approach, and know them as those who, even if higher, were yet like himself, who enjoyed what he enjoyed at its best, and who bade him imitate them in measure and harmony of life. It is true that this region was only for the present life. In the dim light of existence beyond the grave, in the place which they called Ha'des, the Greeks saw little that was attractive. The saying of Achilles long remained true of their feeling: "Rather would I live upon the earth as the hireling of another, with a landless man who had no great livelihood, than bear sway among all the dead that be departed." *The Other Life.*

113. Beginnings of Colonization.—The population of Greece kept increasing steadily after the Dorian migration, and by 750 B.C. it exceeded the power of the little patches of arable land to sustain it. The over-population manifested itself in dissatisfaction with the harsh rule of the nobles and in the severity of the struggle for bare existence. Men needed more land and went abroad to seek it. It was natural for them to assemble at the seaports, where alone they could get transportation to a new world in the north and west which adventurers and merchants were now discovering. Hence, though land hunger was doubtless the main motive of the emigrants, the commercial cities had a leading part in this colonizing activity. *Causes of Colonization.*

114. The Organization of the Colonies.—It was, of course, impossible for men to go independently into strange and often hostile districts. Hence the colony needed to be founded and organized before leaving

The Œcist. Greece. A founder (œcist) was accordingly chosen from the citizens of the port from which the colonists sailed and to him was given absolute power during the formative period of the new settlement. It was usual for him to take with him fire from the hearth of his native city and to secure from the oracle of Apollo at Delphi approval of his enterprise.

115. The Relation to the Mother City.—There was no political connection between the mother city and the colony, but only a weak bond of piety and religion

Each Colony a New State. bound the two together. The world of Greek religion, language and culture was enlarged manifold by the founding of these new communities, but the new states, like the old ones, were cities, small for the most part, and scattered often far apart along the edge of the sea. On the sea ran the ways which kept them in contact with one another.

The Greeks Seize all the Seacoasts. **116. The Distribution of the Colonies.**—The colonists of the eastern Ægean sailed up into the Hel′les-pont and onward, and made the shores of the Black sea Greek territory. Miletus founded Cyz′i-cus, Si-no′pe, Tra-pe′-zus, Olbia and a host of other colonies there. Byzantium, afterward so famous, was Megara's colony. The northern Ægean was settled mainly by men from Chalcis, Eretria and Andros. In the east and south the Greeks pushed out into Cilicia and over to Cyrene. The Eubœans and Corinthians went westward; they founded cities in Sicily, the chief of which was Syracuse, a colony of the latter. They reached the lower coasts of eastern Italy, where they were followed by Achæans who founded

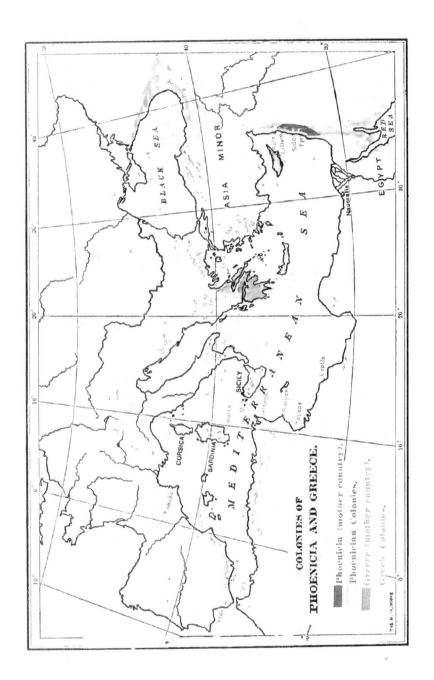

COLONIES OF
PHOENICIA AND GREECE.

Phoenicia (mother country).
Phoenician Colonies.
Greece (mother country).
Greek Colonies.

Croton and Syb'a-ris, Locrians who founded Locri, and
Spartans who founded Tarentum, until so completely
was the region occupied that it was called Magna Græcia,
"Greater Greece." Even on the western coast of Italy
the enterprising Chalcidians settled the city of Cy'me,
while on the coast of Gaul the Pho-cæ'ans, the most vent-
uresome of all early Greek navigators, founded the city
of Massilia, and pressed still farther westward as far as
Spain.

117. Beginnings of New Relations to the Orient.—In
Sicily and Spain the Greeks came into sharp competition with the Phœnicians and Carthaginians (§ 50).
Likewise in the eastern Mediterranean commerce and
colonial expansion soon brought them into contact with
the oriental world. The former lively intercourse
(§ 97), broken off by the Dorian invasion for some
centuries, was now revived. Particularly the native
kingdoms of Asia Minor cultivated relations with the
new Greek world. About 700 B.C. King Midas of
Phrygia dedicated to Apollo of Delphi his golden throne
and Gyges of Lydia a number of costly gold and silver Lydia.
vessels. Under the successors of Gyges the Lydian
kingdom may almost be said to have entered into the
circle of Greek life (§ 75). It began to seek control over
the Greek coast cities of Asia Minor; King Crœsus was
practically the lord of them all, and the closest commercial bonds united them. Soon Greek traders and Egypt.
travellers began to go to Egypt, where King Amasis
(§ 46) received them most graciously and gave them the
city of Naucratis as their trading-post. He himself also
gave gifts to Apollo of Delphi. All these relations came
to be of the greatest moment to the Greeks both in stim-

ulating their own culture and in bringing them within the circle of world-politics. What this latter meant to them we shall see later.

REVIEW EXERCISES. 1. For what are the following places noted: Miletus, Chalcis, Delphi? 2. Who were Amasis, Crœsus, Gyges? 3. What is meant by hexameter, epic, Magna Græcia? 4. Locate from memory on an outline map the chief centres of Greek colonization.

COMPARATIVE STUDIES. 1. Compare the Egyptian idea of the divine world (§ 34) with that of the Greeks. 2. In what respects does the religion of the Greeks differ from that of the Hebrews (§§ 55)?

SELECT LIST FOR READING. 1. The Story of the Argonauts. Bury, pp. 223-231. 2. The Migrations. Bury, pp. 53-64. 3. The Homeric Question. Bury, pp. 65-69. 4. The Rise of the Greek City Republics. Bury, pp. 73-75. 5. Greek Stories of Early Greek History. Bury, pp. 79-84. 6. Life and Institutions of the Middle Age. Bury, pp. 69-75 7. Greek Colonization, Causes, Character and Reaction upon the Mother-Country. Bury, pp. 86-89, 108-110. 8. The Greek Colony of Cyme. Bury, pp. 94-95.

TOPICS FOR READING AND ORAL REPORT. 1. The Labyrinth and the Minotaur. Burrows, pp. 107-110, 121-132. 2. The Homeric Question. Morey, pp 94-97; Capps, pp. 20-22, 114-118. 3. Origin and Early History of the City-State. Morey, pp. 108-109; Botsford, pp. 20-21, Fowler, pp. 5-64. 4. The Life and Institutions of the Middle Age. Botsford, pp 11-17; Morey, pp 98-111; Fowler, pp 64-112. 5. Greek Colonization. Botsford, pp. 30-40 6. Legends of Prehistoric Crete. Baikie, Sea-Kings of Crete, pp 5-16. 7. Life under the Sea-Kings. Baikie, pp. 211-231. 8. Footgear in the Time of Minos. Mosso, The Palaces of Crete and Their Builders, pp 324-342. 9. The Excavations on Crete. Mosso, pp. 17-44.

3.—THE DEVELOPMENT OF CONSTITU-TIONAL STATES

700–500 B.C.

118. The Age of Change.—Thus through commerce, colonization and contact with the larger life of the old world the Greeks were on the threshold of a new and stirring activity. We have seen in part how these stimulating experiences were changing their life at home. Now we turn to trace them more in detail. These changes are seen (*a*) in the new sense of the oneness of the Greek world, (*b*) in the growth of Greek civilization (§§ 129–134), (*c*) in the political upheaval that brought the common people to the front (§§ 135–140).

119. (a) The Sense of Greek Unity.—The physical character of Greece made the union of its states into one political body a difficult thing. But during these centuries of quiet organization there had been growing up a common type of life and a body of ideals and ways of looking at things which went far toward taking the place of a political unity. Now, when the Greek cities extended their horizon and came into contact with peoples outside, they woke up to realize their oneness, their difference in all these respects from the others. They began to feel the value of what they had gained and to develop and improve it. Thus, what we may call their consciousness of themselves appeared. It comes out in various ways. A school of thinkers flourished, who set about organizing the stories of the past into definite and intelligible shape. The most remarkable man among them was He′si-od (about 700 B.C.). His two chief

Seen in Literature

Hesiod.

works are the *The-og'o-ny*, in which he traces the history of Greek gods from the beginning, and the *Works and Days*, in which he arranges the successive ages of gods and men, preaches the gospel of salvation by work and tells men how to get on in the world. The stories of the past, as formulated by illiterate and learned men of these and later times, constitute the wonderful Greek mythology. The following are a few of its many tales:

120. The Greek Races.—The early Greeks firmly believed that at first truth and right prevailed in the world, then gradually wickedness of every sort came into being. Finally the whole world became so contaminated with iniquity that the gods in punishment swept the earth with a mighty deluge. The lofty summit of Mt Parnassus alone overtopped the waves. Hither floated the ark containing the only two faithful followers of the gods, Deucalion and his wife, Pyrrha. Their offspring were two sons, Hellen and Amphictyon. From this common ancestor, Hellen, who gave his name to the Hellenic or Greek race, the Greeks usually traced their origin. Hellen's sons, Æ'o-lus and Dorus, and his grandsons, Ion and Achæus, became the ancestors of four great Greek races, the Æolians, the Dorians, the Ionians and the Achæans. The Æolians occupied the northern parts of eastern Greece and of western Asia Minor. The Dorians coming from the highlands of central Greece pushed southward, and overran the greater portion of southern Greece. They drove out the descendants of Achæus, or the Achæans, who fell back into the district afterward known as Achæa. The Dorians found their way, too, to Asia Minor. The Ionians settled central Greece and the corresponding strip east of the Ægean sea. Amphictyon first caused men to come together in fraternal groups for trade and social intercourse, and in this way the Greeks explained the origin of the name of their early leagues, or amphictyonies (§ 128). Some of the Greeks, indeed, believed that they were sprung from the soil itself, or autochthonous, thinking of their ancestor, whom they reverently worshipped, as a child of some god and nymph.

121. Danaus.*—We shall see that the Greeks believed that those stained with crime in this world received just punishment for their sins in the world of the dead None, perhaps, suffered more severely than the fifty daughters of Dan'a-us, an Egyptian king His brother Ægyptus had fifty sons who were ardent suitors for the fifty daughters of Danaus in spite of the latter's indifference. Danaus fled with his fifty daughters to Argos, but Ægyptus and his sons followed swiftly. Escape seemed impossible, and Danaus pretended to consent to the marriages On their wedding night he gave each daughter a sharp dagger and bade them slay their mates. Thus perished forty-nine of the husbands One bride, Hy'perm-nes'tra, fond of her husband, Lyn'ceus, was unwilling to commit the murder The gods, displeased with the maidens, condemned them to carry through all the ages urns of water up a steep and slippery bank in the vain attempt to fill a bottomless cask. Hypermnestra at first incurred the displeasure of her father, but later he forgave her At his death Lynceus succeeded Danaus upon the throne of Argos. In later times Lynceus and Hypermnestra were revered at Argos as heroes, and it is interesting to note that the Argives were often called Danæi

122. Athenian Myths.—It was under the direction of an autochthonous king, called Cecrops, half man, half serpent, that the Athenians fixed their abode on the rocky hill known as the acropolis The land was called after him, Cecropia. Cecrops grouped the people into twelve communities, and introduced the beginnings of civilized life During his reign there arose a dispute between Athena and Poseidon for the possession of the city. The strife was to be decided by a contest as to which could produce the more useful gift to mortals The gods were to act as jurors Poseidon struck the acropolis with his trident and produced a well of salt water; while Athena planted an olive tree. The gods gave judgment that Athena had rendered the greater service and awarded to her the city which was named after the goddess, Athens. Both the olive tree and the well, situated on the acropolis, were revered by the Athenians In later times Erechtheus, half serpent like Cecrops, ruled Attica. In his youth he had been reared by Athena, and so they were both

* The following myths, in which a general impression that is true is embodied, point to early Greek connection with Egypt, Crete, Phœnicia and Lydia.

worshipped in a temple on the acropolis, named the Erechtheum after Erechtheus.

The deeds of Theseus, son of King Ægeus of Athens, rivalled those of Heracles in destroying wicked men and monsters of all sorts. None of his exploits was more famous than that of slaying the dreadful Min'o taur. Athens had been accustomed to pay as tribute to Minos, king of Crete, seven maidens and seven youths at stated intervals. These were sacrificed to the Minotaur, a monster, half man, half bull, kept in a labyrinth at Cnossus. Theseus went of his own accord as one of the seven youths. Upon his arrival in Crete, A'ri-ad'ne, the daughter of King Minos, fell in love with Theseus and gave him a sword—with which he slew the Minotaur—and a clue of thread by which he made his way out of the confusing windings of the labyrinth. Upon his return Theseus became king of Athens. Previously Attica had been broken up into independent townships. Theseus put an end to this, for he abolished the separate council chambers and governments making of Attica one state. In recognition of this the Athenians celebrated yearly a festival in memory of the man who made Athens the chief city of a united state (§ 107).

123. **Theban Myths.**—A-ge'nor, king of Phœnicia, could not be reconciled to the loss of his daughter, Europa, whom Zeus had stolen away. For many years his son, Cadmus, searched for her without success. Finally in obedience to the Delphic oracle Cadmus gave up the quest and followed the wanderings of a cow. The cow led him a long distance and at last lay down in Bœotia. According to the direction of the oracle he founded here the city of Thebes, but not till he had sown dragon's teeth in the earth as a voice commanded him to do. Gradually there appeared from the surface a strange crop,—warriors all armed. Straightway they fell to fighting till all save five were slain. These made peace and joined with Cadmus in building the city of Thebes. In later times the first Theban families proudly claimed descent from these five warriors. Cadmus is said to have introduced the alphabet from Phœnicia and to have taught his countrymen to read and write.

A curse of the gods upon Œd'i pus, king of Thebes, brought bitter grief upon his family. King Œdipus married Queen Jocasta unaware that she was his mother. When the queen became aware of the truth, she hanged herself in grief; while King Œdipus putting

out his eyes left his kingdom and never returned. But the wrath of
the gods still rested on this unhappy family, for the king's two sons,
E-te'o-cles and Pol'y-nei'ces, quarrelled about the succession to the
throne Eteocles expelled his brother, Polyneices. Polyneices invited help from A-dras'tus, king of Argos, who equipped an army, led
by seven famous chiefs. From this fact the expedition is called that
of "the seven against Thebes." Fearful were the combats before
the walls of the city. The two brothers perished in a deadly duel,
and an edict was issued by Creon, who had succeeded to the throne
of Œdipus, forbidding the burial of their bodies. All obeyed this
harsh command save An-tig'o-ne, a sister of Eteocles and Polyneices.
But Antigone braved the wrath of Creon and buried the body of
Polyneices. The story of Antigone forms the subject of a play of
that name by the Athenian dramatist, Soph'o-cles.

124. **Pelops.**—The Argive myths tell of a Lydian hero, Pelops,
who won the hand of Hip'po-da-mei'a, daughter of Œn'o-ma'us,
king of Pisa, in a chariot race extending from Olympia to the Corinthian isthmus. The terms were: a suitor to be successful must
defeat the king, but, if vanquished in the race, one must forfeit his
life. Thirteen defeated charioteers had perished when Pelops made
trial of his skill. Pelops was much disheartened when he saw the
heads of his conquered predecessors fixed above the door of the king,
and so he devised the plan of enlisting the help of Myr'til-us, the
charioteer of Œnomaus. Myrtilus did not properly fasten the wheels
of the chariot of the king, who was in this way upset during the race
Thus Pelops won the race and his bride, and later he became the
founder of a family that ruled in more than one Argolic city. Among
his grandsons were the famous Greek chieftains, Men'e-la'us and
Agamemnon. The fame of Pelops spread far and wide, and men
took delight in calling southern Greece the Peloponnesus, after the
hero, Pelops, who had driven his victorious chariot from the centre
of the Peloponnesus to the isthmus of Corinth.

125. **Heracles.**—Another hero whom the Greeks greatly admired
and generally worshipped was Heracles, a son of Zeus. Hera plotted continually to overthrow the offspring of her rival. Two serpents were sent by the goddess to destroy the baby in his cradle, but
the infant Heracles strangled each with his tiny hands. Later the
hero was bound out to serve his cowardly cousin, Eu-rys'theus, king of

Argos Before he could again be free he must accomplish twelve
great tasks placed upon him by Eurystheus. These all called for
courage, strength and skill and were such as would have daunted
any mortal man. They included the slaying of wicked men and
dreadful monsters. The last task required that Heracles should descend to Hades and bring to the surface the triple-headed dog, Cer-
berus With the successful completion of the twelve labors the
hero was free from his bondage to Eurystheus. He performed
many other brave deeds during the remainder of his life, and when
he died he was borne away to Mt Olympus to live forever with the
immortal gods.

126. The Heracleidæ.—The descendants of Heracles were kept
out of their hereditary throne of Argos for three generations The
sons and grandsons of Heracles failed to regain their ancestral
possessions, but the hero's three great-grandsons, Te'men-us, Cresphontes and A'ris-to-de'mus were more successful. As the leaders
of a great horde of Dorians they crossed the Corinthian gulf at Naupactus and overran the Peloponnesus By the casting of the lot Te-
menus received Argos, Cresphontes Messenia, Aristodemus Laconia.
Aristodemus soon died leaving twin sons, Eu-rys'the-nes and Procles.
The Spartans decreed that the sons should rule jointly and so Sparta
came to have two kings.

127. The Argonauts.—Ath'a-mas, a Thessalian king, put away
his wife, Neph'e-le, who, fearing danger to her son and daughter,
invoked the help of Hermes. The god gave her a ram with a golden
fleece to convey the children out of harm's way. The ram with the
children upon his back flew eastward. All went well till they were
crossing over the strait separating Europe and Asia when the girl,
Hel'le, frightened at the sight of the waves far beneath, fell from the
ram's back into the body of water since called the Hellespont.
Her brother, Phrixus, reached Colchis where he was kindly received
by king Æ-e'tes. Phrixus sacrificed the ram to Jupiter He hung
the golden fleece on a tree, placing it under the care of a sleepless
dragon. Now it happened that king Æson, who also ruled over a
kingdom in Thessaly, had surrendered temporarily the cares of government to his brother, Pelias, on the understanding that he should
hold the power only till Jason, son of Æson, came of age When the
years were fulfilled and the time for Jason to rule was at hand, the

young prince hastened to his uncle and boldly demanded the crown. Pelias did not deny his request, but suggested that it would be a glorious adventure for the young man to recover the golden fleece, which he artfully pretended belonged to Jason's family. Jason accepted the challenge, and began the construction of a vessel, called the "Argo" (the Swift), capable of holding fifty men. He invited heroes from all Greece and many bold youths joined him There were Heracles, Theseus, Orpheus and many others From the name of their vessel they were called Argonauts. After many adventures and troubles they reached the distant shores of Colchis. King Æetes promised to give up the golden fleece if Jason should plough a field with two fire-breathing bulls and sow it with dragon's teeth The king's daughter, Me-de'a, who was a sorceress, helped Jason, the understanding being that he should marry her When the terrible bulls rushed forth breathing out fire, Jason, following Medea's directions, soothed their rage and forced them to go beneath the yoke. Next, when he had planted the dragon's teeth, a crop of giants, all clad in armor, came forth. The hero was for an instant filled with dismay, but he rushed on the warriors with sword and shield. Following the advice of Medea he cast a stone into their midst with the result that the giants attacked one another and soon none were left alive Finally Medea showed Jason how by magic skill to outwit the dragon that kept guard over the golden fleece. In the night she led Jason to the fleece and sent the dragon to sleep, and when his great eyes were shut in slumber, the hero seized the prize. With his companions and Medea Jason hastened to his good ship "Argo," and, although the swift oarsmen of king Æetes tried to overtake them, they were not successful. After many wanderings and adventures, Jason and Medea and their companions came in safety to Thessaly

128. The Epics Serve the Cause of Unity.—The work of the Epic poets (§ 109) had done much to cement Hellenic unity. The dialect in which they sang, the heroic figures and deeds they pictured and the gods they celebrated became the common property of the Greek world. Some of the splendid divine beings of the epics were honored everywhere. Zeus and Apollo became

Delphi.

universal Hellenic gods.   The shrine of Apollo at Delphi was a kind of centre of religious life.   The noblest religious leadership of the time was given by his priests there; it became the custom to obtain from him his sanction for many enterprises.   At Delphi the god spoke through his priestess in utterances called oracles.   No colony could be sent out without Apollo's oracle; kings from the world without sought his wisdom and sent him

Olympia.

rich gifts (§ 117).   What Apollo did for Greek unity at Delphi, Zeus in a different way did at Olympia.   There every four years a festival in honor of the god was celebrated from the earliest times, in connection with which athletic contests were held.   All the Greek cities sent contestants thither.   The list of the victors was preserved. The tradition makes this list date from 776 B.C., which is the first year of the first Olympiad, or four years' period, on which Greek chronology was based for a long time. During the festival, literary works by poets and historians were read in public and works of art exhibited.   Any Greek was eligible to compete.   Though the reward was only a crown of olive leaves, the glory of the victor was

Amphictyonies.

the applause of all Greece.   Religion also encouraged the union of districts in what was called an am-phic′ty-o-ny. Usually a sanctuary was the meeting-point where deputies met at regular intervals in an amphictyonic council, and the affairs of the god and his worshippers were the matters discussed.   During its sessions peace ruled over the whole territory.   In connection with these amphictyonies appear the names of many states afterward famous. In middle Greece the Bœotian amphictyony was formed; on the island of Delos that of the Ionians; most famous of all was that which met at Delphi and in which the

Thessalians were the leading spirits. Of the influence of this union we learn from the two obligations resting on its members: no city belonging to it was to be destroyed, nor, in case of siege, could running water be cut off from a city. Thus a kind of beginning of international law, applying in a limited circle, was made.

129. (b) Growth of Civilization.—The second way in which the new life appeared (§ 118) was in the progress of thought and manners—what we call Civilization. Two most important things came to Greece through commercial life—the use of money and the art of writing. The old form of exchange was by natural products. Cattle were often the standard of value, as the Latin word for money indicates, *pe-cu'ni-a* (from *pecus*, "cattle"). But such means will not do for commercial life. Metals soon came in—at first bars of copper or iron. Later the precious metals were used, as in the east (§ 23), and soon they were coined into money. The Lydians are said to have first coined money, in the seventh century. The state guaranteed the weight and fineness according to a fixed scale and stamped the piece of gold or silver with a sign or mark of genuineness. From Lydia the custom crossed to Greece; in Ægina, it is said, the first Greek coins were made. In the case of writing it seems that the Greek merchants also introduced that art into Greece. They borrowed the alphabet from the Phœnicians (§ 53) and improved it. At first it assumed a variety of forms according to the commercial cities that adopted it. Finally the Ionic alphabet became the standard. In the eighth century men began to employ writing for public purposes—for the lists of officials and of the Olympian victors (§ 128). A century after it ap-

Use of Money.

Art of Writing.

pears on gifts to the gods and on monuments. Finally,
toward the close of the age comes its general use in literature.

130. Interest in Living Men and Their Doings.—Another mark of the higher life of the time is seen in the
greater interest felt in the present, and in the thoughts
and feelings of living men. Homer sang of the deeds
of the heroes of old; he says not a word about his own
time. But Hesiod, although he laments the misery of
his day, calling the present the "iron age," still talks
and reflects upon it. And now appeared poets who, in
verse called *e-le-gi'ac* or *iambic*, dwelt upon events of their
own day, expressing in satire their disgust at their rulers,
calling to a nobler life or urging some political reform.
Such poets were Ar-chil'o-chus of Paros (648 B.C.), and
Lyric Poets. The-og'nis of Megara (540 B.C).   Others became famous
by their poetic expression of feeling, in lyrical songs of
love and marriage, of feasting and social joys, of war
Music. and victory or of praise to the gods.* Accompanying
this outburst of reflective and passionate poetry was a
development of the art of music by the discovery of the
octave and the lyre of seven strings which opened up a
great variety of harmonies. All this means that knowledge was broadening, thought was awakened, pleasures
were becoming finer and higher, life was growing fuller
and man felt himself of more worth in the world.

131. Interest in the Problem of Origins.—As we have
seen (§ 119), men had already begun to think more about
the world in which they lived—how it came to be and

---

* The most celebrated were Al-cæ'us (600 B.C.) and Sappho the poetess
(610 B C.), both of Lesbos, A-nac're-on of Ionia (530 B.C.) and Alcman of
Sparta (660 B.C.).

what kept it in being   Religion, naturally, was first called
on for the answer to these questions, and told how the
power and will of the gods made all things to be.   To
Hesiod all beginnings were divine.   First came Chaos and
Earth and Heaven and Night and Day, and Sea, and Time
and Love—all gods.   Earth was peopled with mighty destructive beings called Titans, against whom Zeus waged
war and won the victory, thus bringing order and harmony
into the world.   Then the gods created man and endowed
him with power to rule all things on earth.   The earth Cosmog-
was thought of as a curved disk with Greece in the mid- ony.
dle and Mt. Olympus, where the gods dwelt, in the exact
centre.   It was divided into two parts by the Mediterranean and all round it flowed the Ocean stream.   The
earth was the centre of the universe; above it was the
ethereal region of Olympus; beneath it was Hades, the
underworld; at a yet deeper depth was Tar'tar-us, where
were imprisoned the wicked immortals, chief among
whom were the Titans.   The resemblance of this scheme
to that of the eastern world is obvious (§ 33); it may have
been in part derived from that source.

132. Dawn of Science and Philosophy.—But when
Greeks began to travel, to come into contact with strange
countries and peoples outside of the former horizon of
Greek life, they were not satisfied with this purely religious
explanation.   They began to study nature itself and find
the secrets of its origin and life in material things.   Thus,
in the Greek world appeared philosophers and scientific
men who drank in eastern wisdom and exercised their
own keen wits on the problems of nature.   Tha'les of Thales of
Miletus (600 B.C.) was a student of mathematics and Miletus.
physics; he calculated an eclipse   measured the height of

the pyramids of Egypt by their shadow, and knew the lore of the heavens. He held that everything in the universe came from Water. To An-ax-im'e-nes (550 B.C.) this foundation principle was Air. To Her'a-cli'tus (500 B.C.) it was Fire. He did not believe that there was anything permanent in the world. "All things flow," he said, or, "all things are burning." The only reality is the fact of change. These Ionic thinkers found worthy companions in the philosophers of Greater Greece, where Py-thag'o-ras (540 B.C.) sought the source of all things in Number, and Xe-noph'a-nes of E'le-a (575 B C.) saw at the heart of the universe one God directing all things by the might of his reason. In all these, to us, crude ways of thinking, we may see the working of the fine Greek intelligence. These thinkers were not satisfied with ideas that prevailed only because they were handed down from of old. They must find for themselves what was really and finally true.

Heraclitus.

The Spirit of Inquiry.

133. Interest in Practical Life.—As these Greeks began to study nature, so they also came to study man and his duties. Hesiod in his *Works and Days* wrote on how to be a successful farmer. Others followed him in this teaching of wisdom, of practical life in state and society. About the year 600 B.C. in the Greek world the most distinguished of these teachers were known as the "Seven Wise Men." * Sometimes they expressed their thought in proverbs like "Nothing too much," "Unlucky is he who cannot bear ill-luck." "Wisdom is the finest possession," "Know thyself."

The Seven Wise Men.

---

* They were Thales of Miletus, Pit'ta-cus of Mytilene, Bias of Pri-e'ne, Solon of Athens, Cle'o-bu'lus of Lindos, Cheilon (Ki'lon) of Sparta and Periander of Corinth.

134. Changes in Religion.—We may be sure that religion also partook of the new spirit of the times. The Olympian gods became everywhere the guardians of state and society. Temples began to be built in their honor and richly decorated; their praise in song and dance became more stately and splendid; the sculptures in tomb and temple show increasing mastery of art in the service of this religion of divine life and beauty. But by the side of this public or official religion appears another which appealed to the individual and sought to meet his need of divine favor. This faith centres about deities who had not been prominent in the Olympian circle—Di'o-ny'sus and De-me'ter. To Dionysus, the god of the vine, giver of joy and ecstasy, and to Demeter, the nourishing mother-earth, bestower of life and food to all, an enthusiastic popular devotion was poured out. One great reason for their worship was its outlook into the life beyond the grave. The changes that were coming over the face of the times did not in all respects bring happiness and peace to men; they created problems the solution of which was uncertain and unpromising. Naturally, men sought consolation in the hope of the world beyond. Little there was of this in the old faith. But the new faith had a new message on this subject. To him who with a pure heart took part in the ceremonial of worship of these gods was promised a brighter world beyond, where there was freedom from care and sin. This ceremonial was called the *Mysteries*. What it consisted of we do not know exactly, but we do know that those who took part in it were pledged to a life of purity and enjoyed the hope of an immortal life. It was an appeal to the heart, not to the head; it was a religion

Temples.

The New Popular Faith.

The Mysteries.

for the people; mystical and enthusiastic as it was, it became a power for good and a spring of some of the noblest forms of Greek life.

135. (c) Political Changes.—We have kept the political changes of the time to the last (§ 118). They show most simply and clearly the influence of the new forces; it was in them and through them that the other changes could come to the surface and work themselves out. They form also the connecting link between this and the following periods. We have seen how everywhere the aristocracy had gained possession of Greek politics (§ 106). In many states they not merely ruled the citizens; they were the citizens. But commerce had now made many besides the aristocracy wealthy and influential. It had brought individuals everywhere, no matter what their station in life was, to a larger knowledge of the world and their own place in it (§ 130). While some had grown rich, others had become poor; the farmers, especially, suffered through borrowing money from usurers at ruinous rates of interest; for being scarce and much in demand money was exceedingly dear, and an unpaid loan rapidly doubled and tripled in amount. Thus disturbances and difficulties appeared on every hand in Greek political life. The aristocracy, feeling its power threatened, did as those frequently do who feel that their position is growing weaker—they used all means to keep it; they acted unjustly and despotically. This only made matters worse, and they were finally forced to yield to the storm.

New Sources of Wealth.

Decline of Aristocratic Governments.

136. Rise of the Lawgivers.—One chief cause of complaint was that they alone knew the law and administered it according to their own will. Hence, the de-

mand arose for the publication of the law. It was
secured in a truly Greek fashion. One man was chosen,
the best man in the state, to whom all power was given
that he might prepare, publish and administer a code
of law which should be binding upon the people. Thus, The Cod--
of Law.
almost every Greek state of the time had its lawgiver,
or in later days traced its law-code back to some great
man who was thought to be its author. Such famous
names were Za-leu′cus of Locri, Lycurgus of Sparta, Pit-
tacus of Mytilene, Solon of Athens. As a result, people
knew what the law was and could fix the responsibility
for crime and injustice. The broad and deep meaning
of such a measure should not be overlooked. That the
state owed it to the citizens to do justice on the basis of a
public code of laws, that the best man in the state should
prepare these laws, and that, once put forth, it was the
citizen's duty to obey them—these were principles which
no ancient people had before so fully realized.

137. Appearance of the Tyrants.—The publication of
the laws had saved the aristocratic rule for the time,
but it had not been accompanied with any larger political rights to those outside the circle of the nobles. Hence
arose a new struggle. All who were dissatisfied with
aristocratic rule joined together in opposition to it; the
whole body was called the *de′mos*, the "people," and
their aim was the overflow of the ruling powers. They
succeeded. Here and there men put themselves at the
head of the revolutionary movement and by it gained the
supreme power for themselves. These men were called
tyrants. They were really kings, reviving the old mon-
archy, with larger powers. They destroyed the rule of Splendor of
Their Rule
the aristocracy and governed their states with vigor

and splendor. All over the Greek world, so far as it was progressive, in these days (about 650 B.C.) tyrants appeared and in some states continued to rule down to the last Greek age. They favored commerce and trade, grew rich from their skilful management of affairs, adorned their cities with magnificent buildings, encouraged art and literature, and with much political wisdom guided their states in new paths of progress. The people, by whose aid they had gained their place, were not, indeed, given any political rights, but the satisfaction of having rid themselves of aristocratic rule and the enlarged prosperity and comfort enjoyed were sufficient for the time to satisfy them.

138. Some of the Tyrants.—One of the first tyrants was Thras'y-bu'lus of Miletus, a shrewd and energetic ruler, who was able to keep his city independent of Lydia (§§ 75, 117). In Corinth the aristocracy was overthrown by Cyp'se-lus, whose father was a commoner, but his mother of a noble family. His son Periander followed him (625–585 B C.). He was a friend and ally of Thrasybulus.

Herodotus relates a characteristic story of their relations: "He sent a messenger to Thrasybulus and asked what settlement of affairs was the safest for him to make, in order that he might best govern his state: and Thrasybulus led forth the messenger who had come from Periander out of the city, and entered into a field of growing corn; and as he passed through the crop of corn, while inquiring and asking questions repeatedly of the messenger about the occasion of his coming from Corinth, he kept cutting off the heads of those ears of corn which he saw higher than the rest; and as he cut off their heads he cast them away, until he had destroyed in this manner the finest and richest part of the crop. So having passed through the place and having suggested no word of counsel, he dismissed the messenger.

When the messenger returned to Corinth, Periander was anxious to hear the counsel which had been given, but he said that Thrasybulus had given him no counsel, and added that he wondered at the deed of Periander in sending him to such a man, for the man was out of his senses and a waster of his own goods—relating at the same time that which he had seen Thrasybulus do. So Periander, understanding that which had been done and perceiving that Thrasybulus counselled him to put to death those who were eminent among his subjects, began then to display all manner of evil treatment to the citizens of the state; for whatsoever Cypselus had left undone in killing and driving into exile, this Periander completed."

139. Corinth under Periander.—But Periander was more than a despot and a butcher. He raised his city to the leading place among the states of his day in continental Greece. Her power on the sea was mighty. The first war-ships with three banks of oars—called triremes—were built at Corinth. With his fleet Periander subdued Corcyra in the first recorded sea-fight of Greek history. He was a patron of letters. The poet Arion was said to have been an ornament of his court, and tradition has made the tyrant one of the "Seven Wise Men" of Greece (§ 133). Another famous tyrant was Cleisthenes of Sicyon who freed his city from the influence of Argos, put down the nobles with a strong hand and took vigorous part in the general affairs of Greece.

Maritime Enterprise of Corinth.

140. Decline and Fall of the Tyrants.—The new spirit of Greece, which had raised the tyrants to the throne, would not let them remain there long. The nobles were always hostile to them; the demos, still deprived of political rights, grew dissatisfied. Then the tyrants * in their turn grew more despotic, and ruled by force

* Owing to this later form of the tyranny our word "tyrant" has a bad meaning.

and fear, until all parties united to put them down. The tyranny usually lasted no longer than the second generation. It had accomplished one result—the universal rule of the aristocracy had perished and the way **Timocracy.** was opened for the advance of the people. When it fell, its place was taken usually by citizens prominent because of their property, and the change was accompanied by making more of the people citizens. Such a government was called a timocracy (from the Greek *ti-me*, "value") and was a step toward putting the control of affairs in the hands of the citizens—the form of government called democracy (from the Greek *demos*, "peo-**Rise of** ple"). Democracy, the special contribution of Greece **Democracy.** to political progress, was worked out in the next period.

REVIEW EXERCISES. 1. For what are the following famous: Theognis, Thales, Hesiod, Pythagoras, Alcæus, Amasis, Anacreon? 2. What is meant by amphictyony, mysteries, Hellenes, elegiac, penteconter, trireme? 3. What is the date of the First Olympiad?

COMPARATIVE STUDIES. 1. Compare the early Greek idea of the form of the world with that of the Egyptians and Babylonians (§ 33). 2. Compare the political effects of commerce and trade upon the Greeks with their effect upon oriental peoples (§§ 20, 23, 50-53).

SELECT LIST FOR READING. 1. Greek Ships. Bury, pp. 109-110 2. The Games and the Oracles. Bury, pp. 139-144. 3. The Greek Temple. Bury, p. 152. 4. The Lyric Poets. Bury, pp. 118-119. 5. Hesiod and His School. Bury, pp. 107-108. 6. The Lawgivers. Bury, pp. 144-146. 7. The Tyrants. Bury, pp. 146-157.

TOPICS FOR READING AND ORAL REPORT. 1. Greek Ships. Dicts. of Antiquities, articles "Ship" or "Navy." 2. The Games and the Oracles. Morey, pp. 150-153; Botsford, pp. 98-103; Zimmern, ch. 2 3. How Reduce Olympiads to Terms of Our Chronology? Abbott, Skeleton Outline, p. 18. 4. The Ionic

Philosophers. Morey, pp 161–164; Botsford, pp 92–96   5. The
Greek Temple. Morey, pp 154–158   6. The Lyric Poets.
Morey, pp 159–161, Botsford, pp 89–90, Capps, pp. 141–172;
Shuckburgh, pp. 27–29, Jebb, p 491.   7. Hesiod and His School.
Botsford, pp. 87–88; Murray, pp. 53–62; Capps, pp. 129–140;
Jebb, pp. 40–46.   8. The Tyrants. Botsford, pp. 64–70.

4.—SPARTA AND ATHENS

141. The Two Leading States of the Time.—Among
the city-states that from time to time have appeared in
the history of these centuries, two come forward prominently as we draw near the close of this age—Sparta
and Athens. They show the influence of the forces which
have been described, and they became later the leading
states of Greece. The story of their rise and early history, therefore, properly preludes the period of Greek
greatness.

142. Sparta Conquers Laconia.—The Dorians who
occupied Laconia (§ 102) settled down in villages, extirpating the earlier Greek population here, fusing with it there.
The old centre, Amyclæ, was not occupied, but not far
off on the opposite side of the Eu-ro′tas river five little
villages developed in close proximity to one another
These five formed the city of Sparta; and in a few generations prior to about 720 B C. its inhabitants subdued
all the other villages of Laconia. *[Mixture of Peoples.]*

143. The Helots.—The people whose property lay in
the rich river valley the Spartans reduced to serfdom, taking from them their lands and arms and denying to them
liberty to organize or to move away from the plots which
they tilled. About one-half of the yield the conquerors
took for themselves. The subject people were called *[Serfs]*

Helots, and lived a life of miserable dependence upon the moods of their conquerors.

144. The Periœci.—With the villages which lay on the hill slopes around "hollow Lac-e-dæ'mon" the Spartans dealt quite generously. They left them their private property, their communal organization and citizen rights. They could engage in whatever occupation they pleased and possessed full liberty of movement. On the other hand they were required, like the Roman colonies, to serve in war with the Spartans at the call of the latter and could not enter into negotiations with foreign cities except through Sparta. From the way in which their towns and land lay in a circle all round the valley in which the Helots were massed they were called Per'i-œ'ci —dwellers round about. They served at once to keep the Helots from escaping abroad and foreigners from giving arms to them or inciting them to revolt. They shared in the glory of the Spartans and always supported them loyally.

Dependent Allies.

145. First Messenian War.—About 720 B.C. the Spartans conquered Messenia and transferred over the Tayg'e-tus mountains the system of classes already in existence in Laconia. The Messenians in the river valley became Helots. Periœc towns surrounded them on all sides except on the coast near the island of Sphacteria. Here was a stretch of rough grazing land where straggling Helots tended the Spartan herds. The final annexations made by Sparta were in the district at the headwaters of the Eurotas (Sciritis) and the tract beyond Parnon (Cynuria). When this was accomplished there were about 12,000 Spartans, 60,000 Periœci and 180,000 Helots. The Spartan state was thus an inverted pyramid.

Spartan Expansion

146. Revolt of Messenians.—In the third generation after the conquest the Helots of Messenia tried to overturn this ill-balanced combination. In their revolt they had the support of all the Peloponnesian cities which felt menaced by the expansion of Sparta. Of these the most important was the Dorian city Argos At this time a vigorous king called Pheidon was on the Argive throne (about 660 B.C.) He was in hearty sympathy with the new life of the day, as is shown by a system of weights and measures introduced by him, which spread all over Greece; it was called the Æ'gi-net'an system. To check Sparta's victorious progress, he joined with two other Peloponnesian states, Arcadia and Pisatis, and, in connection with the rebellion of the Messenians, entered on a conflict with Sparta, which is called the Second Messenian War (about 650 B.C.). Yet, though the struggle was long and fierce, Sparta was finally victorious here also. *[margin: Pheidon of Argos]*

147. Spartans Become Professional Soldiers.—But though the extremity of the danger was safely past, the number of the Spartans was so small and the number of their Helots so great that the slightest relaxation would bring about a recurrence of the peril Hence the Spartans continued for year after year to declare war upon their serfs, and required young men, organized as a secret police (Kryp-tei'a), to move about among them and slay all who seemed restless or over-ambitious. This did not suffice, however. Henceforth, the whole Spartan population of military age remained constantly in readiness to take the field at a moment's notice Their tents were pitched on Hyacinth street midway between the five villages. *[margin: Krypteia.]*

Tent Life.

148. The Messes.—Each tent was occupied by a mess (syssitia). In the tents the several companies of the army lounged and slept, and ate the famous black broth. There they had their arms. At a moment's notice they could form in battle line and meet all attempts of the Helots, however well contrived, "to rush their lager." Out in the villages lived the women, the young girls, the men over sixty who were past the time of active service and the infants of both sexes under seven years of age.

149. The Spartan Women.—Since their fathers, husbands and brothers were constantly absent in the barracks and dare not be seen by daylight in the village, the women moved about freely and had a chance to manage things

Heroism.

in a way not known elsewhere in Greece. The military ideal dominated their life also; they were doubtless a rough burly lot, but they produced a race of vigorous warriors, and were wont to tell those dearest to them on their departure for war to return "with their shields or on them."

Spartan Ideals.

150. Spartan Education.—At the age of seven the boys were taken from their homes and put with other youths of their own age in "pens" and "herds" whom the grown men between twenty and thirty years of age drilled and "fagged." They had to live by their wits. They got scraps from the men's tables, but were left without a roof at night so that they had to make for themselves out-of-door beds of Eurotas reeds. What they lacked for food they got by stealing, and the thief who was not detected was held to have done nothing dishonorable.

151. The Dorian Phalanx.—All their lives, both while boys and after they were elected into the ranks of the men, and after, at the age of thirty, they had become full citizens, the Spartans spent in gymnastic exercises and in drill; for they had to take their places in the compact Dorian phalanx, the great military machine which the Spartans invented and which proved so efficient that the loose-formation single-combat mode of fighting, characteristic of the age of the nobles, became rapidly antiquated. The heroes and knights disappeared and the closely massed infantry of spearmen in which the middle classes served became the main dependence of all prosperous states. Nowhere was the new system so effective as at Sparta.* _{The Middle Classes Form the Army}

152. The Decay of Spartan Culture.—Now that the Spartans had become professional soldiers, in camp from twenty to sixty, they ceased to have other occupations or interests. Up to about 650 B.C. Sparta had not been different from other Greek cities; it had intimate commercial relations with the outside world; it produced poets like Alcman and Tyr-tæ'us; it patronized musical innovators like Terpander; it had sculptors and architects. A great temple to Athena—Athena of the brazen house— was constructed, and the state was hospitable to all the new ideas and inventions which were breaking down the régime of the Middle Age Henceforth, however, the ring wall of Periœci shut out all foreign life. Foreigners who worked their way through were rounded up at intervals and forcefully ejected. The only money current in Sparta was of iron and of small denomination. The only music tolerated was the march, the only poetry the war-song. Their words were few; they preferred deeds.

All Interests Cease Except Warfare

---

* In later times the Spartans ascribed this constitution of theirs to a lawgiver named Lycurgus and wove a story about him and his doings. In fact he was a god whom they had once worshipped and whom they turned into a man and made the founder of the system. It really sprang up in the natural way just described.

There were no more poets or sculptors or architects. The laws remained unwritten, since few could read them Sparta ceased to be a place of high culture and relapsed into primitive barbarism, redeemed only by the habit of unhesitating obedience to the officials.

Kings.

153. The Government of Sparta.—The supreme authorities in Sparta were two kings, the office being hereditary in rival families—the leaders in time of war, once the chief civil magistrates also; the council of elders

Gerusia.

(gerusia), made up of thirty members, including the kings. The elders were chosen from the retired veterans on the basis of popularity as shown by the applause with which they were greeted when they presented themselves

Ephors.

before the army. In addition there were the ephors, whose original duty was to see that all the citizens, the kings included, obeyed the prescriptions of the common military life, but who used the power thus given to direct the whole

Apella.

domestic and foreign policy of the state. The army met as a body in the Apella and had power neither to discuss nor to amend, but simply to say yea or nay to the proposals submitted to it by the kings, ephors and elders

154. The Peloponnesian League.—Next we find Sparta pushing northward up the Eurotas valley against the neighboring city of Te'ge-a. Against these Arcadian mountaineers not much headway was made; whereupon Sparta adopted a new political policy. A treaty was made, whereby Tegea, in return for being left in peace, agreed to contribute a force to the Spartan army when an offensive or defensive war had been undertaken by mutual consent and to make Sparta's friends her friends. Otherwise she remained a free city and had entire control over her own action even in foreign affairs. This plan worked so well that Sparta proceeded to extend it to other cities, until finally, on these conditions, a league of all the Peloponnesian states except Argos was formed under Spartan leadership By 550 B.C. Sparta was the greatest Greek state; besides her own territories, Elis, Corinth, Ægina, Megara and Sicyon were members of the league. Foreign powers coming into contact with Greece sought her alliance. Thus she joined with Lydia and the other eastern states against Cyrus (§ 75). Outside the Peloponnesus she was involved in relations with other Greek communities, particularly with the growing state of Athens. To understand these larger complications we must turn aside to follow the rise and early history of Athens.

155. Athens.—Attica, of which Athens was the chief city, was a rough, poorly watered and unproductive peninsula, jutting out into the Ægean and cut off from the rest of Greece by Mt. Par'nes, an offshoot of the Cith-æ'ron range. The city lay in a little valley through which the Ce-phis'sus flowed to the southwest into the Saronic gulf. Dwellers in the plain had early gathered about a lofty isolated mass of rock, the Acropolis, so easy of defence as to be marked out for the centre of a city. The plain sloped gently to the sea and was itself protected by mountains on either side. The community worshipped the goddess Athena, its patron and defender, who gave the name to the city. The prevailing race-type was Ionian. At the end of the Middle Age Athens had united all the inhabitants of the peninsula in one city-state (§ 107).

156. Early Organization.—Moreover, when we come to know Athens, the aristocracy was already in control. Traditions told how kings had once ruled, but these had gradually been restricted in powers and in dignities,* until hardly more remained to remind one of them than the name "king" applied to the chief minister of religion. In their place came yearly officials called archons, nine in number, for the conduct of civil, military, religious and financial administration. The tribal council took two forms: (1) a body composed of forty-eight, the representatives of local districts, each of which supplied a war-ship (*naus*), and hence was called a Nau-cra′ri-a, and (2) a body made up, it seems, of ex-officials charged chiefly with judicial powers, called the Council of the A-re-op′a-gus (the "Hill of Curses").   Of course, both officials and councils were limited to aristocrats, who also controlled, if they did not make up, the public assembly.   As elsewhere, so especially in Athens, there was a large number of freemen who, under aristocratic administration, were entirely outside of public activities.   The members of noble houses, like the Me-don′ti-dæ and the Alc-mæ-on′i-dæ, were all-powerful; none could break into their close circle.   Their heads were leaders and their members were citizens of the state.   The army was organized in three divisions: first, the knights (hippeis), the aristocrats who could afford to have war-horses and fine weapons; second, the heavy-armed footmen (zeugitæ, *i.e.*, who had farms big enough to employ a yoke of oxen); third, the light-armed troops (thetes, *i.e*, petty land-owners and farm laborers).   All the people of Attica were divided

Aristocrats in Control.

---

*Another version tells how the Athenians abolished the kingship considering no one worthy to succeed Codrus.   At the time of a Peloponnesian invasion, King Codrus, they said, visited the enemy's camp dressed in peasant clothes, and, provoking a quarrel, was slain.   This sacrifice of his own life he made to save Athens, for an oracle had affirmed that either the king or the city must perish   This story is a late invention.

into four phylæ, each with its chief, each at once a regiment and an electoral division of the popular assembly.

157. Tyrants and Lawgivers.—But, in time, the aristocratic state was affected by the new life. A certain noble, Cylon by name, a son-in-law of The-ag'e-nes, tyrant of Megara, attempted to make himself tyrant (about 635 B.C.), but without success. Commerce was making some men rich and others poor; farmers were in debt and many were being sold into slavery. The demos was rising. A lawgiver (§ 136), Dra'co, was appointed (about 624 B.C.). His legislation gave Athens written provisions for settling business and other disputes, thus limiting the power of the magistrates in recognizing cases, conducting trials and imposing penalties. The most durable of these drew a noteworthy distinction between the penalty for different sorts of murder. Heretofore, all killing had been murder and its penalty death at the hands of the relatives of the dead man (§ 105). Now, accidental or justifiable homicide was distinguished in its punishment from wilful murder. As Draco's laws were chiefly a collection of the old customs of the land, they seemed to the later Athenians exceedingly severe and were said to have been "written in blood." Another trial of a lawgiver was made in 594 B.C., by the choice of Solon as sole archon of the state with unlimited authority in the settlement of affairs; and to him Athens owed in addition to a new constitution a second code of civil law which was a vast improvement on that of Draco.

Draco.

Solon.

158. Early Athenian Expansion.—Athens had already begun to enter heartily into the commercial activity of the time. Pottery was manufactured; olive oil—the chief

Commerce of Attica.

natural product of Attica—exported and, possibly, grain imported; colonizing entered upon. An important station on the trade route to the Black sea was secured—Si-ge′um on the northwestern coast of Asia Minor. A great hindrance was Megara's possession of Salamis, the island at the very gates of Athens. A struggle to secure it for Athens had been crowned with victory through the inspiring war-poetry of Solon. He was, therefore, a prominent man; an aristocrat, but a friend of the people, eager to deliver them from their distresses and to give them a place and a part in the state.

159. Constitution of Solon.—The measures of Solon were vital and thorough-going. The fundamental thing he did was to make all free native-born people really citizens. Second, he relieved them from their chief burdens by remitting all debts contracted on their lands or secured on the person or family of the debtor. Third, he gave all some part in the conduct of the state. All the citizens, rich and poor alike, were made members of the public assembly. All over thirty years old and of good moral character were eligible to membership in a new court of justice called the Hel-i-æ′a, which was the final court of appeal. The Council of the Areopagus was constituted as a criminal court and given supervision of the laws. The other council was transformed by being increased to four hundred members and called the Boule or senate. Its chief function was to prepare business for the public assembly. The higher magistracies, those of archon, treasurer, etc., were open only to men of the largest wealth; the lesser offices could be occupied by the less wealthy citizens. The distribution of administrative positions, while in principle based on wealth, resulted in

Cancelling of Debts.

The Council of 400.

actual practice in giving the highest offices to the most influential hippeis, and in dividing the rest of the places between the other hippeis and the zeugitæ. No thetes were eligible for the magistracy The state, therefore, remained aristocratic in administration, although the peo- ple at large were given political rights never before pos- sessed; these in time were certain to be emphasized and enlarged. It may be truly said that Solon was the founder of the Athenian democracy. The Moderate Spirit of Solon's Constitu- tion.

160. **Pisistratus, Tyrant.**—The constitution made by Solon prepared the way for progress, but it did not act- ually bring relief to the state. Conflict and distress con- tinued. Finally, by the aid of the peasants (chiefly thetes), a nobleman called Pi-sis'tra-tus was able to usurp the government in 561 B.C , and though driven from power, regained it about 545 B.C., and was tyrant until his death in 528 B.C. By him, the poor peasants, who had been relieved of their debts and given citizenship by Solon, were granted land and money to set up farming and to become self-supporting and useful citizens. They could not exercise political rights, but became econom- ically comfortable Pisistratus favored commerce, which brought increasing wealth to the state. His court, like those of the other tyrants (§ 137), was brilliant; literature and art were encouraged. It is said, probably without warrant of fact, that Homer's poems were first written down under his patronage and that he established a li- brary at Athens. A temple to Athena, the patron god- dess of the city, was built, another to Zeus begun, and in general he fostered the worship of the national Homeric gods at the expense of the local clan cults. An important part of the religion of the Athenian peasants had long - His Admin- istration.

His Court.

Religious Festivals.

been the village festivals of the god Dionysus (§ 134), and there existed already in Athens the Flower Festival of the early spring (in February) and the Vintage Festival of the winter (in December). To these Pisistratus added another, the Great, or City, Dionysia (in April), at which he introduced the sacred play in which scenes in the life of the god were exhibited—the Tragedy or Goat-song. It is worth remembering that in 535 B.C. Thespis produced the first tragedy at Athens in connection with this festival. The theatre there was a part of religious worship. The foreign politics of Pisistratus were successful in making Athens a power in the Greek world. He controlled the approaches to the Hellespont and was in alliance with the Thessalians and with Argos. By his services to the sanctuary of Apollo on the island of Delos, a favorite Ionian centre, he became a leader among the Ionians of the Ægean. On his death (528 B.C.) he was succeeded without opposition by his son, Hip′pi-as, who ruled in close partnership with his younger brother, Hippar′chus.

His Foreign Politics.

161. Tyranny Overthrown.—But the tyranny was to have as short a life at Athens as it had enjoyed elsewhere (§ 140). The same reasons for its overthrow existed there. The first blow for liberty, however, was struck as a consequence of a private quarrel in which Hipparchus was assassinated by Harmodius and Ar-is-to-gei′ton. Thereafter Hippias, in fear of a like fate, ruled suspiciously and tyrannically. Exiled nobles, at their head the Alcmæonidæ, intrigued constantly against him, and on one occasion they tried to expel him from Athens by their own strength. Failing in this they turned to Sparta, whose league had now reached the frontiers of Attica, and by

Sparta Aids the Alcmæonidæ

the influence of the oracle at Delphi, which the Alcmæonidæ had won over by great generosity in the rebuilding of the temple of Apollo, this ambitious state was induced to send an army under King Cleomenes to drive Hippias out (510 B C). After he was gone the Spartans attempted to set up an aristocratic government, but after a struggle the Athenian people under the leadership of Cleisthenes, the head of the family of the Alcmæonidæ, a friend of the demos, was able to gain control of the state (508 B.C.). Cleisthenes immediately set about a reorganization of the state on the basis of the constitution of Solon with the purpose of correcting the defects and guarding against the dangers of the former legislation. Two evils had not been met by the Solonian constitution—the people could not exercise the rights given them because of aristocratic influence, and parties based on local self-interest rent the state. To meet these difficulties Cleisthenes made some fundamental changes. He organized the people into ten tribes. Each tribe was made up of three parts taken by lot from each of the three local divisions of Attica, the upland, the plain and the coast, where dwelt respectively the peasants, the landed proprietors and the merchants. Thus all interests and all parties were likely to be represented in each tribe. The unit of each tribe was the deme, or township; to be a citizen one must be enrolled in a deme; it elected its officials, who revised its list of citizen members from time to time and probably cared for the taxes. At the same time a large body of new citizens was created by the admission of strangers (metics) and freedmen resident in the land. The council (Boule) was increased to five hundred members, fifty from each tribe, chosen in the demes according

Legislation of Cleisthenes.

The New Tribes and Demes.

The Prytany. to the number of citizens in each deme. ' The year was divided into ten parts, and each body of fifty senators presided over public business for a little over a month. As such it was called a prytany and was lodged and fed at the public expense during that time. Ten generals (strategoi) were chosen (501 B.C.), one from each tribe. The other officials were appointed as before. A new device **Ostracism.** for guarding against tyranny was ostracism. Every year the citizens were given the privilege of voting as to whether any prominent man was dangerous to the state. If six thousand citizens voted, a majority of votes recorded against any one upon the pieces of tile (*os'tra-ka*) used for the purpose, compelled him to leave the state for ten years, though neither his property nor his citizen rights were lost.

162. **The Victory of Liberal Government at Athens.**— Thus Athens became a definitely constitutional state. Solon had established the citizen body in its political rights; Pisistratus had given the poor people opportunity to become self-supporting and respectable; Cleisthenes made it possible for the great middle class of farmers and merchants to use their power in the actual conduct of the state, and since the tyrant's guiding hand was now removed the ecclesia asserted its right henceforth to determine for itself the chief questions of public policy. A notable political experiment was now tried for the first time in history. The opportunity was soon to come in which it would be seen whether liberal government was equal to meeting the strain of war and suffering. The Persian war-cloud was hanging over the eastern horizon (§ 84). With its swift approach the era of Greek beginnings drew to its close (500 B.C.).

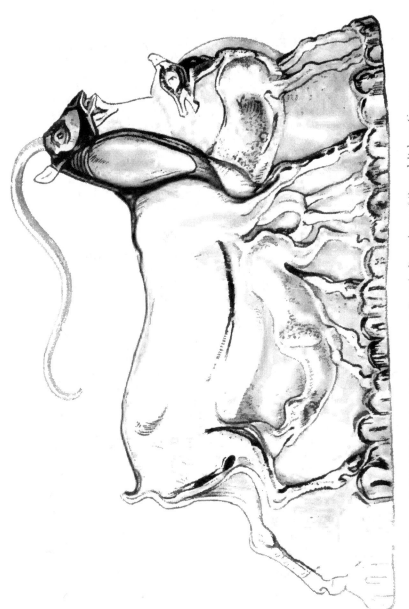

Faience Relief: Wild Goat and Young. From Temple Repository of Second Palace, Cnossos

CRETAN ART OF THE TWENTIETH CENTURY B. C.

REVIEW EXERCISES. 1. What is meant by deme, gerusia, prytany, Helot, Acropolis, Periœci, Heliæa, Boule? 2. Who were Pheidon, Thespis, Dionysus, Cleomenes, Lycurgus? 3. Locate from memory on an outline map all the cities and countries mentioned in §§ 141-163. 4. What is the date of the Second Messenian War? of Solon? 5. What was the character of the conquest of Laconia by Sparta? 6. Describe the condition of the Helots and Periœci. 7. What was the cause of the decay of Spartan culture?

COMPARATIVE STUDIES. Compare the manner in which Sparta built up her power in the Peloponnesus with the manner in which the eastern states built up their power (§§ 11-15, 37, 62-64).

SELECT LIST FOR READING. 1. Cylon's Rebellion. Bury, pp. 175-179. 2. The Cretan Constitution Compared with that of Sparta. pp 136-139. 3. Sparta's Origin, Organization and Expansion. Bury, pp 120-129 4. Early History of Athens. Bury, pp. 163-180 5. Solon's Constitution. Bury, pp 180-189. 6. Pisistratus. Bury, pp 192-202 7. The Reforms of Cleisthenes. Bury, pp 210-215

TOPICS FOR READING AND ORAL REPORT. 1. The Story of Solon. Plutarch, Life of Solon. 2. Sparta's Beginnings and Organization. Morey, pp. 112-117, Botsford, pp 27-29, 56-63; Shuckburgh, pp. 30-45; Zimmern, ch 3 3. Sparta's Expansion. Morey, pp. 118-120; Botsford, pp. 77-80 4. Early History of Athens. Morey, pp 120-125, Botsford, pp 25-27, 41-48, Shuckburgh, pp 55-68 5. Solon's Constitution. Morey, pp. 125-129; Shuckburgh, pp 68-86, Botsford, pp. 48-56. 6. Pisistratus. Morey, pp. 129-131, Botsford, pp. 70-77; Shuckburgh, pp. 81-88. 7. The Reforms of Cleisthenes. Morey, pp. 131-134; Shuckburgh, pp 88-93, Botsford, pp. 81-86.

163. Summary of the Period.—The beginnings of life in the Ægean world are unknown. The oriental peoples were already far advanced in civilization when the first light breaks on this region. But by 2000 B.C. a high culture was produced in Crete under Egyptian influence, probably by a pre-Greek people. About 1500

B C. this culture was diffused over the Ægean world, modified in many respects, and possessed by the Greeks who had migrated into Greece from the north. This so-called Mycenæan age was brought to an end by the descent of rude tribes from the north, which is called the Dorian migration. This cut off Greece from the outer world and set in motion new forces of political and social organization. Changes from tribal life to local settlement created the city-state and put at its head the aristocratic government. When the new-comers had adjusted themselves to their new homes, commerce began to revive on the shores of the Ægean. The cities on the Asia Minor coast came forward. New relations with the orient arose. Wealth gave leisure and opportunity for the new growth of literature and art and religion. Epic poetry reached its height in Homer. The Greeks began to know themselves as one people, the Hellenes, and to form their ideals of social, religious and political life. The Olympic gods (§ 112), the religious games (§ 128), the Delphic oracle, the amphictyonies, were signs of the times. Commerce led to a wide and enterprising colonial activity in the Mediterranean world. All this new life reacted upon the Greeks to produce (1) dissatisfaction with aristocratic rule, leading to the appointment of lawgivers, the appearance of tyrannies and the rise of constitutional government; and (2) larger relations with the outside world, particularly with the oriental empires now being rapidly merged into the Persian empire. Two states rose above the others as the age drew to an end. Sparta illustrates the tendency to maintain and harden the old tribal system with its equality and its military bent. It grew by conquest, until it occupied two-fifths of the Peloponnesus and formed a political league embracing almost all the rest. Thus it was the leading Greek state. Athens went to the other extreme. Its lawgivers, Solon and Cleisthenes, led the way in the establishment of popular government. Pisistratus, the Athenian tyrant, gave the state a leading place among the commercial powers of the time. Thus by 500 B.C. the Greek world had reached a point at which, its political institutions fixed and its states firmly established, it was prepared to take its place and do its work in world politics. This place and work in the world were opened to it in the rapidly approaching complications with the Persian empire.

GENERAL REVIEW OF PART II, DIVISIONS I-IV

TOPICS FOR CLASS DISCUSSION. 1. Trace the development of political institutions through the first three epochs of this period (§§ 98, 105-108, 114-115, 135-140). 2. Note the various stages in the development of literature and art in this period (§§ 94-95, 98-99, 109, 110, 119, 128. 152, 160). 3. Show how the literature and art of each epoch corresponds to the political history of that epoch. 4. Give a history of the Greek king (§§ 98-99, 105, 106, 107, 137, 156). 5. Compare the history of Sparta and Athens as they were affected by the general political development of Greece (§§ 152-153, 157-162). 6. Trace the influence of commerce on the life of the Greeks during this period (§§ 97-98, 108, 113, 129, 135, 152, 158). 7. On what occasions during this period did the Greeks come into contact with outside peoples? Who were these peoples and what did the contact mean for Greece (§§ 91, 97, 103, 116, 117(75), 132)? 8. Enumerate the influences (1) that kept the Greeks separate, and (2) that united them, during this period (§§ 87, 106, 107, 115, 119, 128)

MAP AND PICTURE EXERCISES. 1. On an outline map of Greece place (1) the physical features of Greece, (2) the peoples and cities of the first epoch, (3) those of the second epoch, (4) those of the third epoch—using, if possible, different colored pencils or inks to distinguish the epochs—(5) then, with

the general map of Greece before you, note the peoples and
cities which have not yet played a part in the history. 2.
Compare the oriental scenes in Plates III, IV and VIII with the
Greek scene found in Plates XIV and XV and make observa-
tions from the point of view of grace, strength, simplicity,
technical skill, etc. Compare, for further illustration, the
plates in Tarbell, pp. 132, 137, 146, 151, 156.

SUBJECTS FOR WRITTEN PAPERS. 1. The Olympian Games.
Bury, pp 140-142; Grant, Greece in the Age of Pericles, pp.
26-33; Duruy, History of Greece, II, pp 378-394, Diehl, Excur-
sions in Greece, ch. 7 2. Greek Oracles, especially Delphi.
Bury, pp 159, 161, Grant, Greece in the Age of Pericles, pp. 20-
26; Duruy, History of Greece, II, pp 318-330. 3. Mycenæan
Art. Tarbell, ch. 2; Bury, pp. 11-30, Tsountas and Manatt,
Mycenæan Age, chs. 5, 9. 4. The Story of the Founding of a
Greek Colony. Botsford, ch. 3; Bury, ch. 2, Duruy, History of
Greece, II, pp. 165-173; Greenidge, pp. 36-45. 5. Write the
story of the "Iliad" in a thousand words. Capps, pp 22-74.
6. Write the story of the "Odyssey" in the form of an autobiography of Odysseus. Capps, pp 75-110. 7. History of a
Tyrant; Cleisthenes of Sicyon. Herodotus, V, 67-69; VI, 126-
131; or, Polycrates of Samos. Herodotus, III, 40-47, 54-56,
120-125 8. The Legends of the Chief Gods of Greece. Grant,
Greece in the Age of Pericles, pp. 12-18, Guerber, Myths of Greece
and Rome; Fairbanks, Mythology of Greece and Rome. 9. Heracles and the Dorian Invasions. Bury, pp 80-82; Duruy, History
of Greece, I, pp. 273-281. 10. The Greek Temple. Mahaffy,
Old Greek Life, pp. 19-24; Tarbell, ch. 3

5.—THE GREEK EMPIRES: ATHENIAN, SPARTAN, THEBAN AND MACEDONIAN

500-336 B.C.

164. The Menace of Persia.—The victory of Cyrus
over Lydia (§ 75) had brought the Ionian cities under the
Persian power. This authority had been strengthened
and extended over the islands by succeeding rulers until
practically the whole coast was subject. The Scythian

expedition of King Darius (§ 84) had been followed by the extension of Persian authority throughout the northern Ægean, where a new satrapy was formed. It was clear that the Great King would not stop until all the Greek peninsula acknowledged his sceptre. Some Greek communities were already reconciled to this prospect and had sought the aid of Persia in the settlement of their difficulties. Among these were Thebes and Argos; the Delphic oracle steadily favored submission, and even Athens in the year 497 B.C. offered to do homage. It seemed that the lack of Greek unity, set over against the mighty centralized power of Persia, would make successful defence impossible.

165. The Ionian Revolt.—But events beyond the control of the Greek states made a conflict unavoidable. In 499 B.C. the Greek cities of Ionia under the leadership of Miletus rebelled against the Persians and sought help from Sparta and Athens. The former refused, but Athens sent twenty ships and Eretria five.

The Greeks Hesitate.

The story of the rejection of the petition in Sparta is told by Herodotus as follows:

"Ar-is-tag'o-ras spoke thus, and Cleomenes answered him saying: 'Guest-friend from Miletos, I defer my answer to thee till the day after to-morrow.' Thus far then they advanced at that time; and when the appointed day arrived for the answer, and they had come to the place agreed upon, Cleomenes asked Aristagoras how many days' journey it was from the sea of the Ionians to the residence of the king. Now Aristagoras, who in other respects acted cleverly and imposed upon him well, in this point made a mistake; for whereas he ought not to have told him the truth, at least if he desired to bring the Spartans out to Asia, he said in fact that it was a journey up from the sea of three months; and the other cutting short the rest of the account which Aristagoras had begun to give of the way, said.

Sparta Re-
fuses to
Help the
Ionians.
'Guest-friend from Miletos, get thee away from Sparta before the sun has set; for thou speakest a word which sounds not well in the ears of the Lacedemonians, desiring to take them a journey of three months away from the sea.' Cleomenes, accordingly, having so said went away to his house; but Aristagoras took the suppliant's branch and went to the house of Cleomenes; and having entered in as a suppliant, he bade Cleomenes send away the child and listen to him; for the daughter of Cleomenes was standing by him, whose name was Gorgo, and this as it chanced was his only child, being of the age now of eight or nine years. Cleomenes, however, bade him say that which he desired to say, and not to stop on account of the child. Then Aristagoras proceeded to promise him money, beginning with ten talents, if he would accomplish for him that for which he was asking, and when Cleomenes refused, Aristagoras went on increasing the sums of money offered, until at last he had promised fifty talents, and at that moment the child cried out. 'Father, the stranger will do thee hurt, if thou do not leave him and go.' Cleomenes then, pleased by the counsel of the child, departed into another room, and Aristagoras went away from Sparta altogether, and had no further opportunity of explaining any further about the way up from the sea to the residence of the king.''

The allies opened the campaign by seizing and burning Sardis, the Persian capital of Asia Minor, but while returning to the coast they were defeated near Ephesus by the Persians; whereupon the Athenians abandoned the enterprise. A long and desperate struggle ensued. The Battle of
Lade. decisive factor was the dissension which arose among the Greek cities and it was to this that the great defeat which they sustained in the naval battle of La'de (494 B.C) was due. Even in the midst of the engagement the Samians and Lesbians sailed away, abandoning their comrades. Another disaster of appalling magnitude followed. Destruction
of Miletus. Miletus—at that time the largest and most cultured city in the entire Greek world—was taken by storm and

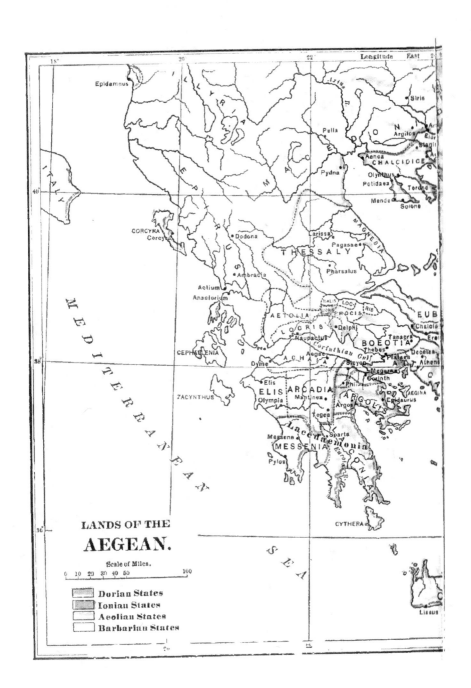

LANDS OF THE

AEGEAN.

Scale of Miles.

0 10 20 30 40 50   100

Dorian States
Ionian States
Aeolian States
Barbarian States

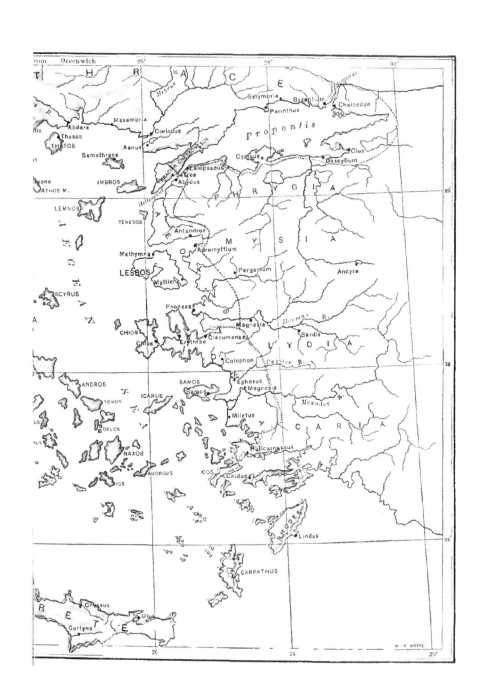

razed to the ground. Persia immediately set about punishing the Greeks of the peninsula for their interference, while Sparta and Athens, with a boldness born rather of ignorance and assurance than of real knowledge, awaited the attack The first expedition commanded by Mardonius, the king's son-in-law, consisted of a land army and a fleet. It started southward from the Persian possessions on the north Ægean through Macedonia in 492 B.C. But the fleet was shipwrecked off Mt. Athos and the expedition returned in disgrace. A second attack was made in 490 B.C by a force which sailed straight across the sea bound for Athens. It consisted of about 20,000 men, chiefly foot-soldiers. After stopping at the island of Eubœa and sacking Eretria, the army was landed on the Attic coast in the hill-girt plain of Marathon. The Athenian citizen force of 10,000 heavy armed men (hoplites), aided by 1,000 troops of the neighboring city of Pla-tæ'a, occupied the heights through which the road passed before descending to the city. The ten strategoi, with the war archon at their head, were uncertain whether to meet the Persians there or to await them behind the walls of Athens. The Persians were equally in doubt as to what to do. Finally, after some days, the persuasions of one of the strategoi, Mil-ti'a-des, were successful in inducing the Athenians to remain. The Persians also decided to advance On the decisive day the war archon handed over the chief command to Miltiades. He extended his force until it equalled the Persian front, strengthening his wings at the expense of the centre, and hurled the army on a run against the advancing Persians. The strategy was successful, for, while his centre was broken, the wings were victorious and

First Persian Expedition.

Second Persian Expedition.

Miltiades.

closed in upon the Persians, who fled to their ships.   The
bows and arrows and light wicker shields of the Persians
proved child's weapons against the spears and metal
armor of the Greeks.   Six thousand four hundred Persians were slain and seven ships were taken; of the Athe-

Marathon. nians one hundred and ninety-two fell.   The rest of
the enemy escaped upon the ships, and, after an attempt
to surprise Athens while denuded of its defenders had
been foiled by the rapid march home of the victors of
Marathon, they returned to Asia Minor.   Two days
after a Spartan force, for which the Athenians had
despatched a swift messenger, arrived on the scene.

166. **Significance of the Victory.**—The victory of
Marathon had no effect upon the Persian king beyond
making him more determined than ever to conquer

Temporary Greece.   To him it was only a temporary check; a small
Check to
Persia.   force had been defeated in a somewhat rash enterprise.
For the Greeks, however, the victory meant everything,
now at last they had no fear of Persia and were ready
to meet any attack however formidable.   To Athens
especially it was most significant.   At one bound she
sprang to the front as the defender of Greek freedom.
Miltiades shared in the glory and became the first citizen
of the state.   Under his leadership a fleet was sent out
against the island of Pa'ros.

167. **The Ten Years' Respite.**—The Persians were
delayed ten years before attacking again.   While Darius
was making his preparations, the province of Egypt rebelled (486 B.C.).   He himself died the next year and was
succeeded by his son Xerxes   During this time important changes were taking place in the political situation
at Athens.   A failure of Miltiades in his naval expedition

brought him into disgrace with the Athenians, he died while under condemnation by the people The democratic movement was greatly aided by a change in the constitution by which the archons were appointed by lot (487 B C.)   In this arrangement those who had hitherto been the chief administrative officers of the state were henceforth men of mere average attainment.   Hence the people found new leaders in the strategoi (§ 161) who were still elected, not chosen by lot.   It was arranged that henceforth, while nine strategoi were elected by the tribes, one, the chief strategos, should be chosen by all the people.   To this position, therefore, the chief man (the demagogue, "leader of the demos") in the state, was usually elected, and the archons fell into obscurity.

Democratic Progress at Athens.

The Leader of the Demos.

168. **Aristides and Themistocles.**—Under this arrangement two men came prominently forward with very different political ideas Aristides, a man of exceptionally high character, thought the safety of Athens and her greatness lay in emphasizing the importance of her heavy armed citizen soldiery that had won the battle of Marathon. Themistocles, the opposing statesman, claimed that there was no hope of deliverance except in the creation of a naval force which could meet the Persians on the sea and beat them off.   He urged also a commercial policy as the true source of wealth and progress for Athens.   When in 493 B.C. Themistocles had been archon, he had induced the Athenians to change their harbor to the roomy and protected bay of the Pi-ræ'us, and now he urged his naval policy more vigorously.   He persuaded the people to devote the income of their silver mines on the promontory of Laurium, usually distributed among the citizens, to the building of the navy.   Opposition was overthrown

Policy of Themistocles.

by the "ostracism" of Aristides in 482 B.C., and in 480 B.C. a fleet of nearly two hundred triremes was ready. This step was one of the most important ever taken by Athens. It marked out her future career. Had Aristides won, Athens would have remained a state in which the landholders and the people of property, who made up the citizen army, would have been the chief element in the state. The new policy turned Athens toward the sea.

Its Result It brought into prominence and importance the merchants and tradesmen; the mass of the poor and landless people, hitherto without influence in the state, were made as necessary for the fleet as the hoplites for the army. Hence, the policy was a step forward toward true democracy within the state and toward giving Athens a leading place in the greater world without

Great (Third) Persian Expedition. **169. The Expedition of Xerxes.**—The preparations of Xerxes for the invasion of Greece were begun by 483 B.C. The plan adopted was the same as that of 492 B.C. (§ 165). To avoid the dangers of shipwreck off Mt. Athos a canal was cut through the peninsula on which it stood. Bridges were thrown across the streams and magazines of stores were established. An army and a fleet, which represented the full strength of the empire, were collected. Xerxes himself took the command. The Greeks estimated the total size of the army at something short of two millions. A very conservative estimate makes the number of first-class fighting men, exclusive of camp-followers, about one hundred thousand The fleet numbered about a thousand ships, great and small In the spring of 480 B.C the Hellespont was crossed, and by July the fleet and the army were moving southward to the borders of Thessaly.

170. Dark Outlook for the Greeks.—The outlook for the Greeks was dark. To the demand for submission which Xerxes had made, through heralds sent up and down the land, a number of states had yielded The Thessalian nobles, Thebes and the Bœotian cities under her influence, Argos and some lesser tribes, were either openly or secretly on the Persian side. The oracle of Delphi had lost all hope and its utterances in response to anxious inquiries from the different states were gloomy and discouraging.

Its attitude is explained by Herodotus in the following passage:
"For the Athenians had sent men to Delphi to inquire and were preparing to consult the Oracle; and after these had performed the usual rites in the sacred precincts, when they had entered the sanctuary and were sitting down there, the Pythian prophetess, whose name was Aristonike, uttered to them this oracle·

The Unpatriotic Counsel of Delphi.

"'Why do ye sit, O ye wretched?   Flee thou to the uttermost limits,
Leaving thy home and the heights of the wheel-round city behind thee!
Lo, there remaineth now nor the head nor the body in safety,—
Neither the feet below nor the hands nor the middle are left thee,—
All are destroyed together; for fire and the passionate War-god,
Urging the Syrian car to speed, doth hurl them to ruin.
Not thine alone, he shall cause many more great strongholds to perish,
Yea, many temples of gods to the ravening fire shall deliver,—
Temples which stand now surely with sweat of their terror downstreaming,
Quaking with dread, and lo! from the topmost roof to the pavement
Dark blood trickles, forecasting the dire unavoidable evil.
Forth with you, forth from the shrine, and steep your soul in the sorrow!'"

"Hearing this the men who had been sent by the Athenians to consult the Oracle were very greatly distressed; and as they were despairing by . . . .

Timon the son of Androbulos, a man of the Delphians in reputation equal to the first, counselled them to take a suppliant's bough and to approach the second time and consult the Oracle as suppliants. The Athenians did as he advised and said: "Lord, we pray thee utter to us some better oracle about our native land, having respect to these suppliant boughs which we have come to thee bearing; otherwise surely we will not depart from the sanctuary, but will remain here where we are now, even until we bring our lives to an end." When they had spoken these words, the prophetess gave them a second oracle as follows:

"'Pallas cannot prevail to appease great Zeus in Olympos,
Though she with words very many and wiles close-woven entreat him.
But I will tell thee this more, and will clench it with steel adamantine:
Then when all else shall be taken, whatever the boundary of Kekrops
Holdeth within, and the dark ravines of divinest Kithairon,
A bulwark of wood at the last Zeus grants to the Trito-born goddess
Sole to remain unwasted, which thee and thy children shall profit.
Stay thou not there for the horsemen to come and the footmen un-
    numbered;
Stay thou not still for the host from the mainland to come, but re-
    tire thee,
Turning thy back to the foe, for yet thou shalt face him hereafter.
Salamis, thou the divine, thou shall cause sons of women to perish.
Or when the grain is scattered or when it is gathered together.'"

Union for Resistance. A council of the states that proposed to offer resistance met at Corinth. The Peloponnesian league under Sparta's headship was naturally the chief power; Athens and other states loyally accepted her leadership. The council agreed that in the face of the pressing danger all feuds between Greek states should cease and a general **Gelon of Syracuse.** invitation was extended to all to unite for defence. A special request for help was sent to Gelon, tyrant of Syracuse, who ruled over the cities of Sicily and possessed military resources beyond those of any other state in the

Greek world. But Xerxes had made an alliance with Carthage (§§ 52, 117), whereby she was to attack the Greeks of Sicily. He gained thereby a valuable ally. For Carthage had now drawn under her control all the Phœnician settlements in the west, and, having possession of western Sicily, Sardinia, the coast of Spain and North Africa, she had succeeded in converting the sea which they enclosed into a Carthaginian lake. Within these waters she had established a commercial monopoly and had drawn from it fabulous wealth. This enabled her to maintain a powerful fleet and, whenever she wished, to take into her employ a host of mercenary troops. She now advanced to the conquest of all Sicily Gelon was, therefore, unable to render assistance even if he had been willing to do so. The plan of campaign proposed to the council of Corinth by Themistocles was adopted; it was simple and masterly. On land, where the Persian army was so much larger, a battle was to be avoided as long as possible; a naval battle was to be sought as soon as possible, for on the sea the opposing forces were more nearly equal. It was thought that, if the Persian fleet were destroyed, the army of the Great King would not be able to remain in Greece. Having made these preparations, full of heroic courage and undaunted purpose, the representatives of the various states separated and the conflict began.

Carthage Joins Persia

The Greek Plan of Campaign

171. Thermopylæ.—In accordance with the plan, a small force was sent forward to block the enemy's advance at the northern mountain border of Thessaly. It was found, however, that there were too many passes through the mountains to make a defence possible at this point, and, abandoning Thessaly, the Greek force took

its stand on the heights south of the Thessalian plain.
Here the narrow and easily defended pass of Ther-mop'y-
læ forms the only entrance into middle Greece. The
Greeks were under the command of the Spartan king
Le-on'i-das and consisted of about seven thousand men,
the kernel of which was a corps of three hundred Spartans.
Xerxes occupied Thessaly without opposition, and by
August, 480 B.C., advanced to Thermopylæ to force the
pass   The battle raged for two days, the flower of the
Persians attacking the Greeks in the narrow defile in
vain.   On the third day, a troop was sent around on the
heights above the pass, and the battle was renewed from
front and rear. Retreat had been possible earlier and
the bulk of the defenders had retired, but Leonidas and
his Spartans remained and at last perished, overpowered
by numbers. After the war was over, a monument was
raised upon the hillock where the last stand was made,
a lion carved in stone with the inscription:

Leonidas and the 300.

> Stranger, report this word, we pray, to the Spartans, that lying
> here in this spot we remain, faithfully keeping their laws.

172. The Greek Fleet.—Meanwhile the Persian fleet,
sailing southward, had encountered a storm which de-
troyed some four hundred ships. The remainder, still
a formidable host, advanced to the Pag'a-sæ'an gulf. The
Greek fleet was gathered at Artemisium on the north
of Eubœa. Several encounters took place without decisive result, when the news of Thermopylæ decided the
Greeks to withdraw to the Saronic gulf. The results
thus far were distinctly unfavorable to the Greeks. The
defeat of Thermopylæ opened middle Greece to the
Persians, while the Greek fleet had not gained any com-

Artemi- cium.

pensating advantage. The decisive struggle still to come was transferred now to the very heart of the peninsula.

173. Salamis.—Xerxes moved down into Bœotia and took possession of the whole middle region. The Greeks still pursuing their original plan, offered no resistance, but awaited the Persians at the isthmus of Corinth, where they built a wall from one side to the other and

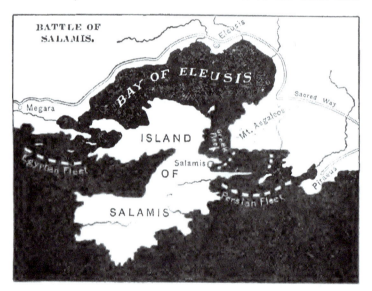

BATTLE OF SALAMIS.

stationed the Peloponnesian army under the command of Cle-om'bro-tus of Sparta, brother of Leonidas. Athens, therefore, was quite unprotected, and measures were immediately taken for abandoning the country and transporting the inhabitants to Salamis, Ægina and the Peloponnesus. Soon the Persians came down and occupied the city. The Greek fleet of about three hundred ships was now drawn up between Salamis and the Attic shore. There was great uncertainty among the commanders

Athenians Abandon Attica.

whether to fight the oncoming Persian fleet then and there, or to retreat to the Peloponnesian shore in order to keep in touch with the army Themistocles, who desired a battle where the Greeks then were, sent a messenger to Xerxes to warn him of the intended flight of the Greeks. The Persian king immediately sent two hundred Egyptian vessels to block up the western outlets, while the main fleet was stationed in front of the Greeks on the eastern side of the island. When the news was brought by Aristides, who had been recalled from exile, that the western passage was occupied, the Greeks saw themselves forced to give battle. It was well for them that the battle was fought here, for, in the narrow straits, their lighter ships and smaller numbers counted for much more, while the larger Persian fleet was crowded

Defeat of Persian Fleet. and hampered. About the 28th of September, 480 B.C., the fight began at break of day, and by night the Persians were completely beaten. Xerxes, whose throne had been set up on the slope of Mt Æ-ga'le-os, witnessed the discomfiture of his navy. The next morning the remaining ships bore away to the eastward and disappeared.

174. Effect of the Battle.—Salamis was the first of the battles with Persia that can properly be called a decisive victory. Its consequences appeared at once. The Greeks were now masters of the sea. The Persian army, without the support of a fleet, and in an enemy's country, must depend upon itself for support and success. A defeat would be ruin. Moreover, should the Greeks sail to the Hellespont, they could cut Xerxes's communications with his own land, stir up the Ionian cities to rebellion and force the Persian army to return home. That was precisely what Themistocles desired the fleet to do immediately after the battle, but the other commanders were unwilling to venture so far away from home. Xerxes was not slow in grasping the situation. He decided to go back at once to Asia, leaving Mardonius with the bulk of the army to push forward the campaign next year.

175. Platæa.—The Persian army withdrew from Attica and went into winter quarters in Bœotia. The Athenians returned to their fields and rebuilt their homes. As spring (479 B.C.) came on, however, it was clear that unless the Peloponnesians advanced beyond the isthmus, Attica would again be laid waste by the Persians. But in spite of the appeals of the Athenians, the Spartans failed to move, and Athens again abandoned was burned to the ground. Only the threat of the Athenians that they would make peace with Mardonius, who had given them all kinds of promises, forced the advance of the Peloponnesians. As they came out of the isthmus, the Persians retired from Attica and took up a position in the vicinity of Platæa. Mardonius was said with gross exaggeration to have an army of three hundred thousand men, well organized and equipped, and might reasonably hope for victory over the Greeks. They were numbered at about one hundred thousand men, drawn from the various Peloponnesian states and from Athens, under the command of Pausanias, the Spartan. The two opponents manœuvred for some days before Platæa, both sides being unwilling to lose the advantage of a defensive position. Finally, however, having caught Pausanias in the midst of a movement to change his base of operations, Mardonius hurled his finest troops upon the Spartan force. But the Spartans maintained their steadiness and discipline in the face of the enemy until ordered

to charge. As at Marathon, so here, the onset of the
hoplites was irresistible. They tore the opposing Persian force in pieces; Mardonius was killed; the Persian
camp stormed. The Persian general, Ar-ta-ba'zus, succeeded in getting away into Asia with less than a fifth of
the army. Thus, as Herodotus said, "was gained by
Pausanias the most famous victory of all those about
which we have knowledge."

175. Himera and Mycale.—During these years two
other battles were fought which completed the discomfiture of the Persians. In the west, Gelon of Syracuse
(§ 170), who was attacked by the Carthaginians in alliance
with Persia, defeated them decisively in the battle of
Him'e-ra (480 B.C.), said to have been fought on the very
day of Salamis.* The Greek fleet, which had been in-
active since the victory of Salamis, sailed in 479 B.C. over
to Asia Minor, where the remnant of the Persian fleet was
protecting the coast. On the approach of the Greeks
the enemy's fleet was drawn up under protection of the
army, on the shore of the promontory of Myc'a-le. Here
the Greeks attacked them and won a complete victory
(479 B.C.) and thus gained control of the Ionian coast.
Not a Persian ship was to be found on the Ægean sea.
After capturing the city of Sestos, one of the keys to the
Hellespont, the fleet returned to Greece.

*Gelon's chief ally in this war was Theron of Ac'ra-gas. Under the
rule of these two tyrants and that of Hi'e-ron, who succeeded his brother
Gelon in 478 B.C., Sicily enjoyed a period of great power and prosperity.
There was no more brilliant society in the world than that of the two
island courts. To them went the most distinguished poets of the eastern
cities, Pindar and Æs'chy-lus (§ 179), Si-mon'i-des and Bac-chyl'i-des.
The greatest exploit of Hieron was the destruction of the Etruscan maritime power by his naval victory at Cyme in 474 B.C.

Marginal notes:

Defeat of Persian Army.

Def'at of Carthage.

Attack on Asia.

PLATE XVI

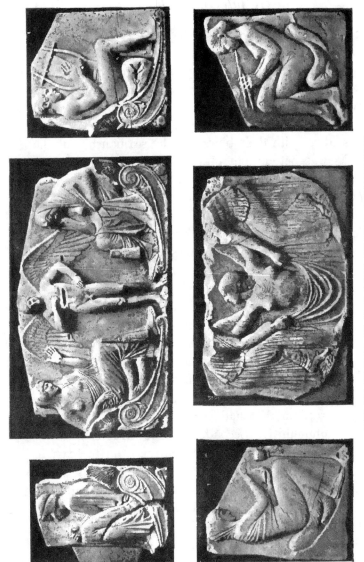

ART OF GREECE IN THE TIME OF THE PERSIAN WAR

177. Reasons for Greek Success.—Thus closed the critical years which resulted in warding off the Persian attack and triumphantly defending the independence of Greece. How it was all achieved, the Greeks themselves hardly knew. We see that (1) the Greek infantry with its long spears was more than a match for the Persian foot-soldiers with their bows, (2) the seamanship of the Greeks was better than that of the Persians, while (3) the strongest part of the Persian army, the cavalry, had no chance in the narrow valleys and mountain passes of Greece. (4) The union of the Greeks, limited and defective as it was, and (5) the consummate statesmanship of Themistocles, in creating and enlarging the navy of Athens and emphasizing the importance of the control of the sea, had no small part in securing victory

178. Twofold Result of the Struggle.—The result of the conflict may be said to have been twofold. First, it emphasized and glorified all those elements of Greek life which the past centuries had been building up—the consciousness of Greek unity in the face of the outside world, the sentiments of independence, of patriotism and of freedom that had come to be the life of every Greek community. Second, it made Greece a world-power, transferred political supremacy from the east to the west and created among the leading Greek states aspirations after wider political influence and authority for which opportunities opened on every side.

Greece the Greatest Power in the World

179. The Literary Echo.—Two poets of the time revealed this sense of the power and glory of victorious Greece. Pindar, of Bœotia (about 522–448 B.C.), mightiest of the lyric poets (§ 130), gained his chief fame by his choral *Odes*, glorifying the victors in the national

Pindar.

games (§ 128). They were sung by a chorus of dancers on the return of the hero to his native city. In them he celebrated all those characteristic qualities which the Greek revealed in the Persian struggle—his manly vigor, his love of beauty, his deep piety, his heroic temper, his joy in his splendid past, his freedom and moral independence, his serene faith in the higher powers, untroubled by doubt or fear. Æschylus (about 525–456 B.C.), the tragedian of Athens, himself fought at Marathon and Salamis, and celebrated the victories in his *Persæ*, a tragedy brought out in 472 B.C., in which he depicts the doom of the arrogant king who sets himself up against the Almighty. Æschylus was the real founder of tragedy; he introduced the novelty of having two actors and a chorus, thus securing effective dramatic action. In his plays he uses the mythical and legendary tales of the heroes of old; *Pro-me'theus, Agamemnon,* the *Seven against Thebes,* are some of his titles. He is the poet-preacher of righteousness, of the punishment of pride, of the supremacy of moral law over all beings, divine and human, of the inevitable payment for sin wherever committed. He moves in a superhuman world of grand, heroic, sinful, suffering beings over whom hangs the penality of violated right and truth. The gods, who are jealous of the overweening might of the Great King and have brought him to ruin, are on the watch to avenge themselves upon such a spirit everywhere. So he warned, while he uplifted, the souls of his generation, and spoke words that live forever.

Æschylus.

180. **The Birth of Greek Imperialism.**—We have seen that the Greek states assumed new political importance in the world as the result of their victory. This was

certain to transform Greek politics Not the petty Greek
communities, but only the leaders could enter into the
race for world-power In the struggle of these leaders
with each other could Greek unity be preserved or Greek
independence be maintained? These were the problems
that sprang up when the fight for freedom from Persian
supremacy was won. Thus it came to pass that Greek
imperialism was the child of the Persian Wars.

REVIEW EXERCISES. 1. For what are the following noted:
Persepolis, Miletus, Marathon, Laurium, Mt. Athos, Hellespont, Platæa, Mycale, Himera? 2. Who were Mardonius,
Cyrus, Æschylus, Leonidas, Gelon, Aristides? 3. What is
meant by tragedy, strategos, lyric poetry, mythical, legendary,
imperialism, ostracism?

COMPARATIVE STUDIES. 1. Compare the attitude of the Lydians and the Persians toward the Ionian cities (§ 117). 2.
Compare the growth of the Persian empire (§§ 74, 75, 81, 84)
with that of the Greek states. 3. Compare the relation of
the Persian armies to the Persian government (§ 81) with
that of the Greek armies toward their governments. 4. Plan
an attack on Greece by Persia and the Greek means of resistance to the attack. 5. Read Browning's "Echetlos" as an
interpretation of Greek spirit.

SELECT LIST FOR READING. 1. The Ionian Revolt. Bury, pp.
241-247 2. The Campaign of Marathon. Bury, pp. 247-257.
3. Themistocles and His Policy. Bury, pp. 263-264 4. The
Campaign of Xerxes. Bury, pp 265-296. 5. Sicily in the Persian Wars. Bury, pp. 296-304.

TOPICS FOR READING AND ORAL REPORT. 1. The Ionian
Revolt. Morey, pp 174-176, Botsford, pp 110-115, Shuckburgh, pp. 111-123. 2. The Campaign of Marathon. Shuckburgh, pp. 128-136; Zimmern, pp 141-147. 3. Themistocles
and His Policy. Plutarch, Life of Themistocles, Botsford, pp.
124-126; Morey, pp. 181-184, Shuckburgh, pp. 138-142 4.
The Campaign of Xerxes. Botsford, pp 127-136; Morey, pp.
184-192; Shuckburgh, pp 142-171, Zimmern, pp. 148-191 5.

Incidents of the Battle of Salamis. Herodotus, VIII, §§ 10–
42, 49–96. 6. Æschylus. Capps, ch 8, Jebb, pp. 73–83, Murray, pp 109–116. 7. Sicily in the Persian Wars. Botsford, pp.
136–139.

181. The Maritime Power of Athens.—Out of the
struggle against the Persian invaders two Greek powers
came forth to reap the fruits of victory. Sparta, as the
head of the Peloponnesian league, had been officially
recognized as the leader in the conflict; but the heroic,
determined and far-sighted activities of Athens during
the wars had given her a foremost place in the estimation of all patriotic Greeks Hence, the coming years
reveal her as the rival of Sparta for the headship among
the Greek states.

Athens the Rival of Sparta.

Herodotus testifies to the service of Athens in the great struggle
as follows "If a man should now say that the Athenians were the
saviors of Greece, he would not exceed the truth For they truly
held the scales; and whichever side they espoused must have carried
the day They, too, it was who, when they had determined to maintain the freedom of Greece, roused up that portion of the Greek
nation which had not gone over to the Medes; and so, next to the
gods, *they* repulsed the invader."

Predica-ment of Sparta.

182. Sparta Loses Naval Command to Athens.—The
first task which awaited the victors was to drive the Persians from the coasts of the Ægean sea and deliver the
Asiatic Greeks from Persian domination. The Greek
fleet under the Spartan king Pausanias (§ 175) undertook this task. That, as things were, it must prove too
great an undertaking for a state like Sparta with not
more than four thousand citizens, who, moreover, lacked
money, ships and maritime experience, and had, besides,
to stand on guard at home against a serf population of

sixty thousand males, was foreseen by both Pausanias and the authorities at home; but whereas the latter were loath to conduct naval operations in far distant Asia, the over-ambitious victor of Platæa was set on keeping his own country at the head of all Greek enterprises, even though to do so he must secure the assistance of Persia. He accordingly offered his services to the Great King as satrap of Greece and conducted himself as the master and not as the leader of the forces serving under his command. His arrogance together with the indifference of the ruling powers at Sparta, however, provoked a prompt reaction which resulted in the transference of the leadership to the Athenians under Aristides (§ 168). They had by far the largest number of ships and hence an irresistible claim to naval command. The work was brilliantly accomplished With the exception of a few isolated cities, the Greek settlements on the entire Ægean coast and in the eastern Mediterranean as far as Cyprus were made free.

183. The Delian Confederacy Formed.—It was clear, however, that this freedom could be maintained only by presenting a united front to the enemy. Hence, a new league sprang into being under the headship of Athens—a league of the Ægean cities. Large and small alike, they banded together to furnish a fleet for defence and offence against Persia (478 B C). Those who were unable or unwilling to furnish ships contributed yearly a sum of money. The amount of the contribution in each case was left to Aristides to determine, according to his judgment of the resources of each city. The pre-eminence of Athens was also recognized by giving her the command of the united fleet and by arranging

Aristides the Just.

that the yearly contributions should be collected by her. The total sum assessed upon the cities amounted to four hundred and sixty talents. The money was placed in the sanctuary of Apollo on the island of Delos. There the representatives of the various cities met to deliberate upon common interests. Hence the league received the name of the Delian Confederacy.

184. Athens Rebuilt.—Meanwhile the Athenians at home under the guidance of Themistocles were making rapid strides forward. He saw clearly into the political situation—the opportunity for Athens to take its place at the head of the Greek world. If Aristides was the active agent of the advance of the city abroad, he supplied the vital energy for the forward movement. Under his inspiration Athens rose again from her ruins larger than before and was surrounded by a strong wall. The Spartans, wishing to have Athens defenceless, tried to prevent the building of the wall, but Themistocles, going to Sparta, deceived them by a clever ruse * until the wall had reached such a height that interference was impossible. The Piræus, the port of Athens, was fortified and its harbors protected by moles. Some years afterward (458 B.C) the city and the port were joined by Long Walls, a device which freed Athens from fear of assault by land and gave her unhindered access to the sea. Thus she became independent of Spartan interference and was able to direct all her energies to establishing her maritime supremacy.

Themistocles the Statesman.

185. The New Commercial Situation.—The revival and extension of Greek commerce assisted in bringing about Athenian predominance. With the driving of

* See Thucydides, I, 90 f.

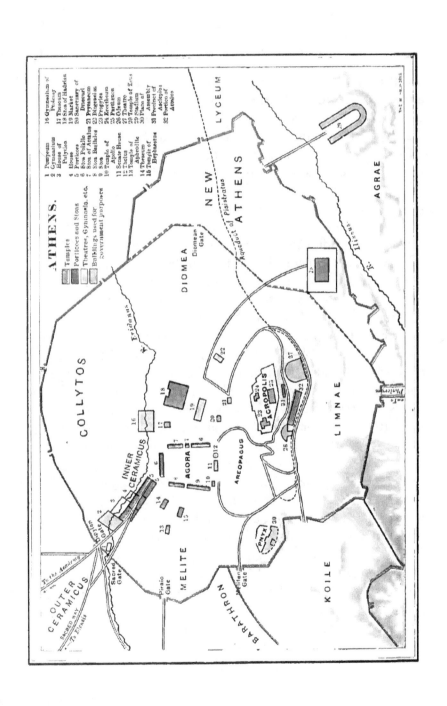

ATHENS.

Temples
Porticoes and Stoa
Theatres, Gymnasia, etc.
Buildings used for
Government purposes

1 Pompeum
2 Gymnasium
3 House of
   Polytion
4 House
5 Porticoes
6 Stoa Poikilo
7 Stoa of Attalus
8 Stoa Basileios
9 Stoa
10 Temple of
   Apollo
11 Senate House
12 Tholus
13 Temple of
   Aphrodite
14 Theseum
15 Temple of
   Hephaestus

16 Gymnasium of
   Ptolemy
17 Theseum
18 Stoa of Hadrian
19 Market
20 Sanctuary of
   Dionosus
21 Prytaneum
22 Biogeneion
23 Propylaea
24 Erechtheum
25 Parthenon
26 Odeum
27 Theatre
28 Temple of Zeus
29 Stadium
30 Place of
   Assembly
31 Precinct of
   Asclepius
32 Portico of
   Attalos

the Persians from the Ægean and—it might almost be added—from the Mediterranean, the sea-trade, already in Greek hands, increased enormously. It was natural that the bulk of this trade should centre about Athens. The cities of the Asia Minor coast were cut off from trading with the interior because of the hostility of Persia. The other towns on the Ægean were small. All were inclined to follow the lead of Athens in commercial as in political matters. Thus the immense increase of Greek commerce contributed to her upbuilding. She became the chief mart where ships gathered from the entire Greek world. The only formidable rival was Corinth, whose connections with the west were many and close. Athens's commercial supremacy naturally opened the way for her political predominance. She made many commercial treaties with her allies, an important condition of which was that a great many of the difficulties rising out of trade should be adjusted in the Athenian law-courts in accordance with Athenian law. From this it was natural to go on to require that other disagreements should follow the same course, until finally the majority of the cases at law among the members of the league were tried at Athens. The advantages of this system were great. One code, and that the best in all Greece, was extended over many communities whose sense of justice had not become so fine and high as that of Athens. Yet it meant for them the giving up to Athens of one of the sovereign powers of the state—the administration of justice—and placed Athens in a position in which she became greater than a mere ally.

Commerce Favors Athens.

Political Primacy of Athens in the Confederacy.

186. Development of Athens into an Imperial State. —Other things tended to push her forward The Per-

sians were not able to make head against so formidable
a league and ceased to attempt opposition Hence, as
fear of their attacks lessened, the allies began to feel
that union for defence against them was not so necessary.
The yearly contributions were made more grudgingly.
Some cities' were even desirous of withdrawing But
Athens held rightly that as the union of states had brought
about this condition of safety, so only a continuance of
the union could maintain it; hence, that states delinquent
in their contributions should be forced to pay and those
who attempted to withdraw should be compelled to
remain. Thus, when Naxos rebelled in 467 B C. and
Tha'sos in 465 B.C., they were reduced to subjection by
the Athenian fleet. The Delian Confederacy was fast becoming an Athenian imperial state

Athens
Denies
Right to
Secede.

187. Fall of Pausanias and Themistocles.—Naturally,
Sparta had regarded the rise of Athens with disfavor, and
recognizing Themistocles as its author, desired his downfall. Through his diplomacy her opposition to the building of the fortifications of Athens (§ 184) had amounted to
nothing She had been unable to make much headway
because of troubles at home occasioned by the ambition of
King Pausanias. He recklessly aimed at making himself
lord of Sparta and thereby of all Greece. He had entered
into treasonable correspondence with the Persians: now
he intrigued with the Helots (§ 143) to induce them to
rebel At Athens, moreover, the influence of Themistocles began to wane before that of Cimon, the son of
Miltiades, the hero of Marathon He was a high-born,
rich, genial, successful general who had succeeded Aristides in the command of the Athenian fleet. He was no
far-seeing statesman like Themistocles, but, for that very

Rise of
Cimon.

reason, was nearer the majority who failed to follow the greater leader in his radical plans for Athenian empire. Cimon's policy was conservative. He favored continuing war on Persia and renewing friendship with Sparta. In the end Themistocles was ostracized (471 B C.). Later, when the Spartans got rid of their difficulties with Pausanias by putting him to death, they claimed to find evidence in his papers that Themistocles had joined in his treasonable plans. The exile was forced to find refuge with the Persians, where he died some years after. Cimon's leadership of Athens was marked by a splendid victory over the Persians at the Eu-rym'e-don (466 B.C) and by his bringing aid to the Spartans in their struggles with the Helots of Messenia who had taken advantage of an earthquake at Sparta to try again to regain their liberty (§ 146). But the Spartans discourteously discharged the troops which he had brought to help them in their siege of I-tho'me, where the Helots had entrenched themselves, and he returned in disgrace

Cimon, Leader of Athens (470–461 B C).

188. Democracy Popular in the Greek World.—Another cause of Sparta's suspicion of Athens, besides that occasioned by her sudden rise to power, was the influence of her democratic constitution. Her vigor and heroism in the Persian struggle had rightly been attributed to her democratic spirit, and, along with her advancement, democratic ideas and institutions had begun to be popular elsewhere. When the Ionian cities were freed from the Persian yoke, they set up democratic governments. The impulse spread to the Peloponnesus, where Argos, Arcadia and Elis became democratic. In the far west the cities of Sicily followed the same example; Syracuse established a democracy on the death of the tyrant

Hieron (467 B.C.), the successor of Gelon (§ 176). In almost every city of Greece, even in aristocratic states like those of Bœotia, a democratic party appeared which followed in the footsteps of Athens and looked to her for **Sparta** support. It was not strange that Sparta, which had been **Opposes De-** steadily growing more aristocratic as her pure-blooded **mocracy.** Spartan citizens grew fewer and fewer in number, should view this state of things with increasing uneasiness, and take a firmer stand in favor of oligarchy against democracy in general, and especially against Athens, its exemplar.

189. Growth of Democracy at Athens.—During these years the government at Athens was coming more and more into the hands of the people. The provisions of the constitutions of Solon and Cleisthenes (§§ 159, 161) were broadened or changed in their interest. But the council of the Areopagus (§ 156), by possessing the sole right to pass upon the legality of acts and propositions and to supervise the magistrates, was a check to their power in public assembly and law-courts. Its organization out of a special class of ex-officials and its self-perpetuating character were likewise inconsistent **Rise of** with popular government. Hence, new leaders of the de-**Pericles.** mocracy, Eph-i-al'tes and Pericles, induced the people to pass a law which deprived it of these powers (462 B.C). **Fall of** This was in direct opposition to the policy of the con-**Cimon.** servatives under Cimon, and the victory of the democracy, aided by the failure of his Spartan policy (§ 187), was followed by his ostracism (461 B.C.). The powers taken from the Areopagus were divided between the council of five hundred (§§ 159, 161), the heliæa (§ 159) and the public assembly. To the Areopagus was left simply the trial of murder cases. A little later, in 457 B C., the office of archon was opened to the less wealthy citizens, the zeugitæ (§ 159), and from this time on few differences in respect to political privileges or opportunities separated the rich from the poor, the noble from the ignoble.

Fall of the Areopagus.

190. The Athenian Council (Boule).—In general, the government was undertaken by the citizens themselves in public assembly (ec-cle'si-a). The ecclesia imposed certain limitations upon its own activity. All measures, whether dealing with foreign affairs or simply administrative acts, must first pass through the council and be presented by it to the ecclesia. The council, however, was as close a miniature of the ecclesia as could possibly be constructed. It consisted of 500 men designated by lot from the entire population of Attica (§ 161), each of the 170 villages or wards (demes) being given the number of representatives to which its population entitled it. Accordingly, all interests and localities could get their desires known in the council. This served, therefore, to admit all popular measures and yet to provide the ecclesia with a programme of business which did not contain a lot of ill-considered, unseasonable or useless propositions. The Athenians knew that it was suicidal for the general assembly to waste time considering such proposals.

A Miniature of the Ecclesia.

191. The Athenian Administration.—Moreover, the ecclesia, which met at intervals of about a week, could exercise only intermittent control over the administration; hence the council was empowered to act for it in this matter also. Since no man could serve in the council for more than two terms, and since its members were designated by lot, it was always a body of average citizens without any special fitness or experience. Hence it took orders readily from the ecclesia. Such a body could not supervise the work of officials, if these were strong men, of long service, and unrestrained by colleagues. Hence the Athenians intrusted their civil administration for single terms of one year only to a large number of committees of ten members each, whom the lot designated. Seven such committees had to do solely with the receipt and distribution of public moneys, which private contractors collected; three others had to act as inspectors in the market-place. All were directed in their routine business by the council to whose auditing committee they had to give a monthly accounting; all took instructions on matters of general policy from the ecclesia to whose three auditing committees they had to render an account of the whole year's transactions. Upon this account the heliæa must finally pass before the officials received an honorable discharge. So many new senators and new magistrates were required every year that it was difficult for an Athenian to escape either of these duties. Hence the citizens generally gained an intimate acquaintance with the details of government, which enabled them to perform their duties as members of the ecclesia with knowledge and rapidity. Without keeping in mind the fact that, as Grote puts it, the intelligence and experience of the average Athenian citizen was as great as that of the members of the British House of Commons, it is impossible to understand how a general assembly of from five thousand to fifty thousand men could manage the affairs of a great empire.

192. The Athenian Ecclesia.—The ecclesia, however, did not act without putting further checks upon its own authority. Thus all alterations in the law-code of Solon,

Marginal notes:

Administrative Committees Chosen by Lot.

The Audit.

which was the nearest equivalent in Athens to a written constitution, must be finally approved by the heliæa. Moreover, to keep citizens from making vicious or wilful changes the regulation was made that anyone who proposed a new law or decree was liable to prosecution, if it was found to be contrary to existing law. Yet, even with these limitations, the power of the ecclesia, both in its direct administrative activity and its indirect authority over all officials, was very great. It declared war, made peace, controlled finance, directed commerce, maintained and guarded religion, determined home and foreign policy.

The Ecclesia Was the Government.

193. The Athenian Law-Courts.—As the citizens in public assembly governed the state, so in the law-courts or heliæa they administered justice directly. Most cases, whether civil or criminal, came before them. For practical work the whole body was divided into sections called dicasteries, each numbering from two hundred to one thousand citizens or even more. Those who came before the court pleaded their cause themselves. No lawyers were permitted to speak, though soon a class of men appeared who wrote speeches for delivery by the pleaders. As the same citizens acted as judges and legislators, it was presumed that they knew the law and passed judgment according to it. And though the dangers of prejudice and ignorance were not always avoided, the legal system and the judicial fairness of the law-courts of Athens were superior to those anywhere else in the world.

Absence of Lawyers.

194. The Citizens as Officials.—This active conduct of the state by its citizens meant that all had a part in it. It has been estimated that each man was brought into the service of the state as an official at least once

in sixteen years, besides taking part in the law-courts and
the ecclesia.   Much time was required for these duties,
and this could be spared with difficulty from daily work.
Hence, pay for certain kinds of state service was intro-

Indemnity for Public Service. duced.   Members of the council received a drachma—
twenty cents—a day, and the jurors in the heliæa two obols
—six cents—a day.*   Attendance at the assembly was not
paid nor did the military officials receive any indemnity.

195. The Strategos.—But who was to lead the citizens
in their public assembly and suggest lines of policy and
courses of action?   In theory this was the privilege of any
citizen.   But the Athenians had not developed that confidence in themselves as individuals, nor had they entirely
lost that dependence upon the aristocratic families, which
would permit them to turn their theory into practice.   We
have already seen that the strategoi occupied the most
honorable positions in the state (§ 167) and that the chief
strategos was elected by the public assembly.   The man
elected was regularly the head of the strongest party in
Athens, and in this dual capacity he took the position

The Leader of the Demos. of leader of the demos, "demagogue "   His position was
entirely unofficial.   It gave him no legal power.   He led
the people because he was able to persuade them that his
plans and policy were the best.   Themistocles, Aristides
and Cimon are examples of such leadership.   And at this
time came forward another who, by virtue of his descent,
personality and character, guided the history of Athens

Pericles the Leader of Athenian Politics. for thirty years.   This was Pericles, a member on his
mother's side of the noble family of the Alcmæonidæ to
which Cleisthenes had belonged.   In the conflicts about

* It must be remembered that the purchasing power of money was
much greater then than now.

the overthrow of the Areopagus, Ephialtes had been murdered, and with his death Pericles stood alone as the leader of the democracy. The changes that have been described, which turned the government into a practical rule of the people, were made under his direction. Though he was an aristocrat who knew and maintained his distance from the people with a dignity that often seemed coldness, he nevertheless took their cause to his heart, awed and convinced them by his incorruptible and lofty ideals, and swayed them by his clear and glowing eloquence. Trusted and followed by the citizens, he ruled them as their servant, and moulded the destiny of the state as no king or tyrant could ever do.

REVIEW EXERCISES. 1. What events are connected with the names of Pausanias, Cimon, Themistocles, Aristides? 2. For what are the following places noted Delos, Eurymedon? 3. What was the date of the founding of the Delian Confederacy; of the ostracism of Themistocles? 4. What is meant by Areopagus, heliæa, ecclesia, drachma, dicastery, Helot? 5. What weight had the ecclesia in legislation?

COMPARATIVE STUDIES. 1. Compare the Delian Confederacy with the Peloponnesian League (§ 154). 2. Compare Athens in the years 500 B C and 476 B C

SELECT LIST FOR READING. 1. The Confederacy of Delos. Bury, pp 328-330 2. Themistocles and the Recovery of Athens. Bury, pp 330-334. 3. Fall of Pausanias and Themistocles. Bury, pp. 324-326, 334-336 4. Athens and the Confederacy. Bury, pp 336-342 5. Cimon. Bury, pp. 342-345.

TOPICS FOR READING AND ORAL REPORT. 1. The Confederacy of Delos. Morey, pp. 205-207; Shuckburgh, pp 173-176. 2. Themistocles and the Recovery of Athens. Morey, pp. 202-205, Zimmern, 192-197. 3. Fall of Pausanias and Themistocles. Shuckburgh, pp. 178-181; Zimmern, pp 198-204. 4. Athens and the Confederacy. Botsford, pp. 151-153 5. Cimon. Plutarch, Life of Cimon, Morey, pp. 207-209, Zimmern, pp. 205-213, Botsford, pp 152-156.

196. The Age of Pericles.—The thirty years (461–431 B.C.) of the leadership of Pericles is the supreme period of the Athenian state. It reached the highest place of wealth, culture and power. To Pericles and his wise direction of affairs this state of things was largely due, and the period is properly called the "Age of Pericles." As the scene includes the whole of Greece, we shall take advantage of it to study, with Athens as the central point: (*a*) the inner life of the Greek world in its general features, and (*b*) the political condition and course of affairs, as they prepared the way for the civil wars which gave Greece her death-blow.

197. The Inner Life of Greece.—The chief characteristic of the age is the growth of city life. The attempts of Solon and Pisistratus (§§ 159, 160) to better the lot of the Attic peasants had broken up many of the large estates and made Attica a country of small farmers. But at the same time, with the improvement of agricultural conditions, the opportunities for making a living in the city and enjoying life there grew greater, and multitudes of countrymen flocked thither. The attractions of trade also brought large numbers of foreigners to reside more or less permanently in Athens and other cities. The result was that city populations reached their highest point. According to probable estimates, Athens numbered upward of 150.000 people; Syracuse was not far behind; Corinth and Ægina reached about 60,000; Sparta and Argos were much smaller, and there was a goodly number of the cities of the Ægean in which from 10,000 to 30,000 people lived.

Growth of the City.

198. Extension of Trade and Industry.—Trade and industry became the chief activities in the largest of these cities. The wants of the large populations must be sup-

plied. Many people set up little shops in which they
manufactured and sold goods directly to customers. The
state needed many hands for its growing public business,
and many others found their bread in working on the
public buildings which were everywhere put up on a
scale of splendor corresponding to the increasing wealth
and importance of the communities. Manufacturing
on a large scale was not uncommon, and many workmen

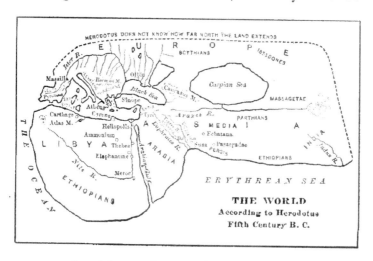

THE WORLD
According to Herodotus
Fifth Century B. C.

were employed in turning out the various articles which
the rapidly advancing commerce required for export to
all parts of the Greek world. The mercantile activity
of the Piræus, the port of Athens, grew with tremendous
strides. Ships from all sides brought food for the support of the population—grain and fish from the Black
sea, meats from Thessaly and Sicily, fruits from Eubœa,
Rhodes and Phœnicia. Costly woods came from Crete,
ivory from Libya, carpets from Carthage, incense from
Syria and books from Egypt. "The fruits of the whole

Athens the
Commer-
cial Centre
of the East-
ern Medi-
terranean.

earth," said Pericles, "flow in upon us; so that we enjoy the goods of other countries as freely as of our own."
The incorporation of the cities of the Delian Confederacy
into the Athenian empire still further stimulated commerce
at Athens if not throughout the various cities. One law
and one system of coinage and of weights and measures
governed most of their transactions with one another.

199. Increase of Wealth.—Thus opportunity was offered for a large increase of wealth. We have seen the
older idea gradually passing away, that true property
was property in land (§§ 135, 140). Now, although the
aristocracy still cherished the notion and took pride in
their estates, manufacturing, trade and dealing in money
afforded to the many the largest opportunity for acquir-
ing property and the best standard for estimating it.
A thoroughly organized system of coinage was in opera-
Coinage. tion. The principal silver coin was the drachma (nearly
twenty cents), there were also two, three and four
drachma pieces. Of smaller coins the chief was the
obol (about three cents); six of them made a drachma.
A copper coin, the chalkous, was one-eighth of the obol.
The standard of monetary exchange was the talent (about
$1,180), containing sixty minas (the mina about $20);
the mina contained one hundred drachmas. Gold coins
were usually those of foreign countries. Later, the gold
stater, in value perhaps equal to twenty drachmas, was
coined. Money had a greater purchasing power than
at present, and therefore the large fortunes of that day
seem small to us. A capital of from $12,000 to $15,000
placed one in the ranks of the rich. Such men of wealth
found abundant opportunities for loaning their money,
since all sorts of manufacturing and commerical enter-

prises needed capital. The usual rate of interest on good security was about twelve per cent.

200. Greeks Not Great Capitalists.—It seems clear, however, that in general the Greeks had no such comprehension of business, nor did they so fully recognize the importance of encouraging trade, as did the ancient Babylonians. They were slow to see that "money-making" was a desirable activity. It was enough that all should live according to their station and serve the state as service was required. Even though to be a land-holder was by that time not regarded as indispensable to good social standing, wealth did not of itself make its possessor a man highly regarded. On the contrary, a merchant or trader, however rich he might be, was looked down upon. The ordinary citizen, living on the modest proceeds of his daily work, or supported by the scanty dole of the state for his public service, was more honorable. Hindrances were put in the way of commerce, and limits were assigned to the profits to be gained. Yet commerce grew and thrived in spite of public sentiment. Only because the advantages of having money could not be denied did the struggle for it continue to absorb more and more of the energies of the citizens. Yet it never approached the importance and prominence which it has to-day. The Greek thought more of what he was than of what he had; to serve the state and to enjoy life as well as to enlarge his opportunities of doing both, these were more desirable in his eyes than absorption in business and the pursuit of wealth.

Greek Attitude toward Money.

The result of this was that the business of Athens was carried on chiefly by foreigners who were permitted to settle in the city; they were called metics. The

Foreigners in Business.

leaders of the state saw clearly the advantages of en‹ couraging them to pursue their businesses, and they were more liberally dealt with at Athens than elsewhere. Apart from having no citizen-rights and being compelled to pay a tax to the state, they were on an equality with other freemen. The same laws protected them; the same privileges were granted them. As a result many of them were found at Athens, and in this period they numbered about thirty thousand persons.

201. The Slave.—From an economic and social point of view the most important class of the population was the slaves. Their unpaid labor was employed in tilling the great estates, in working the mines, in turning out manufactured articles and in doing all sorts of household service. They made it possible for such citizens as owned them to obtain the leisure necessary to perform their political duties and to enjoy the opportunities for culture which the state afforded. But they took the bread from the mouths of the tens of thousands of citizens who had to work for their living. As the activities of the cities en-

Economic Evils of Slavery.

larged, the number of slaves also increased. The slave-trade became more important; the supply from the north Ægean and Black sea region was abundant; captives in war were sold. Every city had a large slave population; that at Athens has been estimated at about one hundred thousand and the other large cities had proportionate numbers. They formed, one might say, the foundation of the economic structure, but were not an unmixed blessing.

202. The Family.—Another social element, the family, throws an instructive side-light upon Greek life. The quality and freedom which reigned in the best public life of the time had no place in the life at home. The husband was ruler in his household, and his wife was a social nonentity. He spent little time at home; she seldom left it. Here the Greek was far behind the oriental of Babylonia and Egypt (§ 25), where woman had a relatively high place in society. Indeed, in some respects, the cultured and free Athenian did not respect woman as highly as the rude Spartan, who gave her much larger liberty. In the earlier ages of the aristocratic rule the wives of the nobles seem to have had greater influence, but it is one of the strange inconsistencies of Greek life that the new democracy and the larger city-life both worked to lower the social activities of woman. The wife did not always have charge of the household, which, in the case of a well-to-do man, was managed by a steward. She usually brought a dowry to her husband, which in case of divorce had to be repaid to her father. On the whole, nowhere is the limitation of the Greek ideal of life more distinctly manifest than in the position of woman and the contribution of the family to society. The Greeks thought of marriage chiefly as a means of raising up citizens for the state; an interesting illustration of this idea is seen in the law introduced in Pericles' time, that only he could be accepted as a citizen whose father and mother were Athenians by blood. Naturally, girls were not as desirable as boys, and little attention was paid to them beyond keeping them indoors. The boy, however, was very carefully reared. Grammar, music and gymnastics were the three parts of his education. By the first was meant the learning of his own language and the study of Homer and the other early poets, not merely as a means of training in forms of speech, but

Woman

Education.

as sources of knowledge about life, duty and religion. In music, he was taught how to sing, and to play on musical instruments. Gymnastics included running and wrestling, practice in the use of weapons, riding and other similar exercises for the finest bodily development and skill in arms.

203. The House.—Greek society then was chiefly a society of men whose main interests lay in public life. The house, for example, was ordinarily small and unattractive. It faced directly on the street, often with no opening except the door which swung outward, a fact suggestive of the preference of the Greek for the open air. The women's apartments were separate and secluded. Indeed, the house served the Greek chiefly for sleeping purposes, the storing of his goods and the keeping of his household From it he sallied out very early in the morning, after a taste of wine and bread, if it were the day of a festival or the meeting of the ecclesia, to meet his friends, or take part in the public business in the assembly or elsewhere. Toward the middle of the day he took breakfast or lounged about and gossiped in the public walks or porticoes. The gymnasium occupied him in the afternoon as a place of exercise or of intercourse with friends, whence he returned home for dinner, the chief meal of the day. If a poor man, he went early to bed; if well-to-do and socially inclined, he spent the evening at a banquet with his friends. If, on the other hand, it were a common work day, a rich man would busy himself with looking after his slaves and other investments, a farmer would plant his crop or tend his orchard, an artisan would hie to his shop or factory, a seaman or fisher would turn to his avocation much as in

Life Varies with Classes and Days.

any modern state There were, however, about one hundred and ten days of a fête or a public assembly in every year in Athens.

204. High Plane of Living.—The Athens of Pericles offered the finest type of this manner of life to be found in the fifth century.   The pursuit of wealth was subordinated to the joy of making the most of life among one's fellows and in public activity.   The "glorification Idealism. of cultivated human intercourse" was the ideal toward which men strove.   The pinch of want was removed by the stipend sufficient for simple living which the state paid its poorest citizen for his work in its service.   Orphans and cripples were cared for at public expense.   Public lands, obtained as the outcome of war, were assigned to citizens who were willing to go and live upon them. Two features of this life which had an especially important bearing on the material welfare of the citizen and his higher culture deserve special mention: the public buildings and the religious festivals.

205. Public Buildings.—In Greece, as in ancient Babylonia (§ 31), the chief buildings of every city were its temples.   They were the centres of public life, of business as well as of religion.   They were the places of deposit for money or treasure of any sort.   Although, in the Greek states, the growth of popular government and the emphasis on the independence of the individual had made the political predominance of the priest impossible and his influence on public affairs unimportant, yet religion continued to be glorified by stately and beautiful temples, adorned with the highest artistic skill.   The The Athenian temples had perished in the successive on- Athenian Temples. slaughts of the Persians, and it was a duty as well as a

pious delight on the part of the citizens to restore them.
Cimon had begun the work on a noble scale, but Pericles
continued the task and carried it through in a fashion
that has immortalized his own name as well as that of
Athens.   An artist of the highest genius was at his hand
in the person of Phidias, who was assisted by other men

The Par-
thenon.

of uncommon ability.   The principal scene of this architectural and artistic display was the A-crop'o-lis (§§ 122,
165); and the building in which it reached its height was
the temple of A-the'na the Virgin (*Parthenos*), hence
called the Par'the-non.   Unlike the famous structures of
the ancient east, it was not the immense size of the Parthenon, but its beautiful proportions, exquisite adornment
and ideal sculptures that made it memorable.   It was
100 feet wide, 226 feet long and 65 feet high, built of
marble and painted in harmonious colors   A row of
forty-six Doric columns surrounded it, and every available space above the columns, within and without, was
carved in relief with scenes representing glorious events in
the religious history of Athens.   A wonderfully sculptured
frieze, extending for more than 500 feet around the inner
temple, depicted, with a variety and energy never surpassed, scenes in the Panathenæa, the festival in honor of
the patron goddess, Athena.   In the temple stood a statue
of the deity, the masterpiece of Phidias, made of ivory
and gold, 38 feet in height including the pedestal.   Though
the statue has long since disappeared and the temple
itself is but a ruin, the remains of it illustrate supremely
the chief features of Greek architecture—"simplicity,
harmony, refinement," the union of strength and beauty.

206. The Religious Festivals of Athens.—Nowhere in
the Greek world were the religious festivals celebrated

PLATE XVII

Erechtheum.

Parthenon.

Temple of
Victory.

Statue of Athene.

Propylæa.

THE ACROPOLIS OF ATHENS (RESTORED)

with so great splendor and beauty as in the Athens of
Pericles. In addition to the ancient Dionysiac festivals
already mentioned (§ 160), there was the new one established by Pisistratus, the Great or City Dionysia,
celebrated in April. The contests in tragedy and comedy were its central feature. Here, before the Athenian The Plays
public, some of the most glorious productions of human
genius were produced. Here Æschylus (§ 179) had
taught his tremendous lessons of righteousness and hu-
mility. He was succeeded by Soph'o-cles (about 496– Sophocles.
406 B.C.), who won the prize over his older competitor
in 468 B.C., and gained it many times thereafter. He
represents the high, free and glad spirit of the Athens of his
day. His most famous play is the *An-tig'o-ne*, in which
is brought out the victory of duty over the fear of death,
of the higher law of God over the visible law of man.
Antigone buries the body of her brother, though the king
has forbidden it under pain of death. The serene soul of
the poet is marvellously shown in the beauty and dignity
of his style. He sang of men as they ought to be, reveal-
ing and idealizing human character, which, at its best, is,
in his inspired vision, harmonious with the blessed will of
God. So he interpreted the supreme ideal of the age of
Pericles and lived it himself. "He died well, having suffered no evil." A later poet, imagining him in the other
world, described him as "gentle" there, "even as he was
gentle among us."

207. The Eleusinian Mysteries.—Another famous, festival was that of the Mysteries (§ 134) of E-leu'sis. Eleusis lay twelve miles away from Athens, and every year
early in September multitudes gathered in the capital
to make in solemn procession the journey to the Eleu-

sinian temple to be initiated into the mysteries or to
renew the celebration of them. A day of purification
by washing in the sea preceded the moving of the procession, which passed along the sacred way to the splendid temple at Eleusis, rebuilt by Ic-tin'us under Pericles'
direction. Here those secret acts of worship and devotion to the goddess Demeter were performed, which exercised so deep, wholesome and hopeful an influence
upon Greek life Yet by far the most splendid of all
festivals was the Pan'a-the-næ'a, celebrated with peculiar
magnificence every fourth year, a festival which glorified
at the same time the goddess Athena, and the city of her
joy and glory. For nearly a week contests in music,
song and recitation, in gymnastics, races and warlike
sports, were held, and all was concluded with a solemn
procession to the temple of Athena on the Acropolis,
where a costly robe woven by the maidens of the city was
given to the goddess. That procession, made up of the
flower of the Athenian citizens, of resident aliens and
colonists, was depicted on the frieze of the Parthenon
(§ 205) and formed the finest picture of Athens in the
days of its highest splendor

The Panathe-næa.

208. **Herodotus.**—At a Panathenæan festival in the
days of Pericles, Herodotus is said to have recited his
History, the first prose work of genius that Greece produced. Herodotus (about 484–425 B.C.) was a native of
Hal'i-car-nas'sus in Caria, but after the days of his youth
found a second home at Athens. He travelled, with eyes
and ears wide open, all over the world, from the capitals
of Persia to Italy, and from the Black sea to the southern
border of Egypt. The results of his investigations he
gathered into a work which finds its motive in the Per-

The Father of History.

sian wars. As he portrays successively before us the rise of Persia, the conquest of Babylon and Egypt, the past history of these peoples, the Scythian expedition, he leads up to the great, the supreme struggle between this mighty, world-conquering empire and the petty Greek states. Then he describes the wars in detail. The whole is a prose poem, pointing the moral of Æschylus (§ 179). Scattered through this broad field are innumerable anecdotes, traditions, legends, which enliven while they do not break the single impression (§ 29). Devoted to Athens, he glorified the part taken by the city in the war; he loved her institutions and enjoyed her society. His work shares in the artistic, keen and genial spirit characteristic of her best days, and while descriptive and not critical, its originality and charm have given it a permanent place in literature.

209. The Education of the Athenian Citizen.—We are ready to understand now how Athens realized the ideal of "the glorification of cultivated human intercourse" (§ 204), the elevation of a body of men possessed of social and political equality to a common height of intelligence and general culture never reached before that day, or probably since. All beheld daily these marvels of architecture and art, and many took part in their erection. All joined in these splendid festivals, witnessed or contended in the athletic, musical and literary contests. The state paid to the citizens who claimed it a fee for attending the theatre, so that all were able to see and hear the plays of Æschylus or Sophocles. It must be remembered that these theatrical exhibitions were also contests between rival authors, in which the people themselves were judges. Thus a standard of

The Diffusion of Culture.

taste and appreciation was set at a very high mark.
The participation in public life, the decisions on points of
state policy which lay in the hands of the citizens, were
all means of training. The popular law-courts cultivated
the judicial faculty. The administration of the affairs
of the state awakened and trained executive ability.
Thus the higher powers of the great body of citizens
were educated to an extraordinary degree; the experience
made the Athenians the most splendidly intelligent of all
Greeks. Such an atmosphere of breadth and freedom,
that encouraged higher thought, invited to Athens from
all over the Greek world men who were eager to know
and to teach. As a consequence the best that was
thought and said and done in art and politics and literature was found at Athens. Therefore, it was no vain
boast of Pericles, but sober truth, when he said, "Athens
is the school of Greece, and the individual Athenian in
his own person seems to have the power of adapting himself to the most varied forms of action with the utmost
versatility and grace."

Athens the Teacher of Greece.

210. Sources of Athenian Revenue.—But whence
came the money to meet the expenses of this highly and
richly organized system of government? Athens had
various sources of revenue: rent from state lands, including especially the silver mines, tolls for markets,
and harbor dues, the tax on resident foreigners, the
receipts from the law-courts in fees, confiscations, etc.,
and in case of great necessity, a direct assessment upon
the people of property. The costs of the splendid exhibitions at festivals were borne by the free-will offerings
of rich citizens, and some offices were without salary.
The entire income from all sources was about one thou-

Rents, Taxes, Tolls, Gifts and Tribute.

sand talents yearly. Besides this, the receipts from the allied cities of the league amounted at this time to about six hundred talents. Athena also possessed a great sum of money in her temple from gifts of the pious, her share of the booty in war, etc., and she was called upon to contribute her share to the upbuilding of the state, as well as to lend money when required. From all these sources Pericles drew the money needful for the various departments of the administration and for the public buildings with which the city was adorned.

211. Greek Politics in the Age of Pericles.—From this sketch of the inner life (§§ 197–210) we pass to the foreign relations of Athens under the leadership of Pericles during the same period (461–431 B.C.). The fall of Cimon (§ 189) was accompanied not only by the victory of democracy at home, but also by an attack upon Sparta's supremacy in continental Greece and upon the Persian possessions in Cyprus, Phœnicia and Egypt. Alliance was made with Argos and Thessaly; Megara was drawn away from the Peloponnesian league. A naval station was secured on the Corinthian gulf at Naupactus where the Athenians settled the Messenian Helots who had held out at Mt. Ithome since 464 B.C. (§ 187) and had surrendered upon the condition that they leave the Peloponnesus. These movements threatened the commerce of Ægina and Corinth, and a great war broke out in 459 B.C. Corinth was beaten; Ægina was subjected and compelled to enter the Delian league. Then Sparta took a hand in the war, by entering Bœotia with an army, on the pretence of punishing the Phocians, but really to organize Bœotia against Athens. Though the Spartans defeated the Athenians at Tan'a-gra in 457 B.C., they accomplished

Athens Tries to Dominate the World

War with Sparta.

nothing. Two months later, however, the Athenians crushed the Bœotians decisively at Œ-noph'y-ta, and by restoring the aristocratic exiles, substituted their own suzerainty for that of Thebes in all the Bœotian cities. Phocis and Locris also submitted to Athens. Soon after, the Achæan cities on the southern coast of the Corinthian gulf joined her. Thus Athenian influence on land extended over a wide territory. But it was also very unstable. Accordingly, when Argos concluded a thirty years' peace with Sparta in 450 B.C., a five years' truce was also arranged by Athens. Three years later, however, Bœotia revolted, whereupon Megara, Locris and

Phocis as well as Eubœa fell away. While Pericles was absent with the army in Eubœa the Peloponnesians invaded Attica, but retreated on the receipt, it is alleged, of a bribe; and so, in the end, though Eubœa was recovered, the vigorous and costly attempt of Athens to build up a

great land power in Greece signally failed. Finally, in 445 B.C., between Athens and Sparta and their respective allies a peace was made that was to last thirty years. Athens renounced her control of central Greece. The allies of each were determined and included in the treaty. Each party agreed not to seduce the other's allies, but neutrals were left at liberty to join either side at will. All future differences were to be settled by arbitration.

212. **The War with Persia.**—Meanwhile, Athens had been carrying on the war with Persia (§§ 182, 187, 211). Though no Persian ships appeared in the Ægean, the Athenians determined to cripple the power of the Great King still further by aiding a rebellion against him in Egypt. In 459 B.C. they sent a strong fleet to the Nile.

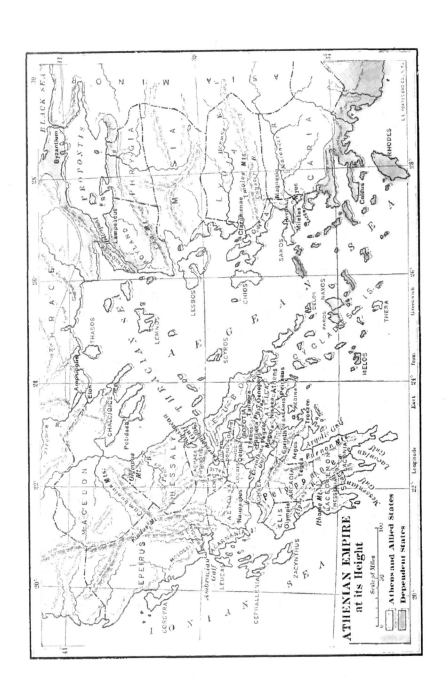

ATHENIAN EMPIRE
at its Height

Athens and Allied States
Dependent States

Scale of Miles

Though at first successful, the rebellion was finally crushed and the Athenian force destroyed (455 B.C). This serious blow brought hostilities to an end until 449 B.C , when Cimon, who had been recalled from exile, was sent with a fleet to Cyprus, where the Persians were attacking the Greek cities. He died while on the expedition, but the fleet gained a brilliant victory by which Persia was again driven from the sea. These conflicts had cost Athens dear in men and money without corresponding results, so that just as she had come to an agreement with her enemies in Greece, it seemed wise to make peace with Persia. Negotiations were entered upon by sending Callias to Susa, and though the Great King would not formally agree to yield his claim upon cities that had rebelled against him, yet practically he consented, henceforth, not to molest Greek cities or Greek ships. This so-called peace is known as the peace of Callias (448 B.C.).

Egyptian Expedition

Death of Cimon.

The Peace of Callias.

213. The Athenian Empire.—Thus Athens in 445 B.C. was at peace with all the world. She had learned the folly of attempting to conquer Greece and Persia at the same time, and now set about recovering her strength and developing her legitimate field, that of commerce and control of the seas. The decisive steps were taken which turned the Delian league into the Athenian empire. In 454 B.C., after the Athenian disaster in Egypt, the treasury of the league had been removed for greater security from Delos to Athens. And now, although all fear of Persia was removed by the peace of Callias, the imperial city continued to require the yearly contributions from the allies and dealt with the money according to her own will. The decision to treat the allies in this way was not reached without a struggle between the parties at Athens. The

The Allies Become Subjects.

opponents of Pericles were led by Thucydides, son of
Me-le′si-as, the ostracism of whom in 443 B C settled the

matter. Samos, Chios and Lesbos alone remained on
the old footing of furnishing ships to the fleet. All the
others were subject and paid tribute. Athens collected
the tolls in their harbors, interfered in their local affairs
in the interests of democracy, had garrisons in many of
their cities, sent out inspectors among them, required
many to destroy their walls. Colonies of Athenian citizens, called cleruchi, were sent out to occupy lands which
had fallen into the hands of the Athenian state, and thus
constituted a body of faithful friends in the midst of restless subjects. The entire body of cities thus dependent
on Athens was divided for administrative and financial
purposes into five districts: Ionia, Caria, the Hellespont,
Thrace, the Islands. Thus a stately imperial system

arose with its centre in democratic Athens. The chief
reason for censuring Athens because of this transformation of the old Delian league is that she took no steps to
attach her subjects to herself otherwise than by fear.
No doubt she gave them protection, better government
and higher culture, but she had robbed them of their independence without granting them citizenship in the new
community or a voice in the state. This blind selfishness
and unblushing arrogance of power provoked Samos to
revolt in 440 B.C. when the aristocratic faction getting
control of the city withdrew it from the empire. There
was a grave danger that the outbreak would spread and
indeed Byzantium followed the lead of Samos. Hence
Pericles stamped out the insurrection vigorously, razed
the walls of Samos, and forced it to pay the costs of the
war.

214. Wide Extent of Athenian Influence.—Far beyond the bounds of the empire Pericles sought to extend the commercial influence and activity of Athens. The Persian peace opened the ports of the eastern Mediterranean, and traders from Athens now frequented them in quest of the wares of the orient. Many of the distant Greek cities of the Black sea acknowledged Athenian authority. The commercial importance of the imperial city grew continually in the west and opportunity was found to establish political relations there. In 443 B.C., under the leadership of Athens, the city of Thurii was founded in southeastern Italy. On its west coast Athenian merchants began to gather the trade into their own hands. The leading people of that region, the Etruscans, bought Attic vases and sold their curious metal-work in the Athenian market. Rome, a city on the river Tiber, which held a dominating place in its own district of Latium, was already preparing for the mighty part it was to play in the centuries to come. In 454 B.C., it is said, the Romans sent an embassy to Greece to study its systems of law. They came to Athens and thence transplanted parts of the legislation of Solon into Roman soil.

Enterprises in the West.

Embassy from Rome.

REVIEW EXERCISES. 1. For what are the following significant: Tanagra, Corcyra, Eleusis, Piræus, Halicarnassus? 2. What is meant by cleruchi, talent, Acropolis, Dionysia, Panathenæa, Antigone? 3. What are the dates of the age of Pericles, of the peace of Callias, of the thirty years' peace?

COMPARATIVE STUDIES. 1. Compare Athenian democracy in the time of Cleisthenes with that in the age of Pericles. 2. Compare the law-courts of Athens with those of your own city. 3. Compare the Athenian empire with the Persian (§§ 77–84).

SELECT LIST FOR READING. 1. Life at Athens in the Age of Pericles. Bury, pp 337–338 2. The Rise and Fall of the Athenian Land Power. Bury, pp 352–363 3. Imperial Athens. Bury, pp 278–284, 363–367 4. The Acropolis. Bury, pp 367–375 5. The Mysteries. Bury, pp 311–316 6. Athens, the City. Tucker, Life in Ancient Athens, pp. 20–52 7 The Athenian Citizens. Tucker, pp 61–68, 78–81. 8. Slavery at Athens. Tucker, pp 69–78. 9. The Position of Athenian Women. Tucker, pp 81–85, 155–167 10. The Furniture of an Athenian Home. Tucker, pp. 101–104 11. The Down-Town Day of an Athenian Citizen. Tucker, pp 120–135 12. An Athenian Dinner-Party. Tucker, pp 139–152. 13. The Athenian Boy's Education. Tucker, pp. 182–189 14. Religious Worship at Athens. Tucker, pp 210–218. 15. A Day at the Theatre. Tucker, pp 231–242. 16. An Athenian Trial. Tucker, pp 258–263.

TOPICS FOR READING AND ORAL REPORT. 1. Life at Athens in the Age of Pericles. Zimmern, pp 224–235, Morey, pp. 251–261 2. The Rise and Fall of the Athenian Land Power. Zimmern, pp. 219–224; Botsford, pp 164–169 3. Imperial Athens. Shuckburgh, pp 213–217, Botsford, pp 169–172. 4. The Acropolis. Shuckburgh, pp. 201–204; Morey, pp. 232–239, Botsford, pp. 179–185. 5. Herodotus. Capps, ch 12, Murray, ch. 6; Jebb, pp 103–106 6. The Mysteries. Encyclopedia Britannica, article "Mysteries", Dyer, The Gods in Greece, ch 5, Diehl, Excursions in Greece, ch 8. 7. Sophocles. Morey, pp. 245–247; Capps, ch. 9, Murray, ch. 11, Jebb, pp. 83–88. 8. Pericles. Plutarch, Life of Pericles

215. The War of Corinth and Corcyra.—Another movement of Athens in the interest of her commercial and political position in the west was the occasion of a serious rupture in the peaceful relations that had been maintained for ten years between Athens and Sparta. In 436 B.C. a quarrel arose between Corinth and Corcyra. The latter state, although it possessed a fleet of more than fifty ships, could not hope to equal the resources of Corinth in a serious conflict.   Hence it sought an alliance with Athens. This proposal put the Athenians in a difficult position. Should they reject it, Corcyra would make terms with Corinth, her naval force and commercial influence in the west would be thrown against Athens and seriously endanger Athenian naval supremacy. Should they accept it, their superiority on the sea would be irresistible, their commercial position in the west strengthened and Corinth, their only commercial rival in the Peloponnesian league, put out of the race. But, on the other hand, they would risk war with the league. It was finally decided to agree to a defensive alliance with Corcyra, whereby Athens was not required to join in an attack on the Corinthians. As might have been expected, this half-way measure roused the enmity of Corinth, whose future now depended on the weakening of Athens. Her only hope for this was in stirring up the Peloponnesian league to war. This was not difficult to do. The Spartans had long been jealous of the growing power of Athens. The years of peace had been irksome to this vigorous and warlike people. Athens, on the other hand, under the influence of Pericles, would not yield. He felt certain that war could be put off only a few years at the most and that Athens was never in a better condition to defend herself against her jealous and ambitious enemies. He was willing to arbitrate the whole matter, but not to compromise. At last, at a council of the Peloponnesian league held at Sparta in 432 B C, it was voted that Athens had broken the peace This was equivalent to a declaration of war. Athens accepted it as such and the conflict began in 431 B.C. With this a new period in the history of the Greek states is begun and we may pause to look back over a finished era.

The Inter-vention of Athens.

Gives Occa sion for War with the Pelo-ponnesian League.

GENERAL REVIEW OF PART II, DIVISION 5; §§ 164-215

500–431 B C

TOPICS FOR CLASS DISCUSSION. 1. An outline of the events
of these periods arranged so as to bring out the chief historical
movements and forces. 2. Illustrate the progress of Athenian democracy by the successive policies of Miltiades, Aristides, Themistocles, Cimon, Pericles (§§165, 168, 177, 183, 184,
187, 195). 3. Trace the growth of the Athenian empire from
500-431 B C 4. Justify the policy of Themistocles from the
events that followed. 5. The various stages in the war with
Persia (§§ 165, 167, 169, 176, 182, 187, 211-212). 6. A comparison
of Æschylus with Sophocles to illustrate the difference in
the periods to which they respectively belong (§§ 179, 206).
7. A list of the most important dates in these periods.

MAP AND PICTURE EXERCISES. 1. Make an outline map
of the Athenian empire in 456 B C, inserting all the places
mentioned in the text. 2. Make a map and plan of Pylos and
discuss the battle on the basis of your drawing. 3. Study the
heads of Sophocles and Pericles in Plate XVIII and compare
with those of Hammurabi and Ramses II in Plate II. Indicate
the artistic and historical resemblances and differences. 4.
Compare the Greek temples in Plate XXIV with those in Plate
VI. Observe the differences in form and arrangement. How
do these differences throw light on the different characteristics
of the oriental and Greek peoples? 5. Note the likenesses and
unlikenesses in the bucolic scenes of Plates XV and XXI.

TOPICS FOR WRITTEN PAPERS. 1. The Privileges and Duties
of an Athenian Citizen in the Age of Pericles. Fowler, The
City State, ch. 6. 2. A Visit to the Acropolis of Athens—a
description of Plate XVII. See references above, § 214; Diehl,
Excursions in Greece, ch 4 3. Herodotus, the Man and His
Book (see the references above, § 214) 4. The Story of a Day in
Athens in the Age of Pericles. Mahaffy, Old Greek Life, Grant,
Greece in the Age of Pericles 5. The Greek Theatre—the Building and the Play. 6. Styles of Greek Architecture. Tarbell, ch 3 7. The Architecture of Greek Buildings as Compared with that of Buildings in Your Own City. 8. The Story
of Sophocles' "Antigone." Translation by Palmer.

216. The War Unjustifiable, yet Unavoidable.—The war, called the Peloponnesian war, which now ensued and with intervals of peace lasted for more than a quarter of a century (431–404 B.C.) was one of the most melancholy wars of history. In one sense it was utterly unjustifiable and unnecessary. Athens and Sparta might have gone on peacefully, each in her separate way— the one a strong land power, the other the mistress of the seas. Both had every reason to avoid a conflict which was sure to be long and costly and the outcome of which was quite uncertain. The grounds on which war was declared were not sufficient to justify the declaration. Passion and prejudice forced the decisive step. But, from another point of view, the war was unavoidable. Beneath all reasons on the surface of the situation, the deeper cause was the imperial ideal of Athens. In building up her empire, Athens had come into conflict with the long-established idea that every Greek state had, as its deepest right, the right to political independence. The Spartans, in opening the war, declared that they waged it on behalf of Greek freedom against the tyrant. The majority of the states naturally sympathized with this spirit. We are to see in the Peloponnesian war, therefore, the conflict of two mighty forces—the one, the purely Greek idea of the separate and independent existence of city-states; the other, the world-ideal of empire, which had its rise in the dawn of human history. These two forces could not long exist together; sooner or later they must grapple one with the other in a life-and-death struggle. Nor was this the only ground for an "irrepressible conflict." In all the cities of both the Athenian and Spartan confederations there

The Struggle of Two Sets of Principles.

were two factions, a democratic and an aristocratic—the one drawn as by a magnet to Athens, the other to Sparta. Each of the leaders had its partisans in the other's camp whose action might at any moment precipitate a general war

217. Comparison of the Combatants.—The situation of the combatants was peculiar. Neither could be attacked in its strongest point. Athens's supremacy by sea was safe from its enemies, unless they had money to build ships and hire sailors, and money was scarce in the Peloponnesus   The Peloponnesians were strong on land, and Athens had no infantry that could stand against them.   For the Peloponnesians there was but one thing to do—invade Athenian territory.   But Athens itself was too strongly fortified to be taken, and it could not be starved into surrender so long as supplies could be brought in by sea.   The fields could be laid waste by the invaders, but that was all.   For the Athenians the plan of campaign, required by the situation and outlined by Pericles, was chiefly a defensive one.   The country people, on the approach of the enemy, should leave their farms, cheerfully accept the spoiling of their goods, and dwell in the city during the month or more of the invasion.   The Peloponnesians would then be forced to return home by lack of supplies and the necessity of tilling their fields, whereupon the Attic farms could be reoccupied by their owners and the damages repaired.   Resistance to the enemy by land battles would be avoided, but the Athenian fleet would sally out to strike at exposed points on the enemy's coast and to ruin the commerce of cities like Corinth and Megara.   The commerce of Athens, on the contrary, would remain undisturbed by the conflict.

The Plan of the Peloponnesians.

The Plan of Pericles.

Hence, the war would resolve itself into a question of Its Advan-
tag-. endurance, and Pericles was confident that Athens, supported and enriched by its enlarging trade, would at last emerge triumphant. The resources of the Peloponnesians would be exhausted in striking fruitless blows, and before long they would cease the unprofitable conflict.

218. The First Period of the War.—This plan of Pericles was followed in the main, during the first ten years of the war (431–421 B C), and these were the years of Athenian success. All Attica gathered behind the walls of Athens during the spring months of the first two years, when the Peloponnesians were abroad in the land. In the third year they omitted their raid and fell with all their force upon Platæa, an Athenian ally, whose isolated position in Bœotia doomed it to eventual destruction. Nevertheless, it beat off the attack made in 429 B.C, and Fall of
Platæa. only fell two years later when starved into submission. All the defenders who survived were executed without mercy. Years brought no impairment of the spirit of the Athenians. Even a fearful visitation of the plague, which car- Plague at
Athens. ried away nearly a third of the citizens in the second and third years (430–429 B.C.), shook their resolution for but a moment. The worst blow was the death of Pericles, Death of
Pericles. who fell a victim to the epidemic in 429 B C. With the removal of his wise counsel and powerful personality it was difficult for the democracy to keep to any fixed policy. Two parties sprang up. One party, headed by The Parties Nicias, a wealthy contractor and capitalist, who in dis- Nicias. position was cautious, moderate, grave and pious, a fair general and a serious politician, was inclined to bring the war to a close as soon as it could be done without dishonor to the state. The other party was led by Cleon, Cleon.

a rich manufacturer. He was in favor of prosecuting the war much more vigorously than the defensive policy of Pericles would have permitted. By his persuasive speech he obtained the leadership of the radical democrats. The mass of the citizens inclined first to one side and then to the other, with the result that Athens now embarked in rash and sometimes unfortunate enterprises, now did little more than stand on the defensive.

219. The Revolt of Lesbos.—A good illustration of the vacillation of the Athenian assembly was given on the occasion of the revolt of Mytilene, which in 428 B.C. shook off the control of Athens. There was no dispute between Nicias and Cleon as to the necessity of suppressing the outbreak vigorously, since otherwise the whole empire would be dissolved. Hence, resort was had to the direct property tax to raise funds, and in 427 B C., after a winter's siege, the rebellious city had to surrender. It was in the treatment to be accorded to the vanquished that opinions differed. Di-o'do-tus of Nicias's party urged clemency as the best basis for future co-operation with the allies, while Cleon, affirming that terrorism alone upheld the empire, recommended that all the adult males of Mytilene be put to death and the women and children be sold into slavery. This harsh policy the Athenians accepted one day, but on the next, repenting of their cruel decree, they compromised and condemned to death the ringleaders alone. A swift trireme sent after the ship which bore the command for a general execution barely arrived in time to save the innocent population.

Clemency vs. Terrorism.

220. The Pylos Affair.—The high-water mark of Athenian success in the ten years' war was reached in 425 B.C. In the spring of that year a fleet was sent out

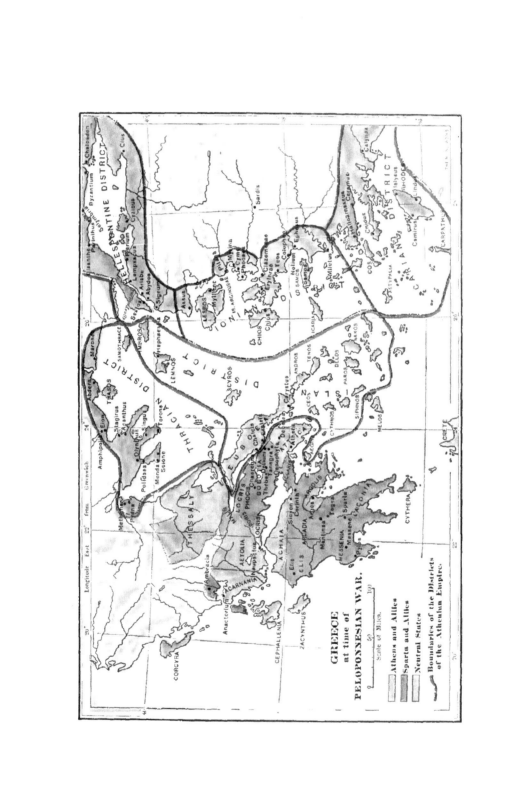

GREECE
at time of
PELOPONNESIAN WAR.

Scale of Miles.

Athens and Allies
Sparta and Allies
Neutral States
Boundaries of the Districts
of the Athenian Empire.

to the west. On their way the ships put in at the bay of Pylos, on the west of the Peloponnesus in Messenia. Here, De-mos'the-nes, Athens's most brilliant general, was landed with a small force and fortified the promontory of Pylos. On hearing of this the Peloponnesian army, already in Attica engaged in its yearly devastation of the land, hastily re-

PYLOS AND SPHACTERIA.

1 Mile

turned. A Spartan force, supported by a fleet, attacked the Athenians, who defended them-selves valiantly. A body of Spartan hoplites took pos-session of the long narrow island of Sphac-te'ri-a, which, from the point of Pylos, stretched away to-ward the south and formed the outer side of the harbor. Suddenly the Athenian fleet reappeared and drove the Spartan fleet upon the shore, thus cutting off the four hundred and twenty Spartan hoplites on the island from their fellows on the mainland. These men made up about one-sixth of the citizen body of Sparta, and the Spartan authorities made every effort to save them, even sending ambassadors to Athens to ask terms of peace. Thus the Athenians had the opportunity to end the war with a brilliant triumph, but under the persuasions of Cleon the ambassadors were denied a fair hearing, and the war went on. On the promise of Cleon that he would bring the Spartan hoplites prisoners to Athens in twenty days, he was given troops and sent as general to Pylos. He was himself no skilful soldier, but he took with him reinforcements with which Demosthenes was able to force the Spartans to surrender within the specified time. This success lifted Cleon into the highest favor with the people, and his policy of bold, aggressive warfare was approved. The most favorable moment for making peace had been allowed to slip. Accordingly, in the following year (424 B.C.) the Athenians made an attack with full force upon Bœotia, Demosthenes advancing from the Corinthian gulf, Hip-poc′ra-tes, with seven thousand hoplites and twenty thousand light-armed troops, advancing from Attica The Bœotians were prepared for the invasion, and the two attacks were not delivered at the same moment. Hence, Hippocrates was assailed near Delium by the main Bœotian army and completely defeated. The judgment of Pericles was vindicated. Athens was unequal to her enemy on land.

Cleon's Rash Policy.

Battle of Delium.

221. Brasidas and His Plan.—In the meanwhile the Peloponnesians had done little more, year by year, than make invasions into Attica or ward off as best they might the advances of Athens upon the mainland. But in the year of the Bœotian victory at Delium they scored a success which augmented the weight of that disaster. This they owed to the Spartan general Bras′i-das, the ablest officer that had yet appeared on their side. Without a fleet the Peloponnesians could make an attack on the Athenian empire outside of Attica at only one point.

The genius of Brasidas perceived and struck at that one point—the Athenian possessions in Macedonia and Thrace. Hurrying north with a small force, he appeared before the city of A-can'thus, and, with the plea that he had come to secure freedom from the Athenian tyrant, he induced the city to rebel. The Athenians were taken unprepared, and before they could collect themselves the important city of Am-phip'o-lis had fallen. The failure in Bœotia and the losses in Thrace now gave the peace party the ascendancy in Athens, and in 423 B C. a year's truce was arranged for the purpose of concluding a permanent peace. The negotiations, however, came to naught, and in 422 B.C. Cleon sailed to the north to recover the cities lost in that quarter. In a skirmish at the gates of Amphipolis, both he and Brasidas were slain. Death of Cleon and Brasidas

222. Peace of Nicias.—With Cleon out of the way, there was opportunity at Athens for the lovers of peace to carry through their programme. Accordingly, in 421 B.C., a treaty was signed for a fifty years' peace between Sparta and Athens. The war had closed with the advantage entirely on the side of Athens. The fundamental article of the treaty was that both powers should give back what they had conquered from each other during the war. This meant for the Spartans the loss of the cities in the north and for the Athenians the setting free of the Spartans taken at Pylos. But the Athenian empire remained practically undiminished, and Corinth's sea power and commerce had been shattered, while Athens had enlarged and strengthened her possessions. On the other hand, the purpose of the Peloponnesian league to destroy the Athenian empire had utterly failed and the members of Result of the Ten Years. Athens in the Ascendant.

the league were themselves at odds one with another. Athens was mistress of the situation.

223. Changes in Athenian Temper and Spirit.—We must pause here to note some changes in Athenian life, which had their root in the time of Pericles, but bore fruit during the years of war. We have seen (§§ 189–195) how democracy under Pericles was perfected. The people ruled directly, and politics became the passion of the citizens. To guide the people successfully one must persuade them in public assembly, he who would win them to his way of thinking and acting must be able to argue better than his opponents. To be a good orator was indispensable for a politician. To meet this demand teachers sprang up who professed, among other things, to make one skilful in the art of persuasion. These were the rhetoricians and the sophists. They were immensely popular at Athens. Men learned from them how to present arguments and to weigh them, to put ideas in a taking way in public speech, and to reply to opponents successfully. It was not so important that the cause urged was good or bad, or that the arguments presented in favor of it were right or wrong—they must be such that the people, hearing them, would think them sound and vote accordingly. As this skill grew, the people grew more critical also. The public assembly became a school of debate, where sharp-witted politicians contended before a keen and excited audience. Fine points were applauded and dulness hissed. But the result of this was to put truth and justice below shrewdness in debate, to make adroitness and popular oratorical skill more important than character and honor in a political leader. The Athenians fell into this fatal error.

Rise of Rhetoricians and Sophists.

The Debating Fever and Its Effect.

224. Comedy as an Illustration of the Times.—This condition of things is illustrated in the comedy of the times. Comedy, like tragedy (§ 160), arose in connection with the religious festivals and dealt familiarly with the scenes and events of common life. In Athens, where the main interest was politics, it found its congenial subjects in the political leaders, who were held up to unmeasured ridicule amidst the unrestrained laughter of the audience. The greatest comic poet of the day was Ar-is-toph'a-nes (about 450–385 B.C.). In his *Knights* he satirizes the Demos as an ill-natured old man, who is the prey of his villainous slave, the leather-worker (meaning Cleon, who was a tanner). The *Clouds* jests at the new learning of the time. The *Wasps* makes fun of the Athenian law-courts by a mock trial in which justice is parodied. The *Birds* pictures a bird-city "Cloudcoockootown" where the bustle and excitement of Athens are kept out. The *Frogs* describes the adventures of Dionysus, who goes to Hades (the underworld) to find a poet, and is in doubt whether to bring back Æschylus (ĕs'kĭ-lŭs) or the favorite dramatist of the time, Eu-rip'i-des. He finally decides for the former. All these and the other comedies of Aristophanes are, in spite of their coarseness and personal abuse, works of permanent power because of their rollicking humor and vigor, interspersed with passages of wonderful lyric beauty. The strange thing is that the Athenians were willing to listen to such satires on their life and such caricatures of their statesmen, to laugh at their leaders one day and follow them the next.

Aristophanes.

225. Effect of Culture on Morals and Religion.—The culture of Athens, fed by architecture, painting and sculpture, by the spectacles of the tragic and comic stage, and stimulated by the stirring political activity, could not fail to have its influence on religion and morals.

It is true that most men were too busy about business and politics to trouble themselves as to whether their notions about the gods would stand the test   But a few could not avoid questioning   Pericles gathered about him men like the sophist An-ax-ag'o-ras, who, following after the earlier thinkers (§ 132), thought of the world as formed not from a single source, but from several original elements, one of which is "mind," that puts all things together.   He regarded the sun and moon as great balls of stone   The speed of the sun had turned it into a glowing mass.

Such ideas—an integral part of the "new learning" which the sophists were bringing within the reach of everybody in the later Periclean time—were shocking to pious people; no less so the teachings of the greatest of all the sophists, Pro-tag'o-ras of Ab-de'ra, which may be formulated in the following statements: "Man is the measure of all things." "In regard to the gods I am unable to say whether they exist or do not exist, for many things hinder such knowledge—the obscurity of the matter and the shortness of human life." Such ideas overturned the old faith.   Those who held them tried to find solider ground to stand on than was supplied by the religion of the day and to clear men's minds from its superstitions.   Pericles sympathized with this aim, but he did not carry the citizens along with him.   The old religion was sacred to most of them and they feared and hated the

philosophers who attacked it.   Anaxagoras was banished from Athens in 434 B.C. for his "impiety," and nearly twenty years later Protagoras escaped persecution only by fleeing from the city.   During the whole time of the

Peloponnesian war Athens was torn by a fierce religious controversy centring round the doctrines of the sophists. In fact, these ideas did not make men better, because they shattered faith in religion, on which people depended, and put nothing in its place. Nor did the prevailing interest in politics help; it rather harmed. Men grew hard and grasping in their ambitions, their love of country made them selfish in her defence and for her glory. Some one has called attention to three dark spots upon this enlightened Athenian society: (1) The putting of slaves to torture before taking their testimony in a court of law; (2) the ruthless slaughter of prisoners taken in war, and the selling of captive women and children into slavery; (3) the want of respect for old age. We have already observed the position of woman (§ 202). In all this we must not judge too harshly, but rather remember that people do not go forward in all things at one time. In Athens the new learning was breaking down the old customs before building up new ones. While the childish things of the old religion and morals were being put away, more reasonable ideas were slow in gaining ground.

Dark Side of Athenian Character.

226. Characteristic Figures.—Four great men of this period illustrate the spiritual temper of Athens in its lighter and darker sides.

227. Thucydides Compared with Herodotus.—Thucydides* (about 471–399 B C.) was the Athenian general who, failing to keep Brasidas out of Amphipolis (§ 221), was banished from Athens and was in exile for twenty years. He improved this time in gathering materials for and writing a *History of the Peloponnesian War*. He wrote during

* Not the same as the son of Melesias (§ 213).

the latter years of Herodo.   § 208), but a whole world separates their histories from one another.   Herodotus describes; Thucydides gives the inner meaning.   Herodotus tells a story because of his interest in it; Thucydides tells nothing but what he knows to be true.   Herodotus enjoys his work and wants others to be entertained also; Thucydides writes for the instruction of men who take things seriously.   In other words, Thucydides has no sentiment or humor; he is intensely keen and hard.   He reveals what is base and selfish, true and heroic in his characters in a masterly fashion, but without praise or blame.   Everything he handles is treated from the purely political point of view.   You learn nothing directly of the religious, economic or social life of his day   His style is strong, concise, sometimes obscure, often eloquent.   The history reaches its height in the account of the expedition to Syracuse in the seventh book.

A Scientific Historian.

228. Euripides.—Euripides (about 480–406 B.C.) was the supreme tragic poet of the war-time.   He had thought deeply upon all the problems raised by the new learning and used his wonderful imaginative power in presenting them through his tragedies.   He was the poet of democracy, but of a glorified democracy which had a deep feeling for woman and the slave   Woman's heroism and devotion form the kernel of his *Iphigenia* and *Alcestis*.   The tragedy of common life is seen in the *Electra*.   He introduces the slave and the beggar to show that they, too, have hearts that can bleed.   Toward the popular religion he stands in an attitude partly of abhorrence and partly of sympathy.   His *Bacchæ* is a powerful picture of the madness and sublimity of the worship of Dionysus (§ 134).   Men were at once charmed by the magic and

"Euripides, the Human"

PLATE XVIII

Sophocles

Pericles

Socrates

The Aphrodite of Melos

Alexander

An Alexandrian Greek

TYPICAL GREEK HEADS

pathos of his poetry and repelled by the boldness and novelty of his thoughts. In all this he reveals himself as a son of his time—of the restless, passionate, practical, sensitive, brutal Athens of the war.

229. Socrates.—One of the most picturesque personalities of the time was Socrates (about 469–399 B.C.). Of a burly, ungainly figure, with bulging eyes, flat nose and thick lips, he could be seen at all times on the streets, as he gathered about him a delighted group whom he engaged in conversation, drawing them on by simple questions to consider the deepest problems of life. He had taken the step which all Athens needed to take— from the enjoyment of material prosperity and the passion for politics to the search for right living. Athens had learned the goodness of greatness; he would teach her the greatness of goodness. He found true knowledge A Moral Philoso-pher. in the study of his own heart and the testing of his own ideals. The old motto, "Know thyself," was the text of all his preaching. In this work he felt himself commissioned from above; a divine spirit goaded him on and inspired him. By his sharp and searching talk he irritated the self-satisfied democracy, whose leaders hated to be made fools of by him. He claimed that skill in government was a result of training just as was skill in shoemaking, and thought that it was absurd to distribute offices by lot. "Politicians," he cried, "all flatterers, His Contempt for Democracy cooks, confectioners, tavern-keepers, whom have they made better? They have filled the city with harbors, docks, walls, tributes and such trash, instead of with temperance and righteousness." For his own time he was a prophet crying in the wilderness; one excitement the more for sensation-loving Athens. But his work, although undertaken too late for the salvation of his own generation, was destined to abide for all time.

230. Alcibiades.—Among those who gathered about Socrates, professing discipleship, was the most brilliant young Athenian of the time, Alcibiades. All the vices and virtues of the Athens of the war were summed up in him; he is the exemplar at once of her glory and her shame. With him we pass from the spiritual forces of the time to one of its most potent political leaders, and therefore take up again the thread of the history. A relative of Pericles, a true aristocrat, wealthy and handsome, Alcibiades was the hope of the friends of that statesman and the natural heir of his ideas. He took up the interests of the people, posing as a radical of the radicals. His education was the best the age could offer, and he shared in all the advanced opinions of his day. He was the idol of the people, yet respected nobody but himself; the teaching of Socrates accomplished little for him beyond confirming him in his egotism without leading him on to self-improvement. On the death of Cleon (§ 221) he sprang into the vacant place as leader of the radical democracy.

Unites the New Learning with Politics.

231. The Years of the False Peace.—The long-desired peace with the Peloponnesian league (§ 222) was followed by a union between Sparta and Athens, from which the allies of Sparta were excluded, because they refused to accept the peace. Apart from the two powerful states now at one, they could do nothing. Hence, a long period of rest and recovery from the waste and turmoil of war seemed at hand. But the prospect was not realized; the fifty years' peace was dead from its birth. Formally, it endured for six years, years in which there was constant turmoil and fighting somewhere in Greece. The causes of this were threefold: (1) In 450 B.C. Sparta and Argos had concluded a thirty years' peace, which now was just at an end   Argos, left alone during these years, had grown strong and was ready to enter the political field.   The other Peloponnesian states, abandoned by Sparta, entered into a league with the new power and prepared to turn against their old leader.   (2) The Spartans failed to carry out the terms of the peace, as they did not give back to Athens the captured cities. This caused dissatisfaction at Athens.   (3) The strife of parties at Athens was intensified by Alcibiades, who, as leader of the war party, sought to destroy the good understanding between Sparta and Athens established by the peace party.   Alcibiades hoped, by renewing the war with Sparta, to place himself at the head of affairs, bring victory to Athens and glory to himself.   He induced the Athenians to ally themselves with the Argive league. Finally, Sparta came to a battle with the league at Mantinea, and defeated them (418 B C.); the league was forthwith broken up.   Yet, even now, Athens and Sparta did not begin to fight.   Each was at heart not unwilling to keep the peace.   Each was ready for a convenient opportunity for war.

Causes of Trouble.

Mantinea

232. The Athenian Expedition against Syracuse.— The opportunity was offered by Athens.   In the year 416 B.C. she made a brutal use of her naval supremacy, and, seizing Doric Melos by violence, she slew or enslaved the inhabitants, and divided their land among Attic cleruchi.   This was, however, but the prelude to a still more daring enterprise.   Her commercial activity in the west had long been hindered by the rivalry of

Melos.

Syracuse. Just at this time the rapid extension of the. power of Syracuse induced some neighboring cities of Sicily to call on Athens for help Alcibiades persuaded the assembly, despite the persistent protests of Nicias, to send against Syracuse an expedition, which set sail in 415 B.C. It was the finest fleet Athens ever put upon the sea and taxed her resources heavily. It consisted of 134 triremes, 20,000 seamen and an army of 6,430 soldiers. The command was not intrusted to Alcibiades alone, but was divided between himself, Nicias and Lamachus. One morning, just before the fleet sailed, the Athenians were startled to find that the sacred images, called Hermæ, which stood along the streets of the city, had been wantonly disfigured. The attempt was made to fasten the guilt for this outrage, and other similar sins against religion, upon Alcibiades and his friends, but a decision on the matter was postponed till he returned.

Condemnation and Flight of Alcibiades. However, he had hardly reached Sicily when he was ordered to come to Athens to stand trial. Fearing for his life, he escaped, and after a short time found a refuge at Sparta, where he sought every means to bring ruin upon his native city.

233. Renewal of the War.—At last, in 414 B.C., under the impulse of the war spirit, the Athenians took the bold step of making a descent upon Spartan soil. This decided the Spartans for war. They sent a small force to the aid of Syracuse under a valiant and able general named Gy-lip'pus and prepared again to invade Attica.

234. The Disaster at Syracuse.—Meanwhile the expedition against Syracuse was faring badly. Lam'a-chus was dead and Nicias was left in sole command. He sent back to Athens for reinforcements. In spite of

some unpleasant surprise at this news, Athens could
not draw back, and her most brilliant general, Demosthenes, was sent out with seventy-three ships and an
army of twenty thousand men gathered from all parts
of the Athenian empire. But his help was in vain
The honest but incompetent Nicias had lost his oppor- Incompe-
tency of
Nicias.
tunity to capture the city by assault and attempted a
siege. The Syracusans gathered courage and strength
with the coming of Gylippus. After a vain attempt to
storm their works, Demosthenes urged a retreat, but
Nicias delayed until it was too late. At the last the
Athenian army was scattered, the two generals captured
and put to death, the soldiers thrown into the stone-
quarries, where many perished of hunger; the survivors
were sold as slaves (413 B.C.).

235. Its Vital Significance.—The Syracusan expedition was the crisis of Athens. With its failure the
Athenian empire was doomed The plague had swept
away about one-third of the citizens; the disaster in
Sicily cut the remainder in two The astonishing thing
—and it exhibits the spirit and resources of the city most
clearly—is that Athens fought the Peloponnesians ten
years longer before she fell.

236. Spartans at Decelea, 413 B.C.—The Spartans,
on the advice of Alcibiades, now occupied a permanent
stronghold in Attica at Dec'e-le'a. fifteen miles north of
Athens, at the head of the valley of the Cephissus.
Thereby the city was in a permanent state of siege; the Flight of
Slaves.
income from the country was cut off; the slaves, to the
number of more than twenty thousand, escaped to the
enemy, and all work suffered correspondingly. This was
in itself sufficiently serious. Then came the awful news

from Syracuse. In three particulars its effects were at once felt.

237. Persia Joins in the War.—In the first place, now that the Athenian navy was destroyed, Persia thought the time come to make good the losses sustained between 480 and 448 B C. Hence she determined to take a hand in the war. Artaxerxes I, the maker and lover of peace, was dead, and his son, Darius II, was on the throne (424–404) B.C. His satraps, Pharn-a-baz′us and Tis-sa-pher′nes, were directed to recover the Great King's possessions on the coast of Asia Minor. Persia had what the Spartans lacked—money. With money the Peloponnesians could build, equip and maintain a fleet and meet Athens on the sea.

Appearance of Persia on the Scene.

238. Revolt of Allies.—In the second place the Athenian allies broke out in revolt the moment a hope of success presented itself. This meant to sever the main artery of the state; for now that Attica was lost it was from the empire alone that Athens drew its revenues, from their transmarine investments and commerce that the citizens gained their livelihood. The loss of revenues meant inability to keep a fleet, and it was solely through having in the treasury a reserve of one thousand talents which Pericles had set aside for such an emergency that a navy could be built at all.

Athens Loses Her Revenues.

239. Rule of the Four Hundred.—In the third place the disaster in Sicily brought the democracy, which had authorized the expedition, into such discredit that a successful attempt was made by its opponents to set it aside (411 B C.). At a packed meeting held in the suburb of Colonus during a reign of terror occasioned by the assassination of prominent democrats, the con-

Democracy Overthrown.

stitutional safeguards of popular sovereignty were first abolished. The payment for all public services of a civil character was suspended during the continuance of the war and a government of four hundred men with power to legislate, conduct foreign negotiations and appoint military and other magistrates was substituted for the government of the ecclesia, the understanding being that Alcibiades, now at odds with Sparta and tired of living in Persia, where, on his arrival he had become the confidant of Tissaphernes, would, if restored, win for Athens the financial support of the Great King. Alcibiades did, in fact, return from exile, but he did not bring Persia with him, and it was to the fleet, which had refused to acknowledge the new government, that he came. The government of the four hundred then tried to betray Athens to Sparta, whereupon it was set aside by a general movement headed by The-ram'e-nes, one of its own members; and after a year's interval, during which the propertied classes alone had the franchise, the complete democracy was restored.

240. Fall of the Athenian Empire.—The first fleet built by the Peloponnesians was not financed liberally by the Persian satraps, who, while inclining to Sparta and setting her up on the sea, also gave sufficient help to Athens to enable her to continue the struggle. The design was to weaken both sides until Persia could step in and overpower both. This scheme was frustrated by a brilliant victory gained by Alcibiades at Cyzicus in 410 B C., and had the Athenian distrust of this versatile man not sent him again into exile when his fleet suffered a slight defeat at Notium during his temporary absence, the war might still have ended favorably for Athens.

First Peso-Spartan Fleet.

Cyzicus.

The disaster of Sparta at Cyzicus was made good when Lysander, of whom we shall hear more later, was given charge of its naval operations, for he persuaded Cyrus, the Great King's younger son, who had superseded Tissaphernes in command of the Asia Minor provinces, to take definitely the side of Sparta, the consideration being that Sparta acknowledged Persia's claim to the Greek territory in Asia Minor. So long as the second Perso-Spartan fleet was under Lysander's command it was successful, but his successor, Cal-li-crat'i-das, was badly beaten in 406 B.C. off the Ar-gi-nus'æ islands by a new navy which the Athenians, making a last desperate effort, put on the sea in that year. The complete demoralization of public life at Athens was manifested at this time in two incidents. In the first place, at the instance of Theramenes, the citizens illegally condemned and executed their successful admirals for failing to rescue some shipwrecked sailors; and in the second place they again, as after the battle of Cyzicus, at the instance of Cleophon, the "boss" of the ecclesia at this time, rejected honorable proposals of peace made by the discouraged Spartans. The people would have the whole of their former empire or nothing. In the meanwhile they again controlled the sea; but once more Lysander and Cyrus built and equipped a new fleet. This the Athenians in the year 405 B.C. followed to the Hellespont. They took their station on the shore of the Thracian Chersonese over against Lamp'sa-cus at Æ-gos-pot'a-mi, an open beach without harborage, and repeatedly offered battle to Lysander. He chose his own time, however, and falling unexpectedly upon the Athenian navy captured it and its crew almost without a blow. This was followed by the surrender of Athens (404 B.C.),

Margin notes: Second Perso-Spartan Fleet. / Third Perso-Spartan Fleet.

the entrance of the Peloponnesians and the pulling down of the Long Walls—a day of triumph for Sparta, heralded as "the beginning of freedom for Greece."

241. Character of Lysander.—The two chief actors during these years were the Athenian Alcibiades and Lysander the Spartan. The unprincipled conduct of the former has been described already in the narrative

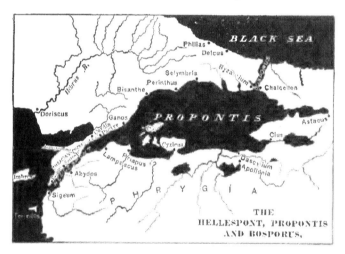

THE HELLESPONT, PROPONTIS AND BOSPORUS.

of the war. Shortly after it was over, he was murdered by the Persians among whom he had taken refuge. Lysander was the Spartan Alcibiades, a brilliant, cruel, selfish politician and general. His purpose was the same as that of his Athenian contemporary, to help his state with the idea of making himself the first man in it. As the friend of Cyrus, he wielded Persian influence in behalf of Sparta and won the final victory which brought Athens low. At the close of the war, he was the greatest man in Greece, and all his ambitions seemed about to be fulfilled.

242. Failure of Democracy in Foreign Politics.—
Nothing in history is more amazing and heartrending

than the spectacle of Athens during these ten years. It
is amazing to see the democracy struggling on with stern
determination against an inevitable fate, spending their
last resources to equip a fleet, and on its destruction
making yet another desperate effort to face their foes,
and yielding only when the treasury was empty, the citizen body reduced to a fraction of its numbers, the subject cities lost, the food supply cut off, the people perish-
ing from famine. However admirable this exhibition of
heroism may be, we are bound to recognize that as the
war progressed the Athenian demos lost a just appreciation of the relative material strength of itself and its adversaries. To its inability to decide on peace when peace
was necessary; in other words, to its inability to choose
the right policy in foreign affairs we must attribute a large
share of the responsibility for the fall of its brilliant empire.

243. Internal Evils of Democracy.—There were, indeed, serious defects in the Athenian constitution, the
chief of which was the inequality of the burdens borne
by citizens. The rich were called on for large contributions for the support of the state (§ 210), while the poor,
having equal rights, were paid for their service. The
attitude of Athens toward her subject cities was also a
fundamental weakness in her foreign policy (§ 213), so
that in her dire extremity they deserted her. But none of
these things, not Athenian democratic institutions, nor
the superiority of Sparta, nor the money of Persia, brought

her low. The want of uprightness and honesty in her
leaders; the preferring of cleverness to character; the
placing of self and party above country and duty; in a

word, the social and political demoralization incident to the long war—this was the dry-rot at the heart of Athens that finally brought the imperial structure to ruin. Far more instructive than any lessons from the eastern empires are the magnificent achievement and the pitiful collapse of the Athenian empire.

244. Terms of Athens's Surrender.—The terms on which Sparta received the submission of Athens were these; the fortifications of the Piræus and the Long Walls were to be pulled down; all the ships but twelve were to be given up; all exiles were to return, the supremacy of Sparta was to be acknowledged; the friends and foes of the Spartans were to be Athens's friends and foes, and war contributions of money and men were to be made when Sparta demanded them. These conditions reveal the Spartan programme: (1) to secure for all Greek cities freedom from outside interference—for this purpose Athens was made powerless, (2) to establish Sparta's headship over all these cities in the spirit of the old Peloponnesian league (§ 154).

The Spartan Programme.

REVIEW EXERCISES. 1. For what are the following famous: Nicias, Demosthenes, Brasidas, Gylippus, Thucydides, Socrates, Euripides, Cyrus the Younger, Lamachus, Protagoras? 2. What events are connected with the following: Amphipolis, Mantinea, Decelea, Ægospotami? 3. What is meant by Sophist, Hermæ, demos, "all things flow"? 4. What are the dates of the three periods of the war? of Pylos, Syracusan expedition, Ægospotami? 5. Explain the attitude of the Athenian assembly on the occasion of Lesbos's revolt. 6. How did the news of the disaster at Syracuse affect Athens? 7. What were the reasons for Athens refusing Sparta's honorable proposals of peace after Cyzicus?

COMPARATIVE STUDIES. 1. Compare Themistocles (§§ 168, 184, 187) and Alcibiades as political leaders. 2. Compare the

Athenian method of declaring war, making peace and appointing generals with our own.

SELECT LIST FOR READING. 1. The Peloponnesian War: Preliminaries and First Period. Bury, ch 10 2. The Second Period: the Sicilian Expedition. Bury, pp 458–484 3. The Third Period. Bury, pp. 484–505 4. The Sophists. Bury, pp 385–389 5. Socrates. Bury, pp 576–581

TOPICS FOR READING AND ORAL REPORT. 1. The Peloponnesian War: Preliminaries and First Period. Zimmern, ch. 15; Shuckburgh, pp 217–235, Botsford, pp 190–205. 2. The Second Period: the Sicilian Expedition. Zimmern, pp 270–282; Shuckburgh, pp 238–248, Botsford, pp 208–216 3. The Third Period. Zimmern, ch 17; Botsford, pp 227–238, Shuckburgh, pp. 248–259. 4. The New Thought at Athens. Botsford, pp. 217–227. 5. Aristophanes. Jebb, pp 95–100, Capps, ch. 11; Murray, pp. 280–293. 6. Thucydides. Jebb, pp 106–109, Capps, pp 317–330, Murray, ch 8. 7. Euripides. Jebb, pp 88–94; Capps, ch. 10; Murray, ch 12. 8. Socrates. Jebb p. 125; Shuckburgh, pp. 264–266, Murray pp 170–177; Morey, pp. 290–291

245. Other Imperial Attempts.—Sparta's headship naturally carried with it the reappearance everywhere of that class of citizens and of that form of government with which Sparta was in sympathy. The aristocracy took charge of affairs, destroyed democracy and established oligarchies in the place of the democratic governments that characterized Athenian rule. The usual form of these oligarchies was the decarchy, or the rule of ten aristocratic citizens. A peculiar form was that at Athens, where thirty men reorganized the government.

Renewal of Oligarchy.

246. Failure of the Programme.—But it was impossible to combine the two parts of the Spartan programme (§ 244). The events of the last fifty years made it difficult to force the demos back into obscurity, and Sparta's aristocratic friends were compelled to depend on Spartan help to sustain them in office. Moreover, Sparta had been infected by Athens with the imperial fever; her great general, Lysander, openly worked to secure Spartan supremacy. Thus, in many cities the decarchy had by its side a Spartan harmost, or overseer, at the head of a body of troops, who represented the real power of the state. Supported by this military authority, the aristocrats took bloody revenge everywhere for the wrongs of years, killing the democratic leaders and seizing their property, while the Spartan commander looked calmly on or aided the avengers.

Sparta Supports Oligarchies.

247. The Thirty at Athens, 404-403 B.C.—At Athens a regular reign of terror was carried on by the "Thirty" with the support of a Spartan garrison on the Acropolis. Strictly they were appointed at the instigation of Lysander to frame a new constitution. Chief among them were Critias, one of the exiled nobles and a disciple of the "new learning," and Theramenes, the leader of the moderate wing of the aristocratic faction at the time of the four hundred. The thirty had no thought of bringing in a new constitution, but their intention was to prolong their term of rule indefinitely. To this end they soon began to expel their opponents, especially the prominent democrats. Numbers were slain that their property might be confiscated. In these murders and confiscations Critias and Theramenes at first agreed, but on the question of the continuation of this extreme policy Theramenes deserted his colleague. To break the force of his agitation Critias broadened the government so as to include three thousand men in a list of privileged citizens. However, this half-way measure did not remove discontent. An open rupture occurred between Critias and Theramenes, the latter being denounced as

Theramenes "the Trimmer."

a "turncoat." Theramenes defended himself valiantly, but the brute force of his adversary prevailed, and he was compelled to drink the fatal hemlock. Meanwhile, the exiles whom the thirty had banished were increasing in numbers. Many found refuge in Thebes, and of these a group under the lead of Thrasybulus seized Phy'le, on the slopes of Mt. Par'nes. The thirty were beaten in an attempt to dislodge them; nor were they more successful when in the spring of 403 B.C. they tried to recover the Pıræus which Thrasybulus and his comrades had occupied by surprise. Critias was among the slain. Even then another oligarchy would have been set up had not Pausanias, the Spartan king, who was hostile to Lysander, secured for the Athenians freedom to reorganize their government as a somewhat conservative democracy.

248. Lysander's Imperial Policy.—Elsewhere Lysander set up decarchies and planted Spartan garrisons, sailing up and down the Ægean sea, levying tribute and practically subjugating, instead of freeing, the cities. Thus the Greek world found that the victory over Athens resulted only in the setting up of a heartless and narrow-minded power, whose aim was a supremacy more thorough and selfish than ever. This could not fail to be clearly seen, when it became known that the condition on which Persia had taken Sparta's side was that Sparta should hand the Greek cities on the Asia Minor coast over to Persia. Not only the Spartans then—the Spartans and the Persians were lords of the Greek states.

Persia, the Ally of Lysander.

249. Affairs in Sicily.—In sympathy with Sparta was yet another power in the Greek world. Ever since the successful defence of Syracuse against the Athenians the Greek cities of Sicily had been living in peace, with increasing wealth and prosperity, under democratic constitutions But Carthage, the Phœnician metropolis of north Africa, who had kept her hands from Sicily since the defeat of Himera (§ 176), took advantage of a local quarrel to invade Sicily in 409 B.C. In the struggles which followed, it seemed as if all Greek Sicily would fall under the Carthaginian supremacy. Deliverance was wrought by a citizen of Syracuse, of humble origin, but of remarkable political and military gifts, Dionysius. He made himself tyrant of Syracuse, and in a series of wars with the Carthaginians forced them back and confined their possessions to the western end of the island. During his long reign (405-367 B.C.), Syracuse became the greatest city of the Greek world. Dionysius fortified it strongly, adorned it magnificently and made it the centre of an empire which embraced a large part of Greek Italy, as well as islands and colonies in the upper Adriatic sea. His help was sought and obtained by the Spartans. He was desirous of entering into close relations with the eastern Greeks, who both admired and feared him as a powerful but dangerous tyrant. His nature was cold and hard; he did little for higher culture, although he wrote tragedies and thought himself most fortunate to have won the first prize at Athens in a tragic competition. His merit was primarily political—to have saved the Greeks of the west from destruction. His empire lasted only a few years after his death.

The Carthaginian Problem

The Empire of Dionysius

250. Growth of Greek Imperialism.—The half-century that followed the close of the Peloponnesian war (404-355 B.C.) is occupied with the history of the attempts of the leading Greek states, one after the other, to rule over the Greek world. In each of these states were ambitious men whose ideals were, like those of Alcibiades at Athens (§ 230), centred on the supremacy of their

own cities under their personal headship. Such a man was Lysander of Sparta, who, despite the fact that there were now not more than two thousand Spartiatæ whereas there were three or four million Greeks, wanted to make Sparta the ruler of Greece and himself the ruler of Sparta. The first of these aims he was accomplishing by supporting dependent oligarchies in the various cities with Spartan harmosts and garrisons. The other he hoped to gain by making the new Spartan king, A-ges-i-la'us (399 B.C), a man small, lame and apparently without force, subservient to himself.

251. The Conflict at Sparta.—But already symptoms of discontent with Lysander's selfish, unscrupulous, policy had shown themselves at Sparta. The liberation of Athens from the thirty tryants by Pausanias (§ 247) is an illustration. Especially the abandonment of the Asia Minor cities to Persia was felt to be unworthy, and their deliverance was loudly called for. The decisive step was forced by an unexpected event. The death of Darius II of Persia in 404 B.C. brought his

eldest son, Artaxerxes II, to the throne. But Cyrus, the younger son, whose union with Sparta had brought Athens low (§ 240), gathered an army of some ten thousand Greek mercenaries and one hundred thousand Asiatics and started from Asia Minor to contest the throne (401 B.C.). The king met the invaders in Babylonia at Cunaxa (401 B.C.), where the Greeks carried all before them, but Cyrus himself was killed. With his death the rebellion collapsed, the Asiatics deserted to the king and the Greeks were left alone in the heart of the empire. But, though deceived and harassed by the Persians, and their generals treacherously slain, they forced their way back to the west through the northern mountains and reached the Black sea. They had challenged the Great King at his very gates and he had been unable to punish them.

252. Xenophon.—Among the Greeks who accompanied Cyrus was a young Athenian, Xenophon, a friend of one of the Greek generals. It was he who encouraged the Greeks after the loss of their generals and inspired them to defy the king and attempt the return march. He has written an account of the expedition in his *Anabasis*, one of the most attractive books in Greek literature. *The Ten Thousand and Xenophon.*

253. War between Sparta and Persia.—When Cyrus planned his rebellion, he sought and obtained the aid of Sparta. The failure of his attempt brought down Persian wrath upon her. She was thus driven to break with Persia and strike a blow for the freedom of the Asia Minor cities. War began in 400 B.C. In 396 B.C. Agesilaus, with a strong army, started for Asia Minor, accompanied by Lysander, who expected to control the expedition. But Agesilaus, though insignificant in body, was vigorous in purpose and ambition; he soon showed himself the real, as well as the nominal, master, and Lysander's supremacy was past. *Agesilaus in Asia Minor.*

254. Sparta's Difficulties in Greece.—The war with Persia ran on feebly for ten years longer (396–387 B.C.). Worthy as was Sparta's motive in waging it, she could not escape the consequences of her arbitrary treatment of Greek states at home. Corinth, Argos and Thebes, who had suffered from her tyranny, joined with Athens; *Corinthian War (395–387 B.C.).*

all threw themselves on the side of Persia, and a struggle began in 395 B C. which is usually called the Corinthian war. Its first incident was the death of Lysander in an attempt to take Hal-i-ar'tus. He was an able man whom only the unfitness and disinclination of Sparta for empire prevented from being uncrowned sovereign of Greece for a long time. The conflict was carried on at sea also where a Persian fleet under the leadership of Conon, an Athenian admiral, operated against Sparta. Agesilaus was called back from Ionia and won a victory over the Thebans at Cor'o-nei'a in 394 B.C., but the same year the Spartan fleet was destroyed at Cnidos. The Ionian cities fell into the hands of Persia. The Persian fleet sailed over to Greece, where Conon rebuilt the Long Walls of Athens, and thus the opportunity was given her to become again an independent sea power. In 392 B.C. the Spartans suffered a startling defeat when the Athenian I-phic'ra-tes, with a body of light armed troops of an improved model (peltasts), defeated for the first time in Greek experience one of their heavy armed regiments. It soon became clear that Sparta could not make headway against the Greeks and Persians combined. Hence she gave up the double contest and sought peace from Persia on terms most advantageous to herself. The Great King dictated the conditions to her ambassador, An-tal'ci-das, and in 387 B C the King's peace was established throughout the Greek world.

Coroneia and Cnidos.

The Peace of Antalcidas.

The royal decree which gave the terms of peace read as follows: "King Artaxerxes thinks it right that the cities in Asia and the islands of Clazomenæ and Cyprus shall belong to him; further, that all the other Greek cities, small and great, shall be independent, except Lemnos, Imbros and Scyros, which shall belong to Athens as formerly. If any refuse to accept this peace, I shall make war on them, along with those who have the same mind, both by land and sea, with both ships and money."

255. A Virtual Victory for Sparta.—To Sparta, as head of Greece, was given the task of maintaining the peace as the king's deputy. The result was practically to restore Spartan supremacy. For whatever cities had organized leagues or subjected other cities would be forced by Sparta to give independence to those under them, while Sparta herself had a free hand in establishing her own power everywhere. The Asia Minor cities were, however, definitely handed over to Persia.

256. The Centralizing Tendency.—It remained to be seen whether Sparta's diplomatic triumph could be maintained in the face of the tendency to unite states, which was steadily making headway in the Greek world against the old-time principle of independence (§ 216). Everywhere leagues were forming, new and larger states were rising; tyrants were appearing and gaining wider power. By the peace of Antalcidas Sparta was empowered to check these movements in her own interest. The real problem was whether she was strong enough to stop them and make herself mistress of Greece. She bestirred herself with energy. The opposition in the Peloponnesus was put down. A league of the Chalcidian cities under the leadership of Olynthus was broken up (382–379 B.C.). A check was put on the Bœotian league by throwing a Spartan garrison into the Cadmeia, the citadel of Thebes (382 B.C.)—a manifest breach of the King's peace. An attempt was made to seize the Piræus, which the Athenians had not yet fully fortified (378 B.C.), but without success.

Checked by Sparta.

The Cadmeia Affair.

257. Revolt at Thebes.—But such high-handed measures provoked intense opposition. A conspiracy at Thebes, aided by the Athenians, succeeded in driving out the Spartan garrison and uniting Bœotia against Sparta (379 B.C). Athens also declared war and swept the Spartans from the sea. And behind the barrier which Bœotia presented to Spartan advance northward, Jason, tyrant of Pheræ, an energetic, clever, highly educated, unscrupulous man, succeeded in bringing all Thessaly under his control. As *tagus* of the whole land, he came to possess an army of eight thousand cavalry and twenty thousand hoplites—by far the strongest force under single

Leuctra
and Its
Lesson.

command in eastern Greece. When, in 371 B.C., the Spartan army under King Cleombrotus entered Bœotia, the Bœotians met them at Leuctra and inflicted upon them a smashing defeat. The king himself was slain and a thousand Lacedemonians with. him. The prestige of the Spartan soldiery was destroyed. All Greece was astounded. The pious Xenophon wrote of it as follows: "The Lacedemonians, who swore to leave the cities independent, seized the citadel of Thebes, and they were punished by the very men, single-handed, whom they had wronged, though never before had they been vanquished by any single people. It is a proof that the gods observe men who do irreligious and unhallowed

Jason of
Pheræ

deeds." For a moment it seemed as though Jason, the ostensible friend of Thebes, would dominate victor and vanquished alike, but his assassination a few months after Leuctra ended the Thessalian peril.

258. Grounds for Theban Success.—The victory of Thebes was the result, not of a sudden outburst of irresistible wrath at Spartan oppression, but of long military training and a new system of military tactics devised and carried through by leaders of genius and enthusiasm. Two great men had been created by the Theban situation—Pe-lop'i-das and E-pam'i-non'das. The former was the leader in the band of conspirators that drove the Spartans out of Thebes, an intense fiery nature, of genial and bold temper; he gathered the Theban youth into the "Sacred Band," one hundred and fifty pairs of friends, skilled in war, bound by the holiest of ties to fight side by side to the death. Epaminondas balanced the passionate enthusiasm of his friend by a philosophic temper and the deep insight of political and military genius.

Two Men of Genius.

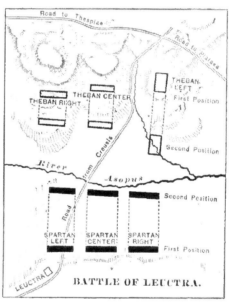

BATTLE OF LEUCTRA.

It was he who developed the new tactics that won at Leuctra. Ordinarily, in a Greek battle the attack was made with the right wing, which sought to outflank the enemy's left wing and throw it back upon the rest of the line. But Epaminondas reversed this order by making his left wing the fighting wing, arranging it fifty men deep instead of the usual twelve, and hurling it first upon the enemy's fighting wing, letting the rest of the line follow and complete the overthrow.

New Military Tactics.

259. The New Theban Policy.—The plans of these
two leaders contemplated not merely the freedom of their
city from Spartan control, but the establishment of Theban supremacy over Bœotia, and even the substitution of
Thebes for Sparta in the hegemony of the Greek world.
They had nothing to fear from Dionysius (§ 249), who
died in 367 B.C., and whose successor, Dionysius II, had
little of the genius and vigor of his father. With Bœotia
consolidated, they must gain control over the Peloponnesus, northern Greece and the sea. To this task Thebes,
under these leaders, gave herself for ten years (371–362
B.C.). In the north the tyrants of Thessaly were subdued, but in the struggle Pelopidas was slain (364 B.C.).
The attempt to control the sea brought Thebes into conflict with Athens and led to no result. In the Peloponnesus a better outcome seemed possible. The defeat
of Sparta opened the way for the cities, which she had
oppressed, to make themselves free. The Arcadians,
hitherto split up into petty villages, united in a common
state life with its centre at a new city, Megalopolis, and
found protection and support from Thebes. Epaminondas marched down into the Peloponnesus, almost
captured Sparta, freed the Messenians and set them up
as a separate state with Messene, a new city planted on
Mt. Ithome, as their capital. But eager as these states
were for freedom, they were not ready to hold it under
Theban direction. They turned against their deliverer,
and when Epaminondas came down, in 362 B.C., to re-
establish Theban authority he found Spartans, Arcadians, Athenians and others in the army that confronted
him. The battle was fought at Man'ti-ne'a. His military genius again gave him the victory, but he himself

was sore wounded and died on the field. With his death
the Theban supremacy was shattered. What Thebes
had accomplished was to break up the Peloponnesian
league—to carry into the peninsula the isolation of the
various city-states existent elsewhere in Greece. She The Result
had overthrown Sparta's supremacy; her own she could
not establish in its place. Greek unity, so urgently
needed and so steadily aspired after, seemed farther off
than ever.

260. Revival of Athenian Ambition.—Could Athens
bring this about? Such had been the ambition of the
restored democracy from the beginning of the fourth century. Various attempts had been made to recover her
power over the Ægean cities. Early in 377 B.C. a con- Second
federacy of Greek cities under Athenian leadership was Athenian
Empire.
proposed, with the purpose of forcing the Spartans to
leave the Greeks free and independent. No possibility
of Athenian encroachment upon the rights and powers
of the allies was permitted. They united as independent
states, about seventy in number, with Athens as the political and military head. The purpose of the league was
accomplished so far as it sought the overthrow of Sparta's
sea power, but it was too loose a confederation to satisfy
Athens or to meet the needs of the time In 366 B C.,
therefore, Athens made a vigorous attempt to turn it
into something more like an empire. Under Ti-mo'-
theus, the son of Conon, and Iphicrates, fleets were sent
out which reduced Samos to subjection and established
Athenian supremacy in the Hellespont and on the Chalcidian peninsula But opposition was found on every Athenian
side. Thebes contested the Athenian claim to the sea Failure to
Dominate
(§ 259). A new king in Persia, Artaxerxes III (Ochus), It.

came to the throne in 359 B.C., and his energetic activity restored Persia to something like unity and strength.

Difficulty with Macedonia. The Athenian advance in the north had disturbed Macedonia, where, in 359 B.C., Philip had become king. By clever diplomacy he outwitted Athens and began to secure the Greek cities which occupied the coast of his kingdom and exploited it to their own advantage and that

The Social War. of Athens, their suzerain. This he could do the more easily in that in 357 B C. the most important of the dependencies of Athens revolted and the Social War which ensued absorbed the energies of that city completely. Thus, the difficulties of maintaining an empire were too great for Athens. In 355 B.C. she made peace with her rebellious allies in the east by renouncing her authority over them; she contented herself with the few possessions which remained in the north, where her trouble with Philip was not yet settled. Greece was in confusion still, and no one could see the end.

261. Review of the Situation.—As we look back over the fifty years that came to a close with 355 B C, we notice, in comparison with the fifth century, some significant characteristics. The facts of the history narrated

Conflict between Old and New Political Ideas. in the preceding sections show very clearly that it was a time of change and conflict, without any clear aim or satisfactory outcome. The brilliant career of Athens with its imperial aspirations had been brought to naught by the determined opposition of states representing the old Greek principle of the separate independence of the several cities. The victory of Sparta strengthened everything that gathered about that principle—the aristocratic class, the old religion, the dislike of democracy, the preference for constitutions like that of Sparta, which restrained the freedom of the individual citizen in the interest of the state. On the other hand, imperial Athens, though fallen, handed on the influences and ideals which she had cherished, and they continued to fight for supremacy in the political and social life of the time. The imperial idea was seized by Sparta and Thebes; the impossibility of turning Greece into a mass of petty, independent cities was emphasized by the various leagues which constantly sprang up; the new thought was asserting the importance of the individual man and his demands upon life, upon the state of which he was a citizen, upon the world in which he lived. Thus everywhere it was conflict between return to the past and progress along new paths.

262. Changes in the Art of War.—Everywhere appeared signs that this was a time of transition. The art of war was changing. The heavy-armed footman, the hoplite, ceased to be the one strong force of the army; the light-armed soldier, the peltast, was found to be more and more useful. As we have seen, it was a great shock to the military science of the time when the Athenian Iphicrates, in 392 B.C , set upon a regiment of Spartan hoplites with his peltasts and nearly destroyed them all. Cavalry also became more important and no army was complete without a strong corps. The new tactics of Epaminondas were likewise revolutionary. Equally striking is the almost universal employment of mercenary soldiers. The long years of the Peloponnesian war bred a generation who knew one thing well—how to fight. Many of them had no other occupation; and since those who were engaged in business and agriculture gradually lost the humor for fighting and preferred to

Mercenaries.

pay others to do it for them, it soon became impossible
to send out sufficiently large armies of citizens; hence
soldiers were hired and the practice of selling oneself for
war was a very profitable trade. Generals, too, let themselves out for hire to conduct campaigns. As money was
scarce in all the Greek states, and the funds for the payment of mercenaries were soon exhausted, opposing generals avoided decisive battles and sought to prolong the
manœuvres until the opposing force was disbanded for
lack of funds. Thus war was carried on quite scientifi-
cally and with much less bloodshed.

263. Confusion in Politics.—Another illustration of
this time of change is found in the politics of the day. It
is a mixture of petty conflicts and local problems with
great plans and large ambitions. The imperial strivings
of each of the greater states were checked by the obstinate opposition of smaller states. Each state had its
own war of factions—aristocrat against democrat. The
complicated politics of the time was due to the ceaseless
intrigues of these little cities, now swinging to this side,
now to that. Fear and jealousy, ambition and conserv-
atism, were contending impulses in every community.
At the same time the problems of these states were of the
pettiest order. They were all reduced in population and
resources. Sparta's legitimate citizens at the end of the
Peloponnesian war numbered only about two thousand.
Athens was hard pressed to keep up her citizen body
which had sunk to about twenty thousand—a figure at
which it remained fixed during the whole of the fourth
century B.C. The difficult question of finance was a
pressing one. Athens was constantly on the verge of
financial exhaustion, although she had a fairly prosper-

PLATE XIX

THE HERMES OF PRAXITELES

ous commercial activity. When they had the opportunity, recourse was had both by Athens and Sparta to plundering defenceless regions and forcing contributions from weaker cities. Piracy was not uncommon. Sometimes the baser expedient of robbing temples was tried. Hence came the importance of the alliance with Persia, for that meant Persian gold.

264. Art and Literature Flourish.—The brightest side of the life of the time appears in the higher spheres of art and literature. During these years of turmoil they went steadily forward. Even in the Peloponnesian war, sculptors could put forth such splendid creations as the ·*Nike* ("Victory") by Pæonius, set up by the Messenians at Olympia. The greatest sculptor of the age was Prax-it′e-les, whose only extant work, the Hermes, reveals the chief note of progress. It consists in the freer expression of human emotion, the delineation of man as an individual with his special traits and feelings, contrasting thus with the more restrained and heroic ideals of the age of Pericles (§ 205). His most famous statues—the Cnidian Aphrodite, the Satyr, the Eros, have perished, and only copies of them, like the *Marble Faun* of Hawthorne, have come down to us. And his contemporaries, Scopas, whose faces always had an alert, far-away look, and Ly-sip′pus, whose works were all in bronze and who alone among sculptors, it is said, was permitted to make portraits of Alexander the Great, have fared no better. A good copy of one of the latter's productions is the famous Apoxyomenus—or athlete using the strigil to scrape the sweat and oil from his arm—now in Rome. As the Parthenon is the finest example of Periclean architecture, so the tomb of Mau-so′lus, satrap and king

The New Sculpture

Architecture

of Caria, reveals for this age the union of sculpture and
architecture at its highest point. The greatest artists of

Painting. the time notably Scopas, worked upon it. Painting, also,
took a place in the art of the day never attained before
The houses of the rich were adorned by frescoes and

**Enrich-
ment of
Life.** the works of great painters. Indeed, everywhere greater
luxury, a finer taste in private life, appeared, illustrated
in the pursuits of hunting, in enjoyment of the country and agricultural activity, and even in cookery, all of
which were studied as arts and on which books were
written that have come down to us.

265. Intellectual Life at Athens.—Athens was the
bright star in the world of literature and thought. Shorn
of her imperial position in the political world, she laid
her hand of power upon the higher realm of letters and
philosophy, and won an unquestioned triumph. What
Pericles had claimed (§ 209) now came true. Athens
was the teacher of Greece   At the opening of the fourth
century B.C., however, things had seemed to point in the
other direction. The backward look toward the past,
so characteristic of this age (§ 261), tended to the sup-

**Execution
of Socrates.** pression of the new learning. Indeed, one awful blun-
der, worse than a crime, was made by this reactionary
spirit in 399 B.C., when Socrates (§ 229) was put to death

**His
Disciples** as an impious and pernicious man. But disciples, inspired by his teaching, took up his work and carried on
the new learning to higher flights. One of the most
attractive of these men was Xenophon (434–354 B.C.).

It is said that Xenophon, when a young and handsome boy, was
one day halted in the streets of Athens by Socrates, who asked him
where various articles of merchandise could be bought   He politely
told him. Then Socrates asked, "But where can one get good and

honorable men?" When the boy could not answer, the philosopher replied, "Follow me," and Xenophon became his disciple

It was not altogether with the approval of Socrates Xenophon. that Xenophon joined the army of Cyrus (§ 252), and the outcome of that expedition, while it brought honor to the young leader, ruined his career as an Athenian. As a friend of Sparta, he was banished from Athens and went to live on an estate in Elis presented to him by the Spartans. There he wrote many books. The most important are the *Memoirs of Socrates*, a worthy record of his master's career and teachings; the *Cyropedia*, a kind of historical romance glorifying the elder Cyrus of Persia (§ 79); the *Anabasis*, which has already been referred to (§ 252); and the *Hellenica*, a history of Greece from the point where Thucydides left off (411 B.C.) to the battle of Mantinea. Xenophon is a typical man of his time, a conservative, clear-headed, sensible, healthy nature, roused into vigorous thinking by the spur of Socrates, but unwilling or unable wholly to yield to the impulse of his master—a son of progressive Athens taking halting Sparta for his foster-father.

266. Plato.—A far abler disciple was Plato (428-347 B C), one of the most brilliant philosophers of all time. He is an example of the contradictions of this troubled age. Born into the circle of Athenian aristocracy, one of the company of brilliant young men that surrounded Socrates, he would have nothing to do with the politics of democratic Athens; yet he was passionately devoted to the study of politics, and even went to Syracuse, in the time of Dionysius II, to introduce his theories into actual practice. Of course they failed. He gathered about himself in Athens a body of disciples. In opposition to

the material and often sordid activities of his city and
age, he taught them the doctrine that things on earth are
faint and faded copies of perfect spiritual realities above
this world, abiding, pure, divine. The perfect life is that
which comes into harmony with these. The death of
Socrates inspired him to write his *Apology of Socrates*,
an endeavor to present in substance the defence which
Socrates uttered before the court that condemned him.
His writings took almost always the form of dialogues.
They deal with a variety of philosophical and political
subjects and are written in a poetical prose of wondrous
refinement and fascination. The *Republic* pictures his
ideal commonwealth, the most noticeable features of
which are the division of citizens into three classes—the
rulers, the guardians and the traders and producers;
the establishment of a communism of property, women
and children; and the requiring men and women to engage in the same occupations. The *Phædo* offers an
argument for the immortality of the soul. The *Sympo-
sium* discusses love as the supreme element in the universe. From the vicinity of his home to the gymnasium of Academus, his school is called the "Academy."

267. **Isocrates.**—While possessing nothing like the
genius of Plato, more truly a child of his age is I-soc'ra-tes
(436–338 B.C.). Indeed, more fully than any other
writer or thinker, he represents the Athens of the fourth
century, its culture, its doubts and its hopes. He sought
no public activity, yet devoted himself to the training of
men for public life. He taught them rhetoric, philosophy,
science and character, and sought to form public opinion
by issuing political brochures in the guise of orations.
His was the most popular school and he the best-known

sophist in the Greek world. As a literary man he was the creator of a classical prose style, smooth, liquid, pure —possibly lacking in strength and fire. As a political philosopher his view was broad and high. At first he hoped, like so many men of his time, that the old union of Sparta, the land power, and Athens, the sea power, of the Greek world might be revived to be the salvation of - Greece. Such was his plea in his *Panegyricus*, delivered at Olympia on the occasion of the hundredth Olympiad (380 B.C.). He rose to a higher ideal, the union of all Greece under a single leader and the advance of united Greece against Persia—the recovery of Greek unity and honor. The trouble was he could get no leader—he summoned one after another of the states to this task. But as his long life drew to a close, one did appear, and Isocrates could look forward hopefully to the realizing of his ideal. That leader was Philip, king of Macedon, whose career is a turning-point in Greek history.

268. How Can Greece Be Revived and United?— Our study of the oriental empires has shown how with the decay of the nations of culture there appear new peoples, rude and strong, to overrun and rule their weaker but more highly developed neighbors, absorb their culture and carry the world a stage farther in the march of progress (§ 35). Such was to be the solution of the problem of the Greek world. In the western and northern parts of the Greek peninsula was a mass of peoples on the borders of civilization, becoming slowly affected by it, forming out of loose tribal conditions states of a steadily increasing strength and unity. Some had already been drawn into the circle of Greek politics and war, like Ætolia, Acarnania and Ambracia. And now, even beyond these, in the wild region of Epirus, occupied by a mixture of races, kingdoms like that of the Molossi began to emerge. A new Greece was rising as the old Greece declined.

269. Rise of Macedonia.—It was in the northeast, rather than in the west, however, that advance was more rapid. This was to be expected, since the eastern coast of Greece had been the scene of the most vigorous life from the earliest period Here, lying back from the northwestern Ægean and cut off from Thessaly by lofty mountains, lay Macedonia. Its people was a strange complex of races: to the north and west Illyrian, to the east Thracian, mixed with the purer Greek blood, but all paying uncertain allegiance to a line of kings whose capital was at Ægæ, far in the interior, at the head of the great plain that stretched down to the Thermaic gulf. These kings, handing down their throne from father to son, steadily grew in power and importance.

Relation to Greece. The position of Macedonia drew them early into the circle of Greek politics; it is their lasting merit that they saw and valued the importance of cultivating relations with the Greek states. The first of the kings to come into historic light took the side of the Greeks in the first Persian wars. They encouraged Greek settlements on their shores. They even claimed descent from the Greek god and hero, Heracles, and the claim was acknowledged by the privilege conferred upon them of contesting in the Olympic games.

The First National Problems. **270. Growth of Macedonian National Life.**—Brought thus into close contact with the intense spirit of Greek national life and culture, the Macedonian king and his people naturally were inspired to develop their own nationality. Two things were necessary for this result. First, the loose attachment of the tribes in the west and north must be turned into a firm allegiance to the sovereign. Second, the sea-coast must be secured. The first of these was undertaken in a series of military operations carried on by king after king with very moderate success. The second meant obtaining supremacy over the flourishing Greek cities which, for centuries planted on the peninsulas of Chalcidice, had monopolized the rich trade with the interior. As most of the cities belonged to the Athenian empire, the kings were involved in difficulties with Athens. This complication bound them up even more closely with the political and military movements of the Greek world. Thus, little by little, Macedonia was being prepared to grapple decisively with the problem that Athens, Sparta and Thebes in turn had laid down.

271. King Philip.—At this crisis Philip was on the throne, a man in genius and energy fully equal to the situation. He brought to a successful end the unifying of his kingdom. By a series of tremendous campaigns in west and north and east, he broke down the resistance of the rude and warlike Illyrian tribes, drove back or absorbed the Thracians and welded all into a living and concordant unity The nation that sprang into full life was animated by a common spirit of military zeal and personal loyalty to the king A new army was His Army formed and trained to a perfection never before reached. He drew the Macedonian peasantry into military service, and by joining them as infantry to the aristocratic cavalry he at one stroke doubled the strength of his army and freed himself from dependence upon his nobles. All

told he controlled an army of three to four thousand
horse and twenty-five thousand hoplites. The foot-
soldiers were formed in close array somewhat deeper
than the ordinary Greek hoplite army and armed with
longer spears. This was the Macedonian phalanx. The
chief reliance was the cavalry, both light and heavy
armed, made up of the nobility, men in the prime of
physical vigor and of high spirit. In a battle their charge
upon the enemy's flank, made as one man with tremendous force, usually decided the day. All advances in the
art of war made by the Greeks during the preceding
years were brought together by Philip in his military organization. He had an abundance of light-armed troops
and a splendid siege-train. He himself was the animat-
ing soul, the directing genius of the whole organization.
All the soldiers were called "companions," and the word
well expresses the relation to their head which he was
able to inspire. The new Macedonia was a nation under
arms.

272. The Advance to the Coast.—Philip was equally
successful in the second of the tasks laid upon the Macedonian sovereign—the securing of the sea-coast. By a
combination of skilful diplomacy and vigorous warfare
he proceeded to wrest from Athens the cities under her
influence and to reduce the others to subjection. With
the fall of the most important of them all, Amphipolis
(357 B.C.), he was master of the central trade-routes; the
gold mines on the northeastern border were secured; the
city of Philippi was built to guard them; a small navy
was begun. By 348 B C. every Greek city on the coast
of Macedonia was in his hands. The capital of his kingdom was removed from Ægæ and established farther

Conquest
of the
Greek
Cities.

down the plain at Pella. The completion of these tasks invited him to the other and greater achievement—the leadership of Greece.

273. **Philip Secures a Foothold in Greece.**—The opportunity came in an outbreak in middle Greece. The Amphictyonic council (§ 128) had proceeded against the Phocians on a charge of doing violence to the rights of the temple at Delphi. On their refusal to submit, the council declared war against them. They seized the temple and borrowed its treasures to hire soldiers for their defence. Little by little all Greece was drawn in. The active members of the Amphictyonic council were Thebes, Locris and Thessaly. For Phocis were Athens and Sparta. The Phocians also succeeded in gaining the tyrants of Thessalian Pheræ to their side; this led the rest of the Thessalians to ask Philip to lead them. Thus Philip crossed the border of Greece and became master of Thessaly (353 B C.), the possession of which, among other advantages, more than doubled the number of his cavalry. The full meaning of the new situation soon became clear. Greece was on the verge of a greater struggle than the petty "sacred war." Philip had come within her gates, and he would have entered central Greece at this moment had not Athens, Sparta and their allies placed an army of twenty thousand men in the pass at Thermopylæ to prevent his farther advance.

The "Sacred War."

Gains Thessaly.

274. **His Attitude toward Greece.**—It is important to observe Philip's ideals and ambitions. He was a true Macedonian, a fearless, impetuous, relentless, unsparing warrior, a deep drinker and reckless reveller, yet devoted to the upbuilding of his kingdom and utterly unscrupulous as to the means of accomplishing it. At

the same time he cherished a strong admiration for Greece, was immensely proud of his Greek descent, and estimated the favor and recognition conferred by Greece above almost everything else in the world. Greek culture, long welcomed at the Macedonian court, had deeply impressed him. For some years he had resided at Thebes as a hostage in the hands of Epaminondas, and had studied, not in vain, the political situation   He aspired to be the leader of Greece, not merely for his own glory and that of Macedonia, not that he might plant his foot on the neck of Greek freedom, but rather because he was, in a kind of romantic reverence for her ancient fame and her immortal culture, conscious of the dignity and glory to be gained thereby.   This feeling seemed to concentrate on Athens.   Although Philip was constantly at war with that city, he was ever ready to make peace with her, to excuse the hostility and perfidy with which she dealt with him and to spare her at the last.   Thus the leadership which he craved was for the purpose of securing peace among free Greek communities.   He would have them recognize in him their arbiter and friend.   He went a step farther, and saw in the unity of Greece, secured by him, the means for carrying out the ideal which Isocrates had already described (§ 267), the punishment of Persia for its lordship over the Greek states.   It was with purposes like these, in which the lust of conquest was mixed with the higher ideals of Greek unity and supremacy, that Philip set foot upon Greek soil and began to push steadily southward.

275. The Old Problem Revives.—Who, after all, could or would oppose him? Had not everything been moving in the direction of unity—Athens, Sparta, Thebes

[marginal note: His Ideal for Greece.]

[marginal note: What His Leadership Meant]

seeking to bring it about? Why not hail his coming as a relief from the half-century of turmoil that had just passed? The answer to these questions is the same as that which was given to Athens, Sparta and Thebes— Greece will not submit to the authority of one. Independence for the separate states—the principle of autonomy—was now to clash again with the impulse to unity. Strange to say, the leader in this last struggle for Greek freedom was Athens. There were, indeed, men in this city who were not averse to Philip, men who looked to Macedonia for the relief from democratic oppression which they had earlier sought from Sparta—namely, the rich aristocrats. The spokesman of this group was the orator Æschines (es′kĭ-nēz), but he had with him ordinarily only a small minority of the citizens. Isocrates, too, received the rise of Macedon with pleasure. We have already seen how Philip's successful activities in securing the Macedonian sea-coast had brought him into conflict with the Athenians (§ 270) A vigorous campaign in 352 B.C. had made him master of Thrace, where he threatened the Athenian possessions on that coast. The "sacred war" (§ 273) had embittered the situation still more. Thus far, however, Athens had done little more than defend herself against Macedonian aggression. But now she entered upon a new activity under the leadership of Demosthenes, the most famous orator of the ancient world.

Athens against Philip.

Æschines on His Side

276. Demosthenes.—Demosthenes (384–322 B.C) began the study and practice of oratory under I-sæ′us, one of the leading practical lawyers of Athens, in order to recover his property, of which in his orphaned childhood his guardians had robbed him. He overcame all his many natural defects by persistent toil, and in the process became not only a wonderful speaker, but a successful politician. His orations against Philip—called Philippics—and his other speeches, of which many have been preserved, show a combination of close logic, intensity of spirit and beauty of language which are without parallel. The most renowned of them is the *Oration on the Crown*, delivered in defence of his policy on the occasion of a proposal to the people to offer him a crown in reward for his public service (330 B.C.).

277. He Champions the Anti-Macedonian Policy.— Demosthenes had already advocated a more vigorous war policy than the defensive one which had hitherto prevailed, and had, in fact, carried the Athenians with him in his plan to preserve Chalcidice against Macedon. But by stirring up a revolt in Eubœa Philip kept the Athenians employed nearer home, while he himself invaded Chalcidice, took its towns partly by bribery and partly by force and finally captured Olynthus and sold its inhabitants into slavery (349–348 B.C.). Now the realm of Philip stretched unbroken from Thermopylæ to the *hinterland* of Byzantium. After these brilliant successes Demosthenes had agreed to a peace in 346 B.C., the so-called peace of Philocrates, which was sorely needed by Athens. But when Philip desired to enter into closer relations of friendship with Athens, Demosthenes induced the Athenians to hold back. Meanwhile, Philip was elected a member of the Amphictyonic league in the place of the Phocians, and thus was entered legally among the Greek powers. This was the opportunity taken by Demosthenes to launch his new enterprise— the aggressive union of all the Greek states against the

The Philippics.

Fall of Olynthus.

dangerous Macedonian enemy. He had some success; states in the Peloponnesus and on the northern Ægean entered a league. At last, the Amphictyonic council, unsupported by Athens and Thebes, invited Philip to lead another "sacred war." This brought matters to a head. The Thebans joined the anti-Macedonian union and prepared to resist Philip's march. The decisive battle was fought in Bœotia at Chæroneia (kĕr'ō-nē'a) (338 B.C.). The Macedonian cavalry was led by Philip's son Alexander, then eighteen years of age. Demosthenes served as a heavy-armed soldier in the Athenian ranks. The result was the complete victory of Philip; the Thebans were cut to pieces; the Athenians were routed and ran away.` *Chæroneia*

278. **Result: Philip at the Head of Greece.**—The victory of Chæroneia meant the supremacy of Macedonia and the Macedonian king over the Greek world. The Greeks had fallen into the hands of no city-state among their own number, but found a master in the monarch of a kingdom which they regarded as outside their circle and had only grudgingly admitted among them. But Philip had no intention of playing the tyrant. He wanted to be the acknowledged head of free communities united of their own accord under his leadership. Accordingly, he summoned the states to meet at Corinth and form a confederacy. The Greek cities were to wage no wars against one another and to have internal liberty, but to acknowledge the suzerainty of Macedon by electing Philip their commander-in-chief in the war which he announced against Persia. It was necessary, however, to establish Macedonian garrisons in strategic points; for the Greeks were unwilling even now to accept *Congress of Corinth.*

Macedonian supremacy. The outcome, however, was certain, since the power of Philip was too great to be successfully resisted. Opposition to it could only end in disaster, in the renewal of strife, which was ruinous to the states themselves, and could not accomplish anything except bring down the wrath of Philip and sorer punishment at his hands.

REVIEW EXERCISES. 1. For what are the following noted: Cunaxa, Coroneia, Olynthus, Megalopolis, Epirus, Pella, Chæroneia? 2. Who were Lysander, Dionysius, Agesilaus, Conon, Pelopidas, Iphicrates, Mausolus, Xenophon, Isocrates, Demosthenes, Critias, Theramenes, Jason of Pheræ, Scopas? 3. What is meant by harmost, autonomy, peltast, academy, phalanx, amphictyony?

COMPARATIVE STUDIES. 1. Compare the Spartan imperial rule with that of Athens (§§ 185, 186, 213). 2. Compare Epaminondas with Pericles. 3. Compare the battle of Chæroneia with that of Marathon.

SELECT LIST FOR READING. 1. The Thirty at Athens. Bury, pp. 507–513. 2. Art and Literature at Athens. Bury, pp. 571–590. 3. The Empire of Dionysius. Bury, pp. 638–666. 4. Epaminondas and Thebes. Bury, pp. 625–626. 5. Macedonia. Bury, pp 683–688 6. Philip and Demosthenes. Bury, pp. 687–737 7. The "Anabasis" of Cyrus. Bury, pp 517–530.

TOPICS FOR READING AND ORAL REPORT. 1. Spartan Im- perialism. Morey, pp. 277–281, Shuckburgh, pp. 260–273; Botsford, pp 250–268, Plutarch, Lives of Lysander and Agesilaus. 2. Xenophon. Jebb, pp 109–114, Capps, pp 330–338, Murray, ch. 15. 3. Plato. Jebb, pp 126–129, Capps, ch. 15; Murray, ch 14. 4. Isocrates. Jebb pp. 119–120, Capps, pp 345–347, Murray, pp. 341–352. 5. The Empire of Dionysius. Botsford, pp. 239–245; Morey, pp 284–286. 6. The Theban Uprising. Botsford, pp. 268–274 7. Epaminondas and Thebes. Shuckburgh, pp 274–278, Zimmern, ch 19, Botsford, pp 275–283, Plutarch, Life of Pelopidas 8. Macedonia. Morey, pp 300–302, Shuckburgh, 280–282; Botsford, pp. 297–302. 9. Philip and Demosthenes. Shuckburgh, pp 283–291; Zimmern, ch 20 10. The "Anabasis" of Cyrus. Zimmern, pp. 301–307; Bury, pp. 517–530

279. The Passing of Greece.—Thus the brilliant chapter of Greek independent political life came to an end. Beginning with petty communities growing up in secluded valleys, the Greeks came to value above all else the blessing of freedom, the glory of the independence of separate states, each working out its own problems. They learned, also, how to give to each citizen a place and a part in the common life. But situated as the Greek peninsula was, midway between east and west and open to the influences of oriental civilization, its states were drawn together by the unifying forces of commerce and international politics. A heroic war of defence against the conquering empire of Persia made them one for a season, and the resulting political conditions gave the opportunity to one of their states—Athens—to take a commanding position in the Ægean sea. Thus the impulse to union was strengthened and took on an imperial form. But the new tendency to empire clashed with the old principle of autonomy, and the conflict dominated succeeding Greek history Athens fell, only to be succeeded by Sparta and Thebes, each following in her steps. A similar movement was made in Sicily, where Dionysius extended his personal rule over a wide territory. But in the fierce conflict of old and new all these imperial endeavors perished. The consummation of the centuries of troubled progress toward unity was at last realized in Philip of Macedon, with whose victory at Chæroneia the importance of the separate city-states came to an end. Their endeavors after empire were swallowed up in a

Summary of Its Career.

mightier imperial achievement which now appeared on the horizon—the empire of Alexander.

GENERAL REVIEW OF PART II, DIVISION 5; §§ 216-279
431-331 B.C

TOPICS FOR CLASS DISCUSSION. 1. The fundamental political issue of the Peloponnesian war traced through the various stages of the war (§ 216). 2. The growth of imperialism as illustrated in the history of the states of the time (§§ 180, 186, 213, 250, 259, 260, 267). 3. The policy of Athens in the Peloponnesian war as illustrated in the leaders Pericles, Cleon, Nicias, Alcibiades. 4. The policy of Sparta in the war as illustrated in the leaders Brasidas and Lysander. 5. The new learning as illustrative of the spirit of the times (§§ 223-230). 6. A list of the ten greatest men of Greece, from 431-331 B C. 7. The part played by Persia during the period from 431-338 B C. 8. The relation of Macedonia to the Greek states historically traced down to 338 B.C. 9. The part played by sea power in the Peloponnesian war. 10. The divisions of the Greek world which were chiefly the scene of the Peloponnesian war.

MAP AND PICTURE EXERCISES. 1. Make a map of Greece during the Peloponnesian war and locate the chief land battles. 2. Make a map of the Ægean and locate on it the chief naval battles of the Peloponnesian war. 3. How did it happen that statues like the Hermes (Plate XIX) and buildings like the Parthenon (Plate I) were produced by the Greeks and not the oriental peoples? 4. Study Plate XXII to observe how superior the Greek sculpture is to the Egyptian in composition. What has the Egyptian which the Greek lacks?

SUBJECTS FOR WRITTEN PAPERS. 1. The Weaknesses of Athenian Democracy as Illustrated in the Peloponnesian War. Fowler, The City State of the Greeks and Romans, pp. 176-183, 245-260. 2. A Play of Euripides, e.g., the "Electra" or "Bacchæ"—the story of the play and its testimony to the times. Coleridge, Translation of Euripides 3. A Talk with Socrates Regarding His Condemnation by the Athenians. Plato, the Apology 4. A Study of the Character of Alcibiades. Plutarch, Life of Alcibiades 5. Why the Greeks were Able to

Drive Back the Persians and yet Fell under the Macedonian Power. Fowler, The City State, etc , chs. 9, 11. 6. A Description of the Disaster at Syracuse. Jowett's Thucydides. 7. A Report of the Discussion in the Athenian Assembly Concerning the Punishment of Mytilene. Jowett's Thucydides.

6.—ALEXANDER THE GREAT

336-323 B.C.

280. Alexander King of Macedonia.—Hardly had Philip organized his new Greek confederacy when, in connection with troubles in the Macedonian court, he was murdered (336 B.C.). His son Alexander succeeded to his throne and his plans. The son was, in many respects, the image of his father—of splendid physical constitution and fascinating personality, possessing the same combination of unyielding will and romantic sensibility; both were too much alike, indeed, to get on well together, and it was said that the father had little notion of permitting the son to succeed him. But Alexander's training had been such as to prepare him to rule. His education had been conducted under Greek teachers; his tutor was Aristotle, the keenest and most learned mind of the time. His military training had been gained in his father's school of arms, and Philip was the first soldier of his day. Now the victories of Philip had put into his hands a united Macedonia and the leadership of the Greek world; he was the general of a magnificently organized and equipped army of fifty thousand men; the splendid project of the deliverance of the Asiatic Greeks from the Persian sway was left to him for realization. He, the young man of twenty years, stood on the threshold of an incomparable

His Preparation for the Throne.

career; on his action hung the destiny of centuries to
come.

281. **His Settlement with Greece.**—His first task was
to establish his position in Greece. Here the death of
Philip was followed by attempts to throw off Macedonian
supremacy. Two expeditions were sufficient to settle
matters. In the first, Alexander was acknowledged by
the states assembled at Corinth as head of the Greek

Destruction
of Thebes.
confederacy. In the second, a Theban rebellion was
nipped in the bud and Thebes was levelled to the ground
as a punishment (335 B C.). Athens, though equally
offending, was spared. During the same time the king
made two campaigns upon his northern borders; in the
one he subdued the Thracians and crossed the Danube;
in the other he routed the Illyrians in the northwest.

282. **His Purpose against Persia.**—Already to the daring ambition of the youthful Alexander, Philip's plan
to deliver the Greek cities of Asia from Persia had become too small. His purpose was nothing less than to
strike at the heart of the empire itself and to take full
vengeance for the wrongs which it had inflicted upon the
Greeks. To the fulfilment of this purpose he now set
himself. His main dependence rested upon his Macedonian army with its trained soldiery and its skilful
generals, all alike devoted to himself; but he had to leave
the half of it behind him with his trusty general, Antipater, who was deputed to maintain Macedonian au-

The Start.
thority in Greece during the absence of the king. The
co-operation of the Greeks had indeed been promised,
and, in fact, of the army of some 30,000 infantry and
4,500 cavalry with which he set forth across the Hellespont in 334 B.C., 12,600 were of that nationality. But

none the less the slightest reverse meant a general insurrection in Greece.

The spirit and purposes of the king and his generals are illustrated in the anecdote preserved in Plutarch On the eve of his departure he distributed among his friends who were to accompany him a great part of his royal property Whereupon Per-dic'cas asked him what he left for himself He replied, "My hopes ' Then Perdiccas said, "Let us be your partners in these," and refused to accept the king's gift.

283. Condition of Persia.—The Persian empire, although it had sadly declined from the spirit of its founders, and the luxury and corruption of the court had undermined the vigor and efficiency of the rulers, was still a mighty and formidable state. Artaxerxes III (§ 260) had been very successful in putting down rebellions and had restored imperial prestige. But court intrigues made way with him in 338 B.C. and with his son after him. Now there sat on the throne Darius III Darius III (Codomannus), a noble not of the royal line, a high-minded and generous ruler, but able, neither in intellect nor in circumstances, to cope with the situation that faced him Neither he nor his counsellors realized that they were no longer contending with a divided and inefficient Greece, whose leaders they had been accustomed to corrupt with their gold, or render powerless by stirring up difficulties at home.

284. Alexander in Asia Minor.—Accordingly, Alexander found himself confronted with an army, not much larger than his own, led by the Persian satraps of Asia Minor. A battle took place in June, 334 B C , at the Granicus. river Gra-ni'cus, on the farther bank of which the Persian army was posted in a strong position. Alexander swept across the river with his heavy cavalry and fell upon the enemy's cavalry. On their rout the Macedonian phalanx followed and engaged the Persian infantry in front, while the cavalry attacked their flanks—the favorite military tactics of Alexander. They could not stand, and when they fled the battle was won. The rest of the year was occupied in winning back the Ionian cities and the other strongholds of western Asia Minor. The most obstinate resistance was encountered at Halicarnassus where the Persian commander-in-chief, Memnon, took up temporary headquarters after his defeat. With its capture the first part of the task was accomplished.

285. Issus.—In the spring of 333 B.C. Alexander set out from Gordium in Phrygia, by a rapid march seized the passes into Cilicia and captured Tarsus, its capital. After being delayed here for some days on account of a nearly fatal illness, he marched forward along the coast toward Syria. Meanwhile, Darius with his army had advanced into Syria, and failing to find his enemy, had marched through an upper road into Cicilia and descended to the plain of Issus in the rear of Alexander. The latter immediately turned about, and the second great battle was joined at Issus. Again, as at the Granicus, the Persians stood on the defensive at the bank of a river and Alexander sprang like a tiger upon the enemy with his heavy cavalry, followed by his foot-soldiers. The struggle was much more fierce; once the phalanx seemed to be broken; the light cavalry on the left were hard pressed. But again Alexander's rush carried all before it; the phalanx recovered and the Persians broke in flight for the mountains. Darius barely escaped, leaving his tent, personal baggage and household to fall into the

Escape of
Darius.

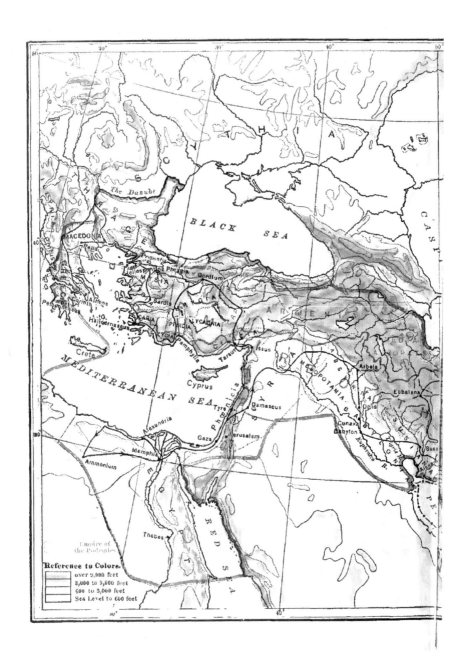

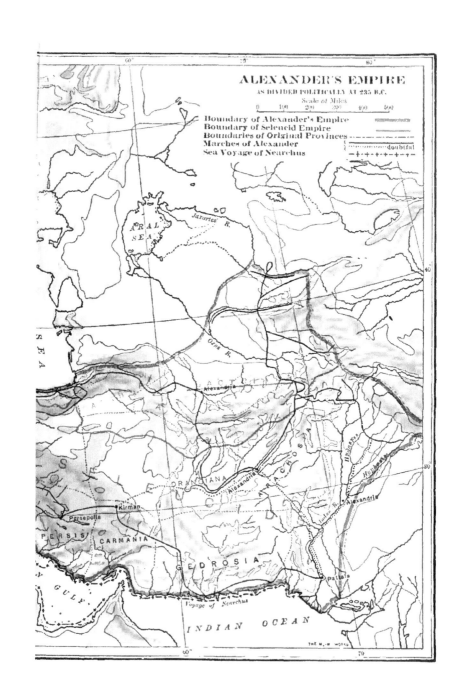

PLATE XX

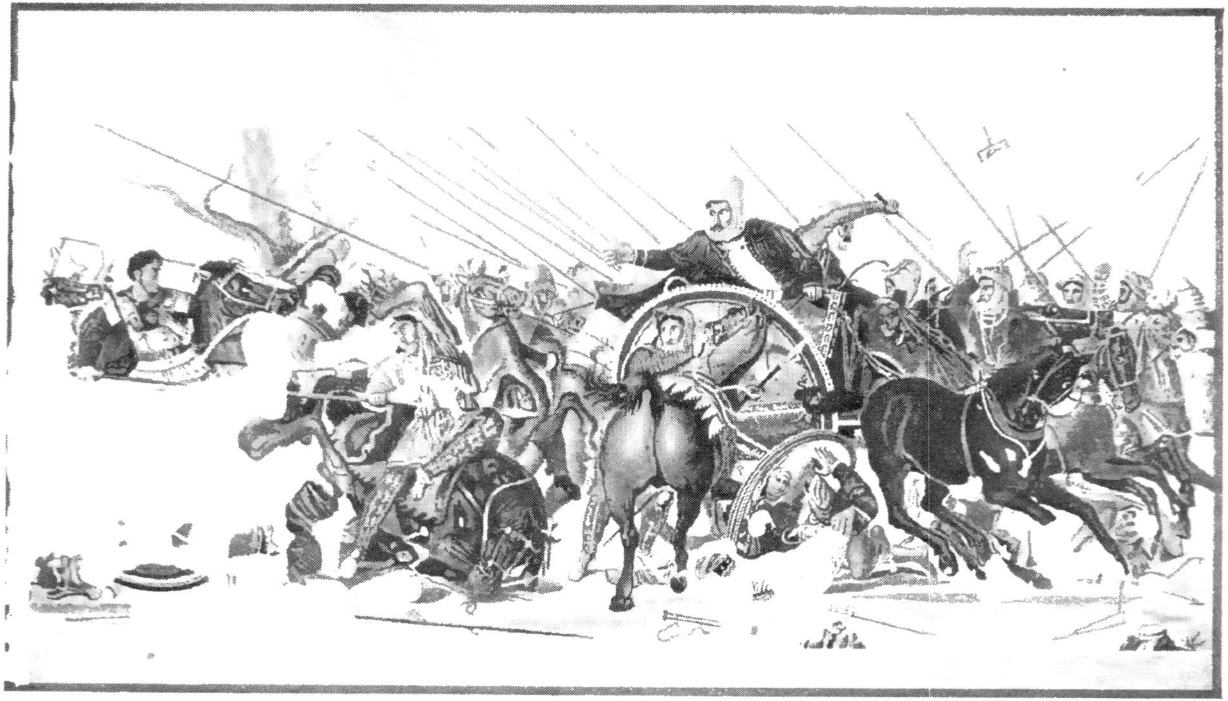

FROM THE HISTORY OF THE WORLD. BY PERMISSION OF DODD, MEAD & CO.

THE BATTLE OF ISSUS; MOSAIC FROM POMPEII

enemy's hands. The way was now open for the conquest of western Asia, and Alexander descended into Syria.

286. Alexander Moves Southward.—Leaving Darius to continue his flight to the east unhindered, Alexander

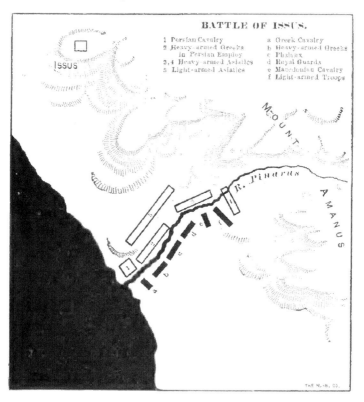

BATTLE OF ISSUS.

1 Persian Cavalry
2 Heavy-armed Greeks in Persian Employ
3, 4 Heavy-armed Asiatics
5 Light-armed Asiatics

a Greek Cavalry
b Heavy-armed Greeks
c Phalanx
d Royal Guards
e Macedonian Cavalry
f Light-armed Troops

moved southward to take possession of Phœnicia, Palestine and Egypt. In the meanwhile the Persian fleet, which was master of the sea, had failed in its mission to recall Alexander by stirring up revolt in Greece as Conon had done in 394 B.C. It was made up chiefly of Phœnician vessels, and could be subdued only by getting pos-

session of the Phœnician seaports.   City after city sub·
mitted until Tyre was reached.   Situated on an island,
strongly fortified, it held out for seven months in one of
the greatest sieges of history.   The king built a mole to
the island half a mile into the deep, and, by the aid of
the fleets of the cities of Phœnicia and Cyprus that had
yielded to him, finally carried the city by assault.   A
similar siege at Gaza was successful; the way was open
to Egypt, which he occupied without a battle.

287. **The Jews.**—While on the way down the coast, as
the story is told by Josephus the Jewish historian, he
visited Jerusalem.   After the overthrow of their kingdom and their exile to Babylon (§ 80), the Jews had been
permitted by Cyrus to return and rebuild their city and
temple (538 B.C).   Since that time they had been under
Persian rule and had devoted themselves to the upbuilding of their religious system under the leadership of their
high-priests.   They had suffered much from their neighbors, the Samaritans, but were faithful to the law of
Moses as their teachers enlarged and explained it.   As
Alexander advanced to the city, the high-priest with his
attendants came forth to meet him.   The king, who was
at first inclined to be angry with the Jews for not taking
his side, was led by a vision which he had seen some time
before to give them special favors.

288. **Egypt.**—In Egypt Alexander's chief work was
the founding of a city at the western mouth of the Nile,
between lake Mareotis and the island of Pharus.   Joining the island with the mainland by a causeway, he
made two fine harbors for the city, which he named after
himself and destined to take the place of ruined Tyre as
the commercial centre of the western Mediterranean.

This destiny was fulfilled, for Alexandria became one of the most important cities of the ancient world.

289. To the East.—A visit to the temple of Zeus Amon in the western desert, where the god declared him his own son and therefore, in the eyes of the Greek world, a god, was followed by the organization of the govern-

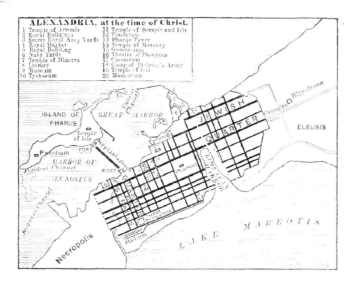

ment of Egypt. By the spring of 331 B.C. Alexander started for the far east. In September he found the Persian king awaiting him with a vast army, east of the Tigris, near the old Assyrian city of Ar-be'la. This city, or the nearer village of Gau'ga-me'la, has given the name to the battle which was joined on the first of October. Over against the Macedonian's 40,000 foot and 7,000 horse were said, with gross exaggeration, to be arrayed 1,000,000 foot and 40,000 horse under the command of the Great King—a motley host, mighty only by sheer weight

Arbela.

and momentum. Alexander's tactics were directed to the breaking up of this tremendous mass and the routing of the enemy's centre, where Darius had taken his stand. A cavalry charge led by Alexander himself was the decisive stroke, and by nightfall the Persians were in flight. The king escaped into the eastern mountains, but his empire over the Mesopotamian valley was utterly lost. Alexander never had to fight another great battle against the Persians. He marched southward to Babylon, which opened its gates without a struggle, then eastward into Elam and the old Persian land (§ 77), where he captured the cities of Susa and Per-sep'o-lis—capitals and treasure-cities of the Persian king. One hundred and twenty thousand talents ($140,000,000) were said to have been obtained from the latter city.

Capture of the Persian Capitals.

290. **Pursuit of Darius.**—In 330 B.C. the conqueror marched northward into Media in pursuit of Darius. He arrived at Ec-bat'a-na, the old Median capital, only to find that the Persian had fled eastward. Alexander was now at the parting of the ways. He had taken vengeance for the Persian invasion of Greece. He had torn from the Persian king the fairest of his dominions—the richest, most famous and cultured districts of the oriental world. To the east lay the vast regions, deserts and mountains, whence the Medes and Persians had come to conquer the world. Why should he advance farther? Only because a new purpose had taken shape in his mind—that he would be not only king of Macedonia and captain-general of the Greeks, but also lord of the Persian empire. To unite the west and the east under his own sway was now his ambition. Hence, at Ecbatana, he dismissed those of the Greeks in his army who desired to return

The New Problem and Its Solution.

home and loaded them with presents. Some of them, on his invitation, remained and re-enlisted as his own soldiers. With an army which no longer represented the Greek states, but obeyed him alone, he advanced to the conquest of the far east.

291. Death of Darius.—Darius, meanwhile, had fallen into the power of his satraps, who were hurrying him eastward, where he might make a new and final struggle against the conqueror. Alexander put forth every effort to capture him, followed on his track day and night with his best soldiers, only at last to come upon him dead, killed by his own people What remained was to make a systematic campaign against the eastern provinces. It required three years (330–327 B.C.) of strenuous, heart-breaking warfare among deserts, through wintry tempests, over lofty mountains. At last the work was fairly done and he was Persian emperor in very fact, lord of the last foot of ground that had once acknowledged the authority of the Ach'e-men'i-dæ

Conquest of the Far East.

292. Alexander's Plan to Unite Greeks and Persians. —Alexander's purpose to be ruler of Persia did not mean to substitute Greek ideas and customs, or Greek officials, for those of Persia, but rather to unite the two peoples in a common life. He placed Persians in charge of the civil affairs of the provinces, while he reserved the military authority to the Macedonians. He began himself to assume something of the gorgeous state of a Persian emperor; he surrounded himself with the splendors of an oriental court He married Roxana, the beautiful daughter of a chieftain of the far east. He settled his veterans in cities which he planted in these regions and gave them orientals as fellow-citizens. All this could not be pushed through without rousing the anger of those bold and loyal Macedonian nobles who had followed him through all perils as their national leader and who disdained the orientals whom they had conquered. Discontent grew into secret plotting or open opposition on the part of Alexander's captains and counsellors. He

stamped it out with merciless rigor. Parmenio, Philip's chosen general, his son's chief of staff, now left behind in Ecbatana with a powerful force holding Alexander's main line of communications, had to be put to death when his son Phi-lo'tas was discovered in a conspiracy and executed. When Clitus, Alexander's foster-brother, at a drinking-bout boldly expressed the unspoken dissatisfaction, the king ran him through with a spear. Cal-lis'the-nes, the philosopher and historian, refused to do obeisance in the oriental manner to his Macedonian lord, and not long after was punished with death. He could not escape responsibility for a plot formed against Alexander among the pages in the king's own household. These young men, who were sprung from the best Macedonian families, resented their degradation to the position of menials which the monarch's new attitude entailed Such disturbances, with their bloody vengeance, speak loudly of the tremendous changes which were coming over the face of the world and not less over the character and position of Alexander himself.

293. Campaign in India.—One more step remained for him to take. Greece and the Persian empire were not sufficient for his ambition. He aspired to be conqueror of the world In 327 B C he crossed the mountains into India, whither the Persians had already gone before him (§ 84). He overran the valley of the river

Indus, won a victory on the banks of the Hydaspes from the Indian king Porus, and would have marched eastward to the river Ganges had not his army stopped at the Hy′pha-sis river and refused to follow him into these unknown and distant regions. Returning, he moved down the Indus to its mouth, and made a voyage into the Indian ocean. At this point he divided his forces. One part he sent with his admiral, Nearchus, to sail for the

Defeat of Porus.

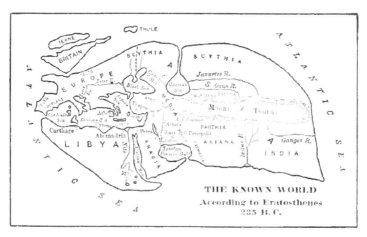

THE KNOWN WORLD
According to Eratosthenes
235 B.C.

head of the Persian gulf; his main army made a long détour inland through Dran-gi-a′na, while he himself took the rest up the coast in a march of terrible difficulty, and after joining his other divisions at Kirman reached Susa early in 324 B.C.

294. Development of Imperial Ideas.—Hardly had he returned from his Indian campaign when he plunged into the task of organizing his empire on the lines which he had planned. The union of Macedonians and Persians was encouraged by his taking as another wife the daughter of Darius, and inducing his nobles likewise to

The Great
Marriage
at Susa.
marry Persian women. Thus, in 324 B.C., a great marriage fête was held at Susa, when not only Alexander himself took a Persian wife, but eighty of his officers and,

Fusion of
Greeks and
Persians.
it is said, ten thousand of his soldiers did likewise. The army was also recruited from Persians; a large number of their young men were trained in Macedonian tactics and in the use of Greek weapons. Their best horsemen were drafted into the cavalry; some were even enrolled in the crack Macedonian regiments. Hostility to Alexander's view that Macedonians and Persians were all alike his subjects had been already encountered among the nobles. It now flamed out at Opis among the common soldiers, when the king proposed to send ten thousand worn-out Macedonian veterans home to their native land. Thereupon the whole army cried out to be sent home rather than be levelled down to the Persians. But the uproar was soon quieted. They were too much attached to their leader to stand out against his will.

295. Alexander at Babylon.—Alexander went to Babylon in 323 B.C. and was met by embassies from Carthage, the Phœnician colonies in Spain, the states of Italy, from the Ethiopians and Libyans, from the outlying peoples of the north, all of whom, it seems, expected sooner or later the advent of the conqueror upon their borders. He himself was planning an expedition to the coast of Arabia, with the design of developing trade routes from India and Babylonia to Egypt and the Mediterranean. But, after a night of feasting and drinking, he was taken

His Death.
ill. The fever increased, and on the 13th of June, 323 B.C., he passed away in the thirty-third year of his age.

296. Alexander Supreme among Greek Heroes.—Alexander is the flower of the Greek race, the supreme figure in its gallery of heroes. In physical strength and beauty, in mental grasp and poise, in moral purpose and mastery, he was pre-eminent among the men of his time. Of high, almost sentimental, ideals of honor, a warm-hearted, genial companion and friend, the idol of his troops, fearless even to recklessness in the day of battle, he knew how to work tirelessly, to hold purposes with an iron resolution, to sweep all opposition from his path, and to deny himself pitilessly for the fulfilment of his plans To reach so high a station, to stand alone at the summit of human achievement, was for so young a man almost fatally dangerous. Alexander did not escape unharmed. Power made him sometimes arbitrary and cruel. Opposition drove him to crimes which are without excuse. Yet in an age of license he was chaste; though given to Macedonian habits of deep drinking, he was no drunkard. In thirteen years of incessant activity he mastered the world and set it going in new paths. While accomplishing this task he made his name immortal.

297. His Military Genius.—The greatness of Alexander as a general is clearly revealed in the full accounts of the battles he fought and the campaigns he carried through to success. He was the mightiest conqueror the world had ever seen. But it has been reserved for modern scholars to emphasize the most splendid and enduring elements of his career: his genius for organization, his statesmanship, his far-reaching plans of government and administration. Like all his great predecessors in the field of arms, he was no mere fighter for the sake of fighting, nor did the lust of acquisition spur him on to useless and empty conquests. The crowning and deci-

His Statesmanship.

sive proof of this is seen in the cities which he founded.
No conquest was complete until he had selected sites for
new settlements, and these sites were chosen with an
unerring insight into the opportunities for trade as well
as for defence. Sixteen Alexandrias all over the east go
back to him as founder, the greatest of which was the
Egyptian metropolis (§ 288). It is said that he founded
in all some seventy cities. Many of them were so wisely
planted that they exist to this day as flourishing centres
of commercial life.

298. Aristotle.—Alexander's interest in the establishment of new city-states is one of the many bonds which
unite him to his great teacher A′ris-tot-le This extraordinary man had come to Athens upon his pupil's accession to the throne, and from 334 B.C. to 323 B.C. he
taught philosophy in the Ly-ce′um in that city. He had
been a pupil of Plato (§ 266), but in his temperament,
his method and his conclusions he departed widely from
his master. Plato was a poet, full of imagination, aiming after lofty ideals which he saw by a kind of inspired
vision. Aristotle was a cool and cautious thinker, seeking the meaning of the world by a study of things about
him, not satisfied until he brought everything to the test
of observation. Thus he investigated the laws which
governed the arts of rhetoric and poetry; he collected
the constitutions of many Greek states and drew from
them some general principles of politics; he studied animals and plants to know their structure; he examined
into the acts and ways of men to determine the essence
of their right and wrong doing. He set his students to
this kind of study and used the results of their work
Thus a new method of investigation was created and new

light thrown on all sides of life. A most learned man, he had a passion for truth and reason; one of his most famous sayings is "Plato and truth are both dear to me, but it is a sacred duty to prefer truth." His works, especially his *Politics, Ethics,* and *Poetics,* have had vast power in guiding the thinking of men since his day. His style is usually dry and difficult, though his *Constitution of Athens,* discovered in an Egyptian papyrus in 1890, is more readable. His interest in universal knowledge was in harmony with the wider world-view opened by the conquests of Alexander; in this respect he is a true son of his times. _{His Writings} _{His Breadth.}

299. Alexander and Aristotle.—His *Politics,* the last word of Greek political science on matters affecting the state, taught that a civilized life was impossible when people lived otherwise than in cities organized on the Greek plan. Yet in Asia—the realm, for the government of which Alexander had assumed full responsibility—a great part of the people lived either in unorganized villages or scattered over a wide district, destitute of political rights, and either lawless, like the nomads on the desert and the wild mountaineers, or subject to the will of priests, princes or officials. It was one purpose of the many foundations of Alexander to provide homes for his veterans and for the surplus population of Greece which flocked into the Persian empire behind the conqueror's army; it was another purpose to civilize the natives, to bring them into urban communities along with the immigrants from Europe, to fuse the new and the old into a new stock above all by forcing them to meet together in general assemblies, councils and executive committees for the transaction of public business. More-

The Purpose of the New Cities.

Fusion of Peoples.

over, the maintenance of the city-states already in existence and the founding of new ones settled for Alexander
the troublesome question as to the administration of his
empire He gave to the cities responsibility for the preservation of order, administration of justice and collecting
of taxes within their several territories and looked forward
to the time when his entire realm would be a honeycomb
of little urban communities such as Aristotle thought
ideal In the meantime he had to assume the burden of
administering the unorganized tracts which lay between
the cities. This he did by using the Persian instruments,
satraps, both for the supervision of the work of the towns
and for the direct government of the interurban districts.

**Adminis-
tration.**

300. The Deification of Alexander.—The sole point
in which his scheme might have done violence to Greek
thinking was in the supervising power assumed by himself; yet nothing was more necessary, since otherwise
struggles were sure to arise among the cities, and individually they would fall an easy prey to foreign attacks.
This difficulty Alexander met by a genial application of
a principle which he had received from Aristotle, that
when a man of supreme political capacity existed in a
state it was unjust to him and disadvantageous to the
community that he should be bound by the laws, which,
though they helped average people, fettered genius.
Such a person Aristotle had taught should be made permanent ruler and treated as a god. As we have already
seen, Alexander had had himself greeted as a son of Zeus
by the oracle of Amon, which enjoyed a great repute
in the entire Greek world in the fourth century B.C.
In 324 B.C. he demanded that each city should enrol him
in its circle of deities. This was done reluctantly in some

places, as in Athens and Sparta, but in general it was done with enthusiasm; for henceforth the cities could take orders from Alexander without loss of self-respect. To obey their gods was a duty, while on the other hand, to acknowledge the authority of an outside king would have been humiliating to places which in theory were free and self-governing. This was the way in which Alexander organized his vast empire; and his first and at the same time his last general command in his new capacity was that all the cities restore their exiles. Otherwise his realm must be disturbed indefinitely by the discontent of lawless and homeless men. . This order the Athenians protested against and the Ætolians defied; and there the matter stood when the whole world was shocked by the news of the death of its lord, the departure to Olympus of its god.

The Political Convenience of Deification.

REVIEW EXERCISES. 1. For what are the following famous: Granicus, Issus, Arbela, Tyre, Alexandria, Persepolis, Indus? 2. What is meant by Achemenidæ, high-priest, phalanx? 3. What is the date of the founding of Alexandria, of the death of Alexander? 4. What principle of government is taught by Aristotle's politics? 5. Did Alexander follow Aristotle's teaching in organizing his empire?

COMPARATIVE STUDIES. 1. Compare Alexander with Alcibiades. 2. Compare the empire of Alexander with that of Assyria or Persia; with the Athenian empire. 3. "No single personality, excepting the carpenter's son of Nazareth, has done so much to make the world we live in what it is as Alexander of Macedon."—Can you justify this assertion?

SELECT LIST FOR READING. 1. Alexander's Campaigns. Bury, pp. 747-821. 2. Alexander's Empire. Bury, pp. 785-786, 793-794, 815-816. 3. Alexander. Bury, pp. 821-822

TOPICS FOR READING AND ORAL REPORT. 1. Alexander's Campaigns. Zimmern, ch. 21, Shuckburgh, ch 20; Mahaffy, Alexander's Empire, pp 12-42; Morey, pp 309-314 2. Alexander's Empire. Mahaffy, pp. 1-3, Morey, pp 322-323 3. Alexander. Plutarch, Life of Alexander, Morey, pp 314-316, 320.

7.—THE HELLENISTIC * AGE

323–200 B C.

301. Revolt of the Greeks.—By the Greeks in the far east the report of Alexander's death was received with fear and trembling, and gathering together from their cities to the number of twenty-three thousand they made a vain effort to force their way back to the Mediterranean. To their kinsmen in the home land, on the other hand, the news brought jubilation and at the initiative of Athens and Ætolia a general outbreak for independence occurred. The war which ensued is called the La'mi-an war because of the fact that An-tip'a-ter (§ 282), who tried to stem the tide of insurrection with inadequate forces, sought refuge in the Thessalian town of Lamia and there stood a siege. Greek success depended upon preventing reinforcements from arriving from Asia, but for this the Athenians, whose navy at first controlled the sea, were too weak, and a defeat first in the Hellespont and then in a decisive battle at A-mor'gos opened the way for army after army to cross from Asia into Europe to Antipater's rescue. Thus reinforced Antipater defeated the Greeks at Crannon, whereupon the league which they had formed dissolved and Athens, threatened by sea and land, surrendered unconditionally. The democracy was over-thrown, an oligarchy established and a governor put in the Piræus. Among the democratic leaders whose person was demanded was Demosthenes. Rather than yield to certain death he committed suicide. "Had but the

Lamian War (323-322 B.C.).

Battle of Amorgos.

Demos-thenes' Death.

---

* By Hellenistic we mean the period which fell between Alexander's death and the last great revolt of the Greeks at the time of Mithridates (88 B C.).

strength of thy arm, Demosthenes, equalled thy spirit,"
ran a contemporary epigram, "never would Greece have
sunk under the foreign yoke."

302. The Regency.—In the meantime an attempt was
being made by the device of a regency to hold the vast
empire together in the interest of Alexander's family
—his half-witted half-brother, Philip Ar-rhi-dæ'us, and
the child, called Alexander, whom Roxane, Alexander's
queen, bore shortly after his death. Three regents followed one another in rapid succession. The first, Perdiccas, erred through assuming too much power; the
second, Antipater, let matters take their course and contented himself with the control of Macedon. The third,
Pol-y-per'chon, found a rival for the possession of Macedon in Antipater's son, Cas-san'der, and a contestant for
his title to the regency in An-tig'o-nus, surnamed Cyclops,
or the one-eyed, governor of Phrygia. By 316 B.C. Cassander had gained Macedon and Antigonus had defeated
and slain Eu'me-nes of Cardia, a brilliant Greek who had
been Alexander's secretary and who supported Polyper-
chon through loyalty to his master's son. The regency
came thus to naught.

303. Antigonus Struggles for Unity.—During the
following thirty years (316–286 B.C.) Antigonus and his
son, De-me'tri-us, surnamed Pol-i-or-ce'tes, or "taker of
cities," made three vigorous attempts to hold the empire
together, not for Philip, who was murdered in 317 B C., nor
for the young Alexander, whom Cassander put out of the
way in 310 B.C., but in order to substitute their own
dynasty for that of the conqueror. The first attempt began when in 316 B.C. Antigonus set aside the satraps of the
far eastern provinces, even Se-leu'cus of Babylon being

(marginal notes: The Young Alexander; The Three Regents; Antigonus I.; First Struggle (316-311 B.C.).)

forced to run for safety to Egypt. This drastic action was
followed up by a proclamation that all Greek cities were
free, which caused trouble for Cassander in Greece; this
in turn by the construction of a fleet—for without sea
power unity was impossible—and by the reduction of
Syria and Phœnicia. The crisis came in 312 B.C. In the
spring of this year Antigonus stationed his son, Demetrius,
at Gaza with instruction to hold Ptolemy, ruler of Egypt,
in check while he himself had his main army massed on
the Hellespont in order to support the operation of the
fleet with which he had already opened an attack on

Battle of Gaza. Macedon. His plan of campaign was foiled by the in-
subordination of Demetrius, who instead of remaining on
the defensive risked a battle and was defeated decisively
at Gaza. Antigonus had to return to drive the Egyptians
out of Syria. This he did with ease, since Ptolemy retreated without a contest, too wise to risk in a fight what
the natural defences of Egypt made tolerably safe. But
in the meanwhile Seleucus had slipped off to Babylon
and installed himself in his old satrapy.

A peace—of which one condition insisted upon by Antigonus was that the Greek cities should be free—now put

Second Struggle (307-301 B C.). an end to the war for four years. But in 307 B.C. Antigonus began his second attempt for world-empire. This
time he singled out Egypt for his main attack, but in order
to keep Cassander employed he sent Demetrius with his
fleet to free Greek cities—particularly Athens, where during the previous ten years a certain Demetrius of Pha-
ie'rum, a pupil of Aristotle and The'o-phras'tus, had
governed as Cassander's agent. From Aristotle the Phalerian got his scheme of government, from Theophrastus
the main ideas for a new law code: he was the patron of

the great comedian Me-nan'der, and of scientists and
artists generally, as well as the head of a gay and clever
court.

304. New Comedy.—The New Comedy, unlike the political plays
of Aristophanes (§ 224), took as its theme the affairs of every-day
life and handled them in a spirited, keen, sympathetic and delightful
way   The shady side of contemporary manners was usually shown
up, but in a fashion to ridicule vice and applaud virtue.   Its chief *Menander.*
representative was Menander (342–292 B.C.), only fragments of
whose plays have been preserved.   So sure was his touch and so
true to reality that the ancients said of him: "Menander and life,
which of you is the imitator of the other?"

305. Demetrius the Taker of Cities.—During his regency the Athenians were exceedingly prosperous and
were much admired and envied.   None the less, they welcomed the "taker of cities," expelled the Phalerian and
fought stoutly against Cassander for the following three
years.   Meanwhile Demetrius had turned his attention to
the main war.   In 306 B C. he vanquished the fleet of
Ptolemy in a great naval battle off Salamis in Cyprus,
whereupon, after assuming the regal title, he by sea, his
father by land, attacked Egypt.   They failed to break *Failure of*
down the defence of its monarch, however, and reverting *the Attack on Egypt*
to the plan of 312 B C.—Ptolemy was now innocuous— *and on Rhodes.*
Demetrius returned to continue the war in Greece.   On
his way he laid siege to Rhodes—now the most progressive
commercial centre in the Ægean—but the Rhodians defended themselves with such vigor and skill that despite all
his efforts he failed to take their city before he was forced
to hurry on to his destination in order to prevent Athens
from falling into Cassander's hands   Athens saved, he occupied Greece in 303 B.C. and was pushing Cassander hard

in Thessaly when he was obliged to return to Asia Minor
to help his father; for the danger of Cassander had so
alarmed the other monarchs, who now called themselves
kings too, though in the sight of Antigonus they were
but rebellious satraps, that a general attack was concerted
against the common foe. At the outset Ptolemy invaded
Palestine and Syria: to be sure, he withdrew on the false
report of the defeat of his partners and contributed nothing to the issue Not so Seleucus who, having mastered
all the eastern provinces and concluded a treaty of peace
with the king of the Punjab, now made a great march
with horse, foot and elephants to Asia Minor and there
effected a juncture with a new enemy of Antigonus. This
was Ly-sim'a-chus, king of Thrace, who after over twenty
years of persistent effort had come to be definitely master
in his own unruly country and was now in a position to
take part in general affairs. Antigonus recalled his son
at this point; part of Cassander's army came to the assistance of the allies, and in 301 B.C. at Ipsus in Phrygia
the greatest battle yet fought in European history took
place. On each side were upward of eighty thousand
trained men. The impetuosity of Demetrius determined
the issue. Having routed the enemy's cavalry, he pursued them too far and returned to find the infantry beaten
and his father slain. With the death of Antigonus disappeared the most important figure which the war of the
diadochi (successors) produced. He was a great, powerful man, kingly in mind and disposition. He formed
his plans carefully, was an accomplished strategist and
worked tirelessly to secure his ends He was the one man
in the whole group who inherited the spirit of Alexander.
His son, Demetrius, was still ruler of the sea, and with

Battle of Ipsus.

this as a starting-point in 294 B.C. he took Macedon from the incompetent sons of Cassander, who had died in 297 B C. Not content with the kingdom Alexander had inherited, Demetrius made great preparations to reconquer the world. The third attempt for the union was forestalled by those whom it menaced. At the same time in 288 B.C. Pyrrhus, king of Epirus, and Lysimachus of Thrace invaded Macedon, and Ptolemy of Egypt despatched a great fleet to secure control of the sea. The coalition was successful: Demetrius got across to Asia and undertook a wild march into the interior, but, defeated and deserted by his troops, he was captured by Seleucus in 286 B C., and died three years later. The thirty years' war, accordingly, resulted in the definite dissolution of Alexander's empire into a number of separate states. Its issue was as disastrous as was that of the Peloponnesian war

The New (Third Struggle for Unity (294-286 B.C.).

Fall of Demetrius

306. Lysimachus and Seleucus.—The spoils had fallen largely to Lysimachus of Thrace who got Asia Minor after Ipsus, half of Macedon after the expulsion of Demetrius and the remnants of the latter's fleet when he had struck into the interior in 287 B.C. In 283 B.C. Lysimachus reunited Macedon by expelling Pyrrhus from its second half, and was about to seize Greece, which Demetrius's son, Antigonus II, inherited, when he in turn was assailed by Seleucus, his rival in Asia. In 282 B C. the two great monarchs met at Cor-u-pe'di-on in Lydia, and Lysimachus was defeated and slain. Thus, by accident almost, Seleucus got the greater part of the distracted empire, but within a year of his victory he was foully murdered by Ptolemy Ce-rau'nus, the disinherited oldest son of the king of Egypt, to whom he had given hospitality.

Battle of Corupedion.

The murderer seized Macedon and Thrace, but his title was at once challenged, not only by Seleucus's son, Antiochus I, but also by Demetrius's son, Antigonus II; and a new struggle began.

307. The Celtic Migration.—At this moment the factious Macedonian kings were rudely reminded that they were not the only ones who coveted the rich world which they were weakening by their struggles. Behind the Alps, stretching from the mouths of the Rhone and Rhine to the middle Danube, the loose conglomerate of Celtic tribes had been massed for over a century. Now finding advance south checked by the unification of Italy and Rome's advance into the Po valley (§ 376) which they had occupied in about 390 B C. (§ 369), they turned their attention eastward, and in 280 B.C. a great avalanche of barbarians overwhelmed Macedon. Ptolemy Ceraunus put himself hastily in their way but lost his life and his army, and for three years the Celts pillaged and murdered in the land of Alexander. In 279 B.C. Brennus led one division of them south into Greece, but though it reached Delphi it was destroyed chiefly by the energy of the Ætolians. About the same time another division went east and occupied Thrace. The credit for breaking the onset of the barbarians belongs to Antigonus II, who first defeated decisively a great body of them near Ly-si-mach'i-a in 277 B.C., then expelled them from Macedon and made himself its king. Thrace, however, was lost altogether; the civilizing work of Philip, Alexander and Lysimachus in this region was undone, and this whole district lapsed back into the barbarism of central Europe. Moreover, the Celts crossed the Hellespont into Asia Minor, where after a career of plunder they settled down in the heart of the

The Celts
Hold
Thrace and
Galatia.

peninsula and forced the adjoining cities and principalities to buy immunity from pillage by paying them tribute. Their territory was called Galatia

308. Alliance of Macedon and Asia.—When Antigonus occupied the throne of Macedon he and Antiochus ceded away their claim to each other's territory and formed a political and matrimonial alliance which was the basis for common action between Macedon and Asia during the rest of the third century B C

309. Egypt under the Ptolemies.—They were forced to co-operate, moreover, by the policy of Egypt. The first Ptolemy had kept Egypt free from invasion and given it an opportunity to prosper, he had constructed a great fleet, and with it finally gained control of the eastern Mediterranean, dominion over its islands and a claim to suzerainty in Greece and rule in Palestine, Phœnicia and Syria. He had, in fact, formed the policy of converting the sea east of Sicily into an Egyptian lake, and by controlling the harbors and coast towns from Gaza to Maro-nei'a in Thrace, he aimed to concentrate all maritime commerce in Alexandria. The benefits of this wise and energetic policy were enjoyed by his son, Ptolemy Philadelphus, who came to the throne in 283 B.C. Down the Nile came the results of the labor of the seven million laborious inhabitants of Egypt and in addition the products of the Soudan, Abyssinia, Arabia and India. A great light-house built on the island of Pharus directed to its mouth all the cargoes of Greece and the Levant.

Sea Power of Egypt.

Ptolemy II Philadelphus.

310. Alexandria.—Hence Alexandria grew with marvellous rapidity and soon had a population of five hundred thousand. It was the one great Greek city in Egypt. The Ptolemies made no attempt to civilize,

Ptolemies
Leave
Native
Customs
Unchanged.

i.e., Hellenize, the natives. The Egyptians, accordingly, were not brought into city centres, self-government being denied to them altogether; they had no interest in politics, their ideal life being satisfied by religion; and the Ptolemies had no scruples of conscience about fostering the native cults, building new temples for the native gods and posing generally as the successors of the Pharaohs.

311. The Government of Egypt.—For the goverment of the country they used a vast bureaucratic system.

A Bureau-
cracy.

By means of officials carefully divided into departments of justice, police, finance, for example, and carefully graded according to rank, the wishes of Ptolemy and of his prime ministers were carried from Alexandria to the smallest village in the valley of the Nile; and by the same agencies the taxes were collected. The chief function of the native population was, in fact, the payment of taxes to the government, and it was by the control of ample revenues drawn from this source that Philadelphus was able to make Alexandria the seat of the most brilliant court in the world.

312. Alexandrian Culture.—Festivals and processions were organized on a colossal scale, and nothing indicative of luxury or provocative of lust was neglected by the

Theocritus.

pleasure-loving monarch. The two greatest poets of the age lived in Alexandria in his time—The-oc'ri-tus, the writer of idylls treating of idealized country life, and

Callim-
achus.

Cal-lim'a-chus, a kind of literary dictator, and the composer of finished epigrams and elegies   In the realm of poetry Theocritus discovered a new and rich field called pastoral.   In his delicately wrought background of Sicilian country life, with its fountains, shady oaks, stalwart

PLATE XXI

Pastoral Scene

An Ancient Cake-Walk

REALISTIC AND ROMANTIC ART OF HELLENISTIC AGE

shepherds, graceful maidens, vineyards, woodland flowers and murmuring bees, he set his simple scenes of
rustic love. In them the worldly and sated Alexandrians
found intense delight and refreshment. Following Theocritus as his model, Vergil, two hundred and fifty years
later, in his *Bucolics*, brought the fragrance of the country
to the equally worldly and sated Romans of the age
of Augustus.

313. **Hellenistic Art.**—Similar themes were handled
by one group of Hellenistic sculptors, who carved little
scenes of outdoor life with shepherds and shepherdesses
or mythological personages grouped in the foreground.
They were used as panels in the decoration of houses.
Doubtless, similar paintings also existed   In this work the
tendency toward realism which characterizes Hellenistic
portraiture is also noticeable. The portraits were not, Realism.
however, grossly realistic; the face had to possess some
charm or nobility even though it ceased to be quite accurate. The classic restraint which limited the expression of feeling to suggestion and left much to the sympathetic imagination of the observer was now abandoned
altogether, and particularly in the Rhodian and Anatolian
schools faces were carved contorted with pain or tense
with excitement   Examples of these are the La-oc'o-on
Group and the Battle of Gods and Giants from the
great altar of Zeus at Per'ga-mon. Action, not repose,
was preferred, and the artists liked to achieve dramatic
effects perhaps inappropriate to work in stone. There
was in this age boundless confidence in the powers
of human beings; men became gods and overturned
all the arrangements of society and states; they shrank
from no tasks however difficult. Hence statues of super-

human magnitude like the Colossus of Rhodes were attempted.

314. Alexandrian Science.—Nowhere was the realistic tendency of this age better manifest than in science, of which Alexandria was the most famous centre. For the accommodation of scholars the Ptolemies built and endowed the Museum—or Academy—of literary and natural sciences. To its equipment belonged a great library for literary and a garden for zoological and botanical research. For the support of the workers the government provided salaries. Thus aided, science, the dominant passion of the Hellenistic age, made remarkable progress, and its greatest names prior to the eighteenth century A.D. appear in the annals of this epoch. E'ra-tos'the-nes computed the circumference of the earth at twenty-eight thousand miles, which is surprisingly near the correct figure. A'ris-tar'chus of Samos showed that the sun, not the earth, was the centre of this planetary system and that the earth revolved on its own axis, thus anticipating Ga'li-le'o and Co-per'ni-cus. He-roph'i-lus foreshadowed Harvey's theories of the circulation of the blood, and Ar'chi-me'des of Syracuse is said to have used the integral calculus long before it was rediscovered by Leibnitz and Newton. Even if this is not the case, his contributions to mathematical physics are sufficiently noteworthy. Euclid wrote at this time his text-book on geometry. All this shows that the constructive imagination of men had free play as well as large bodies of new material with which to operate, and that the world of thought like the world of action was vibrant with fresh life.

315. Alexandrian Philology.—The work of the Alexandrian scholars in literary criticism and interpretation was no less remarkable than in natural science. It was necessary now that a new common speech was extirpating the dialects, and now that a new age was rapidly pushing the world of the little city-states into a distant antiquity, that the older literature—the Ionian epics and the Lesbian and Dorian lyrics—as well as the comedies and orations which dealt with local persons and situations should be interpreted or else abandoned. Besides, the Greek language, which was now used generally for public business, literature and diplomatic and commercial intercourse, had to be organized so that the conquered populations might learn it. Hence grammars and lexicons were compiled, authoritative editions of the classic authors issued and learned commentaries on them published. Epoch-making in this respect was the work of Callimachus and Aristarchus of Alexandria on Homer. Our Iliad and Odyssey date from their revision of the text. All this literature was bookish and learned; it was meant to appeal only to the initiated and hence made little popular impression. It requires a long time to popularize scientific ideas and methods

316. Ptolemy II, Philadelphus.—Philadelphus was a statesman and diplomat, not a soldier or general; hence he remained in his luxurious court at Alexandria and sent out his admirals and paid out his money freely in support of his foreign policy.

317. Antigonus II.—His chief rival was Antigonus II of Macedon. Antigonus was a pupil and patron of Zeno, the great founder of the Stoic philosophy, and from this stern creed the king derived his sturdiness of character, his devotion to duty and his preference for a life of old-fashioned simplicity. It became clear to him that he could not be at peace in Macedon and rule Greece so long as Philadelphus held the islands of the Ægean and by the use of money and promises kept stirring up trouble for him in his realm. Hence he determined to gain for himself the control of the sea which since 287 B.C. had been securely Egyptian.

The New
Battle-
ships.

318. Struggle for the Eastern Mediterranean.—Accordingly, he built a fleet of the great new-fashioned battle-ships characteristic of this age, vessels rising high above the water with sometimes as many as sixteen banks of rowers, powerful artillery and crews of thousands of men   They may have had on occasion a capacity of upward of four thousand tons. With this navy he began a duel for sea power with Egypt in about 256 B.C. which lasted with interruptions until about 241 B.C.   In its course Antigonus won two sea fights, one at Cos and the other at Andros, the first against the admirals of Philadelphus, the second against the admirals of Ptolemy III, Eu-er'ge-tes, who took his father's place in 247 B C ; the first in alliance with Antiochus II of Asia, the second

The
Rhodians.

in alliance with the Rhodians, who, having first defended their freedom against Demetrius, the "taker of cities," now refused to be subservient to their old ally Egypt.   Thus they won a position of general respect.   Much of the banking and carrying trade of the eastern Mediterranean was their reward.   Shortly after the second victory Antigonus died (239 B.C.), and Macedon became involved for ten years in a destructive war in Greece.   At the same time a dynastic struggle—the first of many—broke out in Asia, but none the less Euergetes failed to rebuild his fleet, and without it his far-spread empire was merely a shell which could be crushed by the first strong pressure from without.

319. The Seleucid Empire.—Its existence, however, crippled the economic and political power of the kingdom of the Seleucids in Asia; for it deprived the great continental empire of its coast lines, and prevented it from drawing freely from Greece the men who were needed to colonize its vast waste tracts and to reinforce the Hellenic element in the settled districts. The Seleucids were the real heirs of Alexander the Great. They made it their mission to realize Alexander's vision of a realm honeycombed with self-governing cities of the Greek type. Thus the founder of the dynasty is said to have planted seventy-five cities; his son, Antiochus I, is known as a great founder also; and the work was still in progress when the Romans came into Asia. What they accomplished was to carry the Greek language, ideas, forms of government, art and drama as far as the eastern limits of the Persian empire, and, indeed, as recent discoveries show, far beyond, into distant India and northeastward through Eastern Turkestan to China. Naturally, the interests of the dynasty in Hellenizing these kingdoms provoked native reactions; but these were not serious till Antioch IV interfered with the native religions; then revolts broke out, notably in Ju-de'a, where the Mac'ca-bees took up arms for Jehovah against Zeus and after a long struggle succeeded in establishing the independence of the Jewish community. All the native religions were not so obstinate, however, and, in fact, at the same time that the Jews resisted Hellenization they translated their sacred books into Greek for the use of the Jewish community in Alexandria; but, unlike the oriental cults in general, they modified their beliefs and altered their rituals so slightly that it needed a religious revolution in Judaism

Founding of Cities.

Hellenizing of Natives.

before it could become a rival of the Se-ra′pis-I′sis cult of Alexandria, the At-ar′ga-tis cult of Syria or the Great Mother cult of Asia Minor for the suffrages of the Hellenistic and Roman world. These latter were the aggressive oriental cults in the Hellenistic period. The instruments for their dissemination were religious associations (*thiasi*) formed by their votaries in the cities of the old Greek world. These clubs were made up at first of foreigners and provided social entertainment in the shape of a monthly dinner which was at once a banquet and a sacrifice. They also provided the assurance of decent funeral obse-

Oriental Cults in Greece. quies as well as business facilities to their members. In time the native Greeks became interested, entered the associations and finally got the new deities enrolled in the circle of their native deities, whereupon all the citizens became at once votaries of the oriental god or goddess. It was in this way that Isis, the Syrian Goddess (Atargatis) and Cyb′e-le (the Great Mother) made their triumphal progress through the late Hellenistic world.

320. **Greece—the Achæan and Ætolian Leagues.—** The policy and aggressiveness of the Ptolemies were also fatal for the stability of Macedonian government in Greece, and during the struggle of the two monarchies for power in the peninsula the Greeks had a chance to look out for themselves. To be sure the country suffered through frequent wars; but in this respect it was no worse off in the third century than in the fourth and fifth. It was a gain that its surplus population was

Shifting of Commercial Centres. provided for in the new world of the east. The serious consideration was that through the opening of the Persian empire to European enterprise the centres of commerce and industry ceased to be situated in Greece. Athens

and Corinth, accordingly, sank in size and wealth as
Ephesus, Rhodes, Antioch and Alexandria rose. Thus
Greece tended to revert to an essentially agricultural
country, and impoverishment and depopulation eventually set in. Less injury was, of course, sustained by the
districts which had never been commercial and it was in
them that most progress and vitality survived in the
third century The conviction came ultimately to be
established among them that the little city-states were
unable to protect themselves by individual action; hence
from two centres, one in Achæa in the Peloponnesus, and
the other in Ætolia in central Greece, movements for a
union of the whole country in a federal league began.
A large territorial state such as defence demanded was
thus created without resort to monarchical government.

321. **Federal Government.**—The plan adopted was
to delegate to federal authorities the conduct of negotiations and war, the preservation of peace between the
cities and the protection of individuals while abroad,
leaving the raising, paying and officering of troops, the
levying of the taxes, the maintenance of order within
the cities and the whole round of municipal business to
the local governments. Citizenship was to be common;
also money and weights and measures, and monarchical
rule was not permitted. In Achæa the federal authorities The
were an annually elected general who was at once mili- Achæan
tary and diplomatic leader, a hipparch, admiral and League.
secretary; a college of ten *demiurgi*, who formed a sort
of inner council, a great council made up each year of
a different fraction of the citizens of each constituent city,
and a general assembly of all the Achæans. This latter
body met at least annually at Aé-gium for the election of

officers, but it might meet oftener for the settlement of peace or war at the call of the officials. Each city had one vote in the general assembly regardless of size. This gave the smaller states undue influence. The constitution of Ætolia was similar. A difference between the two was caused by the difference in the character and habits of life of the peoples. The Ætolians were a country, mountain people, active, fond of fighting and inclined to freebooting; the Achæans were more civilized, had urban life well developed, and were averse to making sacrifices in war time. The one was warlike and the other peaceful In both the control of the general assembly tended to fall to the propertied classes who alone could attend the sessions in considerable numbers.

322. Growth of the Leagues.—The Ætolians began to expand first; they seized Delphi in about 292 B.C., and controlled the Amphictyony from then on; they seized first half, then all of Acarnania, including Ambracia; for a period they absorbed Bœotia; while a considerable portion of Thessaly was finally in their control. They remained a free people till the Romans conquered them in 189 B.C.

Aratus of Sicyon. The Achæans became of importance for the first time in 252 B.C. when A-ra′tus, who had just seized the government of Sicyon, his native city, in place of making himself tyrant with the backing of either Antigonus II or Philadelphus, added it to the ethnic confederacy which some thirty years earlier had been revived among the towns of Achæa. From this time on Aratus, a skilful politician and adroit leader in guerilla warfare, but a very incompetent general, was the real head of the confederation, and for every second year but one between 245 B C. and

PLATE XXII

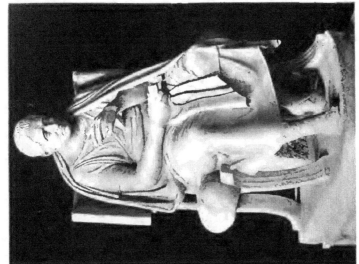

Posidippus the Athenian

Khafre, Pharaoh of Egypt

TYPICAL SCULPTURED FIGURES

213 B.C. he was chosen their general. The normal attitude of the Ætolians and Achæans was one of hostility,
but during the reign of Demetrius II, who had succeeded
Antigonus II in 239 B.C. (§ 318), they joined in a war
against Macedon, and at its issue, with the death of their
adversary in 229 B.C., they both reached the summit of
their power. The Achæan league then included most of
the Peloponnesus.

323. **Athens and Sparta.**—Outside of these stood
Athens and Sparta, neither of which would subordinate
itself to the federal authorities. In 229 B.C. Athens
threw off the Macedonian yoke, but despite the entrea-
ties of Aratus, decided to remain henceforth neutral. It Isolation
asked from the powers and in fact got a position of of Athens.
complete isolation, its internationalization being guaranteed first by Egypt and then by Rome. It was still
the seat of the finest Greek culture, and in the world of
Hellenistic change it remained an oasis of classicism.
Its art, for example, was dominated by the style of Prax-i'-
te-les and Scopas and to its school belongs, perhaps, the
celebrated Aphrodite of Melos. (Pl. XVIII.) In one department of spiritual life alone it had preserved its emi-
nence—in philosophy.

324. **Philosophy in Athens.**—The city became in the
third century the real university of the world, whither
students flocked to study philosophy. Two leading Schools of
schools of thought divided their suffrages. The one Philosophy
was founded by Zeno (333–261 B.C.), who taught in the
Stoa poikike or "Painted Porch," in the heart of the city,
a way of life and thought which was called Stoicism.
He held that, in the midst of the seeming confusion of The Stoic.
things about us, there was a real order, governed by un-

changeable laws; that the secret of life consists in seeing
this order and obeying it.   The chief word of this philosophy was "virtue," and he is the "wise man" who strives
after it.   Everything else is unimportant, even life itself
is not worth living, if virtue cannot be realized.   Virtue
can be found in one's own soul, in that "reason" which is
man's way of expressing the order of the universe.   All
men everywhere in whom "reason" or "virtue" rules

The Epi-
curean.

are brothers.   On the other hand, Ep'i-cu'rus (341–270
B.C) taught that true virtue is found in "happiness,"
everything that contributes to make man happy should
be sought, while all that is disturbing should be avoided.
Hence, to him religion, which spoke of reward and
punishment from the gods above, was harmful and
should be abolished.   This philosophy was called after its
founder Ep'i-cu-re'an-ism.   Its emphasis of pleasure and
its indifference toward the gods brought it into popular
discredit both in later Greece and in Rome.   And, in
fact, as interpreted by many of its professed followers it
was an excuse for sensual indulgence.   Both systems are
illustrations of the broad cosmopolitan spirit of the age,
which recognized no bounds of city or race.   They had a
very wide influence in this age and in the centuries following

Restora-
tion of the
Ancient
Régime.

325. Cleomenes and the Revival of Sparta.—Sparta
met the advance of the Achæans not by an appeal to
the powers, but by resort to the sword, and it happened
that it possessed at this time a remarkable king, Cle-om'-
e-nes by name, who defeated the Achæans repeatedly and
roused the old city into new life by setting aside the government of the ephors (§ 153), redividing the land in such
a way that instead of seven hundred there were four

PLATE XXIII

THE LAOCOON GROUP

thousand Spartiatæ, and re-establishing with antiquarian precision the old tent life which had fallen of late into disuse. Then he pushed the Achæans so hard that Aratus was forced to submit to either Spartan or Macedonian hegemony; he chose the latter alternative and in 222 B.C. the Macedonian king, Antigonus III, crushed Cleomenes on the battle-field of Sel-la'si-a, and became overlord of Greece—Ætolia alone excepted. Subsequently the Achæans were never free agents, but had always to do the bidding of somebody else.

326. Pergamon.—It was in the interval of dynastic strife in Asia and of fierce conflict in Greece and Macedon (§ 318) that Pergamon became the chief among the second-rate powers of the eastern world. Its third prince At'ta-lus I (241–197 B.C.) refused to pay tribute to the Celts of Galatia, and thus became involved in a long struggle with them, at the end of which he found himself for a short time the paramount power in Asia Minor. This position he lost in a few years, however, when unity of rule was at length restored to the Seleucid empire. Under Attalus Pergamon became a rival of Alexandria as a seat of culture, and the king was a liberal patron of philosophers, scientists and artists. It was at his initiative that the sculptors of Greece got a new theme when they undertook to immortalize in stone the victories of the monarch over the Celts. The famous "Dying Gaul" is the outcome of this undertaking. A little later a great altar to Zeus was erected at Pergamon, the frieze of which, now in Berlin, is the best monument extant of Hellenistic sculpture. It deals with the struggle of Gods and Giants. Full of vigor and vitality, it is inferior to the work of the classic age only in the lack of simplicity and grace.

Art of Pergamon

327. The Crisis of Hellenistic History.—About 220
B.C. three young men came to the thrones of the three
great Hellenistic monarchies. Philip V, the new king
of Macedon, became at once involved in a fierce struggle
with the Ætolians, which he abandoned (after Cannæ)
to join Hannibal against Rome. Till 205 B.C. he was
fully employed by the war with the Ætolians and Attalus
of Pergamon which the Romans stirred up against him
to keep him employed while they fought it out with
Carthage. In that year, however, he became free by
making a peace with the Italian republic. The young
king of Asia, Antiochus III, the Great, opened his reign
by an attack on Egypt, and but for a revolt in his eastern
provinces, which gave his adversary time to prepare, the
defeat which he sustained at Raphia in 218 B.C. might
have been a victory. For thirteen years thereafter he
was actively employed in reasserting his authority in his
own empire, which a long dynastic struggle and foreign
embarrassments had paralyzed; but in 205 B.C. he returned to the Mediterranean at the end of a campaign
which covered nearly the same territory as Alexander's
famous march, with a well-trained army and a desire for
further action. Two years later Ptolemy Phi'lo-pa'tor,
the fourth Macedonian king of Egypt, died leaving as his
successor a mere child. He had neglected all the vital
problems of national defence; his court had been governed
by his mistress and her clique, and the native Egyptians
who had fought in his army at Raphia were in revolt.
Hence Egypt was ready for the spoilers. By her wealth
and her maritime power she had preserved a balance of
power in the Hellenistic world since 277 B.C., and in 274
B.C. she had formed a relationship of peace and friendl-

Philip V and Rome.

Antiochus the Great.

Decay of Egypt.

ness with Rome. Now that the Hannibalic war was
drawing to a close, it was clear to Philip and Antiochus
that in the event of a Roman advance into the east
Egypt would be her ally; hence they determined to take
the opportunity, while Rome was still employed elsewhere, to divide the Ptol-e-ma'ic empire between them
In 202 B.C. Philip attacked the possessions of Egypt in the
Ægean world including neutrals like Athens and Rhodes
which had maintained their freedom by Egyptian support,
and at the same time Antiochus assailed the Asiatic dominions of Egypt. Henceforth the Hellenistic world was
to have two great states, not three. The battle of Za'ma
(202 B.C.) and the treaty of Rome with Carthage (201 B C)
came too soon, however, for this project to be completed.

REVIEW EXERCISES. 1. What events are connected with the
names of Antipater, Seleucus, Demetrius of Phalerum, Antigonus Gonatas, Ptolemy Philadelphus, Menander, Zeno,
Poliorcetes, Cleomenes, Antigonus the one-eyed? 2. For what
are the following noted: Galatia, Pergamon, Rhodes, Epirus,
Athens? 3. What is meant by the Museum, Epicureanism,
pastoral poetry, the Dying Gaul, the Painted Porch? 4. What
is the era of Seleucus? 5. The significance of the year 280
B C 6. What was the course and what the outcome of Antigonus's struggle for unity? 7. What was the time and character of the settlement of Galatia? 8. Explain the conditions
existing in Egypt during the Hellenistic age. 9. Describe the
growth and prosperity of Alexandria. 10. The characteristics
of Hellenistic art. 11. The naval victories of Antigonus II.
12. Describe the form of government in the Achæan and
Ætolian leagues.

COMPARATIVE STUDIES. 1. Compare Eratosthenes and Herodotus in respect to their views of geography. 2. Compare
the leagues of this period with the Peloponnesian and the
Delian leagues.

SELECT LIST FOR READING. 1. Greece under Alexander and His
Successors. Bury, pp. 823-833 2. Aristotle. Bury, pp 833-835

TOPICS FOR READING AND ORAL REPORT. 1. The Struggles of Alexander's Generals. Mahaffy, pp. 43-75, Plutarch, Lives of Eumenes and Demetrius 2. Greece under Alexander and His Successors. Bury, pp 823-833; Shuckburgh, pp 300-305. 3. The Kingdoms of Alexander's Successors. Mahaffy, pp 89-95, 111-141, 156-162; Morey, pp. 317-319. 4. Pergamon and the Artistic Life of the Time. Morey, pp 323-328. Tarbell, pp 259-267. 5. Aristotle. Bury, 833-835, Capps, ch. 16; Jebb, pp. 129-135, Murray, pp 373-376. 6. The Moral Philosophers. Mahaffy, ch 11; Shuckburgh, pp 306-307 7. Alexandria and Egyptian Culture. Mahaffy, pp. 120-131, 142-155, Capps, ch. 18, Botsford, pp 320-322, Morey, pp 330-332 8. The Celtic Terror. Mahaffy, ch 8 9. The Leagues of Greece. Mahaffy, ch 18. Botsford, pp 323-325, Shuckburgh, pp 311-324 10. Pyrrhus of Epirus. Plutarch, Life of Pyrrhus; Mahaffy, ch. 2. 11. Conditions under Macedonian Rule in Athens. Ferguson, Hellenistic Athens, pp. 207-236. 12. The Régime of Demetrius of Phalerum. Ferguson, pp 38-94.

8.—THE WESTERN GREEKS. THE TRANSITION TO ROME

350-275 B C.

Danger of the West Greeks.

328. Timoleon.—The dissolution of the empire of Dionysius II in 357-346 B C. had brought with it anarchy in Sicily and grave peril in Magna Græcia. What the likely consequences were Plato, the philosopher, foresaw when in a letter written in 352 B.C. he said: "Should things continue, no end is attainable until the whole population is ruined, the Greek language disappears from all Sicily and the island falls under the dominion of the Phœnicians or the Italians." The impending disaster was postponed for over two generations, however, by help given time and again by the eastern Greeks. The first rescuer was the Corinthian Ti-mo'le-on who came on the invitation of the Syracusans in 345 B.C. to free the

PLATE XXIV

The Greek Temple at Pæstum

A Roman Temple in Gaul

CLASSICAL TEMPLES

Sicilian cities of adventurers who had used the anarchy to make themselves tyrants. He was needed also to unite the island in a common effort against the invading Carthaginians. Some of the tyrants joined Timoleon, others were deposed He relieved Syracuse of the enemy's leaguer, and, after defeating a great Carthaginian army which had been sent over to Sicily to check his progress at the Crimi'sus river in 340 B C , he made peace with Carthage, established an aristocratic government in the Sicilian cities and bound them together in a league with Syracuse at the head. Order within and defence against foreign attack being secured, large numbers of new colonists from old Greece were encouraged to settle in the devastated tracts of the island, and after seven years of successful rule Timoleon retired into private life in 337 B.C. with the blessings of all Sicily. He was one of those rare persons who combined singleness of purpose and absence of personal ambition with devotion to duty and high capacity.

(margin note: Battle of the Crimisus.)

329. Italians Assail Magna Græcia.—Magna Græcia had been less fortunate in its deliverers. The first, King Archidamus of Sparta (343–338 B c.), had accomplished so little that in 334 B c. Alexander, the powerful king of neighboring Epirus, was asked by Tarentum to come to its assistance against its aggressive Italian neighbors, the Lucanians, Messapians and Bruttians. Alexander did, indeed, perform his mission in brilliant style, and subdued most of Italy south of Campania and Samnium and, in fact, kept the latter employed in a defensive war while Rome was consolidating its power in the former. The trouble was that he came not as a leader, but as a master, hence Tarentum took the first opportunity to withdraw its support, whereupon he fell

(margin note: Alexander of Epirus.)

in a desperate struggle to preserve his authority over both his confederates and his subjects. Tarentum, however, was able to stand by itself for the following generation, the energy of the Italians being involved between 327 and 304 B.C. in the great struggle between Rome and the Samnites. When this ceased for a time in 304 B C. Tarentum came again in peril and got assistance from Cle-on'y-mus of Sparta and A-gath'o-cles of Syracuse successively; but on its resumption in 298 B.C. a second respite was given. The decisive victory of Rome in 290 B.C. brought a new and greater peril, however, and in 282 B.C. Tarentum was forced to look abroad for a new and, as it proved, a last deliverer.

330. Agathocles of Syracuse.—In the meantime Sicily had been the battle ground of a fierce struggle between the Greeks and Carthaginians. It had been occasioned by the breakdown of Timoleon's system during struggles of the masses to set aside the rule of the aristocrats. The victory of the populace in Syracuse elevated a certain Agathocles to tyranny in 316 B C. He was a man of great physical and mental ability, one of those "super-men" which the Hellenistic age produced—ready of speech, quick in decision, rapid in execution, at once an accomplished demagogue and general, and, according to Scipio Africanus, one of the two greatest men of action that had ever lived. He had to fight for his position at once against aristocratic emigrants and the other Greek cities in Sicily which feared the revival of Syracusan supremacy, but with the assistance of the Carthaginian general on the island he effected a reconciliation with his domestic adversaries and made his city supreme (313 B C) With this result the Carthaginian government

Struggle for Power.

at home was dissatisfied and in 311 B C. it joined Agathocles' old enemies in an effort to put him down. The
coalition forced the tyrant within the walls of Syracuse, and since no relief from without was thinkable,
Agathocles seemed doomed to destruction. It was in
this crisis that he put his army, twelve thousand strong,
on board sixty ships and, giving the Carthaginian fleet
the slip, sailed for Africa. The Libyans revolted, a
second army came to his aid from Cy-re'ne, even Utica
was captured, but the walls of Carthage defied assault
and the sea was open. Moreover, Agathocles could not
be in two places at once, and while he was at home in
Sicily on a necessary visit his army was destroyed in
Africa, and on his return the remnant lost confidence
in him and mutinied. Agathocles escaped to Sicily, however, and, unable to make head against both Carthage
and his Sicilian adversaries, he made peace with the
former, which feared the result should he be destroyed
altogether, and forced the latter to submit. Thereupon,
in 306 B C he took the title of king and till his death in
289 B C. ruled Sicily gently and wisely. He even developed an empire in Magna Græcia and on the shores of
the Adriatic.

331. Pyrrhus.—On his death, however, the old disorder was renewed, and in 278 B C. the Carthaginians
were again dominant on the island and Syracuse was
in imminent danger of falling into their hands. Some
two years earlier Pyrrhus, king of Epirus, on losing his
control of Macedon and Thessaly, had sought glory and
empire in the west by accepting the call of Tarentum to
protect it against Rome He had defeated the Romans
in two battles, and had for the moment, at least, freed the

Pyrrhus in
Sicily.

Greek cities from danger. He was now entreated to
rescue Syracuse, and, crossing to Sicily, he was joined by
everybody and rapidly expelled the Carthaginians from
all points except the great fortress of Li-by-bae'um, the
Gibraltar of the island (277 B.C.). This he was unable
to take, and, since the Greek cities viewed his mission
as accomplished, and wished to be rid of their protector who could so easily become their master, he found
himself rapidly deserted by his allies and forced to
assume the defensive. Hence, in disgust he left Sicily
to resume his operations against the Romans (276 B.C.).
He is said to have stated in other words the thought of
Plato that Sicily was destined to be a fine battle-ground
for Rome and Carthage.

GENERAL REVIEW OF PART II, DIVISIONS, 6, 7 AND 8

336-200 B.C.

TOPICS FOR CLASS DISCUSSION. 1. The main purpose moving the leaders of world-history from 336-200 B C : how far
was the ideal realized in actual events? 2. A comparison as
to origin, leaders, aims, problems and historical development
of the three kingdoms rising out of Alexander's empire.
3. Course of the history of Greece proper from 336-200 B C.
4. The great epochs of contact between Persia and Greece from
500 B C to the fall of the Persian empire. 5. The dates of not
more than six of the most important events of this age, with
reasons for so regarding them. 6. How Aristotle, Theocritus,
Zeno and Menander represent their age and its spirit. 7. The
various important epochs in the history of Sicily. 8. The
history of King Pyrrhus of Epirus as illustrative of the age.

MAP AND PICTURE EXERCISES. 1. Draw a map of Alexander's empire and place on it three cities founded by Alexander; explain the advantages of their location. 2. Compare the Laocoön (Plate XXIII) with the Hermes (Plate XIX).
What are the differences—which is higher art—how does each
represent the times in which it was produced? 3. Comparing

Plate XXI with Plates XV and XVI, where do you observe differences and resemblances? 4. Study the Greek coins (Plate XXVII). Observe the development in them—what facts for Greek life and history in them—select the finest, with reasons for the selection.

TOPICS FOR WRITTEN PAPERS. 1. What Alexander's Empire Meant for World-History. 2. A Day in Alexandria, 250 B C. Kingsley, Alexandria and Her Schools, Mahaffy, Alexander's Empire. 3. Alexander as a General. 4. A Visit to the Philosophical Schools of Athens in the Year 275 B C Capes, University Life in Ancient Athens 5. Alexander's Cities. 6. A Sketch of Alexander's Campaign in India. 7. The Career of Aratus. Plutarch, Life of Aratus. 8. A Visit to Pergamon. Mahaffy, Greek Life and Thought, ch. 14. 9. A Study of the Constitution of the Achæan League. Mahaffy, Greek Life and Thought, ch. 16, Freeman, History of Federal Government, see index 10. Write a series of notes explaining the allusions to Greek history in Byron's "The Isles of Greece."

III. THE EMPIRE OF ROME

350 B C.–A D 800

PRELIMINARY SURVEY

332. Italy and the Eastern World.—The appearance of Rome in the east about the year 200 B.C. shifts our attention from the lands which have hitherto occupied us and centres it upon the peninsula of Italy. From an early period this land had come within the circle of ancient history. Back in the fifteenth century its sea-rovers may have reached the shores of Egypt and from that time took service in the armies of the Pharaohs.

Phœnicians.

The Phœnician merchants visited its coasts and established trading posts round about it in Africa, Sicily, Sardinia and Spain (§§ 50–52).

Greeks.

Soon the Greeks found it out and drew its people into the sphere of their life and culture. They planted permanent settlements in Sicily, established a line of cities on its southeastern coast and even founded colonies on its western shore whence they exchanged their goods and gave their civilization to its peoples (§§ 116–117). The foot of Italy was called Greater Greece, and a Greek empire sprang up about the Sicilian city of Syracuse (§ 249). The wars that shook the eastern world were felt in Italy; part of the Græco-Persian struggle was fought in Sicily (§ 176), the strength of the Athenian empire was broken by the disaster of Syracuse (§ 234). It is said that Alexander contemplated the conquest of Italy. We have seen how Sicily and Magna Græcia were regarded by the Carthaginians and Italians as their fair prey (§§ 328–331), and how Pyrrhus attempted in vain to carve out for himself an empire on Italian soil (§ 331). The series of circumstances which led the states of the east to draw the Romans into their political entanglements has already been referred to (§ 327). Thus, in turning to Italy, we turn not to a new and hitherto unknown land, but to one already attached to the larger historic world. Italy simply takes the central place; the former leaders become the followers; the west becomes the seat of the dynamo that supplies power to drive politics and civilization to higher achievements in a wider world.

333. Physical Features of Italy.—In its physical geography Italy combined the characteristics of both the orient and Greece (§ 85), having level and broad plains intersected by stretches of wild mountain country, girt about and bathed by the sea on every side. It may be divided into four zones or belts, three running side by side, the fourth placed straight across their top. The central of the three parallel belts is the great bow of the Apennine mountain range, some eight hundred miles long, the backbone and determining feature of all the rest. Starting far to the left at the head of the northwestern sea, it moves at first to the east, but soon swings to the south, broadening and rising as it advances, until, in the centre of Italy, its summits reach the height of more than nine thousand five hundred feet and it becomes a highland of mingled valley and mountain fifty miles wide. Thence it narrows and declines, as it sweeps toward the south and west, and is continued in the westward ranging mountains of Sicily and the projecting

The Four Zones

The Apennines.

highlands of North Africa, less than a hundred miles away. Parallel to this long Apennine bow, on either side of it, are the two belts of eastern and western coast-

The Eastern Slope.

land. The eastern belt in its upper and middle parts is narrow; the sea lies close to the mountains, which fall off steeply into it; the rivers are mountain torrents; harbors there are none, and the stormy winds of the Adriatic sweep along the inhospitable shores. To the south, as the mountains draw away, the plain widens out into a broad upland. The sea has broken into it from the south along the mountain-side and left a broad promontory gently descending into the Mediterranean to the

The Western Slope.

southeast. The western belt, occupying the concave side of the bow, has an exactly opposite character. Its upper and middle parts make a widening plain through which flow two considerable rivers, the Arno and the Tiber. The mountains slope off in gradual terraces to the sea;

The Northern Plain.

good harbors are found. Only in the lower portion, as the Apennines draw toward the southwest, does the plain narrow and at last disappear. The upper Apennines, in their eastern trend, form the southern boundary of the fourth belt, which lies east and west across the top of the other three. To the north of this belt runs the wall of the Alps, the western end of which is washed by the Mediterranean and its eastern slope by the head-waters of the Adriatic. Through the district thus marked out between the Alps and the Apennines flowed two rivers. Far in the west rose the Padus (Po), which gathered the mountain streams from south and north and swept in ever-increasing volume eastward to the Adriatic. From the northern Alps came down the Ath'e-sis (Adige) and reached the Adriatic not far north

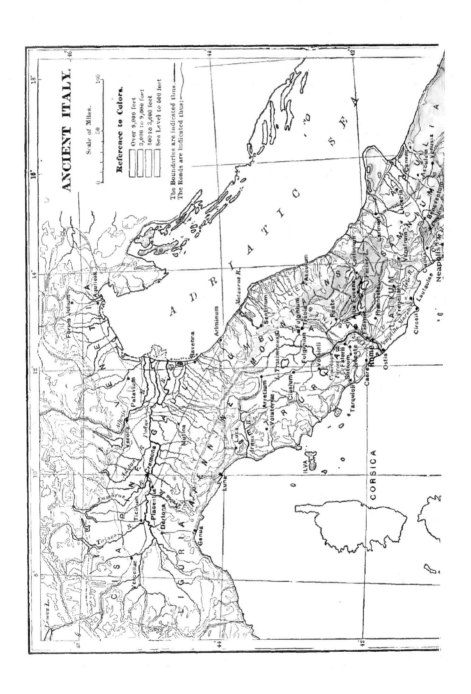

ANCIENT ITALY.

Scale of Miles.

Reference to Colors.

Over 9,000 feet
3,000 to 9,000 feet
500 to 3,000 feet
Sea Level to 500 feet

The Boundaries are indicated thus:
The Roads are indicated thus:

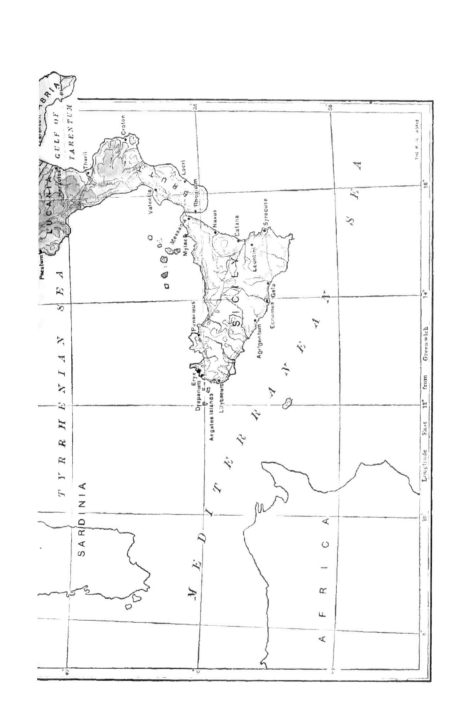

of the Po. Thus a rich and extensive basin was formed,
a little world in itself, cut off from the north by the Alps
and from the south by the Apennines. Entrance into it
from west and north was not easy, but in the east the
mountain streams pouring into the Adriatic had brought
down soil which they deposited in the sea, pushing it
steadily back until a broad and open pathway had been
made, through which outsiders might come from the
region of the Balkan peninsula. It was, perhaps, by this
approach that the Italian peninsula was entered and
settled by its historic inhabitants.

334. The Peoples of Italy.—History has preserved no
record of this incoming. Only a comparison of the languages spoken by the peoples reveals their relationship
The historically unimportant Ligurians, occupying the Ligurians
northwestern mountains about the Mediterranean, are
set apart as a separate people, as are also the Etruscans, Etruscans
a strong and progressive race, who filled the wide upper
plain on the inside of the Apennine bow from the mountains to the sea southward as far as the Tiber. The
great mass of the remaining peoples spoke the dialects of
a common speech which allies them to the historic inhabitants of the Balkan peninsula and Greece, the Indo-
European (§ 5). On the lowest extremity of the eastern Illyrians.
slope, Illyrians from across the sea had settled under the
name of the Iapygians in the districts of Apulia and
Calabria, while others of the same stock reached Italy at
the north and settled as the Ven'e-ti at the head of the
Adriatic. It was possibly in their van, and across the Italians.
sea where it is narrowest, that the Italian stock entered
their historic home. The rest of the peninsula was in
their possession at the dawn of history. Of them there

were several branches.   Of that in the lowlands of the
west and south the most famous was the Latin people
in the plain south of the Tiber; the inhabitants of Sicily
belonged to the same branch.   The mountaineers formed
another vigorous branch called, from their chief peoples, the Umbro-Sabellians.   The Umbrians lived in the
northern Apennines overlooking Etruria; the Sabellians
were split into many tribes occupying the mountain
valleys of the centre and south.   The most vigorous and
numerous stock among them was the Samnites.   The
northern plain of the Po was the seat of mixed populations, a kind of vestibule, perhaps, for peoples to enter
and mingle before pushing southward to permanent
homes.

335. **Influence of Italy's Geography on Its History.**—
Italy, thrust like a limb from the trunk of Europe down
into the Mediterranean, was given by its position an
important part to play in the Mediterranean world.
Like Greece, it was in the pathway of history advancing
westward.   Yet, unlike Greece (§ 86), it did not invite
and embrace its opportunity, but rather repelled it.   Its
eastern coast is inhospitable with forbidding mountains
and an absence of harbors.   To get at Italy you must

The West-
ern Door.
reach its western coasts; it faces the setting sun.   On that
side are the broad plains and the harbors   Hence, west-
ward-moving civilization was slow in getting round the
barrier; it lingered long on the southeastern shores and
in Sicily before moving up to the heart of the peninsula.
Yet it is evident that the power which was to move Italy
must be situated on its western side.

336. **The Problem of Defence.**—In spite of the grim
eastern shore, there was an abundance of easy approaches

to Italy. In the north, passes led down through the Alps,
to the valley of the Po. The long coast-line of the west

and south was open. This made a problem for Italy—
the problem of defence against attacks from without

which every political power that has held Italy has had to solve. How different was Greece in this respect. For Italy the solution of the problem depended on unity within and command of the sea.

337. Contrast of Highland and Plain.—But unity within Italy was made difficult by the opposition of highland and plain. The wide Apennine region was the home of vigorous tribes who envied the prosperity of the plain and sallied out from time to time to obtain their share in it—a proceeding which the plainsmen did not relish and from which they must defend themselves until the time came to settle once for all which should be master.

338. Origin of Rome.—Out of conditions such as these Rome emerged, a city on the bank of the Tiber, in the southern part of the western plain, equidistant from the sea and the mountains. It was made up of villages of Latin stock united by mutual necessities and interests in a common city-state. Its origin and early history are veiled in mists of myth and legend through which actual history vaguely glimmers. But, from the first, the chief interest for the student of ancient history centres in the relation of Rome to surrounding peoples in ever-widening circles. These varying relations make the framework about which gathers the stately structure of its brilliant history.

Its Historic Secret.

338a. The Grand Divisions.—The grand divisions of this period are therefore the following.

1. The Making of Rome, 1200(?)–500 B.C.
2. Rome's Defence against Her Neighbors, 500–390 B.C.

3. The Unification and Organization of Italy, 390–264 B C

4. The Struggle with Carthage for the Western Mediterranean, 264–200 B C.

5. Rome's Conquest of the East, 200–133 B C.

6. The Decline of the Roman Republic, 133–44 (27) B C.

7. The Roman Empire (Principate), 27 B.C –A D. 284.

8. The Later Roman Empire (Despotism), 284–395 A D.

9. The Breaking Up of the Roman Empire and the End of the Ancient World, A D 395–800

REVIEW EXERCISES. 1. Name the chief rivers of Italy and trace them on the map. **2. Make** a chart of the peoples of Italy, showing their relationship. **3. Draw** up a list of the early relations of Italy and the east, look up the references and discuss them in detail.

SELECT LIST FOR READING. 1. The Geography of Italy. How and Leigh, ch 1. **2. Italian Peoples.** How and Leigh, ch 2.

TOPICS FOR READING AND ORAL REPORT. 1. The Geography of Italy. Dionysius in Munro, p 2, Shuckburgh, ch. 2; Botsford, p. 15, Myres, ch. 1. **2. Italian Peoples.** Shuckburgh, ch. 3, Myres, ch. 2. **3. Divisions of Roman History.** Shuckburgh, ch. 1.

BIBLIOGRAPHY *

For bibliography for advanced students and teachers, see Appendix I

ABBOTT. *Roman Political Institutions* Ginn and Co. The best single book on the subject in moderate compass

BOTSFORD. *A History of Rome.* Macmillan Co. (To Charlemagne.) Well written and illustrated. The best book of its size covering the whole field

CARTER. *Religion of Numa* Macmillan Co. The best little book on the subject.

* For previous bibliographies, see §§ 5a, 80a.

FOWLER *The City State of the Greeks and Romans.* See § 89a.

FOWLER. *Social Life at Rome in the Age of Cicero* Macmillan. A charming book Useful.

HOW AND LEIGH *A History of Rome to the Death of Cæsar.* Longmans. Illustrated. Contains vivid characterizations and descriptions.

JOHNSTON. *The Private Life of the Romans.* Chicago Scott, Foresman and Co. A much more elaborate work than that of Wilkins

LAING *Masterpieces of Latin Literature.* Houghton, Mifflin and Co. A serviceable single volume of literary extracts with scholarly introductions.

MACKAIL. *Latin Literature.* Scribners. Of the same type as Murray's Greek Literature (§ 89a). A little above a beginner.

MOREY. *Outlines of Roman History.* American Book Co. A brief sketch, well organized, with useful helps.

MUNRO. *A Source Book of Roman History.* D. C Heath and Co An indispensable collection of historical materials covering a variety of phases of Roman life. English translations.

MYRES *A History of Rome* Rivingtons (To the death of Augustus)

PELHAM. *Outlines of Roman History.* Putnams. The best proportioned, compact and generally reliable summary in English.

PLUTARCH *Translation* by Dryden, edited by Clough 5 vols. Little, Brown and Co , or by Stewart and Long. 4 vols. Bohn.

SEIGNOBOS *History of the Roman People.* Holt. Covers the whole period. Picturesque, anecdotal, simply written.

SHUCKBURGH. *A History of Rome to the Battle of Actium.* Macmillan Co.

WILKINS. *Roman Antiquities* (History Primer). American Book Co. An excellent brief summary of the essentials.

WILKINS. *Roman Education.* Cambridge Univ. Press.

1. THE MAKING OF ROME

1200 B.C.(?)–500 B.C.

339. Its Geographical Position.—Rome lay on the south bank of the Tiber, the chief navigable river of the western slope. It skirted the Etrurian plain and opened a way into the highlands of the central and upper Apennines An easy ford near by the city was the natural

crossing from the Latin to the Etrurian country. These
facts made Rome a place where roads met, through
which traders passed, they gave it some *commercial*
importance. At the same time it was midway between
the sea and the mountains, far enough away from the one
to be protected from the sea-rovers that preyed upon commerce, and sufficiently distant from the other to have
timely warning of the raids of the mountaineers. The
city was also placed on a series of low hills, which fringed
the northern border of the Latin land; the rude fortifications on their summits were sufficient to guard the inhabitants against attack and to enable them to control the
land round about. Thus the city was not only commer-
cially important, but had an *independent* position. It
was central and yet isolated, in the midst of the plain and
yet secure from interference—an ideal site destined to
greatness. A river, a ford, a fortress—these were the
chief physical factors contributing to the making of Rome.

340. The Seven Hills.—Rome is said to have been
built on seven hills. The central and most important
one, called the Palatine, stood isolated. It was almost
square, with its corners turned to the four points of the
compass, and almost directly opposite the river ford.
Back of it and away from the river, standing side by side,
were other hills, called, respectively, the Cælian, the
Es'qui-line, the Viminal and the Qui'ri-nal. On their
eastern side they fell away to the plain. South of it,
overlooking the river, was the Aventine hill; north of it
the Cap'i-to-line, isolated and steep Across the river,
lying over against the ford, was the ridge called the Jani'-
cu-lum. In the narrow ravines and valleys between
these hills were the roads and open spaces which came

to be famous in history. Thus, between the Aventine and the Cælian ran the Appian Way; the Circus Maximus (where the public games were held) lay between the

The Forum. Aventine and the Palatine: the Forum (the market and

1 Arx
2 Temple of Jupiter Capitolinus
3 Temple of Ceres
4 Temple of Quirinus
5 Basilica Fulvia
6 Comitium
7 Temple of Portunus
8 Temple of Juno
9 Temple of Luna
10 Temple of Flora
11 Temple of Mercury

EARLY ROME.
＿＿＿Rome Quadrata
＿.＿.The Septimontium
.......Additions made by Servius

place of citizen-assembly) to the north of the Palatine; where the Tiber makes a great bend, the low stretch between it and the Capitoline, the Campus Martius (the "Field of Mars," where the army exercised).

341. Earliest Period.—This site had, in all probability, been occupied by men since the opening of the neolithic age; and at a time perhaps six hundred years before the

PLATE XXV

Ashurnatsirpal of Assyria   Trajan, Roman Emperor

TYPICAL SCULPTURED FIGURES

rule of the Tarquins it came into the possession of the Latins. What happened to the earlier inhabitants we do not know. If they were not extirpated altogether, they had fused with the Latins long before our knowledge begins. Nor do we know anything definite about the long six hundred years which followed, except that in this interval the Latins were influenced, slightly, it seems, by the Phœnicians, much more strongly, however, by the civilized peoples who settled first north (Etruscans) and then south (Greeks) of them.

342. Social and Political Organization.—In these circumstances progress was accelerated   The villagers in the vicinity of the Seven Hills formed a single city, Rome, to which now belonged all the land in the vicinity (Campagna).   Some families became rich, owning large estates.   In time their members stood as nobles (patricians) over the neighboring peasants, who had become their clients or serfs.   In all the families the father (*pater familias*) had power of life and death over its members, his wife and sons and unmarried daughters included; and with their discipline or offences the state had no concern whatever.   Groups of rich families bound together by intermarriages, and by the bonds of factional war, and claiming descent from a common ancestor, to whom they owed their common name, formed a clan or *gens*.   Of these as many as one hundred or one hundred and fifty appeared, varying, of course, in size and influence.   Examples are the gens Fabia, Cornelia and Claudia.   The members of the gen'tes were the patricians.   That portion of the population which did not belong to the gentes and was not dependent upon them remained free.   It is called the plebs.   The traders

The City-State.

Patricians.

The Gentes

Plebeians.

and artisans resident in Rome belonged to it, as did a body of small farmers who owned their own lands. As the power of the patricians increased the power of the ancient head of the state, the king, waned, and the power of his council of elders, called the senate, in which the nobles congregated, became paramount. There was, of course, a general assembly (*co-mit'i-a cur-i-a'ta*) of the citizens (*quir-i'tes*) to be considered, and from of old it had met for legislative and military purposes in *curiæ* (brotherhoods or phratries). Now this, too, was threatened by the power of the nobles, and in fact it ultimately ceased to be of any account and the curiæ, of which there were thirty, ceased to have any real function to perform; but before this occurred, Rome as we shall see in a moment, like the rest of La'ti-um, and for that matter all the lowlands as far south as the Greek city of Cumæ, near the bay of Naples, was seized by bands of Etruscan nobles and their retainers. The dynasty which occupied the town by the Tiber was that of the Tarquins, who came, perhaps, from Tarquinii, one of the chief Etruscan cities.

The Comitia Curiata

343. The Legends of Rome's Beginning.—About this natural and prosaic origin of Rome * the Romans wove a variety of picturesque stories which were preserved and put in order by Livy and other historians many centuries later. In these legends the Roman people were connected with Æneas, one of the heroes of Troy (§ 110), who wandered to Italy and married Lavinia, daughter of Latinus, king of Latium One of his descendants, Rhea, gave birth to twin sons, Romulus and Remus; their father was the god Mars. Shortly after

* The later Romans dated the founding of the city in 753 B C. Thus A.U.C (anno urbis conditæ, "in the year of the founding of the city," or "ab urbe condita," "from the founding of the city") corresponds to our A D. (Anno Domini, "in the year of the Lord").

their birth, their wicked uncle, the king, ordered them to be thrown into the Tiber, but the river yielded them up to a herdsman, who brought them up as his children On growing up, they discovered their real origin, killed their uncle and proceeded to found a city. A quarrel arising between them, Romulus killed his brother and became founder and king of the city, called Rome after his name He gave the city its laws and religion, invited all men desirous of change and advancement to become its citizens, and appointed one hundred of them senators In order to secure wives for his people, he proclaimed a festival and invited neighboring peoples to the spectacle; when they had gathered, on a signal his men seized their daughters and took them as wives A fierce war arising in consequence, Romulus defeated all his enemies except the Sabines, who were induced, by the intercession of the Roman women, their daughters, at the crisis of a hot battle, to make peace and join the new community. Romulus, not long after, was carried away into heaven. He was followed in the kingship by the wise and pious Sabine, Numa Pompilius, whose achievement it was to organize the religion and civilization of Rome His wife was a goddess, the nymph E-ge'ri-a, whom he was wont to meet and consult in a grove whence a spring flowed. Tullus Hostilius, a Roman, succeeded him, a warrior who fought with Alba Longa and overthrew the Albans In this war there were on one occasion three twin brothers in either army, the Roman Horatii and the Alban Curiatii, who agreed to fight a combat, the issue of which was to determine the war. The Horatii conquered, one brother surviving On his return home, his sister, who was betrothed to one of the slain Curiatii, lamented grievously This so enraged the victor that he slew her About to be put to death by the judges for this crime, he appealed to the people, who acquitted him. Tullus was followed by the Sabine, Ancus Marcius, a grandson of Numa, who won considerable victories over the Latins and added people and territory to the city Such, according to the legends, was the origin and early history of Rome.

344. Italy Makes Rome.—During all this time Rome was a city of Latium, the land of the Latins. The cities of Latium had long formed a league, and the Romans naturally formed part of it. The league had its centre

Latium and Its League.

the city of Alba Longa, where representatives of thirty cities met yearly, united in worship of the god, Jupiter, and deliberated on affairs of common interest. Thus an opportunity was offered Rome of taking part in the life of a larger world. Second, the various civilizing and progressive influences of the east had long been affecting the Italian communities of the west coast and creating a new and vigorous social and political life.

The Etruscan Development. Of all these communities, the Etruscans had been most capable of profiting by such influences. They had, at a very early period, expanded their borders southward to the Tiber and eastward to the Apennines; they had seats in the valley of the Po, and from the sea coast made voyages throughout the Tyrrhenian sea to Corsica and Sardinia The Phœnicians brought them the products of the oriental civilization, and the Greeks gave to them their own rich and splendid achievements in art and culture. Egyptian seals and Greek vases have been found in Etruscan graves. Etruscan art took such objects as models and developed skill in the making of weapons of war and objects of trade. The commerce of their cities grew; they **The Greek Influence.** became rich and powerful. As the Greeks began to settle in Italy, their merchants brought along with their wares the intellectual riches of the mother-country. From the Greek colonies Etruria learned the art of writing, the names and worship of Greek gods and Greek arts of life. **Etruscan Expansion and Rule of Rome.** The Etruscans were thus good exponents of the culture of the eastern Mediterranean world when the Tarquins seized Rome.

345. Etruscan Kings —During the reign of Ancus Marcius— the Roman legends go on to relate—there came to Rome from Tarquinii in Etruria a man whose name was Lucius Tarquinius Priscus It was said that on the journey to Rome an omen of his future greatness was given; an eagle flew down, took off his cap, circled about him and replaced it   He grew in wealth and influence and was appointed guardian of the king's children.   On the king's death he sought and obtained from the people election to the throne.   To strengthen his position he added one hundred men to the Senate.   He fought vic: toriously with Latins and Sabines; he laid out the Circus Maximus and exhibited games there; he began to wall the city, to drain its hollows by sewers and to lay out the space for a temple to Jupiter on the Capitoline Hill.   But the sons of Ancus Marcius, who sought revenge for having been supplanted by a foreigner, plotted against the king and brought about his murder.   They failed, however, to secure the throne.   A young man, Servius Tullius, a captive and slave, had been favored by the king and betrothed to his daughter. It is said that the king's attention had been drawn to him by a strange portent, as the boy lay asleep in the palace, his head suddenly flamed with fire, which disappeared when he awoke   On the king's murder, before it was widely known that he was dead, Servius assumed his duties and at last seized the throne and established himself firmly. He was a wise and vigorous ruler   Under him the Roman state was reorganized   He instituted the census, or classification of the people in classes and centuries on the basis of property, chiefly for purposes of war.   The citizens thus organized numbered eighty thousand.   He enlarged the city and surrounded it with a wall and a moat   After a long reign he was slain by Tarquinius, the son, or grandson, of Priscus, urged on to the crime by his wife, the daughter of Servius, who was eager for royal power   Tarquinius, called Superbus, "the proud," because of his haughty and unbending temper, ruled with energy and success.   He gained for Rome greater influence in the Latin league, warred with the mountaineers and won the city of Gabii. At home he made many improvements in the city; built the great sewer, erected seats in the Circus and began a splendid temple to Jupiter upon the area marked out by Priscus.   But a series of events followed which brought about his overthrow and the disappearance of kings from Rome

346. Growth under Etruscan Rule.—It is clear that under the Etruscan kings Rome entered upon a new career.   All sides of its inner and outer life received fresh impulse. But of their temples, fortifications and sewers little or nothing remains, since they were replaced at a later date by new constructions such as the Clo-a'ca Maxima which drained the Forum and the so-called walls of Romulus and Servius. The Roman power made itself felt in Latium. The headship of the Latin league fell into the hands of these kings. The extension of Etruscan power throughout the western plain contributed to the spread of commerce and trade. A larger share of these fell to Rome and brought increased wealth and culture from the east, as well as a greater population to take advantage of the larger opportunities

New Wealth.

347. Roman Religion.—Two spheres of Roman life, affected by the Etruscan domination, deserve special mention; the religious and the political organization. Roman religion was a very simple and practical affair, befitting a farmer-folk without culture. They believed themselves surrounded by spirits who were active everywhere in nature and in the affairs of men. These spirits dwelt in animals, in trees, in fountains and the like. The farm life had its special divine patrons, worshipped in rude festivals occurring at set times, sowing or harvest. By ceremonies suitable to the occasion—the procession of farmers with their farm animals around the fields, or a rustic feast with boisterous games and rough horse-play—the worshippers appeased the higher powers and secured their help in the growing and ripening of the crops. The farm-house had its deities—Vesta, the guardian of the hearth, and Janus, the spirit of the doorway. As life in the city supplanted life in country villages, these powers took up their home there, and their worship was organized. Some spirits became patrons

The Spirit World.

of private life, as the La'res, who were guardians of the families, and the Pe-na'tes, who presided over the provisions. There was still much indefiniteness as to the names and power of the spirits. The Romans thought more of what they did than of what they were called and how they looked. Yet, as the public life became more regular, the more important gods came to have special names and a suitable worship (§ 100). So we have Jupiter, *The Great Gods.* the sky god, Diana, the forest goddess, Ceres, the mother of agriculture, Venus, goddess of fruitfulness and love, Mars, god of war, Neptune, of the sea, Vulcan, of fire and mechanic arts, Juno, goddess of motherhood and patron of families and clans. The world of the dead was regarded as beneath the earth and had its deity, Dis-pa'ter. King Numa stood in the tradition as the prime organizer of the Roman state-worship of the various gods. To him was ascribed the appointment of *Religious Officials.* the chief body of priests, called pontifices, at the head of which was the pontifex maximus; of the Vestal virgins, six in number, who kept the fire ever burning in the shrine of Vesta—the hearth goddess of the state; of the flamens (lighters) who kindled the fire on the altar and performed the sacrifice to the great gods, Jupiter, Mars and Quirinus; of the fet'i-a'les who declared war by hurling a spear into the enemy's territory and solemnized peace by swearing on a sacred stone brought from the temple of Jupiter Fe-ret'ri-us and thus pledging the faith (*fides*) of the people; and finally of the Salii who guarded the shield of Mars which had fallen from heaven, it was said. As a matter of fact no one knows how or when these sacred offices originated. The sentiment of law and order, which was so characteristic of Roman life everywhere, had full sway in religious matters and led to a very careful arrangement of the relations between gods and men. Though the Romans were not on familiar terms with their gods—they feared rather than loved them—and did not imagine them beautiful beings, as did the Greeks (§ 112), yet they believed one thing firmly and strongly about them, that they would be as honest and as faithful to their agreements as were their worshippers. Thus, attention was directed to learning the terms on which the gods would live at peace with men and prosper them; and having learned this, having come to terms with the gods, the Romans faithfully and scrupulously kept their part of the contract and expected in turn that the gods would do their part. Honest fulfilment of definite obligation, this was man's duty toward the gods. This made the old Roman strong and strenuous in his daily work at home and abroad.

348. Etruscan Influence on Religion.—The Etruscan period brought in new gods and new religious forms.

Minerva.　The most important new deity was Minerva, goddess of wisdom, patron of trade and commerce. New temples were built; particularly the state temple on the Capitoline, where Jupiter, Juno and Minerva were worshipped together and thus became the chief deities of the city.

Omens.　But the principal result of Etruscan influence was to aid Roman religion to determine more clearly the will of the gods by a system of omens. An "omen" was an indication of what the gods wanted or how they felt; it could be deliberately watched for, or it could be a seemingly chance event in the natural world, such as the actions of animals—a rat running across the path, for example, a case of epilepsy or a thunder-storm. The

Etruscans were experts at devising means to this end. The meaning of such things had been studied, and a system of laws discovered, by which the gods revealed themselves to the one who knew how to interpret these signs, called *auspicia*. Such a development of their religion was natural and acceptable to the Romans and became an essential part of it. Officials, called augurs and ha-rus'pi-ces, were set apart to study, put in order and practise this system, to learn and interpret the auspices. Thus the religion became more and more rigid and formal, yet also more definite and concrete. Its name indicates its character—*religio*—that which "binds" gods and men to keep their word, to fulfil a contract, the terms of which are known and acknowledged by both parties. The corresponding word for man's attitude toward the gods—the honest doing of duty as prescribed in definite law and ritual—was *pietas*.

The story went that once the Sibyl visited Tarquin the Proud and offered to sell him nine books by which the will of the gods could be interpreted The price was high and the king refused She burned three of them and offered him the rest for twice the price. Again he refused. She burned three more and again doubled the price for the three that remained The king reflected and finally paid what she demanded. These three Sibylline Books came to be most precious possessions of the state and were consulted at critical moments in its history. *The Sibylline Books.*

349. Etruscan Political Influence on Rome.—Roman political organization underwent important changes in the Etruscan period. As these kings were foreign conquerors, they could deal with the political arrangements of the state as they liked. There was need of change. During Rome's progress in commercial and political importance, while the original basis of citizenship (§ 342) had remained, the population of the city had greatly

The Army Reorganized. altered. A rearrangement, ascribed to King Servius Tullius (§ 345), brought the people into the service of the community by making them a part of the army. This was done by making the possession of property the sole condition for military service. An entire reorganization of the military arrangements of the state was thus made necessary. A larger and more efficient army was created, the strength of the state increased and the power of the king heightened by the devotion of the people, thus honored by him. It cannot be proved that a king named Servius Tullius ever lived, much less that he reordered the army in this fashion. Still we know that an arrangement of the soldiers in centuries on the basis of property dates from at least the fifth century B.C.

350. The Classes and the Centuries.—The traditional account of the arrangements of Servius, as preserved by later Roman writers

The Early Roman Army. and interpreted by modern scholars, is as follows: The very richest of the people were appointed to the cavalry (equites or knights) This cavalry force was divided into eighteen companies called "centuries" or hundreds The rest of the people made up the infantry They were organized into five "classes," grading down according to property. Each class * was made up of a certain number of centuries The first class, composed of men whose wealth was estimated at one hundred thousand asses,† had eighty centuries of fully armed soldiers; the second class, men worth seventy-five thousand asses, the third class, men worth fifty thousand asses, and the fourth class, men worth twenty-five thousand asses, had each twenty centuries and were armed in less complete fashion; the fifth class, men worth

* The term "class" here has the meaning of "calling out," *i e.,* "Levy."
† The *as*, of bronze, was the unit of value in Roman currency. In the time of Servius the property was in land; the estimate in money value is the work of a later time Compare the similar organization of Solon (§ 159).

eleven thousand asses, in thirty centuries, were slingers The land-less formed one century Four other centuries were made up of artificers and trumpeters The cavalry and the men of military age in the first five classes constituted the army in the field. The infantry was drawn up in two bodies, each called a *Legio* (legion) These were made up of men of the first three classes; the fourth and fifth classes supplied the light armed troops. The legion was drawn up six men deep with a front of 500 men; with its light armed troops, there-fore, it numbered 4,200 Two such legions made up of those be-tween 17 and 46 (juniors) constituted the field army Two other legions, held at home to protect the city and made up of men past military age, raised the total military force of Rome to 16,800 men

351. The Roman Reaction.—It seemed as though the influence of the Etruscan kings among the people and their pre-eminence in Latium would secure to them a long and firm hold upon Rome. But it did not so turn out. The noble families grew stronger; the sentiment of nationality opposed the rule of strangers; at last the Etruscan rulers were driven out, with them went the power of the kingship itself. The process was, no doubt, much the same as in Greece (§ 106). Remains of the kingly dignity survived only in the religious sphere. The *rex sacrorum*, "king of sacred things," became the highest priestly representative of the state in certain non-political religious exercises, and the *Regia*, "royal palace," was turned into a holy place where priests dwelt and sacri-fices were performed. The aristocracy took control of affairs and Rome became an aristocratic state. The date traditionally set for this change was 509 B.C. The transformations brought about in connection with it, both in the life of Rome and in its relations to Italy, are so important as to make it a turning-point in Roman history, the beginning of a new period.

Fall of Etruscan Kings and End of the Kingship.

352. **Legend of the Expulsion.**—The Roman legends describe the growing arrogance of Tarquin the Proud and his family, under which the Romans were impatient but submissive. Finally a gross act of violence was inflicted by Tarquin's son upon Lucretia, wife of the noble Collatinus; under the shame of it she killed herself in the presence of her husband and his friends   The king was at the time absent from the city, waging war   They raised a rebellion, the gates of the city were closed against him, and the kingship was formally abolished by the citizens.

REVIEW EXERCISES. 1. How did the Tiber and the Palatine affect the early history of Rome? 2. What is meant by gens, patrician, plebeian, omen, religio, pietas, equites? 3. What was the traditional date of the founding of Rome? of the expulsion of the kings?

COMPARATIVE STUDIES. 1. In what was the early organization of Rome (§ 342) like and unlike that of the Greek communities of the Middle Age (§§ 105–107)? 2. Compare the origin of Rome with that of Athens (§ 107). 3. Compare the geography of Greece and Italy and show how differently the history of each land was thus affected. 4. Compare the reforms of Servius with those of Solon (§ 159).

SELECT LIST FOR READING. 1. Sources and Trustworthiness of Early Roman History. How and Leigh, pp 34–37. 2. The Reforms of Servius in Some Detail, with a Diagram. How and Leigh, pp. 28, 46–47. 3. The Early Roman Legends and Their Value. How and Leigh, pp 34–37. 4. Origin and Growth of Rome, the City. How and Leigh, pp. 37–39 (see map, p 38). 5. The Institutions of Early Rome. How and Leigh, pp 40–45.

TOPICS FOR READING AND ORAL REPORT. 1. Sources and Trustworthiness of Early Roman History. Munro, pp. 3–5; Shuckburgh, pp 54–60; Myres, pp. 38–41; Seignobos, pp. 33–35   2. Stories of the Kings from Romulus to Ancus. Plutarch, Romulus and Numa; Munro, pp. 66–68; Seignobos, pp. 15–20. 3. Stories of the Etruscan Kings. Seignobos, pp. 21, 27. 4. The Reforms of Servius in Some Detail, with a Diagram. Munro, pp. 45–47; Shuckburgh, pp. 43–49; Myres, pp. 56–63; Abbott, pp. 20, 21. 5. The Curiæ and the Comitia Curiata. Abbott, pp. 18–20. 6. Sanitary Conditions of Ancient Rome. Lanciani, Ancient Rome in the Light of Recent Discoveries, pp 53–73. 7. The House of the Vestals. Lanciani, pp. 134–177. 8. The Auspices. Botsford, Roman Assemblies, pp. 100–118.

2.—ROME'S DEFENCE AGAINST HER NEIGHBORS

500-390 B C

353. The New Government.—The growing power of the noble houses had resulted in the overthrow of the kingship. Into the place of the monarchy stepped the aristocracy, to whom fell the organization and conduct of the state. They occupied the offices, made and administered the laws and determined the policy. Two officials, called *prætors* (later consuls), were appointed for the administration. In taking office they were given the *imperium*, which was equivalent to the possession of kingly powers; they led the armies, pronounced judgment and performed the chief public religious services. But the aristocracy had no idea of substituting new kings for the old. The powers of the consuls were carefully limited They were elected for one year only; they must be aristocrats; their powers were equal and hence each could nullify the acts of the other. When, however, unity of command was necessary, a dictator was nominated by the consuls and for a term of at most six months he had absolute power over both citizens and soldiers. He nominated a master of horse to exercise under him the command of the cavalry. The consuls also appointed assistants (quæstors) to help them in collecting the revenues and in searching out foul crimes. An important change took place in the citizen body. The army, as reorganized in the centuries attributed to Servius (§ 350), may have helped the aristocracy in accomplishing the revolution; it was now more than ever necessary in maintaining the state. Very naturally, therefore, it was the most important body of the people; all its members became active citizens and were organized as a new assembly for the election of consuls and the making of laws. It was called the *co-mit'i-a cen-tu'-ria'ta* and soon put the old curiate assembly (§ 342) in the shade. The

Senate

latter continued to meet, but was insignificant. The senate was the real power in the new state. It was composed entirely of aristocrats. It practically dictated the election of consuls, determined their policy and indicated what laws should be passed by the people.

354. Difficulties with Neighbors.—The dangers that confronted the new government were sufficiently alarm-

With the Latins

ing. With the passing of the monarchy, the Latin cities rejected the leadership of Rome; indeed, it is probable that they also put off Etruscan domination and set up for themselves in the same fashion as did Rome. The rivalry thus created might have proved disastrous had not a new danger driven them back to the old alliance. This was the invasion of the mountain tribes, long held in leash by the strong Etruscan power in Latium. The Latin league was said to have been re-established by

With the Mountaineers.

Spurius Cassius in 493 B.C. Thereupon, Rome led the plainsmen out against the invading mountaineers. From the east the Sabines and Hernici were advancing, from the south the Æqui and Volsci. But the Hernici were secured as allies, and thus the eastern and southern invaders were separated. Yet the conflict was long and trying. From time to time the hillsmen swept down to the very gates of Rome, raiding and burning the fields and homesteads.

355. With the Etruscans.—An even fiercer struggle was forced by the Etruscans, who would not willingly

yield up their hold on Rome and Latium. We have
rumors of a struggle in which Rome succumbed for a time
to the superior strength of Lars Por'se-na of Clusium;
of another in which Aruns, his son, was defeated by the

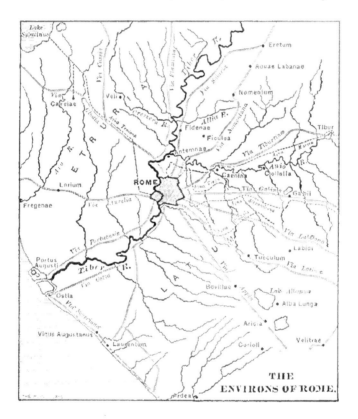

THE
ENVIRONS OF ROME.

combined forces of Cumæ and the Latins; and of still
a third in which the Fabian *gens* fought alone against Veii
on behalf of Rome. Still the Romans gradually got the
better of their antagonist, owing not more to their own
valor than to the general decline of the Etruscan power,

Decline of
Etruria.

which was being attacked on all sides.   Thus in 474 B.C.
the fleet of Etruria was destroyed in the harbor of Cumæ
by Hieron of Syracuse—a blow which apparently carried
with it the loss of the Tyrrhenian sea; and a generation
later the settlements in Capua and its neighborhood fell
before the invading Campanians.   Moreover, a new enemy in the north, the Celts (Gauls), was pushing down
upon them; it drove them out of the Po valley and compelled them to stand on the defensive.   In this situation
they could not concentrate their waning strength on
Rome.   At last Veii, a strong Etruscan city, situated a
few miles to the north, fell before a Roman assault
(396 B.C.).   The Romans advanced into the heart of
Etruria and took possession of the southern half of the
land.

Capture of
Veii.

356. The Legends of These Struggles.—Many stories
of heroic exploits were told about these early wars of
Rome with its neighbors:

1. The
Etruscan
Wars.

When the gates of the city had been shut against him, Tarquin the
Proud immediately set about recovering his power.   At first a plot
was formed within Rome among the noble youth who felt that they
were under restraint in the new conditions.   But just as they were
about to spring their trap, they were betrayed by a slave who over-
heard their treasonable communings.   Even though the sons of the
consul, they were not saved from summary execution inflicted under
their father's direction.   Whereupon Tarquin, having solicited aid
from the cities of Etruria, came against Rome with an army from
Veii and Tarquinii.   In the battle, Brutus, the consul, and Aruns,
Tarquin's son, found death in single combat.   Help was then sought
by Tarquin from Lars Porsena, king of the powerful city of Clusium, who led down from the north a mighty host against Rome.
He would have forced a passage over the Sublician bridge had not a
brave warrior, Horatius Cocles, supported by two companions, held
the entrance against the enemy, never retiring until the Romans cut

Porsena.

down the bridge behind him; then plunging into the Tiber he swam safely back to his friends   Porsena brought the city low by a blockade; he was persuaded to give up his hostile endeavors only through the heroic act of Mucius, who, in disguise, entered the Etruscan camp in order to kill the king.   By a mistake he killed the king's secretary and, when arrested and brought before Porsena, he declared that there were three hundred other Roman youth, like himself, sworn to kill the king   In proof of his determination, he thrust his right hand into the fire that was lighted for the sacrifice   Hence he was afterward called Scæv'o-la, "the left-handed "   Porsena, moved with admiration and fear, dismissed the youth unharmed   Soon he made peace and retired.

But the people of Veii continued to war with Rome, harassing them with frequent raids.   On one occasion, the noble family of the Fabii offered to proceed against them and conduct the war.   So they marched out three hundred and six strong amid the prayers and praises of the people.   Arrived at a strong place at the river Crem'e-ra, they fortified it, and for a time fought the Veientes with great success. But, at last, growing confident and careless, they were ambushed by the enemy and cut off.   Only one of them, and he a child, was left to represent his family.   A few years after, peace for forty years was declared between the two states.   Then the war broke out again with the going over of Fi-de'næ, a Roman colony, to Veii.   In the battle that followed, Aulus Cornelius Cossus slew, with his own hand, Tolumnius, king of Veii, and hung up the royal spoils beside those dedicated by Romulus in the temple of Jupiter Feretrius Not long after, Fidenæ was taken by storm.   But the war continued with varying success, until the other Etruscan cities decided to give no more help to Veii.   Then the Romans resolved to lay siege to the city.   For ten years their armies lay before it, but the city was defended with vigor   In despair the Romans sought an oracle from Delphi (§ 128), and were told that victory depended on letting out the waters of the Alban lake   When this was done, Marcus Furius Ca-mil'lus, the dictator, solemnly invited Juno, the goddess of Veii, to abandon the doomed city and come to Rome; then the assault was made and Veii fell.

News came to the Romans that thirty Latin cities had entered into alliance against them under the leadership of Octavius Mamil-

The Fabii

Siege of Veii.

2 The Latin Wars

ius It was said that Tarquin the Proud, now an old man, had in-
stigated this movement and was present in the hostile army. So great
was the terror of the Romans, that now, perhaps for the first time,
they appointed a dictator who superseded the consuls in carrying on

Battle of Lake Regillus. the war. The armies met at Lake Regillus, and the battle was long
and fierce. The supporters of Tarquin charged with great fury. In
the thick of the fight, twin heroes, mounted on white horses, were
seen leading on the Romans. Under their inspiration the leader of
the enemy was slain and his army routed Strange to say, immediately after the battle, the heroes disappeared and were seen at
Rome with foaming horses, bearing the news of the victory. They
were soon recognized as the twin gods, Castor and Pollux, and a
temple was built in their honor by the fountain in Rome where they
appeared Soon after, the Latins made peace and entered into a
league with the Romans.

3. Wars with the Hill-Folk. In one of the many wars with the mountain tribes the Roman
army had been surrounded by the Æqui and was in danger of de-
struction. News was brought to Rome Hope was found only in
the appointment, as dictator, of the first citizen of the state, Lucius
Cincin-natus. Quinctius Cincinnatus The messengers found him at work cultivating his little farm of four acres across the Tiber. He wiped the
sweat and dust from his face and, just as he was, received the congratulations of the messengers and their announcement of his appointment The desperate situation was explained, he came into
the city, raised an army, defeated the enemy, and delivered his
countrymen. Sixteen days from the time of receiving his appointment he gave it up and returned to his farm.

Coriolanus. Caius Marcius, surnamed Cor'i-o-la'nus, from his valor at the capture of the city of Corioli, incurred the hatred of the plebeians by
his arrogant behavior and was condemned He retired to the
Volsci, and, being kindly received by them, became their leader.
Led by him the Volsci brought the Romans to the brink of ruin
He took his stand a short distance from the city and devastated the
country far and wide All overtures for peace were rejected by the
general, until his mother and wife, leading his children, came to him.
As he rose to embrace his mother, she reproached him with his
treachery to his native land, saying, "Before I receive your embrace,
let me know whether I have come to an enemy or to a son." These

words and the lamentations of the women overcame his resolution
He withdrew his army and Rome was saved.

357. Division of Powers among New Officials.—In
the centuriate army, if not in the centuriate assembly,
the middle-class farmers, who formed the most considerable element in the plebs, and who lived for the most
part in the city of Rome along with the plebeian artisans
and traders, were obviously so numerous and indispensable that they did not long endure their exclusion from
the government. During the troubled years of the fifth
century B C., to hold its course successfully between the
ambitions of individual nobles and the demands of the
aggressive plebeians was no easy task for the aristocratic
government. The account of the events, which was
handed down from these early times, has sadly mixed
up the activities of the patricians in both these directions.
But it is clear that with the increase of public business
new magistracies were created whose very existence
weakened the power of the consuls by distributing it
among other officials. The most important of these Censors.
officials were the two *censors*, whose duty it was to keep a
roll of the citizens, to decide as to the political status of
each citizen and to determine the taxes each should pay.
They supervised public and private morals; indeed, the
censorship was a kind of national conscience, deciding
as to what was good or bad citizenship and punishing
breaches of good order. Two *quæstors* already existed Quæstors
to have charge of the public treasury; they received and
paid out money on the order of the senate. Two other
quæstors were now elected to perform similar duties with
respect to the military chest. Two *æ'diles* were elected by
the plebeians to care for the temple (*æ'des*) of Diana on

the Aventine and other popular shrines. A little later two others—the so-called curule ædiles, were chosen by the people to look after public buildings and streets and preserve order and decency at all public festivals. Thus, important functions were performed, but not by the con-

suls. At the same time, whenever anyone seemed likely to be rising too high in the state and aiming at supreme power, the government made away with him. We are told of the ambitions and the fall of Spurius Cassius, of Spurius Mælius and of Coriolanus,

As the story goes, the consul Spurius Cassius, who had deserved well of the Roman people by bringing the Latins back into union with Rome, devised a scheme for dividing certain conquered lands equally among the Romans and the Latins. This excited grave disturbances within the state, and the patricians tried to stir up the people against him. He, in his turn, sought to gain them to his side by refunding to them certain moneys which rightfully belonged to them. But they suspected him of aiming at royal power and refused the bribe. As soon as he went out of office, he was condemned and put to death.

358. Growing Power of the Plebeians.—It seemed as if the government had nothing to fear from the plebeians, since all powers were in the hands of the patricians. But the plebeians could not fail to have their part in Rome's new wealth and importance. Some of them grew rich, and all were necessary in the wars which the state was waging. Indeed, they found themselves suffering most from the hardships which the wars brought with them. The raids of the mountaineers bore hard on the poorer farmers who could not care for their fields while fighting in the armies. The chains of debt and slavery hung the more heavily about them and their families. The patricians had no mercy upon them. The aristocratic government administered the law with merciless severity to suit the privileged class   When this yoke became unendurable, the plebeians rose in rebellion. Of their uprising nothing is known except the result— that in 471 B C. four tribunes of the plebs were chosen, one apparently as the leader of each of the four tribes (tribus) into which the urban population of Rome was at that time divided   The electorate consisted of the plebeians; and, in order to protect their officials against the magistrates, who were patricians, they consecrated to the infernal gods by a solemn curse anyone in private or official position who injured them or interfered with them in their work.   Such a person could be slain with impunity, and the tribunes themselves were obligated to have him thrown from the Tarpeian rock.   The work of the tribunes was in the first place to protect individuals who appealed to them against the injurious action of the magistrates; and that they might be at hand when needed they sat by day on a long bench in the market-place (forum), while their houses had to be open at all times to suppliants and they could not leave the city overnight. Outside the city they were powerless, and within it they could act only when appealed to personally.   Their work in the second place was to serve as the executive officials of the assembly of the plebeians which elected them. This was organized in such a fashion that the tribes were the voting groups.   Hence it was called the *comitia tributa*.   In each tribe every man's vote was equal to every other and the majority of votes determined the vote of the tribe.

Rebellion (471 B C).

Plebeian Tribunes.

The Comitia Tributa.

359. Number of Tribunes Increased.—The tribes did not long remain four in number.   At some point in the

next twenty years sixteen new tribes were organized in
the district lying in the immediate vicinity of Rome—the

so-called rustic tribes.   Since each of these received its
name from a *gens*, the probability is that in it lay the
estates of the interrelated noble families of which the
gens was formed, and that the essential feature of the
change is the admission of the clients or serfs to the assembly of the plebeians.   Henceforth, there were only
patricians and plebeians in Rome.   At the same time,
probably, the number of tribunes was raised from four to
ten, so that henceforth each pair of tribes had one tribune.
There was nothing to exclude the patricians from the comitia tributa, but it is only natural that they at first disdained
to attend its meetings, and that at a later time attempts
were made to exclude them, without success, however.

The organization of the "masses" (plebeians) in the

comitia tributa under the leadership of tribunes is the
most striking feature in the constitutional growth of
Rome.   The natural outcome of such an uprising, and
the one regularly reached in the cities of Greece (§ 137),
was either that the aristocracy suppressed it and continued to govern as before, or that it overturned the government and substituted a tyranny for the rule of the nobles.

360. Increasing Power of the Tribunes.—In Rome,
on the other hand, the temper of the people and the political sagacity of the senate prevented such extremes, and
the outcome was that the revolution was recognized, its
meetings tolerated, its officials allowed to do their work,
not without interference doubtless, but none the less ef-
fectively.   No tyranny issued in Rome, but the power of
the tribunes collectively speedily became tyrannical in
urban affairs.   The order and circumstances of the rise

of the tribunate are not known: we are simply told that
from interfering with the magistrates in their harsh treatment of the citizens individually, they acquired the right
to veto proposals for new, and possibly harsh, laws made
by the magistrates to the comitia centuriata; and since
all laws were required to be presented and enforced by
the magistrates, the tribunes became thus masters of
the sovereign assembly. The senate chamber, into which
only members and magistrates were admitted, was at first
closed to the tribunes, but they drew their bench to the
door of the building—no one daring to interfere with
them—and listened to the discussions from without; and
after a time they went so far as to draw it into the
chamber itself and to interpose their veto on the propositions laid by the magistrates before their advisers. At
this stage the only thing which prevented the tribunes
from controlling Rome was the fact that the senate had
already made the tribunes its own tools.

361. The Senate: Plebeians Admitted.—This was possible through the fact that the senate had ceased to be
an exclusively patrician body. It was recruited from
ex-magistrates, who in turn were elected by the comitia
centuriata. In this assembly the plebeians had always
had a considerable representation though not enough to
overcome the majority of centuries which was controlled
by the patricians. Besides, the elections were subject
to the veto of the senate. Clearly, it was the sagacity
and patriotism of the senate which made possible the
admission of plebeians to the magistracies and to its
own membership.

362. Reorganization of the Army.—The fact was that
in the first half of the fourth century B.C., owing to the

The Three
Lines and
the Mani-
ples.

stress of the foreign wars, the organization of the army
was changed, and instead of the solid phalanx of spearmen ranged in ranks according to wealth and equipment,
there came the distinctively Roman formation by lines
(*hastati, principes and triarii*) and maniples. Henceforth,
a man's position and value were determined solely by his
skill and experience. In other words, the army became
a democracy, the rules of its iron discipline, to which the
patricians were subject like the others, being the equivalent of the laws in a constitutional state. The comitia
of centuries did not become at the same time a comitia
of maniples; but the army and the assembly were so
closely associated in men's thinking that merit and
distinction acquired by humble persons in war could not
be ignored at elections. Hence distinguished plebeian
soldiers were elected officers and generals, and at the
expiry of their terms were enrolled in the senate, which
came in consequence to consist of *patres et conscripti*.

363. Plebeian Gains.—A plebeian was elected general for the first time in 400 B.C., but after 366 B.C. one
consul was regularly, and the second not infrequently,

Plebeians
Are Elected
to Magis-
~acies.

a plebeian. During the second half of this century
plebeians got elected to the dictatorship, censorship,
prætorship and curule ædileships, and at its close in
300 B.C. they were admitted to the priestly colleges by the
Lex Ogulnia. They probably formed a large part of the
senate at this date, so that this body now represented
not the patricians or the plebeians, but a new class formed
by their matrimonial and social fusion—the so-called
office-holding nobility, and it was to this altered senate
that the tribunes became subservient.

The increase in the powers of the tribunate had been

accompanied by an increase in popular rights. In the first place (451 B.C.) there came the codification of the law which, besides facilitating business, limited the caprice of the magistrates in conducting trials and inflicting penalties.

364. The Decemvirs and the Law of the Twelve Tables. —A commission of ten men, the decemviri, was appointed to draw up a code which was later known as the law of the Twelve Tables and became the foundation of the Roman legal system. The procedure was the same as that of the appointment of the lawgivers in Greece (§ 136) and was probably copied from that. The old magistracy, the consuls and even the tribunes, ceased to be; the decemviri were given the entire direction of the state. They were to be elected yearly. But after two years the experiment did not succeed and the old administrative officers with the tribunes returned.

Codification of the Law.

Some of the laws of the Twelve Tables are as follows:

One who has confessed a debt or against whom judgment has been pronounced shall have thirty days in which to pay it.

Unless he pays the amount of the judgment, or some one in the presence of the magistrate interferes in his behalf (as *vindex*), the creditor is to take him home and fasten him in stocks or fetters. He is to fasten him with no less than fifteen pounds' weight or, if he choose, with more. [After he has been produced in court on three market days and no one has appeared to help him, let the creditors on the third occasion] cut him into pieces. Should they cut off more or less than their several shares the division is none the less legal.

Its Brutal and Formal Spirit.

If a father sells his son three times, the son shall be free from the power of the father.

Whenever a contract or conveyance is made, as it is specified by word of mouth, so let it be binding.

(The owner of the land) must take care of the road. If he does not pave it, (the one having the right of way) may drive his team where he pleases.

If a man maims a limb (of another), unless some agreement is arrived at, he shall be subject to retaliation (*i e.*, his limb shall be broken).

Women shall not scratch their cheeks or inflict any wound (on themselves) on account of a funeral (*i.e.*, not show excessive grief).

If a patron defrauds his client, let him be accursed.

365. The Lex Valeria.—More important still in this respect was the Lex Valeria of 301 B.C., by which all citizens were guaranteed the right of appeal from the judicial decisions of the magistrates when the death penalty, scourging or a fine exceeding thirty cattle and two sheep was involved.   Strictly this made the tribunate no longer necessary, but it was indispensable to the senate for the control of rebellious magistrates and was retained—to become later on the scourge of its master.   After 301 B.C. all greater crimes were turned over to the quæstors, who brought them for trial to the comitia centuriata, while the tribunes served to impeach and prosecute political offences.   The comitia centuriata was accordingly the chief judicial and electoral assembly at Rome. It could legislate still, but did so infrequently since this power was acquired in 287 B.C. by its less cumbrous rival the comitia tributa.

The Victory of the People over the Magistrates.

366. Further Gains of the Plebeians.—The way for the equalization of the resolutions (plebiscita) of the tribal assembly with the laws of the centuriate assembly had been paved by the growth of the power of its executive, the tribunate, and by the fusion of the plebeians and patricians.   The process, moreover, was aided by the partial loss of veto power over election and legislation which the senate sustained when in 339 B C. (Lex Publilia) it was required to give its approval in advance of popular action.

Plebiscita Become Laws.

The final step was taken in 287 B C. when the "masses" rose up and, seizing the Janiculum, held it against the government. They were suffering from the malpractices of the money-lenders, which various laws against usury had failed to check. The rich city men had much influence in the centuriate assembly because of their wealth, but were at a disadvantage in the tribal assembly in that they voted with the city multitude in four only of the tribes. What the "masses," who were obviously the peasants, wanted and what they got through their "secession" was an alleviation of debt, the concession of full legislative power to the comitia tributa and the abolition of the veto power of the senate. With this the constitution of the matured republic was practically complete

The Secession of the Plebs.

367. The Traditional Series of Laws.—The later Roman traditional story has arranged this struggle of the aristocracy with their opponents in the state in a series of legal enactments secured at specific times under known magistrates. While, probably, the progress was in reality much more irregular and uncertain, this arrangement has value as showing how the Romans thought of the struggle between the patricians and plebeians. It is as follows:

509 B C. The right of Appeal was carried through the comitia centuriata by Valerius Poplicola (Lex Valeria).

494 B.C. The First Secession of the plebeians and the appointment of tribunes.

Livy (§ 491) tells* how the plebeians, driven to despair by their debts and the unjust exactions of the military service, rose in revolt and marched in a body to the Sacred Mount, beyond the Anio river, three miles from the city. Here they threatened to found a new city. Then

* II, 32 f.

the senate yielded and sent as an ambassador to the plebeians Menenius Agrippa, a man acceptable to them He told them the following fable: "At a time when the members of the human body did not, as at present, all unite in one plan, but each member had its own scheme and its own function, the other parts were provoked at seeing that the fruits of all their care, of all their toil and service, were applied to the use of their stomach, and that the stomach meanwhile remained at ease and did nothing but enjoy the pleasure provided for it. Whereupon they conspired together that the hand should not bring food to the mouth, nor the mouth receive it, if offered, nor the teeth chew it. While they wished by these harsh measures to subdue the stomach through hunger, the members themselves and the whole body were reduced to the last stage of decay. From this it appeared that the office of the stomach was not confined to slothful indolence; that it not only received nourishment, but supplied it to the others, conveying to every part of the body that blood on which depend our life and vigor by distributing it equally through the veins after having brought it to perfection by digestion of the food." Applying this fable to the present case, the plebeians saw that their interests and those of the patricians were identical. A reconciliation was made between the two orders upon the basis that the plebeians should have officers of their own, known as tribunes, invested with inviolable privileges, who should protect them against the consuls, and that it should be unlawful for any patrician to hold this office.

471 B C. The Publilian law (of Publilius Volero) gave the assembly of the plebeians a legal status and the tribune the right to propose resolutions for adoption there.

451 B.C. The decemvirs were appointed

Livy tells* the story of the decemvirs in the following manner:

368. The Decemvirs.—As the patricians alone had knowledge of the laws which they interpreted to their own liking, no plebeian got justice before the magistrates. The constant disputing about the laws was brought to an end by an agreement that they be published. First commissioners were sent to Greece to bring back a report of its laws and customs. When these had returned and set

* III, 32 *f.*

forth the Greek codes of law, the people decided they would appoint no magistrates of any kind for one year, but intrust the entire government to ten men, known as decemvirs, who should administer the state and compile the laws of Rome   The leader of the decemvirs **Appius** was Appius Claudius who was consul at the time of their appoint- **Claudius.** ment.   During the first year the ten drew up ten tables of the law and placed them in the Forum where every man might see them A report was now spread abroad that two tables were lacking and so it would be wise to elect decemvirs (a second time) instead of other magistrates.   This the people did; but now the real character of Appius Claudius stood forth and his conduct toward the plebeians became infamous.   Indeed, the entire board of decemvirs set aside every principle of law and justice.   They plundered and robbed some plebeians; they even scourged others and put them to death. They frequently came into the market-place attended by lictors carrying the axes bound up within the rods signifying the power of life and death.   There was a certain centurion, Virginius, an estimable plebeian, who had betrothed his daughter to one Icilius who had once been a tribune of the plebs.   The extraordinary beauty of this maiden, Virginia, excited the lust of the decemvir, Appius Claudius, who determined to possess her.   To carry out his foul plan he ordered one of his clients to claim the girl as his slave.   The **Virginia.** day following, as Virginia passed through the Forum on her way to school, she was seized by this agent of Appius who tried to lead her away.   At once a great tumult arose among the commons, for her father, Virginius, and her betrothed, Icilius, had many friends. Whereupon the girl was summoned before the tribunal of the tyrant, Appius, who was compelled against his will to postpone proceedings in the case until Virginius could be summoned.   In the meantime two of his loyal friends hastened with all the speed their horses could make to the camp where Virginius was defending his country.   The anxious father hastened to the Forum where a vast crowd of citizens had assembled at daybreak.   Here he begged them for their support, reminding his countrymen of the fact that he was daily fighting in the defence of their wives and children.   Icilius, too, spoke so feelingly that the hearts of all were deeply stirred.   But to these just appeals the heart of Appius was hardened.   Indeed, he did not permit the father to make any proper presentation of his case, but gave judg-

ment straightway that the maiden should be given over to the cus
tody of his client till the final decision was made.   The wretched
Virginius, drawing his child aside, snatched a butcher's knife from
one of the stalls hard by and spoke thus to his daughter:

"The time is come.   See how he points his eager hand this way!
See how his eyes gloat on thy grief, like a kite's upon the prey!
With all his wit, he little deems, that, spurned, betrayed, bereft,
Thy father hath in his despair one fearful refuge left.
He little deems that in this hand I clutch what still can save
Thy gentle youth from taunts and blows, the portion of the slave;
Yea, and from nameless evil, that passeth taunt and blow—
Foul outrage which thou knowest not, which thou shalt never know.
Then clasp me round the neck once more, and give me one more kiss;
And now, mine own dear little girl, there is no way but this."
With that he lifted high the steel, and smote her in the side,
And in her blood she sank to earth, and with one sob she died.*

After this dreadful deed Virginius calling down curses upon the
head of Appius rushed forth to the army which now rose in revolt

The Second Secession. and elected as chief magistrates tribunes instead of decemvirs.   But
the decemvirs would not yield their power and refused to resign till
the army and the plebeians crossed the Anio to the Sacred Mount in
a second secession.   Nor would they readily abandon their idea of
founding a new city there.   Finally, two patricians, Valerius and
Horatius, whom the plebeians trusted, were able to effect a compromise.   They arranged that the tribunes be restored and respected,
and held out as further relief a series of enactments which came to
be called after the negotiators the Valerio-Horatian laws.   Then the
seceders returned   Some of the decemvirs were banished, while
Appius and one colleague were thrust into prison where some men
said they died by their own hands.

449 B.C   The Valerio-Horatian laws re-enacted the right of
appeal and gave the comitia tributa power to enact legislation
binding on all the people.

445 B.C.   The Canuleian law permitted intermarriage between
patricians and plebeians.

* Macaulay, *Lays of Ancient Rome*, "Virginia."

444 B C. Consular tribunes, who might be elected from plebeians as well as from patricians, were substituted for consuls elected from patricians only. This arrangement continued till 366 B C

366 B C   The laws proposed by Licinius and Sextus provided that there should be no more consular tribunes, that at least one consul should be plebeian and that ten priests should have charge of the Sibylline books (§ 348), half of whom should be plebeians.

Interest already paid was to be deducted from the principal and the balance to be paid in three equal annual installments. Of the public land no citizen was to occupy more than 500 jugera (300 acres) and no one was to pasture on it more than 100 cattle and 500 sheep. A certain proportion of the laborers employed on an estate were to be freeman.

REVIEW EXERCISES.   1. The main divisions of the new period with dates. 2. What is meant by imperium, century, connubium, right of appeal? 3. State briefly the position and power of the censor, the quæstor. 4. Distinguish between the two periods in the history of the tribune. 5. What was the traditional date of the Decemvirate? 6. What was the work of the tribunes? 7. Give reasons for the increase in numbers and powers of the tribunes. 8. Explain the principles governing the reorganization of the army. 9. Summarize the gains of the plebeians in their struggle with the patricians up to 287 B C.

COMPARATIVE STUDIES.   1. Compare the laws of the Twelve Tables here given with those of the code of Hammurabi (§ 15). 2. Compare the Decemvirate with the Greek lawgivers (§§ 135, 136) in origin, purpose and results of work.

SELECT LIST FOR READING.   1. The New Aristocratic Republic: General View of Its External History. How and Leigh, chs. 7, 10. 2. The Consul. How and Leigh, pp 47–50 3. The Decemvirate. How and Leigh, ch. 8.

TOPICS FOR READING AND ORAL REPORT.   1. The New Aristocratic Republic: General View of Its Constitutional History to 390 B.C. Shuckburgh, ch. 8, Abbott, pp. 24–34. 2. General View of Its External History. Shuckburgh, chs. 6, 7. 3. The Consul. Shuckburgh, pp 203–205; Abbott, p 25. 4. The Tribune. Abbott, pp 196–202. 5. The Decemvirate. Abbott, pp. 30–31. 6. The Roman Citizen, His Rights and Duties

Morey, pp. 63-64. **7. The Centuriate Assembly.** Abbott, pp.
26-27, 253-259. **8. The Question of the Comitia Tributa.**
Abbott. pp 33, 259-261, Myres, p. 77 (note) **9. The Twelve
Tables.** Munro, pp. 54-55 (source); Shuckburgh, pp. 101-104.
**10. The Social Composition of the Roman People: A Common-
Sense View.** Botsford, Roman Assemblies, pp. 38-45. **11. Ju-
dicial Cases before Comitia Centuriata.** Botsford, Roman
Assemblies, pp. 248-260.

3.—THE UNIFICATION AND ORGANIZATION OF ITALY

390-264 B.C.

369. The Celtic Invasion.—During the latter part of
the preceding century swarms of Celts had been pouring

Celts
Occupy
Valley of
Po.

down from central Europe over the Alpine passes into
the valley of the Po.   They filled it to overflowing, drove
the Ligurians back into the western hills and the Etruscans into the western plain and began to push southward
over the Apennines.   We have already seen them forcing their way into Greece and Asia Minor, though at a
later period (§ 307).   They were rude, savage warriors,
of huge bulk, with mighty weapons, attacking their opponents with an impetuous fury that usually carried all
before it.   Soon they appeared in the western plain, attracted by the fertility of the soil and the wealth of the
inhabitants.   Etruria was overrun; a bold band appeared

Burning
of Rome.

in the vicinity of Rome, defeated the Roman army in a
disastrous battle at the river Allia, captured and burned
the city (about 390 B.C).

The story goes that Roman ambassadors, sent into Etruria to
treat with the oncoming Celts, had joined with the Etruscans in
fighting against them Incensed at this, the Celts under their

chief, Brennus, advanced rapidly on Rome. The Romans, unprepared, hastily gathered a force and met the invaders eleven miles from Rome, at the river Allia, and were utterly defeated. A few escaped into the citadel, leaving the gates of the city open The Celts entered the city which was abandoned by all except the defenders of the citadel and the senators sitting in state in their porches. The city was set on fire and the citadel besieged. Once it was almost captured by night, only the sacred geese by cackling and clapping their wings aroused the defenders in time. The scattered Romans were united under a leader, Camillus, who was made dictator. The Celts were driven out. Then the city was rebuilt.

370. Rome's Rapid Recovery.—Rome's day of power seemed over. It might have been so had the Celtic fury burst upon her alone. But other states had suffered in north and south. When Rome recovered and had rebuilt the city, she was still as strong as her neighbors and was soon ready to fight again with the invaders. The danger from the Celts was serious. Their bands were constantly coming over the Apennines. It was the question of questions whether they would not overpower all Italy. For over forty years, from 390 to 348 B.C., the peril was pressing. The Romans stood in the breach and, on two occasions within this period, they met and repulsed great Celtic raids. Thus the Romans really saved all that Italy had gained in political power and civilization from being destroyed. The other states recognized this; Rome came to be regarded as the defender of the states of the western plain against attacks. People outside of Italy heard of it. The Greek philosopher Aristotle (§ 298) knew of her gallant defence against the Celts. From this time on, she ceased to be a mere petty state, fighting with neighbors, and stepped into the larger history of the world.

Stands as Defender of Italy.

371. Etruria Won.—During those forty years Rome finally overcame the neighboring states with which she had fought so long. Etruria, as far north as the Ciminian forest, including the city of Cæ're, the Latin cities and even the Volsci, were united under Roman leadership. The river Li'ris was Rome's southern boundary. Of decisive importance was Rome's treatment of its old friend and ally, Cære. What it valued in the Roman state—social and commercial equality with Roman citizens—it got; what it valued in its own institutions, it preserved—its own franchise and offices, its own laws and cults. From the Roman point of view its inhabitants were Roman citizens who lacked the right of voting and holding office (*cives sine suffragio*). Naturally, they were required to fight in the Roman army and to sustain all the other burdens imposed upon Roman citizens. Hence they were called *municipes* (burden-bearers), and their city a municipality. The relation thus formed was so satisfactory to both parties that Cære was the first of a considerable group of cities which Rome incorporated with this status. Such places were said to have "Cæritan rights."

The Origin of the Municipal System.

372. Wars with the Samnites.—The advance of the Celts southward had affected not only the people of the plain, but also the mountaineers. They had been pushed on and had crowded the southern tribes. Chief among the people that felt this pressure were the Samnites, a strong and warlike confederacy, possessing greater power and unity than any mountain peoples hitherto met by Rome. They naturally fell upon the plain beneath them, the populous and fertile Campania. The Campanians appealed to Rome for aid and offered to accept Roman

Conflict over Campania.

PLATE XXVI

Gladiators

Knight in Full Dress

WALL PAINTINGS FROM CAMPANIAN TOMBS

authority. Commercial interests united with ambition to lead the Romans to accept the offer and oppose the Samnites. The war that followed was long and trying, broken by intervals of peace; it lasted for half a century (343–290 B.C.) and drew almost all the states of central and southern Italy into its toils.

The first contest was short (343–341 B.C.); the peace that followed gave Rome the headship of Campania. First Samnite War.

373. The Latin Revolt and the Organization of Latium, 340-338 B.C.—The next three years saw the crushing of a rebellion of the Latin league, the cities of which began to fear that Rome was growing too strong. This sentiment was also shared by the Campanians who joined in the outbreak. A fierce struggle followed, the details of which are mostly legendary. Equal in respect of arms and military experience, the rebels were inferior in unity of purpose and organization. Hence they succumbed, and the league was dissolved. Some of its cities were deprived of local government and ruled by prefects set over them by Rome (*præfecturæ*); others were made municipalities, like Cære. A few specially favored cities remained allies, and retained their independence. A perpetual and irrevocable treaty (*fœdus*) bound them to furnish troops to Rome and to abstain from diplomatic intercourse with one another or with other nations. All their foreign affairs were to be managed by Rome. This was the form of treaty by which Rome brought subjected communities into her federation as allies. In 330 B.C. her territory extended from the Ciminian forest to the bay of Naples and from the sea to the Apennines. It included Rome and Capua, the two greatest non-Greek cities in Italy, and Rome Masters the Southern Lowlands.

had a population of more than half a million. Its inhabitants were all of Etruscan or Italic stock.

374. **The First Greek Ally.**—In 327 B.C. a new element
was added when the first Greek city was brought into the
federation. This was Neapolis, which, trusting in its
fleet and its strong walls, defied its formidable neighbor
and only consented to become an ally of Rome after a
troublesome contest. Into this the Samnites entered
bringing aid to the Greek city; and therewith the great
second Samnite war began. Rome had the advantage of
allies in Apulia and in the central Apennines among the
mountain tribes there who feared their active Samnite
neighbor. Hence she was able to conduct operations from
both the eastern and western lowlands. The contestants
were evenly matched and the struggle long and obstinate.

The
Caudine
Forks.

375. **The Second Samnite War, 326-304 B.C.**—After
a severe defeat at the battle of the Caudine Forks (321
B.C.), where their soldiers were compelled to pass under a
yoke made of three spears as a token of disgraceful submission, the Romans steadily gained, but in 315 B.C.,
while their main army was operating in Apulia, the Samnites advanced through Campania to Latium and defeat-

Lautulæ
and the
Revolt of
Capua.

ed the Romans at Laut'-u-læ. Capua, thereupon, went
over to the enemy, but came back in the following year
after the main army of the Romans had routed the Samnites. The Samnites stirred up the peoples of the north
who feared Rome's growing power; the Etruscans joined
them and the Umbrians of the upper Apennines; but a
Roman army advanced up the Tiber into Etruria and
carried such consternation into the whole district that the
Etruscans made peace. The decisive factor in the struggle
was, however, the systematic Roman operations of the last

decade. By a series of fortress colonies (Latin) placed at The Latin Colonies.
the exits from Samnium on the Liris and Volturnus rivers
the area of war was limited to the enemy's country, and in
order to bring the Roman troops quickly to the main
scene of action a great highway, the famous Via Appia, The Via Appia.
was built from Rome to Capua. Thus hemmed in
and assailed, the Samnites finally sued for peace in 304
B.C. By the treaty then made Rome held all its conquests.

376. The Third Samnite War, 298-290 B.C.—The reappearance of the Celts stirred up the third struggle, in
which Etruscans, Umbrians, Lucanians and Celts united
under Samnite direction for a final attempt to break Ro-
man headship (298 B.C.). The culminating point was The Crowning Victory of Rome at Sentinum
the battle of Sen-ti'num (295 B.C.), in Umbria, where the
soldiers of the alliance were beaten by the Romans (§ 396).
The treaty which ended the war in 290 B.C. settled Rome's
superiority. The Etruscans and Gauls (Senones and
Boii) then felt the weight of Rome's hand, and in 285–283
B.C. they were crushed and forced to acknowledge Rome's
hegemony. Roman authority was now supreme from the
upper Apennines to the foot of Italy. The mountaineers
would never more trouble the plain.

377. Difficulties with Magna Græcia.—Rome's sphere
of influence now bordered on the territory of the Greek
cities in southern Italy. The influence of Greek culture and political life upon Rome had already been considerable and the opportunities of commercial intercourse had brought both parties into friendly relations.
Some time before 300 B.C. a treaty between Rome and
Tarentum had been made. Thus, when the mountaineers, defeated in the western plain, began to make in-

roads into Magna Græcia, it was natural that several of
the Greek cities should look to Rome for defence. But
Tarentum was not so inclined; as Rome gained headship over the other Greek cities by relieving them from
their enemies, she took offence. How she gained the
help of the valiant Pyrrhus of Epirus has already been
told (§ 331). In the war that followed (281–272 B.C),
the skilful Greek general at first defeated the Romans
at Her-a-clei'a in 280 B.C. and at As'cu-lum in 279 B.C. by
his elephants and his cavalry. It was the first meeting
between the Roman legion and the Macedonian phalanx.
In the interval between these engagements he had advanced to within three days' march of Rome, but on
receiving no support from the western lowlands he returned to Tarentum to winter quarters. Now, wishing to
get rid of his obstinate adversary in order to embark on
his Sicilian enterprise (§ 331), Pyrrhus entered into negotiations with Rome and sent Cineas, an eloquent rheto-
rician, to present his case to the senate. Cineas was pro-
foundly impressed by the dignity and incorruptibility of
the senators, and, indeed, if it is true that the old blind
senator, Appius Claudius (§ 379), came to the meeting in
his litter and made an impassioned appeal to his colleagues
never to make a pact with an enemy on Italian soil, he had
some reason for the opinion which he expressed to his
master that the Roman senate was an "assembly of kings."
The mission of Cineas was frustrated by the intervention
of Carthage whose offer of a defensive and offensive alliance against Pyrrhus the Romans accepted. None the
less, Pyrrhus departed for Sicily. On his return he was
beaten at Beneventum (275 B.C) and returned to Epirus,
leaving Tarentum to make terms with Rome as best she

Marginal notes:

War with
Pyrrhus.

The
"Assembly
of Kings."

could. She submitted and Roman power soon became supreme over all the southern coast of Italy (270 B.C.).

378. Political Changes.—This period of more than a century, in which Rome extended her sway in Italy, was marked by important changes in her inner life. These have been already described in §§ 360–366 above. The outcome, as we have seen, was the ascendancy in the Roman state of the farming part of the population. This result was not reached without opposition, however; for in the last stage of the struggle between the patricians and the plebeians we find traces of a keen contest for political power between the city and the country.

379. The Policy of Appius Claudius.—The great champion of the urban elements was Appius Claudius, the censor, in 312 B.C. (§ 397). To him they owed the first of the wonderful Roman aqueducts. He enrolled in all the tribes those whose property was not in land and even freedmen, thus giving to them the same citizen rights as the landed proprietors. But in the following censorship they were again restricted to the four city tribes and the city population was thus unable, even if it flocked in full force to the Forum where the assembly met, to vote down the relatively few farmers who formed the usual delegation from each of the country tribes. It had been long since the rule that, though all citizens were eligible for office, only the rich landed proprietors were actually chosen. The officials when their term of office expired went into the senate,* which, therefore, was a body of wealthy squires who had experience in political and mili-

Rise of Other Dis tinctions.

---

* The right of ex-officials to be considered first in the choice of senators was established by the Ovinian law, by which also the censor was substituted for the consul as the official who appointed the senators. This law dates t ı · · tııı lı ı · ·

tary affairs. Wealth, coupled with wisdom, has the best chance for leadership; hence it very naturally came about that the senate took the direction of affairs, although the people had the power. The oligarchy of wealth and official position occupied the place of the oligarchy of birth; the people accepted the change and continued to be led.

380. Roman Organization of Italy.—No less remarkable than the gradual extension of Roman power over the territory of Italy was Rome's organization of the lands acknowledging its headship. Rome's membership in the Latin league at the beginning of its career was a determining factor in its policy toward neighbors; the city stood as a chief among equals, not as a conqueror ruling subjects.

381. Incorporation of Conquered People as Citizens. —In harmony with this fundamental idea the Romans, first of all, made many of the communities they absorbed parts of the Roman state and their people citizens. These were the municipalities already described (§ 371). Since they got all the solid advantages of Roman citizenship and were not deprived of their own institutions which they cherished highly, their status was an attractive one and nearly all the larger cities in the western lowlands entered the Roman state in this way. Less fortunate were the districts of which the cities like Veii were destroyed, or on which there had been no urban centres prior to the conquest. These were assigned to Roman settlers, and their inhabitants, so far as they remained, were compelled to become Roman citizens. Still less fortunate was a group of maritime cities in which Rome placed as a garrison (cle′ru-chy) to secure the harbor a colony of

A New Oligarchy.

The Principle.

Roman (Maritime) Colonies.

normally three hundred Roman citizens who settled as an aristocracy in the midst of the local inhabitants. In return for garrison duty they were exempted from service in the Roman legions. As a result of these various measures, groups of Roman citizens were found scattered all over Italy. At the end of this period, those with full rights numbered not far from three hundred thousand men and occupied about a third of all the territory of Italy. They were organized into thirty-five tribes, meeting and voting in the comitia. As for the local government of such communities as possessed it, this was largely in their own hands and was formed on Roman models. But in the case of the administration of justice, prefects were sent out from Rome to hold court in the municipia at regular times, since Roman law was new to them. Likewise, where districts in which no cities existed were taken into the Roman state, Roman prefects were placed in charge. Prefects

382. Latin Allies: Colonies.—The rest of the communities in Italy were the "allies." There were two kinds of them. The most favored allies were those given rights enjoyed formerly by the old Latin league, which had now disappeared. The members could trade with Rome and, when specially favored, marry into Roman families.* These were the colonists sent out from Rome and Latium to occupy land taken in the conquest. Like the Greek colonies in general they were established as new city-states having their own laws, magistrates and citizenship. Since they were usually planted in strategic positions in the midst or at the edge of a hostile country, they were normally quite large, one, Venusia, being twenty Allied States.

* These rights were technically called *commercium* and *connubium*.

thousand strong.   Unlike the Greek colonies, they were bound to the metropolis by an indissoluble tie of interest as well as by an inviolable treaty.   These were called "Latin Colonies."   A Roman who went out to join a "Latin colony" gave up his citizenship, and he could regain it on returning home only when he had left a son behind to keep his place in the garrison-colony.   In addition to the privilege mentioned, he could share in the booty of Roman wars and claim his part of the public land.   In course of time these privileges were somewhat restricted, but the "Latin colony" was always on a higher plane than other allied communities.

383. The Italian Allies.—Next below these were the Italian allies, each of which had a separate treaty with Rome defining its status.   All allies of whatsoever status could have relations with each other only through Rome. While they had independence so far as home politics was concerned, Rome decided on all foreign affairs, matters of war and peace and questions relating to their commercial interests.   Each ally was bound to furnish troops to the Roman army, or ships to the Roman navy, but paid no tribute.

384. Italy United under Rome.—Thus was slowly and steadily built up a united Italy with its centre and soul in Rome.   The state itself, made up of the capital city, the Roman colonies and the municipia, was bound up closely with the allies, both those given the Latin right and those having separate treaties with Rome.   The interests of all gathered about the capital, yet a large share of local independence preserved the sense of freedom and the power of initiative.   The system of public roads leading from the city to strategic points aided in

(margin note: Latin Colonies.)

(margin note: Roads.)

binding these cities to Rome   It is not to be wondered at, therefore, that, as this period drew to a close, a common name arose both for land and people.   The defence against the alien Celts stimulated this sense of oneness.   The land was now called Italy, and the people of Italy, distinguishing their common dress from that of the Celts, were called "men of the toga."

385. Military Reorganization.—During the years in which the union of Italy was accomplished, important advances were made in the Roman military organization.   The old Servian system (§ 350) was not equal to the new demands, either in its conditions of service or its organization (§ 362).   Instead of requiring the citizen to equip and support himself, the state now supplied him arms and rations and paid him for his service.   He was also usually granted a share of the booty, although in theory all that was taken belonged to the state and was turned into the public treasury.   As respects organization, the arrangement of the men in the legion according to property gave way, as we have seen, to that according to valor, ability and experience.   The solid phalanx on the Greek model was found unable to stand the fierce rushes of the Celts and the Samnites, and was altered to a loose formation.   The legion was divided into three lines (*hastati, principes* and *triarii*) separated sharply from each other, the first two armed with the *pilum* for hurling and the sword, the third with the pike or spear for mass action.   Each line was made up of ten companies called maniples.   Each maniple of the first two lines had a front of twenty men and a depth of six men (the third had a depth of three men), and each was separated from the other by a space of at most its own width   The maniples of the second line were placed so as to face the spaces made by the first line, and those of the third line faced the spaces left by the second. In battle, the first line (*hastati*), if beaten back, could retire into the space left in the second line (*principes*), which then took up the attack, while the third line (*triarii*), which was composed of the most able and experienced veterans, could if necessary advance through the openings and permit the other lines to retire. Behind each line was a body of maniples of light-armed troops two men deep, making four thousand two hundred men in the legion. The soldiers were armed with helmets, cuirasses and shields for defence, and with swords, pila, pikes and darts for attack. The allied troops fought on each side of the legion. The cavalry, placed outside the wings, was insignificant in numbers and played no great part. To avoid a sudden attack a Roman army made a fortified camp whenever it halted for the night. Every voting citizen between the ages of seventeen and forty-six was liable to be levied for military service; he must take the solemn military oath before the gods and was then entirely under the authority of the commander, who exacted absolute obedience and had the power of life and death. The discipline was exceedingly severe. A great victory was the occasion of celebrating a triumph, providing that the senate gave its consent. In solemn and splendid procession, attended by magistrates and senators, the spoils of war before him, the victorious general, seated on a chariot, a laurel crown on his head, and his face painted red like the gods, rode into the city at the head of his troops to the temple of Jupiter, where he offered thanksgiving.

The Camp.

The Oath.

The Triumph.

REVIEW EXERCISES. 1. For what were the following noted: Sentinum, Cære, Beneventum, Aristotle? 2. What is meant by "men of the toga," Licinian laws, maniple, cleruchy, hastati, principes, triarii, municipalities?

COMPARATIVE STUDIES. 1. Compare a "Latin" with a "Roman" colony. 2. Compare both with a Greek colony (§§ 113–115)

SELECT LIST FOR READING. 1. The War with Veii and the Legend of Camillus. How and Leigh, pp 80–84. 2. The Dissolution of the Latin League. How and Leigh, pp. 97–99, 102–105 3. The Samnites and Sabines Submit to Rome. How and Leigh, pp 114–120, 130 4. The Affairs of Rome and Tarentum. How and Leigh, pp 122–130 5. Organization of Italy. How and Leigh, pp. 133–135.

TOPICS FOR READING AND ORAL REPORT. 1. Camillus and the Story of the Celtic Invasion. Plutarch, Life of Camillus, Seignobos, pp. 60–64. 2. The Samnite Wars. Myres, chs. 10–11 3. The Latin Revolt. Shuckburgh, pp. 131–133. 4. Pyrrhus from the Greek and from the Roman Point of View (§§ 331, 377) 5. History of the Plebeian Struggle after 390 B C. Abbott, pp 34–53; Shuckburgh, ch 13; Myres, ch 9; Fowler, City State, ch 7. 6. The Licinian Laws: Special Study. Munro, pp. 57–60 (sources), Botsford, pp. 85–86, Abbott, pp 36–37, 7. Roman Organization of Italy. Abbott, pp 57–60; Botsford, pp. 62–63, Myres, pp. 146–149. 8. The Roman Army. Seignobos, ch 7, Shuckburgh, pp 214–218. 9. Political Prosecutions before the Comitia Tributa. Botsford, Roman Assemblies, pp. 319–325

386. The Old Roman Life.—This age saw old Roman life at its highest point of strength and achievement. It was to suffer an almost complete transformation as Rome expanded. We may pause, therefore, to sketch some of its characteristic features.

387. Occupations.—The Roman was devoted chiefly to agriculture. At first, cattle-raising, later, the growing of grain, occupied him. The product of his farm was principally wheat, but he also grew vegetables and fruit

<small>Agriculture.</small>

The olive was widely cultivated   Of domestic animals he had cattle, horses, sheep and hogs.   The farmer with his sons did the work, for the farms were usually small. Every eighth day was a market-day, when the farmer went to town with his produce.   In the city industry was well advanced.   The workingmen had already organized into unions or guilds for the purpose of handing down the secrets of their craft from generation to generation. Eight of these unions are known—the goldsmiths, the coppersmiths, the dyers, the fullers (laundrymen), the shoemakers, the carpenters, the potters and the flute-blowers.   Trading and commerce were profitable employments, but the retail traders, the seamen and the artisans were not highly regarded by the Romans.   The same was true of the Greeks (§ 200) and to a certain extent of all civilized peoples.   But in Rome the true gentleman was always a farmer.   This fact shows how dear to the Roman heart were the pursuits of agriculture.   Yet the profits of commerce attracted the better classes who had capital and wanted to increase it rapidly; unwilling to mix in commerce themselves, they employed slaves or dependent freedmen to carry on such pursuits in their interest.   Thus the business of Rome fell largely into the hands of such classes and became still more unworthy of freemen.

Industry

Business.

388. Money.—The standard of business value in the earliest time was cattle, as is shown by the Latin word for money, *pecunia* (from *pecus*, "cattle").   But soon a change to copper took place; it is witnessed to by our word "estimate" (Latin *æstimare*), from *æs*, "copper"   A pound of it cast in a mould was called an *as* and became the unit of Roman coinage.   When Rome had united all

PLATE XXVII

TYPICAL COINS

PLATE XXVIII

TYPICAL COINS

Italy, a silver coinage was introduced. In 268 B.C. the silver *denarius*, equal to ten asses, appeared.*

389. The House.--As might be expected of a community composed chiefly of farmers, Roman life was simple and rude. The house originally consisted of one room, the *atrium*, in which all the family lived. It had no windows and but one door. Opposite the door was the hearth. An opening in the centre of the roof let the smoke out and the light and rain in. The latter fell into a hollow in the floor just beneath the opening. In time, this primitive house was enlarged on the sides and in the rear. The walls were built of stone or sun-baked brick covered with stucco; the floor was of earth mixed with stone and fragments of pottery pounded down hard; the roof of thatch, shingles or tile. A couch, table and stool constituted the furniture. The lamp was a flat, covered vessel holding oil; through a hole in the top a coarse wick was drawn, whence came a feeble, flickering light. In cold weather a box containing hot coals supplied heat. At meal-time the family sat on stools around the table. Dinner was served in the middle of the day. The chief food in early times was ground meal boiled with water. Thus the Roman, like the Scotchman, grew strong on porridge. Pork was the favorite meat; eight Latin words for hog and half a dozen for sausage testify to this. Bread of wheat or barley was baked in flat, round cakes. Olive-oil, cheese and honey were used with it. The usual drink was water or milk. Wine

margin: Furniture

margin: Food.

* Later, from about 217 B C to the time of Nero, the denarius was equal to sixteen asses. The *sestertius* was one-fourth of the denarius. A sum of money equal to one thousand sestertii was called *sestertium*. The denarius, like the attic drachma, was equal to about twenty cents of our money.

was not common. When drunk it was mixed with water. Various vegetables, such as beans, onions, cabbages and turnips, and fruits, such as figs, apples, pears and plums, were cultivated. The frugality of the Roman in his food **Dress** was matched by the simplicity of his dress. About his loins he wore a strip of cloth over which he drew a short-sleeved woollen shirt or tunic reaching to his knees. This **The Toga.** was the ordinary dress while at home When he appeared in public, he threw over this shirt a gracefully folded blanket of white wool called a *toga*. It was this which became his characteristic garment, distinguishing him from all other men. In bad weather or on a journey a cloak might be worn. The women's garments consisted of two tunics for the house and a wrap (*palla*) for the street. Neither sex wore hats or stockings. The feet were protected by sandals or shoes. The hair and beard were worn long in early times, but, later, men shaved their faces and cut their hair close. Professional **Jewelry.** barbers appeared in Rome about 300 B.C. Every citizen wore a seal-ring on the joint of the finger; women were granted greater privileges in the matter of jewelry and they were very fond of display. Their hair was put up elaborately; they had fans, parasols and all sorts of rings, bracelets, chains and breastpins.

390. Amusements.—Amusements had also their place in old Roman life. Babies played with rattles; children **Athletics.** with dolls, carts, tops and hoops. When childish sports were put away, the young Roman found his amusement in the athletic exercises of the Campus Martius, in running, wrestling and feats of arms. These were, however, training for citizenship and service; it has been well said that the Romans had no idea of sport for sport's sake.

Life was too stern and strenuous. For relaxation they turned to exciting spectacles, of which the chief were the chariot races. They were run in the Circus Maximus, which lay between the Palatine and the Aventine, over a narrow elliptical course covered with sand; seven laps, about four miles, were run; the turns were sharp and dangerous; chariots were liable to be smashed and drivers killed; all this raised excitement to fever heat. But no Roman participated except as a spectator; freedmen or slaves acted as charioteers. The same was true of the theatrical exhibitions. The stage in the Circus was occupied by persons whom the Romans regarded as disreputable; to dance or to play in public was the part of foreigners or slaves. To the unbending, respectable, dignified Roman the point of view of the Greek (§ 160, 179, 209) regarding all these things was incomprehensible and disgraceful. He would condescend to laugh, but would not dream of taking part.

391. **The Family.**—The centre about which old Roman life revolved was the family (§ 342). Its head was the *paterfamilias* ("father of the family"), the oldest male member, who had absolute power over the person and property of the other members, whether wife, sons and their families, or unmarried daughters. A newborn child was laid at his feet, and by taking it up he decided that it should be received into the family. Otherwise it was carried away and abandoned. When a daughter was married, she passed under the authority of her husband's father. A son must marry at the bidding of his father; his position in the state was dependent on the father. Of course these powers of the father were practically limited; a wife could not be divorced

The Races.

The Theatre.

The Father's Power.

nor a child put to death by him without good cause and after consultation with other members of the family; nor could the family property be disposed of arbitrarily.

Marriage. Marriage was a religious as well as a civil affair; a solemn betrothal preceded, sealed by a ring placed on the third finger of the left hand; the consent of the bride was required; the marriage ceremony consisted of the joining of hands, the signing of a contract, sacrifices by the religious officials and other ceremonials. On the wedding-day the mother dressed the bride, who wore a veil; the husband went through a form of taking her by force from her father's house; a wedding-feast and a bridal procession were features of the affair. The bride brought a

The Mother. dowry to her husband A matron at Rome, in contrast with Greek custom (§ 202), held a very important position. She managed the household, trained her children, received her guests in person, was honored in public and was given a special place at entertainments. She engaged in special religious festivals and could give testimony in the courts. It has been said that marriage gave the Roman woman "a position unattained by the women of any

Children. other nation in the ancient world." Children, particularly sons, were highly prized and carefully trained. On the son depended the future of the family. The day of the giving the boy his name* was a festal time in which an amulet (*bulla*) was hung about his neck and presents

Adoption. were made. If a family had no son, one might be formally adopted and he became in all respects a member

---

* First of all, he bore the name of the house (*gens*): this was the *nomen*, e g , Tullius. Preceding this came the personal name (*prænomen*) given a few days after birth, *e.g.*, Marcus. Following the *nomen* was the *cognomen* or family name, e g , Cicero.

of the family and took the family name in addition to his own.

392. Importance of the Family in Roman Life.—All these facts help us to see how fundamentally important the family was at Rome. In the case of the nobles it included the dead as well as the living, all bound together in one solemn unity. On the preservation of the family depended the continuance of the sacrificial rites in which living and dead were thought to join. Hence the birth and rearing of children was all-important. In the atrium (§ 389) stood the wax images of the dead to remind the living of the abiding tie of relationship. The paterfamilias received his authority over the family as its representative, the trustee of its property, the pledge of its continuance. Thus the importance of any individ- *Superior* ual member was subordinate to and sunk in the higher *to the Individual.* unity of the whole. Obedience and service were the watchwords, devotion to the interests of the family was superior to all personal advantage. No wonder that under this training men of honor and fidelity, women of discretion and purity, grew up to serve and glorify their fatherland.

393. Education.—Education corresponded to the thoroughly practical bent of the Roman character Up to seven years of age the children were trained at home by the mother. Then the boy was sent to school, while *Of Girls.* the girl was kept at home to be further instructed in domestic arts. Roman women were not highly educated, yet the liberty they enjoyed, the companionship of their husbands and family and the respect shown them in society were in themselves an education. It is said that they spoke the best and purest Latin. Boys were sent to *Of Boys.*

private schools. They were attended by a slave (called "pedagogue") and were taught by slaves or freedmen the rudiments of education in reading, writing and arithmetic. Work began before sunrise. The teacher was paid a small fee and the discipline was harsh. No text-books were used, except that the code of the Twelve Tables (§ 364) was read, written and committed to memory It is claimed that, although higher subjects were not taught, the elements at least of education were more generally diffused among the Romans than elsewhere in antiquity, except in Athens and other Greek cities.

394. Public Life.—The participation in public life was also educative. The youth at about seventeen years of age attained his majority and began his public career; he laid aside his *toga prætexta* and assumed the *toga virilis;* surrounded by his family and friends he went to the Forum and, amid congratulations, his name was enrolled on the list of citizens and he was free to attend the several comitia. On a favorable day the comitia convened by order of the magistrate. The proper sacrifices were made The magistrate made known the purpose of the assembly; only those could speak to whom he gave permission Each citizen gave his vote orally in the group to which he belonged; the decision of the majority in the group determined its vote, which then was counted as one in determining the final vote of the groups. The meeting closed before sunset and could be adjourned by the magistrate at any time, should he regard the omens as unfavorable. The citizen was constantly under the strict surveillance of the authorities. The censor (§ 357) examined into his private life and punished any breaches of social custom by fines or even

Admission to Citizenship.

The Assembly.

The State Superior to the Individual

suspension from civic rights. In the administration of justice he appeared before judicial officers, such as the prætors; no lawyers existed; plaintiff and defendant must plead their own causes; the magistrate acting under the written law of the Twelve Tables interpreted its application and handed the case definitely formulated over to the *judex* for judgment. An appeal in criminal cases might be taken to the comitia. Private persons (*judices*) were regularly appointed by the magistrate to hear cases and give decisions. Out of all this procedure came in course of time the body of public and private law which is one of Rome's chief glories.

395. Science: Its Practical Character.—In the higher ranges of art and science we must not expect old Rome to excel. Its science was practical like all the rest of its works. The year consisted of twelve months; it began in March. The days of the month were indicated by their relation to the moon's changes. All the days of the year were given a special religious significance, either good or bad. Business could be done only on the good days, which made up more than two-thirds of the year In 304 B.C. a calendar on which the character of the days was indicated was published. The whole arrangement was quite imperfect. In architecture the most characteristic achievements were the roads, the bridges and the aqueducts, which began to be built on a grand scale. The arch had a great history at Rome. The chief priesthood had a name which connected it with bridge-building (pontifices). The solidity of the Roman character was already reflected in the architecture. In decorative and plastic art but a few beginnings had been made. The bronze wolf in the Forum and the bronze Jupiter of the

Capitol date from about 290 B.C.; the stone sar-coph'a-gus
of Scipio, from a little later time, was a simple but strong
work. A beautiful casket of like date illustrates as do
the other works of art the source of the artistic impulse,
Greeks were the teachers of Rome in these things. The
beginnings of painting belong also to this same age.
Literature. Literature was even less advanced. The laws of the
Twelve Tables constituted the one Roman book. Bal-
lads and heroic poems in a rude metre were sung. Some
public records, lists of magistrates, religious rituals and
the like—these alone constituted the barren Roman literature of the time.

   396. Morals and Religion.—The rude, severe and
scrupulous temper of the old Roman is revealed in his
moral standards and religious life. Much of it has appeared in what has already been told—the power of the
father, the subordination of the individual to family and
state, the exposure of new-born children, the position of
Sense of the slave in the household, a mere unhuman chattel. In
Duty. its worthiest manifestation this old Roman spirit showed
itself in the conviction that everyone had his place and
work in the community. Let a man do his work in the
sphere in which he is born; be it father, son or slave, be
it patron or client, be it consul or soldier in the ranks—
let him not seek to be above his place and work or fall
Form and beneath it. Religion was still of the type which has
Spirit of
Religion been described (§§ 347–348); but an important change
had taken place in the character of the gods. On coming into close relations with the Greeks the Romans
found that this people possessed deities not unlike their
own. Jupiter was, accordingly, equated with Zeus, Juno
with Hera, Minerva with Athena, Mars with Ares, Venus

with Aphrodite, Diana with Artemis, and so on. At once
the Roman deities ceased to be vague figures and got the
forms and personalities of their Greek counterparts, so
that they could be plastically conceived and represented
in marble and bronze. The Romans, too, were saved the
pains of working out a sacred history for their gods and
goddesses by these identifications, since they applied to
their native deities the whole rich circle of Greek mythology. Where, finally, Greece had a desirable deity for
which Rome lacked an equivalent, the Sibylline books
were consulted and the foreign deity was formally introduced into Rome. Thus came As-cu-lap'ius, the Greek
god of healing, in 293 B.C None the less old Roman
habits and feelings persisted; everywhere the divine
powers were present and their relations to man were
worked out in great detail and their favorable action
secured by complex rituals. Still lived the profound
faith in the fidelity of the gods to their word and the
corresponding obligation and opportunity of man to do
his part toward them. This reaches its highest point in
the voluntary self-sacrifice of the individual for the interest of the state—the *devotio*, as it was called.

In the decisive battle of the Samnite war (Sentinum) the consul,
Publius Decius Mus, saw his legions broken and fleeing before the
enemy. Whereupon he called to himself the priest and charged him
to utter the solemn formula whereby a victim was devoted The
words having been uttered, he cried out that he drove before him fear
and fright, slaughter and blood and the wrath of gods above and below, and that with the contagion of the Furies, ministers of death, he
infected the standards and the arms of the enemy. With this curse,
and conscious that he offered himself as a victim to ward off the peril
from his country, he spurred forward his horse where the enemy's
force was thickest and found death at the points of their spears

397. A Type of a Progressive Roman: Appius Claudius.—The broadening of life, as this period draws to a close, is shown in one of the famous men of the time, Appius Claudius, the censor. It was he who built the first Roman road, the Appian Way, which led southward to Capua; the first aqueduct, likewise, was his work. He was also a patron of letters; to him are ascribed written speeches, wise maxims and the first collection of legal decisions. Even the study of grammar looks back to him. Other men followed in his footsteps. Rome, the head of Italy, rose from provincial manners and customs to be a cosmopolitan city. She was at the turning of the ways. Soon Greek learning and manners would come in like a flood and the old Rome disappear forever

REVIEW EXERCISES. 1. What light on Roman life is thrown by the following: pecunia; toga virilis; devotio? 2. What is meant by denarius, censor, atrium, nomen?

COMPARATIVE STUDIES. 1. Compare the Greek (§§ 200, 201) and Roman estimate of business life. 2. In what did the Roman idea of amusement differ from the Greek (§§ 109, 128, 160, 203, 206, 207, 209)? 3. Compare the Roman idea of the family with the oriental (§ 25) 4. Would a Greek have acted as did Decius Mus (§ 396)? State reasons for or against.

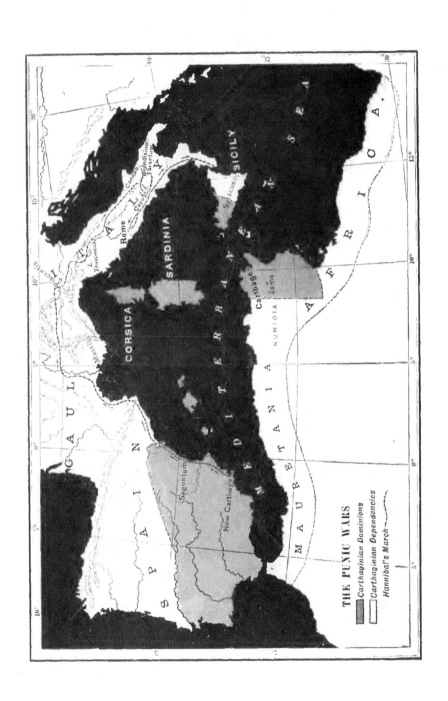

THE PUNIC WARS
Carthaginian Dominions
Carthaginian Dependencies
Hannibal's March

4.—THE STRUGGLE WITH CARTHAGE FOR THE WESTERN MEDITERRANEAN

264-200 B C

398. Roman Responsibility for Italy.—Rome was now head of the Italian land, unifier and protector of its peoples. But this high position involved responsibility (1) for the defence of its coasts and (2) for the protection of its commerce. Dangers in both of these directions appeared on account of the power of the African city, Carthage. The founding of Carthage and its commercial activity in the western Mediterranean have already been mentioned (§§ 352, 170). North Africa as far as the Atlantic was under its authority, as was also a goodly share of Sicily. In that island Carthage had waged long wars with the Greeks for supremacy (§§ 170, 176, 249, 328-331). Its ships had contested the trade of the Adriatic sea with the Greeks of Magna Græcia, and were found in every port of the west. Corsica, Sardinia and portions of the Spanish peninsula were its possessions; while the trade of all Spain was in its hands. Such commercial influence and activity brought immense wealth to the city, and for centuries had given it easily the leading position in the west.

Threatening Power of Carthage.

399. Change in Relations of Rome and Carthage Unavoidable.—As long as Rome was an inland and provincial city, occupied with local affairs, interested in local trade, relations with Carthage had been friendly. Indeed, when Italy had been threatened by the Greeks, led by Pyrrhus (§§ 331, 377), Rome and Carthage had formed an alliance. But now the situation was changed.

Threaten-
ing In-
crease of
Roman
Power.
Rome had taken into its possession the Greek cities of Italy and was bound to protect their interests. Thus at this point it came into touch with Carthage's commercial activity. Nor could Carthage, on its part, accept willingly a limitation of its commerce. It is indispensable to every such community to enlarge and strengthen its trade. The one region remaining in the west which could thus be exploited was Italy. Accordingly, it is not strange that Carthaginian pressure upon the Italian peninsula grew greater just at the moment when Rome's duty of protecting Italy became clear to her statesmen. In these circumstances a conflict of interests leading to open war was unavoidable.

400. Sicily the Scene of the First Breach.—The occasion that opened the breach was insignificant. Its scene was the contested ground of Sicily. There, after
The
Mamer-
tines.
the death of Agathocles of Syracuse (§ 330), a band of his mercenaries, calling themselves Mamertines ("Sons of Mars"), had seized Mes-sa'na, the Sicilian town nearest Italy, and for the following twenty-five years were the scourge of the northeastern part of the island. While
Hieron of
Syracuse.
waging war against them a Syracusan officer named Hi'e-ron obtained such prominence that in 269 B.C. he overturned the republican government with the aid of his army and made himself in that year tyrant of Syracuse and five years later, after a great victory over the Mamertines, king of Sicily. Unable to hold out against him, the Mamertines appealed to Rome. While the appeal was being considered, a faction also asked help of Carthage and the Carthaginians seized the town. The Roman senate hesitated to become embroiled in a war outside Italy, but the comitia centuriata in which prior

to *ca.* 241 B.C. the commercial interests had large influence finally decided to help the Mamertines and despatched a force which expelled the Carthaginian garrison. Thus war with Carthage was declared (264 B.C.).

401. The First Punic War, 264-241 B.C.—This war, called the First Punic* War, lasted for nearly a quarter of a century.

402. Rome and Carthage Contrasted.—It was not unlike the great struggle between Athens and Sparta in that Carthage avoided meeting the much superior land army of Rome and Rome at first conceded to Carthage control of the sea. Rome had under it a population of about five million, Carthage, with a city population of about half a million, had in its empire about five million people also; but whereas Rome could put for years at a stretch one hundred thousand men in the field, Carthage was mainly dependent upon mercenaries and seldom was able to employ more than thirty thousand of them. The main asset of Carthage was its wealth. Its revenues were far greater than those of Rome, which was weak financially; but the first consideration in Carthage was the fleet in which it had on occasion as many as three hundred and fifty vessels, most of them the huge top-heavy quin'que-remes which became the normal battle-ships in the third century B.C. (§ 318). To maintain such a fleet, however, strained to the limit even the enormous resources of Carthage.

Population and Military Resources.

403. Dependencies and Allies of Rome and Carthage.—Carthage had no hope from the start of evening up conditions on land with Rome, since it could not de-

* "Punic" is a form of "Phœnician." Carthage was a Phœnician or Punic colony.

pend upon the loyalty of the native population of Libya, or of its other dependencies, which it exploited ruthlessly for its own profit, and which were a source rather of military weakness than of strength to their masters; nor could it use its own urban population for foreign warfare because in the first place the masses were of little service and in the second place they would fight only for their own protection. Rome, on the other hand, controlled, along the eastern and southern coast of Italy and in Sicily, many Greek cities which it treated with singular generosity and which had fought Carthage to a standstill on the sea for generations before they had entered into the Italian federation. The government of both countries was in the hands of an intelligent aristocracy, the one of merchants, the other of landed proprietors. That of Carthage stood at the head of a peaceful people absorbed in commercial and industrial occupations; that of Rome at the head of a warlike peasantry flushed with victory after victory in Italy, keen for fresh booty, and stoutly loyal and devoted to its leaders. The incompetence of these for the conduct of systematic campaigns and dangerous naval operations was the signal weakness of Rome; for Carthage had long since reached the point of giving charge of its armies and fleets to approved officers and keeping them in command for year after year in succession, whereas Rome entrusted its armies to amateur generals and changed them annually. This was the main reason for the length of the struggle.

Govern-
ment.

A Mercan-
tile vs an
Agrarian
Aristoc-
racy.

404. The Roman Fleet: Mylæ.—The first advantage was gained by Rome when it got its army safely over to Sicily and with it forced Hieron of Syracuse to enter its alliance   All that seemed now necessary was to take the fortified cities into which the Carthaginians withdrew, and, indeed, after a long and difficult siege, the chief place held by them in Greek Sicily, Ag-ri-gen'tum, was captured in 261 B.C. It was practically starved into submission. This could not be done in the case of the Phœnician towns on the coast, Pa-nor'mus, Lil-y-bæ'um and Drep'a-na. Hence Rome decided to use its naval resources and gain possession of the sea. A fleet of one hundred quinque- remes and twenty triremes was, accordingly, despatched to Sicilian waters in 260 B.C under the command of the consul Gaius Duilius. It was contributed, manned and financed mainly by Greeks, but on each ship sailed a body of Roman soldiers. The plan was to drop a newly invented "boarding bridge" with spikes at the end on the deck of the Cathaginian ship whenever two vessels came to close action, and thus to turn the sea fight into a land engagement. The plan succeeded admirably and on the high sea off Mylæ Duilius gained the first naval victory for the Romans and captured sixty of the enemy's ships. This was the opening of a long duel for the mastery of the western Mediterranean, and it was fought out at the same time that the other African power, Egypt, was en- gaged in a similar duel with Macedon for the possession of the eastern Mediterranean (§ 318).

The First Roman Fleet.

405. Regulus in Africa.—Despite Mylæ Rome made no progress with its operations against Panormus, Lily- bæum and Drepana. Hence in 256 B C. the senate decided to carry the war into Africa, which the invasion of Agath- ocles fifty-four years earlier had shown to be the weak place in the Carthaginian armor. First, however, the Punic fleet, three hundred and fifty ships strong, which put itself in the way of the Roman-Greek navy with the army of invasion on board, had to be dealt with. The great sea fight took place at Ec'no-mus, the contestants being about equal in strength. Victory rested with the Romans, and the landing in Africa was made successfully. At this point one of the consuls returned with the fleet to Italy, the other Regulus remained with fifteen thousand men to conduct the war in Africa. In 256 B.C. he defeated the Carthaginians and seized Tunis almost in sight of the huge city, but in the next year he and his army were overwhelmed; and while taking the remnants back home the Roman fleet was destroyed by a storm.

406. Both Parties Exhausted.—The struggle was again centred round the Phœnician forts in Sicily, and in 253 B.C. the Romans gained a great success in the capture of Panormus, but on the return to Italy a second Roman fleet was destroyed by storm. The trouble with the great lofty quinqueremes was that they tended to turn turtle in a rough sea. The ignorant Roman admirals, moreover, took unnecessary risks. Upon the other two places, Lilybæum and Drepana, the Romans made little impression; and when in 249 B C. P. Claudius lost one Roman fleet in action off Drepana, and when in 248 B.C. L. Junius lost another in action off Cam-a-ri'na, the

war came to a standstill. Both contestants were exhausted; and for seven years the only interest the struggle possessed was in the brilliant guerilla warfare conducted by Ha-mil'car, surnamed Barca ("the lightning"), in Sicily. Finally the Romans roused themselves to new action; the funds for a new navy were provided, as usual, by advances of money made to the government by

its patriotic citizens This fleet the consul Cat'u-lus led to victory at the Ægatian islands in 241 B.C., whereupon

Carthage was compelled to ask for peace. It was granted on these terms: Carthage retired from Sicily and the islands between Sicily and Italy; she promised also to pay during a period of ten years three thousand two hundred talents (241 B.C).

407. The Mercenary War, 241-237 B.C.—But the strength of the Punic city was by no means exhausted; the conflict was sure to break out again when time and resources were favorable to its renewal. It was, indeed, deferred for the moment by the horrible "truceless" war (241-237 B C.) between Carthage and its mercenaries— whose pay was greatly in arrears—in which only the genius of Hamilcar Barca saved his country from destruction. But it was made inevitable in that at the crisis of this struggle Carthage had to suffer a further humiliation in the seizure of Sardinia by the Romans and an additional payment of one thousand two hundred talents (238 B.C.). A remonstrance was met by a threat of war which helpless Carthage bought off only by the cession of Sardinia and Corsica. The two islands together formed the second Roman province. Rome, also, had other difficulties on hand which occupied its attention.

Seizure of Sardinia and Corsica.

408. The Gallic Wars.—The Gauls in the north of Italy were causing trouble, and when the tribune Flamin'i-us carried a law to assign to citizens the public lands along the coast of Umbria the Gallic tribes already irritated rose in revolt. The struggle could have but one result; the Gauls were crushed and the Latin colonies of Placentia and Cremona were placed in the conquered territory. A road from Rome to A-rim'i-num, called the Via Flaminia after its builder, Flaminius, brought this restless district within striking distance of the capital. The land between the Alps and the Apennines was called Cisalpine Gaul. The annoyance caused by Illyrian pirates to Roman commerce in the Adriatic brought on Illyrian wars (229 and 219 B C), in which due punishment was inflicted on the aggressors, friendly relations established with the Greek states and the Adriatic made an Italian sea.

409. The Punic Power in Spain.—The occasion for the second struggle with Carthage appeared in an unexpected quarter. One of the most skilful Punic generals, Hamilcar Barca, animated by an inextinguishable hatred for Rome, retired to Spain after the "truceless" war and there spent nine years in building up a Carthaginian power which might furnish men and money to renew the war with Rome. After his death, first his son-in-law Has'dru-bal (228–221 B.C.) and later his son Hannibal, with splendid vigor and success, carried on his work. The wild tribes south of the river Ebro were tamed, united and organized into an effective force. Money and munitions of war were collected and a plan of campaign, bold beyond all expectation, was devised. The first step precipitated war. Sa-gun'tum, a petty fort in alliance with Rome, was attacked and captured by Hannibal. His surrender was at once demanded and as promptly refused, whereupon a Roman ambassador in the picturesque fashion of the Roman declaration of war "gathered his toga in two folds—'War or peace,' he cried; 'which will you have?' 'Which you will,' was the answer. He shook out the fold of war, and war was accepted by Carthage with a light heart." Then with an army of fifty thousand infantry and nine thousand cavalry, supported by fighting elephants, Hannibal marched north-

Margin notes:

Illyrian Wars.

Hamilcar and Hasdrubal in Spain.

Hannibal.

Declaration of War.

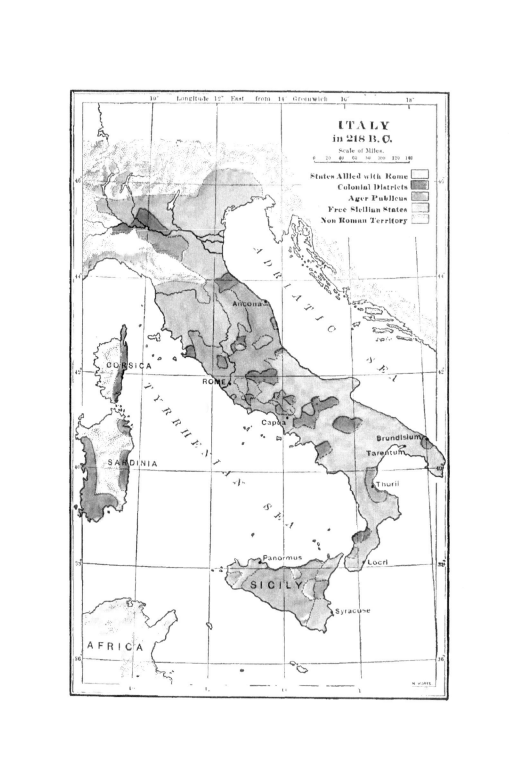

ITALY
in 218 B. C.

Scale of Miles.
0 20 40 60 80 100 120 140

States Allied with Rome
Colonial Districts
Ager Publicus
Free Sicilian States
Non Roman Territory

Longitude 12° East from 14° Greenwich 16°

CORSICA

TYRRHENIAN SEA

SARDINIA

Ancona

ROME

Capua

Brundisium

Tarentum

Thurii

Locri

Panormus

SICILY

Syracuse

ADRIATIC SEA

AFRICA

ward with no less audacious a design than the crossing of the Alps and the descent into northern Italy. After Hannibal Invades Italy. almost incredible hardships, through fightings with wild tribes and the fierceness of winter storms among the high Alps, the army, reduced to less than half its number, stood exhausted, but triumphant, on the plains of Cisalpine Gaul.

410. Hannibal in Italy.—And now began a duel to the death, the Second Punic War (218 B.C.).* The fate of Rome hung on the loyalty of the allied cities of Italy. The newly conquered Gauls soon rose and flocked to Hannibal. The Roman army under the consuls was routed at battles on the banks of the rivers

BATTLE OF CANNAE.
1 Roman Cavalry
2 Cavalry of Allies
3 Roman Light Armed Troops
4 Roman Heavy Armed Troops
a Carthaginian Cavalry
b Numidian Cavalry
c African Infantry
d Spanish and Gallic Infantry

Defeat of Roman Armies.

Ti-ci′nus and the Treb′i-a. The next year (217 B.C.) Hannibal, advancing southward, entrapped and annihilated another Roman army at Lake Tras-i-me′nus in Etruria; the consul Flaminius was killed in the battle. Then the Romans in alarm appointed Quintus Fabius Maximus dictator, known in history as the "shield of Rome." He would not give battle, but followed on the heels of Hannibal as he marched down to the southeast ravaging the country. New commanders, the consuls

* It is suggested that the teacher amplify the sketch of this great war by the aid of graphic passages chosen from Livy and Polybius

Æmilius Paulus and Terentius Varro, and a new and great army of more than eighty thousand men marched out against him in 216 B.C.; again the Romans were utterly beaten at Cannæ in Apulia; one consul, Varro, and ten thousand men survived the slaughter. In this as in all the other Italian engagements of Hannibal the victory was gained or rendered complete by his clever use of his wonderful Numidian cavalry.

411. The Italian Allies Desert.—Rome now appeared on the verge of destruction. The majority of the Roman allies in southern Italy (§ 383) passed over to Hannibal's side—Capua and Tarentum among the rest. In Sicily, Syracuse and its dependencies renounced the Roman alliance. Philip V of Macedonia (§ 327) made an alliance with Hannibal. And, in fact, Hannibal had substantially accomplished his mission, which was not the annihilation of Rome, but the dissolution of the Italian federation and the reduction of its head to its historic position as one among the many petty states of the peninsula. Henceforth, all he had to do was to maintain his position in Italy and prevent the Romans from re-establishing their he-

gem'o-ny. But the heroic Roman spirit remained unshaken. An offer of peace by the victor of Cannæ was rejected. An army sent to Syracuse under the command of Me-tel'lus, "the sword of Rome," captured that city and restored Roman power in Sicily. War was declared against Philip. Energetic efforts were put forth to recover the rebellious Italian cities, while further pitched battles with Hannibal were avoided. The fortified posts occupied by Roman allies all over the land—the Latin colonies (§ 382)—held fast to Rome. Thus gradually the sky brightened, while Hannibal's task grew more difficult.

He lost Capua in 211 B.C , and a dash at Rome in the same year failed. Tarentum was taken by the Romans in 209 B.C. The crisis of the struggle came when Hasdrubal, Hannibal's brother, eluding the enemy in Spain, started for Italy. Already Rome was near the end of its resources. Twelve Latin colonies announced that they could keep up the struggle no longer. If the two Carthaginian armies could unite, their victory was sure. But in 207 B.C. the army of Hasdrubal was destroyed at the river Me-tau'rus, he himself killed and his head thrown over the ramparts of his brother's camp. As Hannibal looked upon it, he is said to have declared, "I behold the fate of Carthage." This battle decided that Hannibal could maintain his position in Italy for only a limited time. Soon his diminishing army was shut up in the region of Bruttium. Peace was made between Rome and Philip. *The Metaurus*

412. **The War in Spain.**—Meanwhile, a tedious war had been carried on in Spain—Hannibal's sole possible source of reinforcements—by the brothers Publius and Gnæus Scipio, who were both finally overthrown and killed (212 B.C.). All Spain seemed lost to the Romans when the son of the slain general, Publius Cornelius Scipio, a brilliant young Roman officer, who earlier than anyone else saw the advantage of fighting the war out in Hannibal's own country, came to Spain with an army (211 B.C.). He did not, indeed, prevent the departure of Hasdrubal for Italy, but after a series of striking campaigns he was able in 206 B.C. to return to Italy leaving Rome master of the Carthaginian part of the Iberian peninsula. Two years later he advanced his project a step further by crossing the sea with an army to carry the war into Africa. *Scipio Africanus*

413. "The War into Africa."—Hannibal was recalled
to defend his country and was overthrown by Scipio at

the battle of Zama (202 B.C.).* The war was over;

Carthage was ruined, and nothing was left but to seek
as favorable terms of peace as possible. They were not
too severe; Spain and the Mediterranean islands were
given up; the kingdom of Numidia was granted its independence under King Mas'si-nis'sa, whose claim to the
throne of all Numidia Rome had espoused, and war upon
it was forbidden; the fleet was reduced to ten triremes;
a payment of two hundred talents yearly for fifty years
was imposed Thus Carthage, while not destroyed, lost
its political and commerical supremacy and became little
more than a dependency of Rome.

414. The Power and Position of the Senate.—During
this long struggle with a foreign enemy the administration
of the Roman state underwent some changes. We have
seen that the political strife of patrician and plebeian
had ended in the victory of the latter and the harmonizing of all interests in a popular government (§§ 362–366).
But when war with Carthage came, it was found that a

strong administration was necessary to conduct it. The
citizens, therefore, let the senate manage affairs, since it
was a compact body of the best men in the state and was
always at hand in Rome on critical occasions Thus
the senate slowly absorbed the powers of government,
which, in theory, belonged to the people. The magistrates, although elected by the people, were guided by
the senate and fulfilled its will. This was to mean much
in the future, but at present it worked successfully. The
firmness and courage with which the senate went about

* From this victory Scipio gained the title Africanus.

its task of carrying on the war, supplying soldiers, encouraging the people, resisting all appeals for peace until the work was done, is worthy of all praise. The only body in Rome which could give this kind of an administration was the senate; hence the government came more and more securely into its grasp.

415. Composition of the Senate.—The strength of this great corporation was due largely to the influence of the men who composed it. On the list of its members the censors were in the habit of registering all ex-magistrates not already enrolled. Only when these did not suffice to fill the vacancies in the aggregate of three hundred did the censors have the liberty to nominate others. Senators held office for life. Only gross misbehavior justified the censors in leaving the names of old members off the list. Accordingly, outside the senate there was rarely anybody who had ever held an important civil or military office; in it were all Romans possessed of knowledge and experience of public affairs.

Ex-Magistrates Enter the Senate.

416. The Senate and the Magistrates.—Moreover, while the people in Rome chose their magistrates, only senators were qualified to be candidates for the higher positions. The reason for this was that the lower offices —such as the tribunate, quæstorship, ædileship—had to be held first, and on holding them men generally became senators. Hence, what the people did was virtually to select from the senate annual committees of senators to hold the prætorships and consulships. Since men were senators for their lifetime and magistrates for only a single year, they did not care to do anything while consuls or prætors to impair the power of the body to which they were to belong permanently. Thus

Higher Magistrates Chosen from the Senate.

the senate was able to retain its control of the higher magistrates.

417. The Senate and the Tribunate.—Should, however, any officer ignore or defy the senate it was always possible for it to get a tribune to veto his actions. A single tribune was able to stop all public business in Rome—to seal up the treasury, suspend the law courts, reduce every magistrate to inactivity, even prevent all votes of the comitia. Hence the senate had an invincible guardian so long as the veto of the tribunes was observed and one of these ten officers was ready to take the senate's point of view.

Tribunes Protect Senate.

418. The Senate and the Assemblies.—The senate, however, was ordinarily able to control the elections and to prevent all but members of the senatorial families from getting elected to the lower offices. It was, indeed, a rare occurrence for a new "man" (*novus homo*) to rise to the prætorship or consulship in Rome. This monopoly of office was preserved largely by the way the electoral divisions were formed. There were now thirty-five tribes and the tribes had each one vote in the comitia tributa and ten centuries in the comitia centuriata. Of the thirty-five only four were open to the urban—landless and freedman—population; so that no matter how many of the residents of Rome flocked down to the Forum or out to the Campus Martius when the comitia met, they could cast only four votes out of thirty-five or forty out of three hundred and fifty. On the other hand, sixteen of the tribes—the so-called "rustic tribes"—lay in the territory immediately around the city. As time passed the land in this district tended to gather in the hands of a smaller and smaller number of great landholders; so that

Senate Controls Elections.

the "rustic tribes" became in a sense "pocket boroughs" of the senators. The other fifteen tribes lay up and down Italy, usually at such a distance from the capital that only men of means and leisure resident on them—men who owned town houses and tilled their estates by slaves —were in a position to appear regularly at the public meetings. The net result was that the land proprietors —"the country gentlemen"—who made up the senatorial or office-holding nobility were able to outvote the masses in the comitia and distribute the offices among themselves as they pleased. Hence the senate could always count on having the support of at least one tribune. A tribune, however, could prevent the magistrates from calling the comitia together; hence to control the magistrates meant ordinarily to control the assemblies.

419. The Constitutional Weaknesses of the Senate.— Should, however, the masses of the countrymen of Italy become dissatisfied and flock to the comitia in tens of thousands to vote for what they wanted; that is to say, should the peasants of Italy want strongly something which the government did not care to give to them, the position of the senate would be in the highest degree perilous. But so long as it was successful in its wars in Italy and abroad, and new land and rich booty were continuously provided for the Roman peasants, so long as the struggle for national honor and existence fired the patriotism of every Roman farmer, the senate was the accepted leader of the agriculturists of the peninsula, and the senator's sons were the men whom the citizens naturally chose to be their officers in the army and in the state.

Success the Chief Asset of the Senate.

420. The Senate's Method of Transacting Business.— The senate was usually convoked by the consuls. The

summons indicated the place and day of the meeting:
the time was daybreak, the place a *templum,* or sacred
enclosure, usually the *curia Hostilia* in the Forum.   The
summons did not disclose the subject upon which the
senators were to tender advice to the magistrates—for it
was solely to advise that the senate existed, not to command or legislate.   Accordingly, there was no opportunity for previous study or manipulation.   It was the duty
of the presiding officer to put the senate into possession
of the facts.   This he did in laying each matter before
the chamber.   The senate did not work with the aid of
committees, except in so far as each pair of magistrates
was its committee; hence no opportunity whatever was
given for the mature consideration of public business
outside the walls of the senate chamber.   The deliberate purpose was that the decisions should be reached in
the senate itself.   That outside pressure might not dis-
turb the equanimity of the senators, all debates were
held behind closed doors.   On either side of the central
aisle, at the farther end of which the magistrates took their
places in their robes of office on their ivory curule chairs,
sat the three hundred senators clad in their white togas
slashed with broad purple stripes.   At one epoch the
tribunes had taken their places at the door of the chamber
and thence heard what they could of the discussion, now
they had drawn their long bench into the room and sat
in the aisle with the magistrates.   At the door crowded
the sons of the senators—the young men destined for a
public life who had not as yet reached the age of office-
holding.   Others were kept beyond hearing by the lictors.

   The senators gave their opinions seated; men rose only
when they voted.   The speeches were short and pithy—

PLATE XXIX

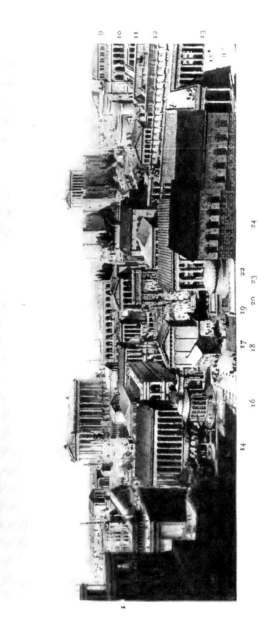

1 Palace of the Caesars.
2 Temple of Jupiter Capitolinus.
3 Temple of Saturn.
4 Tabularium. Temple of Vespasian.
5 Temple of Concord.
6 Arch of Septimius Severus.

7 Temple of Juno Moneta on the Arx.
8 Temple of Mother Venus.
9 Basilica Ulpia.
10 Forum of Trajan.
11 Forum of Augustus.
12 Forum of Nerva.

13 Forum of Vespasian.
14 Temple of Castor and Pollux.
15 Basilica Julia.
16 Temple of Vesta.
17 Temple of Julius Cæsar.
18 Regia.

19 FORUM.
20 Sacred Way.
21 Basilica Æmilia.
22 Temple of Antoninus Pius.
23 Temple of Romulus.
24 Templum Sacræ Urbis.

THE ROMAN FORUM AND THE SURROUNDING BUILDINGS (RESTORED)

the blunt opinions of farmers—and each ended with a motion upon the question at issue. It might simply be an endorsement of an opinion already given. In fact, the only senator who could not escape the onus of giving a formal opinion (*sententia*) was the *princeps senatus*— the oldest ex-censor ordinarily, the man whom the censors on drawing up the list of the senators had put at its head. The others were arranged behind him in accordance with the offices they had held—ex-consuls and ex-prætors having precedence over ex-ædiles. Within each group the place of the individual was decided by seniority. While each senator in turn was expressing his opinion, the voting was in progress. By leaving their places and taking their seats in the vicinity of the man with whose opinion they agreed, the senators kept showing to the presiding officer how they were voting; so that at the end of the process he had to select the opinion he pleased and put it to the whole for a final vote only when more than two popular views had been expressed. The possibility existed for prolonging the discussion indefinitely; for not only was the method of eliciting the will of the senate cumbrous, but the senator when called upon could speak for any length of time he pleased upon any subject he pleased. That, none the less, the enormous amount of public business which arose in Rome, Italy and finally in the entire Mediterranean world, was transacted quickly and wisely is the highest tribute that can be paid to the wonderful political sense of the Roman senators.

421. The Business of the Senate.—The senate could not meet of its own accord, but was dependent upon the magistrates for its corporate existence. It had no

Discussion in the Senate

Voting in the Senate.

legal power to enforce its decrees, and no judicial process could compel any magistrate to follow the advice it gave. It had no judicial authority of any kind except in cases of crisis or emergency. It had no legislative power; and by the Hortensian law of 287 B.C. it had lost all right to regulate or modify the votes of the comitia. None the less, it was the real government of Rome. The business of a state commonly falls into three groups. There are first the regular foreseen tasks which in Rome the magistrates performed: the care of the streets and public buildings (ædiles), the handling of the public funds (quæstors), the settling of disputes (prætors), the handling of the troops and convoking the senate and assembly (consuls), the taking of the census and the imposition of the taxes (censors). With these the senate had no concern. There are in the second place the extraordinary and unforeseen measures affecting the mode of life of the entire people, which in Rome required the action of the comitia: the enactment of a new law, the creation of a new magistracy, the declaration of war, the conclusion of a peace or treaty, the foundation of a colony on the public land, the punishment of a criminal or traitor. Such matters lay beyond the competency of the senate. In the third place there is the great body of extraordinary but foreseen cases where an important decision has to be reached. It might be something unusual in the work of a magistrate, such as the need for levying troops or imposing a war tax; it might be the demand of the people for a new law or a new colony, or a war or a peace; it might be the arrival of an embassy from a foreign state; it might be a strange omen. For the formulation of a policy on such matters the senate was the only proper authority in Rome. Its

The Division of Duties between the Magistrates, the Comitia and the Senate.

province was, in other words, that of the cabinet in the modern parliamentary system.

422. The Roman Assemblies.—The comitia was simply an arrangement of the citizens for convenience of voting. When the comitia was called all discussion ceased. Debate could take place only at unorganized meetings (*contiones*) summoned by the magistrates for that purpose. Only those whom the presiding officers permitted could address the multitude. When the comitia met, it could consider only a programme of business published three weeks in advance by the convening magistrate. Each citizen then went into the compartment assigned to his tribe or century, and on passing out across a bridge told his vote to clerks who recorded it on wax tablets with which they were provided When all had passed out the votes were counted and the vote of the tribe or century declared by the presiding officer. The majority of tribes or centuries determined the issue of the vote. As already explained, this system of group voting permitted the urban population to be "hived" in four-thirty-fifths of the electoral districts; so that the ill-effects of the change which finally occured in the character of the inhabitants of the city of Rome were for a long time obviated. Still, it was a matter of grave concern to the government that as Rome became the capital of Italy and subsequently of the entire Mediterranean world, it ceased to be essentially an aggregate of small and large farmers and came to resemble more and more closely the great cities of the present day. Probably nothing contributed more to the long supremacy of the senate than the fear of all reflecting men that the proletariat of Rome should really exercise sovereign power.

Voting in the Comitia.

Fear of the Mob.

423. The Financial Problem.—The senate's solution of two problems is noteworthy. To procure money and supplies for carrying on the war it adopted a curious plan. Instead of organizing a financial system of its own, it sought the aid of wealthy capitalists and merchants and gave the task into their hands. They supplied the money, the ships, the food, the equipment. The state was thus relieved from a great burden of business; but this relief was dearly bought by bringing the state into bondage to these men of wealth. As their operations widened, the dependence of the administration upon them increased. They began to have an undue influence in shaping its policy. They made the state serve their interests.* But they could not themselves become senators; for a law had been passed in 218 B C. prohibiting "members of the governing class from taking part in foreign trade, as carriers, as manufacturers, or as participants in the great business of the contract for corn which placed provincial grain on the Roman market." Hence those who engaged in foreign commerce and bid for government contracts became the nucleus of a new class —the influential equestrian order.

The
Publicans.

424. The Problem of Conquered Territories.—The other problem was the relation of the newly won territories outside of Italy to the Roman state. We have seen that, in bringing Italy under Roman rule, either the peoples had been made Roman citizens or their relations had been determined by a perpetual treaty (§§ 382–384). But when, at the close of the first Punic war, Sicily and Sardinia became Roman, neither of these

---

* Such men were called *publicani*, "contractors," whence our word "publican." They formed a large part of the equestrian order (§ 439).

methods was adopted, but a prætor (§ 353) was placed in charge of them. This kind of authority, that of a mili-The Province tary magistrate dealing with conquered peoples, was called *provincia*, a name which was also given to the territory thus governed The prætor maintained order and rendered justice in the province, his authority was sustained by a body of Roman soldiers. By this means no new magistrates were appointed nor any new authority created by the Roman administration. The plan worked well enough for a temporary expedient, but the dangers of giving the unlimited authority of a military magistrate to the governor of conquered territories soon became clear as Rome's conquests extended. Of these we shall hear in the coming years.

425. Rome Ruler of the West.—The year 200 B C. saw Rome the ruler of the western Mediterranean. The regions that had been dominated by Carthage—North Africa, Spain, Sicily, and the other islands—passed under Roman sway. The city, which had successfully united Italy and held it firm against the terrific assaults of Hannibal, had now a larger task, the ruling of the west Its imperial destiny was becoming clearer. The New Problems. questions which now pressed for solution were such as these: Was Rome's dominion to be limited to the west? Could Rome succeed in uniting and governing its empire, as it had succeeded with Italy? In these new imperial tasks was Rome itself to remain unchanged? These questions were soon to have their answer.

REVIEW EXERCISES. 1. For what are the following noted: Agathocles, Regulus, Fabius Maximus, Philip V, Zama, Metaurus? 2. Name in order the battles of the second Punic war. 3. What is meant by prætor, quæstor, censor, provincia, Punic,

Latin colony, allied state? 4. What was the duration of this period (dates) and how much of it was taken up with the wars with Carthage? 5. What was the character of the senate during the period of the Carthaginian wars? 6. Explain the position of a tribune in the senate at this time. 7. What was the tribal arrangement? 8. In what state matters had the senate control? Give in detail the method of transacting business in the senate. 9. Describe the system of voting in use in the Roman assemblies.

COMPARATIVE STUDIES. 1. Compare the Roman province with the provinces of Egypt (§ 42), Assyria (§§ 65, 70), Persia (§ 81) and Alexander the Great (§ 299). 2. Compare Hannibal's invasion of Italy with the Persian invasion of Greece (§§ 165, 169–175) 3. "Success is in no way necessary to greatness." Does Hannibal's career justify this assertion?

SELECT LIST FOR READING. 1. Rome and Carthage Contrasted. (a) Rome's Organization, Army and Navy. How and Leigh, pp 131–143. (b) The Organization and Resources of Carthage. How and Leigh, pp. 143–149. 2. The First Punic War. How and Leigh, pp 149–162. 3. The Second Punic War. How and Leigh, chs 21, 22 4. The Battle of Cannæ. How and Leigh, pp. 194–198 5. Hannibal's Character. How and Leigh, pp 171–172.

TOPICS FOR READING AND ORAL REPORT. 1. The Carthaginian Empire. Shuckburgh, pp 223–232, Myres, pp. 149–152; Horton, pp 60–63 2. The First Punic War. Shuckburgh, chs. 18, 19 3. The Second Punic War. Shuckburgh, chs. 22–25; Myres, chs 16–18 4. The Story of Regulus. Seignobos, pp. 92–93 5. Hannibal's March to Italy. Laing, pp. 362–373 (source), Munro, pp 85–86 (source), Horton, pp. 78–81. 6. The Battle of Cannæ. Laing, pp 372–380 (source); Morey, pp. 117, 118; Shuckburgh, pp 323–328. 7. Fabius Maximus. Plutarch's Life of Fabius. 8. Hannibal as a Man. Laing, pp. 360–362 (source); Seignobos, p. 99. 9. Hannibal as a General: His Strategy (a) at Trebia, (b) at Ticinus, (c) at Trasimene, (d) at Cannæ—see the histories as referred to above. 10. The Roman Provincial System. Abbott, pp. 88–91; Horton, ch. 14; Morey, pp. 146–148.

5.—ROME'S CONQUEST OF THE EAST

200 133 B C.

426. Preliminary Survey.—The year 200 B C marks the moment when the separate stream of Roman history merges into the main current of the larger history of the world of the east. How rich and splendid in its culture that Greek world had become, how active and absorbed it was in its imperial enterprises and how fatally it was weakened through its division into three great monarchies, has already been described (§§ 307–309, 318, 322, 327). Rome's progress, at first only indirectly connected with the eastern world, had steadily moved in the direction of closer relations (§ 327). Hardly had the conflict with Carthage been won, when a war broke out with Macedonia. Thus Rome was involved directly with the politics of the east and could not call a halt until the kingdoms of Macedonia, Syria and Egypt, with the lesser powers of Greece and Asia Minor, became either subjects or allies of Rome. Thus was created an empire around the Mediterranean sea, from the Atlantic to the Euphrates river. This splendid conquering career with its effects on Roman life we are now to follow in detail.

427. Wars of Rome with Macedonia, 215-205 B.C.—The war with Philip V of Macedonia that followed his alliance with Hannibal (§§ 327, 411) was brought to an end in 205 B C. by a treaty of peace that was hardly more than a temporary truce. Philip, however, was the first to violate it by attacking Roman allies in Greece and the east; the Romans were not slow to respond by a declaration of war (200 B.C.). The chief powers of Greece, the Ætolian

Marginal notes:
- Preliminary Survey.
- The Eastern Kingdoms.
- Rome Becomes Lord of the East.
- Overthrow of Philip V.

Second
Macedo-
nian War
(200-197
B C).
and Achæan leagues (§§ 320–322), joined with them.
After two ineffectual years, Titus Quinctius Flam-i-ni'nus
led the Roman legions to victory at the battle of Cy'nos-
ceph'a-læ (197 B.C.), in Thessaly, where against the Roman maniples the Macedonian phalanx as a fighting
machine was found wanting. Philip obtained peace at
the price of becoming a dependent ally of Rome, losing
all territory outside of Macedonia and paying one thousand talents. As for Greece itself, the Romans declared
its several states to be, henceforth, independent of the
authority which Macedon had tried to impose on Greece
Greece
Made Free.
since the battle of Chæroneia (§ 277). All Greece was
free once more to work out its own salvation. Rome had
no desire to interfere with its affairs and would see to it
that no other power did so.

428. War with Antiochus, 192-188 B.C.—Antiochus
III, king of Syria, however, viewed with increasing disfavor the appearance of Rome in the east. Roman influence opposed him in Egypt and on the coasts of Asia
Minor. To him Hannibal fled a few years after the fall
of Carthage and kept his anger hot. Now, upon the overthrow of Macedonia, a suitable time seemed to him to have
come to assert his supremacy over Greece. On the invitation of the Ætolian league he entered Greece (192 B.C.).
Antiochus
III
Defeated.
But in the next year he was defeated in the historic pass
of Thermopylæ and driven out of Greece. The following year (190 B C) the Roman army under Lucius Cornelius Scipio,* the consul, who was aided by his brother,
the victor of Zama, crossed into Asia Minor and overthrew the army of Antiochus at Magnesia. The proud
king made a humiliating peace, resigned his possessions in

---

* Because of this victory he got the title Asiaticus.

Europe and Asia Minor and paid an indemnity of twelve thousand talents to the Romans. He further agreed to keep no war elephants and to add no warships to the ten which he was permitted to retain. The treaty called for the surrender of Hannibal, but the great general escaped, only to flee from place to place until, in 183 B.C., he ended his own life by poison. The territories taken from Antiochus were handed over to loyal allies; Eumenes, king of Pergamon (§ 326), received a large share, and his kingdom became, along with Rhodes, a bulwark of Roman influence in the east. The Seleucid empire never recovered from this blow which proved to the subject peoples in Asia that their Greek masters were not invincible. A long series of revolts and dynastic struggles followed which left only a weakened fragment of the once great empire when it fell into the hands of the Romans.

429. The Third Macedonian War, 171-167 B.C.—Eighteen years passed quietly when, in 171 B.C., war broke out a third time with Macedonia. Philip had been followed by his son Perseus, who succeeded in gaining a number of Greek states to unite with him in resisting Rome. They felt that freedom under Roman patronage was not real freedom. Perseus offered a long and vigorous resistance; but in 168 B.C. he was defeated by Lucius Æmilius Paulus at Pydna, where again the Macedonian phalanx was shattered. The king fled with his treasure, but was captured; an immense booty was brought to Rome, where Paulus enjoyed the most splendid "triumph" (§ 385) that the city had ever seen. The state treasury was filled so full that the regular tax upon the citizens was remitted and was not again imposed. Macedonia was divided into four separate independent districts allied to Rome; the

free states of Greece were severely dealt with. The rebellious leagues of Ætolia and Bœotia were dissolved.
The Achæan league, which had stood loyal, had to send
one thousand of its leading citizens to Rome, where
they were unjustly detained in practical exile for many
years. Among them was Po-lyb'i-us, who afterward wrote
a history of the Roman conquest of the world. Even the
loyal allies of Rome in the east, Pergamon and Rhodes,
were treated harshly.

430. The Maccabæan Uprising in Judea.—The next
twenty years (168–149 B.C.) show Rome at a standstill
in eastern affairs. All the eastern powers hung upon the
word of the senate, and their ambassadors thronged the
senate-house. During these years, as we have seen (§§
319, 428), the Jews burst out in rebellion against Antiochus IV of Syria because he had violated the sanctity of
their temple and trampled upon their sacred law. Led
by the valiant family called the Maccabees, they heroically
and successfully fought off the Syrian armies and sought
the aid of Rome, which made a treaty with them, but gave
no actual help. At last they secured their independence
in 143 B. C., under Simon Mac-ca-bæ'us, and set up a kingdom ruled by members of his family The greater and
lesser powers of the east were falling into decay. The
Greek states intrigued and squabbled. The kingdoms
of Syria and Egypt were rent by internal quarrels
Rome stood grimly by and waited, vexed by the continual
appeals for her aid, yet unready to take active steps for
interference.

431. The Roman Attitude toward the Eastern Powers.
--Thus far Rome had been drawn on into the affairs
of the east with hesitation and uncertainty. The troubles

with Macedonia and Syria had not been of her making; she had avoided responsibility wherever possible; the conquered lands had not been absorbed, but left as dependents or allies. Moreover, the weaker powers were constantly seeking her aid or protection against their more powerful and aggressive neighbors. In this Greek world of unending strife and discord, of intrigue and political corruption, the blunt, practical, sober Roman was welcomed as a friend and deliverer by all who looked for protection against the greater powers by whom they were surrounded. How the Romans were looked upon by some of the lesser peoples of the east is strikingly shown by a passage from one of the Jewish books of the time. When the Jews were making their desperate fight for independence they looked about for helpers. The first Book of Maccabees says:

Attitude of the East toward Rome.

And Judas heard of the fame of the Romans, that they are valiant men, and have pleasure in all that join themselves unto them, with their friends and such as relied upon them they kept amity; and they conquered the kingdoms that were nigh and those that were far off, and all that heard of their fame were afraid of them; moreover, whomsoever they will to succor and to make kings, these do they make kings, and whomsoever they will, do they depose; and they are exalted exceedingly· and for all this none of them ever did put on a diadem, neither did they clothe themselves with purple, to be magnified thereby· and how they had made for themselves a senate-house, and day by day three hundred and twenty men sat in council, consulting alway for the people, to the end that they might be well ordered; and how they commit their government to one man year by year, that he should rule over them, and be lord over all their country, and all are obedient to that one, and there is neither envy nor emulation among them.—1 *Maccabees*, viii, 1, 12-16.

432. Rome Slowly Changes Its Attitude for the Worse. —As time went on, however, the temper of the Ro-

mans slowly changed. They could not understand the
politics of the east nor the character of its peoples.
They despised the cunning and weakness of the Greeks,
they were constantly disturbed by the quarrels and intrigues of the various states and by outbreaks against
their own authority. The opportunities for gaining
wealth and influence afforded by the decay of the eastern
Rome powers attracted them. Thus they came to interfere
Becomes
Tyrannical. more and more directly, to make an unrighteous use of
their superior position and power in enforcing obedience
to their will; they became grasping and arrogant, until,
in place of the respect and hope which they had once
inspired, the Greeks began to fear and hate them.

Rebellion **433. Overthrow of Greek Freedom, 146 B.C.**—Things
in Greece.
came to a head by a rebellion in the Macedonian districts (149 B.C.) followed by troubles with the Achæan
league (146 B.C.). The whole country was seething with
discontent now that the freedom accorded by Rome was
found to be a hollow sham. The Roman senate, on the
other hand, had lost all patience with the Greek states,
because of their interminable bickerings. The return of
the hostages taken from Achæa after Pydna fostered the
discontent in that district. Thus out of a petty incident
a pitiful war arose between the Achæans and Rome.
In 146 B.C. the consul Mummius captured Corinth and
order was restored in Greece. Macedonia was made a
province; the Achæan league was dissolved; Greece
was placed under the authority of the governor of Macedonia. In connection with the subjection of Greece,
the city of Corinth was deliberately destroyed and its art
treasures carried to Rome. Thus the last vestige of
Greek freedom perished.

434. Destruction of Carthage, 149-146 B.C.—During these years the Roman name was stained by another act of oppression. The years of peace had raised Carthage to a high degree of prosperity which excited the jealousy of her old rival. The Roman merchants demanded its destruction. The senators took their point of view; none more insistently than M. Porcius Cato, who is said to have ended every speech in that body with the well-known phrase *"Carthago delenda est."* A pretext for war was found in the fact that the Carthaginians in self-protection

had taken up arms against territorial aggressions on the part of their neighbor Massinissa (§ 413). Technically this was a violation of the treaty of 201 B.C. To save themselves from war the Carthaginians sent three hundred of their leading citizens to Rome and even gave up all their arms. Then came the cruel command that they should abandon Carthage and settle ten miles from

Rebellion
in Africa.
the sea. At this, uncontrollable anger led them to resist to the utmost. Two years of fierce fighting followed
Finally the command of the Roman army was given to
P. Cornelius Scipio, a son of Æmilius Paulus, the victor
of Pydna, who had been adopted into the family of
Africanus. He proved a general of capacity, and, in
spite of its heroic resistance, he forced his way into Carthage, destroyed the city, and enslaved the surviving inhabitants. Out of the conquered territory was formed

Disturb-
ances in
Spain.
the province of Africa (149–146 B.C.). In Spain the
wanton injustice and aggression of Roman governors
kept the land continually in uproar. Fierce wars were
waged with the various tribes. An heroic defender of

Viriathus.
Spanish freedom arose in Vi-ri-a'thus, who for nine years
(149–140 B.C.) not only kept the Romans at bay, but
defeated their generals, and was finally disposed of by
assassination. Roman territory in Spain was not secure
till 133 B.C. when Scipio Æmilianus took and destroyed
Numantia. The same year (133 B C) the king of Pergamon, the faithful ally of Rome in the east, died, be-

Addition
of Asia.
queathing his state to the Roman people. Out of it
was made the province of Asia.

435. The Provinces and Their Government.—Thus,
by 133 B C. Rome ruled seven provinces, Sicily, Sardinia
(including Corsica), Spain (divided into two), Macedonia,
Africa and Asia. Strong colonies dominated Cisalpine
Gaul, though it had not yet received a provincial organization. The rapid growth of her foreign domains had
made it impossible for Rome to alter the original temporary form of government given to them (§ 428); it
now became permanent. In addition to the praetors, who
were too few in number or were sufficiently occupied at

home, the government of the province was assigned to
officers on whom was conferred the same authority as that
of a consul or prætor. They were in fact consuls or
prætors whose terms were prolonged by vote of the senate
and who acted in the place of * these magistrates. Hence The Proconsul.
they were called proconsuls or proprætors. A kind of con-
stitution was established for each province, determining The Provincial Constitution.
such matters as the tribute to be paid, the status of the
different communities in the province and the rights and
duties of the provincials. The province was in general
a honeycomb of separate cities whose citizens could not
bear arms or enter into wars, but had in their own hands
almost the entire conduct of local administration. The
proconsul simply supervised the cities, thus taking the
place, in the east, of the Hellenistic monarchs (§§ 299,
319). His rights often depended upon the fact that the
Greek cities added the goddess Roma to their circle of
deities (§ 300) and sometimes the proconsul himself was
deified. His authority was wide, limited only in a vague
general way by the terms of the provincial constitution;
his obligations were equally extensive. He administered
justice, preserved the peace, through a quæstor he directed
the finances and saw to the tribute; he was responsible for
the prosperity and progress of his province. The collection of the taxes was, according to the accepted Roman
system (§ 423), taken over by contractors, the *publicani*,
who assumed the responsibility of paying to the state the
amount it required, and made a profit out of what they
could squeeze from the unhappy provincials over and
above the legal tribute. This "farming out" of the taxes
was thus capable of serious abuse. The success of such

* The Latin word for "in the place of" is *pro.*

a system depended upon the character of the governor, since, left practically alone with powers so large, he could carry out his own will without interference. Appointed for but one year, all that he could accomplish for good or ill must be done in this brief time. It was not strange, therefore, that some of them yielded to temptations to be unjust, selfish and cruel. In 149 B.C. it became necessary to establish a court at home where such injustice could be brought to trial. But, as the accused could not be tried till his term of office was over, and as the court was made up of senators who either had been or might become governors of provinces, the remedy was of little avail.

REVIEW EXERCISES. 1. Significance of the events connected with Cynoscephalæ, Pydna, Magnesia. 2. For what are the following famous: Viriathus, Simon Maccabæus, Polybius? 3. What is meant by proconsul, Achæan league, phalanx, kingdom of Syria, empire of Alexander?

COMPARATIVE STUDIES. 1. Compare Rome's advance into the east with Alexander's (§§ 282, 290, 292, 299). 2. How far was the Jewish praise of the Romans (§ 431) justified in the past history of the Romans? 3. Compare the Greek phalanx and the Roman legion. 4. "I count it glory not to possess wealth but to rule those who do." Show how this reveals the strength and the weakness of the Roman character.

SELECT LIST FOR READING. 1. The East about 200 B C. How and Leigh, pp. 253-260 2. The First and Second Macedonian Wars. How and Leigh, pp 261-265. 3. The Third Macedonian War. How and Leigh, pp. 275-280 4. Scipio Africanus. How and Leigh, pp. 215-216, 273 (a) His character; (b) His Politics. How and Leigh, pp. 300-305.

TOPICS FOR READING AND ORAL REPORT. 1. The East about 200 B C Morey, pp 125-127, Shuckburgh, ch. 27. 2. The First and Second Macedonian Wars. Plutarch, Life of Flaminius, Botsford, pp 116-118, Myres, ch 20, Shuckburgh, ch. 28. 3. The War with Antiochus. Myres, ch 21 4. The

Third Macedonian War. Myres, ch. 22; Horton, pp. 145-158; Shuckburgh, ch. 31; Seignobos, pp 126-130 **5. The Life of Scipio Africanus** (see Index to Shuckburgh, under his name). **6. Change in Roman Policy toward the East.** Seignobos, pp. 130-131; Morey, p 134. **7. The End of Greek Freedom.** Myres pp. 285-289; **8. The Fall of Carthage.** Myres, pp. 289-297; Botsford, pp. 123-126, Seignobos, pp 131-135; Horton, pp. 165-168. **9. Summary of the Period before the Gracchi.** Heitland, Roman Republic, vol. II, pp. 253-255.

6.—THE DECLINE OF THE ROMAN REPUBLIC

133-44 (27) B.C.

436. Changes in Rome's Inner Life.—This extension in Rome's foreign relations, by which she came to take the leading part in the Mediterranean world, was accompanied by a remarkable series of changes in her inner life. The whole process resulted in the transformation of the state. Before proceeding to follow the next steps Causes in this transformation, we stop to study the internal changes which had so large a part in bringing it about.* Two things were chiefly responsible for these changes in Rome; one was the growth of capitalism or money-power, the other the incoming of Hellenistic civilization. Working separately or in unison, they affected every phase of Roman public and private life.

437. Occupations.—Capitalism appeared as the outcome of a process which quite altered the chief occupations of Roman citizens. In this process agriculture, still the prevailing Italian activity, changed its form and, ceasing in the case of the rich to be an occupation, be-

---

* The order of the topics treated will be in the main the same as that in §§ 386-397, thus making comparison easier.

came an investment. The peasant proprietors of small holdings by no means disappeared, but they diminished rapidly in numbers. The rural free laborer gave way to the slave The second Punic war had devastated wide regions and impoverished many farmers. The serious garrison duties in the new provinces and the long booty-less wars in Spain and along the frontiers kept tens of thousands of them absent from their farms for years at a stretch. The new provinces sent in great quantities of grain which the government after 123 B C. distributed at a cheap rate. Italian grain raisers could not compete with this; a bad season brought them to ruin. Thus their land went into the hands of capitalists who organized great estates, manned them with cheap slave labor and used them for the pasturage of vast flocks and herds, or turned them into vineyards and olive groves. Industry and manufacturing might have offered occupation for these farmers, but the competition of foreign workers forbade. The well-developed industrial life of the east (§§ 19, 198, 309), which had now fallen under Roman influence, was far superior to anything that Italy had developed. Such manufacturing as existed at Rome was done largely by slave labor Rome became not a producer of goods, but the centre where goods were exchanged; the Roman merchant flourished on business which he had not created. His chief commodity was money. Banking became a favorite occupation, the possession and investment of capital the main element in Roman business life. The foundation of great fortunes was laid; the Roman capitalist took his place as one of the powers of the time and reached out to control the world's affairs.

The Farmer Disappears.

Rise of Great Estates.

Money and Banking.

438. Social Classes Sharpened.—This era of capitalism brought with it a sharp division of social classes. Already the old equality and unity of Roman life had been threatened by the distinctions conferred by office and wealth (§ 379). In place of the patrician aristocracy had appeared a "nobility," * whose position was gained by these means. The members of these noble families came to regard themselves as alone capable of filling the leading public offices and, therefore, as having a right to them (§ 418). From them came the majority of the senators; the senate, therefore, represented the interests of the nobility.

The Nobility.

439. The Equites.—Not all men of wealth, however, belonged to the nobility. In many cases the capitalists were of lower birth. But their common interests drew them together, and their wealth was so great as to give them entrance to the class of *equites* (§ 423), where they soon came to have the predominance. Thus the equestrian order was sharply marked off from the senatorial class, as representing the wealthy business men The interests of the two orders often clashed and brought trouble into the state.

The Business Men.

440. The City Population.—Beneath these two classes was the rest of the community. The farmers and their families came to the city and helped to swell a poor and restless population, whose chief value was that it could vote. Another element of this population was the freedmen, who absorbed more and more of the petty business of the capital. The slaves became very numerous.

The Slave

* A citizen who held a "curule" office thereby ennobled his family and won for them the right of placing wax masks representing the features of distinguished ancestors in the atrium and of exhibiting them at public funerals of members of the family. Such families were *nobiles*.

Vast numbers of them were bought and sold in the course of the great wars. The fortune of war reduced all classes of conquered peoples, the rich and the poor, the educated and the ignorant, the strong and the weak, under one common yoke; in course of time they were distributed about in the various occupations according to their ability, and their value was thus determined. The average price of slaves ranged from sixty to one hundred dollars. They were employed in the country for farming and herding. They became indispensable in the private houses, in the mercantile and manufacturing activities of the city and as helpers in the state service. Their lot was hard, particularly that of the country slave, who was numbered with the cattle and the dogs.

441. Ways of Living.—Wealth and power wrought a striking change in the living of the upper classes. The old simplicity gave way to luxury. The form was determined by the models of Hellenistic life, which now became the fashion. The house was enlarged by opening a door through the rear and adding a court, which was surrounded by rooms. This was the *per'i-style*, and it soon became the principal part of the dwelling, the a'tri-um being regarded as a kind of front parlor or state apartment. A second story was added and the sleeping-rooms placed in it. The interior was decorated with increasing splendor, elaborate frescoes adorned the walls, mosaics were set into the floor, ceilings were panelled and gilded. Many costly pieces of furniture replaced the former bare and simple furnishings. The sun-dial and the water-clock came from Greece. The bath-room was an indispensable part of the new house. Public baths, also, were established, and grew in number and splendor. The

The House.

Furnishings.

furnishings of the table assumed unusual importance.
New kinds of food were introduced   Wider conquests   Food.
brought new delicacies, nuts and fruits; wild game was
much used; the peacock was a special dainty; fish and
oysters became popular. A slave who was a good cook
was highly esteemed and was worth five thousand dollars.
The stool or bench gave way to the couch, on which
people reclined at dinner. Abundance of silver plate,
costly wines, many courses, rich dresses, music and
dancing—all these show that the abstemious, severe Roman of the early days was yielding to the new opportunities for rich living that conquest and money put in
his way.

442. Amusements.—Roman amusements disclose similar changes. The Greek fashion of having games in   Games.
connection with religious festivals (§ 128) became popular. Greek athletes were often employed. The exhibitions of chariot-driving (§ 390) and wrestling soon over-
shadowed the religious side of the celebration. The
man craving for sensation led to the exhibition of wild
beasts, whose contests were heartily enjoyed. The most
savage animals were imported from the ends of the
earth. Worse than this were the gladiatorial contests,   Gladia-
which first appeared at Rome in 264 B.C. Etruria, not   torial
Greece, was the home of this demoralizing sport, but it   Shows.
found a congenial place in Roman life. At first exhibited
at private funerals, it soon became a part of public life.
In the beginning captives fought for their lives before the
populace; then men were trained for this purpose and
were hired to exhibit their skill in public. The idle and
sensation-loving horde of city-folk went wild with excitement over such displays. Conservative and decent

Gambling.   officials tried in vain to suppress them by law.   Gambling with dice for high stakes was a growing vice of the rich and no legislation could avail against it.   Music and dancing came to be regular accompaniments of luxurious feasts.   The sober sense of the old Roman was shocked by the establishment of a dancing-school, where the children of high and low mingled in dances which were far from becoming.

443. The Theatre.—Greek influence was responsible for the rapid growth of theatrical performances.   Temporary wooden theatres on Greek models began to be erected about 145 B C., though a permanent stone structure was not put up till 55 B.C.   It held at least seventeen thousand people.   The plays were mostly comedies adapted from Greek models.   The actors were mainly slaves, hired from a training master.   Few well-to-do people were present, as they regarded the performances

A Debasing Influence.   as common and improper.   This fact naturally lowered the tone of the theatre.   The plays, lacking in their Roman copies the Greek lightness of touch, were often coarse and vulgar and sometimes made sport of virtue and religion.   Immense throngs of common people attended them and they grew into great popularity.   In course of time their character improved; they came to have some better elements and aided in the growth of culture.

444. Improvement in Education.—It must not be supposed that Hellenistic influence was all for the worse. Roman education, for example, was vastly improved by

Greek Language and Literature Studied.   it.   Greek literature, with its wondrous charm and power, was thrown open to the Romans; all that was necessary was that systematic instruction in the Greek language should be given.   This the multitudes of Greek

slaves could easily furnish. It now became the custom
that every child, whose education was properly attended
to, learned Greek. Soon every educated man could speak
Greek and even make speeches in it. To master another language than one's own is in itself a liberal education, but, in addition to this, the Greek language led
the Roman to the knowledge of an unparalleled literature. Soon other and higher forms of Greek training Philosophy
came to Rome—the schools of rhetoric and philosophy
(§§ 266–267, 324) for the further broadening of the Roman
mind. Thus, in addition to the acquirement of knowledge for practical ends (§ 393), came education for mental
culture. Another educative influence was the wider hori- New
zon which opened before the Roman in the new lands Breadth of
which fell under his sway. Knowledge of other civiliza- View.
tions than his own, of the wonderful east with its treasures
of art and architecture, was possible for him. Young
men were sent out to travel in these lands, either with a
tutor, or attached to a staff of an official or a general.
They came back with a larger outlook on men and things,
no longer limited by their own native town; wider experience gave them sounder judgment and prepared
them for intelligent leadership.

445. Birth of Roman Literature.—Roman literature
and art likewise received a mighty uplift from Greece in
these days. As the Greek school-teacher revolutionized Under
Roman education, so he also produced Roman literature. Greek
Lucius Livius Andronicus (about 250 B C.), a Greek Influence.
from Tarentum, translated the "Odyssey" into Latin,
and this book gradually supplanted the Twelve Tables
(§ 364) as the chief school text-book. He also adapted
Greek plays, chiefly those of Euripides (§ 228), for the

Roman stage. ⊤Gnæus Nævius (about 225 B.C.) and Quintus Ennius (239-169 B.C.) followed in his footsteps in writing Latin plays. Thus the Latin drama on Greek

Comedy. models was established. Latin comedy, founded on the plays of Menander (§ 304), was produced. Here the great names are Titus Maccius Plautus (254-184 B.C.) and Publius Terentius (Terence). The latter was born at Carthage after the close of the second Punic war and taken as a slave to Rome (196-159 B.C.). The plays of the former are vivacious and strong; those of the latter are smooth and elegant. Both Nævius and Ennius wrote historical poems; the one described the first Punic war, the other told the story of Rome from the beginning in rude Latin hex-am′e-ters in Homeric fashion. Prose writing began; the subject was history and the language

History. was Greek. Thus Quintus Fabius Pictor wrote of Roman history down to the second Punic war, in which

Cato the Elder. he himself was an actor. Soon Latin prose appeared, the representative of which was Cato the Elder, who wrote his Roman history, called the *O-rig′i-nes*, about 168 B.C.; by his various writings on agriculture, war and law he made Latin a literary tongue. He is the real founder of Latin prose. It was not long before two branches of literature appeared in which the native Roman genius displayed

Satire. itself supremely—satire and oratory. The founder of Roman satirical poetry was Gaius Lucilius (148-103 B.C.), whose biting couplets were intensely enjoyed by

Oratory. all but their subjects. The first of the great orators were two contemporaries, Lucius Licinius Crassus and Marcus Antonius (about 100 B C.). "To hear both in one day was the highest intellectual entertainment which Rome afforded." At the same time Roman law took a step for-

ward by the legal writings of Quintus Mucius Scævola **Law.**
(sē'v ō lä) (about 100 B.C), who collected and organized
into a series of works the legal material that had been
gathering for centuries   Architecture now had the ser- **Architect**
vices of Greek masters and was based on Greek models. **ure and Art.**
Thus around the Forum arose stately public porticoes
like those of Athens; elsewhere in Rome marble temples
and galleries began to appear.   An era of good taste in
sculpture and painting began as the Romans came in
contact with the masterpieces of Greek art in Syracuse,
Corinth and Athens.   Unfortunately, they were not satisfied with admiring these; they began to covet them and
soon to exercise the right of conquerors by carrying them
off to Rome.   In this field even more clearly than in literature the overpowering effect of contact with Greece is
to be seen.   It is a new Rome that art and literature reveal to us after, and in consequence of, the conquest of
Greece.

446. The Transforming Effects of These Influences.—
Did all these changes take place in Rome without effect
upon the character of her people ?   This is the most important question, and the answer to it reveals as startling
a transformation as has thus far been recorded.   The
change may be stated in brief.   Capitalism and culture
destroyed the old Roman character without putting anything better in its place.

447. Social Ideals Broken Down.—They broke down
the old social equality in which all lived for the good of
the state (§§ 362, 392).   Wealth divided men into classes
and introduced new and strange standards of life.   Selfishness took the place of patriotism.   Men sought to get
something out of the state instead of doing something for

the state. The old Roman idea of doing one's duty in one's place turned into the practice of making the most of one's position and opportunity   Thus each class secured all sorts of distinguishing marks; the senators had special seats at the circus; the citizen had a special dress and a ring to separate him from the foreigner; every successful general sought for some special recognition of his services.   The best side of this change is seen in the influence of Greek culture on the higher class.   The narrow preference of everything Roman passed into a higher appreciation of what other peoples had done in art and literature.   The circle of men that gathered about the younger Scipio* was characterized by a generous and broad culture.   Greek men of letters were welcomed by them.   Thus Polybius, one of the leaders of the Achæan league whom the Romans forced to go to Rome (§ 429), wrote in the spirit of this finer life a *History* in Greek, in which he hailed the union of Greek thought and Roman action as a good omen for the world's future.   It is the first worthy piece of historical literature extant since Thucydides (§ 227).   Yet even this circle, because of its broader life, regarded itself as separated from the common herd.

The Better Side.

Polybius.

448. **Moral Standards Destroyed.**—Capitalism and culture removed the old Roman ideas of right and wrong. Money altered the way in which people thought it proper to live, introducing luxury and show in the place of the former simplicity (§ 389).   Deeds were done for gain

* Publius Cornelius Scipio, the victor over Hannibal at Zama, was given the title of Africanus The adopted son of his son was Publius Scipio, called Æmilianus because he was the son of Æmilius Paulus, the victor at Pydna. He is also known as Africanus the younger·because of his capture of Carthage.

which before would have been despised. The old Roman self-respect and dignity changed to pride and arrogance; these bred brutality in relation to foreigners. The Greeks, with their fine manners and cringing ways, were treated with contempt and abuse. Slaves, now so numerous at Rome, were beneath contempt and often handled with outrageous cruelty. The populace at Rome, once loyal and laborious, were also corrupted by the new spirit of greed and power. The gladiatorial games brutalized them. The low comedies, borrowed from Greece and vulgarized in the process, were as degrading to their morals as they were attractive to their sense. The votes of the citizens began to be estimated by their money value and soon were freely bought and sold. Money even corrupted the home life; Roman matrons and daughters sought to lay up fortunes, and prized gain beyond duty to husbands and fathers. Increasing extravagance and greed led to family troubles. Divorces began to grow in frequency; marriages for money were not uncommon. Thus public and private life was drifting away from the old moorings, and the new ways of living offered no stable anchorage Many, it is true, sought to stem the tide and stood for the old standards. Their foremost representative was Cato the Elder, who fought for the ancient ideals of simplicity and patriotism with fierce denunciations of the novelties of the time. But he had no success, because he had nothing to put in the place of the new. The past was forever gone and no man could bring it back again.

The Conservatives Struggle in Vain.

449. Roman Religion Discredited.—Roman religion, in its old forms and ideals (§ 396), went the way of all the old life. Greek religion had already been discredited by philosophy (§§ 225, 324), and the old Roman faith was less able than the Greek to stand against the keen Greek intellect.   Thus the educated classes lost faith in the ideas that underlay the Roman ritual (§§ 347, 396), and the priests had little confidence in their ceremonials except as necessary parts of the political machine.   The literary men of the time, like Ennius, openly expressed doubts about religion.   The mass of the people caught the contagion, laughed at the jests on sacred subjects in the comedies of the time, and soon ceased to be influenced by the old faith.   Meanwhile, new forms of Greek religion were offered to them, as strange as they were attractive.   Such were the worship of Dionysus (§ 134), called in Rome Bacchus, and Cybele, a goddess of Asia Minor (§ 319), who appealed, not to the old Roman sense of duty, but to the feelings, and led men away into all sorts of superstitions.   The state did not favor these worships, but, offering nothing to take their place, it was powerless to keep the Roman populace from running after them.   Certainly they were better than no religion, and the old Roman faith was decayed and powerless to restrain or to help.   Greek culture could help the educated class here by the teachings of philosophy, and, as time went on, the various schools that had flourished in Greece (§ 324) established themselves among the Romans and found many followers.

New Eastern Cults.

450. **Effect on Public Life.**—Roman public life was deeply affected by all these influences.   They showed themselves in various ways.   A sharp cleavage was made between the public activities of the different classes. The nobles took a tighter grasp upon the public offices and distributed them among their several families.

Nobles Seize Power.

Sometimes one family, like the Scipios, sought to keep them within their own circle. Already it was made illegal for one to be re-elected to an office until a ten years' interval had passed. A law fixed an order in which offices should be held and the age at which one could occupy them.* Hence, it was practically impossible for "new men," as non-nobles were called, to get into office (§ 418). The men of business now began to use the state for their own purposes. It was their influence that dictated the wars of the period; they secured the destruction of rival commercial cities like Carthage and Corinth (§§ 433-434). The faithful allies, like Pergamon and Rhodes, which had been the leading commercial states of the east, were unjustly treated in order to increase Roman business predominance. The greed of the nobles made futile the attempts to revive Italy's peasant class, since they wanted more and more land for their estates. Colonies ceased to be sent out from Rome. The cruel treatment of slaves on these estates led to uprisings, like the slave revolt in Sicily, which threw that province into a state of anarchy from 136-132 B.C. All provinces came to be the prey of capitalistic robbery and extortion. The mass of the citizens, in their turn, began selfishly to shut out others from their privileges. Once citizenship had been a burden; now it was a source of profit, and the faithful allies that had made possible Rome's victory over Hannibal were jealously excluded from it. Indeed, little by little these allies saw their ancient rights withdrawn and themselves treated as subjects. In 177 B C. they were denied their customary share of the spoils of war. Citizens began to expect more in the way of festivals and

Margin notes: Influence of the Money Power.

Civic Selfishness.

* This order was called the *cursus honorum*, the "career of honors "

Bribery.

games from the officials. Their votes were even openly bought. The introduction of the ballot in the assemblies although an improvement on the old method of voting (§ 422), aided bribery. In 156 B C. a magistrate was empowered to dispense with holding an assembly of the people, if the auspices (§ 348) were unfavorable; thus religion became a political instrument to thwart the popular will. All these facts show how the original unity of the Roman state was giving way to factions, each intent on its own selfish interests.

What All this Means.

REVIEW EXERCISES. 1. What is meant by nobiles, auspices, curule office, cursus honorum, peristyle, proprætor, Forum? 2. For what were the following famous: Cato the Elder, Ennius, Lucilius, Appius Claudius, Menander, Dionysus? 3. Explain the difficulties in the problems of the senate in this period. 4. What was the Roman attitude toward military service? 5. Characterize the city of Rome. 6. Explain "failure of popular government" as applied to the period of decline.

COMPARATIVE STUDIES. 1. Compare the origin and purpose of the Roman theatre with those of the Greek (§§ 160, 206). 2. Compare a Roman citizen in this period with one in 350 B.C. 3. What is the difference in the attitude toward money between a Greek of the age of Pericles (§§ 199-201) and a Roman of this age?

SELECT LIST FOR READING. 1. Religion and Politics. How and Leigh, pp 288-293 2. Provincial Administration, How and Leigh, pp 310-313 3. Economic Questions. (a) Land, How and Leigh, pp 305-310. (b) Revenue, How and Leigh, pp 314-315. (c) Business, How and Leigh, pp 318. (d) Slavery and Agriculture, How and Leigh, pp 316-318. 4. Cato the Censor. How and Leigh, pp 302-305.

TOPICS FOR READING AND ORAL REPORT. 1. Roman Life and Manners under Greek Influence. Morey, pp 148-152, Myres, ch 23, Seignobos, ch. 11. 2. Delos and Its Relations with Rome and Athens. William Scott Ferguson. (a) The Rise of Delos in Trade, Hellenistic Athens, pp. 329-333. (*b*) Government and Trade Conditions on Delos Ferguson, pp 346-366, 381-384, 403-409 (*c*) Religious Cults on Delos. Ferguson, pp. 385-399. **3. Corruption of Public Life.** Munro, pp 99-100 (source); Myres, ch. 26; Abbott, ch 5, Seignobos, ch 12; Botsford, ch 6, Morey, pp. 143-148, Shuckburgh, ch. 32. **4. The Beginnings of Roman Literature.** Mackail, pp. 3-38, Laing, pp 1-62 (translation of the Phormio of Terence). **5. Roman Religion under Greek Influence.** Seignobos, pp. 148-251 **6. The Gladiatorial Games.** Johnston, pp 242-252 **7. Cato the Censor.** Plutarch, Life of Cato; Munro, pp 95-97 (source), Shuckburgh, pp 518-521, Seignobos, pp. 156-359, Botsford, pp. 143-146. **8. How far was Cato's claim true that should the Romans come thoroughly to imbibe Greek literature they would lose the empire of the world? 9. The Effect upon the Proletariat of the Rise in the Standard of Living,** Ferrero's Greatness and Decline of Rome, vol. I, pp 79-96. **10. How Money was Made and Spent.** Greenidge, vol. I, pp. 11-25, 30-58. **11. Land Ownership and Control.** Greenidge, vol. I, pp 64-80. **12. The Slaves—a Problem.** Greenidge, vol. I, pp. 80-100. **13. The Thirty-Five Tribes.** Botsford, Roman Assemblies, pp. 51-65 **14. A Summary of Comitial History.** Botsford, Roman Assemblies, pp. 473-477.

451. Difficult Position of the Senate.—The position of the senate became, in fact, more embarrassing from day to day. When the last state which menaced Italy ceased to exist in 167 B.C. the real trial of the government began. There was no longer any great national danger to compel the nobles, the equites and the commons to rally vigorously to its defence. General relaxation followed. Yet the task of the government was greater than ever before. It had not only to keep the provincial magistrates in check; it had to see that officials who changed annually did not misgovern too badly; and it had to guard against the malpractices of contractors upon whom it was dependent for its revenues. Above all, it had to make the most severe military demands upon its citizens and allies without the incentive of pressing danger or expectation of rich booty. Year after year thousands of men had to be stationed in the new provinces or held in service in Spain or in the Alps or in Illyricum or some similar district where hard knocks were more plentiful than spoils. How many soldiers were necessary for these tasks it is difficult to estimate, but Augustus a hundred years later thought three hundred thousand too few. That was more than a fifth of the entire body of men of military age in Italy; and as is known Augustus was able to raise only half of his troops there. It is certain that the senate in 133 B.C. could not raise as many. Yet it doubtless needed more. The wars were not dangerous but they were the hardest kind of wars—guerilla struggles in the mountains, forests and deserts in which victory brought little glory while defeats and delays brought serious loss of prestige. The belief became general that the officers mismanaged the campaigns and that the senate chose its commanders unwisely. There were constant appeals for more soldiers; but the recruiting was again and again stopped in Rome by the veto of rebellious tribunes. The city population, when not exempt from service through lack of property was thus freed from it by the power of the tribunate. This power could not be exercised outside the limits of Rome; hence the small farmers of Italy were made to bear the brunt of the levy, and the burden fell with special severity upon the "allies" whose lack of the franchise prevented them from retaliating upon the officials. The burden of empire thus rested squarely upon the shoulders of the peasants of Italy, who on returning from a cam-

Margin note: Burden of Military Service.

paign after many years of absence often found their farms gobbled up by the nobles for debt or unfit for cultivation through neglect.

452. The Problem of Administration.—The city of Rome was their natural refuge. This had grown enormously in the past century. It may have advanced in population from one hundred thousand to five hundred thousand in this interval. Since it was unable to spread over a large area like a modern city, congestion was the only possible result. The streets were narrow, the houses high; great *insulæ* of little tenements appeared, the menace of fire became horrible, and the preservation of order and decency impossible. What could annually changing ædiles do with such a situation, without a police or fire department? How could such a city be provisioned? In Alexandria the problem was comparatively simple since at its door was the granary of Egypt. Rome, on the other hand, had to import its food from a distance—from Sardinia, Sicily, Africa. For its food supply it was dependent upon the winds and waves, and should the corn ships be delayed by storms, the prices of grain soared in Rome and the urban mob was at once in an uproar. Yet this mob constituted the bulk of the sovereign assembly; it is true that it controlled only four-thirty-fifths of the total vote in the comitia, but in the meetings which preceded the voting it could reign as king riot. The fact was that government by a general assembly of the people was possible, as Aristotle held, only when the citizens were few. It had been developed when Rome was an aggregate of peasants; now that Rome had a population of half a million, made up of restless, discontented men of a great variety

The "Great City."

Failure of Popular Government.

of races, languages and stations—"step-sons of Italy," Scipio Æmilianus called them — it was antiquated. Long since, Alexandria had ceased to be a self-governing city, and had come under the control of permanent officials appointed by the crown. Was Rome to have the same fate? If so, who should wear the crown?

453. The Beginnings of Civil Conflict.—With such a situation in Rome's inner life a conflict of interests and powers was unavoidable. The failure of the leading men to solve the problems of administration was certain to call out attempts from all sides to cope with the difficulties which they were not able to meet. The first attempt, which precipitated a century of struggle, was made in 133 B.C , by the tribune Tiberius Sempronius Gracchus. A member of the senatorial nobility, the grandson of Scipio Africanus, and brother-in-law of Scipio Æmilianus, he was a valiant soldier of the republic and, at the same time, highly educated in the new learning of the times. The miserable economic decay of Italy, the hard fate of the veteran soldiers and the decline of the class available for military service appealed to him, and he sought to restore prosperity by introducing an agrarian law for the distribution of the public lands among the citizens. "The beasts of the field," ran his impassioned plea, "have their holes and their hiding-places, but the men who fight and die for Italy have not a sod which they can name their own. They are called the lords of the whole earth and their generals urge them to fight for their homes and the graves of their ancestors, yet not a parcel of land is theirs." The limit upon the amount of public land to be leased to any one citizen set, it was alleged, by the Licinian laws of 366 B C. (§ 368) had been

The Action of Tiberius Gracchus.

The Land Problem.

disregarded to such an extent that practically all of it had
been taken up in the great estates of the rich proprietors.
The law of Tiberius Gracchus established a commission
of three (*tri-um'vi-rate*) to secure the carrying out of the
new provisions which contemplated reducing the illegal
holdings to their proper limits and assigning the remainder
in equal lots of thirty jugera each to landless citizens.
The proposal created a storm in which the senate placed
itself in opposition to the tribune; even his colleague,
Octavius, interposed a veto. Thereupon Tiberius, sup- Tiberius Appeals to the People.
ported by the country population to whom the prospect
of new lots for themselves and their sons was attractive,
appealed directly to the people, who responded by depos-
ing the obstructive tribune and passing the law. The
commission was appointed and began its work. To
carry out his plans, Tiberius found it necessary to over-
ride the law prohibiting re-election (§ 450) and stand
again for tribune. But the nobles banded against him; His Death.
a riot was raised at election time, the partisans fought in
the streets of Rome, and Tiberius was killed.

454. Rise of Parties.—In his zeal for reform Tiberius
Gracchus had raised issues hitherto unheard of at Rome,
and, no doubt, not grasped by himself. He was the
first to bring new political ideas into the field, which
divided the community into parties The opti-ma'tes,[1]
or aristocrats, and the pop-u-lar'es, or democrats, henceforth struggle for leadership. Men of all classes array
themselves on either side. In appealing to the people The "Sovereign People"
as sovereign in election and legislation without regard
to senate and magistrates, he brought a new doctrine
into Roman politics. This was a Greek idea (§ 191);
at Rome the state depended upon the joint action of

all three and did not go back to any one as supreme. Party struggles led to civil strife, in which reason gave way to force and the state was shaken to its foundations

455. Work of Gaius Gracchus.—Ten years passed; the law prohibiting re-election to the tribunate was annulled, the powers of the land commission were taken from it, but not till the number of registered citizens had

Murder of Africanus the Younger.

increased in six years from 319,000 to 394,000. Scipio Æmilianus, the captor of Carthage, the victor at Numantia, the sturdiest pillar of the best Roman society, the greatest man of his age, was foully murdered and a judicial investigation of the crime was suppressed Then, in 123 B.C., Gaius Gracchus, younger brother of Tiberius, was elected tribune. The senate had put every possible obstacle in the way of his political advancement, but, haunted by a vision of his dead brother and animated by a fierce desire for vengeance on the government which had done the murder, there was no stopping him in the career which he foresaw meant ultimately his own death. Tiberius had been a sincere reformer, and where the evils were so many and complex, what wonder that at

War on the Senate.

times he hesitated? Gaius showed greater resolution, clearer insight and more vigorous leadership; for his main idea was a simple one, to break down the power of the senate at all cost. It is true that each one of his measures has something to be said in its favor, but in their totality they reveal the spirit of the *vendetta*. Thus, too, he overreached himself and perished disastrously.

Court of Ex'ortion Given to the Equites.

He won the support of the urban pro-le-tar'i-at by having grain distributed to it monthly at one-half the market price; he conciliated the country population by restoring the powers of the agrarian commission; above all, he cast

a dagger, as he said, in the midst of the optimates, and
at the same time gained an invaluable backing for himself by transferring the jury courts, which called the
provincial governors to an accounting (§ 435), from the
senators to the equestrians. The powerful financial interest which henceforth for over forty years was virtually in
control of provincial government he further seduced from
its old alliance with the senate by requiring that the contracts for collecting the tithes in the province of Asia
should be awarded in Rome, combined in one, in such a
way that none but the rich financial syndicates of the
capital could undertake them.

456. Attitude of Gaius.—It is true that these two
measures taken together handed over the Greeks of Asia,
bound hand and foot, to the depredation of the tax-
gatherer; but Gaius Gracchus had no thought for the
lessening of provincial oppression. He made it worth
while for the equites to fight for their control of the courts
of extortion and their place of advantage over the senatorial government. That provided for the future degradation of the senate. In the meanwhile he was him- The
self for two years master of Rome. It did not take long Tribune
Masters the
for people to discover that to get things accomplished Govern-
they had to go to him and not as of old to the senate. ment.
Hence, as Plutarch says: "The people looked with
amazement at the man himself, seeing him attended by
crowds of building contractors, artisans, ambassadors,
magistrates, soldiers and learned men, to all of whom
he was easy of access." The appearance, if not the fact,
of a tyranny was there. Moreover, he rejoiced the Colonies.
city population, indeed, by proposing to send colonies
not only to Tarentum and Capua, but also to Carthage;

but this project of transmarine colonization menaced the merchants and bankers of Rome who saw in the new city likely rivals of themselves for the business of the provinces. Finally, in order to get more land to assign he proposed to give the franchise to the Latins (and Latin rights to the Italians) in order to be able, without infringing the rights of allied, and hence separate, states, to confiscate Roman public land which their citizens had occupied without a clear title. This roused the anger of the masses who saw their privileges about to be extended to a large part of Italy; hence the coalition of populace, equites and tribunes went to pieces. The senate put forward Lucius Drusus to propose cheaper corn and more attractive colonies. Gaius failed of election to the tribunate in 121 B.C. and shortly after was set upon by the consul Opimius and slain, with three thousand of his adherents. The agrarian legislation was futile; the work of the commission languished; fields assigned were abandoned, and by 111 B.C. all holders of public land, rich and poor, were confirmed in their possession. But the work of Gaius Gracchus lived after him and the senate never recovered from the wounds he inflicted.

457. The Senate Fails to Manage Affairs.—When the conflict broke out again, party leaders of a different type came to the front and with them a new force took the field. The victorious senate again tried to conduct affairs. They failed in the notable instance of the Ju-gur'- thine war (112–106 B C). The king of Numidia, an ally of Rome, left his kingdom on his death to his three sons. One of them, his illegitimate nephew by birth, his son by adoption only, Ju-gur'tha, sought to secure the

Jugurthine War (112–106 B C)

prize for himself; he killed one brother and made war
on the other, Ad'her-bal by name. The latter appealed to
the senate, which first divided the kingdom anew, giving
to Adherbal the capital, Cirta, but assigning to Jugurtha
the districts of greatest military value; then, when
Jugurtha attacked his rival in his capital, it sent two embassies to expostulate, but did nothing to prevent the fall
of Cirta (112 B.C.). With it fell Adherbal, but, what
was more important, the wild Numidian victors slaughtered a flourishing settlement of Italian money-lenders
and traders who had been plying their opprobrious business in the capital. This roused the equites in Rome to
action, and the populace became unmanageable. War
was declared upon Jugurtha, but the officers put in
charge of it accepted the submission of the king and left
him in possession of all Numidia. The people believed Bribery
that wholesale bribery had been practised by Jugurtha
to secure this end, and, indeed, such was probably the
case. He was, accordingly, asked to Rome to give evidence (110 B.C.). A tribune refused to let him testify, and
he had his only rival for the throne, who had taken refuge
in Rome, murdered; whereupon he was ordered to quit
Italy at once. His parting remark, it is said, was: "A
city for sale, and ripe for ruin, if a purchaser can be
found."

The next news was that a Roman army forty thousand Difficult
strong had been ambushed and forced to capitulate to Conditions
Jugurtha. The senate tried to stem the storm of rage by Marius.
appointing Metellus, an able and honorable man, to the
command and giving him a rising popular hero, the
eques Gaius Marius, as legate (109 B.C.). This meant
serious war, which the senate, alive to the difficulties of

campaigning with infantry in a vast tract of desert and mountains against a nimble and resourceful foe, had tried to avoid. Metellus conducted the war with skill and vigor, but it could not be brought to an end in a year, or even in three; hence in 107 B.C. the democracy took matters into their own hands and made Marius consul for the purpose of bringing the war to a close. This he speedily accomplished. Jugurtha, betrayed by the king of Mauretania, was surrendered to Sulla, Marius's brilliant young lieutenant, brought a prisoner to Rome and died in a Roman dungeon.

458. The Terror from the North.—Meanwhile, a serious danger had been threatening Italy from the north. For a long time the Romans had been making war in Gaul on the other side of the Alps (Gallia Transalpina), and had established a province called Gallia Narbonensis, from the name of the capital city, Narbo.

The Invaders.

Now, down from the distant and unknown north came two peoples, the Cimbri and Teu'to-nes, who sought homes in the more fertile south. With them, in all probability, the Germans make their entrance into history. Breaking their way through the already weakened barrier of Gallic tribes, they came face to face with the Roman armies and defeated them in four successive battles (in 113, 109, 107, 105 B.C.), the last defeat, sustained at A-rau'si-o on the Rhone, being a disaster comparable in loss of life to Cannæ. The route into Italy stood open

Marius Saves Italy.

to them. Dismayed at the prospect, the democracy again stepped forward and elected their hero Marius as consul and defender against this dreaded foe. For four successive years (104–101 B.C.) he was thus chosen. The invaders had separated—the Teutones taking the route from the northwest, the Cimbri passing around the Alps and entering Italy from the northeast. In 102 B.C Marius met the Teutones at Aquæ Sextiæ and defeated them. The next year (101 B.C), joining his colleague, who was facing the Cimbri in the Raudine plains (Vercellæ), he annihilated them. Thus Italy was saved and Marius was its savior. He had gained his success not more by his own valor than by the military reforms he introduced. Doing away with the usual practice of levying soldiers and limiting the levy to men of property (§ 350), he invited Roman citizens to enroll themselves under his banner regardless of property qualifications. As a result he had an army made up of men who wished to fight and were devoted to their commander Moreover, important changes in tactics were made by Marius He took the spear from the *triarii*, and made all three lines alike in weapons; he threw together a maniple of each line to make the tactical unit subsequently used in Roman warfare—the cohort. It had a normal strength of six hundred, and ten cohorts constituted the legion. To this he gave as a standard, what subsequently was its most precious possession, a silver eagle on a staff.

His Military Reforms.

Tactical Changes of Marius

459. The New Situation: Marius and Sulla.—Thus the seed sown by the Gracchi had sprung up and borne unexpected fruit. The democracy placed at its head a military hero behind whom stood an army whose first interest was not loyalty to the state, but devotion to its leader. For the defence of the state abroad and the overthrow of enemies at home the democracy did not hesitate to re-elect its chief to the highest offices year after year. Marius held the consulship seven times. This example was soon followed by the other party. Military

Military
Men
Lead the
People

prowess began to take the place of civic leadership.   He
was strongest who had an army under his command.
Ambition got the better of patriotism and set military
power against civic right.   The conflict of parties passed
into the struggle of individuals occupying positions in
which they controlled armies.

One of these men who had gained his military education under the new captain in Africa and in Gaul was

Sulla.

to outdo Marius on his own field.   This was Lucius
Cornelius Sulla, a man of noble family, an aristocrat in
temper and tastes, who took his stand on the side of the
senatorial party.   Sulla, like Marius, owed his opportunity to the failure of the senate, with its annually changing officials at home and abroad, to preserve order in
Rome and justice and peace in Italy and the provinces.

Marius.

Marius was no statesman.   During his sixth consulship (100 B C.) the democratic leaders, Sat-ur-ni'nus and
Glaucia, plunged Rome into a series of useless civil conflicts.   Finally, the turmoil became so great that the
senate called upon the consul to use the military power
against his allies.   The ideas of Marius were those of the
business interests—the equites—to whom he belonged;
hence he shrank from lawlessness and violence and did
as the senate requested   Saturninus and Glaucia were
seized and put in the senate chamber, but a hostile mob
tore the tiles from the roof of the building and slew them
and their following.   Having abandoned the populares,
Marius was neglected by the nobles after their victory, and
retired to private life a disappointed and embittered man.

460. The Franchise Problem.—The one leading question left unsettled was that of the franchise for the Italian
allies, but with this neither optimates nor populares cared

to deal. Finally, in 91 B. C, from the side of the senate, Livius Drusus, son of the tribune who completed the ruin of Gaius Gracchus, proposed, among other things, to give citizenship to them. The proposal was rejected and Drusus lost his life in the struggle. The long-suffering allies, thus again deluded, rose in arms, renounced their allegiance and undertook the founding of a new Italian state, "Italica," with its capital at Corfinium. This formidable revolt, the Social* War (91–88 B.C.), was ended with a formal victory for Rome, but a virtual success for the allies, since a series of laws, granting citizenship to certain classes among them, was passed during the war and did more than Roman arms to weaken their opposition. Drusus. The Social War.

These laws were the Lex Julia (90 B C), granting citizenship to Italian states not in rebellion, and the Lex Plau'ti-a Pa-pi'ri-a (89 B.C), admitting all Italians without distinction to the franchise on application to the prætor within sixty days. At the same time all the cities of Cisalpine Gaul, not already granted the citizenship, received the Latin right. It seems, however, that the advantages of citizenship were limited from the fact that the new citizens were all confined to eight tribes. Citizenship Granted to the Italians.

461. Rise of Mithridates of Pontus.—During the Social War, Marius came again into action, but his services were eclipsed by the victories of his brilliant rival Sulla, who was elected consul in 88 B C. The situation in the eastern provinces was alarming and a vigorous leader was required to cope with it. Among the states allied to Rome in Asia Minor was Pontus. To the throne of this kingdom, in about 115 B.C., came a remarkable

* So called from the Latin word for allies, *Socii.*

ruler, Mithridates VI, whose ambition contemplated nothing less than the revival of an empire on the model of
Alexander's, which should drive the Romans out of the

east.   Left free to act by the incompetence of the senate
and its eastern representatives, he built up a vast coalition and, taking advantage of a wanton act of aggression
on the part of the Roman officials, he launched his armies
against them, defeated their forces and took possession
of the province of Asia (88 B C).   This victory was
followed by a great revolt of the Greeks everywhere and
by the massacre of all Romans throughout the province
to the number of 80,000, and throughout Delos and the
Ægean islands to the number of 20,000 more.   Such
was the fate of the harpies who, in the employ of the
equites and, as we have seen (§ 455), beyond the reach
of senatorial control, had been plundering and defiling
for thirty-five years the fairest district in the eastern
world

462. Sulla and the Democracy.—Awakened to the
growing danger, the senate had arranged that Sulla should
take the command against Mithridates.   But the democracy, claiming the right to make these appointments,
under the leadership of the tribune Sulpicius, in 88 B. C.,
passed various so-called Sulpician laws, among them one
appointing Marius to the position.   Sulla, who had collected an army for his foreign task and was about to leave
Italy, suddenly marched on Rome, and, for the first time
in Roman history, a Roman army entered the walls and
placed its commander in possession of the state.   Sulpicius was killed, Marius fled, and their partisans were
overawed.   Then, having left his party in power, Sulla
departed with his army for the war with Mithridates.

"The story of the escape of Marius has grown into a romance·
how he fled to Ostia, found a ship and was landed in Circeii, baffled
by adverse winds; how he wandered by the shore faint and half
starved, and just evaded his pursuers by wading and swimming
toward two ships that hove in sight along the coast; how the skippers
refused to obey the summons of the horsemen to surrender him,
and yet, in their fear, abandoned him in his sleep on the land by the
mouth of the Liris; how he hid in the marshes by Min-tur'næ, sunk
to the neck in mud, was discovered and dragged to prison, and there
abashed the Cimbric executioner by the thundering demand, 'Slave,
darest thou slay Gaius Marius?' how the magistrates set him on
ship and sent him away; how he barely escaped with life from the
prætor of Sicily, and landed in Africa hoping aid from the Numidian
king; how the outcast hero sent back the message to the governor
who bade him quit the province, 'Tell your master that you have
seen Marius, an exile, sitting among the ruins of Carthage!' " *

463. First Mithridatic War (87-84 B.C.)—Hardly had
he disappeared when the consul Cinna, with the support of
an army, restored the democracy to power, recalled Marius
and took bloody vengeance on its enemies. But its triumph was short. Marius did, indeed, enjoy a seventh
consulship, but he died soon after his election, and Cinna
headed an embarrassed and incompetent government till
Sulla's return from the east brought it to an end   He had
spent four years in bringing Mithridates to terms (87-84
B.C.). The main struggle was in Greece which the vanguard of the army of Pontus had overrun before Sulla's
advent. On his arrival with 30,000 veterans of the Social
War, these troops took the defensive in the Piræus and
Athens, and kept Sulla at bay for a full year. Finally,
Athens was taken by storm and sacked and the Piræus
evacuated, but the main army of Mithridates had now
arrived in Bœotia. This Sulla routed at Chæronea in

*Party
Conflicts
Continue*

* How and Leigh, *History of Rome*, p. 417.

86 B.C., and he did the same to a second Pontic force at Orchomenus the year after; whereupon the war was carried into Asia and Mithridates sued for peace. He was left in possession of Pontus, but the province of Asia was recovered and its inhabitants forced to pay their arrears of tribute and 20,000 talents besides, a punishment which brought them to financial ruin. The other Greeks who had sided with Mithridates were also punished.

464. The Vengeance of Sulla.—Then Sulla returned home to avenge himself on his adversaries. A decisive victory over the troops opposing him in Italy gave him entrance to Rome, and another in a desperate night battle at the Colline Gate (82 B.C.) over the Samnites, who had joined his opponents and had set forth, 70,000 strong, on a wild march to the capital to destroy "the lair of the Roman wolves," placed him in possession of

supreme power in 81 B.C. He was appointed dictator for the purpose of refounding the republic. His accession was a signal for bloody massacres of his enemies, the confiscation of their property and the enrichment of his followers. Those whom he singled out especially for extirpation were the equites whom he regarded as mainly responsible for the embarrassments of the senate both at home and abroad. Hence, the names of the rich men of business were most numerous in his lists of the proscribed, whom any man might slay and none might harbor.

465. The Sullan Constitution.—His political policy was simple, the restoration of the senate to supremacy and the establishment of its position by constitutional authority. The powers claimed by the people were swept away. The consent of the senate was required before measures could be proposed to either comitia; the trib-

unes were stripped of all but intercessory powers (§ 358)
and those holding the office of tribune made thereafter
incligible for other offices; the courts were restored to
the senators (§ 455); the *cursus honorum* (§ 450) and
the law against re-election to office were revived. But
he did not stop with re-establishing and safeguarding
the government of the senate. He made some important
administrative changes. The trials of criminal and other
offences in the comitia had long since become a farce;
hence at the same time that Sulla transferred the court
of extortion back to the senators, he added six others to
it; so that special courts dealt henceforth with such things
as peculation, bribery, treason, assassination, forgery and
assault and battery. This was a considerable and, as
it proved, a permanent reduction of popular power, and
it gave Rome, for the first time, a permanent judicial
system for criminal cases. Sulla appointed as the presi-
dents of these courts the prætors who did not have the
trial of civil cases and whom he increased from four to
six. There were thus eight prætors, and like the two
consuls, to whom he added the duties of the censors, they
were fully employed with civil matters during their year
of office in Rome and Italy. Hence he arranged that
they should go to the provinces only as proprætors and
proconsuls. Since there were at this time ten provinces
(Sicily, Corsica and Sardinia, Farther Spain, Hither Spain,
Africa, Macedon, Asia, Narbonese Gaul, Cilicia and
Cisalpine Gaul*), there was one ex-magistrate for each.
When a war should arise of such a magnitude that it extended beyond the territory of a single province and hence
beyond the jurisdiction of a single magistrate, it was ar-

* It is unknown when Illyricum became a province.

ranged that the senate should be free to designate for its conduct the best citizen available without regard to his position. This relieved it of the obligation to intrust dangerous wars to the consuls who might or might not be competent generals; but it opened the way for ambitious men to secure in succession all the great commands and thus in time to become indispensable to the senate. One further change Sulla made: he increased the number of the senate from three hundred to six hundred and the number of the quæstors from eight to twenty, ten for domestic finance, one to keep the money chest of each foreign magistrate. Since he arranged that ex-quæstors should enter the senate, provision was thus made for keeping its number at six hundred.

Sulla Dies. These administration changes were the permanent part of Sulla's work. Having thus accomplished his object as he believed, Sulla resigned the office of dictator (79 B.C.), retired to private life and died not long after. The senate was once more in the saddle, this time, as it seemed, legally seated in control.

466. Sulla's Political Reforms Inadequate and Futile. —But, like the work of any man who moves against the **Failure of Provincial Administration.** irresistible current of history, Sulla's political reforms were vain. Rome and its provinces were growing more and more dependent upon one another. The food supply of Italy was largely met by the importation of grain from the provinces The business of Rome stretched over the whole civilized world, and its progress depended upon the peace and prosperity of the provinces. Hence, a government that kept the provinces in order, that secured peace and established justice, was absolutely necessary. But just here the old Roman system was a failure. Rome was a city-state and its government was not organized for imperial rule over a wide domain. Neither senate nor people was equal to the demand. The only way to solve the problem was to give large powers to the extraordinary magistrate, and this way, as we have seen, now lay open before the senate; yet this brought with it the danger that the state had been guarding against for centuries—making the magistrate too powerful, giving him control of the government. We have seen how the state was steadily moving in this direction. Marius and Sulla are examples of the tendency which was growing stronger and stronger. The party conflicts at Rome only opened wider the door of opportunity to the magistrates. Thus the expansion of Rome to an empire brought about the breaking down of the old constitution.

Solution of the Problem.

467. The New Dangers to Rome.—Sulla's legislation was a feeble dam across the current, which soon carried it off Shortly after his death Roman power was being threatened from three sides. (1) The province of Spain was in possession of the adherents of Marius, led by a gallant soldier, Sertorius. (2) A terrible insurrection of slaves in Italy broke out under the leadership of a gladiator, Spartacus. (3) The east was in an uproar owing to the ravages of pirates, having their seats on the coasts and islands of the eastern Mediterranean, especially Cilicia and Crete. They destroyed Roman commerce and even cut off the food supply from Rome. Mithridates, also, was recovering from his defeat and organizing a new coalition to sweep the Romans out of the east.

468. Rise of Pompey.—In the face of these troubles, the senate was forced to find a helper in the person of a young man who had won his spurs under Sulla This was Gnæus Pompeius,* of noble family, whose father had been a successful general. In 77 B.C. he was given proconsular power by the senate though a private citizen at the time, and was sent into Spain, where he overcame, not Sertorius, who had been basely assassinated, but the weakling successor of Sertorius in 72 B.C. Then, returning to Rome, he sought the consulship. When the senate opposed him, he allied himself with Crassus, the richest man in Rome. Crassus was leader of the equites and had already brought the war with Spartacus to an end.

Sulla's Work Over-thrown. The two leaders turned to the democracy and obtained its support by promising to overthrow the constitution of Sulla. Thus, in defiance of the senate, Pompey and Crassus were elected consuls and restored the powers of the tribunes and the comitia tributa. Sulla's political work perished less than ten years after his death. The most important consequence of the restoration of the power of the tribunate was that henceforth the people, on the initiation of a tribune, could virtually appoint the extraordinary magistrate instead of the senate. This was an important step toward monarchy.

469. Gabinian Law; Pompey Sent to the East.— Meanwhile, the war with Mithridates was renewed and the Roman general Lu-cul'lus, a man of ability and worth, was able to win several victories (74–68 B.C.). But the devastations wrought by the pirates continued. Accordingly, in 67 B.C., the tribune Gabinius proposed to the people to give Pompey for three years complete control of the entire Mediterranean and power over its coast for fifty miles inland equal to that of the provincial governors. The next year (66 B C), by the proposal of

---

* The English form of his name, Pompey, will be henceforth used.

PLATE XXX

Julius Cæsar

Cicero

Vespasian

Hadrian

Faustina

Commodus

TYPICAL ROMAN HEADS

the tribune Manilius, the conduct of the war with Mithridates was also conferred upon him; by this "Manilian" law he was given unlimited authority for the settlement of the east. By these two laws Pompey was placed in a position of power which no Roman before him had ever occupied.

470. New Leaders.—In support of these measures two men came forward who were destined thenceforth to play a large part in Roman life—Marcus Tullius Cicero and Gaius Julius Cæsar. Cicero was a countryman, of *Cicero* equestrian rank, who was rapidly rising to the position of the leading orator at Rome and head of the equites. A man of fine personal character and wide culture, he *His Political Ideal* was zealous for the restoration of the old Roman constitution and the revival of the old Roman spirit. This he hoped to secure by giving the Italian element in Roman citizenship a larger place in the state. The people, thus braced and purified by the influence of this worthier and sounder element, he hoped to see unite with the senate in a new and firm government. It was a beautiful dream, and Cicero gave his life to its realization. Cæsar belonged *Cæsar.* to one of the oldest and proudest patrician families. He was a daring and far-seeing spirit, cherishing no dreams, eager to play a leading part in the politics of his day. Related by marriage to Marius, he took the side of the democratic party and from that standpoint sought to re-establish and glorify the Roman name.

471. The Conspiracy of Catiline.—Pompey was in the east five years (67–62 B.C.). During his absence a crisis occurred at Rome which wellnigh destroyed the state. The rapid rise of the democracy encouraged the discontented and the miserable to hope for a change of fortune. A ruined and reckless patrician, Catiline] by name, sought to unite all who were like himself in character and fortune in a conspiracy to overthrow the government and plunder the rich. How widely the plot extended was never known   Even Crassus and Cæsar are thought to have had knowledge of it. To meet the danger feared rather than known, the more conservative citizens, optimates and equites united, elected Cicero as one of the consuls 'for the year 63 B C. He showed uncommon skill and courage in grappling with it, unearthed the conspirators and impeached them. Though Catiline fled, other leaders were seized, and on the authority of the senate put to death by the consul. On January 5, 62 B.C., Catiline, who had gathered an army, was overthrown in battle and died fighting. It was Cicero's one splendid political success in uniting the best elements of the state in its defence, and he looked forward to the speedy realization of his dream (§ 470). But he was soon to be sorely disappointed.

Cicero Overthrows It.

472. Pompey's Victories in the East.—The career of Pompey in the east had been one uninterrupted success. Forty days sufficed for him to clear the sea of pirates; he pursued them to their strongholds and destroyed them. Then he advanced against Mithridates and his son-in-law and ally, Ti-gra'nes of Armenia. A victory in 66 B C. shattered the Pontic power and brought peace with Tigranes. The Parthians also allied themselves with Pompey. Steadily Mithridates was hemmed in, until, in 63 B.C., he fled to his dependency, the kingdom of Bosporus, to the north of the Black Sea, and there killed himself. His kingdom was made part of the Roman province of Bithynia. The kingdom of the Seleucidæ (§ 319) was brought to an end and Syria became a province (64 B.C.). The Jewish king (§ 430) resisted Pompey, who stormed Jerusalem (63 B.C.) and reduced Judea to a Roman dependency ruled by high priests. The Euphrates river became the eastern boundary of the Roman state. Cities were founded, stable government was restored and prosperity revived. Two new provinces, Bithynia-Pontus and Syria* were added to Rome's eastern possessions; the province of Cilicia, which had been established in 102 B.C. at the time of Rome's first operation against the pirates, was enlarged and friendly alliances with the border kings and chiefs were established or renewed. An immense sum was paid into the Roman treasury. Pompey had amply fulfilled his task and now returned to Rome, where he triumphed, in 61 B.C.

473. The First Triumvirate.—The senate took an attitude of criticism and disfavor toward Pompey, and refused to give lands to his veterans or ratify his acts in the east. Looking elsewhere for allies, he joined with Cæsar and Crassus in a coalition which has been called the first triumvirate. It meant that the united influence of all should be used to satisfy the desires of each. They were entirely successful. Cæsar was elected consul for 59 B.C.; as consul he secured for Pompey the things denied him by the senate; also Crassus and his friends were enriched. Cæsar also obtained an appointment as proconsul in Gaul for five years, beginning in March, 59 B C. The compact was followed by the marriage of Pompey to Cæsar's daughter Julia

It turned out that Cæsar's proconsulate in Gaul lasted

---

* Crete was conquered by Metellus and made a province in this same period.

for ten years. When his first term had two years still to
run, the triumvirate met again (56 B.C.) at Luca and
agreed to use their influence to have Pompey and Crassus
elected consuls for 55 B C. The two consuls would then
see to it that Cæsar's term should be prolonged for another
five years, while they themselves were also to have each a
five years' term as proconsul, Crassus in Syria and Pompey
in Spain. The agreement was duly carried out. Crassus
left for Syria in 54 B.C., where he was killed in battle with
the Parthians at Carrhæ the following year. Cæsar remained in Gaul. Pompey lingered at Rome.

474. Rome in Confusion.—Political affairs in Rome
had been going from bad to worse. Intrigue and the
strife of factions filled the city with confusion and turmoil.
Partisan leaders surrounded by armed adherents paraded
the streets and fought with one another. An adept at
this sort of politics was the young and dissolute patrician,
Publius Clodius, a democrat of the type of Catiline, who
succeeded in terrorizing foes and friends alike. As tribune, he proceeded to get Cicero banished in 58 B.C. for
having violated the law of appeal by putting the Catili-
narian conspirators to death (§ 471). A turn of the wheel
brought the great orator back in triumph the next year.
Clodius, finally, was killed in a street fight in 52 B.C.

Pompey had begun gradually to draw away from Cæsar
and incline toward the optimates. Soon after the conference at Luca (§ 473) his wife Julia died and, with the
death of Crassus, the last link that bound him personally
to Cæsar was severed. In 52 B.C. he was made sole consul and introduced measures which revealed his alliance
with the senate and his break with Cæsar. Pompey was
now at the zenith of his remarkable career. He was at

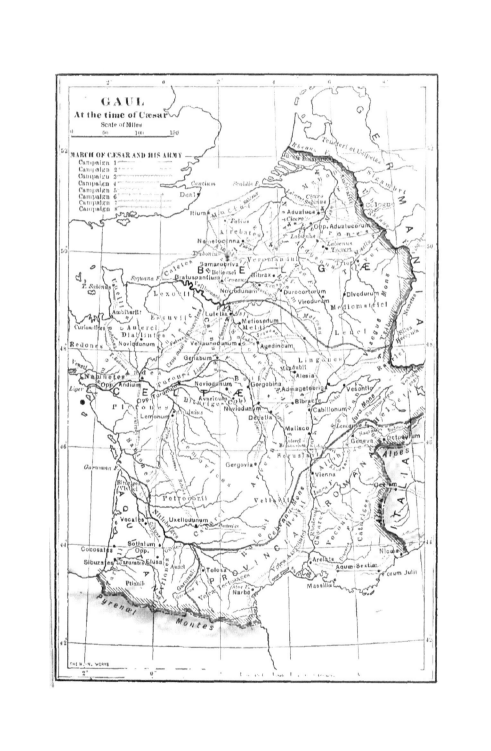

GAUL

At the time of Cæsar

Scale of Miles

0   50   100   150

MARCH OF CÆSAR AND HIS ARMY

Campaign 1
Campaign 2
Campaign 3
Campaign 4
Campaign 5
Campaign 6
Campaign 7
Campaign 8

once sole consul in Rome, proconsul of the two Spains with liberty to govern them through *legati*; he had the right to levy troops in Italy, and was a special commissioner of the corn supply, with unlimited power over the Mediterranean sea and all its coasts and harbors. Such an accumulation of powers was substantially monarchy; if they could be enforced against Cæsar, it was monarchy.

475. Cæsar in Gaul.—Jealousy and fear of Cæsar may have had much to do with the new attitude now assumed by Pompey. For Cæsar's career in Gaul had been remarkable. The ten years now drawing to a close (59–49 B.C.) had been occupied with hard fighting and skilful diplomacy. Assigned the provinces of Cisalpine and Transalpine Gaul and Illyricum, he proceeded at once to protect Roman interests on their borders, threatened by movements among the tribes beyond. The continual tumult caused by quarrels between these tribes was heightened by the incoming of Germans from across the Rhine. Already the Helvetii, a Gallic tribe living in the country about the sources of the Rhone and Rhine, were hard pressed and prepared to move westward. If the pressure were not removed, the Roman province would sooner or later be threatened with invasion. Requests for help from Gallic tribes gave another opportunity for Cæsar's interference. He crossed the Roman border, forced back the Helvetii who had already begun to move, drove the Germans in Gaul over the Rhine and plunged into a series of campaigns which, in successive years, carried his arms to the North sea, across the Rhine, to the shores of the Atlantic and into Britain.* Opposition

---

* For Cæsar's famous campaigns, the student is advised to read his equally famous *Commentaries*.

was crushed or turned by alliance into friendship until the Roman name was supreme throughout all Gaul. No attempt was made to bring the country under the direct rule of Rome, but, following his army, came Roman commerce and culture to transform the people and prepare the way for the addition of Gaul to the empire.

Cæsar's achievement had two results: (1) It turned Gaul into a bulwark of civilization to hold back advancing German barbarism and thus furnished a means for extending this civilization and establishing it in the regions beyond Gaul Thereby all succeeding periods of western history down to our own day have been stamped with Rome's impress. (2) Cæsar gained for himself men and money by which to take a commanding part in the further history of Rome.

476. Cæsar in Conflict with the Senate.—Cæsar had sore need of these things, for Pompey, backed by the senate, was rapidly taking a more hostile attitude. Cæsar's term as proconsul closed in March, 49 B.C., and he could not enter upon the consulship for which he wished to stand till 48 B C.   Meanwhile, he would be a private citizen and could be brought to trial and ruined on charges which he knew would be trumped up against him.   Moreover, he could stand for the consulship only by coming to Rome in person; this he could not do without leaving his province and giving up his proconsulate. He sought to have these conditions waived in his case, but the senate refused.   Finally, after endless negotiations, the senate commanded him to resign his province, and Pompey was called upon to save the state from him as a public enemy.   In response Cæsar crossed the Rubicon, a river which separated his province from Italy, and marched rapidly on Rome with an army (January, 49 B C.). Rome was in alarm, and Pompey, with the majority of the senate and a crowd of nobles, fled to the coast and crossed over to Greece, where he gathered an army from the eastern provinces. Cæsar found himself, without serious opposition, in possession of Italy and Rome. After a hasty expedition to Spain, where he overthrew Pompey's veteran armies under the command of his legates and thus freed his rear from danger during the coming struggle in the east, he was appointed dictator, held the elections, in which he was made consul (48 B.C.), and proceeded to enter upon the war with Pompey and the senatorial party.

He Marches on Rome

Is Master of Italy.

477. Cæsar Wins the Roman World.—The decisive battle was fought at Phar-sa'lus in Thessaly (48 B.C). Pompey was beaten and his army scattered; he himself fled to Egypt, where he was murdered as he sought to land. But lesser commanders held out in the various provinces against the victor and he was compelled to make a series of campaigns against them. First, the east was brought into order. In Egypt, Cleopatra and her brother Ptol'e-my, descendants of the old Greek rulers, were placed on the throne under Roman protection, and Cæsar came under the fascination of the intelligent and charming but morally unscrupulous young queen. A battle at Zela (47 B C) overthrew the son of Mithridates, who attempted to withstand him. It is of these incidents that Byron writes:

Pharsalus

"Alcides with the distaff now he seems at Cleopatra's feet,
  And now himself he beams and came and saw and conquered."

The formidable array of Pompeian generals in Africa was annihilated in the battle of Thapsus (46 B.C) A last stand in Spain was made, only to be overthrown in 45 B.C. at the battle of Munda. After four years of fighting, Cæsar was master of the situation, and the opportunity was open to him of solving the problems of the state, which had been in the balance for nearly a hundred years.

His Death. But early in 44 B.C. (March 15) he was assassinated in

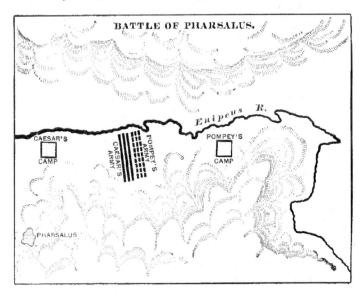

the senate-house by a band of conspirators, led by Gaius Cassius and a favorite friend, Marcus Brutus, and the Roman world again plunged into anarchy.

478. His Work of Reorganization.—In the intervals of his campaigns, however, Cæsar set himself to re-establish public order and civil administration both by his example and spirit and by his laws. (1) His attitude

Its Spirit. toward his enemies was an astonishingly mild one. No murders, no wholesale seizure of property, no gratifying of personal grudges marked his victory; on the contrary

forgiveness of injuries and the employment of vanquished
opponents in state service was the rule. This can only
mean that the welfare of the state and not personal ambition ruled his spirit. (2) He recognized his victory
as the supremacy of the magistracy over the other organs
of state-life. The senate and the people had alike failed
to administer affairs with success. Now it was the turn
of the magistrate. The senate was reduced to its legitimate place as his adviser. To this end it was enlarged
to nine hundred members, made more representative by
being drawn from various ranks of society and districts
of the empire; even "half-barbarian Gauls" were there.
The people exercised its functions of law-giving and election under his bidding and direction. (3) He gathered
all the magisterial powers into his own hand. The particular office by which he ruled the state was that of dictator, but he combined with it consular, proconsular,
tribunician and censorial powers, all of which were conferred upon him by senate and people. (4) The unification of the empire was one of his chief aims. The
centralization of magisterial powers in himself enabled
him to hold all affairs in his own hands and direct them
himself. The chief outward sign of this was his favorite
title, "imperator." As imperator he possessed an *imperium* above and inclusive of that of other magistrates.*
Hence, he alone ruled the provinces and he was head of
the city government. His measures indicate his ideals.
(*a*) Citizenship was conferred on a wider scale than ever
before. The Gauls across the Po, colonies in the provinces and worthy persons among the provincials were
given full rights and the Latin right was conferred upon

The Magistracy Supreme.

He is Sole Magistrate

His Imperial Ideal and Its Realization.

---

* This is called the *majus imperium*

others. (*b*) Municipal government (§ 381) was unified and its institutions and powers determined more precisely. (*c*) New colonies were established at Corinth and Carthage and decaying colonies and towns were revived by new settlers. (*d*) The city populace of Rome was curbed, political clubs were abolished, the number of those receiving state grain was cut down one-half; Rome began to be reduced from the position of a sovereign of subject lands to the place of a leading city, or capital, of an empire. (*e*) The soldiers of his armies were settled on lands obtained without confiscation. Thus law, rights, order and prosperity, common to all, began to

Other Activities. appear throughout the one empire. (5) Outside of political affairs, the activities of Cæsar were notable. He reformed the calendar by substituting for the indefinite lunar year the exact sun year of $365\frac{1}{4}$ days. Public works were undertaken both for the benefit of the state and the employment of needy citizens. Chief among these was the Julian Forum, adorned with the temple of Venus, his patron goddess We are told that he planned other extensive projects for beautifying the city and benefiting Italy, such as erecting a temple to Mars and a theatre, establishing public libraries, draining the Pomptine marshes and the Fucine lake, building a road over the Apennines, codifying the laws; but his death left them uncompleted.

479. Literature in His Day.—Cæsar's genius was many-sided, almost universal. He possessed striking literary power in an age of vigorous intellectual activity. Some of the chief ornaments of Roman literature flourished in his own day, but he shone as brightly as any.

Lucretius. Two Roman poets, Lucretius and Ca-tul'lus, belong to his time. Lucretius is famous for his philosophical poem "On the Nature of Things," dealing with the origin and history of the world and man, on the principles of the Epicurean philosophy (§ 324). Not only is its insight into truth remarkable, but the poetical power displayed is rich and strong. Catullus was a lyric poet who died at thirty, but left behind him poems whose lines are so delicate, original and touching, as to rank him among the greatest lyrists of the world. Supreme in the realm of prose was Cicero (§ 470), who sprang into fame as an orator by his prosecution of Verres, the corrupt Roman governor of Sicily, and advanced it by a long series of legal and political speeches like those against Catiline (§ 471). In another sphere, that of political, literary and philosophical treatises, he wrote works such as those *On Oratory, On the State, On the Nature of God, On Old Age.* These masterpieces are not only notable for their ideas, they are most significant in their marvellous mastery of the Latin tongue, the majestic roll of their sentences, the music of their phrases, the strength and variety of their vocabulary. He made Latin the vehicle of expression for the widest and highest thought, the medium of utterance for generations of scholars and thinkers to come. Among such men Cæsar was also famous. As an orator, there were those who placed him on a level with Cicero. But the world knows him best in literature by his unrivalled narratives of his campaigns. His *Commentaries,* notes or jottings on the Gallic War and the Civil War, are expressed in terse, vivid, clear Latin, "the model and despair of later historians" The only man of the time who approached him was Sallust, one of his younger contemporaries and

Catullus

Cicero.

Cæsar as a Writer.

Sallust.

a trusted officer, whose model for historical writing was Thucydides (§ 227). His chief work was his *History* of his own times from the death of Sulla. Only a few fragments of it remain, but two brief treatises, one on the war with Jugurtha and the other on the conspiracy of Catiline, have survived. They show considerable literary power if not an admirable sense for historic truth. Lesser lights of the time were Cornelius Nepos, the biographer, and Varro, the learned antiquarian, whose treatises on old Roman life and manners, though preserved in fragments, have been of great value to modern students.

480. Cæsar's Supreme Genius Analyzed.—Yet, as soldier and statesman, Cæsar stands pre-eminent. He possessed four gifts to an extraordinary degree. (1) Quickness of insight and an almost preternatural ability to choose the right course to success. (2) A breadth of view which saw things in their widest issues and could devise measures on a scale proportionate to the problem to be solved. (3) Immense capacity for toil. (4) Marvellous power to draw men to himself, to fire them with his own enthusiasm and to set them at work. Any one of these gifts makes a strong man; all of them combined made Cæsar the foremost man of his time and one of the few greatest men of all times. His only parallel in the

The Results of Cæsar's Murder.

ancient world is Alexander of Macedon. His untimely death, like that of his Greek predecessor, changed the whole course of history; for, whereas, Alexander had planned to add the west to his great empire, Cæsar, in the year of his murder, was about to start on a campaign to add the far east to the Mediterranean world, from which it had drawn apart, under Parthian rule, during the decay of the Seleucid empire in the second century B.C. The chance to unite the whole world in one state never recurred. Moreover, Cæsar's idea of a despotic government, and of the degradation of Italy and the Italians to be, like the provincials, his subjects, was not ripe for execution in his time. Certainly, it was not ripe for execution by any one but himself; and since his successor, as we shall see, turned deliberately away from absolutism and sought to preserve intact the imperial position of Italy, Cæsar's career forms but a brilliant episode in a development which continued on its course to issue in the principate of Augustus.

REVIEW EXERCISES. 1. For what were the following important: Drusus, Jugurtha, Sertorius, Luca, the Rubicon, Lucretius? 2. What is meant by triumvirate, Italica, Agrarian law, majus imperium, populares? 3. Who were the two leading Scipios and how did they receive their names of Africanus and Æmilianus? 4. Trace the careers of the following men through the period: Marius, Sulla, Pompey, Cicero, Cæsar. 5. What was the the date of Cæsar's death? 6. What was the spirit of Tiberius Gracchus's reform measures? 7. How did Gaius Gracchus play the game of politics? 8. How were the senate and office of tribune affected by Sulla's legislation?

COMPARATIVE STUDIES. 1. Compare the parties at Rome in origin, aims and character with those at Athens in the fifth century (§§ 168, 189, 218, 223, 239, 243). 2. With what Greek statesman and soldier would you compare Sulla (see Plutarch's choice)? 3. In Plates XVIII and XXX compare the heads of Alexander and Cæsar and draw some conclusions.

SELECT LIST FOR READING. 1. The Land Law of Tiberius Gracchus. How and Leigh, pp. 337–344 2. Gaius Gracchus's Measures and Their Fate. How and Leigh, pp 346–356, 358–360. 3. The Numidian War. How and Leigh, pp 360–371. 4. Military Reforms of Marius. How and Leigh, pp 378–380. 5. The Social War. How and Leigh, ch. 39 6. The Constitution of Sulla. How and Leigh, ch 44. **7. Pompey in the East.** How and Leigh, ch. 46. **8. Conspiracy of Catiline.** How and Leigh, ch. 47. **9. Cæsar in Gaul.** How and Leigh, ch 49. **10. The Legislation of Cæsar.** How and Leigh, ch 52 **11. The Food, Clothing and Employment of the Poor.** Fowler, Social Life at Rome, pp 33–59 **12 The Roman Business Man.** Fowler, pp 69–90 **13. The Roman Matrons.** Fowler, pp. 143–156. **14. The Economic Aspect of Slavery.** Fowler, pp 213–222. **15. Cicero's Country Homes.** Fowler, pp 251–262 **16. A Letter of an Undergraduate in the University of Athens.** Fowler, pp. 199–203.

TOPICS FOR READING AND ORAL REPORT. 1. The Roman Constitution by the Year 133 B C. Munro, pp. 47–52 (source); Horton, ch. 19. **2. The Gracchi and Their Times.** Plutarch, Lives of the Gracchi; Morey, ch. 19; Seignobos, ch 13, Botsford, pp. 151–160; Shuckburgh, ch. 35 **3. The Politics of the Gracchi.** Abbott, pp. 94–98. **4. The Times of Marius and Sulla.** Morey, ch 20, Seignobos, ch 14; Botsford, pp 160–174. **5. The Numidian War.** Myres, pp. 360–368. **6. The Cimbri and Teutones.** Myres, pp 368–372; Horton, ch 23 **7. Military Reforms of Marius.** Myres, 378–380. **8. The Social War.** Shuckburgh, pp. 589–592. **9. The Constitution of Sulla.** Morey, pp. 176–179, Abbott, pp. 104–107, Myres, ch 35. **10. Times of Pompey and Cæsar.** Morey, ch 21, Botsford, pp 175–196 **11. Pompey in the East.** Shuckburgh, ch. 42 **12. Conspiracy of Catiline. 13. Cæsar in Gaul.** Shuckburgh, ch 44. **14. Cæsar, Pompey and the Senate.** Abbott, pp. 129–138; Horton, ch. 30; Morey, pp. 197–200. **15. The Legislation of Cæsar.** Abbott, pp. 114–116. Myres, ch. 41 **16. Roman Literature of This Period.** Laing (quotations and biographies), pp. 63–197; Mackail, pp. 39–88. **17. The Effect of Lucullus's Eastern Campaign upon Financial Conditions in Italy.** Ferrero, vol I, pp. 200–224. **18. The First Triumvirate, a Three-Headed Monster.** Ferrero, vol I, pp. 324–336. **19. How Cæsar became a Demagogue.** Ferrero, vol. I, pp. 250–265. **20. Lucullus in the East.** Heitland, vol. III, pp. 9–10, 13–14, 30–41. **21. Cæsar's Last Ambition.** Ferrero, vol. II, pp 282–302. **22. Jugurtha's Claim to the Numidian Crown.** Greenidge, vol I, pp 321–344 **23. Jugurtha's Visit to Rome: Its Significance.** Greenidge, vol I, pp 346–353 **24. Jugurtha's Capture Closes the War.** Greenidge, vol 1. pp. 465–472. **25. The Trials of Verres and Flaccus.** Heitland, vol III, pp. 18–21, 141–144

GENERAL REVIEW OF PART III, DIVISIONS 1-6

1200(?)–44 B C

TOPICS FOR CLASS DISCUSSION. 1. An outline of the main points of Roman history in chronological order from the point of view of Rome's relation to outside peoples. 2. A similar outline from the point of view of Rome's inner life. 3. The peoples that contributed to Rome's greatness, arranged chronologically with examples (§§ 344, 346, 348, 364, 370–372, 403, 437, 441, 445, 449). 4. The most important dates in Roman history to 44 B C. 5. The changes appearing in Rome's attitude toward outside peoples (§§ 354, 355, 372, 377, 399, 427, 431, 434, 466, 478). 6. Roman farming and the farmer—as illustrating the history (§§ 347, 357, 359, 366, 379, 387, 403, 418, 437, 440, 458) 7. Development of the Roman army (§§ 350, 362, 385). 8. A list of the great men of Rome in the different periods of her history to 44 B C 9. Roman citizenship in the various periods of Roman history (§§ 371, 381, 447, 450, 456, 460) 10. An enumeration of the influences and tendencies that from the beginning of the state led up to Cæsar's supremacy (§§ 419, 423, 424, 435, 451, 452, 456, 459, 466, 469). 11. The history of the influence of commerce on Roman history (§§ 339, 344, 372, 377, 399, 423, 434, 439, 450, 455, 457, 459, 461, 464, 468)

MAP AND PICTURE EXERCISES. 1. Prepare a map of republican Rome to accompany paper No. 3 below. 2. Compare the oriental heads in Plate II with the heads of Cæsar and Cicero in Plate XXX. 3. In the same way compare the two Roman heads with the Greek heads in Plate XVIII. 4. Make a plan of the Roman Forum and use it to illustrate Plate XXIX. 5. Prepare a map of the Mediterranean world to show—by different colored pencils or inks—the expansion of Rome in each of the three periods to 44 B C. 6. On Plate XXVIII study the Roman coins of this age and compare them with the Greek coins of Plate XXVII. (See Appendix II.)

SUBJECTS FOR WRITTEN PAPERS. 1. The Roman Magistrate—His Position, Powers and Duties. Abbott, pp. 150–173. 2. The Ædile—His Powers and Duties. Abbott, pp 202–206. 3. The City of Rome down to 44 B.C. Merivale, ch 78 4. The Roman Senate—its Position, Powers and Duties. Abbott, pp. 220–243; Fowler, City State, ch. 8 5. Rome's Treatment of

Spain as Illustrative of Its Dealing with Conquered Peoples.
How and Leigh, pp 240-245, 464-466, Shuckburgh, pp 458-
463, 538-545. **6. Roman Slavery as Testified to by the Romans Themselves.** Sources in Munro, pp. 179-192 **7. The
Carthaginian Empire.** Mommsen, History of Rome, vol. II, bk
3, ch. 1. **8. Roman Roads.** Dictionaries of Antiquities, articles
"Via" or "Roads", Guhl and Koner, pp. 341-344; Johnston, pp
282-287 **9. The Story of Terence's "Phormio" as Illustrative
of Roman Comedy.** Laing, pp. 4-62. **10. How was Justice
Administered at Rome?** Abbott (§§ 65, 87, 96, 100, 182, 189,
200-203, 222, 236, 251, 309). **11. Some Roman Traditional
Stories:** (a) The Secessions of the Plebeians. (b) The Caudine
Forks. Munro, pp. 74-77 (c) Cincinnatus. Botsford, Story
of Rome; Yonge, Stories of Roman History, Church, Stories from
Livy. **12. An Estimate of Cæsar Written by Pompey. 13. The
Roman Equites (Knights)—History and Privileges.** Dictionaries of Antiquities, under the name, Greenidge, "Roman Public
Life," index under name. **14. The Financial Administration of
the State.** Abbott (§§ 184, 213, 239, 280, Greenidge, pp 229-232,
286-287). **15. "We ought to be thankful to Cæsar every
day that we live."** Justify this remark.

481. Preliminary Survey.—The era of expansion beginning with 264 B.C. had put Rome in possession of the
countries where the main current of historic life had
hitherto run its course. A world-empire had arisen,
stretching from the Euphrates to the Atlantic. The
The Problem and Its Solution. problem, again thrown into the arena by Cæsar's murder, was the administration of that empire; the course
of the following epochs of ancient history is the solution
of that problem—the government of the Roman world.

Divisions of the Period. Thus the history of the period falls into three main
epochs.

7. The Roman Empire (Principate), 44 B.C.-A.D. 284.
8. The Roman Empire (Despotism), A.D 284-395.
9. The Breaking up of the Roman Empire and the
   End of the Ancient Period, A.D. 395-800.

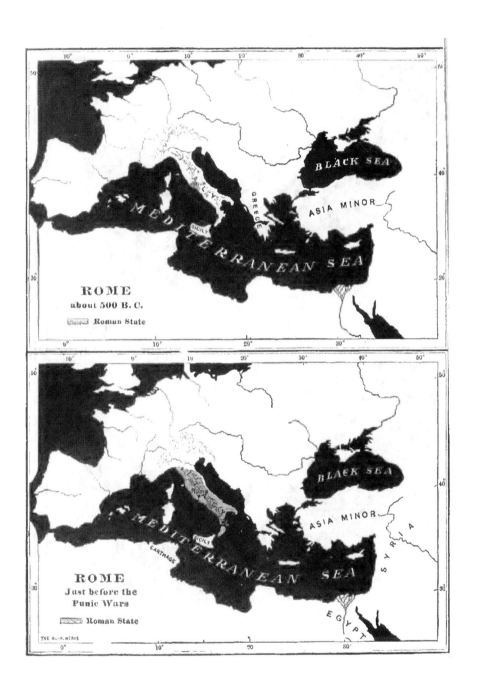

ROME
about 500 B. C.
Roman State

BLACK SEA
ASIA MINOR
MEDITERRANEAN SEA
GREECE
SICILY
ITALY

ROME
Just before the
Punic Wars
Roman State

BLACK SEA
ASIA MINOR
MEDITERRANEAN SEA
ROME
SICILY
CARTHAGE
SYRIA
EGYPT

THE M. N. WORKS

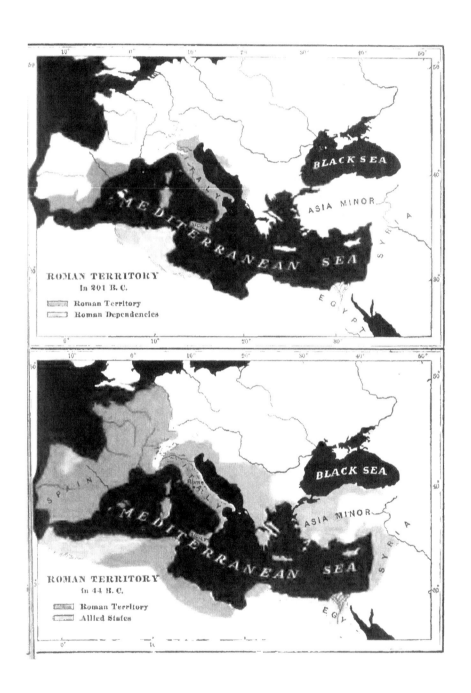

BIBLIOGRAPHY *

For bibliography for advanced students and teachers, see Appendix I

DILL *Roman Society from Nero to Marcus Aurelius.* Macmillan A masterly work. In general suitable only for teachers, but a few passages, judiciously selected, may be helpful for pupils also

BURY *The Student's Roman Empire, to the Death of Marcus Aurelius* American Book Co. Full of matter, well written, an invaluable work of reference, rather too detailed for continuous reading by the beginner

GIBBON. *The Student's Gibbon.* American Book Co This well-known abridgment of Gibbon's *Decline and Fall of the Roman Empire* should be constantly in the hands of the student for the period with which it deals

JONES, H. S. *The Roman Empire.* Putnams Brilliantly written, up to date and reliable   The best single-volume history from Augustus to Augustulus.

MERIVALE. *General History of Rome to 476 A D.* American Book Co. Merivale becomes especially useful in the imperial period, his narrative is full and clear, though the organization of his material is defective.

TUCKER. *Life in the Roman World of Nero and St Paul* Macmillan. Interesting and reliable.

7.—THE ROMAN EMPIRE (PRINCIPATE)

44 B C –A D. 284

482. After Cæsar—What?—The thirteen years (44–31 B.C.) that followed Cæsar's murder were filled with turmoil and struggle. Those who hoped that the senate would resume control of the government were soon undeceived. Antony, consul at the time of Cæsar's death, Antony. came forward as his successor, and Brutus and Cassius, placing no reliance upon the fickle populace of Rome, and finding no enthusiasm for their act in Italy, fled to the east, to provinces assigned to them by their victim. Cicero started to follow at their heels, but plucking up

* For previous bibliographies, see §§ 5a, 89a, 338a.

courage, he returned to Rome; and, taking advantage of a dissension, which split for a time the followers of Cæsar, he roused the senate to action and tried to guide

Octavius.

events on lines favorable to republicanism. This brief restoration of senatorial power was due to the appearance of Octavius, the grandnephew and heir of Cæsar,* a youth who, though but eighteen years of age, showed uncommon prudence and energy. Since Antony declined to recognize his rights, he won over many of Cæsar's veterans by a free use of money, which his friends and relatives provided, and by proclaiming his purpose to be to avenge the murder of the great leader. At the same time, he did not hesitate to co-operate with the senate in its struggle with Antony. Cicero thought he could use "the boy" for his own purposes and then throw him aside. He was terribly mistaken. Once the unnatural partners had defeated Antony in a war at Mu-ti'na and Octavius had shown that he could not be ignored, these two united with themselves Lepidus, whom Cæsar had appointed to the province of Transalpine Gaul, a man of little force or insight. Supported by the legions,

The Second Trium-virate.

they compelled the senate to appoint them a triumvirate for settling the affairs of the state (43 B.C.). Acting in this capacity, they avenged themselves on their enemies in Rome and filled the city with blood. Their most illustrious victim was Cicero, whose brilliant orations † against Antony in the senate, a few months before, had

Philippi.

aroused his hatred. At the battle of Phi-lip'pi (42 B.C.) they overthrew the armies which Brutus and Cassius

---

* As adopted son of Cæsar his name was C. Julius Cæsar Octavianus.

† These orations were called Philippics in recollection of Demosthenes' speeches against Philip (§ 276).

had gathered in the east. Then Antony and Octavius set about their task of settling affairs, Antony taking the east and Octavius the west. Antony failed to manage his share of the empire successfully; he became entangled with Cleopatra, queen of Egypt, and let matters go at loose ends. Moreover, he quarrelled with Octavius, who in the meantime had restored order in Italy, taken the province of Sicily and the rule of the sea from the pirate king, Sextus Pompeius, Pompey's son, shelved Lepidus, found his great general, ⌐A-grip′pa, and his great diplomat and councillor, Mæ-ce′nas, and, in a word, by his shrewd sense and statesman-like conduct won the good-will of all the best Roman citizens. Thus accompanied, the one by failure, the other by success, the two met in battle at Actium (31 B.C.), where Antony was beaten. Octavius alone remained at the head of the state.

Actium.

In the agony of the struggle at Actium, Cleopatra, who had command of the Egyptian squadron of Antony's fleet, raised sail and made off for Egypt. She had bound Antony to herself, as earlier Julius Cæsar, in order to save her kingdom from Roman attack and, maybe, to become queen of the whole world. Now that she foresaw the destruction of her lover, she wished to save herself and her country, if possible, from participating in his fate. What she had not calculated on was the blind devotion of Antony, who, leaving his fleet and army commanderless, sailed away to Egypt with her. Nevertheless, Cleopatra did not despair of getting rid of Antony and gaining the support of the young man who now could deal with Egypt as he pleased. She entered into an intrigue with Octavius as he drew near her country, and carried her treachery so far that, having entered into a pact with her lover to commit suicide together, she issued a false report of her death. Antony at once killed himself. Then the hitherto invincible queen tried her seductions on Octavius, but one glimpse of the cold blue eye and the passionlessly polite mien of the victor told her that she had met her match. Rather than be carried

Cleopatra.

428 *The Principate*

to Rome to grace the triumph of Octavius, she took her own life. Thus perished the last of a long line of Egyptian queens—the last of the Ptolemies Egypt became part of the Roman empire.

483. The Problem of Octavius.—The questions that had faced Cæsar now confronted Octavius—how should the state be reorganized, and what place should he occupy in it? For answering these questions he possessed little of the genius of his uncle, that far-seeing eye, that quick grasp of all the elements in the situation, that daring and enthusiastic spirit which did not shrink from doing in its own way whatever was to be done.   Yet Octavius had what was, perhaps, for his time, a better equipment— caution and coolness, attachment to the past, love of peace and order, an iron will which, however, was ready to use the most available means to gain its way.   With these qualities he could not follow Cæsar's path—break with the past, gather all powers into his own hand and rule the state as supreme magistrate.   Had not that path led to assassination?   He proposed to restore the old order and adjust his own position and power to it. Senate, magistrates and people should play their part as before in the conduct of the state.   On him should be conferred extraordinary powers for the special tasks of administration which so sorely needed attention in the vast domains of the imperial state.

His Fitness to Solve It.

His Plan.

484. Augustus, 27 B.C.–14 A.D.—In the year 27 B.C. the arrangement went into force.   "I transferred the state," he says, "from my power to the control of the senate and people."   He was already consul; now he was given by them the proconsular imperium for ten years and the sacred title of AUGUSTUS.   With this dual power went supreme authority over all provincial governors and sole rule over certain provinces on the frontiers where armies were needed; he was therefore master of the legions. Over these provinces he placed lieutenants (*legati*) responsible to himself. The other provinces were rule l by proconsuls and propraetors appointed by the senate * He already possessed the tribunician power and for some years continued to be elected consul. But, as it was not constitutional to be consul and proconsul at the same time, he laid down the consulship in 23 B.C , although retaining the rank and power, preferring to take part in civil affairs by virtue of his tribunician authority. To represent his place in the state in all its aspects he chose the title of *princeps* or "First Citizen," whence this form of government is called the Principate. Later he was also honored with the title of *pater patriæ*, "Father of his country." From time to time his proconsular power was renewed, as the term for which it was assigned expired; the tribunician power only he held for life. The people elected magistrates and made laws; the senate administered the state through him and other officials appointed by it Thus Augustus proudly declared that he had restored the republic. His conduct was in accordance with his word. In the city he wore the toga of a citizen and lived in his simple home on the Palatine, wearing the clothes woven by the women of his family. No escort accompanied him about the streets except such as became a magistrate, and every citizen could consult him without

The margin notes: The Proconsular Imperium and the Tribunician Power.

The Principate.

The Republic Restored.

---

* The place of Egypt in this arrangement was peculiar. It was assigned as a province to neither, but was regarded as a kind of private possession of Augustus. No senator was permitted to enter it. The reason for this was, no doubt, the monarchical sentiment of the people and the immense importance of Egypt to Rome because of its corn-supply.

ceremony.   His position was, in fact, much nearer that of Pompey in 52 B C. than that of Cæsar in 45 B.C.   It should be observed that Pompey, too, had been called princeps.

485. The Good Results.—The advantages of this arrangement were clear and its beneficial results immediate.   A sense of security and satisfaction was felt everywhere.   Now, at last, peace under constitutional government was obtained.   A proper method of reorganizing the state and meeting the difficulties of administration was reached.   The evils of the time were met with strong remedies.

Italy the Centre.

486. The Empire Organized.—The empire was set in order.   Here the central thought of Augustus was that the heart of the empire was Italy, from the Alps to Sicily.   Over against Italy and dependent upon it were the provinces.   It was the "sacred land."   Its economic prosperity revived; waste lands were peopled and brought under cultivation; disorder was put down; the municipalities were given free scope to organize and govern themselves; public roads were repaired.   The dignity of Italian citizenship was emphasized.   Even the freedmen were given a place in the public life by the institution of the *Augustales*, a body of men, appointed in each community, who at their own expense attended to the worship of Augustus.   To be an Augustal was regarded as a notable distinction by the freedmen, but not by free citizens who could not worship the princeps without admitting their political inferiority.   Italy, thus set apart from the rest of the state, as the model and glory of the empire, was governed by the senate.   The provinces were dealt with in the same thorough way.   Those which were under the direct rule of Augustus were managed

The Freedmen

The Provinces.

by his legates and procurators,* men selected because they were efficient administrators. They were dependent on Officials. him for advancement and honor; hence they sought by good work to obtain his favor. The borders of the empire were protected and the internal affairs of the provinces were regulated. An imperial coinage, guaranteed by the state as pure, was put into circulation. The army, Army. which in the civil wars had reached the enormous size of more than fifty legions, was reduced to twenty-five, or one hundred and fifty thousand men. It was kept on the frontiers constantly under arms, trained and prepared for defence. It was under the direct command of Augustus. After a victory the soldiers hailed, not their own general, as formerly, but Augustus, as imperator. Only Roman citizens could serve in the legions. In addition provincials were employed as auxiliaries to the number of not more than one hundred and fifty thousand. Each legion had its particular name and usually its permanent quarters in a special province. By virtue of being commander-in-chief, Augustus, like other generals, had his body-guard (the *cohors prætoria*); as he lived at Rome, his guard was stationed in the city; it was the "prætorian cohort," and under its two prefects or commanders had much influence in the state. The finances of the prov- Finances inces were established on a firm basis. All the income from the provinces under Augustus came into his treasury, called the *Fiscus*,† and he had sole power over its man-

---

* The procurators were fiscal agents who took the place of many of the *publicani*

† The word means "basket"; in Roman households the money-box was a basket It is also claimed that the Fiscus dates from the time of Claudius. In any case, Augustus controlled the revenues which arose from his own provinces.

agement. Hence, there was no more stealing of public
money by officials. A map of the empire was prepared,
showing the chief towns and roads of every province; a
census was taken of the greater provinces, perhaps of
all. The farming of taxes with all its abominations was
greatly restricted. The land tax and the poll tax, the
two direct taxes levied, were collected by the state; the
"publican" (§ 423) still dealt in the customs and other
like imposts. Thus a business administration was established which saved money and gave the state abundant
revenues. Augustus spent this money freely on imperial
roads and buildings throughout the empire. By these
means he created new bonds of unity which held the
Roman world together as never before and brought about
the extension of Roman civilization from end to end of it.
We can hardly conceive the immense advantage to the
provinces of this stable and beneficent government.

487. Foreign Policy.—The policy of Augustus with
respect to the peoples outside the Roman world was in
The East. general a very prudent one. In the east he had no desire
to follow up the project of Julius Cæsar for a war with
Parthia. He was content by skilful negotiation to obtain the return of the battle-flags lost by Crassus (§ 454)
and to increase by peaceful ways the influence of Rome
The West. beyond the Euphrates. In the west and south he devoted
himself rather to reorganization than to expansion.
Spain was subdivided into three provinces and completely brought under Roman control. A large number
of new colonies was planted in it and every encouragement given for the development of urban (municipal) life.
In fact, Augustus wished to Latinize Spain and Africa,
and provide for their local administration, in precisely

the same way and by precisely the same methods as those followed by Alexander the Great and the Seleucids in Hellenizing Asia (§§ 299, 319, 435). The two districts were to become eventually a honeycomb of municipalities, each with a territory definitely marked off for it and divided into individual holdings by the land surveyors for whom Rome was so famous. The lands between the municipal territories were to be waste or forest lands (saltus) or belong to the public domain. They were a burden and a source of revenue to the central government. In the years to come some of Rome's greatest citizens had their homes in these western lands.

In the case of Gaul, outside the old province of Narbo, quite a different form of organization was adopted. The whole area was, indeed, divided into three provinces, Lugdunensis, Aquitania and Belgica, but unity was preserved in that the revenues were collected from all alike by officials attached to the Rhine army and in that delegates from all met at Lyons to offer worship on the altar of Roma et Augustus. By this act they acknowledged their fealty to the two powers now existent in Italy (dyarchy). They did not control their own tax payments because Augustus neither permitted the foundation of new colonies nor encouraged the growth of municipalities in Gaul. He divided the whole district once for all into sixty-six communities (*civitates*) so that no land was available for colonies; within the communities cantons (*pagi*) were recognized, and also villages (*vici*) but the latter lacked anything like a general assembly, senators (*decuriones*) or magistrates (*duoviri*) such as were found in the municipalities. They were governed from above by officials of the community or canton chosen from the Celtic nobility. Self-government was thus denied to the people in Gaul as it was denied to the people in Egypt; and, indeed, the organizations of these two provinces have many points of similarity (§ 311). *Gaul and Egypt Exceptions*

On the north the problem was first of all a military problem. The dangers from the restless Teutonic peo- *The North.*

ples made necessary an advance into this region until a defensible frontier should be reached and the nations bordering on it brought under Roman influence. The natural boundary in the northeast was the Danube; thither Augustus pushed forward his line. Four new provinces were formed: Mœsia, Pannonia, Noricum and Rhætia, extending from the Black sea to the sources of the Danube. Connecting with these on the north and northwest the shortest boundary would be made by the Elbe Augustus advanced across the Rhine to establish his frontiers on that river. By these means it was felt that the most dangerous border of the Roman world would be safely guarded.

488. The Imperialism of Augustus.—Within the frontier thus defined lay the Roman world; beyond—-to the ends of the earth, to the points reached in the vision of Alexander and Cæsar, Augustus did not venture The fact was that he lacked both the will and the power for further conquest and accordingly stayed the restless advance of Rome to universal dominion. He was no soldier or general and had no passion for adventure. His was the purely intellectual type which lacked physical not moral courage. Besides, his scheme of government placed the burden of imperialism squarely on the shoulders of Italy. From it he demanded one hundred and fifty thousand men for military service, or one-tenth of its entire male population of military age. He could not demand more—the drain on economic activity was almost intolerable as it was Nor could he venture to raise more than another one hundred and fifty thousand in the provinces without bringing the supremacy of the Italians into peril With three hundred thousand men, however,

A Limit Set to Roman Expansion.

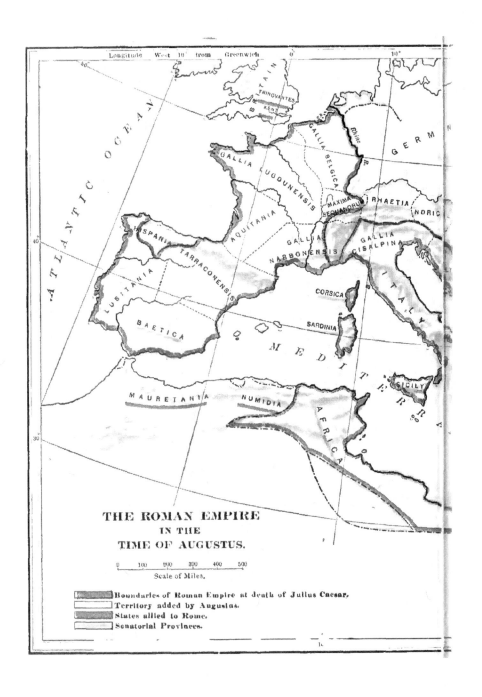

THE ROMAN EMPIRE
IN THE
TIME OF AUGUSTUS.

0 100 200 300 400 500
Scale of Miles.

Boundaries of Roman Empire at death of Julius Caesar.
Territory added by Augustus.
States allied to Rome.
Senatorial Provinces.

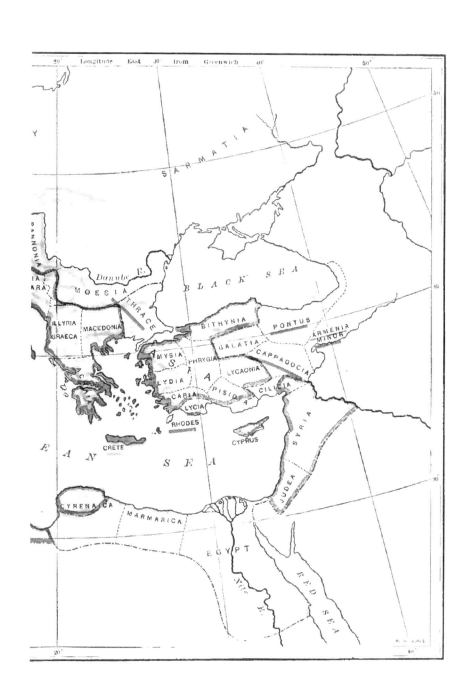

SARMATIA

Danube R.

BLACK   SEA

MOESIA

THRACE

ILLYRIA

GRAECA   MACEDONIA

BITHYNIA

GALATIA   PONTUS

ARMENIA
MINOR

MYSIA

PHRYGIA

CAPPADOCIA

LYDIA

LYCAONIA

CARIA   PISIDIA   CILICIA

LYCIA

RHODES

CYPRUS

SYRIA

JUDEA

CRETE

E   A   N   S   E   A

CYRENAICA   MARMARICA

EGYPT

NILE   R.

RED   SEA

PLATE XXXI

From the Villa Medici and Terme

Terra Mater in the Uffizi

RELIEFS FROM THE ARA PACIS AUGUSTÆ—ART OF THE
AUGUSTAN AGE

he found it impossible to do more than protect defensible frontiers and preserve internal peace.

489. The Worship of the Emperor.—Among the Italians Augustus fostered an aristocracy of senators and knights, the senate being its head. To this the whole administration of the central govern ment of the empire belonged, and of it he was one, its princeps, to be sure. To the Italians belonged the subject world which the aristocracy held and governed primarily for their advantage Of old the sheep had been flayed, now they were to be merely shorn Over the subject world there was established a dyarchy or joint rule of the republic and the princeps. These two authorities divided between them the provinces, the revenues, jurisdiction, administra-tion Their power was absolute That is to say, they were superior to the local officials in Gaul and Egypt, to the city-states in the Greek half and to the municipalities in the Latin half of the Mediterranean world. Yet these lesser authorities, being in theory independent, could not accept orders from foreigners without humiliation. Nor did they need to. *Legalizing Absolutism*

As we have already seen, the Greeks had for generations been in the habit of enrolling their rulers among their deities, and long before the time of Augustus they had accepted as peculiarly their monitor in political affairs a goddess of their own creation—Roma (§ 435). Now Augustus was put by her side, and before the death of the first princeps every province in the empire had its temple or altar to Roma et Augustus. Naturally, Romans could not worship these deities, for to do so meant to become their subjects Hence, in Rome an altar of the "Augustan Peace"—one of the most notable artistic monuments of his age—was erected, no altar or temple of Augustus himself; hence, too, only freedmen, whom Augustus disfranchised in Rome and in the Roman municipalities, could enter into the body of the Augustales who had charge of the worship of Augustus and his successors in these places. Thus the bond which linked the government of the Italians to the provinces was one of religion Cæsar-worship, as it is called, took its place among the recognized religious cults of the time as a natural testimony to the divine char-acter of the new Roman state, which rose high above all other powers, the symbol of universal order and peace

490. Social Life Reformed.—Augustus had clear notions of the spirit which should inspire the state. He proposed to revive the old Roman ideals. The simple life of duty to the gods and service to the state was again to be supreme in Roman society. He encouraged marriage and the rearing of children; divorce, which had grown so alarmingly common, and other forms of immorality, that were destroying the purity of private life at Rome, were sternly repressed   The different orders of society were clearly marked off and fitting tasks were assigned to each. The senatorial order was purged of unworthy members and set at its task of governing its share of the state. From it he chose officials for all the highest positions in the army and in his provinces   The equestrian order he also controlled and reorganized, and from it he chose the great body of his financial officials. As possessed of tribunician power, he guided and curbed the Roman populace, but he had no sympathy for its pretensions, and after some fruitless attempts to make it less of a mob by giving new powers to its ward officials and by arranging for the casting of votes in the municipalities of Italy, he decided to give it as little occasion for assembling as possible and advised Tiberius to deprive it of the electoral power altogether. For Augustus the republic meant the senate, not the comitia. Perhaps his supreme passion was the restoration of the old Roman religion. Ancient temples were rebuilt and the venerable worship was revived in stately splendor. In 12 B.C. he became Pontifex Maximus, the head of the Roman church. New and rich endowments were provided for the priestly colleges. The worship of the Lares (§ 347), which, above all else, was typical of the old faith, and

Margin notes:

Classes of Society Emphasized.

Revival of Religion.

which appealed particularly to the freedmen and slaves, who had little interest in the greater national deities, was revived. Three hundred of their shrines were raised along the streets of the city and twice a year they were adorned with flowers. In each was a pair of little images —the dancing and drinking Lares—and between them was set the representative of the *genius*, or immortal part of Augustus. Thus were the masses taught to reverence the princeps. By all this he sought to show that it was the ancient gods who had raised him to power and had brought peace, order and prosperity to the world. His plans largely succeeded. Religion, as the old Roman conceived it, in its best sense, lived again. The altars smoked anew with sacrifices.

491. Literature Revives.—Corresponding to the glad sense of order and peace, literature and art took on new life. One of the world's greatest poets, Publius Ver- Vergil gilius Maro (70-19 B.C), adorned the Augustan age. His poems, the " Eclogues" picturing pastoral life, the " Georgics", in praise of agriculture, and his chief work, the "Æneid", an epic which glorifies the beginnings of Rome, are all full of the spirit and ideals that inspired Augustus. The religion that made Rome great, the sturdy faith and stalwart patriotism that filled her sons with might—these he hallowed in melodious verse and touching pictures, which gave him wondrous popularity then and have made his name immortal in the world of poetry. His conception of the world-wide mission of Rome, her imperial destiny and the certainty of its success in the hands of Augustus, contributed mightily to the strength of the new régime. He was worthily seconded by the Livy. historian, Titus Livius (59 B.C.–A.D. 17) who used all materials which had come down to him from the past to write his *Roman History* in one hundred and forty-two books, from Rome's beginning to 9 B.C. He idealized the old days and found consolation for the evils of the present only in a return to the sobriety, fidelity and heroism of the past. The legends of early Rome he retells without criticism of their truth, and throws a halo of splendor over the days of the republic. With strong imagination and romantic temper he pictures the noble men and stirring scenes of early times. His style is full and flowing, and he is possessed of a fine literary art which expresses itself in the picturesque grouping of his intensely human characters. Unfortunately, only a small part of his great work Horace. has been preserved. Another literary leader was Quintus Horatius Flaccus (65-8 B.C.), the son of a freedman. In his *Satires* he plays upon the social and literary follies of the Rome of his day; his *Epodes* are even more satirical; he reaches the height of his genius in the *Odes* and *Epistles*. A genial critic of life who sees its weaknesses yet loves it, with few ambitions beyond a glowing fireside, a good wine and a sympathetic friend, a lover of nature who was at the same time a man of the world, he had the unique power of putting his thoughts into precise, telling phrases and of fitting them into lyrical verse of charming delicacy and force Vergil, Livy, Horace—these three have given an enduring fame to the Augustan age, of which they are, each in his own way, the characteristic products.

492. Revival of Art.—Monuments in bronze and marble attested the revival of art in this time. Augustus himself added to the old Forum a new one and built, among other temples, that of Apollo on the Palatine, of marble without, and filled with statues. From him also came the theatre of Marcellus with a seating capacity of twenty thousand persons. Others vied with him in adorning the city. Agrippa, his most trusted officer, built the Pantheon, the temple of Poseidon and magnificent public baths. It is said that Augustus declared with pride: "I received a city of brick; I leave a city of marble." A stately list of the edifices built or restored by Augustus forms a part of the record of his achievements—the Monumentum Ancyranum ("Deeds of Augustus")—which he left at his death, and which is one of our chief sources for his reign.

493. The Culmination.—To show that an old age had come to an end—a century of vast disorder in the state and of ever-present fear for life and property to the individual—and that a new era, one of peace and order, had opened, Augustus chose the celebration of the *Ludi Sæculares,* a festival which was observed every hundred years. This, the fifth time of its observance, in the year 17 B.C., was one of singular splendor. For it Horace wrote a hymn, the *Carmen Sæculare.* *[The Secular Games.]*

494. The Birth of Jesus.—Amid all the splendors of the Augustan age a child was born in one of the most insignificant provinces of the empire whose sway was to surpass in power and extent the wildest dreams of the Cæsars. In the days of Herod, king of Judæa, vassal of Augustus, Jesus Christ* was born in Bethlehem of Judæa. We do not know the year. It was four or five years before the date traditionally assigned. Yet our *[A New Era]*

---

* "Christ" is the Greek equivalent of the Hebrew word "Messiah," the "anointed" (king) whom the Jews expected to appear as their deliverer.

chronology turns upon it, for the years of the world's history are numbered according as they precede the assigned year of his birth or follow it.* Jesus was the founder of Christianity, the religion which was to play a large part in the history of the Roman empire and is professed by the so-called Christian nations of Europe and America.

495. The Shadows in the Scene. Moral Corruption.— But there was another side to all the grandeur of the Augustan age. The people of the city of Rome had too long been a prey to moral corruption to be reformed by example and precept. Unbounded luxury and gilded vice continued to be fearfully rampant among the higher classes. Even Julia, the daughter of Augustus, created scandal by her loose behavior. The lower classes still clamored for free bread and games. To them Augustus had to yield in part, and his doles to them and the shows he exhibited before them surpassed even those of his predecessors. Over against the fine spirit and high ideals of a Vergil must be placed the example and popularity of other poets of the time, among whom the most prominent was Publius Ovidius Naso, better known as Ovid (43 B.C.–A.D. 18). He was not untouched by the nobler memories and hopes of his time, as his *Fasti* show—a gathering up of the ancient Roman religious customs arranged according to the religious calendar. But his *Met-a-mor'pho-ses*, a collection of myths of transformation, his *Art of Love*, his *Love Stories* and other poetical trifles, reveal the gay and profligate character of the society of which he was the pride and ornament. Possessed of a vivid, brilliant and graceful poetic gift, a born

The Aristocracy Corrupt.

Ovid Its Exemplar.

---

* That is, B C , "before Christ," and A.D , *anno Domini*, "the year of the Lord." Christ was crucified in the reign of Tiberius.

story-teller, he used his powers for frivolous and unworthy ends. Banished to Pontus by Augustus because of his intrigues, he exhibits in his *Tristia* the baseness of his spirit by his fawning praise of the princeps who had justly condemned him.

496. Administrative Difficulties.—Augustus's scheme of government did not work altogether as was expected. The balance of power between the senate and himself steadily swung toward his side. The senate showed incompetence in the sphere of administration assigned to it, and he was compelled to take more and more of its proper activities upon himself. In Rome, for example, he took charge of the supply of corn and its distribution to the poor and also of the water supply The police and firemen were also under prefects appointed by him. In Italy and the senatorial provinces he had large powers. All the military forces throughout the empire were under his orders. Sometimes he was compelled to undertake the financial reorganization of a province which had gone bankrupt under senatorial administration Thus it gradually became clear how difficult it was to conduct affairs on this division of powers No wonder that those who had hailed him as the restorer of the republic began to question whether he had not become its master. The nobles murmured. At least three conspiracies were formed against him; though they failed, the motive which inspired them was obvious. That Augustus was able to hold his position for so many years, without falling a victim to the spirit that had killed Julius, is a testimony to his prudence and vigilance. He was fortunate, also, in having two wise counsellors, Mæcenas and Agrippa. Mæcenas was a diplomatist of uncommon tact and wis-

Growth of Power of Princeps.

Conspiracies.

His Counsellors

dom; at the same time he was a man of the world, enormously rich, a patron of art and literature. Agrippa was the man of action as well as of counsel. He won the battle of Actium for Augustus and was intrusted by the princeps with the direction of every critical piece of work in military or civil affairs. Both died before their master, and he was wont to say during the later and darker days of his reign: "This would not have happened had Mæcenas or Agrippa been alive."

497. The Disaster of Varus.—For darker days did come as the long years of Augustus drew to their close. A severe blow was struck at his military prestige, when Varus, the incompetent commander of the legions on the northern frontier, was slain and his army cut to pieces in the Teutoberg forest by the Germans under Arminius (A.D. 9). Augustus decided that it was impossible to keep the frontier at the Elbe and withdrew his forces to the Rhine. He enjoined this policy of cautious defence of the borders upon his successors.

498. Augustus the Only Successful Princeps.—The state of Augustus did not come into existence at one stroke. To conceive grandly and execute promptly was not his way. His motto was "hasten slowly" (*festina lente*), and all his life he kept adding and subtracting—building a new order round his own personality. Augustus and his state became, in fact, a unity, and that was the tragedy of the principate None but a man of Augustus's temperament could make a successful princeps: he must be zealous, yet careless of the appearance of power; he must guide and direct, yet observe all forms scrupulously—was he not simply the first citizen, entitled to influence, of course, but not to command? He must keep the

army in the background and yet dominate it beyond fear
of rivalry; he must be able to mingle freely in the society
of the nobles as one of themselves, yet surpass all in personal dignity.   Around Augustus himself the institutions
of state were moulded.   Where could another Augustus
be found to take his place?

499. Problem of the Succession.—The weakest point
in the arrangement between Augustus and the senate concerned the imperial succession.   If he had received his
appointment as princeps from the senate and people, then
they could appoint as his successor whomsoever they
might choose.   As his was an extraordinary office, they
might decide not to continue it after his death.   But, in
fact, Augustus was determined not only that the princeps
should remain, but that the one whom he should point
out should succeed him.   But how should this successor
be indicated?   Augustus decided to associate with him- The De-
self this destined successor during his lifetime in such a vice of
way as to make his purpose clear.   Whom, then, should Augustus.
he thus designate?   He himself had married twice; his His Family
first wife bore him a daughter, Julia, whom he married to
his friend and counsellor, Agrippa.   Two promising sons
of this marriage died before their grandfather.   The
third son was an impossible candidate.   Agrippa, his
son-in-law, was at one time thought of as the chosen successor, but he, too, passed away in the lifetime of Augustus.   Augustus's second wife, Livia, had been divorced
from her former husband after she had borne him two
sons, Tiberius and Drusus.   Drusus died before Augustus.   Tiberius alone remained.   Though Augustus dis- Choice of
liked him, he was a capable, vigorous man and the choice Tiberius.
was narrowed to him.   In A.D. 4 Augustus adopted him

as his son, and bestowed upon him the imperium for ten years and the power of the tribunate, in A.D. 13 he renewed the command and defined it as equal to his own. Thus there could be no doubt whom the princeps desired to follow him. Having gone thus far, he could not venture farther. The next year he himself died at the age of seventy-five years.

Death of Augustus.

We are told that in the hour of death he called for a looking-glass and bade them arrange his hair and his beard He asked his friends whether he had played well the "farce" of life Then, alone with his own family, he asked after the health of a little child of the family who was ill, then suddenly kissed his wife Livia and expired quietly, breathing out the last words "Livia, live mindful of our union; farewell."

500. The Achievement of Augustus.—The nearly half a century during which Augustus had conducted the plan of administration devised by himself had established it as an abiding work. Herein is his glory, that he founded a new and permanent government for the shattered Roman state. He had done what Julius had failed to do. Order, peace, prosperity, permanence—these things he restored to the Roman world. Defective and illogical as his scheme may have been in some points, it was thoroughly timely and practical It saved Rome from going to pieces; it formed a working basis for unity and progress; it preserved Roman civilization for centuries and gave it the opportunity to expand to the ends of the earth. For these blessings, the results of which we enjoy, we are indebted to Augustus Cæsar

REVIEW EXERCISES. 1. For what are the following famous: Agrippa, Antony, Livy, Varus, Mæcenas, Vergil, Livia? 2. What is meant by princeps, Fiscus, Augustales, Ludi Sæculares, Prætorian Cohort, Pontifex Maximus? 3. What is the date of the battle of Actium, of the death of Augustus, of the birth of Jesus? 4. What burdens did the imperialism of Augustus inflict upon Italy?

COMPARATIVE STUDIES. 1. What ideas of the divinity of man had appeared in the eastern world which resembled Cæsar-worship? 2. Compare the differing conditions in which Vergil and Homer (§§ 104-111) lived as illustrating the differences in their poetry. 3. Compare the political position and ideas of Augustus with those of Alexander (§§ 282, 290, 292, 294, 297-300).

SELECT LIST FOR READING. 1. The Foundations Laid by Augustus for a New Rome. Jones, pp 3-12, 40-41 2. The Military System Reconstructed. Jones, pp 12-18. 3. Augustus's Settlement of the Eastern Question. Jones, pp 21-24, 38 4. The Disappointments of Augustus's Private Life. Jones, pp 19-21, 25-26, 30-33.

TOPICS FOR READING AND ORAL REPORT. 1. The Period of the Second Triumvirate. Morey, pp. 203-212, Shuckburgh, ch 46. 2. The Principate. Munro, pp 143-148 (sources); Abbott, pp 266-273; Myres, pp 545-549; Seignobos, pp. 266-268, Merivale, ch. 51. 3. The Provinces in the Scheme of Augustus. Morey, pp 220-224, Abbott, pp. 283-285; Merivale, pp 409-410, Myres, pp 553-555 4. The Foreign Policy of Augustus. Myres, pp 544-553, Abbott, p 282 5. The Character of Augustus. Botsford, p 218; Morey, pp 228-229, Horton, pp. 316-318. 6. Roman Literature of the Augustan Age. Laing, pp. 198-386 (biographies and quotations); Mackail, pp. 91-168. 7. Social and Financial Rome in the Last Century B.C. Ferrero, vol II, pp 42-54. 8. The Corn Trade of the Ancient World. Ferrero, pp. 321-325 9. The Death of an Aristocracy. Ferrero, vol III, pp 215-226, 229-238 10. New Revenues and Expenditures in Augustus's Reign. Ferrero, vol. IV, pp 159-165. 11. The Vital Elements of Augustus's Policy. Ferrero, vol. V, pp 348-351.

501. The Successors of Augustus—the Julian Line.— Tiberius succeeded his stepfather without opposition. He was the first of four members of the house of Cæsar to occupy the position of princeps. These were:

TIBERIUS (stepson of Augustus), A D. 14–37.

GAIUS, surnamed Ca-lig'u-la (great-grandson of Augustus and grand-nephew of Tiberius), A D 37–41

CLAUDIUS (uncle of Gaius and nephew of Tiberius), A D 41–54

NERO (nephew of Gaius and stepson of Claudius), A D 54–68

502. Tiberius, A.D. 14-37.—TIBERIUS had force of character and genuine ability, but he came to his position when fifty-five years of age, and the weight of administration hung heavy upon him. His originally sensitive temperament had been rendered gloomy and suspicious by bitter experience; now placed at the head of the state, he lapsed into injustice and cruelty when opposed by the senatorial nobility. At the death of Augustus the legions on the Rhine and the Danube rose in revolt hoping to extort booty, lands and other concessions from the new Germani- ruler The Rhenish legions offered to support the nephew cus. of Tiberius, Germanicus, in a contest for the position of princeps. It was a trying time for the newly established principate. The maintenance of imperial authority was due largely to the loyalty of Germanicus, who diverted the thoughts of the legions from treason by a military campaign across the Rhine in which the Germans were punished for the defeat of Varus. Following the cautious policy of Augustus, Tiberius did not try to hold any territory overrun by Germanicus beyond the Rhine. In the east the Parthians required a display of Roman arms, and here Germanicus was sent by Tiberius, but his un-
The timely death ended a career full of promise. Tiberius Provinces. restrained the wealthy, who longed to regain their old liberty of plundering the provinces, thereby earning the gratitude of the subject world. He rebuilt twelve cities of Asia Minor that had been destroyed by an earth-

quake. He was loyal to the principles of Augustus and he even outdid his model in repressing the populace, one of his acts being to transfer to the senate its right of electing magistrates. He established the prætorian guard permanently within the city. The law of treason together with the tribuniciary sanctity of the prince permitted almost any act or word to be construed as lese-majesty (treasonable). Taking advantage of this opening and of the peculiar temperament of Tiberius, a crop of de-la'tors (*delatores*) sprang up who prosecuted with indiscriminate zeal good and bad alike. In Tiberius's old age he fell under the influence of a brilliant but unscrupulous favorite, Se-ja'nus, the prætorian prefect (§ 486). Weary of his social and imperial burden, the old emperor retired for repose to the island of Capri, where he performed only the necessary duties of his position, leaving the conduct of affairs to Sejanus. The latter had already the substance of imperial power, but he wished to have the visible form also. Hence by base deception and intrigue he got the natural heirs of Tiberius put out of the way one after another and eventually formed a conspiracy against the prince himself. Its detection led the unfortunate old man to suspect the loyalty of everybody. Prosecutions thickened. Trials for treason multiplied among the nobility, and amid a reign of terror Tiberius died at the age of seventy-eight

503. **Caligula, A.D. 37-41.**—GAIUS, as a youth, was a universal favorite. The soldiers on the frontier, among whom a part of his childhood was spent, idolized him.* His elevation to the principate, at twenty-four years of

*They called him Caligula, "little boots," because of the soldier's boots which he wore while among them as a child.

(margin notes: Law of Treason / Delators / Sejanus.)

age, was followed by a series of acts which promised well. But hardly a year had passed when he entered upon a course of life unparalleled for extravagance and brutality. The riches which the frugal Tiberius had gathered were dissipated in costly games and wild vice. He heaped contempt on the institutions and representatives of the republic. He proposed to make his horse consul. He demanded worship as a god. It is charity to assume that a sudden illness which fell upon him early in his career had left him a madman. A conspiracy in his palace brought him to his death, and Rome drew a long breath of relief.

504. Claudius, A.D. 41-54.—Up to the time of his becoming princeps, CLAUDIUS was known as a timid, incapable pedant. He was found cowering in the imperial palace by the prætorian guards who had just slain his freakish nephew, and, with the tardy assent of the senate, he was thrust into the highest position in the state at the age of fifty-one. None the less, he showed surprisingly excellent administrative qualities He still pursued his antiquarian researches, made tedious speeches and wrote tiresome books His weakness of character made him as he grew older a prey to designing women and intriguing servants. The government was really in the hands of a trumvirate of freedmen, Pallas, Narcissus and Polybius, able but conscienceless men, who not only managed the emperor, but also filled the imperial service with men of their own class. Freedmen, not senators, were thus running the empire under Claudius. To their influence we may attribute the startling liberality of the prince in extending the franchise to Celtic nobles in Gaul, and perhaps also his abandonment of the foreign policy of Augustus. For Claudius made a notable addition to the empire by

The Rule of the Freedmen.

annexing Britain in 43 B.C. From that time the island, though not entirely subjugated, began to come under the direct influence of Roman civilization. The same ruler enlarged the empire in Africa, where he formed two new provinces. Dependent kingdoms like Thrace and Judæa were turned over to procurators who ruled them as agents of the *Fiscus*. The freedmen were thus imperialists, but Italy was not neglected during their régime; the Fucine lake was drained; a harbor for Rome was artificially constructed at Ostia; two new aqueducts, one the famous Claudian, carried pure water into the heart of the great city. Claudius's ambitious wife, his niece A-grip-pi′na, succeeded in having her own son Nero designated for the succession, whereupon the death of the emperor occurred and it was whispered that he died by poisoning. Annexation of Britain.

505. Nero, A.D. 54-68.—All men hoped the best things from NERO. He was fond of art and literature and had imbibed a taste of wisdom from his tutor Seneca, the philosopher. The latter, with Burrus, the prætorian prefect, guided the first activities of the new ruler, who was a mere youth seventeen years old. His mother, a capable, imperious woman, had a strong influence over him. But the quartette fell out one with another. Nero was encouraged to emancipate himself from his mother's authority, and plunged into wild excesses, while his able ministers conducted public affairs successfully But soon his frivolous, brutal temper, thus roused, played havoc on every side. His mother was murdered. Seneca was condemned and committed suicide. Nero gave himself loose rein. He posed as a poet and public singer Extravagant revels and unending shows wasted the imperial treasures, abominable vices and unspeakable The Reign of the Unprincipled Dilettante cruelties disgraced the court. So low had he fallen in public esteem that a frightful conflagration, which destroyed the greater part of Rome, was laid at his door. Patience was at last exhausted, the legions in the provinces rebelled and Nero fled to die at length by his own hand. His last words were: "That such an artist as I should perish!"

506. The Principate as Tyranny.—During these years the position of the princeps changed. The balance in his favor over against the senate was complete. His powers were, it is true, voted to him by the senate and people, but he had made sure of the position before election. Hereditary descent was recognized as giving a claim to it. The principate, therefore, in theory and form constitutional, was, in fact, a tyranny. The possession of military power was decisive; the princeps was first of all *imperator*—and emperor* we shall henceforth call him. The senate was little more than his tool. Its fear of him was intensified by his assuming the right to accuse anyone of treason; an accusation meant condemnation and was followed by immediate execution at the hands of the soldiery. By this means many of the leading men of Rome were put to death. Yet a section of the proud and independent nobility, though silenced, was not subdued. They knew their rights and steadily

The Senatorial Opposition. opposed the tyranny. The emperor, in turn, knew that constitutionally he was dependent upon the senate, and did not dare go so far as to destroy it and rule alone. As a result, he looked for support to the weapons of his prætorian guard. Such an ally was dangerous; it might in time become the master.

* Emperor is only the English form of *imperator*.

507. Political Progress.—The growth of the princeps' power was an advantage to the empire as a whole. His imperial administration came to be better organized. The emperor's helpers were now to be found in every department and district of the empire. Every great noble had freedmen to manage his private affairs, write his correspondence and keep his accounts. But the emperor's accounts and correspondence were those of an empire, and the men who attended to these became of great importance to the state. Under this improved public service the prosperity of the provinces advanced. The unifying of the empire by a common government and by the spread of commerce and culture went on rapidly. The personal character of the emperors and their doings at Rome, whether good or bad, did not affect the well-ordered system. Egypt, for example, was never so prosperous as under Nero. The same progress is found in relation to the frontier. In general the cautious policy of Augustus was followed (§§ 487, 488). Military roads and fortifications strengthened the Rhine frontier. *Freedmen in Office. Prosperity. The Frontier.*

508. The Flavian Cæsars.—The revolt of the legions, before which Nero took his own life and thus left the principate vacant, was followed by a brief period of anarchy (A.D. 68–69), in which four generals, Galba, Otho, Vitellius and Ves-pa'sian, were proclaimed imperators by their troops and each was recognized by the senate. In the struggle that followed, Vespasian came out victor. He and his two sons who followed him constitute the house of the Flavian Cæsars. They reigned as follows: *The One Long Year.*

VESPASIAN, A.D. 69–79.
TITUS, A D. 79–81.
DOMITIAN, A D 81–96.

509. Vespasian, A.D. 69-79.—VESPASIAN was an ex-perienced commander and administrator. He was of humble origin, the son of a Sabine centurion and money-lender. He brought to the principate shrewd common-sense and practical ability, coupled with unpolished manners and provincial speech, which were a stock subject of ridicule with the Roman nobles. But he knew how to rule wisely and well, joining firmness with justice and forbearance toward his enemies, and restoring the shattered finances of the state by such careful economies that he was thought stingy and sordid. He appreciated the dignity of his office and was worthy of it. When at the age of seventy years the pains of death came upon him, he struggled to his feet declaring that the emperor should die standing.

510. Titus, A.D. 79-81—The early life of his son TITUS led men to expect in him a second Nero They were happily disappointed. He, like his father, sought to live up to his high position; he abandoned his vices and boon companions. To his enemies he was splendidly gracious; to the people lavishly generous. He thought that day lost in which he had not given something away. "The darling of humanity" is the descrip-

tive phrase of a later historian The terrible eruption of Vesuvius, which destroyed Pompeii and Her-cu-la'ne-um (A D 79), a disastrous fire at Rome, a wasting pestilence which devastated Italy, gave him unequalled opportunities for exercising his benevolence, and he was not found wanting. It has been questioned whether in time the vexatious problems of imperial rule would not have changed him for the worse. As it was, after scarcely two years of power, he died, loved and mourned by all.

511. Domitian, A.D. 81-96.—His younger brother, Do-
MITIAN, was a passionate, ambitious character who, held
back by his father and brother during their lifetime, was
all the more eager to rule. People called him a "bald-
headed Nero," but if, like that ruler, he was corrupt and
vicious in his private life, as an administrator he was able
and successful. In many respects he resembled Tiberius,
whom he took as his model. His haughty air and lordly
bearing made enemies for him among the nobility, and
their renewed hostility turned him into a suspicious and
cruel tyrant. He perished by the daggers of his attendants after a reign of fifteen years

512. Political Progress.—Two important political
changes date from the Flavian emperors. (1) They
made much of the office of censor, by which they had
large power over the senate. Domitian held it for life.
By virtue of this censorial authority Vespasian enlarged
the senatorial order (§ 490), which had become thinned
out by civil war and executions He chose new senators
from the most honorable citizens throughout Italy and
the empire. Thus to the old republican nobility, which
had practically died out during the persecutions of the
Julio-Claudian time, was added a new official aristocracy
created by the emperor and friendly to him. (2) Vespasian met the problem of the succession by emphasizing the hereditary right of his oldest son to follow him.
In the same way Titus made his nearest of kin, his brother
Domitian, a colleague. The name Cæsar was taken as an
imperial title, as though these emperors were descended
from Augustus. The result of all these measures was to
raise the dignity and mark the supremacy of the princeps.
The senate had less and less importance; the people none.

Reorganization of the Senate.

The Succession

513. Imperial Advance.—Apart from the reorganization of the finances of the state and the restoration of order and peace by these emperors, three imperial tasks call for special mention. (1) The province of Judæa (§ 472) broke out in a fierce rebellion in A.D 66   Vespasian had been sent against the rebels, and it was while he was fighting there that his legions proclaimed him emperor.   When he went to Rome he left the conduct of the war to Titus.   Among the Jews there were many who preferred Roman rule, but a body of violent fanatics gained the upper hand, destroyed the Roman garrison in Jerusalem and slaughtered right and left.   Finally, Titus shut up the rebels in Jerusalem   For five awful months the Romans besieged and assaulted the city, until at last the rebels held only the Temple hill.   The whole was finally taken by assault and burned to the ground (A.D. 70).   (2) Under the reign of Domitian the empire was extended in the west and north of Britain.   The legions were under the command of an able general, A-gric'o-la, who advanced into Scotland.   His fleet also circumnavigated the island.   (3) On the German frontier Rome advanced across the upper Rhine and a fortified wall more than a hundred miles in length was begun, to connect the upper waters of the Rhine and the Danube. Behind this rampart lay a strip of land called the *Agri Decumates*, which was thus added to the empire.   It was in no sense a change in the defensive policy of Augustus, but a measure of protection for Roman colonists and a stronger means of defence against the Germans.

The Revolt of Judæa

Destruction of Jerusalem.

Britain.

Germany.

REVIEW EXERCISES. 1. Name the emperors of this century in chronological order. 2. What is meant by Agri Decumates, prætorian prefect, the title Cæsar? 3. For what are the fol-

PLATE XXXII

Spoils of the Jewish War

RELIEF FROM THE ARCH OF TITUS IN ROME

lowing famous: Seneca, Sejanus, Jerusalem, Pompeii, Agricola? 4. What is the date of the annexation of Britain, of the fall of Jerusalem? 5. Had Tiberius a definite administrative policy?

COMPARATIVE STUDIES. 1. Compare the policy of the Flavian Cæsars regarding the problem of the succession with that of Augustus. 2. As far as good government goes, how does the first century A D of Roman rule compare with the first century B C? 3. What was the difference between the demands made upon an emperor by the city of Rome and by the provinces? Could they be reconciled? 4. "I wish that the Roman people had but one neck, that I might strike it off with one blow." "I wish to govern the state not as my property, but that of my people." Show how both these sayings are characteristic of a Roman emperor.

SELECT LIST FOR READING. 1. The Difficulties of Tiberius. (*a*) Military. Jones, pp. 44–49; (*b*) The Control of Sejanus. Jones, pp 49–52 2. Claudius's Influence on the History of the Empire. Jones, pp. 61–64. 3. The Contradictions in Nero's Reign. Jones, pp 69–83. 4. The Flavians' Conduct of Roman Affairs. (*a*) Business Administration. Jones, pp. 115–118. (*b*) The Extension and Strengthening of the Frontiers. Jones, pp. 119–124, 139–145. (*c*) The Building in the City. Jones, pp 127, 130, 132 (*d*) A General Estimate of the Flavians. Jones, p 148

TOPICS FOR READING AND ORAL REPORT. 1. The Problem of Tiberius. Munro, pp 149–152 (source); Merivale, pp. 430–436; Abbott, pp. 288–289; Bury, pp 189–195, 209–213. 2 Life and Character of Sejanus. Merivale, pp 438–442. 3. Internal Politics under the Julian Cæsars. Abbott, ch 13. 4. Imperial Politics under the Julian Cæsars. Mor y, ch. 24, Merivale, pp. 430–478, Bury, pp 166–187, 206–209, 238–245, 258–270, 305–321. 5. The Burning of Rome under Nero Laing, pp. 424–431 (source), Bury, pp. 285–288. 6. The Flavian Cæsars—Their Personality and Achievement. Merivale, pp. 501–513; Abbott, ch 14; Bury, ch. 21. 7. The Jewish War. Merivale, pp 495–500, Bury, pp. 366–373. 8. The Destruction of Pompeii and Herculaneum. Lai g, pp 455–460 (source).

514. Social Progress.—The century of imperial Rome closing with the death of Domitian presents a brilliant and instructive picture, when viewed from the side of A Warning social life. In studying it, we must observe, however, that our information comes chiefly from the capital. Rome was the centre of literature, and its life is reflected in the writings which have come down to us. Italy and the provinces contributed but little to the picture, and what little comes from them reveals, in many respects, a notable difference in the purity and simplicity of their life and manners from those that prevailed in the great city.

515. Social Classes.—In social classes and their relations the old Roman distinctions (§ 490), emphasized by Augustus, grew more rigid. At the summit stood the princeps and the senatorial order. The rulers that followed Augustus imitated him in the formal rejection of special titles and in not encouraging an elaborate court etiquette Yet little by little, with increasing powers, The Court. they assumed greater state. A court grew up; "friends" of the emperor paid him formal visits every day; his house became a palace,* and was filled with servants and Senators. courtiers. A similar stateliness appears in the households of the senatorial nobility. Immensely rich and standing next to the emperor, they kept up splendid establishments. A curious feature is the system of clients. The The old Roman client (§ 342) became a mere courtier Client. and parasite. Every morning he visited his noble patron to pay his respects. If a poet, he recited his verses; if a wit, he amused the great man by jests; if a common man, he followed in his train when the senator went out on the street. For these services all expected rewards,

---

* Our word "palace" comes from *Palatium*, the Palatine Hill, where the emperor dwelt.

food or money or patronage of some sort. Beneath the senatorial was the equestrian order (knights), whose members were immersed in business or official duties. They, too, were men of great wealth. Next came the mass of ordinary citizens, divided into a middle class, doubtless respectable and well-to-do, but of whom we know little, and the lowest classes, who were restless and wretchedly poor, dependent on state doles for food and on the public shows for amusement. Then there were the freedmen, who were often wealthy and influential by reason of their positions as confidential servants in the imperial administration, and great houses, or because of their business activities. The various foreigners from the provinces formed another body, a crowd of Egyptians, Syrians, Jews and others, who had sought the capital for the opportunities afforded by it of making an easy living. Beneath all was the enormous body of slaves who performed all sorts of tasks in the household, the manufactories and the mines, on the streets and the farms. A Roman house could not be managed without slaves. In the great mansions they performed all sorts of services for the members of the household. Their duties were carefully specialized; besides a slave to keep the door, or a slave to call the name of the guest, the noble sometimes had a special slave to put on his sandals and a special slave to fold his clothes.

516. Occupations.—In considering the occupations of the period we observe that some activities which hitherto were thought unworthy have risen into favor. Such were teaching and medicine. Citizens became wealthy and distinguished as physicians. An income of ten thousand dollars a year was obtained by one famous

specialist. Other Romans trained themselves as teachers of rhetoric and philosophy and gained large fees. We hear of successful booksellers. The law became a most important profession. The immense extension of Roman business and political interests gave a rich field for the lawyer. To win this case he must be a good speaker, and Roman legal oratory was famous the world over.

Art of Living.

The increase of Roman wealth and the expansion of the Roman horizon resulted in the improvement of the art of living. This is seen in studying (*a*) the house, (*b*) food and dress, (*c*) the amusements of Rome.

517. The House.—The simple one-room house of old Rome (§ 389) had grown into an extensive and magnificent mansion. The improvements of the later day (§ 441) were carried further. The height of splendor was reached in the famous palace of Nero, the "Golden House," "the most stupendous dwelling-place ever built

The Villas of the Rich.

for mortal man." Country-houses were of great size and marvellously adorned. Ivory, marble, gems and gold were lavishly employed for decoration. Even a provincial town like Pompeii (pŏm-pā′é), could boast elegant private mansions. There the house of Pansa occupied an entire square. It had more than sixty rooms on the ground floor, of which half, being on the street and separate from the interior, were rented for shops. Back of the peristyle (§ 441) were five great rooms opening on a long veranda which faced a garden covering a space one-third as large as the house. The most remarkable ornamentation in houses of this age was the mosaic and fresco work Statues, paintings and bric-à-brac abounded; the furniture was highly ornamental and costly.

PLATE XXXIII

A ROOM IN THE HOUSE OF THE VETTII, POMPEII

518. Dress.—Little change is seen in Roman dress except in the costliness of the materials The *lacerna*, or cloak, was often worn in addition to the toga. Garments of silk and linen began to appear. Extravagant display of jewels, a weakness of Roman women (§ 389), is characteristic. The popular gem was the pearl; strings of pearls of great size and purity were highly prized. Caligula's wife had a set of pearls and emeralds valued at nearly two million dollars. The growing refinement of taste in food and the lavish extravagance at banquets, already referred to (§ 441), reached a great height Rare and costly dainties were sought from the ends of the earth; dinners of twenty courses were given. Gluttony became an art and the Roman nobles were unrivalled masters in it. This wanton extravagance, however, testifies to a greater variety of food and a finer taste among all classes of society. Three courses, consisting of kid or chicken with eggs and asparagus and fruit, was probably an ordinary bill of fare for a dinner among well-to-do people and indicated a variety and refinement in eating of which old Rome knew nothing. *Food.*

519. Amusements.—In a society of luxurious wealth and idle poverty amusements are a necessity, and the Romans never plunged so deeply into them as at this time. The number of holidays grew; there were eighty-seven in a year under Tiberius. Two favorite holiday seasons were the *Sat'ur-na'li-a*, beginning December 17, and New Year's Day. The former was a season of riotous fun, when the ordinary conditions of life were reversed. Slaves could do as they liked; crowds thronged the streets, laughing and feasting. New Year's Day was an official and religious holiday. Visits were exchanged *Holidays.*

among friends. The emperor received the people in state. At both seasons gifts were made. All classes of the people were accustomed to give something to the emperor, and in return he made a splendid festival or reared statues and temples. But the chief centres of amusement remained, now as before, the amphitheatre, the circus and the theatre. The splendor of the shows and the races almost surpasses description, while the buildings in which they were held were of extraordinary number and size. Of amphitheatres the greatest was the Col-i-se'um at Rome, built by the Flavian emperors. It covered nearly six acres and accommodated eighty thousand spectators. Here were held the gladiatorial contests (§ 442), which had now become a favorite spectacle. More elaborate methods of fighting were introduced. The whole system occupied a recognized place in Roman life. All sorts of contests were held. Wild beasts were imported to fight with each other or with men. The arena was flooded and naval battles were fought. The shows were advertised, and the entire population of Rome, from emperor to slave, attended and enjoyed the scenes of blood. In the circus the races were almost equally popular. Here organization increased the interest; rival establishments were distinguished by their colors, the red, the white, the green, the blue. The populace, and even the emperors, took sides and great sums were wagered. Successful charioteers, although slaves or freedmen, and without social rank, became popular idols and gained immense wealth. An inscription in honor of one Crescens, who died at twenty-two, tells us that he won forty-seven races and received seventy-eight thousand dollars. The Circus Maximus was enlarged to accommodate the crowds

The Amphitheatre.

The Circus.

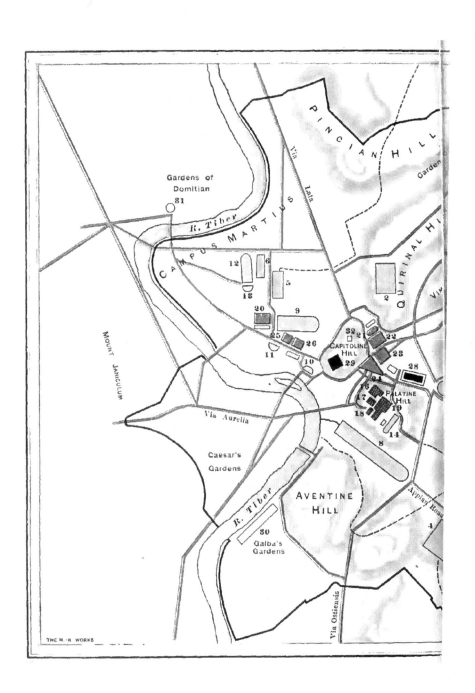

PINCIAN HILL

Garden ob

QUIRINAL HILL

Via

Via Lata

Gardens of
Domitian
○ 81

R. Tiber

C A M P U S   M A R T I U S

12   6

5

13

20   9

25   26

11   10

MOUNT JANICULUM

Via Aurelia

Caesar's
Gardens

R. Tiber

30

Galba's
Gardens

AVENTINE
HILL

Appian Road

4

Via Ostiensis

THE M. N WORKS

32 21   22
CAPITOLINE
HILL
29   23
28
31
16
17   PALATINE
HILL
18   19
14
3

2

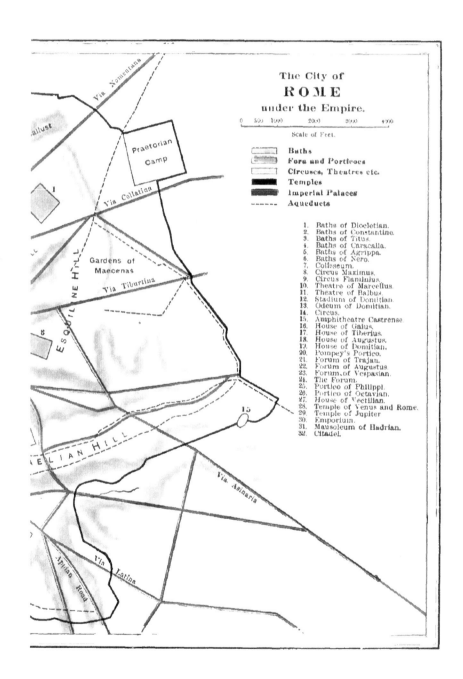

The City of
ROME
under the Empire.

0   500 1000   2000   3000   4000

Scale of Feet.

Baths
Fora and Porticoes
Circuses, Theatres etc.
Temples
Imperial Palaces
Aqueducts

1. Baths of Diocletian.
2. Baths of Constantine.
3. Baths of Titus.
4. Baths of Caracalla.
5. Baths of Agrippa.
6. Baths of Nero.
7. Colisseum.
8. Circus Maximus.
9. Circus Flaminius.
10. Theatre of Marcellus.
11. Theatre of Balbus.
12. Stadium of Domitian.
13. Odeum of Domitian.
14. Circus.
15. Amphitheatre Castrense.
16. House of Gaius.
17. House of Tiberius.
18. House of Augustus.
19. House of Domitian.
20. Pompey's Portico.
21. Forum of Trajan.
22. Forum of Augustus.
23. Forum of Vespasian.
24. The Forum.
25. Portico of Philippi.
26. Portico of Octavian.
27. House of Vectilian.
28. Temple of Venus and Rome.
29. Temple of Jupiter
30. Emporium.
31. Mausoleum of Hadrian.
32. Citadel.

Via Nomentana

Sallust

Praetorian
Camp

Via Collatina

Gardens of
Maecenas

ESQUILINE HILL

Via Tiburtina

ELIAN HILL

Via Asinaria

Via Latina

Appian Road

that flocked to these races until it held four hundred
thousand persons. The theatrical exhibitions were of a
low order; pantomime was the favorite form of acting
and the crowds that attended were amused by vulgar
jests and debasing scenes. Another form of amusement
must be mentioned—the bath. Public bathing-houses,
established at an earlier day (§ 441), became numerous
and splendid People bathed for pleasure several times
a day. Bathers, for a fee of less than one penny, had
entrance to what was practically a luxurious club-house.
In connection with the bath proper were bowling-alleys
and a gymnasium. Colonnades and resting and loung-
ing rooms adorned with pictures, a restaurant, shops
and a library completed the outfit of a first-class bathing
establishment at Rome. Even a daily paper, published by
the government, containing news of the city and official an-
nouncements, was at the service of curious and idle readers

520. Amusements Outside Rome. — The Romans
carried with them these forms of pleasure all over the
world. In Africa, on the Danube and in the borders of
the eastern desert the ruins of amphitheatres and baths
may be seen to-day in the cities where the Romans ruled.
In Pompeii, which was a small Italian town, there were
three bathing establishments, two theatres, seating respectively 1,500 and 5,000 people, and an amphitheatre
with a capacity of 20,000 persons. When we remember
that these admirably built and decorated structures were
for the use and enjoyment of the people at large, we may
realize the place and influence of these amusements in
the life of the Roman world.

521. Art.—Turning to the higher life of the century
we observe first the art and literature. At no previous

period in human history were these so widely diffused.
Cities had their libraries and their fine public buildings
adorned with statues of the emperors and other distinguished men of the past and present.   The private houses,
if we may judge from those of Pompeii, were beautified
with mosaics and wall-paintings; artistic objects, large
and small, abounded.   Rich men were patrons of artists
and writers, and could criticise their productions with
taste and judgment.   A marvellous number of good works
of art have come down to us from these times.   Yet nowhere is there evidence of originality or genius.   The

Portrait Statues.
artists are imitators or copyists of the past.   Yet the
Roman portrait statues are notable artistic successes.   It
was characteristic of the Roman to wish to preserve portraits of his ancestors (§ 392) and the noble art of sculpture
gave him the opportunity to make these portraits enduring in marble and bronze.   While seeking to portray his
subjects to the life, the artist seems sometimes to have permitted himself to idealize them; a portion of the Greek
grace and charm has been joined with the Roman vigor
and literalness.   The long series of the statues or busts

Architecture.
of the emperors is the supreme illustration of this art.   In
the achievements of architecture and engineering the Roman shows his power.   The massive buildings, the enduring roads, the extensive and graceful aqueducts, the ruins
of which remain in all the lands that acknowledged the imperial sway, these are the witnesses of that practical genius
so truly characteristic of the Roman.   That genius reached
its height under the empire in such buildings as the Coli-
seum, the palaces of the Cæsars and the aqueducts of Rome.

Under the Julian Cæsars.
522. Literature.—The literature of the time, like the
art, was widely distributed and highly finished, but it was

not genuine and powerful. Following the Augustan
writers (§ 491) came a variety of authors of whom only
a few strike high. It is remarkable, also, that they hail
mostly from the provinces. To the period of the Julian Seneca.
Cæsars belongs Seneca, the minister of Nero, as its chief

THE WORLD
According to
Ptolemy 150 A.D.

literary star, (A.D. 4 65). He wrote essays and letters
on morals in the spirit of the Stoic philosophy and in an
ornate rhetorical style which is always clear and strong
and sometimes eloquent. His tragedies, while attaining
some fame, are less significant works. Another courtier Petronius.
of Nero, who was also a writer, was Pe-tro′ni-us, who has
the distinction in literary history of having written the
first known novel. The fragments of it which have been
preserved are witty and realistic. One of its characters.
Tri-mal′chi-o, a rich fool, has been the original of many
similar personages in fiction. A richer literary life opens Under the
Flavian
Cæsars.
under the Flavian Cæsars—a period which, in compari-
son with that of Augustus, has been called the Silver Age.
Its chief poet was Statius (about A.D. 45-96), whose epic Statius.

poem, the *The-ba'is*, centring about the mythical wars of Thebes, falls just short of greatness. Martial (43–101 A.D) wrote *Epigrams*, short stanzas, witty, stinging or complimentary, as desired by the patrons to whom he paid court.   They present a vivid picture of Roman life in his day.   Pliny (plin'i), the elder of the name, was the great scholar of the time (23–79 A.D).   He was an imperial official who, in the course of his duties, gathered a mass of information which he condensed into the most important of his works that has been preserved, the *Natural History*. He was a diligent student and careful observer.   While his conclusions are valuable only as illustrating the ideas of his time, the facts he gathered are of the greatest interest to all later students of the geography and history of the empire.   Another learned prose writer was Quintilian, a distinguished teacher of rhetoric.   He gathered the results of his observation and study in a notable work on the *Art and Science of Rhetoric*, which formed for centuries the standard treatise on the subject.   Two subjects treated in it still have living interest, a criticism of the great Greek and Roman writers of the past and a theory of how children should be educated.   Such a work covered in reality the whole subject of education, since the method and subjects of that discipline were based upon what the ancients called rhetoric.   To become a good speaker and writer, to argue your cause skilfully, or to express your thoughts with elegance and force— this was the end of education.

523. **Morals—The Dark Side.**—When looked at from the point of view of its moral and religious life, this century shows strange contradictions.   It seems impossible to believe that a world which ran after amusements such

Marginal notes: Martial. / Pliny the Elder. / Quintilian. / Contradictions.

as the brutal gladiatorial shows, or was wedded to such luxury and extravagance as we have described, could be moved by serious things. Other sides of life disclose like dark pictures. The mad thirst for money led to all sorts of wickedness. The legacy-hunter who paid court to rich old bachelors in order to be remembered in their wills was a recognized character in society. Others did not hesitate to forge wills or to remove by poisoning those who stood in the way of their inheritance. Marriage was now a mere civil contract and the wife retained control of her property. Common and easy as divorce had become, marriage was, nevertheless, regarded as undesirable. A man who married, some thought, was out of his sober senses. He would be much more sought after in society if he remained single.

524. Morals—The Brighter Side.—To offset this dark side, we need to remember that such scenes are found at Rome only and that they are characteristic of a society in which both the rich at the top and the poor at the bottom are idle—a perfectly unnatural state of things. In the provinces a healthy and sober life was the rule, and from them a stream of new strength was poured into the capital. Moreover, the worst phases of Roman life appeared under the Julian Cæsars. In the time of the Flavians a much higher tone of morals is to be observed. In the first half of the century the Romans had gone crazy from excess of power and riches; in the latter half they came back to reason.

525. Moral Philosophy.—The popularity of philosophy in Rome throws a brighter gleam over these times. The moral system of the Stoics was the favorite. When we recall the principles of that school (§ 324), we cannot The Stoics fail to see how they would fall in with the practical bent of the Roman mind. For the old Roman notion of doing one's duty to the state and the gods, the Stoic only substituted a larger obligation to the world, to nature. Virtue came to be a fad, and devotion to virtue even unto death an exquisite delight. Thus suicide was elevated into a sacred duty. The Stoic idea of the brotherhood of man had a softening influence upon the harsh treat-

Seneca. ment of the slave. "Treat slaves," says Seneca, "as inferiors in social rank to whom you stand in the position of protector." The education of the poor was encouraged by free schools, such as Vespasian founded, and many rich men gave donations for free education to their native towns. Humane feeling was roused at the sight of suffering, weakness and helplessness. The disasters and pestilences that afflicted parts of the empire gave occasion for social help and sympathy. Even kindness to animals was approved. Seneca protests against the cruelty of the amphitheatre. But his own actions illustrate the strange contradictions of his day. He preached virtue and encouraged Nero in vice. He commended poverty and was worth millions. Many rich men flung themselves with equal zeal into the pleasures of life and the instructions of virtue. They employed philosophers to teach them the way of right living and received their teachings with enthusiasm, but did not practise them. Yet, after all, the standards of morals and the ideals of life were sensibly lifted by the influence of philosophy.

526. Religion.—The first century of the empire could hardly be said to be deeply religious. The vigorous attempt of Augustus to revive the old Roman faith resulted in little more than giving it an official and formal life.

Not much genuine religious feeling was involved in the worship of the Cæsars, which Augustus had seen grow up in the provinces, and from which Roma (§ 489) had gradually been eliminated, but it continued to meet a popular need for the expression of gratitude, awe and satisfaction felt by high and low alike in view of the grandeur and the beneficence of the imperial organization. Assemblies were organized in the provinces for the purpose of carrying on this worship and holding a religious festival in honor of the emperor. Officials were elected to superintend the affair, and participation in the worship was regarded not only as a privilege, but also as a sign of proper loyalty to the state. Oriental faiths, pre-eminently that of Isis, the Egyptian goddess, which had made its entrance into Rome from the Hellenistic world (§ 319) in the later Republican time, continued to be popular with the lower classes, who found cheer and inspiration for their wretched lives in the emotional appeal of the noisy and startling performances of such cults and in the promise of future happiness which they held out.

Cæsar-Worship Developed

Eastern Cults.

527. Rise of Christianity.—Among these new religions from the east one which began to make its way in the Roman world of this age requires special consideration. Jesus, whose birth in Judæa has already been mentioned (§ 494), began at the age of thirty to preach and teach in Palestine. He proclaimed himself the Mes-si'ah, or Christ, for whom the Jews were looking as a deliverer But he taught a spiritual deliverance from sin as the highest good and would not lead a rebellion against Rome. The Jewish authorities denounced him before the Roman governor, Pilate, and he was crucified after having taught a little more than two years (A.D. 29).

The Crucifixion.

But he left behind him a band of disciples who proclaimed that he had risen from the dead and thus had sealed the truth of his teaching. They, also, were bidden by him to preach the new doctrine of salvation from sin through the risen Christ to all who would hear, with the assurance that he would soon return to earth to rule as supreme lord. Among those who were gained for the cause was

Paul. a Jew named Paul. He carried the name and doctrine of the Christ to non-Jews or Gentiles and gathered companies of believers in the cities of Asia Minor and Greece. These believers were first called Christians in Antioch. Soon assemblies, or churches, of Christians were founded in the west, at Rome and as far as Spain and Gaul. To many of these churches Paul, afterward executed by Nero, wrote letters explaining the doctrines of Christ as he understood them. Soon narratives of the life and work of Jesus were written down and sent about among

The New Testament. the churches. Thus a book of Christian writings was begun, the book we call the *New Testament*. The organization of these churches was very simple at first.

Organization. Each church was a unit, its members managing its affairs and choosing officers to lead—deacons to minister to the poor, elders* to preside at its assemblies.† Admission to the circle was conditioned on confession of faith in Christ as Saviour and submission to the rite of baptism. At stated seasons the members met and partook of bread and wine in obedience to the command of Jesus at his Last Supper with his disciples.

528. Opposition to Christianity.—The new brotherhood soon came under the notice of the imperial author-

---

* These elders appear under two names, both Greek, *presbyter*, or priest, and *episcopos*, or bishop

† See for Hellenistic associations of the same general characte. § 319.

ities. Its secret meetings and ceremonies were suspected of evil designs, and the belief of its members in one God brought them into opposition to the worship of the emperors. The first action against them was taken by Nero, not indeed as Christians, but as malefactors, upon whom he laid the charge of setting fire to Rome. At this time many of them were put to death with horrible tortures They were later accused of evil practices and systematically punished. Gradually the refusal of the Christians to join in the worship of the emperors came to be the chief ground of their punishment. They were regarded as disloyal to the empire and punished as traitors, for that was what refusal to worship Cæsar signified (§§ 299, 435, 489). Thus Domitian is said to have persecuted them cruelly on this account. The empire, therefore, at the end of the first century regarded all Christians as worthy of death. In spite of this, the new religion spread widely, especially in Asia Minor, Greece and Egypt. The city of Rome possessed a flourishing church, and its adherents were found even in the imperial court. The pure morals, the brotherly love, the joyful spirit and the hopeful confidence of the members of this faith commended it to those everywhere who by reason of poverty or sinfulness or scepticism sought light, strength and peace—and many such there were in the Roman world. All who joined it looked forward to the speedy return of Christ to earth; they cared nothing for society and the state; they would not join in heathen worship; they doubted whether it was right to serve in the army. By this separateness they were laying up for themselves hatred and contempt on the part of the people and the empire.

Persecution for Disloyalty.

How Far Justified

REVIEW EXERCISES. 1. For what are the following significant: Seneca, Paul, Crescens, Pliny the Elder, Isis, Martial? 2. What is meant by Messiah, imperial client, Saturnalia, Gentiles, legacy-hunter, Stoicism, New Testament?

COMPARATIVE STUDIES. 1. Compare the Stoicism of Rome with the Stoicism of Greece (§ 324). 2. Why was the craze for amusements in Rome so much greater than in Athens? 3. "As many slaves, so many enemies." How does this saying reveal Roman character?

SELECT LIST FOR READING. 1. The Assessment and Collection of Taxes. Tucker, Life in the Roman World of Nero and St. Paul, pp 85-91. 2. The Life of the Roman Working People. Tucker, pp 244-255 3. An Ordinary Roman Dinner-Party. Tucker, pp 229-237 4. The Household Servants of a Well-to-do Roman. Tucker, pp 200-206 5. Roman Marriages and Matrons. Tucker, pp 292-308. 6. The Roman Woman's Dress. Tucker, pp 308-313 7. The City Streets and Water-Supply. Tucker, pp. 130-137 8. Building Materials and Town-Houses. Tucker, pp. 137-138, 143-163 9. The Lighting and Heating of a Roman House. Tucker, pp 161-162, 186-188 10. The Senate as a Rival of the Emperor. Dill, Roman Society from Nero to Marcus Aurelius, pp 39-57 11. The Position of the Clients and Freedmen. Dill, pp. 93-99, 102-114 12. Municipal Income and Expenditure. Dill, pp. 218-230 13. The Roman Colleges: Their Wide Organization and Influence. Dill, pp 250-286 14. Roman Society Seen through Pliny's Writings. Dill, pp 179-190. 15. The New Stoicism. Dill, pp 301-321 16. The Belief in Immortality among the Romans. Dill, pp 499-515. 17. The Influence of the Eastern Cults. (a) The Religion of Mithra, Dill, pp 600-610 (b) The Great Mother Dill, pp 547-559.

TOPICS FOR READING AND ORAL REPORT. 1. Social Life at Rome in the First Century. Morey, ch. 25, Botsford, ch. 15; Bury, ch 31. 2. Roman Amusements. Munro, pp 207-216 (sources), Bury, pp 607-626, Thomas, ch 4, Wilkins, ch. 3, Johnston, ch. 9 3. Education of the Time. Munro, pp. 193-197 (sources), Bury, pp. 598-600. 4. Literature of the Silver Age. Botsford, pp 239-242; Bury, pp 457-475; Mackail, pp 171-204 5. The Rise of Christianity. Seignobos, pp. 362-366, Botsford, pp 262-264, 281-282, Gibbon, pp 109-111

529. The Emperors of the Second Century.—Domitian was followed by a series of rulers equal in character and achievement to Tiberius and Vespasian. In the century of their leadership the empire reached its climax. Their names are as follows:

NERVA, A D 96–98
TRAJAN (adopted son of Nerva), A D 98–117.
HADRIAN (relative and adopted son of Trajan), A.D. 117–138.
ANTONINUS (adopted son of Hadrian), A D 138–161
MARCUS AURELIUS (adopted son of Antoninus), A.D. 161–180
COMMODUS (son of Aurelius), A D 180–192.

530. Nerva, 96-98 A.D.—On the death of Domitian the senate chose as princeps, NERVA, a senator of more than sixty years. An aged, kindly ruler, his chief service to the state during his short reign was the selection of TRAJAN as his successor.

531. Trajan, 98-117 A.D.—TRAJAN was a Spaniard by birth and an able general. As princeps, he showed himself equally vigorous in the management of the empire. He was a tall, strong, handsome man, of genial manners, not highly cultured, but with a broad and active mind. He selected his officials wisely and won their respect, yet kept careful watch upon their doings and required minute reports from them. During long periods he was occupied on the various frontiers with military campaigns. In them he gained brilliant victories and enlarged the empire. In this respect he struck out a new path. He died in Asia Minor while returning from a victorious war in the east.

532. Hadrian, 117-138 A.D.—HA'DRI-AN, his successor, is a most interesting character. A tried soldier, he proved himself also a practical administrator. But his

Cosmopolitanism.

most striking trait was his wide interest in all the affairs
of politics and life. He was well educated and dabbled
in literature, art and philosophy. He travelled into every
nook and corner of his wide domains. He was not attracted by military glory. A peaceful reign, with the
opportunity it gave him for consolidating and improving
the state and for following out the bent of his eager inquiring spirit, was his ambition. He was the first emperor to wear a beard, and his love of letters gave him
the nickname of "Greekling." He had no capacity for
personal friendship; men respected, but did not love
him. The Roman world was his pride and joy; he left
it happier and stronger than it had ever been before. In
the hour of death he composed the famous poetic address
to his soul, two lines of which are characteristic of the
man.

> "Whither wilt thou hie away,
> Never to play again, never to play"

533. Antoninus Pius, 138-161 A.D.—A senator of Gallic descent, AN'TO-NI'NUS, became his successor at the
age of fifty-two. From his name, he and his two successors are called the Antonines. He was a quiet, frugal
ruler, without striking qualities, yet sustaining with
dignity and honor the duties of his position. So econom-
ical was he in the finances of the empire that he was called
the "cheese-parer" His devotion to religion was particularly marked. From this trait he received the name
Pius, "devout."

**Juris-
prudence.**   " It was in the field of jurisprudence, and there only, that the reign
of Antoninus could show any positive achievement We have already
seen that Hadrian had formed a school of jurists whose most eminent

PLATE XXXIV

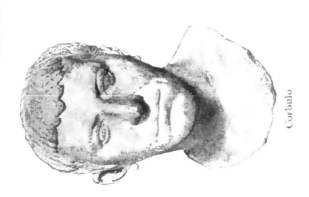

Corbulo

Antoninus Pius, in the British Museum

ROMAN PORTRAITURE

members had seats on his privy council and exercised a marked influence on legislation. Their labors continued to bear fruit under his successor, and Roman law was modified in many particulars by the principles of equity upon which the dominant philosophy of Stoicism laid stress A wide conception of humanity found expression on the provisions which facilitated the enfranchisement of slaves and limited the use of torture. It should be noted also that the Antonine jurists did much to give to Roman law the systematic form which it had hitherto lacked, and to present it in a compendious form to the student "

534. Marcus Aurelius, 161-180 A.D.—In this respect he prepared the way for MAR'CUS AU-RE'LI-US, the most extraordinary man who occupied the imperial throne. From his youth Marcus had been a student of moral philosophy of the Stoic type (§ 324), and in his exalted station he sought only to carry out his high ideals. Much of the activity of an emperor was distasteful to him, but he was proud that everywhere he did his duty as a philosopher should He sought to carry into practice the sentiments of love for mankind which he cherished. Severe toward himself, he disdained luxury and preferred hardship in spite of the fact that he was always in poor health. Though he loved peace and desired to relieve suffering, his reign was darkened by a series of disastrous wars and a terrible pestilence. His family life was not pleasant, perhaps through his own fault. His son was unworthy of him. His sole joys were found in the circle of his fellow-philosophers and in his own thoughts which he expressed in his lofty *Meditations*. He died at the age of sixty, while campaigning against barbarian invaders on the Danube.

The Philosopher on the Throne.

535. Commodus, 180-192 A.D.—His worthless son, COM'MO-DUS, followed him at the age of nineteen and brought the happy age of the Antonines to a sorry end. Cruel and depraved in tastes, weak and vain in disposition, he preferred games to government. His highest glory was to win in the gladiatorial contests and to be hailed as the Roman Hercules. To his prætorians only was he attentive and they were the bulwark of his rule. He was strangled by a wrestler after eleven years of folly and disorder.

536. Political Progress.—The emperors of the second century received their position through election by the senate. Hence they were constitutional rulers. So far as election went, therefore, the principate was practically restored. These emperors ruled also in harmony with the senate It was an era of good feeling in the state. Some measures were even brought before the comitia of the people. But each emperor took care to indicate his successor. The method chosen was that of adoption and association in government. The senate never failed to elect the successor thus indicated.

Emperors Constitutionally Chosen.

The Succession.

537. Advance in Organization.—In the imperial organization two notable advances are seen. (1) The offices of Cæsar's household, formerly filled by freedmen (§ 504), were now given to members of the equestrian order. Thus Cæsar's administration was dignified and an honorable public career in the civil service was opened to equestrians. (2) The emperor gave to the counsellors, who had been called in from time to time to advise him, a more official and stable character. They constituted the imperial council, made up of officials and senators. (3) The edicts of the prætors were collected and arranged in a code—the so-called Perpetual Edict. From time immemorial the officials had taken

Civil Service Reform

PLATE XXXV

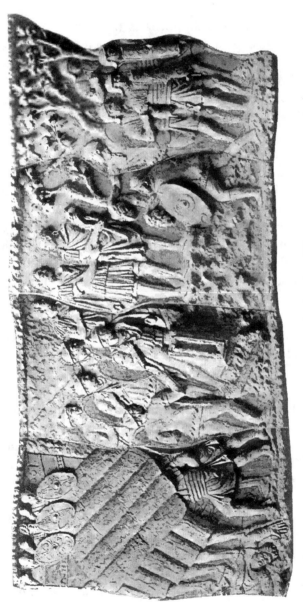

Scene in the Dacian War

A RELIEF FROM THE COLUMN OF TRAJAN

account of the law of other peoples (*ius gentium*) in administering justice in Italy and the provinces. Thus a body of legal decisions had grown up alongside the law of the Twelve Tables. Now this ill-defined mass was classified and withdrawn from the control of magistrates. All of these changes were the work of Hadrian.

538. Imperial Progress.—The second century was a stirring period in the external history of the empire. Two epochs of special importance are to be observed. (1) The reign of Trajan marks a significant extension of the empire in north and east. After completing the rampart begun by the Flavian emperors protecting the Agri Decumates (§ 513), Trajan proceeded to deal with a formidable danger that had arisen on the Danube. Here just across the river the Dacians had established a kingdom under an able ruler, De-ceb'a-lus. He had already been able to make terms with Domitian, and his strength menaced the security of the Roman frontier. Trajan determined to crush him. Two campaigns were necessary, each taking two years (A.D. 101–102; 105–106). The struggle was fierce and desperate. Only on the death of Decebalus in battle did Dacia submit and become a Roman province. The splendid victory is commemorated in the Column of Trajan raised at Rome to the height of a hundred feet and decorated with sculptured scenes of the war. In the east the question of the relation of Armenia to the empire was reopened; Trajan determined to take issue with Parthia and settle it. He took the field in A.D. 115, overcame Armenia, advanced southward into Mesopotamia and did not stop till he reached the Persian gulf. The Roman arms were supreme in the seats of the oldest civilization. Three new

Enlargement of the Empire

Conquest of Dacia.

The Eastern Question.

provinces were created, Armenia, Mesopotamia and Assyria; the Parthian king received his crown from the hand of the Roman emperor. Already the province of Arabia Petræa had been created. Thus the entire oriental world was under the authority of Rome, and the Roman empire had reached its greatest extent. What would have been the verdict of time on these eastern conquests we cannot know, for hardly had Hadrian come to the throne when he voluntarily withdrew his troops, abandoned the provinces of Mesopotamia and Assyria and restored Armenia to its position as a dependent kingdom. It seems likely that Rome would not have been able to maintain them permanently against Parthia, however important they were to the protection of the older Roman provinces in the east. (2) The other epoch was a much less brilliant one. In the reign of Marcus Aurelius Teutonic peoples began pressing down to the Danube and seeking peaceably or by force to enter the empire. Chief among these were the Mar'co-man'ni, and in the endeavor to drive them back, Marcus Aurelius was involved in a series of fierce conflicts. The invaders were finally overcome and driven across the Danube. The importance of the struggle lies in the fact that it was the pressure from behind that forced these barbarians into the empire, the beginnings of those movements which in the coming centuries were to break it in pieces.

539. Organization.—The changes in internal organization were all in the direction of more unity under the imperial administration. The emperor and his officials were everywhere active. Hadrian is the great example of this. His visits to the provinces, which covered a dozen years, were not simply for pleasure, but for the

Marginal notes:

Hadrian's Change of Policy.

Appearance of Barbarians.

Its Significance.

Administrative Activity.

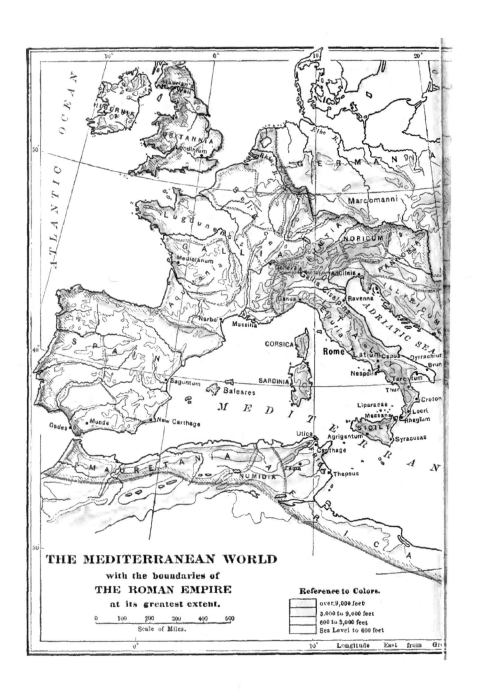

ATLANTIC OCEAN

HIBERNIA

Hadrian's Wall

BRITANNIA

Londinium

GERMANIA

Elbe

Marcomanni

Lugudunum

GALLIA

Mediolanum

NORICUM

PANNONIA

Genava

Aquileia

ILLYRICUM

Gallia Cisalpina

Genua

Ravenna

ETRURIA

ADRIATIC SEA

Narbo

Massilia

CORSICA

Rome

Latium

Capua

Dyrrachium

Brun

SPAIN

Saguntum

SARDINIA

Neapolis

Tarentum

Thur

Baleares

Croton

Liparaeae

Locri

Gades

Munda

New Carthage

M E D I T E R

Messana

Rhegium

SICIL

Syracusae

Agrigentum

Utica

Carthage

Thapsus

R A N

MAURETANIA

NUMIDIA

Zama

AFRICA

THE MEDITERRANEAN WORLD
with the boundaries of
THE ROMAN EMPIRE
at its greatest extent.

0 100 200 300 400 500
Scale of Miles.

Reference to Colors.

over 9,000 feet
3,000 to 9,000 feet
600 to 3,000 feet
Sea Level to 600 feet

Longitude East from Gr

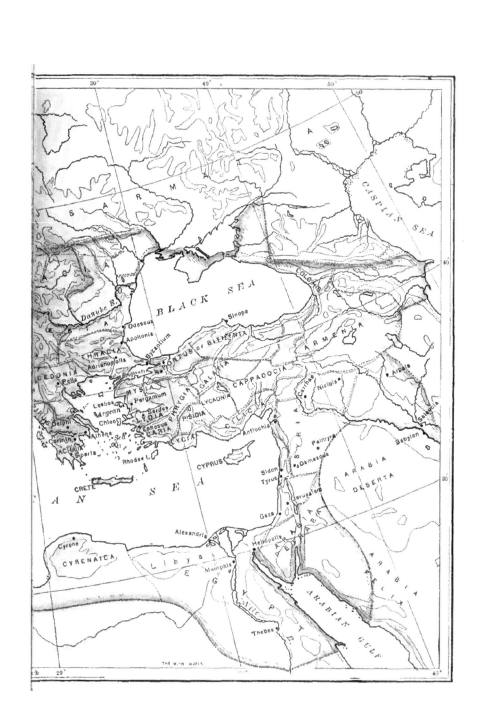

purpose of inspecting their resources and organization. As a result of them, a more careful and minute supervision of the details of administration was introduced. Imperial officials were appointed to look after the affairs of the municipalities which were thus taken up directly into the structure of the empire. Hadrian built many fine buildings for these cities and brought their finances into order. The chief benefit of such measures was that they consolidated the powers of the state and its interest, bringing all under the guidance of a central authority, produced greater efficiency and stimulated the life of the members. A wider extension of the franchise was natural in these circumstances, but this was not followed by greater zeal for the state and a patriotic devotion to it. Citizenship was rather looked upon as a personal honor and prized because it gave special privileges. In this imperial administration Italy began to stand on the same basis as the provinces, and Rome itself was treated like any other municipality. The use of barbarians in the legions still further relieved the citizens from military service. Likewise the extension of imperial courts of justice throughout the Roman world and the supremacy of Roman imperial law which was characteristic of the time, while it was a bond of union, served as another means of making individuals and local communities dependent on the central government. *Its Good and Bad Sides.*

540. Social Life.—Society breathed more freely under the emperors of the second century, and as a result new life sprang up on all sides. Trajan and Hadrian were mighty builders. The finest memorial of the former is his Column at Rome, already referred to (§ 538). Hadrian's three chief buildings at Rome were the temple of Venus *Art and Architecture.*

and Roma, the largest and most magnificent of all Roman temples; the Pantheon—originally the work of Agrippa—a temple of all the gods; and a massive mausoleum which he built on the other side of the Tiber, now known as the Castle of St. Angelo. Yet, most characteristic of the times was the stately villa of Hadrian at Tibur, conceived on a grand scale and filled with works of art; a theatre, libraries, temples, porches and gardens found place in it. From it have been taken statues, reliefs, mosaics and silver ornaments sufficient to stock several museums.

541. The Literary Revival.—Literature flourished under the liberal patronage of the emperors and in the free atmosphere of the times. A striking sign of the unity in the world of letters under the empire is the fact that as many works of lasting fame were written in Greek as in Latin. One of the greatest historians of antiquity, Cornelius Tac'i-tus, belongs to this century. His chief works are the *Histories* and the *Annals*, which deal with the empire under the Julian and Flavian Cæsars. Unfortunately, large parts of these works have been lost, but what remains is our chief source of knowledge for the times. Tacitus aspired to bring back to life and power just the ideas and institutions which the history of the empire had shown to be fruitless and hopeless. He sought to exalt the senatorial nobility as over against the princeps, Rome and Italy as over against the provinces. But so keen is his insight into characters and manners at Rome, and so brilliant his way of expressing his estimates of them, that his bitter and one-sided judgments have colored all subsequent views of the times. Two lesser works of his are the *Agricola*, an appreciation

Tacitus.

PLATE XXXVI

CASTLE OF ST. ANGELO: HADRIAN'S MOLE

of his father-in-law, the general of Domitian, and the *Germania*, a description of the Germans, in which their simplicity and purity of life are favorably compared with the depravity of imperial Rome. Side by side with Tacitus stands Juvenal, the satirist of the empire. What the former condemned as an historian, the latter held up to scorn and ridicule in his powerful verse. Hypocritical philosophers, parasitical clients, rich fools, ostentatious luxury, fortune-hunting and the trials of poor men of letters are painted in strong and vivid colors. Suetonius wrote the *Lives of the Twelve Cæsars*, a gossipy work, yet very helpful as a source for the reigns of the early Cæsars including Domitian.

Juvenal.

Suetonius

542. Plutarch and Lucian.—Of Greek writers the most famous is Plutarch (A D. 46–125), who wrote the *Parallel Lives*, forty-six in number, setting the biography of a Roman hero over against that of a Greek. He was a diligent collector of anecdotes and used them shrewdly to show the traits of his characters. The book has ever been a storehouse of information and at the same time a hand-book of morals—history teaching by the examples of the greatest men of the ancient world. Not so well known, but a brighter, keener mind than Plutarch, was Lucian (about A.D. 125–180). His career was typical of the time; he was a travelling lecturer. His peculiar gift revealed itself in the writing of witty and satirical dialogues. The weaknesses and inconsistencies of the religion of his day are daringly ridiculed in his *Dialogues of the Gods*, while similar keen and amusing criticism is passed on various types of people of his day in the *Dialogues of the Dead*.

Greek Writers.

543. Representative Men of the Times.—Two men may be chosen to represent the higher life of this century: Pliny the Younger and Marcus Aurelius, the emperor. Pliny was a trusted official of Trajan and reveals himself and his times in a series of *Letters* to friends. In these he appears as a cultivated gentleman, such as might be met among us to-day. He takes long walks in the woods and delights in the beauty of nature. He discusses the latest books. With a modesty that approaches vanity, he tells of his gifts to his native town in behalf of education. He entertains his guests by taking them around the grounds of his villa and inviting their admiration. He gives public readings from his works, and we feel him tremble as he gets on his legs before his cultured audience. A good-natured, indulgent master to his slaves, a devoted husband, an upright, earnest, if somewhat commonplace, character, he exhibits the Roman gentleman produced by the broad, serious and refined culture of the early second century

544. Marcus Aurelius, Emperor and Philosopher.— On a higher plane we meet with the impressive and melancholy figure of the emperor-philosopher, Marcus Aurelius. From his youth he was a Stoic in word and deed. His *Meditations*, which he wrote down in Greek from time to time wherever he happened to be, in the camp or in the palace, reveal to us his thoughts. He aspired to be a perfect man and he thought it possible to attain his ideal by the old Stoic rule of following nature (§ 324). His philosophy was tempered by practical experience, and hence he insisted much on the duty of a true man to society. From his experience, perhaps, came also his sense of the need of divine help. He turned his thought into life; this separates him from the professional philosopher and makes him interesting, for he passed his life on the throne. A sober and high-minded personality, he did his duty in this high sphere and came near to practising what he preached.

545. Religion.—Yet this emperor persecuted the Christians! Such are the contradictions of history. The growing popular hatred of the Christians is not remarkable. We have already suggested a reason (§ 528). As Tertullian, a Christian writer, said: "If the Tiber rises, if the Nile does not rise, if the heavens give no rain, if there is an earthquake, famine, or pestilence, straightway the cry is, 'The Christians to the lions!'" The imperial authorities in some cases sought to stand against the mob and protect the Christians from unwarranted violence. Trajan wrote Pliny not to search out Christians for death, but only to deal with cases that were brought before him. Marcus Aurelius was more severe, and under his command Christians were hunted down and put to death. He regarded their refusal to join in the religion of the empire as "mere obstinacy" and thought it a part of his duty to punish those who professed what Pliny called "a degrading and unreasonable superstition." The Christians, in their turn, went willingly in great numbers to death, which they called "martyrdom," that is, "witnessing" to their faith. Yet they grew in numbers and in unity, impelled both by persecution from without and by the false doctrines that some within the fold were teaching. Among them appeared literary defenders, some of whom addressed to the emperors what are called *Apologies*, or arguments in defence of Christianity as a reasonable and worthy religion; others wrote books maintaining the true or "orthodox" doctrine against the false doctrine or "heresy." Thus out of the

[margin: Persecution of Christians]

[margin: Their Progress.]

various churches all over the empire was slowly forming the Church, the one body of believers in Christ, standing over against the empire and the heretics. It was soon to make its power felt in both directions.

REVIEW EXERCISES. 1. What is meant by mausoleum, heretic, Imperial Council, martyrdom, dyarchy, apology? 2. Name the emperors of this century in chronological order. 3. For what are the following famous: Hercules, Pliny the Younger, Decebalus, Tacitus, Plutarch?

COMPARATIVE STUDIES. 1. In what were Marcus Aurelius and Solomon alike? 2. Compare the empire of Augustus in extent with the empire of Trajan. 3. Compare Pliny the Younger with Cicero in ideals, activities and character. 4. Why is Juvenal more a type of this period than of Athens in the fifth century? 5. What reasons may be given for the famous saying of Gibbon quoted below? *

SELECT LIST FOR READING. 1. An Estimate of the Character of the Good Emperors. Nerva, Jones, p 149, Trajan, Jones, p 156, Hadrian, Jones, p 179, Antoninus, Jones, pp 196–197, Marcus Aurelius, Jones, pp. 204–208   2. The Eastern Conquests. Jones, pp. 164, 170–172, 175, 203, 208, 212. 3. The Barbarians Threaten the Empire. Jones, pp. 221–228. 4. The Material Welfare of Italy. Jones, pp 165–168, 171, 180–182. 5. Eastern Ideas Triumphant Over Western Ideas. Jones. pp. 212–220

TOPICS FOR READING AND ORAL REPORT. 1. The Empire in the Second Century. Seignobos, ch. 22; Botsford, pp. 243–256; Morey, ch 26, Merivale, pp 513–542; Gibbon, ch 1. 2. The Inner Politics of the Empire. Abbott, ch. 15   3. The Dacian Wars of Trajan. Bury, pp. 421–430. 4. Personality and Work of Hadrian. Merivale, pp. 524–529   Bury, ch. 26. 5. Marcus Aurelius. Merivale, pp. 538–539; Bury, ch. 28, Munro, pp. 176–178 (source)   6. The Literature of the Second Century. Botsford, pp. 256–262, Bury, pp. 475–487   7. Pliny and the Christians. Laing, pp 468–471 (source); Munro, pp 165–167 (source);

* "If a man were called upon to fix the period in the history of the world during which the condition of the human race was most happy and prosperous, he would, without hesitation, name that which elapsed from the death of Domitian to the accession of Commodus "

Bury, pp. 445-448. 8. Tacitus the Historian. Mackail, pp 205-220; Laing, pp. 399-424. 9. "As an emperor I am a Roman, but as a man my city is the world." How does this saying reveal the spirit of the time?

546. Septimius Severus, 193-211 A.D. —The prætorians, after the death of Commodus, held the succession to the empire in their hands. Having finally sold it to the highest bidder, they were met by the opposition of the three frontier armies on the Rhine, the Danube and the Euphrates, who proclaimed their own commanders as emperors. In the civil war that followed, SEP-TIM'I-US SE-VE'RUS, of an African family, general of the army on the Danube, secured the throne and ruled with vigor as the first military emperor (A.D. 193–211). He reorganized the prætorians by substituting his own soldiers for the Italians, and by drawing troops from the regular army into Italy he increased its military establishment from ten thousand to forty thousand. He extended the empire by recovering Mesopotamia, abandoned by Hadrian (§ 538). He ruled as a practically absolute monarch, disregarding the prerogatives of the senate. By taking the name of Antoninus he sought to attach himself to the previous dynasty, while he appointed his sons as his successors. The centralization and extension of the power of the princeps were his manifest aims, the vigor and prosperity of his administration were evidences of his success. Yet the military basis of his throne was unsound and dangerous.

The Prince Rules in the Interest of the Army.

547. Caracalla, 211-217 A.D.—His son CAR'A-CAL'LA was a cruel and wasteful ruler who was murdered by the prefect of the guard. Two achievements have made him famous: (1) the building of the " Baths of Caracalla " at

Rome, a colossal and elegant series of public baths; (2) his edict, of which the beginning has been recently found in an Egyptian papyrus, bestowing citizenship upon all the inhabitants of the empire except the *dediticii*, that is to say, those destitute of rights in some one of the organized municipal or city-states (A.D. 212). This last act was intended by him to facilitate the supervision of local government by making it more uniform, to increase the number of citizens, from whom alone was collected a tax on inheritances and on sales which went to provide pensions for the veterans, and to bring to completion the long process of civilizing by means of urban institutions which Alexander the Great—the model of Caracalla —had begun (§ 299).

548. Alexander Severus, 222-235 A.D.—ALEXANDER SEVERUS a distant relative of the house of Septimius, was no soldier. Indeed, his reign marks a reaction toward constitutional rule. Though young, he had an earnest and serious spirit and sought to conform his life to the highest models. An oriental by birth and sentiment, he was deeply religious. In a sanctuary in his palace he placed statues of Abraham, Orpheus, Apollo and Jesus. But such a temper did not attract the legions. His campaigns were unsuccessful and he was slain by a mob of his own soldiers.

549. The Golden Age of the Jurists.—Under the emperors of the house of Septimius Severus the importance of the jurists is notable. The prefect of the prætorians had come to have charge of the administration of justice under the emperor. He was, therefore, chiefly a great lawyer and only secondarily a military man. Under these emperors he became the chief minister and adviser of the crown. Since he was a "knight," and not a senator, his elevation meant the elimination of the highest aristocracy from all but the chief military positions, and, indeed, the Severi began, what Gal'li-e'nus (253–268 A D) completed, the removal of the senators from the army also. The glory of their reigns were the prefects Papinian and Ulpian. To them the emperor was the source of justice and law, the supreme authority. Thus they gave a new theory of the Roman constitution. They gathered the imperial judgments ("decrees"), instructions ("rescripts") and orders ("edicts"), and brought them into harmony according to the highest ideals of the time. This they did by writing commentaries on the decisions of the emperors, by giving official legal interpretations (*responsa*) and discussing doubtful points of law. Thus was prepared the way for a code of imperial law. The spread of the Græco-Roman civilization reached its acme in the age of the Severi. It is true that the empire was a trifle greater in territorial extent in the last year or two of Trajan's reign; but the growth of new municipalities, which is the mark of expanding culture, continued to its culmination in the epoch now under consideration.

The Old Aristocracy Ceases to Furnish the Officials.

The Harmonizing of the Civil Law.

During the régime of the jurists, moreover, the ties of law which bound the municipalities to the central government were perfected, and the various officials already established—notably by Hadrian—to check their extravagance and to remedy defects in their administration of justice were as yet interfering only in a salutory way with local freedom. There is no clear evidence for a lessening of a healthy interest in municipal politics It is true that men of wealth did not always volunteer for public officers, but this was nothing new. Seeing that rich men paid their taxes by holding offices, they had been compelled to become candidates for the magistracies since the time of the republic.

Supervision of Municipal Government.

For over two hundred and fifty years a territory, which has to-day a population of over one hundred and ninety millions, and which may have had one-third of that number in antiquity, had seen no great war or serious disturbance of economic production.

550. Growth of Municipalities.—The results were apparent in the existence of many thousand towns and municipalities in which the peasants as well as the traders and citizens lived. These were well equipped with sewers and aqueducts, streets and sidewalks, temples and amphitheatres which stand in their ruins to-day, sometimes far out in the desert, as impressive testimonials of the achievements of the "Roman peace."

551. The People Not Warlike.—Around the frontiers ran, where a natural barrier was wanting, the great *limes*, a wall here, a chain of forts there, along which lived the soldiers, now permitted by the Severi to have wives and homes in the towns which had grown up at the military posts. Only these men on the border had weapons, military organization and knowledge of war. Two centuries and a half of relaxation and peace had converted a population almost every man of which at the time of Julius Cæsar had been potentially a soldier into a great flock of sheep of which the soldiers were the watch-dogs. In return for their services they received pay while in the army, and pensions and immunity from municipal taxes after their discharge. They were really the masters of the world, and during the time of the Severi they became conscious of this fact. Accordingly each great army corps now sought to gain for itself the possession of the empire; they left the frontiers and setting out for the capital engaged in a

The Soldiers the Masters.

protracted war (235 A.D to 270 A.D.) with one another, while in their rear the barbarians whom they had held in check swept over the *limes* and plundered and harried at will.

552. The Break-up of the Roman Empire.—During this horrible welter of civil and foreign war Franks and Alamanni invaded Gaul and pushed south into Spain and Italy. Goths swept from beyond the Danube to the Mediterranean, and taking ship crossed the Black sea and ravaged Asia Minor. They even sailed the entire length of the Mediterranean, plundering Greece and Africa on their way. The Sassanids, who in 227 A.D. had set the Parthian dynasty of the Arsacids aside and re-established a Persian empire in Asia, claimed all the territory once ruled by Cyrus, and again and again sacked Asia Minor and Syria. Even Antioch was twice captured by them. Down the Nile came the Arab Nomads; into Numidia swarmed the Moors. The whole civilized world was at one time or other overwhelmed by the barbarians. A horrible plague broke out which raged in the empire for fifteen years. Great cities like Alexandria fell to half their size. Whole towns were left without inhabitants, and in every direction stood tumbled-down houses and deserted farms. This frightful period culminated in the reign of the unhappy GALLIENUS (253–260 A.D.). *Barbarian Invasions* *The Plague* *Gallienus*

553. The Thirty Tyrants.—One of his predecessors, his father, DECIUS, was slain in battle against the Goths; another, VALERIAN, was made prisoner by the Sassanian king AURELIAN (A D. 270–275) had better success. He restored the unity of the empire by overthrowing Queen Zenobia, who had set up an independent kingdom in the east with its capital at Palmyra, and Tet'ri-cus, the head *Aurelian.*

of a similar kingdom in Gaul. The barbarians were beaten back, Rome was fortified with the so-called Aurelian wall and a splendid "triumph" was held in the city. He was compelled, however, to abandon Dacia to the invaders. PROBUS (A.D. 276-282) was equally successful against the barbarians. He thrust them back from the northern frontiers and restored the wall connecting the Rhine and Danube. He transplanted numbers of these tribes into the empire as settlers and added many to his armies. This desperate measure was necessary to strengthen the waning size and vigor of the Roman military and civic body. Both he and Aurelian, however, were at last slain by their own soldiers while in the field, but not till the one had restored the unity of the empire and the other cleared it of the invaders. It remained for a more adroit and fortunate man to build anew a wonderful imperial system. But he could not undo what had been done in the generation between Alexander and Aurelian—the age of the Thirty Tyrants, as it is sometimes called; for in that awful time the noble culture of antiquity perished beyond the hope of restoration. The barbarian invasions of the third century with their attendant wars and calamities were more far-reaching in their effects upon ancient life than were the Germanic movements of the fifth century.

554. Religion.—It is not surprising that religion had a large place in the life of this age of disaster. The troubles and woes of the time led men everywhere to look to the heavenly powers for mercy and help. All sorts of religions found favor. Magic and astrology were very popular with all classes. In Alexandria a new school of philosophy sprang up called "New Platonism," because

PLATE XXXVII

THE PANTHEON, ROME

From a photograph by R. Moscioni

THE WALLS OF AURELIAN

it revived the ideas of Plato (§ 266) and sought to find comfort and a rule of life in them. The soldiers had their religion and, as they were the leading force of the time, it spread widely. This was the worship of Mithra, a Persian deity, represented as a young hero slaying a bull or bearing it off on his shoulders. He had his priests and his temples; he promised victory over sin and immortal happiness to his followers. The worship of the sun as the source of all life, the unconquerable lord, was a popular cult. The emperors of the time were very favorable to these various religions; they saw in them a source of strength for the hard-pressed Roman world.

Mithraism.

555. Christianity.—Only against one faith were all alike opposed. Christianity had to battle with them for her life and no one could foresee the result. Yet she grew through all the century, undismayed by persecution. The effect of her independent position, opposed as she was by the state and attacked by the people, began to appear. Her organization became more centralized. Among the elders or bishops of the churches, here and there, a leader appeared who stood at the head of the Christians of the city and became *the* bishop; the elders or presbyters became "priests"* under the bishop's authority; churches of a district united for the settlement of questions common to them by sending their priests to a synod, presided over by a bishop. Thus a distinction between the clergy and the lay members began to arise. Bishops in such centres as Antioch, Alexandria or Rome, where the Christians were many, were called archbishops or metropolitans. The church at Rome came to have a special position. It was thought

Growth of Organization.

The Hierarchy.

The Roman Church.

---

* The word "priest" is a contracted form of the word "presbyter."

that Peter, the leader of Jesus' disciples, was its founder and thus gave it leadership over the other churches. Its bishop was thus led to make peculiar claims to headship in the Church. In all this advance of the Church we see it begin to shape itself on the model of the imperial organization and to stand up over against it. Leaders of thought began to come forward. In Alexandria, a school of Christian teaching was formed, the most brilliant ornament of which was Origen. In North Africa, Christianity was particularly strong. Here the great names were Tertullian and Cyprian, who by their writings defended the Church against enemies within and without A Christian art began to appear. Upon gravestones and chapels the dove, the good shepherd and the lamb, favorite symbols of the new faith, were rudely carved or painted.

Christian Writers

Art.

REVIEW EXERCISES. 1. Name the chief emperors of the third century. 2. For what are the following significant: Zenobia, Ulpian, Origen? 3. What is meant by coloni, priest, New Platonism, edict, Sassanian? 4. What is the date of the Edict of Caracalla? 5. Describe the conditions existing on the Roman frontier in the third century. 6. From what regions did the invaders come into the Roman territory?

COMPARATIVE STUDIES. 1. Compare Greek religion in the sixth century B C. (§ 134) with the religion of this age—what similar conditions and results? 2. How do the barbarian invasions resemble those that afflicted the oriental world (§§ 12, 16, 35, 48, 71, 74)?

SELECT LIST FOR READING. 1. The Concessions of Severus to the Military Element. Jones, pp 244-249. 2. Two Opinions upon the Edict of Caracalla. Jones, pp 256-257 3. Ten Years of Respite under Severus Alexander. Jones, pp. 268-276. 4. Strife between the Senatorial and Military Orders. Jones, pp 280-286, 306-310 5. Aurelian, One of the Great Commanders. Jones, pp 318-335

THE STORY OF JONAH: EARLY CHRISTIAN ART

TOPICS FOR READING AND ORAL REPORT. 1. The Empire in the Third Century. Gibbon, pp. 21-83; Morey, ch. 27, Merivale pp 542-569, Seignobos, pp 373-390 2. The Emperor and His Administration. Abbott, pp 329-334, Botsford, pp 276-278 3. The Jurists of the Empire. Seignobos, pp. 383-384, Botsford, pp 269-270 4. Severus Alexander. Gibbon, pp 37, 38; Merivale, pp 555, 556. 5. The Sassanian Kings. Gibbon, pp 39-42, Botsford, pp 271-272. 6. Zenobia and Palmyra. Gibbon, pp. 70-73.

8.—THE LATER ROMAN EMPIRE (DESPOTISM)
A.D. 284-395

556. The Empire Reorganized.—The new organization of the state which was demanded by the times was started by an emperor at the close of the century. Among the able lieutenants that the valiant emperors Aurelian and Probus gathered about them and trained in the fierce battles with Goths and Persians were Di'o-cle'tian and Max-im'i-an. The legions chose DIOCLETIAN as emperor (A.D 284-305) to defend and restore the decaying empire. He responded by a new plan of imperial organization to meet the difficulties of the times. (1) To solve the problem of the succession he associated with himself as colleague MAXIMIAN, giving him the title of Augustus, and took as assistants GALERIUS and CONSTANTIUS, giving them the title of Cæsar. Hence, there was always one at hand to succeed to the throne. (2) To meet the necessity of defending so great an empire from its enemies, he assigned Maximian to Italy and the western provinces with Constantius under him in charge of Gaul, Spain and Britain, and himself took the east with Galerius under him in charge of Illyricum. His cap-

Diocletian (284-305 A D).

The Plan of Reorganization.

ital was at Nicomedia in Asia Minor; that of Maximian at Milan in Italy. Thus there was no general of a large army who was not already a member of the government. (3) For a better administration of the state, he split up the provinces, making one hundred and sixteen in all. These were united into twelve "dioceses." (4) To guard against misuse of power, he separated the military from the civil authority. Governors of provinces were civil officers. Generals (counts and dukes) had charge of the soldiery. (5) A very complex organization of the officials of the state was introduced; all were closely bound together, each dependent on the one above him in rank, until the culmination was reached in the emperor Each rank of officials had its appropriate title. The supreme emperor was far above all other mortals and surrounded himself with oriental pomp and form; he wore a diadem and was called *Dominus*, "lord"; the subject was *servus*, "slave." This kind of a government had existed in Egypt since the time of the Ptolemies (§ 311).

557. A Despotism.—Thus by these measures the principate perished and an absolute monarchy took its place. The republic with its constitution and magistrates, princeps, senate, assemblies, citizens became as insignificant as titles of nobility in a modern republic. The pre-eminence of Rome and Italy vanished. All that had been built up by Augustus with such marvellous skill, and, for three centuries, had, in form at least, been the basis of Roman government, passed away. That it should perish was proper, for it had done its work and was unequal to the new demands. But the meaning of the change now introduced must not be overlooked. The empire of Rome was essentially transformed. The

Bureau-cracy.

End of the System of Augustus.

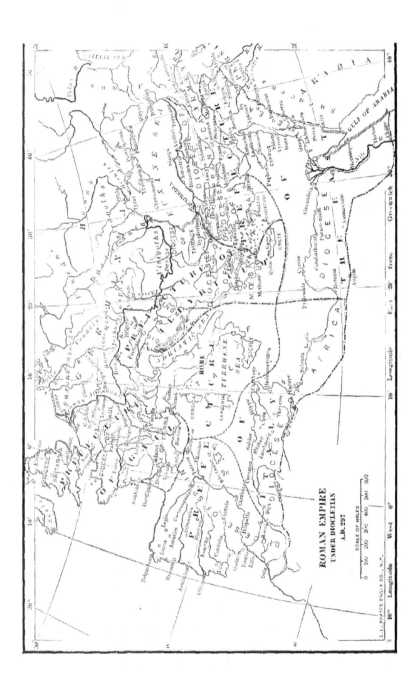

ROMAN EMPIRE
UNDER DIOCLETIAN
A.D. 297

SCALE OF MILES
0   100   200   300   400   500   600

L.L. POATES ENG. CO., N.Y.

experiment in government, which sought to combine republican institutions with effective administration of an empire, was over.

558. The Personality of Diocletian.—His plan of reorganization proves Diocletian to have been a wise and practical statesman, as well as a skilful soldier. He was of humble origin, the son of a freedman of Dalmatia, and had worked his way up from the ranks. Tall and spare of body, he had a clear mind, reflected in a face with finely cut features, and an attractive personality which made firm friends. With a strong will that pursued its way resistlessly, and used all men to further its designs, he had one weakness common to his age—a vein of religious superstition which caused him to set much store by omens and signs, and to pay passionate heed to the utterances of magicians and astrologers

559. Good Results of the New Plan.—Under his skilful ministration the exhausted empire was revived and leaped to its feet. The coinage was improved and finances restored. New taxes were imposed, but their burden was unwisely distributed among the various classes of society. Military reforms, particularly the Concentration of creation of a field-army in addition to the legions on Troops. the frontiers, available wherever the need was greatest, brought the disturbed frontiers into order. Laws were issued bearing on all sides of life; it was even attempted to regulate prices by legislation Imperial cities were adorned with new and splendid buildings, and old foundations were renewed. Inscriptions of the time hail the period as the "happy era" of general betterment.

560. Bad Results of the New Plan.—The complicated administrative system of Diocletian, while it preserved the empire as a structure, sapped its inner life. The cost of maintaining so great a body of officials was an enormous drain. Taxation grew by leaps and bounds accompanied by scarcity of money, increase of poverty and decline of population. Class distinctions still further weakened the effectiveness of the body politic. The senatorial class was rich and powerful and was exempted from many civic burdens. These fell largely on the next lower class, called the curials or decurions. All who possessed at least twenty-five acres of land were included in this class. They were responsible for the collection of taxes, deficiencies in which they must make up out of their own **Ruin of** private fortunes. These obligations were hereditary; a **Free** **Citizens.** son of a curial entered the order at the age of eighteen; severe laws were passed to prevent any from avoiding the civic burdens, which often proved their ruin. As the result of wars and taxation many small freeholders lost their liberty to migrate and became coloni on the estates of the nobles, to be sold with the land to which they belonged. The artisans formed a separate class to which all members were likewise perpetually bound. The result of all these arrangements was that the imperial machine with its rigid system and universal sweep was crushing the life out of the middle classes, destroying all civic patriotism and individual ambition, in the praiseworthy endeavor to hold the state together.

561. Persecution of Christians.—The religious policy of Diocletian brought upon him a serious conflict. In his zeal for the revival of the ancient Roman worship, he sought to suppress the Christians. Although they were in his court and his legions and formed an influential and progressive element in the state, his unrelenting, almost fanatical, spirit did not flinch from the struggle. He did not use bloody means; his plan was rather by destroying churches, silencing leaders and seizing property to bring Christianity gradually into contempt and weakness. He failed. His edict against the faith was only partially respected in the west, and down to the end of his reign the struggle went on. During his own lifetime—after his abdication (§ 562)—his successor, Galerius, issued his Edict of Toleration (A.D. 311), which gave the Christians freedom to worship in public and private on condition of paying due respect to the laws. Its Failure

562. Difficulties of the Succession.—A more remarkable weakness in his system revealed itself. Worn out with his incessant labors, Diocletian determined to retire from his imperial position. In A.D. 305, after twenty-one years of rule, he abdicated and retired to Dalmatia to spend in private the remainder of his life. He persuaded his colleague, Maximian, to follow his example. The Cæsars stepped into their places and new Cæsars were appointed. But without Diocletian the system would not work. His successor as senior Augustus lost control of the situation, and a year later the son of Constantius, CONSTANTINE, was proclaimed imperator by his legions in the west. The Roman world saw the emperors involved in conflict with each other for the supremacy. The outcome was the victory of Constantine, who in A.D. 323 became sole emperor (A D. 323–337). · Abdication of the Augusti.

563. Constantine, 306-337 A.D.—Constantine was at this time about forty years of age, a man of heroic stature, handsome and strong. Tradition tells of his piercing eye and commanding dignity. A brave warrior, His Personality.

he won many of his battles by his own personal courage and strength in single combat. Shrewd and self-
contained, never thrown off his guard, quick to seize an
opportunity, with a religious sense akin to Diocletian's
and a love of praise and pomp which he gratified by the
oriental splendor of his dress and court, he carried out
the spirit of Diocletian's policy to the end. From the
men of his own time and from succeeding ages he has
won the title of "the Great." Of all his achievements
two have given him this special claim to remembrance:
(1) his transference of the imperial capital from Rome
to a new city on the Bosporus, named from him Constantinople; (2) his reconciliation of the empire with
Christianity.

His Two Contributions to Progress.

564. The New Capital.—Constantinople was placed
on the site of the Greek city of Byzantium. It was most
wisely placed for the capital of an empire that extended
from the Euphrates to Britain. From it the emperor
could survey his domain on either side and most easily
control its several parts. Commerce found it a most convenient centre and its harbors were unsurpassed. It lay
near, yet not too near, to the Danube, the frontier whence
danger from the barbarians was most pressing. It was
easy of defence by land and sea, lying on seven hills and
protected on three sides by water. The emperor proposed to call it New Rome, and, although the name com-
memorating its founder has been preferred by after ages,
the result contemplated by him took place—the supremacy of old Rome passed to its new rival. Here the court
was set up, here magnificent palaces were built, from
here the imperial administration ruled the Roman world.
Rome sank to the level of a provincial city, mighty in

Advantages of the Site.

PLATE XXXI

The Arch of Constantine at Rome

A Roman Aqueduct in Gaul

CHARACTERISTIC ROMAN ARCHITECTURE

its past alone, until it rose again to be the capital of a spiritual state, the seat of the Roman Church.

565. Recognition of Christianity.—Already, before he became sole emperor, Constantine had seen how great a power Christianity had become, and by his friendly attitude won the Christians to his side. His father, though never breaking with the old religion, had inclined to the worship of the Christian god, and the son followed his example. In A.D. 313 he published the Edict of Milan, by which Christianity was put on a par with the other religions of the Roman empire. As time went on and he became the lord of the Roman world, his favor was shown more clearly by his edicts and by his personal kindness to Christian bishops. He read the Scriptures. He presided at a famous council of Christian bishops at Ni-cæ'a (A.D. 325), where an important theological question was decided—whether Jesus Christ was the same as God or only like him.* In the hour of death he was baptized into the Church, and thus personally confessed Christianity. But, as emperor, he refused to take sides; if he granted favors to Christians, he also consecrated temples and gave privileges to priests of the old Roman cult. Nor was his conduct ever deeply influenced by Christian teaching. He sought to reconcile all worshippers of every god and use them for the upbuilding of the empire. Yet his personal attitude toward Christianity was more potent than his official neutrality. From his reign dates the beginning of the victory of Christianity over the ancient faiths of the Roman world and the union between the Church and the empire.

Constantine as a Christian.

* Those who held the latter view were led by the Bishop Arius and were hence called Arians. The question was decided against them in the Nicene Council.

Eu-se'bi-us, the Church historian and friend of Constantine, tells us, in his life of the emperor, that Constantine, before he became sole emperor, while marching against one of his rivals, uncertain as to his duty to God, beheld a wonderful vision. As the day was declining, he saw the representation of a cross of light in the heavens, above the sun, and bearing the inscription, *Conquer by this!* At this sight he himself was struck with amazement, and his whole army also, which followed him on the expedition and witnessed the miracle. While pondering on the vision, he fell into a sleep in which Christ appeared to him with the same sign and bade him make a likeness of it as a standard for his army. He obeyed, and produced what was called the Labarum, a banner hung from a cross-bar on a spear, at the top of which was a wreath containing in its centre a monogram for the name of Christ   From this time forth Constantine was at heart a Christian

566. Successors of Constantine.—On the death of Constantine, his three sons followed him as emperors in the east and west (A.D. 337–353) until one of them, CONSTANTIUS, became sole emperor (A.D. 353–361). After him came another member of the house of Constantine, JULIAN (A.D. 361–363). His death on the eastern frontier was followed by the elevation of several generals of the armies, one of whom was the unfortunate Valens (A D 364–378), until a vigorous and successful warrior, THE'O-DO'SI-US (A D. 379–395), at first emperor in the east, succeeded in uniting the empire again. The renewal of barbarian invasions after his death on a scale hitherto unparalleled, and the establishment of their independent states in the empire, has made the year of his death, A.D. 395, a significant turning point in history.

567. Christianity and the Empire.—While the inroads on the Danube and the Rhine continued, and the Persians in the east were constantly threatening the Roman provinces, the uppermost question in the history

of this half-century was the relation of the empire to
Christianity. The Church, superbly organized under
its bishops, and having its greatest strength in the cities,*
offered itself as a useful ally to the imperial power.
A fierce conflict about the doctrine which had been in
dispute at the council of Nicæa (§ 565) was rending the
Church in twain. Arianism sought to reassert itself
against its opposing view, which being accepted in that
council was called Orthodoxy or the "right doctrine"
The sons of Constantine had been reared as Christians,
but Constantius accepted the Arian view. Hence, the
Arians sought to obtain his help to gain their victory.
Although, as emperor, he sought to remain, like his
father, neutral in religious matters, he could not help
being drawn into the struggle. The empire took the
side of Arianism. Over against him as representing
orthodoxy was Athanasius, the brilliant and unscrupulous bishop of Alexandria. The result of the conflict
was the triumph of Arianism by the aid of imperial
authority. The moment was full of meaning, not because of the triumph of this or that doctrine, but because
it brought the union of the empire and the Church a long
step nearer. Julian, who sought to revive paganism
and repress Christianity, was an interesting character,
but his attempt was futile. In Christian annals he is
branded as "the apostate." The emperors who followed
favored the Church more and more. One of them,
GRATIAN, withdrew all imperial support from the public

*The War of
Doctrines
in the
Church.*

Its Effect.

---

* A remarkable illustration of this are our words "Pagan," which
means "dweller in a village," and "Heathen," "dweller on the heath"
or "country." Christianity made its way very slowly among the country
people. Hence "Paganism" and "Heathenism" are used to signify the
non-Christian religions of the ancient world

worship of the heathen gods. In A.D. 392 Theodosius
issued an edict forbidding all practice of the old religion.
This date marks the formal downfall of paganism and
the victory of Christianity in the Roman world. At the
same time, this emperor exalted the orthodox doctrine;
he forbade and punished Arianism and all other false
teachings of the true faith. He practically made Christianity the religion of the empire. Henceforth bishops
and emperors joined hands for the rule of the Roman
world.

568. **Union of Empire and Church.**—Let us stop a
moment to consider what this meant. In the ancient
world, the part of religion was to serve the state. It was
one of the elements of public life which made up the
state. The ruler was the head of the religious system.
But Christianity had grown up outside public life; it
obeyed no earthly ruler; Jesus Christ, the son of God,
was its supreme master. Hence, in uniting with the
state, it came in as an equal, nay, rather, as representing
a Lord to whom the emperor, too, must bow. Therefore,
the union of Christianity and the empire brought with it
the victory of the Church over the empire. Before the
authority of its Christ there could be no equal power.
Hence, this moment in history reveals to us that we are
approaching the border of a new age. The ancient world
is passing away.

The position occupied by the Church is illustrated by the famous
"penance" of Theodosius He had been stirred by a rebellious act
of a mob in the city of Thessalonica to order the massacre of the
inhabitants. At least seven thousand people perished. Ambrose,
the bishop of Milan, was horrified by this crime. When Theodosius
approached the church to worship, he was met by the bishop, who

forbade him entrance and laid before him the conditions on which God's pardon could be obtained. Taking off his royal robes, he must appear in the church as a penitent and beg for mercy from God. The emperor submitted, and, after eight months of probation, Ambrose absolved him from guilt and restored him to the communion of the Church

REVIEW EXERCISES. 1. What is the meaning of bishop, diocese, Orthodoxy, pagan, New Rome, labarum? 2. For what are the following famous : Ambrose, Gratian, Athanasius, Julian, Mithra? 3. What is the date of the Edict of Toleration, of the Council of Nicæa?

COMPARATIVE STUDIES. 1. What circumstances and conditions existed at this time to justify and make possible the despotism which did not exist in the time of Augustus? 2. Compare the position of Christianity in the state under Constantine to that of religion in the ancient oriental states (§§ 34).

SELECT LIST FOR READING. 1. Diocletian's System : Its Success. Jones, pp. 354-362. 2. Diocletian's Reorganization of (a) The Army, Jones, pp. 365-369 (b) The Finances, Jones, pp 369-372. (c) Espionage of Officials, Jones, pp 372-373. 3. Constantine's Attitude toward Christianity. Jones, pp 385-386, 388-389 4. A New Capital. Jones, pp 389-390. 5. The Tax System and Municipal Administration. Jones, pp 392-396. 6. The New Social Orders. Jones, pp. 396-398.

TOPICS FOR READING AND ORAL REPORT. 1. The Reorganization of the Empire. Morey, ch 28, Botsford, pp 278-280, 285-288; Merivale, ch 70, Gibbon, pp 91-95. 132-143; Seignobos, pp 390-392, 406-409 2. Constantine and Christianity. Munro, p 175 (source); Botsford, pp. 282-283; Merivale, ch 71, Gibbon, pp 120-240 3 The Edicts of the Emperors in Relation to Christianity. Munro, pp 174-176 (sources), Gibbon, pp. 118-119 4. The Council of Nicæa. Seignobos, pp. 400-401. 5. Julian and Pagan Learning. Merivale, ch. 73; Seignobos, pp. 412-413; Gibbon, ch 12. 6. Theodosius. Merivale, pp. 616-623; Seignobos, pp 416-420; Gibbon, pp 207-221. 7. Constantinople and Rome. Munro, pp 236-237 (source); Gibbon, pp. 123-132; Botsford, pp. 283-285; Merivale, pp 587-590; Seignobos, pp 403-404 8. Society in the Fourth Century. Davis, An Outline History of the Roman Empire, pp 192-195.

9.—THE BREAKING UP OF THE ROMAN EMPIRE AND THE END OF THE ANCIENT PERIOD

A.D. 395-800

569. The Last Four Centuries of Rome.—The four centuries A.D. 400-800 form the last great era of transition in the history of the ancient world. Everything was in confusion; everywhere ancient races were yielding to fresh and vigorous peoples, old and established forms of organization were breaking down and new institutions were forming to correspond to the new life. The struggle was long, the changes slow in taking place, but the end was the transformation of the old world into the Middle Age.

BIBLIOGRAPHY *

For bibliography for advanced students and teachers, see Appendix I.

CHURCH. *The Beginning of the Middle Ages.* Scribners. Not a new book, but by an admirable scholar and of permanent value for the period A D. 400–800.

DILL. *Roman Society in the Last Century of the Roman Empire* Macmillan An interesting and helpful work, particularly for teachers.

EMERTON. *Introduction to the Middle Ages.* Ginn and Co The clearest and the most illuminating account of the transitional period.

ROBINSON. *History of Western Europe.* Ginn and Co. An excellent book, especially strong on the social elements of the history.

THATCHER AND SCHWILL. *A General History of Europe.* Scribners. The early chapters have a full and spirited account of the decline of the empire and the rise of the barbarian kingdoms.

570. The Barbarian Deluge.—The death of Theodosius placed the administration of the empire in the hands of his two sons. ARCADIUS received the eastern

* For previous bibliographies, see §§ 5a, 89a, 338a, 481.

portion, HONORIUS the west Both were young and incapable. Meanwhile the flood of Germanic invasion
which in the course of the following century was to overwhelm the fairest provinces of the western empire had
already begun. The Visigoths (West Goths), fleeing
before the Huns, who had already conquered the Ostrogoths (East Goths) settled for a time in Dacia, but
with the consent of the Roman officers they crossed the
Danube in the reign of Valens. Feeling misused by
their hosts, they rose in rebellion and in the bloody battle
of Adrianople (378 A.D.) they slew the emperor himself
and destroyed his army. The best that Theodosius could
do was to leave them in Mœsia where only his strong arm
restrained their further movements. Meanwhile, Vandals, Suevi, Burgundians, Alamanni and Franks burst
into the western provinces. The very year of the death Visigoths.
of Theodosius (A.D. 395), the Visigoths rose under Alaric, their chieftain, and marched into Greece. Seven
years later they attacked Italy. Stil'i-cho, the general of
Honorius, successfully resisted them, until, out of jealousy and fear, he was murdered by his royal master.
Then Al'a-ric was able to overrun Italy and even to capture Rome (A.D. 410). It was in this crisis that the Roman legions departed from Britain, leaving it exposed to
the attacks of the Picts and Scots. The Suevi had pene- Vandals.
trated into Spain, where they were followed by the Vandals. Upon the death of Alaric, the Visigoths left Italy
and moved westward into Spain, where they set up a kingdom (A.D. 412) which was to last for three hundred years.
The Vandals retired before them into Africa (A.D. 429),
where they captured Carthage ten years later and therein
established a kingdom under their shrewd and enter-

prising leader Gai'ser-ic. As if this were not enough, the cause of this tremendous upheaval of the German tribes now appeared on the scene in the advance of the Huns, a people of alien race and strange manners, wild savage warriors, rushing down out of the far northeast from their homes in Central Asia. Under their king, At'ti-la, they were united and organized into a formidable host, which included also Germans and Slavs. Attila had no less a purpose than to overthrow the Roman empire and set up a new Hunnish state upon its ruins. "Though a barbarian, Attila was by no means a savage. He practised the arts of diplomacy, often sent and received embassies and respected the international laws and customs which then existed." After ravaging the east as far as the Euphrates, he turned to the west, crossed the Rhine and invaded Gaul. There he was met by an imperial army under Aetius and was defeated and turned back in a fierce struggle at the "Catalaunian Fields" (Châlons) in A D. 451, which is justly regarded as one of the decisive battles of history. The next year he penetrated into Italy and the destruction of Rome seemed imminent, but mysteriously the heathen king stayed his advance on the receipt of the message from Pope Leo the Great: "Thus far and no farther." In 453 A.D. he died, and with his death his vast empire dissolved and the Hunnish peril was over.

571. Weaklings on the Throne.—The emperors during this period were weak men and ineffective rulers, often set up and always upheld by their armies, which were made up almost entirely of Germans and led by men of the same race. Stilicho was a Vandal. Ric'i-mer, another imperial general, was a Suevian. The emperors

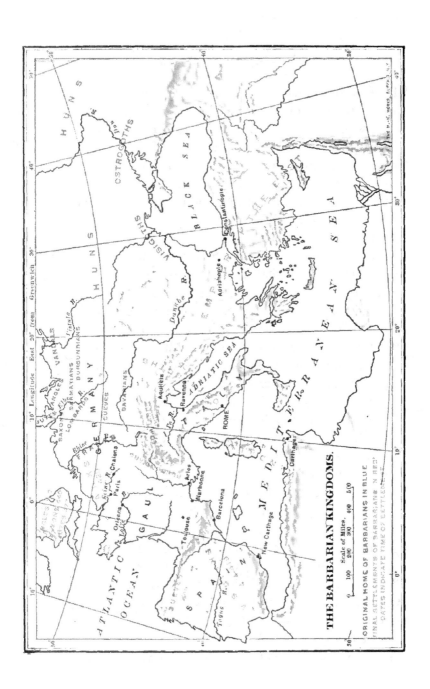

THE BARBARIAN KINGDOMS.

Scale of Miles.

ORIGINAL HOME OF BARBARIANS IN BLUE
FINAL SETTLEMENTS OF BARBARIANS IN RED
DATES INDICATE TIME OF SETTLEMENT

of the west emphasized still more their importance by placing the seat of government at Ra-ven'na, an almost inaccessible fortress on the Adriatic sea. The rest of Italy might suffer from the marches and contests of rival armies, while they were secure. Thus they beheld, in A.D. 455, the capture and sack of Rome by Gaiseric, the Vandal king of Africa, repeated in A.D. 472 by Ricimer. Following Honorius, a succession of nine weaklings kept up a pretence of imperial rule, until ROMULUS AUGUSTU-LUS, a mere boy, was set upon the throne. His Ger- man mercenaries, irritated by a refusal to grant them lands on which to settle, took as their leader O'do-va'car, the Rugian, captured the emperor and forced him to resign his office (A.D. 476). Then the imperial insignia were sent to the emperor of the east, ZENO, who thus be- came sole emperor and appointed Odovacar governor of Italy. In fact the latter ruled Italy as a king, while, as we have seen (§ 570), other parts of the west did not even formally acknowledge the emperor's authority. For this reason the year A.D. 476 is often regarded as a turning point in the history of Rome as marking the fall of the Western Empire.

Fall of Western Empire.

572. Ostrogoths in Italy.—But peace was still far off. The Ostrogoths, who lived an unsettled and warring life in the Danubian provinces of the eastern emperor, set out, under their leader, The-od'o-ric, to contest with Odo-vacar the possession of Italy. The struggle ended with Theodoric as victor and king of Italy. He ruled it for more than thirty years (A.D. 493–526), wisely and pros-perously. "He restored the aqueducts and walls of many cities, repaired the roads, drained marshes, re-opened mines, cared for public buildings, promoted agriculture, established markets, preserved the peace, administered justice strictly and enforced the laws. By intermarriages and treaties he tried to maintain peace between all the neighboring German kingdoms, that they might not mutually destroy each other." * Nominally a subject of the emperor, he was in reality sole lord of Italy.

573. Influence of Rome on Invaders.—It must not be thought that these waves of barbarian invasion completely shattered the structure of Roman politics and society. Such attacks on the borders had been going on for centuries. Multitudes of Germans had already been settled in the provinces. The armies were almost entirely made up of them. They were found in numbers in the offices of the imperial administration and in close touch with the court of the emperor. Not only had the splendor and the strength of the empire, its civilization and its wealth, attracted them, but they had been deeply influenced by it. Many of them had been converted to Christianity. We can, therefore, understand the famous saying of one Gothic chieftain, that once, in his youth, he had the ambition to overthrow the Roman power, but now his highest ambition was to sustain the law and order of Rome by the swords of the Goths. Accordingly, the moment these invaders reached their goal, they fell into the ways of Rome. They came not to destroy, but to enter into the Roman heritage. They were proud to be made the bulwark and support of its civilization and even of its throne. Thus, it was not long before the superior culture, the organizing and civilizing power of old Rome, worked them over and they settled

* Thatcher and Schwill, *A General History of Europe*, p. 27.

down to maintain the most substantial parts of the imperial structure. This appears most clearly in their laws, which were gathered up into codes that show the deep influence of Roman law.

574. The Imperial Reaction.—With the passing of the fifth century, the empire, sorely smitten in the storms of barbarian invasion, raised its head and asserted its ancient authority over the Roman world. A series of able rulers in the east prepared the way for the brilliant and vigorous reign of JUSTINIAN (A D. 527–565). Under him the imperial armies were again victorious, and territories lost for a time were again united to the empire. His able generals were Belisarius, a Thracian, and Narses, an Armenian; under their skilful administration and admirable generalship, the army was reorganized and led out successfully to recover lost territory. In A.D. 534 Africa was won back from the Vandals. In 553, after a long and fiercely contested struggle, Italy was rescued from the Ostrogoths. The Visigoths were deprived of parts of Spain. The German tribes on the Danube, as well as the Avars, who were related to the Huns, were kept in check. The Persians in the east were less successfully resisted.

Justinian

Military Achievements.

575. Peaceful Victories.—The achievements of Justinian in more peaceful spheres were equally splendid. He was occupied with building, with law and theology, with commerce and manufactures, as well as with war. In architecture and painting he is renowned for the wonderful cathedral of St. Sophia in Constantinople. "When one enters into this church to pray," says a contemporary of the great emperor, "one feels at once that it is not the work of human power and industry, but rather the work of God himself; and the spirit, rising up to heaven, understands that here God is quite near and that he rejoices in the dwelling-place which he himself has chosen." In law, he is immortalized in the code which bears his name. To do away with the inconsistencies and contradictions which existed among the laws of the empire, he appointed a commission with Tribonian at its head

The Code of Justinian. to collect, harmonize and arrange them The result was the famous Code of Justinian. "Besides the laws, the opinions, explanations and decisions of famous judges were collected (§ 549). As in the practice of law to-day, much regard was had for precedent and decisions of similar cases, and these were brought together from all quarters in a collection called the Digest (Pandects). For the use of the law students, a treatise on the general principles of Roman law was prepared, which was called the Institutes Justinian carefully kept the laws which he himself promulgated, and afterward published them under the title of Novellæ." *

576. The Continued Influence of the Empire.—Thus once more, under the guidance of Justinian, the Roman empire proved itself a power in the earth. And though its newly recovered provinces were soon lost, it long continued on its way a light and a fruitful source of culture to the world. The wisdom of Constantine's choice of New Rome for its capital was proved. Behind its impregnable walls, the city was able to bid defiance to barbarian assailants and to send forth again and again

Centred in Constantinople. its armies to regain its lost territories. Its unrivalled commercial advantages drew irresistibly the trade of the world, and riches continued to flow into it, while learning

* Thatcher and Schwill, *A General History of Europe*, p. 36.

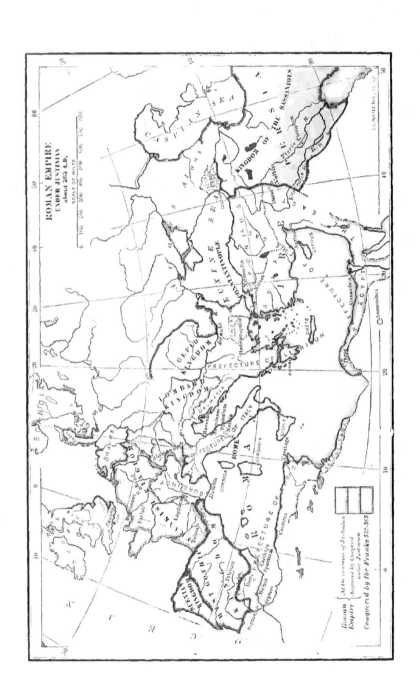

ROMAN EMPIRE
UNDER JUSTINIAN
about 565 A.D.

SCALE OF MILES
100 200 300 400 500 600 700 800

Roman { At the accession of Justinian
Empire { Acquired by Conquest
         under Justinian

Conquered by the Franks 537-565

FROM THE HISTORY OF THE WORLD. BY PERMISSION OF DODD, MEAD & CO.

CHRIST ENTHRONED : BYZANTINE ART

and culture found refuge and encouragement within its bulwarks. When the west succumbed to barbarian invasions and within its borders Roman civilization faded out and disappeared, it was revived and renewed by the influences which went forth from the eastern capital. Its citizens were alert and progressive, combining the gifts of Greek and Roman; its palaces were many and magnificent. Above all, it was the centre of a Christian life and thought, which transformed the hordes of eastern and northern barbarians that settled on its borders. A sense of nationality was aroused among the motley populations that fell under its spell; Byzantine imperialism, by infusing ancient Græco-Roman forms with the Christian spirit brought to the support of the state the fanaticism hitherto existent only for the church.

577. The New Persian Peril.—The occasion for this alliance was the advance to the Mediterranean and even to Cyrene of the great Sassanid monarch, Chosroes (Kŏs'-rōz), who threatened to extirpate both the Græco-Roman state and the Christian religion. The hero of a war which assumed the character of a religious crusade was HERACLIUS (A.D. 610–641) who drove the Persians back into the interior of Asia. His triumph, however, was brief. At this point a new religion appeared in the orient and was spread by force of arms throughout the eastern world. This was Mohammedanism.

578. Mohammed.—In far Arabia, on the southwestern side, near the Red sea, lay the city of Mecca, a sacred shrine of Arabian heathenism and a centre of trade for the wandering tribes of the desert. Here, about A.D. 570, was born, in poverty but of a noble family, Mohammed, who was to be the founder of a religious and a political power of wide extent and influence. As he grew up and came somewhat in contact with the world without, he became deeply impressed with the idolatry and wicked practices of his people. Of a highly sensitive nature, perhaps in early life a prey to some nervous disease, he felt himself in a vision called to be the prophet of Allah, the supreme god of the Arabs. After long trial and struggle, in the course of which, in 622 A.D., occurred the flight (He-gi′ra)* from Mecca to Me-di′na, the Arabs were won for his doctrine. Mohammed founded a church, and his utterances, which Allah commissioned him to speak, were gathered into a sacred book, the Koran, the law and gospel of his followers. He claimed to be the supreme prophet of God, and, therefore, all men were called upon to obey his word. To the emperor and to the Persian king he sent his messengers calling for submission to God and his prophet. When he died (A.D. 632), his followers were ready to go forth to the conquest of the world on behalf of the true faith.

His New Faith.

579. Spread of Mohammedanism.—Despite the vigor of Heraclius the fanaticism of the Mohammedans carried all before it. Syria and Egypt were lost. A Mohammedan capital was established at Damascus, from which the successors of the prophet, called Caliphs, ruled over a wide empire that included Persia, Arabia, Syria and Egypt. They entered Asia Minor, and in A.D. 673 appeared before the walls of Constantinople. They were repulsed, but the empire had forever lost its eastern provinces.

* His followers still use this date as a point for reckoning time as we do the birth of Christ.

Filled with missionary zeal and warlike fury, the Mohammedans pressed westward along the northern coast of Africa and added it to their empire   Thence they crossed over into Spain, and in A.D. 711 overthrew the kingdom of the Visigoths (§ 570). From there they advanced into Gaul.   It seemed as though the western Roman world, like the eastern, was to fall into their power.   But the force that held them in check had been growing strong during these same centuries on Gallic soil.   This was the kingdom of the Franks, to the history of which we now turn.

580. The Franks.—The Franks had advanced but slowly into the empire, appearing first on the lower Rhine.   Thus they kept in touch with their German brethren and renewed their native vigor by constant additions from the old stock.   In A.D. 481 a petty tribal king, Clovis, united the Frankish tribes under his authority, defeated a Roman governor and took possession of upper Gaul.   From here he pushed eastward and conquered the Alamanni.   Still unsatisfied, he drove the Visigoths from southern Gaul into Spain and overcame the Burgundians to the southeast.   At his death, in A.D. 511, the kingdom of the Franks stretched from the Pyrenees and the ocean to beyond the Rhine.   His sons extended the kingdom eastward in Germany to a point beyond the farthest conquests of the Romans.   In time this territory was divided up between members of the royal house, and two kingdoms appeared, Austrasia in the east and Neustria in the west.

Kingdom of Clovis.

581. Rise of Mayor of the Palace.—The Frankish nobility, like many ancient aristocracies in states just emerging from the tribal conditions (§ 106), succeeded in course of time in gaining more and more power over the king. The way in which this took place, however, was peculiar. An important officer of the royal household was the *major domus,* or "mayor of the palace," through whom admission to the king's presence was secured. The noble families were able to put in this position men from their own body and thus to control the king. The *major domus* possessed royal authority though he did not have the royal name. The kings were mere figureheads, "do-nothing-kings."

A contemporary thus describes them. "Nothing was left to the king except the kingly name, with long hair and flowing beard, he sat on the throne to receive envoys from all quarters, but it was only to give them the answers which he was bidden to give. His kingly title was an empty shadow, and the allowance for his support depended on the pleasure of the mayor of the palace. The king possessed nothing of his own but one poor farm with a house on it, and a scanty number of attendants, to pay him necessary service and respect. He went abroad in a wagon drawn by oxen, and guided by a herdsman in the country fashion, thus was he brought to the palace or to the annual assemblies of the people for the affairs of the realm; thus he went home again. But the government of the kingdom, and all business, foreign or domestic, were in the hands of the mayors of the palace."

582. Charles Martel.—One of the mayors of the palace of the Austrasian kingdom, Pippin by name, conquered Neustria and Burgundy, and when he died, left the domains thus gained to his son, Charles Martel (A D. 714), his successor in the mayoral office. The new ruler confronted the advancing Mohammedans and defeated them near Tours in A D. 732. They retreated into Spain, and, owing to disturbances in the Mohammedan empire,

Battle of Tours.

no further attempt was made to extend their power beyond the Pyrenees. The possible fate of western Christendom, if the victory had been gained by the Mohammedans, has placed the battle of Tours among the world's decisive battles.

583. Growth of the Church.—During these centuries, which had seen the barbarian deluge, the establishment of barbarian kingdoms, the revival of the empire and the rise of Mohammedanism, one imperial institution, the Christian church, had suffered the least and perhaps had gained the most. Since its recognition as the religion of the state, it had advanced rapidly. Its ministers became imperial officials and its religious enactments in its great councils had imperial authority. Among its leaders were men of learning and eloquence, Leaders. whose writings have deeply affected the history of Christian thought. John Chrys'os-tom ("he of the golden Chryso's-tom. mouth") was one of the most powerful preachers of his age (A.D. 347–407). As patriarch of Constantinople, he was the idol of the people for his eloquence and the aversion of the court for his fearless denunciation of vice and hypocrisy. He was twice banished by the emperor. Jerome (about A.D. 346–420) was the most learned Jerome. man of his time. His services to the church are twofold: (1) He translated the Bible into Latin so successfully, that with some modifications his translation, called the Vulgate,* remained the accepted version of the Latin church. (2) He aided powerfully the "monastic" move- Monasti cism. ment. Very early in the history of Christianity its followers, coming into contact with the Roman world that in their eyes was evil and that also persecuted them,

* Latin, *Vulgata, i e.,* "in common use."

were moved to flee from it, to hide in the deserts or other
solitary places, that thus they might escape from temptations and trials, and be enabled to live a worthier life.
The men who followed this impulse were called "as-
cetics." When Christianity became the religion of the
empire, the reason for this mode of life changed somewhat. Now it was thought to be the one means of obtaining a higher kind of goodness; it was a method of
reaching perfection of character. Soon such persons,
who had fled from the world, found that they could better
gain these ends by living together in secluded communities. Men and women had separate establishments;
they were called "monks" and "nuns" respectively.*
All the church leaders praised and encouraged this mode
of life and it soon became immensely popular. Jerome
fervently preached and rigorously practised the monastic
life and succeeded in inducing many wealthy and noble
women to take it up. Such persons refused to marry, devoted their wealth to charity, ate coarse and scanty food
and dressed in the simplest way. Jerome went so far
as to denounce the study of heathen literature, even the
Augustine. noblest works of antiquity. The greatest of the Christian leaders of the age was Augustine, bishop of Hippo
in Africa (A.D. 354–430). Trained in the best culture of
the day, he devoted his powerful mind to the defence
and upbuilding of orthodox Christianity. He wrote innumerable books, the greatest of which was *The City of
God*. This book was inspired by the capture of Rome by
Alaric (§ 570), and compared the splendid city of the
empire, now fallen, with the true spiritual capital of

---

* The words "monk," "monastery" and "monasticism" come from
the Greek word *monos*, meaning "alone," "separate."

mankind, the Christian church. Its eloquence and its logic, its splendid survey of the past, and its prophetic insight into the future have given this work a place among the classics of all time.

584. Increased Importance of the Roman Church.— In the general progress of the church especial prominence was secured to the church and bishop of Rome. In the troubles that fell upon Italy this church was foremost in asserting the power of Christianity and in representing its spirit. Its bishops were the friends and helpers of the oppressed, the fearless opponents of injustice and cruelty. They also secured recognition for their own claims to superior position among Christian churches (§ 555). Leo I, the Great (A D. 440–461), Leo the Great. obtained an imperial decree (A.D. 445) commanding all the bishops of the west to recognize the supreme headship of the Roman bishop and to receive his word as law. It is true that a little later a church council declared that Spiritual Authority the bishop of Constantinople was the equal of the Roman and that both were to be superior to all others. But, as the western church, now slowly separating from the eastern, refused to accept this ruling, the Roman supremacy was established. It has been well said that with Leo (§ 570) the history of the papacy began. The Roman bishop became "pope" of the church in the west with the claim to be the head of all Christendom. Likewise, as an Temporal Power. imperial official, he had authority over the territory about Rome, and this he exercised to its fullest extent during the dark years of the fifth century. He "watched over the election of the city officials and directed in what manner the public money should be spent. He had to manage and defend the great tracts of land in different parts cf

Italy which, from time to time, had been given to the bishopric of Rome. He negotiated with the Germans and even directed the generals sent against them." *

Thus, as the empire declined, his power grew in two directions: (1) in spiritual headship over western Christendom; (2) in worldly, or temporal, authority over parts of the empire.

585. Conversion of the Barbarians.—As leader of western Christendom the papacy entered upon the most important task of winning the barbarians for the true faith. Some of these peoples were already Christians, although in the Arian form (§ 567). Others were still pagan. In the work of conversion the popes employed the monks, whose freedom from family ties and zeal for the Gospel made them admirable instruments for this purpose. The leading spirit in this movement was Pope Gregory I (A.D. 590–604), to whom is due the sending of a missionary monk to England. Its result was not merely conversion of the Angles and Saxons who had entered and occupied the land, but their acceptance of the primacy of the pope. Another famous missionary whom the popes sent out was Boniface (A.D. 718), through whose labors the Germans across the Rhine were converted and churches organized among them.

Gregory the Great.

Boniface.

586. The Franks and the Faith.—The Franks, however, were to prove the most potent allies of the popes in their progress toward headship in the west. Clovis embraced orthodox Christianity on the occasion of his victory over the Alamanni (§ 580), and ranged his people on the side of the papacy. Christianity flourished exceedingly among them, although the purity of life among

---

* Robinson, *History of Western Europe*, p. 52.

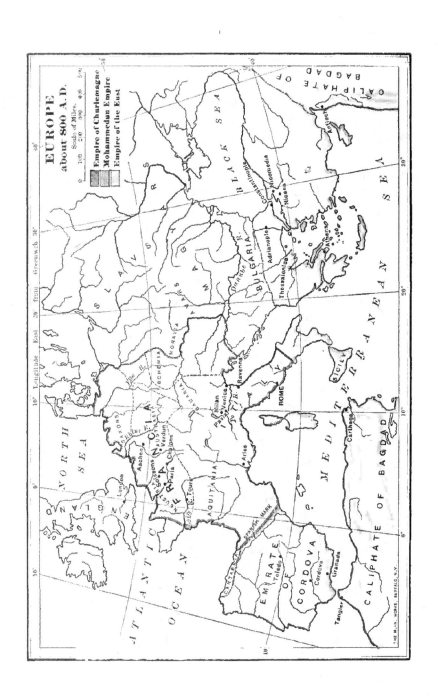

EUROPE
about 800 A.D.

Scale of Miles
0   100   200   300   400   500

■ Empire of Charlemagne
▦ Mohammedan Empire
▤ Empire of the East

the priests and bishops was not on a par with that of the doctrine. When, however, Boniface, having completed his labors among the Germans, sought to reform the Frankish church, he found a helper in Charles Martel. The decisive step was taken in A.D. 748, seven years after this king's death,' when the bishops of Gaul agreed to uphold the orthodox faith and obey the commands of the pope at Rome. Thus the strongest force in the new world was won for Christ and the Roman church. Henceforth the history of the Franks and the papacy were inseparably connected.

Acceptance of Papal Supremacy

When Charles Martel died, his mayorial power was handed on to his sons, Carloman and Pippin. The former soon retired to a monastery, leaving Pippin alone in the office. "Deeming that the time was now ripe, Pippin laid his plans for obtaining the royal title. He sent an embassy to Rome to ask Pope Zacharias who should be king; the one who had the title without the power, or the one who had the power without the title. The pope, who was looking abroad for an ally, replied that it seemed to him that the one who had the power should also be king; and acting on this, Pippin called an assembly of his nobles at Soissons (A D 751), deposed the last phantom king of the older line, and was himself elected and anointed king " *

Pippin, King of the Franks

587. The Lombards.—This alliance between Roman pope and Frankish king soon had practical results. The pope found his temporal authority (§ 584) threatened by the Lombards. This people had entered Italy soon after the Ostrogoths had been overcome by the Emperor Justinian. By A.D. 568 they were in possession of north

* Thatcher and Schwill, *A General History of Europe*, p. 47.

Italy with their capital at Pavia. Then, in separate bands, they spread southward, settling here and there, conquering large parts; only Ravenna, the seat of the emperor's representative, the exarch, and the district about Rome were able to maintain themselves. When, however, the Lombards united under 'a king, the pope found himself hard pressed. He appealed to his over-lord and natural protector, the Emperor LEO, the Isau-rian (A D. 717–740), in the east. But the latter had intro-duced a violent controversy into his realm by command-ing the removal from Christian churches of all images as tending to encourage idolatry. His violence in enforcing this command gained him the name of Iconoclast ("Image-breaker"). The pope refused to obey the de-cree and was supported by the western churches. Thus the fellowship between the two was broken off and no help came from the east. The pope turned to the west and appealed to Pippin to deliver him. "Pippin made two campaigns into Italy and compelled the Lombards to cede to the pope a strip of territory which lay to the south of them (A.D. 755). This marks the beginning of the temporal sovereignty of the pope. He was freed from the eastern emperor, and recognized as the political as well as the ecclesiastical ruler of Rome and its surrounding territory, under the overlordship of Pippin, who had the title of *Patricius*." * The Lombards were made tribu-tary to the Frankish king.

The Pope's Appeal to the Eastern Emperor.

Pippin His Savior.

588. Accession of Charlemagne.—His two sons, Carlo-man and Carl, succeeded to the kingdom on Pippin's death (A D. 768) The former's early death left Carl sole king. He is the first prominent figure of the times

* Thatcher and Schwill, *A General History of Europe,* p 130.

of whom we know something distinct and detailed. The reason for this is not far to seek. With him the old world passed away and the new world stepped into its place. To later ages he was Carl the Great, *Carolus Magnus,* whence the common form, Charlemagne. His personal appearance is described to us by his contemporaries

589. Appearance of Charlemagne.—We copy the admirable condensation of this description made by Robinson· "He was tall and stoutly built: his face was round, his eyes were large and keen, his nose somewhat above the common size, his expression bright and cheerful. Whether he stood or sat, his form was full of dignity; for the good proportion and grace of his body prevented the observer from noticing that his neck was rather short and his person somewhat too stout . . . His step was firm and his aspect manly, his voice was clear but rather weak for so large a body He was active in all bodily exercises, delighted in riding and hunting, and was an expert swimmer His excellent health and his physical alertness and endurance can alone explain the astonishing swiftness with which he moved about his vast realm and conducted innumerable campaigns in widely distant regions in startlingly rapid succession."

590. His Relations with the Pope.—With the details of the organizing activity of Charlemagne or with the way in which he corrected and expanded the frontiers of his empire, the student of ancient history does not need to acquaint himself. The king's relations to Italy and the pope alone require attention A noteworthy feature in this connection is the conquest and Christianizing of the Saxons. The troubles of the papacy with the Lombards continued in his time, until, on the appeal of the pope, he entered Italy, conquered the Lombards, made himself their king (A.D. 774) and restored to the pope his territories. When a party in Rome sought to deprive Pope Leo III of his temporal authority and drove him from the city, he again appealed to Charlemagne, who reinstated him. A service of thanksgiving was held in St. Peter's Church on Christmas Day, A D. 800, at which **Crowned Roman Emperor.** Charlemagne was present. While the king was kneeling before the altar, the pope placed upon his head the imperial crown and hailed him "Emperor of the Romans."

591. Crowning of Charlemagne.—A Frankish chronicle gives the following reasons for this act which seems to have taken Charlemagne by surprise.

"The name of emperor had ceased among the Greeks, for they were enduring the reign of a woman [Irene], wherefore it seemed good both to Leo, the apostolic pope, and to the holy fathers [the bishops] who were in council with him, and to all Christian men, that they should name Charles, king of the Franks, as emperor. For he held Rome itself, where the ancient Cæsars had always dwelt, in addition to all his other possessions in Italy, Gaul and Germany Wherefore, as God had granted him all these dominions, it seemed just to all that he should take the title of emperor, too, when it was offered to him at the wish of all Christendom."

592. What This Act Means.—This assumption of the **Revival.** imperial title by Charlemagne has two aspects. (1) In one sense it is only a continuation of the past. The years of confusion in the west were over and a well-ordered state came into existence, embracing in its unity the old imperial provinces, and ruling in the name of Rome, a name hallowed by centuries of splendid history. So it was looked upon at the time. Charlemagne was regarded as a successor of the line of eastern emperors.* But (2) in a more important sense it was entirely new. A new race, a barbarian people, upheld the imperial

* The Empress Irene was on the throne, and it was regarded as a disgrace that the imperial seat should be occupied by a woman.

throne and were represented in its occupant. The old
Roman blood and institutions were swallowed up in the
Teutonic. Even more significant is the union of this
new imperial people with the Christian church. Moreover, in the east the Semitic Arabs, inspired with zeal
for a new faith, had forced back almost to the walls of
Constantinople the eastern empire, now shorn of its ancient strength. Such a breaking up of the past institu- A New Era.
tions and such a combination of new historical forces
introduces us to a new order and indicates that the ancient world has passed away and another world is rising
on its ruins.

REVIEW EXERCISES. 1. What do Alaric, Attila, Gaiseric,
Theodoric, Clovis stand for? 2. Why are the following im-
portant: Catalaunian Fields, Code of Justinian, exarch,
Tours? 3. What has rendered the following famous: Jerome,
Charles Martel, Gregory, Justinian, Stilicho, Augustine? 4.
What is the date of the fall of the Western Empire, of the
death of Mohammed, of the battle of Tours, of the crowning
of Charlemagne?

COMPARATIVE STUDIES. 1. Compare Charlemagne and Constantine. 2. Compare the origin and growth of Mohammedanism and of Christianity. 3. In what was the relation of
the barbarians to the empire like that of Philip of Macedon
to the Greeks (§§ 272, 278, 279)? 4. Compare the rise of the
Franks with the rise of the Roman state.

SELECT LIST FOR READING. 1. Julian, the Last of Constantine's House. Jones, pp. 403–408. 2. The Arian Controversy.
Jones, pp. 409–417. 3. The Invasions of the Empire. Jones,
pp. 420–424, 429–434 4. The Barbarians as Makers of History.
Boniface, Jones, pp. 436–438, Attila, Jones, pp 440–443; Ricimer
and Odovacar, Jones, pp 444–446 5. The Decay of the Middle Class. Dill, Last Century of the Western Empire, pp. 245–
281. 6. Roman Feeling about Barbarian Invasions. Dill,
pp. 303–345. 7. Relations of Romans and Invaders. Dill, pp.
346–382.

TOPICS FOR READING AND ORAL REPORT. 1. The Germans and Their Culture. Laing, pp 401–409 (source), Seignobos, pp 440, 441; Botsford, pp 293–296 2. The Visigoths and Alaric. Seignobos, pp. 421–425, 442, Gibbon, pp. 226–238, Botsford, pp 297–303. 3. The Ostrogoths and Theodoric. Botsford, pp. 312–315, Seignobos, pp 444–446 4. The Vandals and Gaiseric. Botsford, pp 303–306, Seignobos, pp 429, 442 5. The Conquest of Britain. Botsford, pp 321–322 6. The Huns and Attila. Merivale, pp. 648–651, Seignobos, pp. 427–429; Gibbon, pp. 200–203, 251–263 7. The Lombards. Gibbon, pp. 378–383, Botsford, pp. 319–321, Seignobos, pp 446–447 8. Theodoric. Gibbon, ch 19 9. Justinian and the Eastern Empire. Gibbon, chs 20–22, Seignobos, pp. 449–456. 10. The Decay of Society—Causes and Course. Seignobos, pp. 432–438. 11. The Fathers of the Church. Morey, p 324 12. Rise of the Roman Church. Gibbon, pp 383–384, Seignobos, pp. 460–465 13. The Iconoclasts. Gibbon, pp 428–432 14. Monasticism. Seignobos, pp. 465–467 15. Mohammed. Gibbon, pp 451–465, Seignobos, pp 467–471 16. The Victories of Mohammedanism. Gibbon, pp 465–483, Seignobos, pp 471–475 17. The Rise of the Franks. Seignobos, pp. 443–444, Botsford, pp 322–328, Gibbon, pp 274–277 18. Charlemagne. Seignobos, pp 479–485, Botsford, pp 328–331.

GENERAL REVIEW OF PART III, DIVISIONS 7-9

44 B C–A D 800

TOPICS FOR CLASS DISCUSSION. 1. Follow the different steps in the relation of the emperor to the institutions of the republic (§§ 483, 484, 496, 506, 512, 515, 536, 546, 549, 556, 557). 2. Progress in the administrative organization of the empire (§§ 507, 537, 539, 546, 556, 576) 3. External causes tending to weaken the empire (§§ 487, 538, 552, 553, 570, 573, 577). 4. Internal causes tending to weaken the empire (§§ 496, 498, 499, 523, 539, 551, 560, 568, 571). 5. The problem of the succession in its various stages (§§ 499, 512, 536. 546, 556) 6. Stages in the organization of Christianity (§§ 527, 545, 555, 567, 568, 583, 584) 7. Important dates in the history of the empire. 8. A chronological list of the invasions of the barbarians. 9. Trace the gradual separation of the empire into an eastern and a western part (§§ 556, 562, 564, 565, 567, 570, 571, 575, 584, 586, 587)

PICTURE EXERCISES. 1. With Plate XXV before you, compare the figures and note differences of artistic and historical importance. 2. On Plates XXVII and XXVIII compare coins 6 and 8 with coins 9 and 14. What important differences are seen? 3. Compare coins 11 and 13. Bearing in mind whose coins these are, what historical conclusions can you draw? 4. Compare Plates XXXVIII and XL to register the advance or decline in artistic character. 5. Why have Plates XX and XL decided differences in subject and style? 6. On Plate XXX study head 6, does this style suit the man? How? 7. Why are the illustrations of Plates XXXVI, XXXVII and XXXIX characteristic of Rome? 8. What does Plate XXXIII tell us of Roman life in the first century A D ? 9. Find other pictures like Plate XXXI. 10. Wherein does Plate XXXIV differ from Plate XIX.

SUBJECTS FOR WRITTEN PAPERS. 1. The City of Rome under the Empire. Merivale, ch. 79 2. The Persecutions of the Christians. Munro, pp 164-176 (sources), Univ. of Pa. Translations, Vol IV, No 1, Gibbon, ch 9, Seignobos, pp. 366–372 3. The History of Roman Law. Gibbon, ch. 23. 4. Rome in Juvenal's Time from His Own Report. Laing, pp. 433-449 (translation). 5. What the German Gave to the Roman and Received from Him. See Select List § 592. 6. An Account of the Parthian Kingdom, Its History and Relations to Rome. Encyclopedia Britannica, Article. "Persia" (the part dealing with Parthia). 7. A Letter from Pliny to Tacitus Describing His Own Life and Activities, Interests, Pleasures, etc. Laing, pp. 451-471 (contains translations of Pliny's letters), The Atlantic, June, 1886, Thomas, Roman Life under the Cæsars, ch 14 8. The Gifts of Rome to Human Civilization. Morey, ch 30. 9. An Account of the Historical Event Suggested by Plate XXXIII.

CHRONOLOGICAL TABLE

THE ORIENT

B C

?2980–2475. Old Egyptian Kingdom (Capital at Memphis)· Khufu and the Pyramids; rise of Thebes.

?2160–1788. Middle Egyptian Kingdom (Capital at Thebes) feudal organization; Nubia subdued; contact with Crete, internal improvements; coming of the Hyksos.

?2500. Sargon of Accad

?1950. Hammurabi of Babylon, old Babylonian Empire; code of Laws.

1580–1150. Egyptian (New) Empire (Capital mostly at Thebes). the eighteenth dynasty, campaigns in Asia, first great empire in history, commerce with Babylonia, Syria Ægean; Egyptian remains in Crete and Mycenæ, Seti I (conflicts with the Hittites), Ramses II (wars with the Hittites), great hall at Karnak completed, decadence.

745–727 Tiglathpileser III makes Assyria first power of ancient world

722–705 Sargon II Assyria at its height; captivity of Israelites.

705–626 Sennacherib, Esarhaddon, Ashurbanipal Capital at Nineveh; brilliant age of Assyria; cruel wars.

606. Assyrian Empire ends with destruction of Nineveh.

605–562. Nebuchadrezzar (Chaldean or New Babylonian Empire); building of temples, fortifications, palaces. Babylonian captivity of the Jews

539 Babylon becomes Persian province under Cyrus.

ÆGEAN DISTRICT

?2000–1350. Bloom-time of Cretan Age.

1500–1150. Mycenæan civilization at its best.

1000–700 Epic Age.

776. First Olympiad.

750–550 (about). Period of colonization.

750–650 (about). Period of the nobles at Athens

700–500 (about). Cultural development, lyric poetry and philosophy.

683 Yearly archons at Athens.

650–594. Period of the heavy-armed at Athens.

624 (about). Codification of Draco.

594. Reforms of Solon.

560–510. Pisistratid tyranny.

550. Sparta supreme in the Peloponnesus.
508. Reforms of Cleisthenes.

RELATIONS WITH PERSIA AND CARTHAGE, 500–479

499–494 Ionic revolt· Sardis, Lade, Miletus.
492 First Persian attack under Mardonius
490. Second Persian attack under Datis and Artaphernes (Marathon).
487. Choice of archons at Athens by lot.
480. Third Persian attack under Xerxes (Thermopylæ, Artemisium; Athenians withdraw from Athens, Salamis).
480 Himera (Gelon and the Carthaginians).
479 Campaign of Mardonius (Platæa); Mycale.

THE SUPREMACY OF ATHENS, 479–431

477–454. Delian Confederacy
474 Hieron defeats Etruscans off Cumæ.
462. Cimon goes to help Sparta against the Helots; decline of the Areopagus.
459–445. Athenian Land League Tanagra; Œnophyta; The Thirty Years' Truce (445)
445–431. Golden Age of Athens under Pericles the bloom of art and literature

THE PELOPONNESIAN WAR, 431–404

A The Archidamian War, 431–421.

429. Death of Pericles (rise of Cleon)
427. Revolt of Lesbos, surrender of Platæa.
425 Pylos (peace negotiations)
424 Brasidas and the Chalcidice, Delium.
422. Amphipolis. death of Brasidas and Cleon. `
421. Peace of Nicias.

B. Period of the Sicilian Expedition, 421–413

418. Mantinea (Alcibiades and Nicias rivals at Athens).
416. Fall of Melos.
415–413 Sicilian expedition.

C. The Decelean War, 413–404

412. Alliance between Persia and Sparta; revolt of Chios, etc.
411 The Four Hundred at Athens (recall of Alcibiades).
410 Cyzicus (peace negotiations).
407. Notium (retirement of Alcibiades).

406. Arginusæ (peace negotiations and condemnation of Athenian generals).
405 Ægospotami.
404 Surrender of Athens and end of the war.
405-367 Dionysius I, tyrant of Syracuse

THE SUPREMACY OF SPARTA, 404-371

404-403 The Thirty at Athens
401. Expedition of Cyrus (Cunaxa).
399-394 War between Sparta and Persia Agesilaus and Conon (Cnidus).
395-387. Corinthian War: Agesilaus and Iphicrates, peace of Antalcidas (387).
379. Liberation of Thebes (Pelopidas and Epaminondas).
371. Leuctra (end of the Spartan supremacy).

THE LEADERSHIP OF THEBES, 371-362

371-362. Theban invasions of the Peloponnesus; Pelopidas in Thessaly and Macedonia.
362. Mantinea (death of Epaminondas and decline of Thebes).

THE PERIOD OF PHILIP OF MACEDON, 362-336

357-355. Social War
356-346. Sacred War Philip and Demosthenes; peace of Philocrates (346)
345-337. Timoleon of Syracuse
338. Chaeronea (end of Greek freedom).

ALEXANDER AND THE PERSIANS, 336-323

336-323. Alexander the Great. Granicus (334), Issus (333); Tyre and Alexandria (332), Arbela (331)

HELLENISTIC PERIOD, 323-146

323-322. Lamian War (death of Demosthenes)
323-301. War of the Diadochi, Ipsus (301)

The Separate Kingdoms

(1) Egypt under the Ptolemies, Ptolemy I, Ptolemy II, Ptolemy III.
(2) Syria under the Seleucidæ Seleucus Nikator, Antiochus III.
(3) Asia Minor kingdoms of Pergamon, Bithynia, Pontus; Rhodes.

    (4) Macedonia: the Antigoni.

    (5) Greece.

289.   Death of Agathocles of Syracuse.

280 (251).   Achæan League (Aratus).

222.   Macedonian supremacy restored (Cleomenes III).

196.   Rome declares Greece free from Macedon.

146.   Destruction of Corinth.

Roman History to the Samnite Wars, 753 (?)–343 (?)

753 (?).   Founding of Rome.

510 (?).   Establishment of the Republic two consuls, two quæstors.

494 (?).   First secession two plebeian tribunes, two plebian ædiles.

451 (?)–449 (?).   Decemvirate; twelve tables; second secession.

445 (?).   Canuleian law.

444 (?).   Military tribunes with consular power.

443 (?).   Two censors.

396.   Capture of Veii

390.   Sack of Rome by the Gauls (Allia River).

367.   Licinian laws; prætor; two curule ædiles.

Conquest and Organization of Italy, 343–264

343–341.   First Samnite War.

340–338.   Great Latin War

326–304   Second Samnite War. (Caudine Forks, 321).

300   Valerian law

298–290.   Third Samnite War (Sentinum, 295).

287.   Hortensian law

281–272.   War with Tarentum and Pyrrhus: Heraclea, Asculum, Ben-
      eventum.

First Punic War, 264–241

260   Mylæ

256   Ecnomus (Regulus in Africa)

255–241   War in Sicily.

241.   Ægates Islands. Rome gains Sicily; Sardinia and Corsica (later).

225–222.   Extension of Italy to the Alps

Second Punic War, 218–201

218.   Ticinus and Trebia.

217.   Trasimenus

216.   Cannæ; Hannibal gets new allies, but Syracuse and Capua are
      recovered by Rome.

218–207.   Constant war in Spain.

207. Metaurus (Hasdrubal).
202. Zama. Rome gains Hither and Farther Spain.

Conquest of the East, 201–133

200–197. Second Macedonian War (Cynoscephalæ).
192–189. War with Antiochus III (Thermopylæ and Magnesia)
171–168. Third Macedonian War (Pydna).
149–146 Third Punic War (Destruction of Carthage)
146. Destruction of Corinth
146. Addition of Africa and Macedonia.
133. Addition of Asia.
133. Surrender of Numantia.

Decline of the Republic, 133–27

133. Reforms of Tiberius Gracchus.
123. Reforms of Gaius Gracchus.
120 (about). Addition of Gallia Narbonensis.
111–105. Jugurthine War (Marius).
102. Addition of Cilicia
102. Marius defeats Teutons at Aquæ Sextiæ.
101. Marius defeats Cimbri at Vercellæ
100. Insurrection of Saturninus and Glaucia (decline of Marius).
91. Attempted reforms of Drusus.
91–88 Social War (Sulla).
88. Sulpician laws.
88–84. First Mithridatic War (Cinna and Marius at Rome).
82–79 Sulla's dictatorship: proscriptions and constitution.
81. Gallia Cisalpina added.
79–72 Sertorian War in Spain.
73–71 War of the Gladiators (Spartacus).
70. Consulship of Pompey and Crassus (overthrow of Sulla's constitution).
67. Pompey clears the sea of pirates (Gabinian law).
66–63. Pompey ends the third Mithridatic War (Manilian law). Provinces added: Pontus and Bithynia, Syria, Cilicia (reorganized and enlarged), Crete.
63. Consulship of Cicero (Conspiracy of Catiline).
60. First Triumvirate (Pompey, Cæsar, Crassus).
59 Consulship of Cæsar.
58–51 Cæsar's conquest of Gaul.
56. Conference of Luca.

52. Pompey "sole consul" (Clodius and Milo)
49-45 War between Cæsar and the republicans· Dyrrachium, Pharsalus [Zela], Thapsus, Munda; Cæsar supreme
44. Death of Cæsar.
43 Second Triumvirate (Antony Octavian, Lepidus).
42 Battle of Philippi
31 Battle of Actium

THE ROMAN EMPIRE: AUGUSTUS TO THEODOSIUS 27 B C -395 A D.

The Julian Cæsars

27 B C.-14 A D Augustus: establishment of the principate, the bloom-time of literature.
Provinces added: Ægypt, Mœsia, Pannonia, Rhætia, Noricum, Galatia, Lusitania.

A D.
14-37. Tiberius (Crucifixion of Christ).
37-41. Caligula.

Claudian Cæsars

41-54 Claudius (Britain added).
54-68. Nero.
68-69. Disputed succession.

The Flavian Cæsars

69-79. Vespasian (Destruction of Jerusalem, 70).
79-81. Titus.
81-96. Domitian.

"The Five Good Emperors"

96-98 Nerva.
98-117. Trajan. Provinces added: Arabia, Dacia, Armenia, Mesopotamia, Assyria
117-138 Hadrian
138-161. Antoninus Pius.
161-180 Marcus Aurelius.

Later Emperors

211-217. Caracalla (all freemen become Roman citizens).
270-275. Aurelian (new wall).
284-305. Diocletian (Absolutism).
313. Edict of Milan.

323–337 Constantine sole emperor (further reorganization and council of Nicæa, 325).
378. Adrianople (Visigoths).
395. Final division of the empire (Theodosius).

PERIOD OF TRANSITION, 395–800 A.D.

410 and 455. Sack of Rome by the Visigoths (Alaric, 410); by the Vandals (Gaiseric, 455).
451 Châlons (Attila and the Huns).
476. Odovacar (end of Western Empire).
493. Theodoric (the Ostrogoths) conquers Odovacar.
496. Clovis becomes an orthodox Christian (the Franks).
527–565. Justinian (codification of the law).
622. Hegira of Mohammed
732. Tours (Martel and the Arabs).
800. Charlemagne crowned emperor in the west.

APPENDIX I

BIBLIOGRAPHY FOR ADVANCED STUDENTS AND TEACHERS

I GENERAL WORKS

ANDREWS AND GAMBRILL *Bibliography of History for Schools and Libraries.* Longmans.

BONHAM, ANDREWS AND OTHERS (New England History Teachers Association). *Catalogue of Collection of Historical Materials.* Houghton, Mifflin Co. Information as to maps, charts, pictures, models and other aids to visualizing history.

CUNNINGHAM *Western Civilization in Its Economic Aspects. Ancient Times* Cambridge Univ. Press. Uniquely valuable for its point of view, which is ordinarily overlooked   Covers with special fulness the classical period.

FOSTER, CUSHING AND OTHERS (New England History Teachers Association). *History Syllabus for Secondary Schools.* Heath   An excellent bibliographical aid for teachers   Also useful for class work.

HARPERS *Dictionary of Classical Antiquity* Harper and Bros.

HAZEN, BOURNE AND OTHERS. *Historical Sources in Schools* Macmillan.

HELMOLT. *History of the World.* Vol III, *Western Asia and Egypt;* Vol. IV, *The Mediterranean Countries* Dodd, Mead and Co The most recent and best of the great general histories.

MURRAY'S CLASSICAL ATLAS. For Schools. Edited by G. B. Grundy. London. Murray   Is the most artistic and accurate school atlas published.

SANBORN'S CLASSICAL ATLAS. Edited by J. K. Lord. Boston· Sanborn and Co   A close rival of the Grundy-Murray work.

SEYFFART *Dictionary of Classical Antiquity.* Ed. Nettleship and Sandys. Macmillan.

TOZER. *Classical Geography* (Literature Primers) American Book Co.

II THE EASTERN EMPIRES

Encyclopedia Biblica, edited by Cheyne and Black   4 vols   Macmillan
Dictionary of the Bible, edited by J Hastings. 4 vols   Scribners.
These latest Bible dictionaries have elaborate and valuable articles and maps dealing with the ancient oriental peoples.

HARPER. *Assyrian and Babylonian Literature.* Appletons. A useful collection of accurate translations from these ancient documents.

JACKSON. *Zoroaster.* Macmillan The best account of the founder of the Persian religion.

JASTROW. *The Religion of Babylonia and Assyria.* Ginn and Co. The standard treatise on this subject

McCURDY *History, Prophecy and the Monuments.* 3 vols Macmillan An elaborate survey of the oriental world from the Hebrews as a centre Learned and instructive

MASPERO *History of the Ancient East.* 1 *The Dawn of Civilization.* 2 *The Struggle of the Nations* 3 *The Passing of the Empires.* 3 vols Appletons A most elaborate work by an excellent scholar. Full of illustrations Costly but of great usefulness for school study.

MYRES *The Dawn of History* (Home Univ Library) Henry Holt and Co Especially valuable for the relations established between the land and the people

PATON *The Early History of Syria and Palestine.* Scribners. An admirable little book, well constructed and accurate

PERROT AND CHIPIEZ *History of Art in Ancient Egypt.* 2 vols. *History of Art in Ancient Babylonia and Assyria* 2 vols Dodd, Mead and Co. These are the best works on ancient oriental art, fully illustrated. They are costly, but fully repay constant consultation. The same is true of the other works of these authors.

RAWLINSON. *The Five Great Monarchies of the Ancient Eastern World* 3 vols Scribners Always entertaining and useful, but now largely antiquated by the advance of knowledge.

Records of the Past First Series, 12 vols Second Series, 6 vols (New York Pott) Translations from Egyptian and Babylonian Assyrian documents by various hands. An excellent series

ROGERS. *History of Babylonia and Assyria* 2 vols Eaton and Mains. Besides a good historical survey the book has an elaborate introduction dealing with the history of excavation and the decipherment of inscriptions.

STEINDORFF *The Religion of Ancient Egypt* Putnams An excellent survey by a competent scholar

III THE GREEK STATES

ÆSCHYLUS. Translated by Plumptre D. C. Heath and Co.

ARISTOPHANES Translated by Frere ("Acharnians," "Knights," "Birds," in Morley's Universal Library). Routledge 5 vols.

ARISTOTLE. *On the Constitution of Athens* Translated by Kenyon. Macmillan. *Politics.* Translated by Welldon Macmillan

BECKER *Charicles* Longmans This time-honored scholastic tale of ancient Greece is still useful for reference

BEVAN *The House of Seleucus* 2 vols Arnold A well-written, detailed history of the Seleucid empire

BLUMNER *Home Life of the Ancient Greeks.* Cassell.

BURY. *The Ancient Greek Historians.* Macmillan The best critical appreciation of the less-well-known as well as the famous Greek historians For teachers

CURTIUS. *History of Greece* 5 vols Scribners. See Holm

DAVIDSON. *Education of the Greek People.* Appletons.

DEMOSTHENES. 5 vols Translated by Kennedy. Macmillan. *On the Crown.* Translated by Collier Longmans.

DICKINSON *The Greek View of Life* New Edition. Doubleday, Page and Co. Singularly clear, interesting and instructive.

DIEHL. *Excursions in Greece.* Grevel.

DURUY. *History of Greece* Dana, Estes and Co. Profusely illustrated and written with French clearness and grace. Not, however, the work of a great scholar

EURIPIDES. Translated into prose by Coleridge Bell. In verse by Way. Macmillan.

FREEMAN. *History of Federal Government.* Macmillan. One of Freeman's best works Deals in great detail with the Achæan and Ætolian leagues

GARDNER, E. A. *Ancient Athens* Macmillan The work of an expert in Greek art and archæology.

"   *A Hand-book of Greek Sculpture.* Macmillan.

GRANT. *Greece in the Age of Pericles* Scribners

GULICK. *Life of the Ancient Greeks* Appletons.

HAWES. *Crete, the Forerunner of Greece* Harpers.

HERODOTUS. Translated by Rawlinson, edited by Grant. 2 vols. Scribners.

HOGARTH *Ionia and the East.* Clarendon Press. Lectures on the oriental background of Homer.

"   *Philip and Alexander of Macedon.* Scribners. A stirring exposition of the ideals and achievements of these heroes Especially appreciative of Philip

HOLM. *History of Greece.* 4 vols Macmillan See Curtius Curtius and Holm are very different in point of view and treatment Curtius emphasizes the æsthetic, Holm the political Curtius is the more interesting, Holm is more recent and hence more accurate and satisfactory.

HOMER. *Iliad*. Translated by Lang, Leaf and Myers *Odyssey*. Translated by Butcher and Lang Macmillan Excellent prose versions

JEBB. *Classical Greek Poetry*. Houghton, Mifflin Co

MAHAFFY. *Social Life in Greece*. Macmillan

"   *Greek Life and Thought from Alexander to the Roman Conquest*. Macmillan.

"   *The Silver Age of the Greek World*. Chicago Univ. Press. Largely a reprint of Mahaffy's *Greek World under Roman Sway*.

"   *The Ptolemaic Dynasty* Vol 4 of Petrie's *History of Egypt* Scribners

    Mahaffy's books are stimulating, full of learning, sometimes rather opinionated.

MURRAY, G. *The Rise of the Greek Epic*. New Edition. Clarendon Press. A brilliant work on the Homeric question

PERROT AND CHIPIEZ. *History of Art in Primitive Greece* 2 vols Practically a discussion of Mycenæan Civilization.

PLATO. *Socrates*. A translation of the Apology, Crito and Parts of the Phædo of Plato. Scribners.

SCHUCKARDT *Schliemann's Excavations* Macmillan.

SOPHOCLES *Antigone*. Prose translation by G H Palmer. Houghton, Mifflin and Co *Works* In Prose, translated by Coleridge Bell

SYMONDS. *Studies in the Greek Poets*. Macmillan

THUCYDIDES Translated by Jowett. Clarendon Press.

TSOUNTAS AND MANATT *The Mycenæan Age*. Houghton, Mifflin Co A thorough discussion of recent discoveries in primitive Greece (up to 1897)

WHEELER. *Alexander the Great*. Putnams. The best life of Alexander Well illustrated

XENOPHON *Works* Translated by Dakyns. Macmillan. These are the best translations, but in the Bohn series others may be obtained at less expense

IV. THE EMPIRE OF ROME

ABBOTT. *The Common People of Ancient Rome*. Scribners. A good treatment of a series of related topics, such as "Diocletian's Edict and the Cost of Living," "Corporations," "A Roman Politician "

ANDERSON AND SPIERS *The Architecture of Greece and Rome* Botsford The best volume on this subject.

APPIAN. Translated by White. 2 vols. Macmillan.

ARNOLD. *Roman Provincial Administration.* New Edition. Macmillan. A standard authority

BECKER *Gallus* Longmans. Of the same character as his Charicles

BOTSFORD. *The Roman Assemblies.* Macmillan. A sober, well-informed, detailed treatment

BRYCE *The Holy Roman Empire.* Macmillan. Of great value for the closing epoch of Ancient History.

BURY. *The Later Roman Empire.* 3 vols. Macmillan

CARTER. *The Religious Life of Ancient Rome* Houghton, Mifflin Co. A study in the development of religious consciousness from the foundation of the city until the death of Gregory the Great.

CICERO. *Letters* Translated by Shuckburgh. Bohn.
    "   *Works.* Translated in Bohn's Library.

CUMONT. *The Oriental Religions in Roman Paganism* Open Court Publication Co A fascinating narrative of a great movement.

DAVIS, W S. *Influence of Wealth in Imperial Rome.* Macmillan. Graphic.

DUFF. *Literary History of Rome.* Scribners.

DURUY *History of Rome* 8 vols. Dana Estes and Co. Of the same character as his History of Greece.

FERRERO *The Greatness and Decline of Rome* Putnams. 5 vols. *The Women of the Cæsars.* Century Co. Clever, with many of the qualities of the historical novel; not dependable, however.

FIRTH *Augustus Cæsar.* Putnams. Useful.

FOWLER. *Cæsar.* Putnams.
    An excellent volume in the series "Heroes of the Nations."
    "   *The Religious Experience of the Roman People* Macmillan.
    From the earliest times to the age of Augustus.
    "   *Roman Festivals* Macmillan.

FRIEDLÄNDER. *Roman Life and Manners under the Early Empire.* Translated by Magnus and Freese. 3 vols Dutton and Co. Has long been the standard work on the subject
    "   *Town Life in Ancient Italy.* Translated by Waters. Sanborn. Clear, concrete, picturesque.

GIBBON. *Decline and Fall of the Roman Empire.* Edited by Bury. 7 vols. Scribners.

GREENIDGE. *Roman Public Life.* Macmillan. Fuller than Abbott's Roman Political Institutions; scholarly, valuable.

GREENIDGE. *A History of Rome.* Dutton. The best account of the period from 133 to 105 B.C.

GUHL AND KONER. *Life of the Greeks and Romans.* Scribners.

GWATKIN. *Early Church History to A D* 313. Macmillan. 2 vols.

HEITLAND. *The Roman Republic.* 3 vols Cambridge Univ Press. A recent English work, highly valuable for the period of the revolution

HILL. *Handbook of Greek and Roman Coins.* Macmillan.

HODGKIN. *Italy and Her Invaders.* 7 vols. Clarendon Press.
    "   *Theodoric.* Putnams.
    "   *Charles the Great* Macmillan

HORACE. Translated by Martin. 2 vols. Scribners. Or, into prose by Lonsdale and Lee. Macmillan.

INGE. *Society in Rome under the Cæsars* Scribners.

JOHNSTONE. *Mohammed and His Power.* Scribners. See Macdonald.

JUVENAL. Translated by Gifford. Bohn.

LANCIANI. *Ancient Rome in the Light of Recent Discoveries.* Houghton, Mifflin and Co
    "   *Ruins and Excavations of Ancient Rome.* Houghton, Mifflin and Co.

LECKY. *History of European Morals from Augustus to Charlemagne.* 2 vols. Appletons

LIVY. Translated by Spillan. 4 vols. Bohn

LUCRETIUS Translated into prose by Munro Bell

MACDONALD. *Development of Muslim Theology, Jurisprudence and Constitutional Theory.* Scribners. Johnstone. *Mohammed and His Power.*

    The above two useful works in small compass cover the whole field of Mohammedan history, life and thought.

MARCUS AURELIUS. *Meditations.* Translated with introduction by Rendall. Macmillan.

MAU. *Pompeii, Its Life and Art* Macmillan. The most authoritative work on the subject. Well illustrated

MERIVALE. *History of the Romans under the Empire* 6 vols Appletons. From Augustus to the Antonines. Not a great work, but clear, in full detail and interesting.

MOMMSEN. *A History of Rome.* 5 vols. Scribners.
    "   *The Provinces of the Roman Empire.* 2 vols. New Edition Scribners.

    These seven volumes contain Vols 1–3 and 5 of the German original. The fourth volume of the History, covering tne period from Julius Cæsar to Augustus, was left unwritten.

OMAN. *Seven Roman Statesmen.* Longmans. A good biographical treatment of the revolutionary epoch.

OVID. Translated by Riley. Bohn.

PLATNER. *Topography and Monuments of Ancient Rome* New Edition. Allyn and Bacon. The best work in English on the subject

PLINY, THE YOUNGER. *Letters.* Translated by Melmoth-Bosanquet. Bohn.

POLYBIUS. Translated by Shuckburgh. 2 vols. Macmillan.

PRESTON AND DODGE. *Private Life of the Romans* Leach.

RAMSAY. *The Church in the Roman Empire before A D 170* Putnams. A stimulating discussion by an unusually competent scholar.

SELLAR. *Roman Poets of the Augustan Age.* Clarendon Press A standard treatise on its theme.

SHUCKBURGH. *Augustus.* Fisher Unwin. Has in an appendix a translation of the autobiography of Augustus.

STANLEY *History of the Eastern Church.* Scribners. Vivid pictures of the relations of the Church and the Empire in the fourth and fifth centuries.

STRACHAN-DAVIDSON. *Cicero.* Putnams. Perhaps the fairest of the biographies of the orator.

STRONG *Roman Sculpture from Augustus to Constantine* Scribners. The best work on the subject. Well illustrated

SUETONIUS *Lives of the Twelve Cæsars.* Translated by Thompson-Forester. Macmillan

TACITUS Translated by Church and Brodribb. 2 vols. Macmillan.

TAYLOR *A Constitutional and Political History of Rome.* Methuen. Clear and accurate, somewhat old-fashioned.

THOMAS. *Roman Society under the Cæsars.* Putnams

Translations and Reprints from the Original Sources of European History, Department of History, University of Pennsylvania, Vol 5. No 1. Monumentum Ancyranum, The Deeds of Augustus Translated by Fairley.

VERGIL. Translated into prose by Bryce. 2 vols. Bell.

WICKHOFF. *Roman Art.* Macmillan.

APPENDIX II

NOTES ON THE ILLUSTRATIONS

PLATE I. The Parthenon and its Frieze.—The attempt
is made in this plate to reproduce the effect wrought by the use
of color on Greek temples It is taken from Fenger's work on
the subject. We are looking at the northeast corner of the Parthenon. (See Plate XVII and § 205.) The top of the Doric
column is impressively shown. The sculptured "metopes" in
high relief represent various scenes, the meaning of which is
doubtful On the right side is a knight in battle array and a
combat between footmen. On the other side are female figures.
The refinement, coupled with vigor in the pose and execution of
the figures, should be marked. At the bottom of the plate the
portion of the frieze pictured is taken from that upon the east
side of the building From the right the procession of maidens
bearing sacrificial vessels is advancing toward a group of men
conversing. These are presumably the archons of the city. To
the left, seated facing them, are the gods and goddesses. The
one farthest to the left has been identified with Poseidon, next
to him in order are Dionysus, Demeter (?), Aphrodite with Eros
at her knee. On the sculptures of the Parthenon, see Tarbell,
ch. 8, and Gardner, *Ancient Athens*, ch. 7

PLATE II. Typical Oriental Heads.—1. The portrait of
Hammurabi stands on a limestone slab found near the site of
ancient Accad (§ 11). The king is in the attitude of adoration
with hands uplifted Study the cap, the hair, and the beard as
illustrating the style of dress. 2. The head of Rameses II is
taken from his mummy now in the Museum at Cairo, Egypt
The remarkable profile betokens a man of imperious character.
3. The head of Esarhaddon, the Assyrian, is from a stone tablet
found in Syria. The conical cap betokens royalty The curled
beard and hair are characteristic of Assyrian-Babylonian style,

538

and may be compared with those of head 1. The king holds in his uplifted hand an object which he is offering (?) to his god. The Semitic type of face is evident. 4. The Syrian head is equally Semitic. The thick shock of hair, bound with a fillet, and the beard are characteristic of the Syrian in distinction from the shaven Egyptian and the carefully barbered Assyrian 5. The head of the Philistine illustrates by its unlikeness to the features of the other heads the non-Semitic character of this people The helmet or head-dress (of feathers?) is likewise peculiar. 6. The Hittite is distinguishable from Semitic heads by nose and chin. The hair hangs in a pigtail and the eyes are oblique, suggestive of the Chinese. Heads 4, 5, and 6 are from Egyptian reliefs. Observe that all of these heads are in profile. Why was this characteristic of oriental art? See Tarbell, pp. 33, 38–42.

PLATE III. (1) THE SUMERIAN ARMY IN ACTION.—The phalanx formation of the Sumerians is noteworthy. "The great, rectangular, nail-studded shields, which protect the entire body, form a wall, out of which issue the levelled spears of the front lines. A helmet, probably of leather, with neck-guard, protects the head" The king strides in front, boomerang-like sceptre in hand (below he is about to hurl his spear). The machine passes over the bodies of the slain enemy. Note the bird-like heads of the Sumerian soldiers.

(b) BABYLONIAN CYLINDERS. Round the surfaces of the cylinders ran scenes such as those shown in the plate. They were used to stamp documents (which were made of moist clay) with a seal or a signature. The upper scene on the right comes from the Gilgamesh Epos (§ 28). The scene in the same corner at the bottom shows a lion hunt. Observe in others a god or goddess standing on the back of a wild animal. Observe also the fondness for monstrosities.

PLATE IV. PAINTING FROM AN EGYPTIAN TOMB.—These pictures adorn the wall on the tomb of a noble in the time of the twelfth dynasty (§ 8). At the top is a hieroglyphic inscription giving the usual prayers for the dead. Following in order from top to bottom are represented (1) the making of sandals, (2) the making of arrows, chairs, and boxes, (3) goldsmiths' work, (4) the making of pottery, (5) the preparing of flax and the making of linen, (6) harvesting and threshing, (7) ploughing and sowing The picturing of these on the wall of the tomb, together with the sacred words above, was thought to assure to the dead the enjoyment of such things in the world to come Besides the representation of Egyptian life here, the student has an excellent opportunity to study the merits and defects of Egyptian art.

PLATE V SWAMP-HUNTING IN A REED BOAT (EGYPT).— The Theban tombs have preserved exquisite examples of New Empire painting like "the hunt in the marshes, exhibiting a fine touch of animal savagery in the fierce abandon of a lithe cat as she tramples two live birds beneath her feet and sinks her teeth at the same moment into a third victim."

"In a light boat of papyrus reeds, accompanied by his wife and sometimes by one of his children, the noble delighted to float about in the shade of the tall rushes, in the inundated marshes and swamps. The myriad life that teemed and swarmed all about his frail craft gave him the keenest pleasure While the lady plucked water-lilies and lotus flowers, my lord launched his boomerang among the flocks of wild fowl that fairly darkened the sky above him, finding his sport in the use of the difficult weapon which for this reason he preferred to the more effective and less difficult bow "—Breasted, *A History of Egypt*, pp. 47, 89 *f.*

PLATE VI. BABYLONIAN AND EGYPTIAN TEMPLES — (*a*) This restoration of the temple at Nippur was made by Professor Hilprecht. As one passed through the great oblong tower-gate in the outer wall, he entered the outer court, measuring 260 by 260 feet, containing a small shrine. Through similar but greater gates the inner court was reached. There, directly in front, was the mighty stage-tower, its sides 190 by 128 feet. At the top of the tower was a shrine to the god. Besides the stage-tower was the temple proper, the "house of Bel." It consisted of one-story roofed chambers and open courts Off to the right of the picture is one of the city gates In front of the temple area was the canal.

(*b*) The Egyptian temple lay along the Nile. Leading up to the entrance was a road bordered by sphynxes In front of the gate were two obelisks, symbolizing, perhaps, the rays of the sun-god, and some sitting statues of the kings or gods. A square entrance, flanked by huge buttresses called pylons, admitted to the court, surrounded by a portico upheld by pillars. Through this was the passage by pylon gateways into a covered hall, thence into another pillared court The "holy of holies," the shrine of the god, was in the low rooms at the rear of the long series of courts and halls Thick high walls and lofty pylons shut off entrance except through the front of the temple Light was admitted through the courts The chambers were entirely dark. The length of the whole structure was over 790 feet, its width over 100 feet.

PLATE VII Ancient Systems of Writing.—The Rosetta stone contains in Greek, demotic, and hieroglyphic script a decree of the Egyptian priests passed in 197 B C. It was found by Napoleon in 1802. By its aid Champollion in 1822 deciphered the hieroglyphics The demotic writing (*i e*, the cursive form used in Egypt in the first millennium B C) was first read by Brugsch in 1849. The Brick of Hammurabi is inscribed with Babylonian cuneiform characters. Cuneiform writing was first deciphered by Grotefend in 1802, but it was not till Henry Rawlinson, in 1847, had read the long Behistun inscription of Darius that the key to the language was really obtained. Neither the pictographic nor the linear Cretan writing has been deciphered as yet. These new scripts were discovered by Arthur Evans.

PLATE VIII Typical Assyrian Scenes —(*a*) This relief is cut from the surface of a limestone slab, and was one of a series which lined the walls of the Assyrian royal palace. King Ashurbanipal (§ 65) is galloping after a lion and in the act of discharging an arrow at him An attendant follows with fresh javelins and arrows The energy and life of the scene, as well as the subject, are typical. A study of the dress and, indeed, of the various objects represented, as well as of the excellences and defects of the pose, will reward the student with new light on Assyrian life and art.

(*b*) This relief represents the siege and assault of the city of

Lachish by King Sennacherib (§ 65). See 2 Kings 18:14. A breach has been made in the walls directly in front, where the Assyrian military engines are playing. Torches are being hurled down upon the besiegers, the fire is being put out with pans of water, archers are pouring clouds of arrows on the defenders. Scaling-ladders are raised against the walls. In front, prisoners are impaled on stakes. From one of the towers captives are coming forth with their effects The animation and variety of the scene are only equalled by the grotesqueness of the art. Try to get the artist's point of view and study the details of the scene for the collection of facts concerning ancient military life.

PLATES IX and X. Decoration of a Cretan Sarcophagus.—"On the best-preserved side (Plate IX), at the extreme right, is the erect figure of the dead closely swathed, standing before his tomb, beside which grows a sacred tree. Three persons approach him with offerings, the first bearing the model of a ship, to typify perhaps the voyage of the dead, the other two carrying young calves, which are drawn as if galloping—an absurd and slavish imitation of a well-known Minoan type. On the left a priestess is pouring wine into a large vase standing between two posts surmounted by double-axes upon which birds, probably ravens, are perched. A lady and a man in long rich robes attend the priestess, the man playing a seven-stringed lyre. In the writer's eyes these double-axes are not fetishes, but are emblems referring to the lineage or status of the deceased. The opposite side (Plate X) shows a bull sacrificed, a priestess before an altar, and a man playing a flute, followed by five ladies . . . Whereas the priestesses and offerants on the sarcophagus wear a short skirt of peculiar cut, the lay persons taking part in the religious rites, two men and six women, all wear long rich robes, and the flute-player keeps to the ancient Minoan fashion of dressing his hair in long curls "—*Crete the Forerunner of Greece*, by C H and H. Hawes, pp. 86 *f*.

PLATE XI. Kamares Pottery.—For the time and vogue of this work, see § 94. It seems to have been peculiarly Cretan. The view above to the right is simply the interior of the vessel shown below. Note the similarity in artistic effect with Plates IX and X.

PLATE XII. THRONE OF MINOS AND PILLAR OF THE DOUBLE-AXES —The double-axe, Labrys, seems to have been the sacred symbol of a male Cretan deity—perhaps the Carian Zeus, Zeus of Labraunda. It has been suggested that the name Labyrinth is derived from this word. The symbol is of frequent occurrence in Cretan monuments.

"No more ancient throne exists in Europe, or probably in the world, and none whose associations are anything like so full of interest."—Baikie, *The Sea Kings of Crete*, p. 72.

The connection with Minos is fanciful.

PLATE XIII. LION GATE AND BEE-HIVE TOMB.—In these two Mycenæan structures the aperture over the doorway is to be noted. By means of it the lintel is relieved of the superimposed weight In the case of the gate the slab which filled the aperture is still in place. It is adorned with two lions rampant on either side of a sacred pillar which, in the typical Mycenæan fashion, has the smaller end of the base. The gate is set back in such a way that assailants were exposed to a cross-fire from the wall. Mycenæ was surrounded by walls, such as those which abutted the gate Below we look down the walled passage which led into a bee-hive tomb. The wall at the end continues so as to enclose a conical space. Each ascending tier of stories projects inward until the top is closed by a single slab Inside the bodies of the great dead of Mycenæ were placed, and with them objects which would be needful for a king or queen in the spirit world.

PLATE XIV. GOLD CUPS OF THE MYCENÆAN AGE.— These cups were found at Vaphio, in Laconia, in 1888, and hence are called the Vaphio cups. The upper design represents a hunt of wild cattle. The centre one is caught in a net On the right another is in full flight, while on the left a third has thrown one hunter and is goring another In the lower design the bulls are tame and under the care of a herdsman. The material is beaten gold A sense of abounding life, coupled with some crudity, is the characteristic impression made by these works See Tarbell, pp. 67–69; Tsountas and Manatt, pp 227–228.

PLATE XV. WILD GOAT AND YOUNG—CRETAN ART OF THE TWENTIETH CENTURY B.C.—This plaque was probably applied to a backing of colored plaster. Several examples of it have been found all taken from one mould A vitreous glaze of siliceous composition has been put over a body of porous paste The surface color of the faience is here a pale green with dark sepia markings "The scene is laid on a mountain crag of Dicta or of Ida and the animal here is the Cretan wild goat, or *Agrimi*. The suckling kid is shown in almost identically the same posture as a calf in a parallel design. In front, another kid looks up at its mother and bleats to her its desire, while the mother goat, in an attitude of serene impartiality, seems to chide the impatience of her offspring This design, apart from its beauty and naturalism, is characterized by a certain ideal dignity and balance. . . . In beauty of modelling and in living interest, Egyptian, Phœnician, and, it must be added, classical Greek renderings of this traditional group are far surpassed by the Minoan artist."—A. J. Evans, in *Annual of the British School in Athens*, IX, pp 71 *ff*

PLATE XVI. ART OF GREECE IN THE TIME OF THE PERSIAN WAR —Pieces of a single monument, possibly a pedestal The upper three pieces are in Rome, the others in the Boston Museum of Fine Arts The subject of the composition is Aphrodite, the goddess of love, who is seen rising from the sea. She inspires the flute girl and the lyre player The maiden at the left may be concocting a love potion or simply burning incense. The somewhat realistic figure of an old woman in the upper corner may be a nurse. The central scene above probably portrays the love rivalry of two maidens.

Eros holds the balance. On each weight a man is sketched. The two seated figures sympathize with its movement, the one rejoicing, the other sorrowful, according as the weight inclines toward her or rises away from her.

PLATE XVII THE ACROPOLIS.—This restoration of the buildings on the Acropolis is, like all such attempts, probably not accurate, but it represents the general situation and relation of the different structures (§ 205) The entrance at the western end was by the Propylæa, at the head of which stood the colossal statue of Athena To the right was the Temple of Victory. At the centre of the elevated platform, the Parthenon lay on the right and the Erechtheum on the left. The Parthenon was entered at the eastern end Other smaller temples filled up the enclosure. The Acropolis was about 1,000 feet long by 500 feet wide, it was a sort of oval, with its long axis lying east and west. (See Plan of Athens, facing p. 147.)

PLATE XVIII. TYPICAL GREEK HEADS —1. The first is taken from a full-length statue of Sophocles (§ 206) It is an ideal representation of the poet, no doubt, but it is instructive as illustrating the Greek type The arrangement of hair and beard should be noticed. The failure to work out the detail of the eye gives the aspect of blindness, and is a defect of Greek sculpture Compare some modern statue in this respect. 2. The head of Pericles bears a helmet as a sign of leadership (§ 195) A calm, thoughtful, somewhat reserved expression on the face is discernible 3 The head of Socrates is noticeable for its originality, and offers some instructive comparisons with the preceding. The breadth of the face contrasts with that of the others. 4. The head of Aphrodite is taken from the statue found in the island of Melos. The grace and purity of the face illustrate the Greek ideals of love and of woman It dates from the early Hellenistic Age (§ 323). 5. The head of Alexander is taken from a relief on a sarcophagus now in Constantinople. He wears a lion's head instead of a helmet, and the ram's horn appears, typical of his divine descent from the Egyptian god Amon The characteristic Greek profile is instructive This, too, is early Hellenistic. 6 The last head is taken from a Græco-Egyptian portrait painted on a wooden panel placed in a grave along with the mummy and intended to represent the features of the dead. It is clear that the Greek in Egypt remained in all essential traits a Greek. The thin beard, the oval face, the large eye, the straight nose find their counterparts in the other heads A golden wreath in the hair is exquisitely done.

PLATE XIX. THE HERMES OF PRAXITELES.—This statue was found at Olympia in 1877. The god Hermes has the infant Dionysus on his arm. The god's mantle is thrown over a tree-trunk and he stands with his body gracefully curved, its weight resting on the right leg and left arm It would seem that the right arm held something which was being offered to Dionysus. The material is Parian marble The child is not successfully modelled, but the figure of Hermes is of extraordinary excellence. Forget the mutilation as far as possible. A special study should be given to the head. For a full description, see Tarbell, pp. 221–223.

PLATE XX. THE ALEXANDER MOSAIC.—This mosaic came from the floor of a room in the so-called house of the Faun in Pompeii. In the lower left-hand corner a portion of it has been broken away. It represents probably the battle of Issus (§ 85) at the point where Darius turns to his chariot to flee and Alexander on horseback presses on in his charge. "At the head of the Greek horsemen rides Alexander, fearless, unhelmeted, leading a charge against the picked guard of Darius The long spear of the terrible Macedonian is piercing the side of a Persian noble, whose horse sinks under him The driver of Darius's chariot is putting the lash to the horses, but the fleeing king turns with an expression of anguish and terror to witness the death of his courtier. . . . The grouping of the combatants, the characterization of the individual figures, the skill with which the expressions upon the faces are rendered, and the delicacy of coloring give this picture a high rank among ancient works of art." See May, *Pompeii, Its Life and Art*, p 288.

PLATE XXI. REALISTIC AND ROMANTIC ART OF HELLENISTIC PERIOD.—The bronze statuette to the left formed part of the cargo of a ship which sank off the coast of Africa (Mahdia) in about 100 B.C. while *en route* from Athens to Italy. For the rest of the cargo, see Ferguson, *Hellenistic Athens*, p. 376 The figure is that of a dwarf. She belonged in all probability to an ancient vaudeville troupe. Note the realism evidenced in the choice of the subject and its faithful portraiture.

For the purpose and subject of the relief reproduced to the right, see § 313. This scene should be compared with that of Plate XV The two are alike in theme and use, though one thousand five hundred years fall between their times of composition.

PLATE XXII TYPICAL SCULPTURED FIGURES —(a) The statue of Khafre is of green diorite, a very hard stone The Pharaoh is seated on the royal chair in an attitude of regal composure and majesty The head-dress, false beard, and body garment are characteristically Egyptian. Special attention should be given to the face and the pose The right leg of the statue is badly broken. In judging of Egyptian art the other specimens in Plates III, IV, and V should be taken into account, and also the examples in Tarbell, pp 16-35.

(b) Posidippus was an Athenian playwright of the third century B.C., and the statue is a striking example of the portrait statuary of the period. The easy grace of the pose, as well as the cultured refinement of the face and bearing, are especially worthy of note. The student will be profited by a study of the dress, the chair, and other accessories. It would be well to compare these two figures with each other, and also the face of the Greek with those of the typical heads of Plate XVIII.

PLATE XXIII. THE LAOCOON GROUP.—This group represents the scene described by Vergil in the *Æneid* (II, 199-233), where the priest Laocoön, advising against admitting the Trojan horse into Troy, is, with his sons, slain by serpents. It is a work of the school of Rhodes about 150 B C. The exhibition of horror and agony is the salient feature of the work. The Laocoón has been variously judged. For examples, see Tarbell, 264-267.

PLATE XXIV. CLASSICAL TEMPLES.—(a) The Greek temple at Pæstum, in southern Italy, belongs to the sixth century B C. It is, therefore, an early type A double row of sturdy Doric columns surrounds the shrine. The temple was built of limestone and covered with stucco.

(b) The Roman temple is a modification of the Greek. This temple, 59 by 117 feet, is surrounded by a single row of Corinthian columns 30 feet 6 inches in height It dates probably from the time of Hadrian (A D 122). Changes in certain features of the temple of the Greek type can be clearly seen by comparison of these two structures

PLATE XXV TYPICAL SCULPTURED FIGURES.—(a) The statue of Ashurnatsirpal is the only fully wrought Assyrian statue known The king stands in royal majesty, his arms bare. The right hand holds a sceptre, the left a mace The hair and beard as well as the royal dress deserve notice. See Goodspeed, *History of Babylonians and Assyrians*, p. 202; Tarbell, pp 40, 41.

(*b*) The statue of Trajan represents him probably in the act of addressing his soldiers. He wears a cuirass, and his mantle is draped over his shoulder and around his arm. A series of instructive comparisons may be drawn between the two royal figures on this plate.

PLATE XXVI WALL PAINTINGS FROM CAMPANIAN TOMBS. —Campania was the seat of a rich culture before the Roman conquest. It had learned much from the Greeks, who were settled near by on the Bay of Naples The Etruscans had been its overlords for many generations, and had brought their customs south with them. The art of Campania in the fourth and third centuries B.C., as we see from these grave monuments, was Greek in its general characters. The knights of Campania were famous warriors. To the left one of them rides on his tomb as he often rode in the flesh. Note particularly his plumed helmet. To the right is a bloody combat of gladiators Observe frightful wounds inflicted where the body is unprotected The gladiatorial games arose, we are told, from combats of victims which formed part of funeral ceremonies.

From an early date they were given in the cities along the entire western slope of Italy.

PLATES XXVII and XXVIII TYPICAL COINS.—1. A coin of Lydia of the type of the Babylonian "stater" One of the earliest known coins (§ 129). Date about 700 B C. The material is electrum. 2. A Persian gold "daric" (§ 81) of Darius I. 3. A gold "stater" of Mithridates of Pontus (§ 461). Here is the king himself represented, with hair blown back as though he were driving a chariot The reverse shows a stag feeding A long period of growth in the artistic production of coins lies between 2 and 3. 4. Another oriental gold coin, representing Queen Berenice of Egypt, wife of Ptolemy III (§ 318) Both this and the preceding are noticeable because on them are portraits of the reigning monarchs. 5. A silver medallion of Syracuse. The coins of this city reached the highest artistic excellence. The head is that of Persephone surrounded by dolphins. The reverse shows the victor in a chariot race, over the chair hovers Victory conferring the laurel The design and workmanship of this coin are specially worthy of study. 6. A silver "stater" of the Greek city of Amphipolis and dating about 400 B.C. The head of the god Apollo appears on one side, and on the other a torch such as the racers bore The god's head is remarkable for animation. 7. A silver "tetradrachm" of Athens, about 550 B.C., earlier and ruder than the preceding. On one side is the head of Athena, patron goddess of the city, on the other the olive branch and sacred owl 8. A silver "shekel" of Judæa in the time of Simon Maccabæus (§ 430). A cup, a pot of manna, and triple lily are the emblems, and the letters signify "shekel of Israel," and "Jerusalem the holy." 9. A bronze "sestertius" of Nero. The emperor appears on horseback armed with a spear and accompanied by a mounted soldier carrying a banner. 10. A silver coin of the Roman Republic about 100 B.C. The head of Roma, Victory in a chariot, and an ear of corn are represented The name of the official who coined the piece also appears 11. A gold "solidus" of the Emperor Honorius (§ 570) from Ravenna. The portrait of the emperor is given in the style characteristic of this late age. He wears the diadem and holds the sceptre. 12. A bronze "sestertius" of Antoninus Pius (§ 533). An excellent wreathed portrait-head of the emperor stands on one side; on the other is Roma with the palladium, and the inscription "Roma æterna" 13 A silver coin of Augustus (§ 484). The emperor appears on one side, on the other, one of his favorite symbols, the Sphynx. 14. A silver "denarius" of the Republic (99–94 B.C.). The bust of Roma appears On the other side are three citizens engaged in voting—a typical scene. 15. A silver "argenteus" of the Emperor Caracalla (§ 547). His portrait, with his head surrounded with the sun's rays, is characteristic of the time. (See § 554) 16. A bronze "as" of Rome, weighing one and one-fifth ounces. The symbols are the head of the god Janus and the prow of a galley. The date is just before 217 B.C The symbols are characteristic in view of the date. Why? (See § 404)

PLATE XXIX. THE ROMAN FORUM —This plate represents the Forum and its surroundings in the imperial period. The Forum itself was never very large (§ 340) and was early surrounded by buildings and filled with statues. At the upper end into which we look stood the Rostra. The various public buildings are named upon the plate itself A plate representing the Forum at the present day will be found in Morey, *Roman History*, frontispiece

PLATE XXX. TYPICAL ROMAN HEADS —1. The striking head of Julius Cæsar is that of a man of force and ideas The high forehead, the prominent cheek-bones, the firm mouth, and thin lips reveal the general and the statesman He is also the typical Roman patrician. The sculptor evidently sought to produce an exact likeness 2 Cicero is the typical urbane and cultivated Roman of the middle class. His face has a strikingly modern character, being distinctively Roman, perhaps, in its dignity and the traces of sternness. The chin and nose of both these typical Romans are noteworthy. 3. Vespasian's head illustrates exactly that of the Roman peasant, honest, unyielding, practical. Notice the cropped hair, thick neck, and decided mouth. 4. Hadrian's head and hair are characteristic of the ruler of the later imperial age. His face is of the western type, yet not Roman. 5. Faustina, the wife of Marcus Aurelius, is the typical Roman matron. The features are strong and simple without the ideal grace of the Greek type. Such a woman would naturally accompany her husband on his campaigns. Notice the dressing of the hair. 6. The bust of Commodus represents him as Hercules. The characteristic club is in his hand and the lion's skin on his head. The curling beard and hair, and, indeed, the whole representation, disclose the vain and frivolous weakling. It is a long step from Julius Cæsar to Commodus. The artistic skill of the sculptor is worthy of notice

PLATE XXXI. ART OF THE AUGUSTAN AGE.—"First two *flamines* and behind them a beautiful young figure, with drapery drawn over the head; he is the bearer of the *sacena*, the 'official' axe borne as a symbol of sacrifice, though not actually for use. Behind again comes a stately middle-aged personage (Agrippa?) to whose drapery clings a small boy   A lady in the background (Julia?) places her right hand on the child's head as he looks back at a stately matron.   This second lady   . . fronts the spectator and turns in three quarters to the left. . . . She can be no other than the Empress Livia herself.   Behind Livia come two young men, the first of whom is thought to be Tiberius "— Strong, *Roman Sculpture*, pp. 44 *f.*

"If we study these trains of priests and officials, of proud youths, of beautiful women, and well-bred children, who walk behind the Emperor (Augustus) in long rows, or come forward to welcome him, we must confess that there are few works of art which would have rendered with equal success the consciousness of high worth combined with elegance of deportment.   It is an historical picture of the first order, which shows us the people, who first conquered the world and were then governing it, united together "—Wickhoff, *Roman Art*, pp 31 *f.*

"A woman of gracious mien sits on a rock.   The back of her head is covered by an ample veil which is then drawn round her from waist to ankles.   On her lap is abundance of fruit—apples, grapes, nuts, on the left knee, which is raised, sits a little child whom she holds with her left hand, while a somewhat bigger child scrambles up on her right. . . . To the right and to the left are the fertilizing genii of the earth—Air mounted on a swan and Water figured as a nereid riding a sea monster, . . . while below in the meadows spring the trees and flowers among which the animals pasture "—Strong, pp 44 *f.*

PLATE XXXII.   RELIEF FROM THE ARCH OF TITUS —The Arch of Titus commemorated his victory over the Jews and the capture of Jerusalem (§ 513)   It stood on the Sacred Way Unlike the Arch of Constantine (Plate XXXIX), it had but one central archway and within the vault of this was the relief of our plate.   A group of soldiers lead captives and bear the spoils of the Jewish temple   The golden table of the shewbread and the seven-armed golden candlestick are prominent among them. Laurels crown the heads of the soldiers and they carry Roman military standards   The work is of Pentelic marble, and testifies to the artistic taste and skill of the time

PLATE XXXIII.   Room in the House of the Vettii.—The House of the Vettii at Pompeii was unearthed in 1894 and contains some of the best preserved memorials of Pompeian art.   This room, one of the two dining-rooms, with its variegated marble work, its paintings, and its frescoes, illustrates notably the character of the better Roman house of the time.   The subjects of the paintings are taken from Græco-Roman mythology. On the right is Bacchus coming on the sleeping Ariadne.   On the left are Dædalus and Pasiphæ   The subject of the painting facing us is the punishment of Ixion.   Hermes, who has brought Ixion, is in front, at his feet a veiled figure.   To the right is the goddess Hera, and on the left Hephæstus has just fastened Ixion to the wheel.   See May, *Pompeii, Its Life and Art*, pp 333-334

PLATE XXXIV.   Roman Portraiture.—Roman art is distinguished for the excellence of its portraiture.   Corbulo was Nero's brilliant general in the Parthian wars.   Summoned home treacherously by his jealous master, he was forced to commit suicide.   Compare the other portraits in Plate XXX.

PLATE XXXV.   Relief from Trajan's Column.—The Column of Trajan stood in his Forum (Plate XXIX).   It was 128 feet high and was surmounted by a statue of the emperor twenty feet high.   A spiral staircase of 185 steps led to the top Around the column wound a series of bronze reliefs in twenty-three tiers representing scenes in the Dacian war (§ 538).   The reliefs contained 2,500 figures   In the centre of this relief appears Trajan receiving from his soldiers the heads of Dacian spies. To the left a siege is going on, Roman soldiers advancing to the assault under a testudo.   Observe carefully the dress and weapons of the soldiers.

PLATE XXXVI   Castle of St. Angelo: Hadrian's Mole.—In the front flows the Tiber.   In the rear to the left is St Peter's.   In the foreground rises the huge mass of Hadrian's Mole.   In it were buried the emperors from Hadrian to Caracalla. Begun by Hadrian in 136, it was completed by Antoninus Pius in 139   It was a fortress in the Middle Ages and played an important part in the struggles of the popes for the control of Rome. Its modern name is derived from the statue of the archangel at its summit.

PLATE XXXVII. The Pantheon and the Walls of Aurelian.—The Pantheon was first constructed by Agrippa, in the time of Augustus, but the present dome dates from the reign of Hadrian The portico, supported by sixteen Corinthian columns of granite forty-one feet in height, is part of the original structure. In the rear were colossal baths. As it stands to-day it is one of the most beautiful and impressive monuments of Rome. First a "very sacred" pagan temple, it became in the Middle Ages a Christian church, and is now the tomb of the Italian kings.

Great walls of brick were built in 271, at the command of Aurelian by the Roman guilds of workmen to protect the city from the Germanic invaders. By a desperate Italian campaign the emperor had just saved Rome from sack. They form one of the most conspicuous and picturesque monuments of antiquity to be seen in modern Rome. At intervals towers were set such as those in the plate

PLATE XXXVIII. Early Christian Art.—These scenes from the life of Jonah were painted on the walls of a chamber in the catacombs They are dated about the beginning of the third century A D They are notable not merely for the crudity of their execution, but also for the religious symbolism which they set forth. The experiences of Jonah had a twofold meaning for the Christian (1) they were types of the death and resurrection of Jesus (Matt 12· 39–49), and (2) they encouraged the persecuted believers to persevere in the trials of the present life and hope for the life to come. The "great fish" is thought to be copied after the dragon that figures in Græco-Roman mythology; for example, in the story of Andromeda, representations of which in the art of the time were not uncommon. The symbolism of this picture is further carried out by the mast and yard of the ship, which are arranged to form a cross

PLATE XXXIX. Typical Roman Architecture.—(a) The highly decorative character of this arch is at once evident.

Some of the adornments were taken from other monuments, for example, the four great statues and some reliefs from an arch of Trajan. At the top were originally a chariot and horses, and statues The arch was built in A.D. 315, to commemorate the victory of Constantine over Maxentius in 312. Its proportions are fine and its adaptations of Greek architecture are instructive. Compare it with the Arch of Titus and consider whether it does not lack dignity in comparison with that. See Seignobos, p 322

(*b*) This aqueduct is a remarkable union of simplicity, strength, and beauty. Its length is 882 feet, its height 162 feet. The water channel above is covered with large slabs of stone about fourteen feet wide The character of Roman engineering and architectural work is most fully illustrated by it. It was built for the needs of a Gallic city, the like of which, in size and importance, were to be found scattered all over the Roman Empire The various features of it will reward study.

PLATE XL. CHRIST ENTHRONED.—This fresco stands over one of the doors in the Mosque of St. Sophia in Constantinople, once a Christian church (§ 575) Christ sits on his throne raising his hand in blessing. On either side are Mary, his mother, and Michael, the archangel. Before him lowly kneeling is the emperor in the attitude of a subject. By some this figure is said to be the Emperor Justinian (§ 574). The Greek words signify "Peace be unto you. I am the light of the world " Study both subject and style of execution as characteristic of Byzantine art and the times in which it arose.

INDEX

References are to pages, *f* indicates "following page", *ff.*, "following pages", *n*, "notes"

Ab-de'ra, 186   See map following p 88.

Academy, 218

A-can'thus, 183. See map following p. 66.

A-car-na'ni-a, 219   See map following p. 66.

Ac'cad, 10   See map facing p 3

A-chæ'an cities, 170

A-chæ'an League, struggle with Macedonia, 265, relations to Rome, 366, 368, dissolved, 370

A-chæ'us and A-chæ'ans, 92.

A-che-men'i-dæ, 239.

A-chil'les, 85, 87.

Ac'ra-gas (Agrigentum), 140. See map facing p. 89

A-crop'o-lis, of Athens, 115, 164

Ac'ti-um, 427. See map following p. 66.

Adoption, in ancient East, 19, at Rome, 336 f

A-dras'tus, 95

A-dri-a-no'ple, 503 See map facing p 517

A-dri-at'ic sea, 278   See map following p. 278.

Æ-e'tes, 96 f.

Æ-e'ti-us, 504

Æ'gæ, 220, 222. See map following p 66.

Æ-ga'le-os, mt, 138

Æ-ga'tes, islands, 348   See map following p. 278

Æ-ge'an sea, 41, 65 f   See map facing p. 77.

Æ-ge'ium, 263   See map following p 66

Æ-gi'na, 83, 99, 169. See map following p 66.

Æ-gos-pot'a-mi, 196.

Æ-gyp'tus, 93

Æ-mil'i-us Paul'us, 352, 367.

Æ-ne'as, 287

Æ-ne'id, 437

Æ'o-lus, and the Æ-o'li-ans, 92.

Æ'qui, 300, 304.

Æs'chi-nes, 225.

Æs'chy-lus, 140, 142, 165

Æ'son, 96.

Æ-to'li-a, 219. See map following p 66

Ætolian League, 268, 365 f, 368.

Africa, province of, 372.

Ag-a-mem'non, 95.

A-gath'o-cles, 272 f., 344.

A-ge'nor, 94

A-ges-i-la'us, 204 f

Agrarian problem, in Greece, 104, 117, 119, 163, 172, at Rome, 306, 317, 327, 392 ff, 396.

A-gric'o-la, 454, 478.

Agriculture, in ancient East, 14 f ; at Rome, 331 f., 375 f

A'gri Dec'u-ma'tes, 454

Ag-ri-gen'tum, 347   See Acragas.

A-grip'pa, 427, 441 ff.

A'haz, 50

Al-a-man'ni, 503, 511.

Al'a-ric, 503.

Al'ba Lon'ga, 288 f. See map on p 301.

Al-cæ'us, 100.

555

Al-ci-bi'a-des, 190 ff , 197
Alc-mæ-on'i-dæ, 116, 120, 154.
Alc'man, 101
Alexander, 38, youth and train-
ing, 231, campaigns in Greece,
232; invasion of Persia, 233;
development of plans, 239,
lord of Persia, 239, organiza-
tion of empire, 239 ff , 241 f ;
world ruler, 242; death, 242,
characterization, 242 ff.; Alex-
ander II, 249.
Alexandria, in Egypt, 236 f.;
Egyptian Alexandria under the
Ptolemies, 255 ff ; Christian-
ity in, 489 f , 499, other Alex-
andrias, 244
Al'li-a, 318 See map on p 301.
Alphabet, 21, 42, 99.
Alps, Hannibal's passage of, 351.
Am'a-sis, King of Egypt, 37, 89.
Am-bra'ci-a, 219. See map fol-
lowing p. 66.
Am'brose, 501.
Am'on, god of Egypt, 32 ff.; Alex-
ander and, 237
A-mor'gos, 248.
Am-phic'ty-o-ny, 92, the leading
ones, 94 f ; and Philip of Mace-
don, 223, 226.
Am-phip'o-lis, 183, 222. See map
following p 66.
Amphitheatre, 460.
Amusements, in ancient East, 24,
in Greece, 98, 100, 120, 141 f ,
162 f., 164 f , 167 f., at Rome,
334 f., 379; under the Empire,
459 ff.
A-myc'le, 74. See map facing p. 77.
An-ab'a-sis, of Cyrus, 204 f.
An-ac're-on, 101.
An-ax-ag'o-ras, 186
An-ax-im'e-nes, 102.
Ancient history, earliest seats of,
1, 3, divisions of, 4; end of,
502, 521.

An'cus Mar'tius, 288
An-dro-ni'cus, 381
An'dros, 88, 260. See map fol-
lowing p. 128
Angles and Saxons, 516
An-tal'ci-das, 206
An-tig'o-ne, 95, 165.
An-tig'o-nus I, 249 f.; II, 259 f
An'ti-och, 263 See map follow-
ing p 476
An-ti'o-chus I, 261, II, 260; III,
268, 366, IV, 368
An-tip'a-ter, 232, 248 f.
An-to-ni'nus Pius, 472 f
An-to'ni-us, M , the orator, 382,
the triumvir (Antony), 425 ff.
A-pel'la, 114
Ap'en-nine, mts , 277 See map
following p 278.
A-phro-di'te, 86.
A-pol'lo, 86 f., at Delphi, 88 f., 98
Ap'pi-an Way, 285, 342.
Ap'pi-us Clau'di-us, the censor,
325, 342; the consul, 315 f
A-pu'li-a, 279, 352 See map fol-
lowing p. 278
A'quæ Sex'ti-æ, 399. See map
facing p. 412.
Aqueduct, 339, 342, 462
A-qui-ta'ni-a, 433. See map fac-
ing p 412.
A-ra'bi-a Pet-ræ'a, 2; province of,
476
Arabians, invade Babylonia, 9.
Ar-a-me'ans, original home, 3;
invasions by, 39 f ; Kingdom
at Damascus, 46.
A-ra'tus, 264.
A-rau'si-o, 398
Ar-be'la, 237 f. See map facing
p. 3.
Ar-ca'di-a, early history, 111, 114;
democracy in, 149; united by
Thebes, 210. See map follow-
ing p 66.
Ar-ca'di-us, 502.

Archbishop, 489

Ar-chi-da′mus, 271.

Ar-chil′o-chus, 100.

Ar-chi-me′des, 258

Architecture, in ancient East, 24, 33, Egyptian, 24 f , Assyrian, 51, Persian, 61, Greek, 163 f , Roman, 339, 383, in Augustan age, 438 f ; first century A D , 462, in second century, 477 f , in Constantine's time, 496, in Justinian's time, 507 f

Ar′chon, official at Athens, 116, 131, 151.

A-re-op′a-gus, council of, 116, 118, decline of, 150 f

A′res, 86.

Ar-gi-nu′sæ, 196. See map facing p. 180.

Ar′go, 84, 97.

Ar′go-nauts, 96 f

Ar′gos, early history, 111; in Persian wars, 127, 133, democracy at, 149; takes part in Peloponnesian War, 191. See map following p 66

A-ri-ad′ne, 94.

A′ri-ans, 487 n.

A-rim′i-num, 349. See map following p 278.

A-ri′on, 107.

Ar-is-tag′o-ras, 127 f.

Ar-is-tar′chus, 258.

Ar-is-ti′des, 131 f , 138, 145 f.

Aristocracy, in Orient, 17, in early Greece, 80 f.; decline of, 104; in Athens, 115 f., revival in Greece, 200, at Rome, 286 f , 297, 299, 305 f., becomes oligarchy, 326; the nobility, 377, under the Empire, 453, 456; Frankish, 511 f

Ar-is-to-de′mus, 96.

Ar-is-to-gei′ton, 120.

Ar-is-toph′a-nes, 185.

Ar′is-tot-le, 231, 244 f.

A′ri-us and A′rians, 487 n , 499 f.

Ar-me′ni-a, 40; and Rome, 410, 475 f. See map following p 234.

Ar-min′i-us, 442.

Army. See "Warfare "

Ar′no, 278 See map following p 278

Art, in ancient East, 24; in Mycenæan Greece, 72 ff , in Periclean Athens, 163 f ; in the fourth century B C , 215 f., in Hellenistic Age, 257, at Rome, 339 f , 383, 438 f , 461 f , early Christian, 490, Byzantine, 507 See "Architecture," "Sculpture "

Ar-ta-ba′zus, 140.

Ar-tax-erx′es I, 194; II, 204; III, 212, 233.

Ar′temis, 86

Ar-te-mis′i-um, 136 See map following p. 66.

A′runs, 301.

As, 332.

As-cu-la′pi-us, 341.

As′cu-lum, 324. See map following p 278.

Ash′dod, 42 n.

Ash′ur, 52.

Ash-ur-ban′i-pal, 49; rebellion against, 51, library of, 51 f.; death, 53

Ash-ur-nats′ir-pal, 49.

Asia, province of, 372, 404 f See map following p. 434.

Asia Minor, 33, 42, 49, 89. See map following p. 424.

As′kal-on, 42 n

Assemblies, in Greece, 81; in Sparta, 114, in Athens, 116, 118, 150 ff , 154, 184, at Rome, 287, 300, 307, 309, 338, 356 f , 474, 492, provincial, 467. See "Comitia "

As′sur, city, 13, 48. See map facing p. 3.

As-syr'ı-a, 3, 13; physical features, 48, Kingdom, 13, empire, 49; organızation, 49 f.; cıvılization, 51 f , contribution to history, 52; fall, 53; Roman provınce of, 476. See map facıng p 3.

Astronomy, 25, 101 f. See "Scıence."

Ath'a-mas, 96.

Ath-a-na'sius, 499

A-the'na, goddess of Athens, 86, 93, 115, 164, 166

Athens, geographical position and people, 115, early organization, 115 f., lawgivers, Draco, 117; Solon, 117 f ; tyranny of Pisistratus, and its fall. 119 ff ; legislation of Cleisthenes, 121 f , early expansion, 117 f ; comes in contact with Persia, 127 f ; change in political policy under Themistocles, 131 f ; destroyed by Persians, 139; rival of Sparta, 144, rebuilt, 146; after Persian wars, 144; progress under Themistocles, 146 f , fortified. 146, commercial and political development, 147; growth of imperialism, 147 f , population, 156, the citizen of, 159; income, 168 f ; politics under Pericles, 169, decline of land empire, 170, thirty years' peace, 170, expeditions against Persia, 170 f., empire of, 171 f , interferes between Corinth and Corcyra, 175, war with Sparta, 169 f , plague at, 179, parties at, 179; end of first period of war, 183, spirit of the people during the war, 184. expedition against Syracuse, 191 f , in third period of war, 193 ff.; surrender of, 196; glory and weakness in the war, 198 f., second naval league, 211, intellectual splendor

in fourth century, 216 ff , 244 f.; relations to Philip, 212, 225 f.; to Alexander, 232, literature in third century, 265 t.

Ath'e-sis. 278

Ath'os, mt., 129. 132 See map following p 66.

A'tri-um. See "House."

At'ta-lus 267

At'tı-ca, 117, 118. See map following p 66.

At'tı-la, 504

Au'gur, 295.

Au-gus-ta'les, 430.

Au'gus-tine, 514.

Au-gus'tus, his problem, 428; solution of it, 428 ff ; provıncial admınistration, 429, foreign policy, 432 f , imperialism, 434 f , defects in his scheme of administration, 441 f.; achievement, 444.

Au-re'lı-an, 487.

Au-re'lı-us, Marcus, 471, 473, 476, 480 f

Aus'pi-ces, 295, 388

Aus-tra'si-a, 511. See map facing p 517

Av-a'ris, 30.

A'vars, 507.

Av'en-tıne hıll, 294 f.

Bab'y-lon, 9, under Nebuchadrezzar, 55; Alexander at, 242.

Bab-y-lo'ni-a, physical features of, 1, beginnings. 8, first empire, 10 ff., why so called, 9, new Babylonian empire, 55 f. See map facing p 3

Bac'chus, 386

Bac-chyl'i-des. 140

Bac'tri-a, 58 See map following p 234

Bal-e-ar'ıc islands, Phœnicians in, 41 See map following p. 476.

Baths, at Rome, 461.

Bar-di'ya, 58

Bee-hive tombs, 75

Bel, god of Babylonia, 8, 11, 27.

Bel'gi-ca, 433. See map following p 434

Bel-i-sa'ri-us, 507.

Ben-e-ven'tum, 324. See map following p. 278.

Bi'as, 102.

Bible, 513.

Bishop, 468 n, 489, of Rome, 489 f. See "Papacy."

Bi-thyn'i-a, 410 See map following p. 434

Black sea, 88. See map facing p. 3.

Bœ-o'ti-a, in Persian wars, 133, 137, 139, democracy in, 150, complications with Athens, 169 f. See map following p 66

Bon'i-face, 516 f

Book of the Dead, 28

Bos'por-us, 410, 496. See map following p 128.

Bou'le, of Athens, 118, 121, 151

Bras'i-das, 182 f.

Bren'nus, 319

Bribery at Rome, 385, 388.

Britain, Phœnicians in, 41, Cæsar in, 411 f, under Claudius, 449, under Flavians, 454; Anglo-Saxons in, 516. See map following p. 434

Brut'ti-um, 353 See map following p 278

Bru'tus, 416, 425 f.

Burgundians, 503, 511.

Bur'rus, 449

Business, Greek, 159 See "Merchant," "Industry."

By-zan'ti-um, 88, 496. See map facing p 89.

Ca'diz, 41. See Gades.

Cad-mei'a, 207

Cad'mus, 94

Cæ'li-an hill, 284. See map on p 286

Cæ're, 320. See map following p. 278.

Cæ'ri-tan rights, 320

Cæsar, Gaius Julius, his rise, 409; first triumvirate, 411, in Gaul, 411 ff, conflict with senate and Pompey, 414 f, death, 416; his measures, 416 f, as a writer, 418 f; his work and personality estimated, 420 f

Cæsar, the title, 453, 491.

Cæsar-worship, 435, 467

Ca-la'bri-a, 279. See map following p 278.

Calendar, 25, 339, 418.

Ca-lig'u-la, 447.

Ca'liphs, 510.

Cal'li-as, 171.

Cal-li-crat'i-das, 196.

Cal-lim'a-chus, 259.

Cal-lis'the-nes, 240.

Cam-a-ri'na, 348

Cam-by'ses, 37, 58

Ca-mil'lus, 303, 319

Cam-pa'ni-a, 320 See map following p 278.

Cam'pus Mar'ti-us, 285.

Ca'naan-ites, 3, 44

Canary islands, Phœnicians in, 41

Can'næ, 352 See map following p. 278

Can-u-lei'an law, 316

Capitalism at Athens, 158 f.; at Rome, 362, 375 ff, 383 ff.

Cap'i-to-line hill, 284, 294

Cap'ri, 447. See map following p. 278.

Cap'u-a, 352. See map following p. 278.

Car-a-cal'la, 483 f

Car'di-a, 249

Ca'ri-a, 166, 172. See map following p. 128.

Carl, 518 f.

Carl'o-man, 517 f.

Car'mel, mt , 43

Car'men Sec-u-la're, 439.

Car'rhæ, 412 See map following p 476.

Carthage, founding of, 41; commerce of, 41; in Sicily, 135, 203 f , 271 ff ; expansion in the West, 343 f , early relations to Rome, 344, wars with Rome, 345 ff , becomes a dependent ally, 354, destroyed, 372, Cæsar's colony, 418. See map facing p 89.

Cas'pi-an sea, 49, 57 See map facing p 3

Cas-san'der, 249

Cas'si-us, Spurius, 300, 306, Gaius, 416, 425 f

Cat-a-lau'ni-an Fields, 504.

Cat'i-line, 410.

Ca'to the Elder, as writer, 382, as censor 385.

Ca-tul'lus, 418 f.

Cat'u-lus, 348

Cau'dine Forks, 322. See map following p 278

Cavalry, Persian, 59 f., 141, Macedonian, 221 f., 234; Roman, 296, 330.

Ce'crops, 82, 93.

Celts, 3 , in Greece and Asia Minor, 254 f , in Italy, 302, at Rome, 318 f

Cen'sor, 305, 338 f.; under Flavian Cæsars, 453.

Census, under the Empire, 432.

Centuries, 296 f

Ce-phis'sus, 115 See map following p 66

Cer'ber-us, 96

Ce'res, 293.

Chæ-ro-nei'a, 227 See map following p. 66.

Chal-cid'i-ce, 221. See map following p 66.

Chal'cis, 83, 88. See map following p 66

Chal-de'ans, invasion by, 39, in Babylonia, 51; victory over Babylonians, 55, empire of, 55.

Chal'ons, 504. See map facing p. 517.

Char'le-magne, his personality, 518 f ; achievements, 519, emperor, 520, significance, 520 f

Charles Martel, 512 f , 517.

Chei'lon, 102

Children, 19 f , 60, 112, 161 f., 335 ff See "Education."

Chi'os, 83. See map following p 128

Chos'roes, 509

Christianity, founded, 440, beginnings of, 467 f.; persecutions, 469, 481, 494 f , growth in unity, 481, 489 f , 499, and power, 513; toleration of, 495, recognition of, by Constantine, 487; in the cities, 499 n , religion of the Empire, 498 f.; Julian's attack, 499, as an imperial power, 500 f ; the monastic movement, 513 f ; leaders in fourth century, 513, and the barbarians, 516; and the Franks, 516 ff. See "Papacy."

Chronology, eras of, 98, 287 n., 440

Chrys'os-tom, 513

Cic'e-ro, his rise and ideals, 409, and Catiline, 410, banished and recalled, 412; as an orator and writer, 419, death, 426.

Ci-li'ci-a, 88, 411. See map following p 234.

Cim'bri, 398

Cim-in'i-an forest, 320. See map following p 278

Ci'mon, 148 f., 150, 171.

Cin-cin-na'tus, 304.

Cin'na, 403.

Cir-ce'ii, 403 See map following p. 278.

Circus Max'i-mus, 285, 291, 335, 460.

Cir'ta, 397. See map facing p 493.

Cis-al'pine Gaul, 350, 372, 401. See map following p 278

Ci-thæ'ron, 115. See map following p. 66.

Cit'i-um, 41 See map facing p 89.

Citizen See "Common People," "Franchise."

"City of God," 514

City-state, in Orient, 8, in Greece, 81 ff., culmination in Greece, 156, 167 f.; Rome, 281, 406 f.

Civilization See "Society"

Clau'di-us, 448 f

Cla-zom'e-næ, 206 See map following p 128

Cleis'the-nes, 121, his legislation, 121 f.

Cle-o-bu'lus, 102.

Cle-om'bro-tus, 137, 208.

Cle-om'e-nes, 127 f, 266 f.

Cle'on, 179 ff

Cle-on'y-mus, 272.

Cle-o-pa'tra, 415, 427 f.

Cle'o-phon, 196

Cler'u-chi, 172, 326.

Client, Roman, in early period, 286, in the imperial period, 456

Ch'tus, 240

Clo'di-us, 412

Clo'vis, 511, 516

Clu'si-um, 301 See map following p 278.

Cni'dos, 206. See map following p. 128.

Cnos'sos, great palace at, 73; people, 73 See map facing p 77

Code of Hammurabi. 11 f, of Moses, 43 f., of Justinian, 508

Coinage, of Persian Empire, 59; in Greece, 99, 113, 158, at Rome, 332 f, 431, 493. See "Exchange."

Col'chis, 96 f. See map following p. 476.

Col-is-se'um, 460, 462.

Col-o'nus, 194

Colony, in Egyptian Empire, 35, of Phœnicians, 41; of Greeks, 87 f, Roman, 327 f.; Latin, 328; failure at Rome, 387; Cæsar's colonies, 418.

Col'o-phon, 83 See map following p 128

Comedy, at Athens, 165, 185, 251; at Rome, 382.

Co-mit'i-a, meeting of, 338; under empire, 429, 450, 474, 492; Cu-ri-a'ta, 286, 300; Cen-tu-ri-a'ta, 300, 309, 327; Tri-bu'-ta, 307 f, 313, 327, 408.

Commerce, early Egyptian, 6, 16; early Babylonian, 16, 18; in Kassite Babylonia, 13; of Phœnicians, 40 f; of Damascus, 46; of Assyria, 52; of Mycenæan age, 74 f; of Greek middle (Homeric) age, 83, 89, 104, at Athens, 117 ff, 124 f, predominance of Athens in. 132, 146 f, 156 ff., how regarded in Greece, 79, 156 ff., 159; of Ptolemaic Kingdom, 255 f.; Rome's commercial position, 284, Etruscan, 290, 292, attitude of early Romans toward, 332, development of Roman, 343 f, 387, 406 f.

Com'mo-dus, 471, 473 f.

Common people, in ancient East, 17 f; in Greece, 150 f, 156, 167 f, at Rome, 286 f, 377 f, 440, 457. See "Assemblies"

Con-nu'bi-um, 327 n

Co'non, 206.

Con'stan-tine, 495; his achievements, 496

Con-stan-ti-no'ple, 496 f., 508 f., 510. See map facing p 505

Con-stan'ti-us, elder, 491; younger, 498.

Consul, 299, 305, 310 f , 314, 317, 373, 405, 429, 448.

Consular tribunes, 317.

Co'ra, 86

Cor-cy'ra, 107, 174 f See map facing p 89

Cor-fin'i-um, 401. See map following p 278.

Cor'inth, 83, 88, 106 f , 134, 169, 174 f , 227; destroyed by Rome, 370. See map following p. 66

Cor-i-o-la'nus, 304

Co-ri'o-li, 304. See map on p 301.

Cor-o-nei'a, 206. See map following p. 66.

Cor'si-ca, 343, 349   See map following p 278.

Cor-u-pe'di-on, 253.

Cos, 260   See map following p. 128.

Cosmogony, in ancient East, 26; Greek, 101; Roman, 464. See "World "

Council   See "Senate."

Cran'non, 248.

Cras'sus, 382, 408, 410 ff , 432.

Crem'e-ra, 303   See map on p 301.

Cre-mo'na, 349.

Cre'on, 95

Cres'cens, 460.

Cres-phon'tes, 96

Crete, 42, 72 ff. See map facing p. 77.

Cri-mi'sus, river, 271.

Crit'i-as, 201 f

Crœ'sus, King of Lydia, 56, 89

Cro'ton, 89. See map facing p 89

Cu'mæ, 140. See map following p. 278

Cu-nax'a, 204. See map following p. 234.

Cu'nei-form, 21.

Cu'ri-æ, 287. See "Comitia curiata."

Cu-ri-a'ti-i, 288.

Cur'sus hon-o'rum, 387 n.

Cu'rule, 377 n

Cyb'e-le, 262, 386.

Cy'lon, 117.

Cy'me, 89   See map facing p. 180.

Cyn-os-ceph'a-læ, 366.

Cyp'ri-an, 490.

Cy'prus, 40, 74, 169, 171, 236. See map following p 234

Cyp'selus, 106.

Cy-re'ne, 88   See map facing p. 89.

Cy'rus, of Persia, 56, 58, 236; the younger, 196, 204.

Cyz'i-cus, 88, 195   See map facing p 89.

Da'ci-a, a province, 475, 488. See map following p 476.

Dacian war, 475

Dal-ma'ti-a, 495. See map facing p 509.

Da-mas'cus, 46, 47; overthrow, 50, Mohammedan, 510. See map facing p 3.

Dan-a'us, 93

Da-ri'us, I, organizer of Persian Empire, 59, 61 f , II, 194, 204; III, 233.

David, of Israel, 44 ff.

Deb'en, 18

Debt, law of, in ancient East, 18 f ; in Greece, 117 f , at Rome, 306, 313.

Dec'arch-y, 200 f.

De-ceb'a-lus, 475.

Dec-e-le'a, 193. See map following p 128.

De-cem'vir-i, 311, 314 f

De'ci-us, 487.

De'ci-us Mus, 341

De-la'tors, 447.

De'li-an, Confederacy, organization of, 145 f , growth of Athenian power in, 147 f , becomes an Athenian empire, 171 f

De'li-um, 182. See map facing p. 180

De'los, amphictyony of, 98, Apollo at, 120, treasury of Delian Confederacy, 146 See map facing p 171

Del'phi, Apollo's oracle at, 89. 98, in Persian wars, 127, 133. See map following p. 66

Deme, 121 f.

De-me'ter, 86, 103, 166.

De-me'tri-us, 249 ff.

Democracy, rise of, Greek, 108, 119, 121 f , Solon's service to, 118 f , development at Athens, 131 f , in the Greek world, 149 ff ; the Athenian democracy described, 150 ff., 161, 167 f., its defects, 184, 198, at Rome, in time of the Gracchi, 391 f ; struggles with the senate, 396 f See "Assemblies," "Common People."

De'mos, 105, 107

De-mos'the-nes (general), 181 f., 193, (orator), 225 f., 248 f.

De-na'ri-us, 333.

Deportation, 49.

Deu-ca'li-on, 92.

De-vo'ti-o, 341.

Di-an'a, 293

Di-cas'ter-ies, 153

Dictator, 299, 303, 304, 319, 415

Di'o-cese, 492

Di-o-cle'ti-an, 491 ff.

Di-o'do-tus, 180.

Di-o-nys'i-a, 120, 165.

Di-o-nys'i-us, I, 203, 210, II, 210, 217

Di-o-ny'sus, 86, religion of, 103; at Athens, 120; at Rome, 386.

Diplomacy, meaning of, 35 n

Dis-pa'ter, 293

Do-mi'ti-an, 453, 469.

Do'ri-ans, migration, 76 f , organization, 79 f , Dorus and, 92

Dra'co, 117

Drama. See "Theatre"

Dran-gi-an'a, 241 See map following p 234

Drep'a-na, 347 See map following p 278.

Dress, in ancient East, 23; at Rome, 334, 338; in imperial Rome, 459

Drink, in ancient East, 23.

Dru'sus, 396.

Dy'ar-chy, 433, 435.

Dynasty, 6 n.

E'bro, 350.

Ec-cle'si-a, of Athens, 151 ff See "Assemblies"

Ec-bat'a-na, 57 See map facing p 3

Ec'no-mus, 348 See map following p 278

Edict of Toleration, 495.

Education, in ancient East, 52, 60; in Greece, 161 f , 167 f , at Rome, 337 f , 380 f , 457, 464

Egypt, physical features, 1, first kingdoms, 5 ff., empire of, 31 ff (organization, 35, ruling classes, 36; the army, 36; the priests, 36; splendor, 33 f), under Assyrian sway, 37, conquered by Nubians, 37, conquered by Persia, 37, Greeks visit, 89; revolts from Persia, 130; Athenian expedition to, 171, conquered by Alexander, 235 ff., kingdom of Ptolemies, 225 ff., 258 f ; gradual reduction under Rome, 365, 368, under Augustus, 429 n ;

under Nero, 451. See "Alexandria."
Eighteenth dynasty, 31 f
Ek'ron, 42 n. See map facing p 3
E'lam-ites, home, 3, invade Babylonia, 9, 51; conquered by Assyria, 49.
El'be, 434, 442 See map following p 476
El-e-gi'ac poets, 101
Eleu'sis, 165 f See map following p 66
E'lis, 115, 149. See map following p 66.
Empire, meaning of, 10 n. See "Imperialism"
Engineering, Egyptian, 24 f.; Roman, 462.
En'ni-us, 382, 386.
E-pam-i-non'das, 209 f.
Eph'e-sus, 83. See map facing p. 89
Eph-i-al'tes, 150, 155.
Eph'ors, 114.
Epic poetry, Babylonian, 21; Greek, 84 f., 97, Roman, 437
Ep-i-cu'rus, 266.
Eq'ui-tes, 296, 377, 389, under Augustus, 436, in first century A D., 459; in second century A.D., 474.
Er-a-tos'the-nes, 258.
E-rech-the'um, 94.
E-rech'theus, 82, 93 f.
E-re'tri-a, 88, 127. See map following p 66.
Er'os, 86.
E-sar-had'don, 49.
Es'qui-line hill, 284. See map on p. 286
E-te'o-cles, 95
Et-e-o-cre'tans, 71.
E-thi-o'pi-a, 8. See "Nubia."
E-tru'ri-a, 280, 290 See map following p. 278.

E-trus'cans, 279; at Athens, 173; at Rome, 290 ff; expansion, 290, Roman wars with, 300 ff.; conquest of, 320
Eu-bœ'a, 83, 88 See map following p 66.
Eu'clid, 258.
Eu-er'ge-tes, 260.
Eu-me'nes, 249, of Pergamon, 367.
Eu-mol'pus, 82
Eu-phra'tes, river, 1. See map facing p 3
Eu-rip'i-des, 184, 188 f, 381.
Eu-ro'pa, 94
Eu-ro'tas, 109 f. See map following p 66.
Eu-rym'e-don, 149
Eu-rys'theus, 95 f.
Eu-se'bi-us, 498.
Ex'arch, 518
Exchange, means of, in ancient East, 18, 59, in Greece, 99, 143; at Rome, 332 See "Coinage."

Fa'bi-i, 303
Fa'bi-us Max'i-mus, 351; Pictor, 382
Family, in ancient East, 19 f; in Greece, 160 f; at Rome, 286, 335 ff; decline of, 385; in Augustus's time, 436.
Fa-yum', 8.
Festivals, Greek religious, 98, 103, 119 f, 164 f.; Roman, 292, 459
Feudal government, in Egypt, 7.
Fi-de'næ, 303 See map following p. 278
Finances, at Athens, 168 f., 214; at Rome, 362, 431 f.; under Augustus, 362, 431 f; in later empire, 493.
Fis'cus, 431.
Flam-i-ni'nus, T., 349.
Fla'vi-an Cæsars, 451.
Food, in ancient East, 23; at Rome, 333, 379; in imperial Rome, 459.

Foreigners, in Greek cities, 156, 159 f.; at Rome, 295, 457.

Fo'rum of Rome, 285

Fourth Egyptian dynasty, 6

Franchise, in Greece, 108, 121 f , 214, at Rome, 295 f , 299 f , 325 f , 387 f , 396, 400 f , extension of, by Cæsar, 417; by emperors, 477; edict of Caracalla, 484.

Franks, cross the Rhine, 487, 503; settle in Gaul, 511, kingdom of, 511, "do-nothing" kings, 512; and the pope of Rome, 516 ff.

Freedmen at Rome, 377, 457; under Augustus, 430; as officials under Claudius, 448 f

Future life, belief in, in Egypt, 28, in Babylonia, 28, in Greece, 87, 103, 218.

Ga'bi-i, 291 See map on p. 301

Gabinian law, 408

Ga'des, 41. See map facing p 89.

Gai'ser-ic, 504

Gai'us (Caligula), 447 f

Ga-la'ti-a, 255, 267 See map following p 434.

Gal'ba, 451.

Ga-le'ri-us, 491, 495.

Gal-li-e'nus, 485

Gath, 42 n See map facing p. 3

Gau-ga-me'la, 89.

Gaul, Greek colonies in, 89; Roman province in, 398, Cæsar in, 413 f , divided into provinces, 433, Franks enter, 511, Mohammedans in, 511 f See map facing p. 412

Gauls See "Celts."

Gau'ma-ta, 59

Ga'za, 42 n , 236 See map facing p 3

Ge'lon, of Syracuse, 134, 140

General. See "Strategoi."

Gens, 287.

Ger-man'i-cus, 446.

Germans, enter Gaul, 413; cross the Danube, 476, settled in the Empire, 488, how affected by Rome, 506, conversion of, 516.

Germany, and Augustus, 434, 442; and the Flavians, 454.

Ge-ru'si-a, 114.

Gil'ga-mesh, 21.

Gladiatorial shows, 379, 460.

Gods, of Babylonia, 27, of Egypt, 27; of Israel, 43 ff ; of Assyria, 52, of Persia, 60 f., of Greece, 86, 103, of Rome, 292 ff., 340 f.

Gor'di-um, 234.

Goths, cross the Danube, 487; in the Empire, 503. See "Ostrogoths," "Visigoths."

Grac'chus, Tib Semp , 392 f ; Gaius, 394 ff

Gran-i'cus, 233 See map following p 234

Gra'ti-an, 499

Greece, first appearance in Oriental history, 37, physical geography, 65 f ; relation of its physical geography to its history, 66 f ; people, 68, 71, outline of its history, 68 f , Neolithic Age, 70, colonization, 87 f , contact with the East, 89, Mycenæan age, 71 f , middle age, 79 f ; age of political adjustment and expansion, 91 f ; elements of unity, 91, summary of progress to 500 B C , 123 ff ; significance of victory over Persia, 141; summary of progress to supremacy of Philip, 229, revolt from Macedonia, 248, experiences under Alexander's successors, 248, 250 f , 265 ff , influence on Italy, 290, declared free by Rome, 366, becomes Roman, 370, transformation of Roman life by Greek civilization, 378 ff.

Greg'o-ry, 516
Gy'ges, king of Lydia, 56, 89
Gy-lip'pus, 192 f.
Gymnastics, 161 f.

Ha'des, 87.
Ha'dri-an, 471 f , 476, 478.
Hal-i-ar'tus, 206. See map follow-
　ing p 66.
Hal-i-car-nas'sus, 166, 234　See
　map following p. 128.
Ha'lys, river, 56. See map facing
　p. 3.
Ha-mil'car, 348
Har-mo'di-us, 120.
Har'most, 201.
Ha-rus'pi-ces, 295
Has'dru-bal, 350 f.
Hebrews, home, 3, divisions, 43.
　See "Israel."
Hel-i-æ'a, at Athens, 118, 152 f
Hel'le, 96
Hel'len, and the Hel-le'nes, 92.
Hel'les-pont, 88, 120.
He'lot, 109, 148.
Hel-ve'ti-i, 413
He-phaes'tus, 86.
He'ra, 86, 95
Her-a-clei'a, 324　See map follow-
　ing p 278.
Her-a-clei'dæ, 96.
Her'acles, 86, 95 f., 220.
Her-a-cli'tus, 102.
He-rac'li-us, 509
Her-cu-la'ne-um, 452
Heresy 481
Her'mæ, 192
Her'mes, 86, 96, of Praxiteles, 215
Her'ni-ci, 300
Her'od, 439.
Her-od'o-tus, 8, 41; on Cyrus, 58;
　on the Persians, 60, 106 f., 127 f.,
　133 f , on battle of Platæa, 140,
　on Athens, 144; his work, 166 f ;
　compared with Thucydides, 188.
Her-oph'i-lus, 258

Hes'i-od, 91 f , 100, 102.
Hez-e-ki'ah, 50.
Hi-e-ro-glyph'ics, 21.
Hi'e-ron, tyrant, 150, king, 344.
Him'e-ra, 140
Hip-par'chus, 120
Hip'pi-as, 120.
Hip'po, 514.
Hip-po-da-mi'a, 95.
Hi'ram of Tyre, 45.
Hit'tites, home, 3, invasions, 32;
　kingdom, 33, Egyptian wars, 34
Homer, 84, 100, 119.
Hon-o'ri-us, 503.
Horace, 438 f
Ho-ra'ti-i, 288.
Ho-ra'ti-us Co'cles, 302.
Horse, in Egypt, 31. See "Cav-
　alry "
Hor-ten'si-an law, 360
House, in ancient East, 22 f ; in
　Greece, 162, at Rome, 333, 378,
　in imperial Rome, 458
Huns, 503.
Hy-das'pes, river, 241.
Hyk'sos, 29, 30
Hy-perm-nes'tra, 93
Hyph'a-sis, river, 241.
Hyr-ca'ni-a, 57.　See map facing
　p 3

I-am'bic, 100.
Ia-pyg'i-ans, 279
Iconoclastic controversy, 518.
Ic-ti'nus, 166.
Ikh-na'ton, 32.
Il'i-ad, 84 f.
Illyrians, 279; pirates, 350.
Il-lyr'i-cum, 491. See map follow-
　ing p. 476.
Im'bros, 206.　See map following
　p 128
Immortals, 59
Im-per-a'tor, 450
Imperialism, in earliest history,
　8 f , 10 f , rise in Greece, 142 f.,

its conflict with the opposing Greek ideal, 177, 207, 210, 212 f, 224; defeat of Athenian, 198 f, Sparta's imperial policy, 200 f, 203 f; Theban imperialism, 210, revival at Athens, 211, Isocrates's view, 218 f.; achieved finally by Philip, 227 f, imperialism of Alexander's successors, 249 ff.; of the Ptolemies, 255, Roman, 326 ff, 363, 368 f., 387, 406 f, 420 f, 430 ff., 434 f, 450 f, 476 f, 491 f.

Im-pe'ri-um, 299, 417, 428.

India, Darius I in, 62; Alexander in, 240 f.

Indo-European, or Indo-Germanic, family, 3 f, 54, 279

Industrial activities, in ancient East, 15 f; in Phœnicia, 40; in Crete, 72, 75, in Greece, 79, 157 f., at Rome, 332, 376.

Interest, rate in Greece, 159

Invasions, of Babylonia, 9, 13, of Egypt, 29, 32 f.; by Hittites, 58; by northwestern peoples, 33, 37, 42; by Arameans, 39; by Chaldeans, 39; of Greece by Dorians, 76 f; Barbarians in Roman Empire, 475 f, 487, 498, 502 ff, 517 f; Mohammedan, 510 f, 512

I'on, and I-o'ni-ans, 92

Ionian revolt, 127 f.; cities to Persia, 206.

I-phic'ra-tes, 206.

Ip'sus, 252. See map following p. 234.

I-ran', 57. See map facing p. 3

I-re'ne, 520

I'sis, 262, 467.

I-soc'ra-tes, 218 f.

Is'ra-el, appearance, 43; in Egypt, 43; in the desert, 43; settlement in Palestine, 43, conflicts with Philistines, 43; religion of, 43 f; organization of kingdom, 44 f.; disruption of, 46; kingdom of Israel in the north, 46, destroyed, 50.

Is'sus, 234. See map following p. 234.

I-tal'i-ca, 401.

Italy, the name, 329; physical geography, 277 f., historical contact with the East, 276 f; peoples, 279 f.; historical geography, 280, influence on early Rome, 289 f, union of Italy under Rome, 328 f; economic decay of, 375 f., 387, 390 ff; under Augustus, 430 ff

I-tho'me, mt, 149, 210. See map following p. 66.

Jan-ic'u-lum hill, 284, 313. See map following p 460.

Ja'nus, 292

Ja'son, 96 f., of Pheræ, 208

Je-ho'vah, God of Israel, 43 ff.

Je'rome, 513

Jerusalem, capital of Israel, 44; destroyed by Nebuchadrezzar, 55, visited by Alexander, 236; stormed by Pompey, 411; by Titus, 454. See map facing p. 3

Jesus Christ, 439 f., 467

Jewelry, 25, 334, 336, 459

Jews, deported to Babylonia, 55, 58, restored to Judea, 236, and Alexander, 236; the Maccabees, 368, and Rome, 368, feeling toward Rome, 369, subjected by Rome, 411, Judæa a province, 411; revolt, 454.

Jo-cas'ta, 94

Joseph in Egypt, 36 f.

Jo-se'phus, 29, 236.

Judah, kingdom of, 46; vassal of Assyria, 50, overthrown, 55. See map following p. 434.

Ju-gur'tha, 396 f.

Julia, daughter of Julius Caesar, 411 f , daughter of Augustus, 440, 443

Julian, 498; Julian Cæsars, 445 ff ; law, 401.

Ju'no, 293.

Ju'piter, 289, 293.

Justice, administration of, in ancient East, 11 f., 17, 19, 26, 49; in Greece, 80 f., 116, 153, in Roman Empire, 339, 477, 484 f., 508.

Jus-tin'i-an, 507 f.

Ju'venal, 479

Kal'di, 39 See "Chaldeans "

Ka-ma'res, epoch 72, pottery, 72; painting, 72; frescoes, 72.

Kar'nak, 33.

Kas'sites, in Babylonia, 12 f , 29

Kef'tiu, 71 See "Cretans "

Kha'ti See "Hittites."

Khe-ta'sar, 33

Khu'fu, 24

King. See "Ruler."

Knights See "Equites."

Ko-ran', 510.

Kryp-tei'a, 111.

Lab'a-rum, 498.

Lab'y-rinth, 8, 73.

Lac-e-dæ'mon, 110. See map following p 66.

La'de, 128. See map facing p. 171.

La'gash. See "Shirpurla."

Lam'a-chus, 192.

Lamia and Lamian war, 248.

Lamp'sa-cus, 196 See map following p 128.

Land See "Agrarian."

La-oc'o-on, 257.

La'res, 293, 436 f.

Latin colony, 328

Latins, 280, 286; league of, 288 f , 292, 300, 321.

La'ti-um, 287 f , 322, 327. See map following p 278

Lau'ri-um, 131. See map following p. 66.

Lavt'u-læ, 322.

La-vin'i-a, 287.

Law, importance of, in ancient East, 19, international law in Greece, 99, lawgivers in Greece, 105, at Sparta, 113 n ; at Athens, 117, 150; Greek law at Rome, 173; of Twelve Tables, 311 f , laws securing plebeian rights, 313 ff.; securing franchise to Italians, 401, conferring powers on Pompey, 408 f ; jurists under the military emperors, 484 f.; German laws as affected by Rome, 507; code of Justinian, 508 f See "Justice "

League, Peloponnesian, 114 f ; Delian, 145 f ; leagues in later Greek history, 262 f , 271; Latin, 289, 291, 300, 304, 321.

Leb'a-non mts , 33, 40. See map facing p. 3.

Legion, 297, 329

Lem'nos, 206. See map following p. 128

Leo, pope, 516; emperor, 518.

Le-on'i-das, 136

Lep'i-dus, 426 f

Leuc'tra, 208. See map following p. 66.

Libraries, in ancient East, 22; Ashurbanipal's, 51 f ; at Athens, 119, at Alexandria, 258, at Rome, 418, 462.

Lib'y-a, 346. See map following p 476

Li-cin'i-o-Sextian laws, 317.

Ligurians, 279.

Lil-y-bæ'um, 274. See map following p 278.

Lin'dos, 102 n. See map following p 128.

Li'ris, river, 320. See map following p 278.

Literature, in ancient East, 21, 34; in Egyptian empire, 34, in Assyria, 52; beginnings in Greece, 83 f., development in Greece corresponding to political and social progress, 91 f; great names and periods in Greece, 141 f, 165, 166 f 185, 187 ff., 215 ff., 225 f, 244 f, 265 f; in Alexandria, 256 f, 258 f.; beginnings at Rome, 340, 381 f; in Cæsarian period, 418 ff.; in Augustan age, 437 f., 440 f.; in the first century A D, 462 ff.; in the second century A D, 478 f.; Christian, 468, 481, 490, 513, 514.

Liv'i-a, 443 f

Liv'i-us (Livy), 437 f.; Andronicus, 381.

Lo'cri, 89, 105. See map facing p 89

Lom'bards, 517 ff.

Lu'ca, 412. See map following p. 278

Lu'ci-an, 479.

Lu-cil'i-us, 382

Lu-cre'ti-us, 418 f

Lu-cul'lus, 408

Lu'di Sæc-u-la'res, 439.

Lug-du-nen'sis, 433 See map following p 476.

Lux'or, 33.

Ly-curgus, 105, 113 n.

Lyd'i-a, empire of, 55, 89, 126; kingdom of, 56, coinage of, 99. See map facing p 3.

Lyn'ce-us, 93

Lyric poets, of Greece, 100, 141 f.; of Rome, 419.

Ly-san'der, 196 f, 201 f, 204 ff.

Ly-sim'a-chus, 252 f

Ly-sip'pus, 215

Mac'ca-bees, 261, 368.

Mac-e-do'ni-a, Athenian difficulties with, 212; early history, 220 f.; under Philip, 221 ff, 226 ff; under Alexander, 231 f., under Alexander's generals, 248 ff.; wars with Rome, 365 ff. See map following p 66

Mæ-ce'nas, 427, 441 f

Magistrate, at Sparta, 114; at Athens, 116 ff., 150, 154; at Rome, 299 f, 305 f, 308 f, 310 ff., 314 f, 327, 338 f, 355 ff, 358 ff, 361 ff., 373 f., 388, 389, 393, 405 ff., 408, 417, 429, 433, 441, 450, 453, 492.

Magna Græcia, 89, 271 f.: and Rome, 323 f.

Mag-ne'si-a, 83, 366. See map following p. 128.

Mal'ta, 41.

Mam'er-tines, 344.

Ma-mil'i-us, 303.

Man'e-tho, 6 n, 29.

Man-il'i-an law, 409

Man-ti-ne'a, 191, 210. See map following p 66.

Manufactures. See "Industrial Activities"

Mar'a-thon, 129 f See map following p 66.

Mar-co-man'ni, 476.

Mar-do'ni-us, 129, 139.

Mar-e-o'tis, lake, 236. See map on p 237

Mar'i-us, Gaius, 397 f., 401 ff.

Marriage, in ancient East, 20 ff; at Rome, 336, 465.

Mars, 293.

Mar'ti-al, 464.

Mas-sil'i-a, 89 See map facing p. 89.

Mas-si-nis'sa, 354, 371

Mau-so'lus, his tomb, 215.

Max-im'i-an, 491.

Mayor of the palace, 512

Mec'ca, 510

Me-de'a, 97.

Medes, rise, 53 f ; empire of, 55, overthrow by Persians, 56

Medicine, in ancient East, 26, in imperial Rome, 457

Me-di'na, 510

Mediterranean sea, 1, 9, 10, 31, 33, 40

Me-don'ti-dæ, 116

Medo-Persians, home, 3

Meg-a-lop'o-lis, 210.

Meg'a-ra, 83, 88, 100, 115, 117 f , 169 See map following p. 66.

Me-gid'do, 32. See map facing p 3.

Me'los, 191 See map following p 66

Mem'phis, 6. See map following p 234

Me-nan'der, 251.

Men-e-la'us, 95.

Me'nes, 6

Merchants, in ancient East, 18 f ; in Greece, 159, at Rome, 332

Mes-o-po-ta'mi-a, 2, Roman province, 476, 483 See map facing p 3

Mes-sa'na, 344 See map following p 278.

Mes-se'ni-a, wars with Sparta, 110 f ; alliance with Thebes, 210. See map following p. 66.

Mes-si'ah, 439 n , 467 f

Me-tau'rus, 353 See map following p 278

Met'ics, 159 f.

"Metropolitan," 489.

Mi'das, king of Phrygia, 89

Migrations See "Invasions"

Mil'an, 492, 500. See map facing p 517 •

Mi-le'tus, 56, 83, 88, 101, 127 f. See map facing p 89.

Mil-ti'a-des, 129 ff

Mi'na, 18, 158.

Mi-ner'va, 294

Mi-no'an, periods, 72.

Mi'nos, 73.

Min'o-taur, 94.

Min-tur'næ, 403.

Mith'ra, 489.

Mith-ri-da'tes, 402 ff., 408 ff.

Moe'si-a, 434. See map following p 434

Mo-ham'med, 509 f.

Mo-ham'me-dan-ism, 510 f , 513

Mo-los'si, 220

Mon'arch-y. See "Ruler "

Mo-nas'ti-cism, 513 f.

Mon'ey. See "Coinage" and "Exchange "

Monks, 514

Moors, 487

Morality, in ancient East, 7, 11 f , 19, 43 f , 69 f , in Greece, 86, 103, 142, 165 f , 184, 186 f , 189, 218, 244 f , 266, at Rome, 340, 369, 383 ff., 387, under Empire, 436, 440, 464 f , 480. See "Christianity."

Mosaic, 462

Moses, 43

Motives of progress in Ancient History, expansion, 8 f , 10, 31, 177; religion, 31, 43 f , invasion, 9, 29 f., 39, 71, 76 f , 79 f., 140, 219, 506, commerce, 16, 18, 40 f , 290, wealth, 15, 33, organization, 59 f.. 430 ff , 491 f.

Mu'ci-us, Scæv'o-la, 303, 383

Mum'mi-us, 370.

Mun'da, 416. See map following p. 476

Mu-ni-cip'i-a, Cæsar's law for, 418, in Empire, 430, 477

Museum at Alexandria, 258

Music, Greek, 100, 161 f.

Mut'i-na, 426

Myc'a-le, 140 See map following p 170

My-ce'næ, 72. See map following p 76.

My-ce-næ'an civilization, 71, 74; pottery, 72, houses and fortifications, 74, commerce, 75; respect for dead, 75, religion, 75 f.; decline of, 76

My'læ, 346. See map following p 278.

Myr'til-us, 95.

Mysteries, 103 f , 165 f

Myt-i-le'ne, 83. See map following p. 128.

Na'bu, 52.

Næ'vi-us, 382.

Na'ram Sin, 10

Nar'bo, 398.

Nar'ses, 507.

Nau-cra'ries, Council of, 116.

Nau'cra-tis, 37 See map facing p 89.

Nau-pac'tus, 169. See map following p 66.

Navy, 107, 131, 170 f., 194, 195 f., 235 f , 345, 346 ff See "Commerce"

Nax'os, 148. See map following p. 128

Ne-ar'chus, 241.

Neb-u-chad-rez'zar, 55.

Neph'e-le, 96

Ne'pos, 420

Nep'tune, 293

Ne'ro, 449 f , 469

Ner'va, 471.

Neus'tri-a, 511 See map facing p 517

New Comedy, 251.

New Platonism, 488 f.

New Testament, 468.

Ni-cæ'a, 487, 499 See map facing p 509

Nic'i-as, 179, 192 f.

Nic-o-me'di-a, 492. See map facing p. 509

Nile, 1. See map facing p 3

Nin'e-veh, 48; fall of, 51, 53. See map facing p. 3.

Nip'pur, 8, 13. See map facing p 3

Nobility, in ancient East, 17; at Rome, 377.

Nome, 5

Nor'i-cum, 434. See map following p 434

Not'i-um, 195. See map facing p 180.

Nu'bi-a, 8, 31. See map facing p. 3.

Num'a, 288 f , 293.

Nu-man'ti-a, 372.

Nu-mid'i-a, 354; war with, 396 f. See map following p 434

Occupations of early civilized man, 14 f ; of Greek middle age, 79, of early Romans, 331 f ; change in, 375 f ; under the Empire, 457 f.

Oc-ta'vi-us, 426. See "Augustus"

O-do-va'car, 505.

O-dys'seus, 84

Od'ys-sey, 84 f

Œ'cist, 88

Œd'ip-pus, 94 f.

Œ-no-ma'us, 95.

Œ-noph'y-ta, 170. See map following p 66

O-gul'ni-an law, 310

Ol'bi-a, 88 See map facing p. 89

Oligarchy, 200 See "Aristocracy."

O lym'pi-a, festival at, 98 See map following p. 66.

Olympiads, 98.

O-lym'pus, 86 See map following p 66

O-lyn'thus, 207. See map following p 66

O'men, 294, 338.

O'pis, 242. See map following p. 234.

Oracles, Greek, 98.
Or-chom'en-us, 404 See map following p. 66.
Oriental world, physical features, 1, 2, peoples, 2, its beginnings, 5.
Or'i-gen, 490
Or'tho-dox-y, 499.
O-si'ris, 28.
Os'ti-a, 403. See map following p 278
Os'tra-cism, 122.
Os'tro-goths, 503, 505, 507.
O'tho, 451
Ov'id, 440 f.
O-vin'i-an law, 325 n

Pa'dus, 278. See "Po."
Pæ-o'ni-us, 215.
Pag'a-sæ, 74. See map following p 128
Palace epoch, 72
Pal'a-tine hill, 284, 429, 456 n.
Pal'es-tine, 43, origin of name, 43, under Ptolemies, 252, 255. See map facing p. 3.
Pal-my'ra, 487. See map following p. 476
Pan-ath-en-æ'a, 164, 166 f.
Pan'dects, 508
Pan-no'ni-a, 434. See map following p. 434
Pan-or'mus, 347. See map following p 278
Pan'sa, 458
Pa'pa-cy, 515 ff
Pa-pin'i-an, 485.
Pa-pin'i-an law, 401
Pa-py'rus, 15.
Par-me'ni-o, 240
Par-nas'sus, 92. See map following p. 66.
Par'nes, mt, 115, 202. See map following p. 66
Par'non, mt, 110.
Pa'ros, 130. See map following p. 180.

Par'the-non, 164, 166.
Par'thi-a, 58, and Rome, 410, 412, 432, 475 f ; Sassanid dynasty, 487 See map following p. 60
Parties, in Athens, 179, in Greek cities, 214, rise at Rome, 387, 393
Patricians, 286.
Paul, 468.
Pau-sa'ni-as, 139, 144 f., 148 f ; II, 204
Pa'vi-a, 518 See map facing p 517
Pe'li-as, 96 f
Pel'la, 223 See map following p 66.
Pe-lop'i-das, 209, 210
Peloponnesian League, founded, 114; in Persian wars, 134, 144; and Athens, 169, declares war, 175.
Peloponnesian War, 177 ff.
Pel-o-pon-ne'sus, 65. See map following p 66.
Pe'lops, 95.
Pel'tast, 213
Pe-na'tes, 293.
Per-dic'cas, 233, 249.
Per'ga-mon, 257, 267, 372. See map following p 128
Per-i-an'der, 102 n , 107 f.
Per'i-cles, 164, age of, 156 ff., 168; and Peloponnesian War, 178; death, 179, and the higher life of Athens, 186 f.
Per-i-œ'ci, 110
Perpetual Edict, 474.
Per-seph'o-ne, 86.
Per-sep'o-lis, 57, 238. See map facing p. 3.
Per'seus, 367.
Persia, physical features, 57 f ; empire of, rise, 56, extent, 58 f , 59, organization, 59 f ; people, 60, civilization, 61, expansion, 62, threatens Greece, 127, expeditions against Greece, 129 f.,

132 f., driven from Greece, 140, from the Mediterranean, 140, Athenian expeditions, 170 f , peace of Callias, 171; reappearance in Peloponnesian War, 194, dominating influence, 202; war with Sparta, 205 f , condition at invasion of Alexander, 233, overthrown by Alexander, 239; revival under Sassanians, 487, 507; conquered by Mohammedans, 510 See map facing p. 3.
Pe-tro'ni-us, 463.
Pha-le'rum, 250.
Pha'raoh, title, 6.
Phar-na-ba'zus, 194.
Phar-sa'lus, 415.
Pha'rus, 236
Phei'don, 111.
Pher'æ, 208. See map following p 66
Phid'i-as, 164.
Philip of Macedon, 212, 221 ff ; his ideals and purposes, 223 f ; master of Greece, 227 f , death, 231; V, 268, allies with Hannibal, 352; wars with Rome, 365 f.
Phil-ip'pi, 222, 426. See map following p. 66.
Phil-ip'pics, 426 n.
Phil-is'tines, 40, 42 f.
Philosophy, early Greek, 101, at Athens, 186 f.; in the third century B.C., 265 f.; at Rome, 381, 386; under the Empire, 465 f., 473, 488 f.
Phi-lo'tas, 240.
Pho-cæ'ans, 89
Pho'ci-ans, 169, 226.
Phœ-ni'ci-ans, home, 3; geography of Phœnicia, 40; civilization, 40, commerce, 40 f , service to civilization, 42; empire of, 41; influence on Italy, 290, in Græco-Persian wars, 235 f.

Phrat'ry, 79 f
Phrix'us, 96
Phryg'i-a, 89   See map following p 128
Phy'le, 202. See map facing p. 171
Physical geography, influence on history, 15, 280, 283 f , 494.
Pi'e-tas, 295.
Pi'late, 467.
Pin'dar, 140, 141 f
Pin'dus, mts., 65   See map following p. 66.
Pip'pin, the elder, 512; the younger, 517.
Pi-ræ'us, 131, 146, 157, 199, 202. See map following p. 66.
Pirates, 410
Pi-sis'tra-tus, 119 f , 156.
Pit'ta-cus, 102 n , 105
Pla-cen'ti-a, 349.   See map following p 278
Pla-tæ'a, 129, 139 f , 179. See map following p 66
Plato, 217 f., 244
Plau'tus, 382
Ple-bei'ans, 286, struggles with patricians, 306 ff , victory over them, 313.
Plin'y, the elder, 464; the younger, 480, 481.
Plu'tarch, 479.
Plu'to, 86.
Po river, 278. See map following p 278.
Pol-y'bi-us, 368, 384.
Pol-y-nei'ces, 95.
Pol-y-per'chon, 249.
Pom-pei'i, 452, 461. See map following p. 278.
Pom'pey, 407 f ; victories in the East, 410 f.; first triumvirate, 411; sole consul, 412; conflict with Cæsar, 414 f., death, 415.
Pon'ti-fex, 293, 339, 436.
Pon-ton'o-us, 84.

Pon'tus, wars of Rome with, 402 ff, 410. See map following p 434
Pope, 515 f., 517 ff
Pop-lic'o-la, law of, 313.
Population, of Greek cities, 156, 214, of Roman Italy, 327
Por'sen-a, 301 ff.
Po-sei'don, 86, 93
Præ'tor, 299
Prætorian guard. 431, 450, 483.
Prax-it'e-les. 275
Prefects, Roman, 327, 431.
Pri-e'ne. 102 n
Priesthood, in ancient East, 21, 23, 26 f, in Egyptian empire, 36 f; in Greece, 80, 98, at Rome, 293.
Prin'ceps, 429, growth of power, 441, 451; as tyranny, 453, increasing state of, 456, imperial council of, 474, theory of, by third-century jurists, 485; transformed into absolute ruler, 492.
Pro'bus, 488.
Proconsul, 373
Prophets of Israel, 44, 58
Pro-tag'o-ras, 186.
Provincial government, in Egyptian empire, 35; in Assyrian empire, 49; in Persian empire, 59 f.; origin of Roman provincial system, 362 f; Roman provinces in 133 B C, 372, Roman provincial organization, 372 ff, trial court for governors, 374, defects of, 387; importance of provinces to Rome, 406; reorganization under Augustus, 429; imperial provinces, 430 f; under Julian Cæsars, 451; assemblies, 467, under Diocletian, 491 f
Pryt'a-ny, 122
Psam-met'i-cus, 37.
Ptol'e-my, I, 250 ff., 255, II, 255 f., 259 f.; III, 260; IV, 268

Public land   See "Agrarian "
Pub-li-ca'ni, 362, 373, 432
Pub-lil'i-an law (Vol'e-ro), 312, 314.
Pu'nic wars first, 345 ff, second, 350 ff.; third, 371 f.
Pyd'na, 367.
Py'los, 180 ff, 183. See map following p 66.
Pyramids, 6, 24, 26, 102.
Pyr'rha, 92
Pyr'rhus, of Epirus, 253, in Italy and Sicily, 273 f, 324.
Py-thag'o-ras, 102.

Quæs'tor, 299.
Quin-til'i-an, 464.
Quir'i-nal, 284.

Ram'ses II, 32 ff, 43, III, 33, 42.
Raph'i-a, 268
Rau'dine plains, 399.
Ra-ven'na, 505, 518. See map facing p. 517.
Re, Egyptian god, 27, 34
Red sea, 6, 43 See map facing p 3.
Re-gil'lus, battle of Lake, 303
Reg'u-lus, 347 f.
Religion, in ancient East, 26-28, of Israel, 43 f; of Assyria, 52, of Persia, 60 f, of early Greece, 85 ff., influence of Zeus and Apollo in, 87, 97 f, Greek problems of, 100 f, progress of, as related to growth of civilization, 103, in Æschylus, 142; influence of Greek philosophers on, 186; Stoicism and Epicureanism, 265 f; of early Rome, 292 ff., 295, 340 f; decline of, 385 f; revived under Augustus, 436 f; in the first century A D, 466 f; of Alexander Severus, 484, in third century, 488 f. See "Christianity."
Re'mus, 287.
Rex sa-cro'rum, 297.

Rhæ'ti-a, 434 See map following p 434.

Rhetoricians at Athens, 184, at Rome, 381, 458

Rhine, river, 413 See map following p 434

Rhodes, and Rome, 367 f See map following p 128

Rhone, river, 413. See map facing p 493

Ric'i-mer, 504.

Roman church, 489 f , 515. See "Papacy "

Rome, origin, 281, 287; geography, 283 f ; union of peoples in, 286; a city-state, 286, early legends of, 287 f.; influence of Italy on its origin, 288 f.; under Etruscan Kings, 290 ff ; political reorganization by Servius, 296 f ; overthrow of kingship, 297 f ; struggle with neighbors, 299 ff.; struggle of patricians and plebeians, 305 ff.; the Celtic terror, 318 f ; its result, 319, expansion in Italy, 320 ff.; victory of plebeians, 313 ff , rise of distinctions of wealth and office, 325, organization of Roman Italy, 326 ff , Roman society and manners, early period, 331 ff , relations to Carthage and wars, 343; early embassy to Greece, 173; war with Magna Græcia and Pyrrhus, 323 f ; early complications with Greek world, 273 f.; attitude toward Eastern powers, 368 f , wars with Macedonia, 365; with Syria, 366 f ; Rome an imperial state, 368 ff.; society and manners under Hellenistic influence, 375 ff ; era of party struggles, 392 f ; victory of Cæsar, 416; a world-empire, 424 ff , under Augustus, 427 ff.; under Julian

Cæsars, 445 ff , fire at, 450, under Flavian Cæsars, 451 ff , society and manners in the first century A D , 456 ff ; under the constitutional emperors, 471 ff , under the military emperors, 483 ff ; city fortified, 488, under the Despotism, 491 ff , rivalled by Constantinople, 496, captured by Alaric, 503; by Gaiseric, 505; and the Roman church, 489 f , 515 f.; division into Eastern and Western Empires, 502 f , fall of Western Empire, 505; influence on the barbarians, 506 f ; revival under Justinian, 507 f ; influence of Eastern Empire, 508 f ; Mohammedan attacks, 510; passing of Empire with Charlemagne's accession, 520 f

Rom'u-lus, 287 f.

Rom'u-lus Au-gust'u-lus, 505.

Rox-a'na, 239, 249.

Ru'bi-con, 414.

Ruler, in ancient East, 17; in Egyptian empire, 17; in Persian empire, 61, in early Greece, 74, 80, 81, 82; in Sparta, 114; the Greek tyrant, 105 ff ; king at Athens, 115 f , divinity of, 246; king at Rome, 287, 295 ff.; in Roman Empire (see "Princeps"); absolute monarch, 491 f , Frankish king, 511 f.; caliphs, 510.

Sa-bel'li-ans, 280

Sa'bines, 288, 300

"Sacred Band" of Thebes, 209.

Sacred war, 223, 225.

Sa-gun'tum, 350. See map facing p. 343.

Sa'is, 37.

Sal'a-mis, 118, 137 f See map following p. 66.

Sal'lust, 419 f.

Sa-ma'ri-a, 46; destroyed, 50. See map facing p 3

Sa-mar'i-tans, 236.

Sam'nites, 280, Roman wars with, 320 ff.

Sa'mos, 83, 172. See map following p. 128.

Samuel, 44.

Sap'pho, 101.

Sar-din'i-a, Phœnicians in, 41; Carthaginians in, 343; Romans take, 349. See map following p. 278

Sar'dis, 56. See map facing p 180.

Sar'gon of Accad, 8; autobiography, 9; conquests, 10, his library, 22; his empire, 9; of Assyria, 49

Sas-sa'ni-ans, 487.

Sa'trap, 59 f

Sat-ur-na'li-a, 459.

Saul, 44

Sa\ons, 516.

Scæv'o-la, Mucius, 303; the jurist, 383.

Science, in ancient East, 25, in Greece, 101; at Rome, 339, 464

Scip'i-o, Pub. Cornelius, 353; L Cornelius, 366; the younger, 384, 394.

School See "Education."

Sco'pas, 215 f.

Scribe, in ancient East, 21.

Sculpture, in ancient East, 25, 33 f, Assyrian, 51, Greek, 164, 215 f.; at Rome, 339 f; portrait statues, 462.

Scy'ros, 206. See map following p. 66.

Scyth'i-ans, invade the east, 55; Darius I attacks, 62, 126 f

Se-ja'nus, 447.

Se-leu'cus, 249 f ; kingdom, 261 f., 367, 410 f.

Sel-la'si-a, 267.

Sem'ites, origin and home, 2; distribution, 2 f.; passing of their power, 55

Senate, Greek, 80, 114, 116, 118, 121 f , 151, Roman, origin, 287; early history, 300, practical dominance of, 326, 354 ff ; plebeians admitted to, 309; methods of doing business, 357 ff ; powers of, 359 f ; and the nobility, 377, difficulties of, 389 f.; struggle with the democracy, 392 ff ; failure in administration, 396; legally supreme under Sulla, 405 f.; conflict with Cæsar, 414 f ; reorganized by Cæsar, 417; joint rule with Augustus, 428; Augustus reorganizes, 436, and Augustus, 441, and Julian Cæsars, 450; and Flavian Cæsars, 453, and constitutional emperors, 474; under absolute monarchy, 492.

Sen'e-ca, 449, 463, 466.

Sen-nach'er-ib, 49 ff., and Judah, 50 f

Sen-ti'num, 323. See map following p. 278.

Ser-a'pis, 262.

Ser-to'ri-us, 407 f.

Ser'vi-us Tul'li-us, 291, 296.

Ses'tos, 140 See map following p. 128.

Se'ti I, 32 f

"Seven against Thebes," 84, 95.

"Seven Wise Men" of Greece, 102.

Se-ve'rus, Sep-tim'i-us, 483, Alexander, 484.

Shek'el, 18.

Shir-pur'la, 8. See map facing p 3.

Sib'yl, 295.

Sic'i-ly, Phœnicians in, 41; Greek colonies in, 88, in Persian wars, 134 f , democracy in, 149 f.;

Syracuse and Athens, 192 f , empire of Dionysius, 203, events after its fall, 270 f., 272 ff , Carthage and Rome in, 343 ff , 346 ff ; Roman province, 362 f ; slave wars in, 387. See map following p 278
Sic'y-on, 107, 115. See map following p 66.
Si'don, 40 See map facing p 3.
Si-ge'um, 118. See map facing p 180
Silver Age, 463.
Si-mon'i-des, 140.
Si'na-i, 6, 31. See map facing p. 3.
Si-no'pe, 88. See map facing p 89
Sixth Egyptian dynasty, 6.
Slavery and Slaves, in ancient East, 18; in Egyptian empire, 33, 35, in Greece, 160; at Rome, 377 f., 385, 387, 407, 457, 459, 466; coloni, or serfs, 494
Slavs, 3
Social war, in Greece, 212, in Italy, 401
Society, organization in ancient East, 16 f.; in early Greece, 79 f., 85; in Athens in age of Pericles, 162 f , 167 f.; in early Rome, 331 ff , transformation, 375 ff , 383 ff.; at Rome under Augustus, 436, 440 f , classification of, at Rome in first century, A.D , 455 f , in the second century A D., 479 f.; in the third century, 486
Soc'ra-tes, 189, 216 f
Sois-sons', 517 See map facing p 517.
Solomon of Israel, 45 f
So'lon, lawgiver of Athens, 102, 105, 117 f., his legislation, 118 f ; outcome, 156.

So-phi'a, St , church of, 507.
Soph'ists, 184.
Soph'o-cles, 95, 165.
Spain, Phœnicians in, 41 , Greeks in, 89, Carthaginians in, 343, 350, becomes Roman, 353; under Augustus, 432, Mohammedans in, 511. See map facing p 89
Sparta, primitive organization, 109 f , expansion, 110, wars with Messenians, 110 f ; Spartan character, 112, development of culture and its suppression, 113 f ; final organization of political system, 114 ; headship of Peloponnesian League, 115; in alliance against Cyrus, 115; in Persian wars, 135 f , 139 f., 144 ff.; jealousy of Athens, 148; growth of oligarchy, 150, complications with Athens, 169; war with Athens, 170 ff.; fifty years' peace signed, 183; victory over Athens, 196, terms of peace, 199; imperialistic programme, 200 ff.; war with Persia, 205; peace of Antalcidas, 206, Sparta supreme, 207; revolt of Thebes, 208; later history, 265, 266 f.
Spar'ta-cus, 407 f.
Sphac-te'ri-a, 181 See map following p 66
Spu'ri-us Cas'si-us, 300, 306, Mæ'li-us, 306
Sta'ti-us, 463 f.
Stil'i-cho, 503
Sto'i-cism, 265 f.; at Rome, 465 f.
Strat'e-goi, at Athens, 122, 131, 154, in later Leagues, 263
Succession, problem of, in Roman Empire, 443 f , 453, 474, 483, 491.
Su-e'vi, 503

Sul′la, L. Cornelius, 398, 400 ff , his administration, 404 f , its failure, 406 f.

Sul-pi′ci-us, 402.

Su-me′ri-ans, 8.

Su′sa, 57, 238 See map facing p. 3.

Syb′a-ris, 89. See map facing p 89.

Syr′a-cuse, founded, 88; Gelon, tyrant of, 134 f , wars with Carthage, 135, 203, 270 f ; Hieron, tyrant of, 149 f , democracy in, 149 f., Athenian expedition against, 191 ff ; under Dionysius I, 203; Hieron, king of, 344; complications with Rome, 344 f See map following p 88

Syr′ia, 5, under Babylonian sway, 12 f , under Egyptian sway, 31, empires of, 39-48, under Assyrian sway, 48 ff ; complications with Rome, 366 f ; becomes a Roman province, 411 See map facing p 3

Tac′i-tus, 478 f

Tal′ent, 18, 158

Tan′a-gia, 169 See map following p. 66.

Ta-ren′tum, 89, 271 f , treaty with Rome, 323, war with Rome and submission, 324 f , revolt and subjugation, 353 See map following p. 278.

Tar-quin′i-i, 287.

Tar-quin′i-us, Priscus, 290; Superbus, 291, 295, 302, 304.

Tar′sus, 234 See map facing p. 493.

Tar′tar-us, 101.

Taxes, in ancient East, 17 f.; 35 f , 45, 49, 59, Athenian, 160, 168; Roman, 367, 373; imperial, 432.

Ta-yg′e-tus mts., 110. See map following p 66

Teaching at Rome, 457 f

Teg′e-a, 114. See map following p. 66.

Tel-el-A-mar′na letters, 35

Tem′e-nus, 96.

Temple, in ancient East, 24; in Egypt, 33, of Solomon, 45, at Athens, 163 f.; at Rome, 436, 438 f.

Ten Commandments, 44.

Ter′ence, 382.

Ter-pan′der, 113.

Ter-tul′li-an, 481, 490.

Tet′ri-cus, 487.

Teu′to-nes, 398.

Teu-ton′ic peoples. See "Germans."

Tha′les, 101 f.

Thap′sus, 415. See map following p 476

Tha′sos, 149. See map following p 66

The-ag′e-nes, 117

Theatre, at Athens, 120, 165, 167; at Rome, 335, 380, 461.

Thebes (in Bœotia), in Persian wars, 127, 133, rises against Sparta, 208, imperialistic ideal of, 210, failure, 211; real achievement, 211, destroyed by Alexander, 232. See map following p 66.

Thebes, capital of Egypt, 7, 30, 31, 33 See map facing p. 3

The-mis′to-cles, 131, 138, 141, 146, 148 f

The-oc′ri-tus, 256

The-od′or-ic, 505.

The-o-do′si-us, 498, 500, 503; penance of, 500 f.

The-og′nis, 101.

The-ram′e-nes, 195 f.

Ther-mop′y-læ, 135 f See map following p. 66.

The'ron, 140, 201 f.

The'seus, 82, 94.

Thes'pis, 120.

Thes-sa-lo-ni'ca, 500. See map following p. 66.

Thes'sa-ly, tyrants of, 210. See map following p. 66.

Thirty, at Athens, 201 f.

Thrace, 449. See map following p. 128.

Thras-y-bu'lus, 106.

Thu-cyd'i-des, the historian, 187 f.; on founding of Athens, 82.

Thu-cyd'i-des, son of Mel-e'si-as, 172

Thu'ri-i, 173. See map following p. 278.

Thut'mose, III, 31 f.

Ti'ber, 279. See map following p 278.

Ti-be'ri-us, 443, 445 ff.

Ti'bur, 478 See map on p 301.

Ti-ci'nus, 351. See map following p. 278.

Tig-lath-pi-le'ser, III, 49 f.

Ti-gra'nes, 410.

Ti'gris, river, 1. See map facing p 3

Ti-moc'ra-cy, 108.

Ti-mo'le-on, 270 f.

Ti-mo'theus, 211.

Tir'yns, 74. See map facing p 77.

Tis-sa-pher'nes, 194, 196.

Ti'tans, 101.

Ti'tus, 452.

To'ga, 296, 334, 338

Tours, 512 See map facing p. 517

Trades, in ancient East, 16, at Rome, 332 See "Industrial Activity "

Tradition, meaning of, 10 n.

Tra'jan, 471, 475, 477.

Tra-pe'zus, 88. See map facing p. 89.

Tras-i-me'nus, 351 See map following p 278

Treaty, Ramses and Hittites, 33; Greek, 171, 199, 206 f.; Roman, 323, 328, 343, 349, 354, 365

Treb'i-a, 351. See map following p 278

Tribal system, 79, 511

Tribe, at Rome, 325, 327.

Tri-bo'ni-an, 508.

Trib'une, origin, 307 f , transformation, 309

Tribuniciary power of Augustus, 429, 436

Trib'ute See "Taxes," "Province "

Tri'remes, 107.

Tri'umph, 330

Tri-um'vi-rate, 393; first, 411; second, 426

Tro'jan war, 84, 287

Troy, 74 See map facing p 3.

Tul'lus Hos-til'i-us, 288.

Tu'nis, 348

Twelfth Egyptian dynasty, 7.

Twelve Tables, law of, 311, 338 f.

Tyrants, of Greece, 105 ff.

Tyre, 40, 41, 45; siege by Alexander, 236 See map facing p. 3.

Tyr-rhe'ni-an sea, 290. See map following p 278

Tyr-tæ'us, 113

Ul'pi-an, 485.

Um'bri-ans, 279, 323.

Um-bro-Sa-bel'li-ans, 279.

University, at Athens, 265.

Ur, 8. See map facing p 3

U'ti-ca, 41. See map facing p. 89.

Va'lens, 503.

Va-le'ri-an, 487.

Valerian law, 312

Va-le'ri-o-Horatian laws, 316.

Van'dals, 503, 507

Var'ro, 420

Va'rus, 442

Ve'i-ı 301 ff See map facing p 89

Ven'e-tı. 279

Ve'nus, 293

Ve-nus'ı-a, 327. See map follow-ing p 278.

Ver'gil, 257, works, 437 f

Ves-pa'sı-an, 451 f.; and senate, 453

Ves'ta, 292

Ve-su'vı-us, 452.

Vim'ı-nal hill, 285. See map on p. 286

Vır-gın'ı-us, 315 f.

Vir-i-a'thus, 372

Vis-i-goths, 503, 507, 511.

Vi-tel'li-us, 451.

Vol'sci, 300, 304, 320

Volturnus river, 323.

Vul'can, 293.

Vul'gate, 513.

Warfare, of Sumerians, 8; develop-ment in Egypt, 31, 36, of Philis-tines, 42 f , in Persia, 61 f., naval, 107; at Athens, 116; at Marathon, 129 f ; new tactics of Epaminondas, 209 f.; Greek development in, 213 f ; Mace-donian army, 221 f.; tactics of Alexander, 233 f , 238, 242 f ; army at Rome under Servius, 296 f.; development and reor-ganization, 309 f , 329 f , reforms of Marius, 399, army under Au-gustus, 431, army supreme in Roman Empire, 486 f , im-provements by Diocletian, 493.

Wealth. See "Capitalism "

Woman, in ancient East, 19 f ; in Greece, 161; at Rome, 335 ff , 459, 465.

World, ideas of, in ancient East, 26, in Greece, 100 f.; in Rome, 463, 465 f. See "Cosmogony."

Worship   See "Religion."

Writing, materials, 15; systems of, 20 f ; in Greece, 99; in Italy, 290.

Xen-oph'a-nes, 102.

Xen'o-phon, 205; on Leuctra, 208; his works, 216 f.

Xer'xes, 130, 132, 135 ff.

Zach-a-ri'as, 517

Za'gros mts , 57.

Za-leu'cus, 105

Za'ma, 354. See map following p 476

Ze'la, 415.

Ze'no, philosopher, 259, 265; em-peror, 505.

Ze-no'bı-a, 487.

Zeus, 86, 98.

Zo'ro-as-ter, 60 f.

www.ingramcontent.com/pod-product-compliance
Lightning Source LLC
LaVergne TN
LVHW012209040326
832903LV00003B/207